# Additional Praise for *Terrorism and Tyranny*

"*Terrorism and Tyranny* is not just the best book you'll ever read about the War on Terrorism. It's not just the best Libertarian book of the year. It's one of the most important books of the decade. Whether you support or oppose the War on Terrorism, you owe it to yourself to read it."

—Bill Winter, *LP NEWS*

"The most important book since 9/11 . . . Anyone interested in the War on Terrorism must read James Bovard's newest book . . . He has constructed with precision and scholarly excellence a narrative of all that Bush has done since 9/11 in the name of fighting terror."

—Antiwar.com

"James Bovard forces the reader of *Terrorism and Tyranny* to take a long, hard look at how the current war against terror threatens freedoms. . . . Bovard hits us over the head with a two by four, in an effort to awaken us to the dangers we face if we don't demand that government restrain itself. . . . Bovard pulls no punches. . . . The road map painted by Bovard is not a pretty picture, but it is a true depiction of where we are, how we got where we are, and why we *must* alter our course."

—Former congressman Bob Barr, *American Spectator*

"James Bovard is a one-man truth squad who has combined an astounding amount of research into a fascinating, readable book. . . . Bovard has trapped Bush, Ashcroft and other officials in a string of lies that warrant a serious discussion about regime change in America."

—*Hillsdale Collegian*

"What is so valuable about Bovard's work is that it is just plain, fact-based, footnoted reporting. . . . A sober recitation of the facts set within a philosophical framework that exactly matches that of the Founding Fathers."

—Syndicated Columnist Charley Reese

"Bovard . . . looks at the post-September 11 policies and actions of the government and finds them sorely lacking. . . . Meticulously documented . . . May well leave readers as angry as its author."

—*Publishers Weekly*

"Bovard's new book, *Terrorism and Tyranny*, is like his many other exposés of government power and corruption: clear, dispassionate, factual, and heavily documented. He is the Joe Friday of political analysis: Just the facts, ma'am. And the facts will make your blood boil."

—Richard Ebeling, *The Freeman*

"The book is so provocative, in so many ways, and so right on target. . . . It is a wonderful book . . . I think this is Bovard's best by far."

—David Brudnoy, WBZ, Boston

"The gallows humor of James Bovard, a bright fellow with a sharp wit, helps to underscore the more outrageous blunders and miscalculations that have been committed by the several intelligence communities and law-enforcement agencies, the opportunistic power grabs by high-ranking bureaucrats, and the heavy damage inflicted on the Bill of Rights not by terrorists, but by friendly fire from both the Justice Department and the White House, all under the banner of defending freedom."

—Prof. Harold Cordry, Bookreporter.com

"Bovard's penchant for detailed analysis and fair-minded reporting has created one of the best critiques of post–9/11 policies yet."

—Brigid O'Neil, *Freedom Daily*

"This is an awesome book. . . . There is no filler—every page is 'need to know information.'"

—Doug Basham, KLAV Radio, Las Vegas

## Also by James Bovard
## and Available from Palgrave Macmillan

*The Fair Trade Fraud* (1991)

*Lost Rights: The Destruction of American Liberty* (1994)

*Freedom in Chains* (1999)

*"Feeling Your Pain": The Explosion and Abuse*
*of Government Power in the Clinton-Gore Years* (2000)

## Also by James Bovard

*Farm Fiasco* (1989)

*Shakedown* (1995)

# Terrorism and Tyranny

## Trampling Freedom, Justice, and Peace to Rid the World of Evil

James Bovard

TERRORISM AND TYRANNY
Copyright © James Bovard, 2003.
All rights reserved. No part of this book may be used or reproduced in any
manner whatsoever without written permission except in the case of brief
quotations embodied in critical articles or reviews.

First published in hardcover in 2003 by Palgrave Macmillan
First PALGRAVE MACMILLAN™ paperback edition: September 2004
175 Fifth Avenue, New York, N.Y. 10010 and
Houndmills, Basingstoke, Hampshire, England RG21 6XS.
Companies and representatives throughout the world.

PALGRAVE MACMILLAN is the global academic imprint of the Palgrave
Macmillan division of St. Martin's Press, LLC and of Palgrave Macmillan Ltd.
Macmillan® is a registered trademark in the United States, United Kingdom
and other countries. Palgrave is a registered trademark in the European Union
and other countries.

ISBN 1-4039-6682-6

Library of Congress Cataloging-in-Publication Data
is available from the Library of Congress.

A catalogue record of the book is available from the British Library.

Design by Letra Libre, Inc.

First PALGRAVE MACMILLAN paperback edition: September 2004

10  9  8  7  6  5  4  3  2  1

Printed in the United States of America.

# Contents

# CHAPTER ONE

# Introduction

The war on terrorism is the first political growth industry of the new millennium. After the September 11 attacks on the World Trade Center and the Pentagon, President George W. Bush promised to lead a "crusade" to "rid the world of evil-doers."[1] Unfortunately, the political fallout from the 9/11 attacks could fatally blight both individual liberty and public safety.

After the terrorists killed thousands of Americans, the United States had the right and the duty to retaliate against the perpetrators—the Al Qaeda network—and destroy their ability to ever strike the United States again. Bush's initial response to the attacks received almost universal support among the American public and pervasive support from foreign governments.

But as time passed, the Bush administration continually broadened the war. The response to attacks by a handful of killers is morphing into a campaign to vanquish all potential enemies of U.S. hegemony and to impose American political values on much of the world.

Like a phoenix rising from the ashes, Americans' trust in government soared after the terrorist attacks. In the days after the attack, flag waving and patriotic appeals swept the land: polls showed a doubling in the number of people who trusted government to "do the right thing."[2] The national media rallied to the cause with headlines such as "The Government, Once Scorned, Becomes Savior" (*Los Angeles Times*), "Government to the Rescue" (*Wall Street Journal*), and "Government's Comeback" (*Washington Post*).[3] The government failed—so the government became infallible.

The surge in trust was spurred by a profusion of false government statements in the aftermath of the attacks. The Bush administration did everything possible to portray the United States as a blindsided innocent victim. Yet, from the 1995 warnings from the Philippines that Muslim terrorists were plotting to use hijacked airplanes as guided missiles to attack America, to the warnings to the Federal Bureau of Investigation that Arab students at flight schools were acting suspiciously, to the warning that Al Qaeda operatives had infiltrated the United States, to the failure by the National Security Agency to translate key emails on the pending attack, the feds were asleep at the switch.

After 9/11, the Bush administration rushed to increase the power of federal agencies across the board. Within hours after the attacks, Attorney General John Ashcroft began strong-arming Congress to enact sweeping antiterrorism legislation. Ashcroft's constant shrill warnings of new terrorist attacks resulted in maximum intimidation and minimum deliberation by Congress.

Because of the actions of a handful of terrorists on September 11, federal agents could have more power over all Americans in perpetuity. The Uniting and Strengthening America by Providing Appropriate Tools Required To Intercept and Obstruct Terrorism (USA-PATRIOT) Act treats every citizen like a suspected terrorist and every federal agent like a proven angel. The Bush administration carried off the biggest bait-and-switch in U.S. constitutional history. Rather than targeting terrorists, Bush and Congress awarded new powers to federal agents to use against anyone suspected of committing any one of the three thousand federal crimes on the books.

The Bush administration converted the terrorist assault into a trump card against American privacy. The Patriot Act entitled the FBI to cannibalize the nation's email with its Carnivore wiretapping system. The FBI is crafting a computer virus that can be inserted via email into targeted computers, allowing government access to everything a person types. FBI agents can now easily get warrants to compel public libraries and bookstores to surrender records of what books people borrow or buy. Federal agents have issued over 18,000 counter-terrorism subpoenas and search warrants since 9/11;[4] in many other cases, FBI agents have snared personal or proprietary information via arm-twisting and intimidation, no warrant required. The number of "emergency" searches conducted solely on the Attorney General's command (and approved ex po facto by federal judges) is skyrocketing. Operation TIPS, the Terrorist Information and Prevention System, raised the specter of millions of informants—from truck drivers to letter carriers to cable television installers—reporting any "out of the ordinary" behavior to the feds. The Pentagon's Total Information Awareness surveillance system aims to create a vast database dragnet, potentially creating hundreds of millions of dossiers on Americans containing all their phone bills, all their medical records, and everything they purchase (from books to magazines to plane tickets to guns)—all in the name of preemptively detecting terrorists. The Pentagon is also financing research to track people by their gait and by their odors.

The Patriot Act gave the feds the right to financially strip-search every American. It created new financial "crimes without criminal intent"—empowering the Customs Service to confiscate the bulk cash of American travelers who fail to fill out a government form. The president and federal regulators can now ban any foreign bank or institution from the U.S. market unless it bares its books to U.S. investigators. The Justice Department is exploiting Patriot Act powers to confiscate bank accounts for alleged crimes with no relation to terrorism. Federal officials continually bragged of the total amount of alleged terrorists assets frozen. But there were no press releases confessing that much of the money was later returned after no evidence of wrongdoing could be found.

The Patriot Act created the new crime of "domestic terrorism," defined as violent or threatening private actions intended "to influence the policy of a government by intimidation or coercion."[5] This definition reaches far beyond the box-cutter crowd. It could take only a few scuffles at a rally to transform a protest group into a terrorist entity. This could allow the government to drop the hammer on environmental extremists (even those not spiking trees), anti-trade fanatics (even those not trashing Starbucks), and anti-abortion protesters (even those not attacking doctors). If the violence at a rally is done by a government agent provocateur—as happened at some 1960s anti-war protests—the government could still treat all the group's members as terrorists. Likewise, anyone who donates to an organization that becomes classified as a terrorist entity—be it Greenpeace, the Gun Owners of America, or Operation Rescue—could face long prison terms.

Six days after the terrorist attack, Ashcroft effectively canceled the "Great Writ" of habeas corpus with a decree announcing that the government would henceforth lock up suspected aliens for a "reasonable period." Over one thousand "special interest" detainees were jailed in the months after 9/11; however, no evidence surfaced linking any of those people to the terrorist attacks. Many suspects were locked up and not charged for weeks or months afterwards and effectively held incommunicado. More than six hundred people were deported after secret trials. When a New Jersey judge denounced the government's refusal to release the names of detainees as "odious to a democracy,"[6] Ashcroft responded by issuing an emergency regulation trumping the state court decision. Georgetown University law professor David Cole observed: "Never in our history has the government engaged in such a blanket practice of secret incarceration."[7] Even after the Justice Department released or deported most of the "special interest" detainees, President Bush continued to describe all of them as "terrorists" and "murderers."[8]

Airports have far more potholes after 9/11. Despite the success of all the hijacking attempts on 9/11, Bush raced to lavishly praise Transportation Secretary Norman Mineta and Federal Aviation Administration Chief Jane Garvey. The feds promised to greatly improve airport safety. The result is institutionalized panic-mongering and an unending comedy of errors: hundreds of evacuations and scores of thousands of travelers delayed because of unplugged metal detectors, sleeping security guards, pairs of scissors discovered in trash cans, or other dire breaches of regulations. New search policies have become a Molesters Full Employment Act, with airport screeners obsessing on the underwiring of bras or poking and prodding beyond the bounds of decorum. Federal airport security agents have confiscated more than five million nail clippers, cigar cutters, screwdrivers, and other prohibited items since early 2002. But covert government tests showed that firearms, knives, and dummy explosives have continued to gush through the new improved checkpoints. Congress mandated that more than $5 billion be spent purchasing and installing bomb detection machines that are notoriously unreliable and generate endless false alarms every day. Travelers can now be arrested if they commit the new crime of raising their voice at the federal agent pawing the socks and underwear in their carry-on luggage.

At the same time that Bush is making government more powerful, he is making it much less accountable. The Bush administration seized on the national security emergency atmosphere to erect stonewalls around all federal agencies. On October 12, 2001 Ashcroft announced that the Justice Department was reinterpreting the Freedom of Information Act to make it far more difficult for Americans to discover what the federal government actually does.[9] Bush issued an executive order gutting the Presidential Records Act, which required the routine release of most of a president's papers 12 years after their term ended.[10] (Bush's action will keep secret the actions of his father and many of his own top advisors during the Reagan administration.) White House spokesman Ari Fleischer pressured the news media not to broadcast or even print a transcript of videotapes from Osama Bin Laden, warning that "if you report [the information] in its entirety that could raise concerns."[11] At the same time that the Bush administration rations the truth, it is generous with fabrications. Bush's solicitor general, Theodore Olson, informed the Supreme Court: "It's easy to imagine an infinite number of situations where the government might legitimately give out false information."[12]

While Bush perennially invokes freedom to sanctify his antiterrorism policies, freedom to dissent may be on the endangered list. Ashcroft informed a congressional committee in December 2001: "To those who scare peace-loving people with phantoms of lost liberty . . . your tactics only aid terrorists for they erode our national unity and . . . give ammunition to America's enemies."[13] The federal Homeland Security Department is urging local police departments to view critics of the war on terrorism as potential terrorists. In a May 2003 terrorist advisory, the Homeland Security Department warned local law enforcement agencies to keep an eye on anyone who "*expressed dislike of attitudes and decisions of the U.S. government.*"[14] Such an expansive definition of terrorist suspects is especially pernicious because the Justice Department is advocating the nullification of almost all federal, state, and local court consent decrees restricting the power of local and state police to spy on Americans. Homeland Security officials also urged local lawmen to be on alert for potential suicide bombers who could be detected by such traits as a "pale face from recent shaving of beard." They "may appear to be in a 'trance,'" or their "eyes appear to be focused and vigilant"; either their "clothing is out of sync with the weather" or their "clothing is loose." Perhaps to ensure that there will never be a shortage of suspects, federal experts advised local agencies of another tell-tale terrorist warning sign: someone for whom "waiting in a grocery store line becomes intolerable."[15]

## Perpetual Wars, Endless Enemies

Shortly after 9/11, President Bush announced: "So long as anybody's terrorizing established governments, there needs to be a war."[16] The Bush administration quickly organized what Bush labeled a "freedom-loving coalition"—which included many of the most oppressive governments in the world. But as long as a foreign leader recited Bush's catechism on terrorism, his government was automatically certified as a partner in Bush's crusade against evil.

A week after the 9/11 attacks, Bush proclaimed he wanted Osama bin Laden "dead or alive" and made bin Laden the poster boy for the war on terrorism. Six months later, when asked about Osama at a press conference, Bush groused that bin Laden is "just a person who's now been marginalized" and insisted: "I just don't spend that much time on him, to be honest with you."[17] From the initial targeting of al Qaeda, the enemies list expanded to include Iraq, Iran, North Korea, Syria, Somalia, and Libya, as well as an array of private groups.

The more foreign nations the United States bombs, the more domestic tranquility Americans will presumably enjoy. Bush declared on February 27, 2002: "We owe it to our children and our children's children to rid the world of terror now, so they can grow up in a free society, a society without fear."[18] Bush assumes that there is a fixed sum of terror in the world and all that is necessary is to use enough force to "bring justice" to the culprits. Bush's policies may spawn new terrorists faster than the U.S. military can kill existing terrorists.

Bush proclaimed that "either you're with us, or you're against us in the fight for freedom; either you stand beside this great Nation as part of a coalition that will defend freedom and defend civilization itself, or you're against us."[19] Bush often speaks as if all he need do is pronounce the word "freedom" and all humanity is obliged to obey his commands—as if he were the World Pope of Freedom and his infallible proclamations are sufficient to justify scourging all slackers.

Bush rarely misses a chance to proclaim that the war on terrorism is being fought to save freedom—either U.S. freedom, or world freedom, or the freedom of future generations. On January 31, 2002, Bush proclaimed: "We are resolved to rout out terror wherever it exists to save the world for freedom."[20] Bush contrasts freedom and terror as if they are two ends of a seesaw. Because terror is the enemy of government, government necessarily becomes the champion of freedom. This simple dichotomy makes sense only if terrorists are the sole threat to freedom.

## The Evolution of Terrorism

Terror was first explicitly used as a political tactic during the French Revolution. Terror had been used for thousands of years by despots to crush resistance but the French revolutionaries were likely the first to claim to be idealists for maximizing oppression. Maximilien Robespierre gushed that terror is "justice prompt, severe and inflexible," "an emanation of virtue," and "a natural consequence of the general principle of democracy." For Robespierre, terror tactics exemplified "the despotism of liberty against tyranny."[21] The revolution featured not only the guillotining of thousands of aristocrats, but also the ritualized mass drownings of people in Nantes and the extermination of the populace of entire towns who failed to enthusiastically support the "despotism of liberty." Britain's Edmund Burke, the most eloquent enemy of the French Revolution, denounced "thousands of those hellhounds called terrorists."[22]

By the mid-twentieth century, the term "terrorism" was routinely used to condemn those who attacked politicians, government forces, or established regimes. The Nazis denounced French Resistance saboteurs as terrorists. Terrorism has permeated Middle East conflicts since the 1940s, when Menachem Begin and his Irgun gang helped drive the British out of Palestine by blowing up the King David Hotel in Jerusalem, killing 91 people. In the 1950s, Algerians terrorized Paris and other French cities, eventually driving the French out of northern Africa and ending colonial rule. The United States revved up its military intervention in Vietnam to deal with what the Kennedy administration perceived as a "small war of terrorism and political subversion" by a few thousand Viet Cong.[23] In the late 1960s, Palestinians became the premier terrorists in the Western world; the kidnapping of Israeli athletes at the 1972 Olympics in Munich heralded the era of televised political murders.

After President George W. Bush announced a war on terrorism in the wake of the 9/11 attacks, one British wit declared that this was the first time in history that war had been declared on an abstract noun. Actually, many politicians had declared war on terrorism in the preceding decades—from Germany's Helmut Schmidt, to various Israeli leaders, to Ronald Reagan. Reagan's war on terrorism eventually crippled his administration, as revelations about the Iran-Contra scandal (trading weapons to gain release of hostages held by terrorists) raised the specter of both his impeachment and his senility. The first U.S. war on terrorism ended when a bomb exploded on Pan Am 103 over Lockerbie, Scotland, demonstrating the abysmal failure of the U.S. government to protect American citizens.

While Bush portrays his war on terrorism as a simple question of "good versus evil," the concept of *terrorism* is murkier than many government officials would like to admit. Brian Jenkins, one of the most respected U.S. experts on the subject, observed in 1981: "Terrorism is what the bad guys do."[24]

The U.S. State Department defined terrorism in 1981 as "the use or threat of the use of force for political purposes in violation of domestic or international law."[25] Since government use of force is almost automatically lawful (based on government edicts and sovereign immunity), governments by definition cannot commit terrorist acts. For decades, U.S. representatives to the United Nations have been adamant that "state terrorism" is a near impossibility. Private cars packed with dynamite are evil, while guided missiles launched from government jet fighters that blow up cars driven by terrorist suspects are good, regardless of how many children are in the back seat at the time of the "surgical strike."

A core fallacy at the heart of the war on terrorism is that terrorism is worse than almost anything else imaginable. Unfortunately, governments around the world have committed far worse abuses than Al Qaeda or any other terrorist cabal. By treating terrorism as the supreme evil, and insisting that governments can never be guilty of terrorism, the Bush administration makes the crimes of government morally negligible. From 1980 to 2000, international terrorists killed 7,745 people, according to the U.S. State Department.[26] Yet, in the same decades, governments killed more than 10 million people in ethnic cleansing campaigns, mass executions, politically caused famines, wars, and other slaughters. During the 1990s, Americans were at far greater risk of being gunned down by local, state, and federal law enforcement agents than of being killed by international terrorists.

---

Despite continual victory proclamations out of Washington, there is no end in sight for Bush's war on terrorism. An August 2002 United Nations report announced that Al Qaeda "is, by all accounts, 'alive and well' and poised to strike again how, when and where it chooses."[27] Central Intelligence Agency director George Tenet warned a congressional panel on October 17, 2002 that Al Qaeda has "reconstituted, they are coming after us, they want to execute attacks" and that "the threat environment we find ourselves in today is as bad as it was the summer before September 11."[28] Though the war on Iraq was justified to thwart terrorism, many experts believe that the bombing and invasion of an Arab country actually fueled terrorist fires. The International Institute for Strategic Studies, a British think tank, warned in May 2003 that Al Qaeda is "more insidious and just as dangerous" as before 9/11.[29]

Despite scores of billions of dollars of new government spending, despite the hiring of legions of new federal agents, and despite the U.S. military campaigns to overthrow the Taliban and Saddam Hussein, Americans continue to be at grave risk.

The federal government must vigorously defend America against terrorists. But is the United States suffering more from political exploitation of terrorism than from terrorists? Is the Bush administration's aggression creating more terrorists than it is vanquishing? And what are the prospects for the survival of American liberty from an endless war against an elusive, often ill-defined enemy?

# CHAPTER TWO

# The First American War on Terrorism

You don't want to just carelessly go out and maybe kill innocent people. Then you're as bad as the terrorists.

—*President Ronald Reagan, November 27, 1984*[1]

The President angrily thundered: "Let terrorists be aware that when the rules of international behavior are violated, our policy will be one of swift and effective retribution."[2] The Secretary of State was apoplectic, declaiming that terrorism is "hemorrhaging around the world" and that "international terrorism . . . is the ultimate abuse of human rights."[3]

This antiterrorist rhetoric is not from September 2001 but from January 1981—when Ronald Reagan and Secretary of State Alexander Haig proclaimed that fighting terrorism would be one of the Reagan administration's highest priorities. Amazingly, America's first war on terrorism is now almost completely forgotten. Or perhaps it is no accident that the first war on terrorism has been brushed aside, since it left the Reagan administration in shambles, spurred the killing of hundreds of innocent foreigners, and dismally failed to protect American civilians.

As America avidly continues its second war on terrorism, it is time to examine the lessons of its first war on terrorism.

---

At the time Reagan took office, Western Europe and the Middle East had suffered waves of attacks by leftist guerilla outfits and radical Arab organizations.

The seizure of American embassy personnel in Tehran by an Iranian mob symbolized to Americans the dangers of the new terrorism—even though the subsequent hostage crisis was the result of actions by the regime of Ayatollah Khomeini.

Reagan was determined to make antiterrorism a driving force of American foreign policy. The Reagan Administration revved up its campaign by redefining "terrorist" attacks to include any threat of a terrorist attack—a simple jiggering that more than doubled the number of international terrorist incidents over the previous dozen years, from 3,336 to about 7000.[4] The White House also pressured the CIA to redefine terrorism to include "all acts of violence intended to impact on a wider audience than the victims of the violence."[5] This expansive definition would have placed such American icons as Robert E. Lee and George Washington onto the list of terrorist offenders.

The Reagan administration portrayed Moscow as the terrorist mastermind of the world. FBI director William Webster was the skunk at the party, stating that there was "no real evidence" that the Soviets were instigating terrorism in the United States.[6] Rep Don Edwards (D-Cal.), chairman of the House Civil and Constitutional Rights Subcommittee, observed that terrorism is "not a great threat, in the United States. . . . Terrorism is 17th now on the FBI's list of priorities." But Secretary of State Haig—who became famous for shouting "I'm in charge here!" after Reagan's attempted assassination—was undaunted: "The symptoms of this breakdown—terrorism, subversion and conquest—are already apparent. The ideals and safety of democratic societies are under assault."[7]

Reagan's war on terrorism initially largely consisted of sending money and arms to anti-communist guerillas in Nicaragua and elsewhere. As a 1981 *National Journal* analysis noted, "Haig has blurred the distinction between terrorism and guerrilla warfare by suggesting that all revolutionaries are terrorists unless they are anti-communists."[8] The Reagan administration was understandably anxious to prevent the establishment of new communist regimes, considering the bloodbaths following communist takeovers in Cambodia, Vietnam, and Ethiopia in the preceding years. However, its knee-jerk bankrolling of anticommunist groups led to the slaughter of thousands of innocent civilians in Africa, Latin America, and elsewhere.

The worst terrorist attacks the United States suffered during the 1980s were the result of U.S. involvement in the Middle East. The Israeli-Arab conflict had been festering for almost half a century by the time Reagan took office. In June 1982, a terrorist organization headed by Abu Nidal (the Osama bin Laden of the 1980s) attempted to assassinate the Israeli ambassador in London. Nidal's forces had previously killed many Palestinian Liberation Organization (PLO) officials in numerous bomb and shooting attacks, since they considered Yasser Arafat a traitor for his stated willingness to negotiate with Israel.

Israeli Prime Minister Menachem Begin exploited the shooting in London to send the Israeli Defense Force (IDF) into Lebanon to crush the PLO. Yet, as Thomas Friedman noted in his book *From Beirut to Jerusalem,* "the number of Israeli casualties the PLO guerillas in Lebanon actually inflicted were minuscule (one death in the 12 months before the invasion)."[9] The Israeli invasion was originally scheduled for the previous summer but was postponed after U.S. envoy Philip Habib negotiated a ceasefire between Israel and the PLO.[10] Defense Minister Ariel Sharon told the Israeli cabinet that his "Operation Peace for Galilee" would extend only 40 kilometers into Lebanon. However, Sharon sent his tanks to Beirut, determined to destroy the PLO once and for all. Foreign Ministry Director General David Kimche announced: "We have no aspirations for a single inch of Lebanese territory. Our sole aim is to free ourselves from the threat of terrorism."[11] As David Martin and John Walcott noted in their 1988 book, *Best Laid Plans: The Inside Story of America's War Against Terrorism,* the U.S. embassy in Beirut "sent cable after cable to Washington, warning that an Israeli invasion would provoke terrorism and undermine America's standing in the Arab world, but not a word came back."[12] The Palestinian Red Crescent estimated that fourteen thousand people, mostly civilians, were killed and wounded in the first month of the operation. (The Israeli government stated that casualties were much lower.)[13]

When Palestinians fought back tenaciously, the IDF responded with indiscriminate bombing, killing hundreds of civilians. The IDF bombed the buildings housing the local bureaus of the *Los Angeles Times,* United Press International, and *Newsweek.*[14] The Israelis cut off the city's water and electricity supply and imposed a blockade. The UN brokered a peace deal by which the United States and other multinational troops entered Beirut to buffer a ceasefire to allow the PLO to exit to ships to transport them to Tunisia, which had agreed to provide a safe haven. The U.S. government signed an agreement with Arafat, pledging that U.S. forces would safeguard civilians who stayed behind: "Law-abiding Palestinian non-combatants remaining in Beirut, including the families of those who have departed, will be authorized to live in peace and security. The U.S. will provide its guarantees on the basis of assurances received from the Government of Israel and from the leaders of certain Lebanese groups with which it has been in contact."[15] Once the PLO withdrew from Beirut, the U.S. troops were pulled out and put back on Navy ships.

Shortly after the U.S. troops withdrew, Lebanese president-elect Bashir Gemayel was assassinated. The IDF promptly invaded Muslim West Beirut, violating the fragile peace agreement worked out with Muslim forces and the government of Syria. Prime Minister Begin declared: "The terrorists cheated us. Not all of them got out. . . . They left behind a considerable number of terrorists together with their arms."[16] The Israeli cabinet announced: "The Israeli Defense Forces have taken positions in West Beirut to prevent the danger of violence, bloodshed and anarchy."[17] The Israeli army encircled Palestinian refugee camps in the area and prohibited anyone from entering or leaving without its permission. An IDF spokesman announced: "The IDF is in control of all key points in Beirut. Refugee camps harboring terrorist concentrations remain encircled and closed."[18] As the New York Times' Thomas Friedman noted, "Although the Israelis confiscated the arms of all of the Moslem groups in West Beirut, they made no attempt to disarm the Christian Phalangist militiamen in East Beirut."[19]

Sharon invited Lebanese Phalangist militia units trained and equipped by Israel to enter the Sabra and Shatila refugee camps. Sharon and IDF chief of staff Gen. Rafael Eitan met with Phalangist commanders before they entered the camp, and, as Sharon later explained, "we spoke in principle of their dealing with the camps."[20] Gen. Eitan told the Israeli cabinet that when the Phalangists went into the camps, there would be "an eruption of revenge. . . . I can imagine how it will begin, but not how it will end."[21] The Phalangists were enraged about the killing of Gemayel, a Christian Lebanese.

The militia entered the camps and over the next 48 hours, more than seven hundred Palestinian women, children, and men were executed; many corpses were mutilated.[22] Palestinian sources estimated that the death toll was much higher. Israeli troops launched flares over the camps to illuminate them throughout the night and provided the Phalangists with food and water during their respites from the killings. Palestinian women sought to escape the slaughter but "the Israelis encircling the area refused to let anyone cross their lines."[23] After the first day's carnage, a Phalange leader reported to the IDF that "until now 300 civilians and terrorists have been killed," according to the Jerusalem Post.[24] After the Phalangists finished, they brought in bulldozers to create mass graves. More Palestinians may have been killed at the two camps than the total number of Israelis killed by the PLO in the previous decade.

The slaughter provoked outrage around the world. The government of Menachem Begin initially blocked proposals in the Knesset for a formal inquiry into the massacre; Ariel Sharon declared that his critics were guilty of a "blood libel."[25] One left-wing Israeli paper, Al Hamishmar, declared: "This slaughter has made the war in Lebanon the greatest disaster to befall the Jewish people since the Holocaust."[26] Former Israeli foreign minister Abba Eban denounced the invasion of Beirut as "the most deadly failure in Israel's modern history."[27]

The massacre at the refugee camps threatened to plunge Lebanon back into total chaos. Two days afterward, the Lebanese government requested that the United States send its troops back to Beirut; in a televised speech Reagan quickly agreed to do so. Reagan repeatedly called for Israeli withdrawal from Beirut and declared: "Israel must have learned that there is no way it can impose its own solutions on hatreds as deep and bitter as those that produced this tragedy."[28] In late 1982 Congress rewarded Israel for invading Lebanon with a special appropriation of $550 million in additional military aid and other handouts, on top of the $2 billion Israel was already scheduled to receive that year from the U.S. government.[29]

The massacres of the Palestinian refugees catapulted the U.S. much deeper into the Lebanese quagmire. As clashes continued between Israelis and Muslims, the situation became increasingly polarized in the following months. On April 18, 1983 a delivery van pulled up to the front door of the U.S. embassy in Beirut and detonated, collapsing the building and killing 46 people (including 16 Americans) and wounding over a hundred others. President Reagan denounced "the vicious terrorist bombing" as "a cowardly act."[30] But the U.S. embassy was a sitting duck for the terrorist assault: unlike many other U.S. embassies in hostile environments, it had no sturdy outer wall.[31] *Newsweek* noted: "Delivery vehicles are supposed to go to the rear of the building. Why Lebanese police guarding the embassy driveway would have made an exception in the case of the black van remained a mystery." Col. James Mead, the commander of the 1,200-man U.S. Marine Corps peacekeeping force in Beirut, declared shortly after the attack: "The embassy was not adequately protected. There was no way an unidentified vehicle with an Arab driver should have been allowed in."[32] The attack lacked novelty value, since the Iraqi and French embassies had been wrecked by similar car bomb attacks in the preceding 18 months.[33] (From the late 1970s until 1982 the U.S. government contracted for embassy security with the PLO; the embassy went unharmed, despite the civil war raging throughout the country.[34])

On April 23, 1983, Reagan announced to the press: "The tragic and brutal attack on our embassy in Beirut has shocked us all and filled us with grief. Yet, because of this latest crime we are more resolved than ever to help achieve the urgent and total withdrawal of all American forces from Lebanon, or I should say, all foreign forces. I'm sorry. Mistake."[35] But the actual mistake was a U.S. policy that would cost hundreds of Americans their lives.

When the embassy bombing victims' corpses were returned to the United States, Reagan proclaimed: "These gallant Americans understood the dangers they faced. The act of unparalleled cowardice that took their lives was an attack on all of us. We would indeed fail them if we let that act deter us from carrying on our mission." But as fighting between Christians and Muslims in Lebanon escalated, the original U.S. peacekeeping mission became a farce. The U.S. forces were training and equipping the Lebanese army, which was increasingly perceived in Lebanon as a pro-Christian, anti-Muslim force. By late summer, the Marines were being targeted by Muslim snipers and mortar fire.

On September 13 Reagan authorized Marine commanders in Lebanon to call in air strikes and other attacks against the Muslims to help the Christian Lebanese army. Defense Secretary Caspar Weinberger vigorously opposed the new policy, fearing it would make American troops far more vulnerable. Navy ships repeatedly bombarded the Muslims over the next few weeks.

At 6:20 A.M. on Sunday morning, October 23, 1983, a lone, grinning Muslim drove a Mercedes truck through a parking lot, past two Marine guard posts, through an open gate, and into the lobby of the Marine headquarters building in Beirut, where he detonated the equivalent of six tons of explosives. The explosion left a 30-foot-deep crater and killed 243 marines. A second truck bomb moments later killed 58 French soldiers.

Reagan administration officials scrambled to persuade the American people that the administration was blameless. White House press spokesman Larry Speakes declared on the day of the attack that the bombing "definitely was a difficult situation for us" since "people come out of nowhere and perform these acts."[36] Vice President George H. W. Bush rationalized: "It's awfully hard to guard against that kind of terrorism." Defense Secretary Weinberger announced that "nothing can work against a suicide attack like that, any more than you can do anything against a kamikaze flight."[37] (Actually, during World War II, the U.S. Navy quickly responded by placing rows of antiaircraft guns on the sides of its big ships.)

A surprise attack on a troop concentration in a combat zone does not fit most definitions of terrorism. However, Reagan perennially portrayed the attack as a terrorist incident and the American media and political establishment accepted that label. It is impossible to understand the first American war on terrorism without examining the political spin after that attack.

In a televised speech four days after the bombing, Reagan portrayed the attack as unstoppable, declaring that the truck "crashed through a series of barriers, including a chain-link fence and barbed-wire entanglements. The guards opened fire, but it was too late." Reagan claimed the attack proved the U.S. mission was succeeding: "Would the terrorists have launched their suicide attacks against the multinational force if it were not doing its job? . . . It is accomplishing its mission." He also warned that a U.S. withdrawal could result in the Middle East being "incorporated into the Soviet bloc."[38] Reagan said the

United States was involved in the Middle East in part to secure a "solution to the Palestinian problem."

Reagan sent Marine Corps commander Paul X. Kelley to Beirut. Kelley quickly announced that he was "totally satisfied" with the security around the barracks at the time of the bombing.[39] Upon returning to Washington, Kelley was summoned to Capitol Hill and bragged to Congress: "In a 13-month period, no marine billeted in the building [destroyed by the truck bomb] was killed or injured" from incoming fire.[40] Kelley inaccurately testified that the Marine guards had loaded weapons and that two of them had been killed in the attack.[41] When congressmen persisted questioning, Kelley became enraged and shouted: "We're talking about clips in weapons, but we're not talking about the people who did it. I want to find the perpetrators. I want to bring them to justice! You have to allow me this one moment of anger."[42]

Even though there had already been numerous major car bombings in Beirut that year and scores of other suicide attacks, Kelley told the committee that the truck bombing "represents a new and unique terrorist threat, one that could not have been anticipated by any commander."[43] Kelley denied the Marines received any warning of an impending attack. However, on the morning of Kelley's second day of testimony, the *New York Times* reported that the CIA specifically warned the Marines three days ahead of time that an Iranian-linked group was planning an attack against them.[44] Kelley responded to this report with a snit: "We have yet to find a shred of intelligence which would have alerted a reasonable and prudent commander to this new and unique threat. . . . I'm not talking about those broad, vague, general statements that they hide behind. I'm talking about specificity, about a truck."[45]

Other military officials involved in Lebanon also insisted that no American could be blamed. Vice Admiral Edward Martin, the commander of the Sixth Fleet, declared: "The only person I can see who was responsible was the driver of that truck."[46] Martin stressed in an interview: "You have to remember that prior to Oct. 23, there hadn't been any real terrorism threat."[47] A *New York Times* investigation, published on December 11, 1983, concluded: "Marine officers in Beirut and the admirals and generals in the chain of command above them did not consider terrorism to be a primary threat even after the embassy bombing, and even though Beirut had been full of terrorists for years."[48] Sen. John Warner (R-Va.), a former Secretary of the Navy, noted, "Since the crusades, every force that has occupied Lebanon has been attacked by terrorists, not conventional forces."[49]

Marines sent to Lebanon had received little or no counterterrorism training, though some of them did receive four days of specialized training on "dealing with the press: how to project."[50] Marines labored under restrictive orders that made it problematic for them even to punch back if they were slugged in the streets of Beirut. The *New York Times* investigation noted, "Several officers said the rules of engagement and their interpretation by the men may have encouraged the truck bombing, because the marines had demonstrated that they were slow to fight back."[51] Guards outside the Marine headquarters were prohibited from carrying loaded weapons. One Marine sentry explained the rules for dealing with suspected car bombers: "First you shout, 'Stop!' Then if he doesn't stop, you can load your weapon and shoot at the vehicle and try to hit the tires. If that doesn't stop him, then you are allowed to shoot at the driver."[52]

The Marines failed to defend all approaches to the barracks. Thomas Friedman reported in the *New York Times* shortly after the bombing: "The marines almost never used the entry from the parking lot south of their headquarters, where the suicide bomber drove in. The area was blocked off to civilian traffic and was used only as a helicopter landing pad. Judging from conversations with marines and Lebanese Army officers, it is clear they thought that because they did not use that entrance no one else would think of it."[53] Berms—earthen walls—are routinely built around buildings exposed to suicide bomb attacks. The hundred-man U.S. Army unit stationed in Beirut to train the Lebanese Army had built berms around the hotel where the troops slept.[54] The Marines also neglected to install the type of speed bumps and metal spikes around their barracks that the British used in Northern Ireland.[55]

After the embassy bombing in April 1983 and before the Marine barracks attack, Neal Koch, deputy assistant secretary of defense and the Pentagon's chief counterterrorism official, headed a team of military experts sent to Lebanon to examine the safety of the Marine deployment. Koch's team made several recommendations that went unheeded. After he resigned in 1986, Koch disclosed that the team's report was ignored because "they were seen as having a Special Operations association; that their report reflected adversely on people who outranked them; and, finally, their work had been submitted with no opportunity for the military system to sanitize their findings. This led to denials, ass-covering, and all-around outrage that the survey had been done at all. Thus, it was decided that there were no problems, and even if there were, they had been fixed. The report was swept under the rug."[56]

A House Armed Services subcommittee report concluded that "irrespective of possible intelligence inadequacies . . . there is no basis for the Marines' differentiating among vehicular threats . . . i.e., car bombs were real threats but a large truck bomb was not."[57] The subcommittee found the blind spot "inexplicable" considering that "an intelligence survey in the summer of 1983 recommended that trucks be visually inspected for explosive devices."[58]

Shortly after the bombing, Reagan appointed a Pentagon commission headed by retired Admiral Robert Long to investigate. The commission report, finished in mid-December 1983, concluded that military commanders in Lebanon and all the way back to Washington failed to take obvious steps to protect the soldiers. The commission suggested that many fatalities might have been prevented if guards had carried loaded weapons.[59] The report stated that the only barrier the truck overcame was some barbed wire that it easily drove over. The commission also noted that the "prevalent view" among U.S. commanders was that there was a direct link between the Navy shelling of the Muslims and the truck bomb attack.[60] (Colin Powell, who was then a major general, commented in his autobiography: "Since [the Muslims] could not reach the battleship, they found a more vulnerable target, the exposed Marines at the airport."[61])

When the White House saw the final version of the commission's report, they issued a stop order. The *Washington Post* reported that the White House "delayed release of the report for several days, allowing Reagan to respond to its criticism before it became public, and then attempted to play down its impact by vetoing a Pentagon news conference on the document."[62] The *New York Times* noted, "A White House official said Mr. Reagan wanted his own statement about the report to come out first to deflect any criticism of the Marines. Mr. Reagan's announcement apparently caught senior officers by surprise as they were meeting to consider possible disciplinary action."[63]

On December 27 Reagan revealed that "we have never before faced a situation in which others routinely sponsor and facilitate acts of violence against us."[64] Reagan sought to make the report "old news": "Nearly all the measures that were identified by the distinguished members of the Commission have already been implemented and those that have not will be very quickly."[65] Reagan announced that the Marine commanders in Beirut "have already suffered enough" and should not "be punished for not fully comprehending the nature of today's terrorist threat."[66] Reagan then effectively declared that no one would be held accountable: "If there is to be blame, it properly rests here in this office and with this president,"[67] he announced, just before leaving Washington for a vacation in Palm Springs, California.

Reagan's remarks were characterized by Pentagon officials as a "blanket pardon" for everyone involved in the debacle[68]—including the officials who gave him the incorrect information he presented in his televised speech. Reagan may have acted to prevent the possibility of an embarrassing military court martial occurring while he was campaigning for reelection.[69]

At the same time that Reagan perfunctorily took responsibility, White House press spokesman Larry Speakes announced that the real source of the debacle was the Carter administration: "We don't quarrel with the fact that the CIA and other intelligence-gathering agencies have been crippled by decisions of the previous administration, and we are in the process of rebuilding capabilities. But it takes time . . . to re-establish our intelligence-gathering methods."[70]

While the Reagan administration abstained from holding any American culpable in failing to prevent the deaths of hundreds of Marines, the White House vigorously responded to a perceived threat to one of their own. In late November 1983 the White House launched an investigation to determine who leaked to the press the fact that National Security Advisor Robert McFarlane strongly advocated U.S. naval bombardments of Muslim forces in Lebanon. The Associated Press noted that "McFarlane was said to have complained that the disclosure of them endangered his life by clearly identifying him as the official responsible for any stepped-up U.S. military activity."[71] The culprit was never discovered. The *Washington Post* later reported comments from "sources" that "the threat to McFarlane's life, though real, may have been exaggerated to encourage Reagan to order the investigation."[72]

Even after two horrific truck bombings of U.S. facilities in Beirut, the U.S. State Department continued to have a lackadaisical attitude toward safety. After the U.S. embassy in Beirut was destroyed in April 1983, U.S. embassy personnel worked temporarily at the British embassy before moving much of the staff and operations to a new embassy site in East Beirut in July 1984.

On September 20, 1984 a van sped by the gate manned by Lebanese guards. The guards followed orders: after shouting at the driver, they fired at the van's tires. The van detonated near the building, killing 2 American military officers and 12 Lebanese civilians and injuring the U.S. ambassador and 89 other people. The damage would have been far greater if a British military policeman, part of the bodyguard for the visiting British ambassador, had not seen the van racing toward the embassy building and fired five shots from his Heckler and Koch machine pistol, killing the driver and preventing him from reaching an ideal position to completely collapse the six-story building.

Martin and Walcott observed that "the annex blast was the most graphic example yet of American incompetence and impotence in the face of terrorism."[73] The *New York Times* noted that prior to the bombing, construction of the annex had proceeded at a "leisurely pace"[74]—even though the Defense Intelligence Agency warned two months earlier that the risk of an attack on U.S. government facilities in East Beirut was "exceedingly high."[75] The State Department had not gotten around to erecting a heavy steel gate to block the road leading to the annex. A blast wall had not yet been erected to protect the building from the usual attacks occurring in that neck of the woods. Shatterproof windows had not yet been installed. And the approach to the embassy annex was guarded by Lebanese militiamen, despite their failure at the U.S. embassy the previous year. U.S. Marines were kept inside the building.

A day after the bombing, Reagan shrugged off the attack as if it had been an act of God: "I think if someone is determined to do what they did, it is pretty difficult to prevent it. Actually, the only defense you have against terrorist activities is if you can infiltrate and intercept and know in advance where they are going to strike."[76] Reagan specifically denied any negligence regarding the defense of the embassy. When asked by a reporter why there were no Marines outside the building, Reagan responded inaccurately: "You can't have exterior guards. That's foreign territory, and there was no need inside the compound for a detachment of 80 marines."[77] Actually, a detachment of 80 Marines had been assigned to guard the embassy but had been withdrawn to ships offshore shortly before the attack.

Two days later, Reagan explained: "We've only been in that building two months, and about 75 percent of all the work that had to be done had been completed. It's true that it was not quite completed."[78] Chatting with reporters at a photo op, Reagan put the delay in perspective: "Anyone that's ever had their kitchen done over knows that it never gets done as soon as you wish it would."[79]

On September 26 Reagan blamed the debacle on Carter administration CIA cutbacks: "We're feeling the effects today of the near destruction of our intelligence capability in recent years before we came here."[80] Reagan falsely asserted that the Carter administration had "to a large extent" gotten "rid of our intelligence agents."[81]

The Reagan reelection campaign decided that the best defense is a good offense. On September 30 Secretary of State George Schultz threw a tantrum on a Sunday talk show, outraged at the idea that "somebody's head has to roll" for the bombing. Schultz hailed the U.S. ambassador in Beirut as a "hero" and declared: "The people out there in Beirut are serving our country in a risky environment . . . and they are doing everything possible to improve their security and it's up to us to help them."[82] The Reagan administration official with primary responsibility for the safety of embassies, Under Secretary of State for Management Ronald Spiers, announced: "I cannot find anything in what happened that's the basis for an adverse judgment against anyone involved."[83]

On October 2 at an airfield mini-press conference, Reagan denounced the "lynch atmosphere" that he said was being shown toward his administration officials. When asked about blame for the deaths at the latest embassy bombing, Reagan declared: "I was responsible—and no one else—for our policy and our people being there."[84] Reagan then announced the final settlement of the embassy annex bombing issue: "We've had an investigation. There was no evidence of any carelessness or anyone not performing their duty."[85] However, the Reagan administration had not yet begun a formal investigation.

A few weeks before the embassy blast "the U.S. government had specific, reliable intelligence warnings that explosives had been shipped into Lebanon and were targeted against American Embassy personnel," the *Washington Post* reported.[86] The House Select Committee on Intelligence issued a bipartisan report concluding that "the probability of another vehicular bomb attack" against U.S. installations in Lebanon was "so unambiguous that there is no logical explanation for the lack of effective security" at the embassy.[87] A report by the Senate Foreign Relations Committee minority staff noted that the State Department officials still "seemed to be concerned with the threats characteristic of the late 70's, namely: mob violence against an embassy."[88]

The terrorist attacks turned the U.S. role in Lebanon into a flash point in the 1984 presidential campaign. In the vice presidential candidate debate on October 11, George H. W. Bush denounced Democratic candidate Walter Mondale and his vice presidential pick, Geraldine Ferraro: "For somebody to suggest, as our opponents have, that these men died in shame, they had better not tell the parents of those young marines."[89] Neither Mondale nor Ferraro had said that the Marines "died in shame." Bush denounced Mondale for running a "mean-spirited campaign": "We've seen Walter Mondale take a human tragedy in the Middle East and try to turn it to personal political advantage."[90] But Mondale's criticisms of the Reagan administration's failures in Lebanon were less strident than Reagan's criticisms of Jimmy Carter for the Iran hostage crisis during the 1980 presidential campaign.

There were few commonplaces that offended Reagan more than the old saying that "one man's terrorist is another man's freedom fighter"—a delusion that Reagan said "thwarted . . . effective antiterror action."[91] As Reagan explained, "Freedom fighters do not need to terrorize a population into submission. Freedom fighters target the military forces and the organized instruments of repression keeping dictatorial regimes in power. Freedom fighters struggle to liberate their citizens from oppression and to establish a form of government that reflects the will of the people."[92] In contrast, "Terrorists intentionally kill or maim unarmed civilians, often women and children, often third parties who are not in any way part of a dictatorial regime," Reagan declared.[93] He especially admired the "Nicaraguan freedom fighters . . . fighting to establish respect for human rights, for democracy, and for the rule of law within their own country."[94] Similarly, Secretary of State Schultz declared in a June 24, 1984 speech: "It is not hard to tell, as we look around the world, who are the terrorists and who are the freedom fighters."[95]

A few weeks before the 1984 presidential election, news broke that the CIA had financed, produced, and distributed an assassination manual for the Nicaraguan contras fighting the Marxist Sandinista government. The manual, entitled "Psychological Operations in Guerrilla War," recommended "selective use of violence for propagandistic effects" and to "neutralize" (i.e., kill) government officials.[96] Nicaraguan contras were advised to lead "demonstrators into clashes with the authorities, to provoke riots or shootings, which lead to the killing of one or more persons, who will be seen as the martyrs; this situation should be taken advantage of immediately against the Government to create even bigger conflicts."[97] The manual also recommended "selective use of armed force for PSYOP [psychological operations] effect.... Carefully selected, planned targets—judges, police officials, tax collectors, etc.—may be removed for PSYOP effect in a UWOA [unconventional warfare operations area], but extensive precautions must insure [sic] that the people 'concur' in such an act by thorough explanatory canvassing among the affected populace before and after conduct of the mission."[98]

This was not the CIA's first Nicaraguan literary project. In 1983, the CIA paid to produce and distribute a comic book entitled "Freedom Fighter's Manual," a self-described "practical guide to liberate Nicaragua from oppression and misery by paralyzing the military-industrial complex of the traitorous Marxist state without having to use special tools and with minimal risk for the combatant."[99] The comic book urged readers to sabotage the Nicaraguan economy by calling in sick, goofing off on their jobs, throwing tools into sewers, leaving lights and water taps on, telephoning false hotel reservations, dropping typewriters, and stealing and hiding key documents (sage advice later followed by numerous high-ranking Reagan administration officials). The comic book also included detailed instructions on making Molotov cocktails, which, it suggested, could be thrown at fuel depots and police offices.[100]

At the time when news of the assassination manual leaked out, the contras had a sordid human rights record.[101] A human rights group, Americas Watch, accused the contras in early 1985 of atrocities against unarmed women and children as part of its "deliberate use of terror."[102] In March 1985, the International Human Rights Law Group submitted a report based on 145 sworn statements from Nicaraguans showing the contras guilty of "a pattern of brutality against largely unarmed civilians, including rape, torture, kidnappings, mutilation and other abuses."[103] The Marxist government was also up to its elbows in blood and oppression and may have killed more innocent people than did the contras.[104]

Reagan administration officials quickly conceded that the CIA manual was "clearly against the law" and violated Reagan's 1981 executive order banning political assassinations.[105] In the final presidential campaign debate, Reagan promised that "whoever is guilty [of preparing the manual], we will deal with that situation and they will be removed."[106] CIA director William Casey sang a different tune, insisting that the goal of the manual was to help guerillas be persuasive in "face-to-face communication"[107] and that the manual's "emphasis is on education, not on turning a town into a battlefield."[108] In a news conference the day after his reelection victory, Reagan dismissed the entire controversy as "much ado about nothing."[109] Reagan administration officials stressed that the manual did not specifically call for assassinations. However, as a confidential 1954 CIA assassination manual warned: "No assassination instructions should ever be written or recorded."[110]

A few weeks later, the White House announced that several "lower level" CIA employees were receiving letters of reprimand or suspensions for "poor judgment and lapses in oversight" because of the manual.[111] Word later leaked out that Casey blocked any punishment of the two senior CIA officials involved with producing and distributing the manual, including one who admitted he was "fully responsible" for the document. In closed testimony to a congressional committee, Casey declared: "There's no reason to discipline them for one little slipup."[112]

In an era when Reagan denounced terrorists as "uncivilized barbarians,"[113] U.S. government policies were not always overly enlightened. The CIA provided other helpful publications to its Latin American friends, including its 1983 torture instruction classic, "Human Resource Exploitation Training Manual." This CIA manual stressed that, when a "new safehouse is to be used as the interrogation site . . . the electric current should be known in advance, so that transformers or other modifying devices will be on hand if needed." An intelligence source later explained to the *Baltimore Sun:* "The CIA has acknowledged privately and informally in the past that this referred to the application of electric shocks to interrogation suspects."[114]

## A License to Kill

In late 1984 Reagan authorized the CIA to covertly train and equip antiterrorist operations/groups in the Middle East. The *Washington Post* later reported that Reagan signed an order on November 13, 1984 that was widely perceived by intelligence officials as a "license to kill"—providing U.S. agents with "go-anywhere, do-anything" authority, according to one former white House official.[115] The *Post* reported that "any actions under the orders would be 'deemed lawful' if conducted in 'good faith.'"

On March 8, 1985 a massive car bomb detonated near the Beirut suburban home of a radical Muslim leader, killing 80 people—mostly women and children—and injuring 200. The bomb failed to kill the Muslim cleric. Supporters of the cleric strung a giant "MADE IN USA" banner across the blast site.

A few weeks after the bombing, one U.S. government official bragged to the *Washington Post* that CIA and U.S. military training of antiterrorist units in Lebanon had "been very successful."[116] National Security Advisor Robert McFarlane, in a speech entitled "Terrorism and the Future of Free Society," announced: "We cannot and will not abstain from forcible action to prevent, preempt or respond to terrorist acts where conditions merit the use of force."[117]

In mid-May 1985 news broke in Washington that the car bomb attack had been carried out by people hired by a CIA-trained group of Lebanese intelligence personnel.[118] The news set off a firestorm of CIA denials and foreign denunciations. *Washington Post* reporter Bob Woodward later wrote that CIA director William Casey told him that he had arranged the bombing via the Saudi government.[119]

On June 14, 1985 two Arab terrorists hijacked a TWA flight out of Athens and forced it to land in Beirut. Robert Dean Stethem, a Navy seaman, was executed by the hijackers and his body dumped out of the airplane. The hijackers repeatedly declared they were striking to avenge the CIA-linked car bomb in Beirut.[120] One hijacker kept shouting "New Jersey! New Jersey!" at the terrified passengers, referring to the U.S. battleship *New Jersey,* which had rained down hundreds of 2000 pound shells on Lebanon the previous year. The U.S. bombardment killed an unknown number of civilians; Navy Secretary John Lehman had predicted the shelling would kill "the odd shepherd."[121] The hijackers demanded that Israel release 700-plus Muslims captured in Lebanon and taken to Israel. After Israel agreed to release many of the captives, the hijackers released the passengers and crew members, 17 days after the heavily televised drama began.

Shortly after the TWA hijacking ended, Reagan, in a speech to the American Bar Association, thundered that Americans "are not . . . going to tolerate intimidation, terror and outright acts of war against this nation and its people. And we are especially not going to tolerate these attacks from outlaw states run by the strangest collection of misfits, Looney Tunes and squalid criminals since the advent of the Third Reich. . . . There can be no place on Earth left where it is safe for these monsters to rest, or train, or practice their cruel and deadly skills. We must act together—or unilaterally, if necessary—to ensure that terrorists have no sanctuary, anywhere."[122]

On December 27, 1985 Arab gunmen attacked passengers outside El Al counters at the Rome and Vienna airports. Twenty people were killed, including five Americans. Reagan was furious, blaming Libyan leader Mohamar Qaddafi and denouncing him as the "mad dog of the Middle East."[123] Israeli defense minister Yitzhak Rabin announced that he believed that Abu Nidal was behind the airport attacks.[124] It was unclear who was responsible for the killings.[125]

On January 7, 1986 Reagan issued an executive order decreeing that Libya's actions and policies "constitute a threat to the national security and foreign policy of the United States."[126] Libya posed no threat to the mainland United States, though its forces had clashed repeatedly with the U.S. Navy when Qaddafi believed U.S. military exercises had violated Libya's territorial integrity. Reagan's executive order made sense only if any foreign leader who defied an American president was automatically a threat to national security.

In March 1986, U.S. and Libyan forces clashed again off the Libyan coast, with Libyan patrol boats getting hammered. On April 5, a bomb exploded in a West Berlin discotheque, killing 1 American soldier and wounding 50 others. U.S. officials stated that intelligence intercepts identified Qaddafi as the source of the attacks. Pentagon counterterrorism chief Neal Koch later noted that other circumstances leading to a U.S. attack on Libya included "the persistent and irritating posturing of Libyan strongman Moammar Gadhafi; growing public and congressional disenchantment with the Reagan administration's failure to deal with terrorism—especially Middle Eastern terrorism; intra-governmental pressures, with elements within the administration at war with each other; and finally, the fact that Libya was simply considered the easiest target among terrorist-supporting nations."[127]

On April 14, 1986 Reagan ordered the U.S. Air Force and Navy to attack Libya. He announced hours after the bombing began that the United States had launched strikes against the "terrorist facilities" and other "military assets" and headquarters of Qaddafi.[128] Reagan declared, "Self-defense is not only our right, it is our duty. It is the purpose behind . . . a mission fully consistent with Article 51 of the U.N. Charter."

One F-111 bomber dumped its load on a residential neighborhood, also damaging the French Embassy. Martin and Walcott noted in their history of terrorism in the 1980s: "The carnage in the Bin Ghashir neighborhood where four 2,000 pound bombs had fallen on residential streets was as ghastly as the scene of any terrorist attack—severed hands lying in the rubble, a father grieving over the body of his three-year-old child, exposed electrical wires crackling in pools of blood, water, and sewage."[129] The Pentagon postponed admitting responsibility for several days: "The weapons officer [aboard the F-111] had realized his error and reported it immediately, but Defense Secretary Weinberger would maintain for days that the damage could have been caused by spent antiaircraft missiles falling to earth."[130] Martin and Walcott noted: "Libya reported that 37 people had been killed and 93 injured. By that count, Reagan had killed more Libyans than Qaddafi had murdered Americans."[131] One F-111 crashed during the operation, resulting in two American deaths.

On the night of the attack Reagan proclaimed in a televised address: "The Libyan people are a decent people caught in the grip of a tyrant."[132] But, while the U.S. government insisted that the killing of civilians was an accident, a Voice of America broadcast that night warned the Libyan people: "The people of the U.S. bear Libya and its people no enmity or hatred. However, Colonel Qaddafi is your head of state. So long as Libyans obey his orders, then they must accept the consequences. Colonel Qaddafi is your tragic burden. The Libyan people are responsible for Colonel Qaddafi and his actions. If you permit Colonel Qaddafi to continue with the present conflict, then you must also share some collective responsibility for his actions."[133] When asked by a reporter whether Qaddafi was "losing his grip" on Libya, Defense Secretary Caspar Weinberger replied, "There may well be some of the people . . . unhappy with him who are trying to take matters into their own hands. In other words, people who have read the lesson that this attack was supposed to administer."[134] The U.S. portrayal of Qaddafi as a near all-powerful dictator—at the same time it did not hesitate to punish his victims for the sins of their leader—set precedents for the treatment of the Serbian and Iraqi people in the 1990s.

Many observers believed the attacks sought to kill Qaddafi, but the White House denied such an explicit goal. Seymour Hersh, writing in the *New York Times Magazine,* concluded that the raid targeted both Qaddafi and his family: "The notion of targeting Qaddafi's family, according to an involved National Security Council aide, originated with several senior CIA officers, who claimed that in Bedouin culture Qaddafi would be diminished as a leader if he could not protect his home. One aide recalls a CIA briefing in which it was argued that 'if you really get at Qaddafi's house—and by extension, his family—you've destroyed an important connection for the people in terms of loyalty.' . . . All eight of Qaddafi's children, as well as his wife Safiya, were hospitalized, suffering from shock and various injuries. His 15-month-old adopted daughter Hana died several hours after the raid."[135]

On the day after the bombing, Reagan announced: "Yesterday the United States won but a single engagement in the long battle against terrorism. We will not end that struggle until the free and decent people of this planet unite to eradicate the scourge of terror from the modern world."[136] A few days later, Reagan urged all nations to rally to the U.S. government's uncompromising war on terrorism: "These vicious, cowardly acts will, if we let them, erect a wall of fear around nations and neighborhoods. It will dampen the joy of travel, the flow of trade, the exchange of ideas." Reagan swore that there must be no "appeasement of evil . . . no sanctuary for terror,"[137] and thundered: "Terrorism undeterred will deflect the winds of freedom."[138]

In the days after the Libyan bombing, Reagan's approval rating hit 70 percent—an all-time high (except for the period after the assassination attempt by John Hinckley in 1981).[139] Terrorists responded to the American bombing by killing several British citizens in Lebanon, wounding an American in the Sudan, and attempting to blow up an El Al airliner. Reagan commented on those attacks: "I think it's a tragedy, but I think it's another example of the fact that terrorism is something that we have to deal with once and for all, all of us together." Reagan administration officials exulted in the bombing. State Department analyst Francis Fukuyama, who later won renown for his "End of History" thesis, bragged in 1987 that the U.S. handling of Libya was "one of the best planned out policies" of the Reagan administration.[140]

---

Especially after the bombing of Libya, terrorism was a good political issue for Reagan. On May 4, 1986 Reagan bragged: "The United States gives terrorists no rewards and no guarantees. We make no concessions; we make no deals."[141]

While Libya caught the most American wrath, many experts believed Iran had done far more to finance and equip international terrorists, including those who carried out the 1983 Beirut attack on U.S. Marines.

In late 1986, Reagan's war on terrorism exploded in a fireball of hypocrisy. News leaked that his National Security Advisor Robert McFarlane, along with National Security Council aide Oliver North and CIA agents, had traveled to Tehran to deliver a chocolate cake to the Speaker of the Iranian parliament—along with a planeload of U.S. antitank missiles and advanced military radar. The Iranians received several other planeloads of U.S. advanced weapons, with Israel as the intermediary. The Reagan administration sought Iran's cooperation in securing the release of four U.S. hostages in Lebanon. The administration at that time was heavily pressuring its allies to embargo arms sales to Iran because of its role in fomenting terrorism.

On November 13, 1986 Reagan denied the reports: "Our government has a firm policy not to capitulate to terrorist demands. That 'no concessions' policy remains in force, in spite of the wildly speculative and false stories about arms for hostages and alleged ransom payments. We did not—repeat—did not trade weapons or anything else for hostages nor will we."[142] On December 6, Reagan fudged, conceding that "mistakes were made" but stressing: "Let me just say it was not my intent to do business with Khomeini, to trade weapons for hostages, nor to undercut our policy of antiterrorism."[143] On January 30, 1987 the White House issued a statement: "To be sure, the linking of arms sales to the release of hostages at several points during this 15-month episode could be interpreted as a trade of arms for hostages, but this was not the policy approved by the President."[144] Investigators later discovered that Reagan did sign an order approving the arms sale for the "hostage rescue."[145]

The debacle became far more politically damaging after it was revealed that the proceeds from Iranian arms sales were laundered to purchase weapons for the Nicaraguan contras. Congress passed a law in 1984 prohibiting U.S. military support for the contras. The Reagan White House ignored the law.

At the end of December 1986 the *Los Angeles Times* proclaimed: "After six years of magic, President Reagan broke the spell. By deceiving the nation, he and those around him badly damaged his presidency."[146] In an initial interview with the Tower Commission, appointed by the president to investigate the debacle, Reagan indicated that he had approved the arms-for-hostage deal but later renounced his admission. In a subsequent written plea to the commission, Reagan sought to exonerate himself by invoking his own mental limits: "In trying to recall events that happened 18 months ago I'm afraid that I let myself be influenced by others' recollections, not my own. . . . I have no personal notes or records to help my recollection on this matter. The only honest answer is to state that try as I might, I cannot recall anything whatsoever about whether I approved an Israeli sale [of arms to Iran] in advance or whether I approved replenishment of Israeli stocks around August, 1985. My answer therefore and the simple truth is 'I don't remember—period.'"[147]

The White House staff was spooked by the specter of impeachment.[148] One Democratic Senate aide summarized the consensus of Democratic senators: "Impeach what? There's nothing left."[149] In his comments on the growing scandal, Reagan came across as confused and inept. Reagan went into such a tailspin after the crisis broke that his new chief of staff, Howard Baker, briefly examined invoking the Twenty-Fifth Amendment to remove Reagan from office because of medical unfitness.[150] Former National Security Advisor Robert McFarlane added to the drama when the former Marine Corps officer took an overdose of Valium in a failed suicide attempt.[151]

The Tower Commission report on the debacle concluded: "The arms-for-hostages trades rewarded a regime that clearly supported terrorism and hostage-taking."[152] Reagan signed off on providing arms to the Iranian government because of his obsession with the hostages in Lebanon. As Martin and Walcott noted, "The President was particularly vulnerable to the pressures of the hostage families because terrorism undercut his image as a strong and decisive leader."[153] A report by a joint congressional committee denounced the "pervasive dishonesty and inordinate secrecy" and "deception and disdain for the law" that characterized the operation.[154] Yet, in mid-1987, at a Washington press conference, Reagan sought to blame the media for any criticism he suffered from the debacle: "I know the damage that's been done to my credibility, but it has not been by anything that has been proven—quite the contrary. It has been the image that has been created by our own, particularly, Washington press corps in describing what took place."[155]

## Minor Misfire

In the wake of the Iranian arms debacle, the Reagan administration sent the U.S. Navy to patrol the Persian Gulf—in part to reassure Arab nations that the U.S. government was not siding with Iran in the Iraq-Iran War. On July 3, 1988, the USS *Vincennes,* the most advanced missile frigate in the U.S. Navy, shot down an Iranian Airbus A-300 flying from Iran to Dubai, killing all 290 passengers and crew on board. After the shootdown of the civilian airliner, *Newsweek* noted that, "the men of the *Vincennes* were all awarded combat-action ribbons. Commander Lustig, the air-warfare coordinator, even won the navy's Commendation Medal for 'heroic achievement,' for his 'ability to maintain his poise and confidence under fire,' enabling him to 'quickly and precisely complete the firing procedure.'"[156] Captain Will Rogers III received the Legion of Merit for his "outstanding service" as commander of the *Vincennes.* *Newsweek* noted that the incident was a "professional disgrace" for the U.S. Navy: "The navy's most expensive surface warship, designed to track and shoot down as many as 200 incoming missiles at once, had blown apart an innocent civilian airliner in its first time in combat." A Navy commission that investigated the incident scrupulously avoided discovering facts or asking questions that would impugn the official explanation. The U.S. government proceeded to lie about the position of the *Vincennes* when it launched its attack (claiming it was in international waters, when it was actually in Iranian territorial waters), claiming the *Vincennes* acted in self-defense (*Vincennes* was the aggressor against a handful of diddly speed boats), claiming the targeted plane was at a lower altitude and descending toward the *Vincennes* (it was higher and rising as would a commercial airliner), and claiming the Airbus was outside the established corridor for commercial flights (it was flying where it was supposed to fly).[157] Two other U.S. Navy ships correctly identified the Iranian plane as a civilian airliner before the shootdown. President Reagan issued a statement on the same day: "This is a terrible human tragedy. Our sympathy and condolences go out to the passengers, crew, and their families. . . . We deeply regret any loss of life."[158] The U.S. government eventually paid compensation both to the survivors and the Iranian government. Vice President George H.W. Bush, on the other hand, who was running for President at the time, declared when asked about the shootdown: "I will never apologize for the United States of America, I don't care what the facts are."[159] Bush went to the United Nations, where he defended the U.S. action by denouncing Iranian aggression. Bush falsely claimed, as *Newsweek* reported, "that the *Vincennes* had rushed to defend a merchantman under attack by Iran."

The U.S. government saw the incident as an accident that, after a few days of unpleasant news, could be swept in the dustbin. The *New York Times* noted in an article ten years after the attack: "For the Iranians, the shootdown still represents one of the most heinous entries on the list of U.S. 'crimes' against their country in the last 50 years—one that became even more monstrous in their eyes when two years later the U.S. Navy decorated two of the vessel's commanders instead of punishing them immediately."[160] Iranian officials continued to denounce the shootdown as "an act of state terrorism."[161]

---

By the Fall of 1988, the war on terrorism was again politically profitable for Republicans. Reagan declared at a Republican Party fundraiser in Boca Raton, Florida, on September 23, 1988: "We know that the menace of terrorism must be challenged when and where it appears. And the history books will say that on April 14, 1986, we sent the terrorists in Libya a message. The message was: You can run, but you can't hide."[162] In stump speeches around the country during the election campaign, Reagan denounced the Democratic Party because "they opposed the raid on terrorist Libya."[163] Reagan was chirping along as if the Iran-Contra scandal never occurred.

On December 16, 1988, barely a month before the end of his final term, Reagan bragged to a student audience: "We adopted a policy of complete resistance to terrorism: no recognition of a country that supported it. . . . When we had the irrefutable proof that Qaddafi of Libya had been responsible for terrorism that took the lives of a number of people at an airport in Europe, including some Americans—we responded. And I'm going to knock on wood—just one more line on that. Since that response, there has been no Libyan terrorist move against any American target."[164]

Five days later, a bomb exploded in a suitcase on Pan Am Flight 103 flying over Lockerbie, Scotland, killing 271 people—including 189 Americans. The U.S. embassy in Helsinki, Finland, received an anonymous telephone warning beforehand that a Pan Am flight out of Frankfurt, Germany, would be bombed before Christmas.[165] Pan Am 103 originated from Frankfurt. Though the warning was not publicly disclosed, it was posted in staff-only areas in U.S. embassies throughout Europe and may have helped some U.S. government employees avoid being killed in the attack.

A Libyan agent was eventually convicted for his role in the bombing. Robert Gates, CIA director under the first George Bush, concluded that "the Libyan bombing of Pan Am 103 in 1988 was in retaliation for the 1986 bombing attack on Libya."[166] As for Reagan's 1986 triumph over Qaddafi, Pentagon counterterrorism chief Neal Koch observed: "Qaddafi barely skipped a beat, changing the communications system that had led to the discovery of his involvement in the Berlin bombings, and enlisting a more competent group of surrogates to continue his actions."[167]

Though Reagan spent his entire time in office warring against terrorism, far more American civilians died in terrorist attacks at the end of his reign than at the beginning. Koch summed up the Reagan record: "The American record in dealing with terrorism has been marked variously by indifference, indecision, vacillation, venality and incompetence."[168] Yet terrorism lost none of its political value as a hobgoblin. The Reagan administration almost totally escaped responsibility for its failures to deliver promised protection to Americans. Now, almost 15 years after Reagan left office, his chroniclers rarely address the failure of an initiative that was, after his successful campaign to quash the Soviet Union, his highest foreign policy goal.

# CHAPTER THREE

# Blundering to 9/11

On November 5, 1990, Rabbi Meir Kahane was giving a speech (characterized by the *Washington Post* as "an anti-Arab diatribe")[1] to the Zionists Emergency Evacuation Rescue Operation at the New York Marriot Eastside Hotel.[2] Kahane was the founder of the Jewish Defense League (JDL), an organization that carried out dozens of bombings and assaults in the United States against foreign embassies, banks, and Jewish organizations considered insufficiently militant. JDL members attempted to hijack an Arab airliner at John F. Kennedy International Airport, and Kahane urged his followers to "kidnap a Soviet diplomat in the U.S." and to "blow up the vacant Iraqi Embassy in Washington." A report on Kahane by the Anti-Defamation League observed: "Kahane consistently preached a radical form of Jewish nationalism which reflects racism, violence and political extremism. Kahane's political ideology . . . centered on rejecting any notion of compromise between Jews and non-Jews in America, and specifically Jews and Arabs in Israel."[3] Kahane vigorously advocated forcible expulsion of all Arabs from Israel and the Occupied Territories. Kahane explained: "I want to remove the Arabs of Israel because I do not want to kill them every week as they grow and riot."[4] When he was elected to the Knesset, the Israeli parliament, in 1984, his supporters had chanted: "Death to the Arabs!"[5] The Knesset subsequently banned Kahane's party for "inciting racism" and "endangering security."[6]

At the end of his speech on that November 1990 night, El Sayyid Nosair, a burly 36-year-old Egyptian immigrant, walked up to Kahane, pulled out a .357, and fatally shot him in the neck. Nosair was captured a few blocks away after he was wounded in a shootout with an alert Postal Service policeman.

Nosair was part of a cabal of Muslims filled with intense hatred toward Israel and the Egyptian government of Hosni Mubarak. When police searched his residence, they carried off 47 boxes of documents, paramilitary manuals, maps, and diagrams of buildings (including the World Trade Center). But, as the congressional Joint Intelligence Committee staff report on federal failures before 9/11 noted in September 2002, "the NYPD and the District Attorney's office resisted attempts to label the Kahane assassination a 'conspiracy' despite the apparent links to a broader network of radicals. Instead, these organizations reportedly wanted the appearance of speedy justice and a quick resolution to a volatile situation. By arresting Nosair, they felt they had accomplished both."[7] An FBI agent informed the congressional investigators that Nosair's legal defense was financed by Osama bin Laden.[8]

The trial of "lone gunman" Nosair, beginning in late 1991, was "marked by rioting outside the courthouse, death threats against the judge and lawyers, calls for 'blood' revenge against the defendant and cries of 'Death to Jews!' from his Moslem supporters."[9] A small band of Muslims paced the sidewalks each day in front of the court, denouncing Israel, the United States, and the supposed persecution of Nosair. As a *Los Angeles Times* July 4, 1993 article, headlined "N.Y. Trial in Rabbi's Death Planted an Explosive Seed" observed: "Out of those loud demonstrations of contempt for the U.S. judicial system would emerge what authorities now say was a clandestine cell of terrorists who conspired to set off the World Trade Center bomb blast, plotted an unparalleled wave of attacks on U.S. landmarks and political figures and shattered America's image of invulnerability to terrorism."[10] Terrorism expert Brian Jenkins noted that the Nosair trial "was a catalyst" for subsequent terrorist action.[11]

The FBI placed an informant named Emad Salem, a 43-year-old former Egyptian military officer, in the midst of the Muslim protestors. Salem insinuated himself and became the bodyguard for Sheik Abdul Rahman, a radical Muslim cleric who preached that "Muslims must kill the enemies of Allah, in every way and everywhere, in order to liberate themselves from the grandchildren of the pigs and apes who are educated at the table of 'Zionists, Communists and Imperialists."[12] The Sheik had been heavily subsidized by the U.S. government while in Pakistan in the late 1980s helping to inspire Muslims to fight the Soviets in Afghanistan.

Legendary leftist attorney William Kunstler became Nosair's lawyer. *National Law Journal* noted that Kunstler "originally planned to base his defense on a claim of not guilty by reason of 'temporary insanity.'"[13] Though the evidence that Nosair killed Kahane was stark, bizarrely, the jury found him not guilty on the murder charge but guilty of a firearms charge—that is, possessing the murder weapon. Judge Alvin Schlesinger denounced the verdict as "devoid of common sense and logic" and Anti-Defamation League chief Abraham Foxman called for "an independent inquiry into jury deliberations."[14] Schlesinger sentenced Nosair to 22 years in prison.

After the trial, Salem continued his work as an FBI informant, receiving $500 a week, plus expenses.[15] Shortly after Nosair was convicted, Salem began meeting regularly with other members of the group of hard-line Muslims who coalesced during the Kahane trial. In mid-1992, Salem repeatedly warned the FBI that the Muslim group was planning to carry off a catastrophic bombing in New York City.[16] FBI supervisors were convinced Salem was concocting tall tales and fired him.

On February 26, 1993, a 1,200-pound bomb in a van exploded in the parking garage beneath the World Trade Center. This was the most destructive terrorist attack carried out on United States soil up to that time, killing six people, injuring over a thousand, and causing half a billion dollars in damage. If the van had been parked a few feet closer to one of the pillars, it could have collapsed an entire tower of the Trade Center, killing tens of thousands.

An Immigration and Naturalization Service snafu contributed to the success of the bombing. One of the key plotters, Ramzi Ahmed Yousef, was stopped at JFK International Airport in September 1992 after an INS inspector recognized that his Iraqi passport was a fraud. Yousef applied for asylum. Because the nearby "holding facility" the INS used for illegal immigrants was full, the INS permitted Yousef to enter the United States.[17] Yousef slipped out of the United States immediately after the bombing. (A 1998 ABC News analysis noted, "Yousef was living in a guest house in Pakistan paid for by bin Laden at the time of his capture—a connection that led the FBI to investigate whether bin Laden was also the mysterious source of money behind the bombing."[18])

The case was quickly cracked when Mohammad Salameh, one of the bombers, repeatedly went to the Ryder rental office in Jersey City and demanded that Ryder refund his $400 deposit for the van, which he claimed had been stolen. Law enforcement agents had already determined from fragments at the World Trade Center that the van was the bomb delivery device. After Salameh was arrested, the FBI quickly snared other plotters. *Time* noted that the FBI "looked supremely capable in speedily rounding up suspects in the World Trade Center bombing."[19] Assistant U.S. Attorney Andrew McCarthy later bragged to a New York jury that the first World Trade Center attack was one of the FBI's finest hours: "To the rest of the world out there, the explosion in all its tragedy was actually a high-water mark for the FBI."[20]

Shortly after the bombing, the *New York Times* reported that FBI agents had been monitoring two mosques in the New York City area, as well as the Sheik Omar Abdul Rahman, though "federal guidelines had limited their ability to tail them or conduct other close surveillance. Nothing suggesting the purchase of explosives or the assembling of a bomb was detected, the officials said. Even close surveillance might not have picked up a surreptitious act, they said."[21] A few months after the attack, FBI director William Sessions declared: "Based on what was known to us at the time, we have no reason to believe we could have prevented the bombing of the World Trade Center."[22]

The FBI initially appeared to have a strong case, buttressed largely by evidence provided by informant Emad Salem. In July 1993, the media learned that Salem had been inside the conspiracy a year before the attack.[23] Rep. Charles Schumer (D-NY), chairman of the House Subcommittee on Crime and Criminal Justice, complained to FBI director Sessions that the FBI's failure to act on Salem's information could represent "an extraordinarily disturbing development in this case—and for counter-terrorism in general."[24]

After the bombing, the FBI quickly rehired Salem and promised to pay him a million dollars to develop evidence of additional terrorist plots. Because Salem did not trust the government to pay up, he secretly recorded his conversations with FBI agents. In August, as the case was heading for trial, news leaked that Salem had made tapes of over a hundred hours of his conversations with FBI agents and handlers.[25] The tape transcripts were not helpful to the prosecution.

In a call to an FBI agent shortly after the bombing, Salem complained that "we was start already building the bomb, which is went off in the World Trade Center. It was built, uh, uh, uh, supervising, supervision from the Bureau [FBI] and the DA [district attorney] and we was all informed about it. And we know that the bomb start to be built. By who? By your confidential informant. What a wonderful great case. And then he [the FBI supervisor] put his head in the sand and said, oh no, no, no that's not true, he is a son of a bitch, okay."[26] After the bombing, Salem anguished to one FBI agent: "You were informed. Everything is ready. The day and the time. Boom. Lock them up and that's that. That's why I feel so bad."[27] On another tape, Salem asked an FBI agent: "Do you deny your supervisor is the main reason of bombing the World Trade Center?" The agent did not deny Salem's charge.[28] Shortly after the bombing FBI agent Nancy Floyd confided to Salem that her supervisors had botched the case: "I felt that the people on the squad, that they didn't have a clue of how to operate things. That the supervisors didn't know what was going on. That they hadn't taken the time to learn the history."[29] It was never clear how much Salem instigated the bombing, as opposed to simply reporting on the plot to his FBI controllers.

Before the bombing, Salem offered to do a switcheroo on the bombers, substituting a harmless powder for the deadly explosives and thereby preventing any potential catastrophe. The FBI spurned his offer.[30] The *New York Times* October 28, 1993 article with this revelation was headlined "Tapes Depict Proposal to Thwart Bomb Used in Trade Center Blast."[31] Salem complained to one FBI agent that an FBI supervisor "requested to make me to testify [in public] and if he didn't push for that, we'll be going building the bomb with a phony powder and grabbing the people who was involved in it. But . . . we didn't do that."[32]

Salem was not the only person on the inside whom the FBI could have used to stop the attack. As *Newsday* reported on October 29, 1993:

> In addition to Salem, *New York Newsday* has learned that the FBI had a second confidential informant who infiltrated the Jersey City mosque where the sheik preached. According to law-enforcement sources, two months before the Feb. 26 Trade Center bombing, the informant was on a military-style training exercise in a New Jersey park with other suspects when he was asked to obtain dynamite for an attack. After the informant told FBI officials, they met for nearly an entire day to consider providing the suspects with inoperative, counterfeit dynamite. But, to avoid the possibility of an entrapment charge, FBI officials instead pulled the informant off the assignment the next day, sources said.
>
> "Instead of trying to stop it they just waited for it to happen, then swooped in and arrested everyone," said an investigator. "It was incredible."[33]

The FBI was also embarrassed by the contents of the 47 boxes it had seized from Nosair and left in storage for over two years. The boxes were ignored in part because no one at the New York FBI office spoke or read Arabic. One note discovered in the boxes declared: "We had to thoroughly demoralize the enemies of God. This is to be done by means of destroying and blowing up the towers that constitute the pillars of their civilization, such as the tourist attractions they're so proud of and the high buildings they're so proud of."[34] One law enforcement official told the *Los Angeles Times* in 1993 that the material "described major conspiracies and provided a road map to the bombing of the World Trade Center and the subsequent plot."[35] Ariel Cohen of the Heritage Foundation observed that "when the translation was finally completed, it was so poorly done that the name al Qaida, was mangled and wound up being interpreted simply as 'the basis.' As a result, FBI agents completely failed to recognize it."[36] Bin Laden formed Al Qaeda in 1989 in Afghanistan, where he had been fighting (with CIA aid) the Soviet Army since the early 1980s. Al Qaeda shifted to Sudan in 1991;[37] by late 1992, bin Laden was hatching schemes to kill American soldiers heading toward Somalia or stationed in Saudi Arabia.

The FBI received far more credit for solving the first World Trade Center bombing than it received blame for the fact that its informant may have helped cause the bombing. In the wake of the FBI's debacle, there were no oversight hearings or investigations by Congress to find out where the feds went wrong. Instead, the FBI was riding high on the laurels of its new director, Louis Freeh, and was still collecting kudos on Capitol Hill for its decisive solution to the Branch Davidian problem at Waco.[38]

Despite the fact that Muslim terrorists came within a few feet of killing thousands of Americans, federal agencies subsequently failed to take seriously the risk of more such attacks. The 2002 congressional report into pre–9/11 failures observed: "The first attack on the World Trade Center was an unambiguous indication that a new form of terrorism—motivated by religious fanaticism and seeking mass casualties—was emerging and focused on America. . . . However, the strategic implications of this shift in lethality do not appear to have been fully recognized."[39]

---

Less than five months after the attack on the World Trade Center, the FBI proudly announced the arrest of eight people "for plotting to bomb a number of New York City landmarks, including the United Nations building and the Lincoln and Holland tunnels."[40] With Salem's encouragement, the eight suspects launched plans to throw the Big Apple into total chaos.[41] The *New York Times* summarized the U.S. government's case: "The prosecution has charged that the 1990 killing of Rabbi Meir Kahane and the 1993 bombing of the World Trade Center were also part of the same conspiracy, intended to punish the United States for its support of Israel."[42] The case went to trial in 1995 and ended in convictions on seditious conspiracy for Sheik Rahman and nine other men.[43]

## Planes as Bombs

In the wake of the World Trade Center bombing, many aspiring Muslim terrorists shifted their scheming towards using airplanes as weapons. As the congressional report noted:

In December 1994, Algerian Armed Islamic Group terrorists hijacked an Air France flight in Algiers and threatened to crash it into the Eiffel Tower. French authorities deceived the terrorists into thinking the plane did not have enough fuel to reach Paris and diverted it to Marseilles. A French anti-terrorist force stormed the plane and killed all four terrorists. . . .

In January 1996, the Intelligence Community obtained information concerning a planned suicide attack by individuals associated with Shaykh Omar Adb al-Rahman and a key al-Qa'ida operative. The plan was to fly to the United States from Afghanistan and attack the White House.

In October 1996, the Intelligence Community obtained information regarding an Iranian plot to hijack a Japanese plane over Israel and crash it into Tel Aviv. An individual would board the plane in the Far East. During the flight, he would commandeer the aircraft, order it to fly over Tel Aviv, and then crash the plane into the city.[44]

Project Bohinka—a plan to plant bombs on and hijack a dozen airliners coming from Asia to the United States on the same day—was the most ominous plot of the mid-1990s. The mastermind of the plot was Ramzi Ahmed Yousef. As the congressional report noted, "In January 1995, a Philippine National Police raid turned up materials in a Manila apartment indicating that three individuals— Ramzi Yousef, Abdul Murad and Khalid Shaykh Mohammad—planned, among other things, to crash an airplane into CIA headquarters. The Philippine National Police said that the same group was responsible for the bombing of a Philippine airliner on December 12, 1994."[45]

Yousef was arrested in Pakistan and quickly extradited to the United States, where he was tried, along with two others, in 1996 and convicted for conspiring to place bombs on a dozen planes, as well as for his role in placing a bomb that killed one person on a Philippine airliner. At the time of Yousef's trial, former CIA counterterrorism chief Vince Cannistraro characterized the plot as "extraordinarily ambitious, very complicated to bring off, and probably unparalleled by other terrorist operations that we know of."[46]

While the plan to use hijacked airplanes as bombs to attack CIA headquarters and other targets was a major portion of the Bohinka plot, federal prosecutors dropped that element when it came time to make final charges. The congressional report noted that its investigators had "located almost no references to the plan to crash a plane into CIA headquarters in the FBI's investigatory files on the case. FBI agents . . . confirmed this focus, stating that this case was about the plan to blow up 12 airliners and that the other aspects of the plot were not part of the criminal case and therefore not considered relevant."[47] As Sen. Richard Shelby (R-Al.), vice chairman of the Senate Intelligence Committee, later commented, "Because the CIA crash plot did not appear in the indictment, however, the FBI effectively forgot all about it." (A few days after the 9/11 attacks, a Philippine government investigator told the

*Washington Post:* "We told the Americans everything about Bohinka. Why didn't they pay attention?")[48]

On April 19, 1995 a truck bomb exploded outside the Murrah Federal Office Building in Oklahoma City, Oklahoma, killing 169 people and wounding hundreds of others. Though initial suspicion focused on Muslims, Timothy McVeigh was convicted in 1997 for the attack and executed in 2001. After the bombing the FBI redirected some of its counterterrorism efforts, shifting to targeting Americans—especially right-wingers and Christians. In 1999 the FBI unveiled Project Megiddo, warning that "the volatile mix of apocalyptic religious and conspiracy theories may produce violent acts aimed at precipitating the end of the world as prophesied in the Bible." (Megiddo is the name of "the hill where the apocalyptic battle of Armageddon is supposed to occur.")[49] The FBI warned that its Project Megiddo initiative "has revealed indicators of potential violent activity by extremists in this country. . . . Certain individuals . . . are acquiring weapons, storing food and clothing, raising funds through fraudulent means, procuring safe houses, preparing compounds, surveying potential targets and recruiting new converts."[50] A coalition of 32 conservative groups called for a congressional investigation of the FBI project, complaining that "only the 'right wing' is referred to and targeted in this report. There is no reference whatsoever to the political Left. . . . One walks away with the impression that members of the Religious Right in America are lunatics who are a danger to society."[51] John Whitehead, president of the Rutherford Institute, warned that the FBI report amounted to "religious profiling—targeting potentially dangerous persons based on their religious beliefs. The truth is that if Jesus Christ were alive today, He would in all likelihood be a target of Project Megiddo."[52]

After Iraq's Saddam Hussein invaded Kuwait in August 1990, President George H. W. Bush sought permission from the Saudi Arabian government to temporarily deploy U.S. troops in Saudi Arabia until Hussein could be defeated. Bush repeatedly promised that the United States would not make the bases permanent.[53] After the war with Iraq was completed, the U.S. government double-crossed the Saudis and kept its troops on Saudi territory. As University of Toronto professor Stephen Clarkson observed, "In defiling Moslem space with permanent military bases in Saudi Arabia, the United States became a greater insult to Koran-steeped fundamentalists than the USSR had ever been."[54] The troop deployment further inflamed Islamic fundamentalists with hatred of the United States. The U.S. military bases would increasingly become both a target and a propellant for terrorist attacks.

On November 13, 1995, a van packed with explosives exploded in Riyadh, Saudi Arabia, killing five Americans. Seven months later, on June 25, 1996, two

Muslims drove a fuel truck up to the perimeter of the parking lot about 80 feet from a U.S. Air Force barracks named Khobar Towers in the city of Dhahran, Saudi Arabia. The two men left the truck and jumped into a car, which sped away. American sentries on the barracks roof saw the danger and sought to sound the alarm. However, the U.S. forces had no operable warning alert system. The residents of the barracks had no evacuation plan, so the sentries went knocking door to door, urging occupants to exit the premise.[55] A massive explosion a few minutes later killed 19 American soldiers and wounded over 350. The CIA had warned that terrorists were surveilling the Khobar Towers site,[56] and an Air Force inspection a few months before the attack warned that the defenses against terrorist attacks were inadequate.

The subsequent Pentagon investigation searched and searched but could find no culpability. Defense Secretary William Perry insisted that no military officer deserved any blame for the American dead. In testimony to a congressional committee three months later, Perry announced: "To the extent that this tragedy resulted in the failure of leadership, that responsibility is mine and mine alone."[57] However, Perry did not resign, forfeit his pay, or ceremonially commit hari-kari: he simply claimed responsibility and assumed that everyone could go their merry way. Perry insisted that the military commanders "have served our country with enormous distinction and considerable sacrifice, and they deserve our gratitude, not our blame." Perry also revealed: "We now know that we face an unprecedented threat."

In December 1996, the Air Force effectively exonerated the general in charge of the housing complex wrecked by the terrorist bomb. Yet an earlier Pentagon inquiry concluded that, though the commanding general "had been warned that the housing would be vulnerable to a bomb-rigged truck outside the fenced compound, he failed to move the fence away from the building or relocate the troops."[58] The *New York Times* noted: "Many leading Democrats and Republicans have expressed outrage that none of the 10 officers responsible for safeguarding the troops in Saudi Arabia got even a mild reprimand, which would be censure enough to doom a career."[59] President Clinton reshuffled his cabinet after winning reelection in November 1996, and the new defense secretary, William Cohen, reopened the case and found Terryl Schwalier, the commander of the unit, at least partially culpable. Cohen punished Schwalier by denying him a promotion from Brigadier General to Major General.[60]

U.S. government officials believed that bin Laden was linked to both of the attacks on U.S. troops in Saudi Arabia, as well as other schemes to kill Americans. In 1996 the government of Sudan offered to seize bin Laden and turn him over to the U.S. government for prosecution. The Sudanese government wanted to patch up its deteriorating relations with the United States. Shortly before its offer to the U.S. government, the Sudanese government captured the notorious terrorist known as Carlos the Jackal and extradited him to France.[61] According to Sandy Berger, who was then deputy national security adviser, the Clinton administration rejected the offer in part because "the FBI did not believe we had enough evidence to indict bin Laden at that time, and therefore opposed bringing him to the United States."[62] Maj. Gen. Elfatih Erwa, the Sudanese defense minister, warned U.S. officials that if bin Laden was not taken into custody, he would go to Afghanistan. Erwa told the *Washington Post* shortly after 9/11 that the high-ranking U.S. officials replied: "'Let him' go to Afghanistan."[63] Timothy Carney, who was U.S. ambassador to the Sudan from 1995 to 1997, noted that shortly after bin Laden left the country, "Sudan gave U.S. authorities permission to photograph two terror camps. Washington failed to follow up."[64] High-ranking Sudanese government officials continually offered to provide information to Washington on terrorist operatives on its soil but the U.S. government spurned the offer. The information the Sudanese offered might have helped detect and prevent several major terrorist attacks on U.S. facilities and forces in Africa and the Mideast.[65]

Shortly after the Khobar Towers attack, Osama bin Laden "issued a public *fatwa*, or religious decree, authorizing attacks by his followers against Western military targets on the Arabian Peninsula. In February 1998, Usama Bin Ladin and four other extremists publicly issued another public fatwa expanding the 1996 fatwa to include U.S. military and civilian targets anywhere in the world. In a May 1998 press conference, Bin Ladin publicly discussed 'bringing the war home to America,'" the congressional report noted.[66]

## Operation Infinite Reach

On August 7, 1998 two trucks loaded with explosives detonated nearly simultaneously, wrecking U.S. embassies in Nairobi, Kenya, and Dar es Salaam, Tanzania.[67] Two hundred and twenty-four people were killed, including 12 Americans, and over four thousand were wounded (many left permanently blind). U.S. ambassador to Kenya Prudence Bushnell, who was wounded in the bomb attack, had repeatedly warned the State Department of the unreliable security at the U.S. embassy in Nairobi.[68] The State Department shrugged off her concerns. After the bombings of the U.S. embassy in Beirut in the early 1980s, Congress passed a law requiring safety upgrades for American embassies around the world. However, the law was often ignored. The 1998 embassy bombings were followed by the usual commission, which concluded, in the words of one official, that "there was a collective failure by several administrations and congresses over the past decades."[69] The State Department had failed to provide any training to embassy staff in Kenya and Tanzania on "how to react to a car or truck bomb."[70]

The U.S. government quickly concluded that the embassy attacks had been an Al Qaeda operation. Twelve days later the Clinton administration launched Operation Infinite Reach. In a failed attempted to kill bin Laden, scores of Tomahawk cruise missiles struck Al Qaeda terrorist training camps in Afghanistan. Thirteen cruise missiles launched from U.S. ships in the Red Sea destroyed the El Shifa factory in Khartoum, Sudan.

President Clinton announced that "our goal was to destroy, in Sudan, the factory with which bin Laden's network is associated."[71] Clinton declared that the attack on the "chemical weapons-related facility" was an "exercise of our inherent right of self-defense . . . to prevent and deter additional attacks by a clearly identified terrorist threat" and that the "terrorist-related facilities in Afghanistan and Sudan" were hit "because of the imminent threat they presented to our national security."[72]

In Washington press conferences on the day of the attack, National Security Advisor Sandy Berger continually referred to the "so-called pharmaceutical plant." When a "senior intelligence official" speaking at a Pentagon briefing was asked, "What is this pharmaceutical facility supposed to make?" he replied: "We have no evidence—or have seen no products, commercial products that are sold out of this facility. The facility also has a secured perimeter and it's patrolled by the Sudanese military."[73]

But the plant was actually wide open to visitors and had been visited by U.S. government officials, World Health Organization officials, and foreign diplomats in the months before the U.S. attack. There was no Sudanese military presence near the plant. On these key elements of the indictment of the factory, the President, the chief of the Central Intelligence Agency, the Secretary of Defense, and the Secretary of State acted with less "intelligence" than a tourist from Muscatine, Iowa, could have gathered in a two-minute stop at the factory during a 24-hour "highlights of Sudan" bus tour. Under Secretary of State Thomas Pickering declared: "It is important to know and understand that we have been aware for at least two years that there was a serious potential problem at this plant that was struck."[74] But the plant had been open for less than two years.

Earlier in 1998, El Shifa had been awarded (with U.S. government approval) a United Nations contract to ship a hundred thousand cartons of a veterinary antibiotic medicine to Iraq under a special exemption to the UN embargo on that country.[75] In the days after the attack, journalists reported that the factory grounds were littered with "melted packets of pain relievers and bottles of antibiotics."[76] Before the smoke had ceased rising from the rubble, it was undeniable that El Shifa was the largest pharmaceutical producer in the Sudan.

The factory was destroyed in part because when CIA whiz kids searched the Internet for information on it, the El Shifa website did not contain a list of drugs the factory manufactured. This supposedly proved the factory was a chemical weapons site that must be destroyed.[77]

Defense Secretary Cohen announced: "We do know that [bin Laden] has had some financial interests in contributing to the—this particular facility."[78] Salah Idris, a Saudi Arabian banker and industrialist, bought the plant five months before the U.S. destroyed it, but the U.S. government was unaware that the factory had changed hands. After Idris contacted the U.S. government to seek to correct its mistaken assumptions about bin Laden's ownership, the U.S. government responded by notifying the Bank of America to freeze $24 million in Idris's bank accounts in the United Kingdom under a U.S. regulation covering "*pending* investigations of interests of Specially Designated Terrorists."[79] U.S. government officials claimed to possess secret evidence linking Idris to bin Laden. Yet, though the freeze was justified based on suspicions that Idris was a terrorist financier, the U.S. government never bothered to officially list him as such.

Cohen announced that "the facility that was targeted in Khartoum produced the precursor chemicals that would allow the production of a type of VX nerve agent."[80] Administration officials stressed that the "only known use [of the precursor chemical discovered] is as a precursor ingredient in the nerve gas VX."[81] In reality, the precursor ingredient—known as EMPTA—is also used in pesticides.[82]

The Clinton administration's smoking gun was little more than a cupful of dirt that a "CIA operative" had scooped up in December 1997 across the street from the factory—60 feet from the factory entrance and on someone else's property.[83] The CIA did not bother to test the soil sample until July 1998.[84] Former CIA official Milt Bearden later observed: "Never before has a single soil sample prompted an act of war against a sovereign state."[85] The Clinton administration refused to reveal the test results from the sample, refused to disclose which lab had done the test, and refused to allow any outside organization to conduct the same test on the same sample.[86]

On the day of the bombing White House press spokesman Michael McCurry declared that "the president acted on a unanimous recommendation from his entire national security team."[87] However, an analysis by the State Department Bureau of Intelligence and Research before the bombing concluded that there was no evidence linking the factory to chemical weapons production. A

CIA analysis warned that the existing evidence on the factory was insufficient and called for further investigation. Attorney General Janet Reno opposed the attack because of insufficient evidence against bin Laden. Four of the five military chiefs of staff were not informed of the plans for the bombing until just before the attacks, and the Defense Intelligence Agency was kept completely out of the loop, as Seymour Hersh reported in the *New Yorker*.[88]

The Clinton administration possessed a much stronger case for attacking the terrorist training camps in Afghanistan than the factory in the Sudan. But, especially with a name like "Operation Infinite Reach," hitting only one country simply would not do. National Security Council official Richard Clarke later explained that since bin Laden showed his "global reach" by bombing U.S. embassies in two countries, President Clinton "obviously decided to attack in more than one place."[89]

In his August 20 announcement, Clinton declared: "Afghanistan and Sudan have been warned for years to stop harboring and supporting these terrorist groups. But countries that persistently host terrorists have no right to be safe havens."[90] Two weeks after the bombing, the Sudanese ambassador to the United States, Mahdi Ibrahim Mahammad, declared that in May 1998 he had "delivered a formal letter of invitation to a senior official in the Federal Bureau of Investigation, offering to establish a joint effort between our two countries to see the possibilities, to explore them, of working together against international terrorism." The United States scorned the Sudanese offer. Mahammad also noted that the government of the Sudan had cooperated with a U.S. request "to liquidate bin Laden's financial holdings." Mahammad was angry that the U.S. government blocked a Sudanese request for a UN investigation of the bombing: "When a country is bombed and immediately goes to the UN and asks for an inquiry, an independent, objective, fair inquiry about the nature of this facility, why shouldn't the UN immediately accept that? . . . Why should the U.S. hide away from this?"[91]

When State Department Under Secretary Pickering was asked why the U.S. government opposed a Sudanese request for an independent investigation headed by former President Jimmy Carter, Pickering replied: "I've just presented the evidence very clearly, I think, on why this was a target. I don't believe that an international investigative committee needs to have an additional role. The evidence, in our view, is clear and persuasive."[92] But the primary evidence presented was the assertion by a government official that the U.S. government possessed secret evidence—which, of course, it could not reveal.

The cruise missile attack came three days after President Clinton, in a deposition with Independent Counsel Ken Starr's legal team, finally admitted he had had an "inappropriate" relationship with White House intern Monica

Lewinsky. Clinton made a brief television address on August 17 during which he seemed nearly out of control with rage. Lewinsky was returning to the grand jury for additional testimony on the day that Clinton bombed Afghanistan and the Sudan—spurring the nickname "Monica's Missiles" for the attacks.[93]

In a speech eight days after the U.S. attack, Clinton bragged to an audience about how he had sacrificed himself to protect innocent Sudanese: "The night before we took action against the terrorist operations in Afghanistan and Sudan, I was here on this island [Martha's Vineyard], up until 2:30 in the morning, trying to make absolutely sure that at that chemical plant there was no night shift. . . . I didn't want some person, who was a nobody to me but who may have a family to feed and a life to live and probably had no earthly idea what else was going on there, to die needlessly."[94] (One factory watchman was killed and ten other people were injured in the attack.) But Clinton did not have a second thought about destroying the largest pharmaceutical factory in one of the poorest nations on Earth. The Sudanese, like many others in the Third World, cannot afford the more expensive drugs produced in Western countries. El Shifa was the largest producer of malaria tablets in Africa. In the months after the attack, Sudanese government officials blamed the U.S. attack for a severe malaria epidemic.[95]

Twelve days after the bombing, Defense Secretary Cohen "insisted that the incomplete intelligence was irrelevant to President Clinton's decision to destroy" the factory, the *New York Times* reported.[96] Cohen told reporters that the U.S. government "did not learn until at least three days after the attack on the plant that it made medicine." This raises questions about government officials' reading speeds, considering that the news was splashed all over the world's media within hours of the attack.[97]

Idris, the factory owner, hired one of the most respected law firms in Washington to file suit to have his assets unfrozen. On the day before the U.S. government was obliged to respond to his claims in federal court, it threw in the towel and permitted Idris to reclaim his $24 million. When Idris filed a second lawsuit to receive compensation for the destruction of his factory, the U.S. government effectively invoked sovereign immunity, refusing its permission to the lawsuit and thereby eliminating any chance for recompense.

Regardless of how many times the Clinton administration adjusted its rationale for the Sudan bombing, everyone was obliged to accept that the latest version was the truth, the whole truth, and nothing but the truth—pending revision.[98] And while Clinton never tired of traveling the country and the world to officially apologize for the past sins of the U.S. government (ranging from the African slave trade to the Tuskegee syphilis experiments), he never had a contrite word for the Sudan.

The U.S. attack on the Sudanese factory exemplified a fatal mixture of bad intelligence and crass politics. When the operation turned out to be a fiasco, there was a total evasion of responsibility. Instead, the Clinton administration preferred to repeat banalities about the evil of terrorists. Clinton portrayed the destruction of the factory as a triumph of American idealism: "Terrorists must have no doubt that in the face of their threats, America will protect its citizens and will continue to lead the world's fight for peace, freedom and security. . . . America is and will remain a target of terrorists precisely because . . . we act to advance peace, democracy, and basic human values; because we're the most open society on Earth."[99] Despite the lofty rhetoric, Clinton's action, at best, did nothing more than protect Americans from Sudanese horse pills.

That Clinton shot at and missed bin Laden in the wake of the 1998 embassy bombings may have been the best thing that ever happened to bin Laden. At the time of the embassy bombings the Taliban were on the verge of expelling bin Laden from Afghanistan; they considered him to be a rude, trouble-making, publicity-hungry guest. But, as a *Wall Street Journal* analysis concluded, the U.S. retaliation "turned Mr. bin Laden into a cult figure among Islamic radicals, made Afghanistan a rallying point for defiance of America and shut off Taliban discussion of expelling the militants. It also helped convince Mr. bin Laden that goading America to anger could help his cause, not hurt it."[100] The *New York Times* concurred, noting that the failed U.S. counterstrike converted bin Laden into a "hero" and a "revered figure" among many Muslims.[101]

By late 1998, evidence was pouring in of a new threat to the U.S. mainland. A December 1, 1998 CIA assessment of Osama bin Ladin warned that he "is actively planning against U.S. targets. . . . Multiple reports indicate UBL is keenly interested in striking the U.S. on its own soil. . . . Al Qaeda is recruiting operatives for attacks in the U.S. but has not yet identified potential targets."[102] On December 4, 1998, CIA director George Tenet sent a memo informing his top deputies: "We must now enter a new phase in our effort against Bin Ladin. . . . We are at war . . . I want no resources or people spared in this effort, either inside CIA or the Community."[103] However, the CIA made few changes to its operations and almost no one in the FBI was informed that the CIA declared war on bin Ladin.

A 1999 Library of Congress report for the National Intelligence Council entitled "The Sociology and Psychology of Terrorism: Who Becomes a Terrorist and Why?" warned that "Al Qaeda's expected retaliation for the U.S. cruise missile attack against Al Qaeda's training facilities in Afghanistan on Aug. 20, 1998, could take several forms of terrorist attack in the nation's capital. . . . Suicide bomber[s] belonging to Al Qaeda's martyrdom Battalion could crash-land an aircraft packed with high explosives into the Pentagon, the headquarters of the [CIA] or the White House." The study concluded: "The new generation of Islamic terrorists . . . are well educated and motivated by their religious ideologies. The religiously motivated terrorists are more dangerous than the politically motivated terrorists because they are the ones most likely to develop and use weapons of mass destruction in pursuit of their messianic or apocalyptic visions."[104] This prophetic report was ignored.

As December 31, 1999 approached, the intelligence community feared that the terrorists might use the arrival of a new Millennium to launch attacks. On December 13, 1999 U.S. Customs inspector Diane Dean, on duty at the border crossing at Port Angeles, Washington, spotted a nervous-looking Arab arriving on a car ferry from Canada. After Customs agents began questioning Ahmed Ressam, he took off running but was quickly apprehended. His vehicle contained 134 pounds of explosives.[105] He was convicted in early 2001 of conspiring to bomb Los Angeles International Airport. The congressional report noted that Ressam's arrest "should have dispelled doubts that al-Qa'ida and its sympathizers sought to operate on U.S. soil, even though most of the masterminds remained overseas."[106]

## Another "Lesson to be Learned"

On October 12, 2000, two smiling Arabs piloted a small boat up to the hull of the USS *Cole*, one of the Navy's newest and most advanced destroyers, which was refueling in the harbor of Aden, Yemen. Moments after sailors waved to the men in the boat, a massive explosion ripped a 40-foot hole in the side of the *Cole*, almost sinking the ship. Seventeen sailors were killed and 39 others wounded.

Yemen was known to be a hotbed of terrorist activity and an Al Qaeda base. The *New York Times* noted: "Yemen was considered insecure enough that the American Embassy there was closed as a security precaution on the day the *Cole* stopped to refuel."[107] Yet the *Cole* was not on maximum alert when it entered the harbor. A *Newsday* investigation revealed: "Three weeks before the attack, the *Cole* was warned that the Saudi accused terrorist Osama bin Laden was planning to assault a U.S. warship with a small boat loaded with explosives. But senior Navy officers thought the warning applied only to the Mediterranean, and no special security precautions were ordered for the *Cole*."[108] The attack on October 12 followed "almost exactly the scenario outlined in a still-classified intelligence message" (based on warnings from Israeli intelligence) sent to *Cole* commander Kirk Lipphold a month earlier.

An investigation by the Navy's Fifth Fleet concluded that the *Cole* commander failed to carry out almost half of the 61 force-protection measures required
to defend Navy ships against terrorists. The *Cole* did not have a single "Arabic
speaker aboard when it pulled into the Yemeni port of Aden to refuel."[109] The
*Cole* neglected almost a dozen "force protection measures" that might have
stopped the attack, including failing to operate "a system of verifying the au-
thenticity of small boats approaching the warship" and failing to have "fire hoses
ready to spray at boats that didn't properly identify themselves and wouldn't withdraw."[110] Vice Admiral C. W. Moore Jr., commander of naval forces in the Middle East, noted: "The watch was not briefed on the plan or their responsibilities,
the bridge was not manned, service boats were not closely controlled, and there
was little thought as to how to respond to unauthorized craft being alongside."[111]

The initial proposal to sanction Commander Lipphold was overruled by
higher-ups and Pentagon brass. On January 9, 2001 at a press conference announcing the results of one report on the attack, Defense Secretary Cohen announced: "I think we owe it to the families of those who were wounded and
those who were lost that accountability at least be looked at."[112]

Ten days later, at 4 P.M. on January 19—in the final hours of the last full
day of the Clinton presidency—Cohen document-dumped a 1,600-page report
on the Washington press corps. The Navy report on the *Cole* attack concluded
that no senior officer was to blame; instead, there were only "lessons to be
learned."[113] Admiral Vern Clark, the chief of naval operations, announced:
"There is a collective responsibility. We all in the chain of command share responsibility for what happened on board USS *Cole*."[114] Secretary Cohen announced: "We have, in fact, identified accountability . . . all the way from the
central commander, right up through to the secretary of the Navy, the chairman
of the Joint Chiefs and myself."[115] And since everyone was responsible, no one
deserved even a wrist slap. Cohen asserted: "We were not complacent, but the
terrorists found new opportunities before we found new protections."[116] On an
upbeat note, Cohen added: "We have learned from this experience that we need
to be more vigorous."[117] Besides, as one Pentagon official explained to the *New
York Times:* "If you have a small boat carrying out a suicide attack, there's not a
lot you can do to stop it."[118]

## Tracking Nonchalantly

In the wake of the bombings of the U.S. embassies in Africa, the CIA vigorously
tracked suspected Al Qaeda operatives. When a "terrorism summit" was held in

Malaysia in January 2000, the CIA arranged to have the meeting's attendees surveilled by the Malaysian government.

Two of the 19 people who would hijack planes on September 11 were at the Malaysian summit. The CIA knew that Al Qaeda's Khalid al-Mihdhar and Nawaf al-Hazmi already possessed visas permitting them to travel to the United States. Yet the CIA failed to place their names on the "terrorist watch list," which would have alerted other federal agencies to the danger and blocked them from entering the United States. Sen. Shelby concluded that the CIA's negligence "allowed at least two such terrorists the opportunity to live, move, and prepare for the attacks without hindrance from the very federal officials whose job it is to find them. . . . The CIA seems to have concluded that the maintenance of its information monopoly was more important than stopping terrorists from entering or operating within the United States."[119]

On August 23, 2001 the CIA finally placed the names of al-Mihdhar and al-Hazmi on the terrorist watch list and notified the FBI that the two men were likely somewhere in the United States. As the congressional report noted, "Other potentially useful federal agencies were apparently not fully enlisted in that effort: representatives of the State Department, the FAA, and the INS all testified that, prior to September 11th, their agencies were not asked to utilize their own information databases as part of the effort to find al-Mihdhar and al-Hazmi. An FAA representative testified that he believes that, had the FAA been given the names of the two individuals, they would have 'picked them up in the reservations system.'"[120]

Once the CIA notified the FBI of the presence in the United States of two suspected terrorists, the FBI could have quickly run a few Internet searches to snare the San Diego residential address of al-Mihdhar. But this step was not taken until after the 9/11 attacks. Both al-Mihdhar and al-Hazmi rented rooms in the house of an FBI informant while they attended flight school in San Diego in 2000. An FBI case agent was aware that his informant had a couple of Saudis staying with him but had no curiosity about the guests.[121] Al-Mihdhar, who piloted the plane that crashed into the Pentagon, made multiple phone calls to a suspected terrorist facility in the Middle East.[122] (The Bush administration succeeded in prohibiting any testimony from the landlord-informant to the joint congressional committee investigating the 9/11 debacle.)

One New York–based FBI counterterrorism agent immediately recognized the danger posed by al-Mihdhar and al-Hazmi. He pleaded with FBI headquarters to be permitted to launch a criminal investigation of the two suspects, which would have permitted the use of far more resources in the hunt. FBI headquarters denied his request, insisting that it could not target the two men because the information regarding them came from the CIA, and it was considered more important to preserve the "wall" between criminal and intelligence investigations. The frustrated FBI agent emailed FBI headquarters on August 29, warning: "Whatever has happened to this—someday someone will die—and . . . the public will not understand why we were not more effective and throwing every resource we had at certain 'problems.' Let's hope the [FBI's] National Security Law Unit will stand behind their decisions then, especially since the biggest threat to us now, UBL [Osama bin Laden], is getting the most 'protection.'"[123]

In the weeks after the 9/11 attacks, FBI and CIA officials repeatedly implied that the hijackers had been so clever and had kept such a low profile while in the United States that it had been effectively impossible for the feds to detect either them or their plot. However, the congressional investigation concluded that "at least some of the hijackers were not as isolated during their time in the United States as has been previously suggested. Rather, they maintained a number of contacts both in the United States and abroad . . . with individuals who were known to the FBI, through either past or, at the time, ongoing FBI inquiries and investigations."[124]

## Planes as Bombs: Cascading Warnings

From the mid-1990s onward warnings piled up that terrorists could use airplanes to wreak havoc. A 1997 National Intelligence Estimates report on terrorism warned: "Civil aviation remains a particularly attractive target in light of the fear and publicity the downing of an airliner would evoke and the revelations last summer [referring to the TWA 800 crash] of the U.S. air transport sectors' vulnerabilities."[125]

As the 2002 congressional report noted,

In August 1998, the Intelligence Community obtained information that a group of unidentified Arabs planned to fly an explosive-laden plane from a foreign country into the World Trade Center.[126]

In September 1998, the Intelligence Community obtained information that Usama bin Ladin's next operation could possibly involve flying an aircraft loaded with explosives into a U.S. airport and detonating it.[127]

In 1998, the FBI's chief pilot in Oklahoma City drafted a memo expressing concern about the number of Middle Eastern flight students there and his belief that they could be planning a terrorist attack. Also in 1998, the FBI had received reporting that a terrorist organization planned to bring students to the United States to study aviation and that a member of that organization had frequently expressed an intention to target civil aviation in the United States. Yet another terrorist organization, in 1999, allegedly wanted to do the same thing, triggering a request from FBI headquarters to 24 field offices to investigate and determine the level of the threat. To date, our review has found that the field offices conducted little to no investigation in response to that request.[128]

In April 2000, the Intelligence Community obtained information regarding an alleged Bin Ladin plot to hijack a 747. The source, who was a "walk-in" to the FBI's Newark office, claimed that he had been to a training camp in Pakistan where he learned hijacking techniques and received arms training.[129] He also stated that he was supposed to meet five to six other individuals in the United States who would also participate in the plot. They were instructed to use all necessary force to take over the plane because there would be pilots among the hijacking team. The plan was to fly the plane to Afghanistan, and if they would not make it there, that they were to blow up the plane. Although the individual passed an FBI polygraph, the FBI was never able to verify any aspect of his story or identify his contacts in the United States.[130]

In April 2001, the Intelligence Community obtained information from a source with terrorist connections who speculated that bin Ladin would be interested in commercial pilots as potential terrorists. The source warned that the United States should not focus only on embassy bombings, that terrorists sought "spectacular and traumatic" attacks, and that the first World Trade Center bombing would be the type of attack that would be appealing.[131]

The congressional report noted: "Despite these reports, the Intelligence Community did not produce any specific assessments of the likelihood that terrorists would use airplanes as weapons."[132]

The Federal Aviation Reauthorization Act of 1996 required the FBI and Federal Aviation Administration "to conduct joint threat and vulnerability assessments of security at select 'high risk' U.S. airports and to provide Congress with an annual report." In a December 2000 report the FBI and FAA concluded: "FBI investigations confirm domestic and international terrorist groups operating within the U.S. but do not suggest evidence of plans to target domestic civil aviation. . . . While international terrorists have conducted attacks on U.S. soil, these acts represent anomalies in their traditional targeting which focuses on U.S. interests overseas."[133]

During the 1990s American flight training schools became a major draw for students from around the world. But some students set off alarm bells among their trainers. Hani Hanjour, who would pilot a Boeing 757 into the Pentagon, attended a flight school in Phoenix. His instructors contacted the FAA, concerned that Hanjour's English was so poor that he was unfit to be a pilot. (English is the international language of aviation.) An FAA inspector came to the school, sat next to Hanjour during classes, and then "offered to find Mr. Hanjour a language tutor."[134] Peggy Chevrette, manager of JetTech flight school in Phoenix, repeatedly contacted the FAA complaining that Hanjour was so inept that he should not be allowed to have the training. The FAA never responded to her concerns.[135] FAA officials also disregarded four separate warnings from a Minnesota flight school about suspect Muslim pilots.[136] Rep. Martin Sabo (D-Minn.) later commented that "the school was clearly more alert than federal officials."[137]

Kenneth Williams, a Phoenix-based FBI agent, sent a five-page memo to FBI headquarters, dated July 10, 2001, warning that an Osama bin Laden support network might be operating in Arizona and could be involved in training pilots to hijack airplanes. Williams urged action: "Phoenix believes that the F.B.I. should accumulate a listing of civil aviation universities/colleges around the country. F.B.I. field offices with these types of schools in their area should establish appropriate liaison. F.B.I. HQ should discuss this matter with other elements of the U.S. intelligence community and task the community for any information that supports Phoenix's suspicions."[138] (Two of the 9/11 hijackers received aviation training in Arizona.) FBI headquarters never responded to Williams' memo. The Phoenix memo "generated almost no interest. . . . No one gleaned from the FBI's own records that other's at the Bureau had previously expressed concerns about possible terrorists at U.S. flight education institutions," the congressional report noted.[139]

Throughout the summer of 2001 fears were rising about a pending terrorist catastrophe. In July, the CIA issued a confidential warning regarding Osama bin Laden: "Based on a review of all-source reporting over the last five months, we believe that UBL will launch a significant terrorist attack against U.S. and/or Israeli interests in the coming weeks. The attack will be spectacular and designed to inflict mass casualties against U.S. facilities or interests. Attack preparations have been made." The congressional investigation noted, "During the spring and summer of 2001 the Intelligence Community experienced a significant increase in information indicating that Bin Ladin and al-Qa'ida intended to strike against U.S. interests in the very near future."[140] On July 5, 2001, National Security Council counterterrorism chief Richard Clarke summoned a dozen top federal officials and warned them: "Something really spectacular is going to happen here, and it's going to happen soon."[141] Clarke "directed every counterterrorist office to cancel vacations, defer nonvital travel, put off scheduled exercises and place domestic rapid-response teams on much shorter alert," the *Washington Post* later reported.[142] (The state of high alert was rescinded a few weeks before the terrorist attack.)

In Eagan, Minnesota, instructors at the Pan Am International Flying Academy became suspicious of a new Arab student who, according to later news reports, wanted to learn how to fly a 747 jet in mid-air—but had no interest in learning how to land or take off. Zacarias Moussaoui, unlike almost all the other students, had no pilot's license or aviation background. But he showed up with $6,800 in cash and a passion to learn a few flying skills as quickly as possible. Moussaoui "was extremely interested in the operation of the plane's doors and control panel, which Pan Am found suspicious," the congressional report noted.[143] Moussaoui also pumped an instructor for information on how much fuel a 747 carried and how much damage it could do when it crashed. While Moussaoui claimed he was from France, he was unable or unwilling to converse with an instructor who sought to speak French with him.

After phoning the local FBI office four times, a flight instructor finally reached the right FBI agent,[144] relayed the suspicions on Moussaoui, and bluntly warned, "Do you realize that a 747 loaded with fuel can be used as a bomb?"[145] The next day, August 16, 2001, FBI agents came and, after ascertaining that Moussaoui's visa was expired, arrested him. The INS agreed to hold Moussaoui for seven to ten days—exploiting the flexibility in its regulations to protect the public from a potentially dangerous alien. When the agents asked to search his possessions and computer, Moussaoui adamantly refused.

Minnesota-based FBI agents notified the CIA and the FBI liaison in Paris, seeking further information; French intelligence sources reported that Moussaoui was "a known terrorist who had been on their watch list for three years."[146] The CIA alerted its overseas stations that Moussaoui was a "suspect airline suicide hijacker" apprehended at a Minnesota flight school who might be "involved in a larger plot to target airlines traveling from Europe to the United States."[147]

On August 18, Minneapolis agents sent a 26-page memo to headquarters warning that Moussaoui was acting "with others yet unknown" in a hijack conspiracy. Three days later, Minneapolis agents notified headquarters: "It is imperative that the USSS [Secret Service] be apprised of this threat potential indicated by the evidence. . . . If he seizes an aircraft flying from Heathrow to New York City, it will have the fuel on board to reach D.C."[148]

But when Minneapolis agents sought FBI headquarters' permission to request a search warrant to check out Moussaoui's belongings, an agent at the FBI's Radical Fundamentalist Unit refused permission. Instead, headquarters insisted that Minneapolis agents file a search warrant request under the Foreign Intelligence Surveillance Act (FISA), a 1978 law that created the Foreign Intelligence Surveillance Court to authorize searches of agents of foreign governments and foreign organizations. FISA sets a much lower, easier, standard for securing search warrants than is required by other federal courts. (The 1978 law was enacted to allow the federal government to surveil suspected foreign agents, creating a parallel legal system that would avoid undermining constitutional protections for Americans not suspected of foreign espionage.) FBI headquarters feared that if Minneapolis agents were rebuffed in their attempt to get a criminal warrant, it would be more difficult to get a FISA warrant. (FBI headquarters agents may have been leery of submitting a FISA request on Moussaoui in part because the FISA court, in a decision a few months earlier, berated the FBI for repeatedly submitting false or misleading statements in pursuit of search warrants.)[149]

FBI headquarters lawyers insisted that FISA required Minneapolis agents to prove that Moussaoui was linked to a foreign power before a search warrant could be issued. French intelligence had hinted that Moussaoui might be linked to Chechen rebels, and Minneapolis agents thought that might be sufficient to meet the FISA standard. However, because the Chechen rebels were not a recognized terrorist group under U.S. law at that time, FBI headquarters insisted that Minneapolis agents find evidence connecting the Chechens to a recognized terrorist group. The congressional report noted that "because of this misunderstanding, Minneapolis [FBI agents] spent the better part of three weeks trying to connect the Chechen group to al Qaeda."[150] This "wild goose chase" did nothing except buy time for the hijackers. The Senate Judiciary Committee concluded in an early 2003 report that "it is difficult to understand how the agents whose job included such a heavy FISA component could not have understood" the FISA law.[151]

An exasperated FBI supervisor in Minneapolis warned FBI headquarters Moussaoui could "take control of a plane and fly it into the World Trade Center."[152] On August 27 an agent in the FBI headquarters Radical Fundamentalist Unit complained that the Minnesota office was getting people "spun up" over Moussaoui.

As FBI agent Coleen Rowley later complained, the FBI headquarters supervisory special agent handling the Moussaoui case "seemed to have been consistently, almost deliberately thwarting the Minneapolis FBI agents' efforts."[153] The Senate Judiciary Committee noted: "Even after the attacks had commenced, FBI Headquarters discouraged Minneapolis from securing a criminal search warrant to examine Moussaoui's belongings, dismissing the coordinated attack on the World Trade Center and Pentagon as a coincidence."[154] The FBI headquarters agent who stonewalled the Moussaoui probe was promoted and received a presidential commendation after 9/11; none of the Minneapolis agents, nor the Phoenix agent who sounded an early alert, received a bonus, commendation, or promotion for their superior efforts. FBI agents in Minneapolis joked among themselves that some FBI headquarters agents "had to be spies or moles, like Robert Hanssen, who were actually working for Osama Bin Laden to have so undercut Minneapolis' effort."[155] Rowley wrote her memo in response to the stream of false and misleading statements coming out of FBI headquarters after 9/11 on Moussaoui; she informed FBI chief Robert Mueller, "I think your statements demonstrate a rush to judgment to protect the FBI at all costs."[156]

The FBI's Moussaoui debacle may have been the most costly delayed search in American history. Sen. Arlen Specter (R-Pa.), former chairman of the Senate Intelligence Committee, declared that the information in Moussaoui's possession provided a "veritable roadmap" to the 9/11 terrorist conspiracy. One document directly linked Moussaoui to the owner of the Malaysian condominium where the terrorism summit was held in January 2000.[157] Investigators also discovered in Moussaoui's notebook the German phone number of a top Al Qaeda operative and proof that Moussaoui had been wired $14,000 by a known terrorist contact "just two weeks before his arrest."[158]

## The Mirage of FBI Intelligence

The FBI budget for counterterrorism rose by almost 400 percent between 1994 and 2001—from $79 million to $372 million.[159] The number of FBI intelligence analysts increased by more than 350 percent from 1992 to 2000—from 224 to 994.[160] Yet, despite the 1993 World Trade Center attack, despite bin Laden's 1998 public proclamation to "bring the war to America," and despite the December 1999 arrest of an Al Qaeda–linked Muslim on his way to blow up Los Angeles International Airport, the FBI had only one employee doing strategic analysis of Al Qaeda's machinations on September 11, 2001.

Much of the increase in FBI "intelligence" was a mirage. Daniel Franklin, writing in the *American Prospect,* observed that FBI "intelligence resources were regularly 'reprogrammed' over to the criminal-investigative side. . . . Intelligence analysts were often removed from their counterterrorism responsibilities and used instead for criminal investigation or, even worse, as secretaries. . . . At the same time, the quality of analysis was hurt by a lowering of the standards governing who could become an analyst."[161] Robert Heibel, former FBI deputy chief of counterterrorism, observed that the analyst jobs became "a reward system for people's secretaries. . . . If you did a good job and you had typing ability and could communicate, you could get promoted to an intelligence analyst.

The system became bastardized."[162] Heibel noted that "when it comes to the correlation of the information and the analysis of the information for intelligence purposes, we have fallen down dismally."[163]

The FBI's ability to decipher terrorist plots was further dissipated by the agency's profound aversion toward modern technology. Between 1993 and 2001, Congress deluged the FBI with almost $2 billion to upgrade its computers. However, many FBI agents have eight-year-old computers that are incapable of searching the web or sending email. As the *Los Angeles Times* noted, "Investigations are still largely paper-driven, and many agents use dinosaur-era computers or even write reports longhand in this era of high-speed Pentium processors."[164] One FBI agent observed that the FBI ethos is that "real men don't type. The only thing a real agent needs is a notebook, a pen and gun, and with those three things you can conquer the world. That was the mind-set for a long time, and the computer revolution just passed us by because of it."[165] The FBI has 42 different databases with incompatible software; it is not possible to run a search in multiple databases. One FBI headquarters supervisor testified to Congress in September 2002 that the FBI's computer "system is very cumbersome, and people unfortunately have just become very frustrated with it, to the point where they have somewhat given up."[166]

Sen. Shelby concluded that the FBI "does not know what it knows, it has enormous difficulty analyzing information when it *can* find it, and it refuses to disseminate whatever analytical products its analysts might, nonetheless, happen to produce."[167] The FBI's electronic messaging system is so unreliable that many FBI personnel prefer to use email—but, since "most offices at the FBI *lack* a classified e-mail capability," internal communication is stifled. Sen. Shelby noted, "There are 68,000 outstanding and unassigned leads assigned to the counterterrorism division dating back to 1995. At the time of our inquiry, the FBI had no idea whether any of these leads had been assigned and dealt with outside the electronic system."[168]

The Senate Judiciary Committee concluded that when the terrorist threat was greatest, "the crucial information being collected by FBI agents in the field was disappearing into a black hole at Headquarters. . . . The FBI's failure to analyze and disseminate properly the intelligence data in the agency's possession rendered useless important work of some of its best field agents."[169] The congressional Joint Intelligence Committee report noted the same problem: "Although the FBI conducted many investigations, senior FBI officials and analysts did not accumulate these pieces into a larger picture. . . . The FBI was not able to gather intelligence from disparate cases nationwide to produce an overall assessment of al-Qa'ida's presence in the United States."[170] Sen. Shelby derided "the FBI's dismal recent history of disorganization and institutional incompetence in its national security work."[171]

The FBI was also slothful in keeping track of suspected terrorists and foreign agents. The Senate Judiciary Committee reported that the "the surveillance of existing targets of interest was often terminated, not because the facts no longer warranted surveillance, but because the application for extending FISA surveillance could not be completed in a timely manner. Thus, targets that represented a sufficient threat to national security that the [Justice] Department had sought, and a FISA Court judge had approved, a FISA warrant were allowed to break free of surveillance for no reason other than the FBI and DOJ's failure to complete and submit the proper paper work."[172]

The congressional investigation concluded that the FBI's "mixed record of attention contributed to the United States becoming, in effect, *a sanctuary for radical terrorists.*"[173] Former National Security Advisor Brent Scowcroft groused that "the safest place in the world for a terrorist to be is inside the United States, as long as they don't do something that trips them up against our laws, they can do pretty much all they want."[174] Deputy Secretary of Defense Paul Wolfowitz complained that "even worse than the [Afghanistan] training camps was the training that took place here in the United States and the planning that took place in Germany."[175]

## Chasing Everything Except Mass Killers

In the aftermath of 9/11, politicians scrambled to assure the American public that fighting terrorists had long been a top priority. However, between 1996 and 2001 federal investigative agencies referred more than a hundred times more drug cases to federal prosecutors than terrorist cases. Terrorism cases amounted to less than one-quarter of 1 percent of the nearly 700,000 criminal cases referred to federal prosecutors between 1996 and 2001, according to an analysis by the Transactional Records Access Clearinghouse (TRAC) at Syracuse University.[176] And prosecutors were more than twice as likely to fail to prosecute terrorist cases as to prosecute other alleged violations of federal law.

The federal government failed to convict more than 50 terrorists in any year prior to 2002. And the terrorists who did get nailed often escaped with less jail time than a two-time drunk driver. TRAC reported that most convicted international terrorists "received no prison time or one year or less. The median sentence—half got more, half got less—was ten months."[177] And much of the "terrorism" the feds prosecuted was ludicrous. Among the supposed terrorists were a tenant who impersonated an FBI agent in a call to his landlord protesting an eviction, an airline passenger who got drunk on a flight from China and demanded more liquor in an unruly fashion, and a guy who asked his shrink for medicine because voices were telling him to kill George W. Bush.[178]

Between 1981, when President Reagan first declared war on terrorism, and September 11, 2001, federal law enforcement resources skyrocketed. The total number of employees of the Justice Department tripled, to over 125,000. Yet in the wake of 9/11, during the 2002 joint congressional hearings, federal agents complained that their agencies were "overwhelmed" before 9/11. While agency resources skyrocketed, the criminalization of everyday life advanced even faster, creating nearly endless new targets for lawmen. In the 20 years before 9/11, Congress added over 150 new crimes to the federal statute book, and federal lawmen took over primary jurisdiction from state and local governments of environmental enforcement, many white-collar crimes, and health care fraud. As planes were smashing into the Pentagon and the World Trade Center, ten FBI agents were working a prostitution investigation in New Orleans. After a year's work and more than five thousand tapped calls, the FBI proudly announced the indictment of a dozen hookers and madams on conspiracy and racketeering charges. The FBI justified the federal investigation in part because some hookers crossed state lines to service clients.[179] George Washington University law professor Jonathan Turley quipped, "Only the FBI could go to the French Quarter and find only a dozen prostitutes after a year of investigation."

FBI agent Kenneth Williams told congressional investigators that "counterterrorism and counterintelligence have always been considered the 'bastard stepchild' of the FBI because these programs do not generate the statistics that other programs do, such as Violent Crimes/Major Offenders or drugs."[180] Former Phoenix FBI agent James Hauswirth declared that terrorism "has always been the lowest priority in the division; it still is the lowest priority in the division."[181]

Since 1981, federal spending on the drug war has increased almost tenfold. The FBI had over two thousand agents detailed to narcotics as of 9/11.[182] The FBI may have had a hundred times more agents devoted to fighting drugs than it had defending the United States against Al Qaeda. Even though CIA chief George Tenet formally declared war on Al Qaeda in 1998, the CIA had only five analysts assigned full time to bin Ladin's network worldwide at the time of the terrorist attack.[183] The CIA likely had scores more employees involved in the war on drugs than were analyzing Al Qaeda before 9/11.

In the wake of 9/11 a CIA agent, testifying anonymously to Congress, complained that "the lack of resources is critical" in the fight against terrorism. Yet, in the years before 9/11, Congress actually gave the CIA more dollars than the

CIA requested to fight terrorism, and the funding had increased "considerably" since the end of the Cold War.[184] (The CIA's budget is classified as a national security secret.) Sen. Shelby noted that "the CIA ended Fiscal Year 2001 with millions of dollars in counterterrorism money left *unspent.*"[185]

The congressional panel concluded: "Prior to September 11, the Intelligence Community's . . . quality of counterterrorism analysis was inconsistent, and many analysts were inexperienced, unqualified, under-trained, and without access to critical information." Though the threat from Muslim terrorists had been obvious for almost two decades, the congressional panel gingerly noted that "the Intelligence Community was not prepared to handle the challenge it faced in translating the volumes of foreign language counterterrorism intelligence it collected." Intelligence agencies had "a readiness level of only 30% in the most critical terrorism-related languages."[186] The federal government lacked any central counterterrorism database. Instead, numerous federal agencies were hoarding their own information, careful to prevent their bureaucratic rivals from seeing their scoops.

## Passionate Denials, Devoted Cover-up

The pervasive incompetence that permeated federal antiterrorism efforts before 9/11 was followed, immediately after the debacle, by pervasive mendacity. Suddenly, nobody knew nothing before 9/11—and besides, it was important for the nation to move forward, not to wallow in irrecoverable losses. The post 9/11 political exploitation of the attacks required a denial of prior knowledge and warnings. Administration officials scrambled to cover all of the government's failures in a shroud of patriotism.

On the day of the attacks, White House spokesman Ari Fleischer declared that President Bush knew of "no warnings" of terrorist attacks. On September 12, 2001 Secretary of State Colin Powell stated, "I have not seen any evidence that there was a specific signal that we missed." On September 14, 2001 FBI director Robert Mueller declared, "The fact that there were a number of individuals that happened to have received training at flight schools here is news, quite obviously. If we had understood that to be the case, we would have—perhaps one could have averted this."[187] A few days later Mueller announced: "There were no warning signs that I'm aware of that would indicate this type of operation in the country."[188] On September 16 Bush declared, "Never did anybody's thought process about how to protect America—did we ever think that the evildoers would fly not one but four commercial aircraft into precious U.S. targets.

Never."[189] In a January 2002 interview, Bush declared, "Never did we realize that the enemy was so well organized. They struck in a way that was unimaginable." In February 2002 congressional testimony, CIA chief Tenet vehemently denied that there had been any intelligence "failure" before 9/11 and asserted, "We are proud of our record."[190]

In May 2002 news leaked out about the memo from the Phoenix FBI agent and the Moussaoui warnings from the Minneapolis FBI agent. Americans also learned that on August 6, 2001, during a month-long "vacation" at his Texas ranch, Bush received a CIA briefing warning that bin Laden was determined "to bring the fight to America"[191]—and that Al Qaeda could hijack planes in the United States. (The White House continues to refuse to disclose the actual content of the briefing, insisting that "national security" would be imperiled if the American people learned what President Bush actually knew before the terrorist attack.) *Time* revealed: "After the strike came, White House sources concede, the Administration made a conscious decision not to disclose the August briefing, hoping that it would be discussed 'in context'—and months later—when congressional investigations into the attacks eventually got under way."[192]

As the "pure ignorance" defense unraveled, the White House launched a counteroffensive against critics. Bush whined to a college football team visiting the White House on May 16, 2002: "Washington is unfortunately the kind of place where second-guessing has become second nature."[193] Vice President Dick Cheney, speaking at a dinner of the New York Conservative Party, warned Democrats "to not seek political advantage by making incendiary suggestions . . . that the White House had advance information that would have prevented the tragic attacks of 9–11;"[194] Cheney declared that such comments were "thoroughly irresponsible and totally unworthy of national leaders in a time of war."[195] House Majority Leader Dick Armey (R-Tex.) denounced the criticism of the White House as "deplorable" and "unconscionable."[196] First Lady Laura Bush announced during a visit to Budapest: "I think it's sad to prey upon the emotions of people as if there were something we could have done to stop [the 9/11 hijackings] because that's just not the case."[197]

White House spokesman Ari Fleischer described September 11 as "a new type of attack that had not been foreseen."[198] National Security Advisor Condoleezza Rice held a press conference on May 16 to stomp proliferating doubts about the administration's credibility. She declared, "This government did everything that it could in a period in which the information was very generalized, in which there was nothing specific to which to react."[199] Rice stressed that the "president received a presidential daily briefing which was not a warning briefing, but an analytic report."[200] But the report Bush received on August 6, 2001, was headlined "Bin Laden Determined to Strike the United States in U.S." Apparently, as long as the president was not pre-notified of the specific names and addresses of the hijackers and the dates and flight numbers of their intended attacks, the administration could claim it received no warning. Rice insisted: "I don't think anybody could have predicted that these people . . . would try to use an airplane as a missile, a hijacked airplane as a missile."[201] Rice also stressed that the briefing that Bush received was only about "hijacking in the traditional sense." Yet a CIA analysis two months after the 9/11 attacks noted that "the idea of hijacking planes for suicide attacks had long been current in jihadist circles."[202] Tom Clancy's 1995 best-selling novel, *Debt of Honor,* featured a cover drawing of a 747 jetliner crashing into the U.S. Capitol; the plane's Japanese pilot was determined to avenge his family's losses from World War II. Also, two months before 9/11 the Italian government "closed airspace over Genoa and mounted antiaircraft batteries based on information that Islamic extremists were planning to use an airplane to kill President Bush" during a G-7 summit, the *Washington Post* reported.[203]

At the same time that administration officials scorned critics, Bush worked to derail a congressional proposal to create an independent panel to investigate how 9/11 happened. Administration officials also issued a barrage of warnings of new terrorist strikes: Vice President Cheney announced that another terrorist strike is "almost certain," Defense Secretary Rumsfeld declared that terrorists would "inevitably" acquire weapons of mass destruction, and Homeland Security director Tom Ridge revealed that additional terrorist attacks are "not a question of if, but a question of when."[204]

## Conclusion

At a time when the government failed abysmally and then lied, politicians succeeded in making "trust in government" the first duty of every citizen. If the Bush administration had not deceived the public regarding pre-9/11 warnings, fewer Americans would have cheered sharply increasing government power.

The Bush administration seems determined to cover-up government foreknowledge and foul-ups prior to 9/11 in perpetuity. The Joint Intelligence Committee completed its report in December 2002, but the Bush administration permitted the committee to release only 10 pages of its 450-page report. The rest of the report was suppressed because of "national security concerns." Some of the details in the report were justifiably kept under wraps. But, as Sen. Bob Graham, (D-Fla.), the chairman of the Senate Intelligence Committee, complained, "There's been a pattern in which information is provided on a classified basis, and then what is declassified are those sections of the report that are most advantageous to the administration."[205] The Bush administration abused its power—falsely invoking national security—to protect its reputation.

In the same week that the White House effectively censored almost the entire 450-page congressional report, Bush nominee Henry Kissinger resigned as chairman of the new "independent" commission that Congress mandated to investigate 9/11. Some commentators were surprised that Bush initially chose Kissinger as chairman, since Kissinger's record on open government was less than stellar during his years in high-ranking positions in the Nixon and Ford administrations. Bush announced on December 13, 2002: "My Administration will work quickly to select a new chairman whose mission will be to uncover every detail and learn every lesson of September 11, even as we act on what we have learned so far to better protect and defend America."[206] Yet Bush had already made it clear that he had no intention of permitting the American people to learn more details of the 9/11 debacle.

In late April 2003 controversy revived over the Bush administration's continuing efforts to suppress almost all of the report by the Joint Intelligence Committee investigation. Some intelligence officials even insisted on "reclassifying" as secret some of the information that had already been discussed in public hearings, such as the FBI Phoenix Memo.[207] The Bush administration also repeatedly erected barriers to prevent the members of the 9/11 commission from accessing classified information on government failings before the attacks. On May 13, Sen. Graham accused the Bush administration of engaging in a "coverup" and said that the report from the congressional investigation "has not been released because it is, frankly, embarrassing . . . embarrassing as to what happened before September 11th, but maybe even more so the fact that the lessons of September 11th are not being applied today to reduce the vulnerability of the American people." Graham warned: "There was information which the administration and its agencies knew before Sept. 11 that was not acted upon. That same information is available today. It's not being acted upon today."[208]

---

"September 11 was the devastating result of a catalogue of failures on behalf of our government and its agencies," said Kristen Breitweiser, whose husband was killed in the attack on the World Trade Center.[209] However, the congressional investigation concluded: "No one will ever know whether more extensive analytic efforts, fuller and more timely information sharing, or a greater focus on the connection between these events would have led to the unraveling of the

September 11 plot. But, it is at least a possibility that increased analysis, sharing and focus would have drawn greater attention to the growing potential for a major terrorist attack in the United States involving the aviation industry. This could have generated a heightened state of alert regarding such attacks and prompted more aggressive investigation, intelligence gathering and general awareness based on the information our Government did possess prior to September 11, 2001."[210]

The congressional report concluded with a warning about the high cost of keeping the American public in the dark: "Prior to September 11th, the U.S. intelligence and law enforcement communities were fighting a war against terrorism largely without the benefit of what some would call their most potent weapon in that effort: *an alert and committed American public.*"[211]

# CHAPTER FOUR

# Patriot Railroad
## Safety through Servility

The terrorists' success supposedly proved that the federal government needed more power over Americans and practically everyone else in the world. Within hours of the attacks, Attorney General John Ashcroft began pushing for legislation to increase federal power.[1] In his address to Congress on September 20 President Bush declared, "We will come together to give law enforcement the additional tools it needs to track down terror here at home."[2]

The U.S. Senate granted new powers to the Bush administration even before the administration formally requested a new arsenal. On Thursday, September 13, the Senate passed with no debate a bill entitled the "Combating Terrorism Act." Sen. Jon Kyl (R-Ariz.) declared: "We are in a race to the finish line with agents of terror. Will we enhance our security and defenses before they are able to strike again?"[3] By voice vote, the Senate unanimously approved a bill empowering federal prosecutors to authorize short-term wiretaps without a judge's approval and to permit the FBI to vacuum up millions of people's email with its Carnivore wiretap system. Judiciary Committee chairman Patrick Leahy (D-Vt.) protested: "Why don't we say what we are doing here? We are going to amend our wiretap laws so we can look into anybody's computers."[4] (Leahy may have been miffed that his committee would lose jurisdiction over the issue if it got rammed through on the floor of the Senate that night.)

But the Bush administration scorned the Senate's offering—since it sought far more power. Ashcroft also rebuffed House Judiciary Committee chairman James Sensenbrenner's offer to discuss legislative remedies in the first days after 9/11.[5] By the end of the week of the attacks, the Justice

Department had a hefty package ready for legislative canonization. On Saturday, September 15, Justice Department officials briefed Senate staffers on the Bush administration's antiterrorism legislative proposal. But the immigration section of the bill was missing.[6] Even though they only showed Senate staffers an unfinished draft, Justice Department officials still expected them to enthusiastically sign onto the deal. The immigration portion of the bill—entitled "Suspension of the Writ of Habeas Corpus"—would turn out to be the most controversial part.[7]

On the Sunday talk shows on September 16, Ashcroft portrayed the Justice Department as a helpless giant in the fight against terrorism. Ashcroft complained, "It's easier to investigate someone involved in illegal gambling schemes than it is to investigate someone involved in terrorism."[8] Ashcroft had been on the Senate Judiciary Committee for six years and was actively involved in the debate and enactment of the 1996 Antiterrorism and Effective Death Penalty Act. Thus, he bore some responsibility for the federal code on terrorism. But this was no time to stop and ask why the federal government feared gamblers more than terrorists before 9/11.

On Monday, September 17 Ashcroft demanded that Congress enact his Mobilization Against Terrorism Act (MATA) by the end of the week—even though his subordinates had not yet finished writing the bill. Ashcroft announced: "In the next few days, we intend to finalize a package of legislative measures that will be comprehensive. Areas covered include criminal justice, immigration, intelligence gathering and financial infrastructure. . . . Now, we will be working diligently over the next day or maybe two to finalize this comprehensive proposal, and we will call upon the Congress of the United States to enact these important antiterrorism measures this week."[9]

Ashcroft sought to have his bill enacted without any congressional hearings. Eventually, he compromised and agreed to appear for one hour each at House and Senate Judiciary Committee hearings.

The Bush administration's antiterrorism bill sought to give law enforcement *carte blanche* to imprison aliens in perpetuity without charges, to confiscate Americans' cash based on mere suspicion, and to intrude into almost every nook and cranny of people's lives. The Fourth Amendment of the Bill of Rights states, "The right of the people to be secure in their persons, houses, papers, and effects, against unreasonable searches and seizures, shall not be violated . . . and no Warrants shall issue, but upon probable cause, supported by Oath or affirmation, and particularly describing the place to be searched, and the persons or things to be seized." The prohibition of unreasonable searches is the key to the Fourth Amendment. The Bush bill sought to radically change the prevailing concept of a "reasonable" search. House Judiciary chairman Sensenbrenner perceived the administration's bill as a "Magna Carta for federal agents," according to *Newsweek* columnist Steven Brill.[10]

Bush also sought to make the American legal system more efficient by preventing judges from interfering with justice. In area after area, the bill sought to strip judges of meaningful oversight of the actions of federal agents. The bill aimed to expand the definition of terrorism to allow federal prosecutors to seek a sentence of life imprisonment for any protestor who broke a window in a government building.[11] Eric Sterling, president of the Criminal Justice Policy Foundation, observed: "Even kids carrying Boy Scout knives who vandalize traffic signs can be labeled terrorists."[12]

The Bush administration exerted maximum pressure on Congress to enact the law with no questions asked. At the same time, the administration issued warning after warning of imminent attack. On September 20 Ashcroft telephoned Boston mayor Thomas Menino and Massachusetts governor Jane Swift to personally warn them of possible terrorist attacks in Bean-town over the coming weekend.[13] Ashcroft publicly announced: "We should live our lives but we should do it with a heightened awareness of a vulnerability that we have."[14] A few days later, Vice President Dick Cheney privately warned Republican senators: "We don't want to look at a future tragedy and say, 'What could we have done differently?'"[15]

Administration officials seemed to enjoy pushing the hot buttons of the American people. In war council discussions over what to include in Bush's September 20, 2001 speech to Congress and the American people, Defense Secretary Donald Rumsfeld suggested mentioning that weapons of mass destruction could be used against America by the terrorists. Rumsfeld favored mentioning this threat because "it's an energizer for the American people."[16]

On September 24, in his opening statement to the House Judiciary Committee, Ashcroft warned: "The American people do not have the luxury of unlimited time in erecting the necessary defenses to future terrorist attacks. Terrorism is a clear and present danger today. . . . The death tolls are too high, the consequences too great. . . . Each day that so passes [before the bill is enacted] is a day that terrorists have a competitive advantage. Until Congress makes these changes, we are fighting an unnecessarily uphill battle."[17] Nothing was more dangerous than failing to immediately increase federal power: "We need to unleash every possible tool in the war against terrorism and do so promptly. . . . This new terrorist threat to Americans on our soil is a turning point in American history."

Ashcroft spun away any concerns about the Constitution: "In the past when American law enforcement confronted challenges to our safety and security from espionage, drug trafficking and organized crime, we have met those challenges in ways that preserve our fundamental freedoms and civil liberties. Today we seek to meet the challenge of terrorism within our borders and targeted at our friends and neighbors with the same careful regard for the constitutional rights of Americans and respect for all human beings."[18] This was the soul of the administration's campaign for new legislation: the Justice Department always had and always would automatically respects citizens' rights, so there was no danger in vastly expanding federal power. Ashcroft's rhetoric echoed J. Edgar Hoover's 1960 declaration that the FBI "scrupulously protects the liberties of the individual. The criminal and the subversive must be defeated, yet the historic rights of the individual must be held inviolate."[19]

Rep. John Conyers (D-Mich.), the ranking Democrat on the Judiciary Committee, asked about the time available during the hearing for Democratic members to question Ashcroft. Rep. James Sensenbrenner (R-Wis.), the committee chairman, replied, "You can use your 17 and a half minutes however you want."[20] The rules of House committee hearings often effectively prevent any sustained examination of witnesses. To allow only 17 and a half minutes to question a cabinet member about a bill that would affect 40 agencies and hundreds of different provisions of the statute book[21]—that would change the rules for immigration, Internet use, financial privacy, international banking, criminal procedures, ad infinitum—was novel.

Rep. Howard Coble (R-N.C.) asked Ashcroft if the 9/11 attacks could have been prevented if the federal government had all the powers Ashcroft now sought. Ashcroft replied: "There is absolutely no guarantee that these safeguards would have avoided the September 11th occurrence. We do know that without them, the occurrence took place."[22]

Rep. Barney Frank (D-Mass.) asked, regarding the Bush proposal for expanded surveillance and sharing of confidential information among law enforcement and intelligence agencies, whether the bill would include a right for citizens who are smeared by false or unauthorized leaks to sue the federal government. Ashcroft agreed that "the inappropriate leakage of classified information. . . . is a crime" but added that "this proposal does not include a private cause of action."[23] This meant that government employees would have de facto legal immunity to disclose confidential information on private citizens.

Rep. Conyers mentioned that the Senate Judiciary Committee could take weeks to finish the bill and indicated that House Democrats would not support a final markup of the bill the following morning. Ashcroft protested: "I think we would be ill-advised to find a reason that someone else might be slowing down. . . . It's our position at the Justice Department and the position of this administration that we need to unleash every possible tool in the fight against terrorism and to do so promptly, because our awareness indicates that we are vulnerable and that our vulnerability is elevated as long as we don't have the tools we need to have."[24]

Rep. Conyers politely inquired: "Attorney General Ashcroft, as you realize, can calculate, there are 11 members on our side who haven't said a single word. Could I appeal to you and your kind consideration, and your very difficult schedule to accommodate at least these members for a couple of minutes of observation or question?"

Ashcroft replied: "I do have a responsibility that I'm required to meet at 3:00" but added that his assistants were allowed to stay for up to another hour after he left. (The Justice Department Office of Public Affairs refused to disclose Ashcroft's schedule for the remainder of that afternoon.)[25]

At the end of Ashcroft's cameo, chairman Sensenbrenner crooned, "Mr. Attorney General, thank you for spending the hour that you have spent with us. I really appreciate your carving time out of a schedule that I know is crushing. . . . And I do think that we're lucky to have the attorney general here for an hour, and he's here because we agreed to accommodate his schedule, because he is in charge of conducting probably the largest law enforcement operation in the history of the world."[26]

After Ashcroft left, Rep. Bob Barr (R-Ga.) challenged Assistant Attorney General Michael Chertoff over the administration's exploiting of the 9/11 attacks: "Why is it necessary to propose a laundry list of changes to criminal law generally and criminal procedure generally to cast such a wide net? And why is it necessary to rush this through? Does it have anything to do with the fact that the department has sought many of these authorities on numerous other occasions, has been unsuccessful in obtaining them, and now seeks to take advantage of what is obviously an emergency situation?"[27]

Chertoff replied: "I think the department was very careful when we put this together not to engage in the temptation to treat it as a laundry list of all the things we wished we could have." Before Barr had a chance to begin dissecting Chertoff's response, Sensenbrenner announced that Barr's time had expired.

The following day, President Bush gave a pep talk to FBI agents at FBI headquarters and demanded that Congress act quickly: "I want you to know that every one of the proposals we made on Capitol Hill, carried by the attorney general, has been carefully reviewed. They are measured requests, they are responsible requests, they are constitutional requests. Ours is a land that values the constitutional rights of every citizen, and we will honor those rights, of course. But . . . in order to win the war, we must make sure that the law enforcement men and women have got the tools necessary within the Constitution to defeat the enemy."[28] In a speech in which he was "pounding a lectern with clenched fists for emphasis,"[29] Bush proclaimed that the terrorists "have awoken . . . a mighty nation that will not rest until those who think they can take freedom away from any citizen in the world are brought to justice."[30] Bush did not have the FBI in mind at that moment.

Also on September 25, Ashcroft made a drive-by appearance at a Senate Judiciary Committee hearing. Prior to his testimony Ashcroft told an aide: "Give me some tangible example I can use that's new and will make headlines, that illustrates what we're up against. We need to put it to them."[31] Ashcroft opened his testimony by warning: "I regret to inform you that we are today sending our troops into the modern field of battle with antique weapons."[32] Ashcroft announced that there was a "clear and present danger" of new attacks: "Today, I can report to you that our investigation has uncovered several individuals, including individuals who may have links to the hijackers, who fraudulently have obtained, or attempted to obtain, hazardous material transportation licenses." Ashcroft's warning caused massive gridlock in New York City as cops swarmed to inspect trucks.[33]

Sen. Orrin Hatch (R-Utah), the ranking Republican on the committee, brought some bona fide Utah logic to the hearing: "If we do not prevent terrorists from taking away our liberties, we will not have any liberties and we will not have the freedoms that we have all taken for granted."[34] Since the terrorists sought to steal American liberties, the Justice Department must strike first. Hatch is the most reliable champion of unbridled federal power in the Senate.

Hatch's questions to Ashcroft sounded as if they might have been written by Ashcroft's staff. Hatch asked: "Do any of the provisions you have requested allow law enforcement agencies to engage in electronic surveillance without getting approval from a federal judge?"[35]

Ashcroft replied: "No, they don't. What we've tried to do is to bring into parity some of the communications and records of communications, not the content of communications, that are on the Internet now that used to be done over the telephone. We've tried to develop a technology neutral framework."[36]

This was hokum. The administration's bill required judges to automatically approve email wiretaps based on an unsubstantiated assertion by a federal agent that the tap was "relevant" to any criminal investigation—not just a terrorist investigation. Judges would never have the right to deny approval: they would merely provide a stamp of legitimacy to the Justice Department's intrusion.

Late in his testimony, in response to comments by Sen. Arlen Specter (R-Pa.), Ashcroft asserted that the 9/11 attacks were "perhaps the most massive hate crime ever perpetrated."[37] Ashcroft did not explain how Osama bin Laden in one morning out-scored twelve years of Adolph Hitler.

Ashcroft's appearances at Judiciary Committee hearings were akin to the king stopping by for the ceremonial opening of Parliament. Ashcroft twice refused to return to Capitol Hill for public testimony, claiming he was too busy. Ashcroft announced on September 27 that the administration was sending new legislation, covering financial matters, to Congress. Ashcroft said that the administration wanted to make it a federal offense to "transport more than $10,000 in interstate commerce with the intent to use the money to commit a criminal offense."[38] The administration bill did not specify how a person might prove to lawmen that he did not intend to spend his own money illicitly. Pervasive abuses have occurred in federal confiscations (known as asset forfeitures) in recent decades because federal agencies create many impediments to prevent innocent owners from reclaiming their property. Ashcroft declared, "We are also asking for Congress to permit federal courts to restrain the assets of a criminal defendant such as a terrorist pending trial in order to prevent the transfer of his or her assets to others in the terrorist network. Current law allows post-conviction forfeiture judgements. We believe it makes sense to allow the freezing of such assets earlier, before a terrorist has the opportunity to protect his assets by transferring them to others." While Ashcroft portrayed this as an emergency response to the terrorist threat, the administration bill would permit prosecutors to freeze before trial the assets of anyone accused of any of the three thousand crimes in the federal statute book. This would radically reduce the ability of citizens to defend themselves against the World's Largest Law Firm, the U.S. Department of Justice.

On Sunday, September 30 Ashcroft turned up the heat on Congress. On CBS's *Face the Nation,* he declared: "We believe that there is the likelihood of additional terrorist activity. . . . That's why this legislation is so important. We need something more than talk."[39] On CNN, he warned, "We need a very serious and expeditious approach to providing the additional tools that are necessary to fight terrorism. Talk will not prevent terrorism. . . . It's very unlikely that all of those associated with the attacks of September 11 are now detained or have been detected."[40]

House leaders renamed their version of the antiterrorism bill the "Providing Appropriate Tools Required to Intercept and Obstruct Terrorism Act of 2001"—the Patriot Act. Rep. Bob Barr quipped that he hoped the bill's supporters spent as much time on the bill itself as they did coining the acronym.[41] Senators renamed their terrorism bill the Uniting and Strengthening America Act—the USA Act.

On October 2 Ashcroft warned at a press conference: "I'm deeply concerned about the rather slow pace [of Congress]. . . . We need to be able to put tools in place that would help us disrupt or prevent any additional terrorist acts to which we might be susceptible."[42] At the same press conference, Sen. Trent Lott (R-Miss.), the Senate Majority Leader, snipped that Democrats should worry that if the terrorists attacked again, "people are going to wonder where have you been in giving the additional tools that are needed to, you know, find these terrorists and avoid plots that may be in place." Sen. Hatch harumphed: "It's a very dangerous thing. It's time to get off our duffs and do what's right."[43] Hatch may have been thumping for the bill in part to escape the onus he earned on September 11 when he repeatedly announced during interviews that the U.S. government had intercepted satellite phone calls between Osama bin Laden's followers that confirmed his role in the attacks—something he learned at a confidential White House briefing.[44] Defense Secretary Donald Rumsfeld publicly denounced the leak as subversive of national security.[45]

Congressional leaders received a confidential White House briefing in early October at which CIA officials told them that there was a "100% likelihood" that Al Qaeda would launch terrorist attacks against the United States in response to the start of the U.S. bombing campaign in Afghanistan. When word of the administration's "100% likelihood" of terrorist attacks hit the news, Bush denounced Congress: "I want Congress to hear loud and clear, it is unacceptable behavior to leak classified information when we have troops at risk."[46] Bush temporarily prohibited intelligence briefings for almost all congressmen as a result of the news. Legendary First Amendment lawyer Floyd Abrams observed that the Bush administration's response "was all wrong. If they're prepared to tell congressmen that there is sure to be retaliation in this country, they should be prepared to tell the public."[47]

Some Republicans had qualms about the sweeping power the Bush administration sought. House Majority Leader Dick Armey observed: "There are a lot of members that are acutely aware of the fact that the agencies don't always exercise due diligence in the way they handle information that is at their disposal."[48] Armey complained to Ashcroft during a meeting that he did "not want investigators to be reading all his e-mails," the *Chicago Tribune* reported. "Dick, we already read all your e-mails," Ashcroft jokingly replied.[49]

The House Judiciary Committee worked through the administration's proposal in good faith and crafted a compromise bill, which passed by a vote of 36–0—a remarkable achievement, considering the committee's ideological polarization. Committee chairman Sensenbrenner commented: "This shows that with respect to conflicting viewpoints and a bipartisan approach, the legislative process works. We are all the winners. The terrorists are the losers."[50]

Ashcroft was indignant that the committee did not grant all his demands. At an October 4 press conference, Ashcroft proclaimed: "These weeks have underscored for all Americans the degree to which we look to law enforcement for our safety and security" and warned that "it would be a tragedy indeed to retreat from . . . seeking to strengthen the arm of law enforcement in the effort against terrorism."[51] Ashcroft promised: "We will propose no change in the law that damages constitutional rights and protections that Americans hold dear. Just as we have provided law enforcement with the tools they need to fight drug trafficking and organized crime without violating the rights and the freedoms of Americans, we are committed to meeting the challenge of terrorism with the same careful respect for the Constitution of the United States and the protections that that Constitution accords to America's citizens."[52]

Like a Soviet historiographer, Ashcroft rewrote the judicial history of the United States and expunged all the court decisions detailing and denouncing abuses by law enforcement. There have been scores of Supreme Court decisions and hundreds of lower federal court decisions condemning outrageous government conduct and abuses of American's constitutional rights in antidrug and anticrime campaigns. From the rash of fatal no-knock drug raids at wrong addresses, to the reams of cases of wrongful seizures of private property on false allegations of narcotics links, to the perpetual unjustified searches based on "drug courier profiles" that authorize the accosting of practically any young black or Hispanic male, the drug war has spawned abuses and oppression at all levels of government.[53] Nor is the recent history of the FBI—the premier federal crime fighters—reassuring. From the coverup and destruction of evidence regarding the unconstitutional "shoot to kill" orders that spurred an FBI sniper to slay a mother holding a baby in a cabin door at Ruby Ridge, Idaho, to the FBI's illegal delivery of hundreds of confidential files on Republicans to the Clinton White House, to the FBI sting operations that sought to destroy the daughter of Malcom X in 1994, to the FBI's framing of an innocent security guard, Richard Jewell, for a pipebomb explosion at Centennial Olympic Park in Atlanta in 1996, to recent revelations that the FBI protected murderers who were informants in the Boston Irish Mafia and was complicit in sending four innocent men to prison for life on murder charges,[54] the FBI has too often oppressed Americans and obstructed justice.

On October 7 Vice President Cheney was hustled back into hiding[55] and the FBI urged local governments to exercise "the highest level of vigilance and be prepared to respond to any act of terrorism or violence." On October 8 Ashcroft warned of pending domestic terror attacks: "I encourage all Americans to have a heightened sense of awareness of their surroundings, and to report suspicious activity to law enforcement."[56] After hyping imminent carnage, he reminded people: "While we must be attentive to the threat, we must not yield to fear."[57]

The Senate leadership caved and gave the Bush administration almost everything it wanted. When Senate Majority Leader Tom Daschle (D-S.D.) sought to push the antiterrorism bill through with almost zero opportunity for debate or amendments on October 9, Sen. Russell Feingold (D-Wis.) objected. Under Senate rules, a single senator's objection can prevent a bill from sailing through untouched. Sen. Feingold stated that he would like to offer four amendments that were not finalized at that moment.[58]

Daschle was outraged: "I think it is asking a good deal of all the Senate that we reserve opportunities for him to offer amendments without having the opportunity to see the amendments themselves. . . . I am very disappointed."[59] Sen. Leahy was greatly distressed, and repeatedly mentioned that he had "gotten up at 3 A.M. this morning in Vermont to try to get back" for final action that day on the terrorism bill. Sen. Harry Reid (D-Nev.), the Senate majority whip, proved the complete unreasonableness of Feingold's position by asking Senator Leahy, "Is it not true that the Senator and Senator Hatch and the staffs have spent hundreds of hours on the bill in the last 5 weeks? Is that a fair statement, hundreds of hours? . . . I know that one of Senator Leahy's key staff members had a long-standing dinner engagement, and he had to dress in the car prior to taking 2 hours off on a Saturday night for dinner because he had worked all Friday night, all Saturday, and he finished dinner and was going back to work."[60] The most telling argument offered by one of the most powerful senators for rushing the bill through was the fact that a Senate staffer had dressed in the car before a Saturday date. The more hours Hill staffers put in on the job, the more damage senators are entitled to inflict on the Constitution.

On October 11, the FBI issued an official warning: "Certain information, while not specific as to target, gives the Government reason to believe that there may be additional terrorist attacks within the United States and against US interests overseas over the next several days. The FBI has again alerted all local law enforcement to be on the highest alert and we call on all people to immediately notify the FBI and local law enforcement of any unusual or suspicious activity."[61] The FBI posted the warning at www.fbi.gov/pressrel/pressrel01/*skyfall*.htm. An FBI spokesman insisted that the address was "just a technical error."[62] Justice Department spokesperson Mindy Tucker announced that "it would be irresponsible" for the news media to suggest that the name of the "skyfall" web address had any significance.[63]

There was a sharp division of opinion among federal experts on whether or not sufficient evidence existed to declare the national alert. President Bush later told journalist Bob Woodward: "We came to the conclusion at this point in time that a national alert was important to let the enemy know that we were on to them." Bush said that the alert was "trying to get in their mind as much as anything else."[64] Regardless of whether Bush succeeded in getting into the terrorists' minds, the alert helped thwart resistance to his political agenda.

Sen. Leahy opened the Senate proceedings on the Uniting and Strengthening America Act on October 11 by assuring his colleagues: "What I have done throughout this time is to remember the words of Benjamin Franklin: 'A people who would trade their liberty for security deserve neither.'"[65] After dutifully invoking Franklin, Leahy led the stampede to sacrifice liberty.

Leahy shrugged off the fact that the Judiciary Committee never had substantive hearings: "I regret that the Attorney General did not have the time to respond to questions from all the Members of the committee either on September 25 or last week, but again thank him for the attention he promised to give to written questions Members submitted about the legislation. We have not received answers to those written questions yet, but I will make them a part of the hearing whenever they are sent."[66] Ashcroft never answered the inquiries prior to the final enactment of the Patriot Act.

Leahy introduced into the record a Bush administration statement gushing over the Senate bill: "This bill contains, in some form, virtually all of the proposals made by the Administration in the wake of the terrorist attacks perpetrated against the United States on September 11th."[67] Leahy explained, "To accede to the Administration's request for prompt consideration of this legislation, the Leaders decided to hold the USA Act at the desk rather than refer the bill to the Committee for mark-up, as is regular practice." The reigning sentiment seemed to be the axiom of Roman Emperor Justinian: "Whatever pleases the prince shall have force of law."

Senators uttered the usual protestations about their devotion to civil liberties. Sen. Hatch proclaimed: "We took into consideration civil liberties throughout our discussions on this bill. I think we got it just right. . . . The fact is that the bulk of these proposals have been requested by the Department of Justice for years, and have languished in Congress for years because we have been unable to muster *the collective political will* to enact them into law."[68] The fact that the government sought power in the past automatically legitimated demands for far more power now. The only thing necessary to sanctify the pursuit of additional power is the passage of time. The previous failures of "collective political will" were simply a refusal to abjectly submit to all the demands of the executive branch. As Steven Osher noted in the *Florida Law Review,* "No restraint was ever placed on government power without a history of government abuse."[69]

Sen. Specter complained that the bill "was negotiated between the chairman and ranking member and the White House. The Judiciary Committee did not take up the bill. We have had ample time. This bill should have been before the Senate 2 weeks ago. If we had moved on it promptly after it was submitted on the 20th, we could have had hearings, perhaps some in closed session. We could have had a markup. We could have had an understanding of the bill."[70] Specter was gravely concerned that the Senate had failed to meet "the standards of the Supreme Court of the United States for a sufficient deliberative process" before enacting major legislation. Specter added that he would vote for the bill in part because it was his understanding "that a terrorist act may happen in the United States or overseas in the next several days."

Feingold opened his pitch for his amendments by observing: "The Constitution was written in 1789 by men who had recently won the Revolutionary War. They did not live in comfortable and easy times of hypothetical enemies. They wrote the Constitution and the Bill of Rights to protect individual liberties in times of war as well as in times of peace."[71] Feingold recognized that some of the powers the Justice Department sought to fight terrorists were common-sense fine-tunings of existing laws. Feingold later commented, "It is entirely appropriate that with a warrant the FBI be able to seize voice mail messages as well as tap a phone. It is also reasonable, even necessary, to update the federal criminal offense relating to possession and use of biological weapons. It made sense to make sure that phone conversations carried over cables would not have more protection from surveillance than conversations carried over phone lines. And it made sense to stiffen penalties and lengthen or eliminate statutes of limitation for certain terrorist crimes."[72]

Feingold offered an amendment to prevent giving the government an unlimited right to covertly surveil computer users at universities, libraries, and workplaces. Feingold noted, "Under the bill, anyone accessing a computer 'without authorization' is deemed to have no privacy rights whatsoever, with no time limit, for as long as they are accessing the computer at issue. Basically, the way I read this, this provision completely eliminates Fourth Amendment protection for a potentially very large set of electronic communications."[73]

Sen. Hatch rushed to disparage the amendment: "Either we have to get serious in this modern society, with these modern computers, about terrorism or we have to ignore it. I, for one, am not for ignoring it."[74] Hatch appeared to understand little or nothing about the computer privacy issue Feingold raised.

Senate Majority Leader Daschle hastened to block the Senate from attempting to improve the bill: "My difficulty tonight is not substantive as much as it is procedural. . . . We have a job to do. The clock is ticking. . . . I hope my colleagues will join me tonight in tabling this amendment and tabling every other amendment that is offered. . . . Let's move on and finish this bill. . . .

Then, let's let law enforcement do its job, and let's use our power of oversight to ensure that civil liberties are protected."[75] Trusting to congressional oversight to correct stark flaws in legislation is like expecting to receive a "get well" card after being brutalized by a mugger.

Sen. Leahy fretted that "if we start unraveling this bill, we are going to lose all the parts we won and we will be back to a proposal that was blatantly unconstitutional in many parts."[76] Since some parts of the current version of the bill were not unconstitutional, it was important not to try to change it because it might be replaced by a bill in which almost all provisions violated the Constitution.

Sen. Feingold complained: "This is the first substantive amendment in the Senate on this entire issue, one of the most important civil liberties bills of our time, and the majority leader has asked Senators to not vote on the merits of the issue." Feingold's first amendment was defeated by an 83–13 vote.

Feingold then offered an amendment to prevent the government from conducting wiretaps on an almost unlimited number of innocent people, simply in hopes of catching the words of one suspect. Sen. Leahy conceded the point: "Senator Feingold's amendment simply assures that when roving surveillance is conducted, the Government makes efforts to ascertain that the target is actually at the place, or using the phone, being tapped. This is required in the criminal context. It is unfortunate that the Administration did not accept this amendment."[77] Leahy's comments vivified how the Senate votes on the Feingold amendments were a mere formality since the Bush administration had already announced it would tolerate no changes to the bill.

Daschle reentered the fray: "I am sympathetic to many of these ideas, but I am much more sympathetic to arriving at a product that will bring us to a point where we can pass something into law. . . . It is too late to open up the amendment process in a way that might destroy that delicate balance. For that reason, I move to table this amendment."[78] Sen. Paul Wellstone (D-Minn.) complained about the "rush to table all of the Feingold amendments."[79] But the die was cast.

Feingold later observed that "few in Congress had even read summaries, let alone the fine print, of the document they so hastily passed."[80] Feingold characterized Daschle's reaction to his amendments as "fairly brutal. . . . When the original Ashcroft anti-terrorism bill came in, they [Daschle and other Senate leaders] wanted us to pass it two days later."[81] Feingold thought there would be time to improve the bill "but then something happened in the Senate, and I think the Democratic leadership was complicit in this. Suddenly, the bottom fell out. . . . The Majority Leader came to the floor and spoke very sternly to me, in front of his staff and my staff, saying, you can't do this, the whole thing will fall apart. . . . He was on the belligerent side."[82]

The Bush-approved bill passed in a 96–1 cliffhanger. (Feingold cast the sole nay vote.) The White House then squeezed the House leadership to scuttle the bill that had been painstakingly worked out by the House Judiciary Committee. In the early morning hours of October 12, House Speaker Dennis Hastert agreed to require the House to vote on the Senate bill later that day.[83] The bill was rushed to the floor under a rule prohibiting any amendments. Instead, it would be an up-or-down vote on whether the members favored George Bush or Osama bin Laden.

Helping set the tone for the day's legislative achievements, a *Washington Post* front page headline on October 12 blared "Terrorist Attacks Imminent, FBI Warns."[84] Vice President Dick Cheney announced during a PBS *Newshour with Jim Lehrer* interview: "There's no reason for us to operate on the assumption that [September 11] was a one-off event that's never going to happen again. In fact, we have to assume it will happen again. . . ."[85]

Rep. Sensenbrenner, the floor manager for the Republicans, opened the proceedings by assuring everyone that "the bill does not do anything to take away the freedoms of innocent citizens. Of course we all recognize that the Fourth Amendment to the Constitution prevents the government from conducting unreasonable searches and seizures, and that is why this legislation does not change the United States Constitution or the rights guaranteed to citizens of this country under the Bill of Rights."[86] Sensenbrenner used the old charade of claiming that legislation could not possibly violate constitutional rights because that would be unconstitutional—as if the mere existence of the Bill of Rights automatically prevented Congress from violating citizens' rights. This is like arguing that because automobiles have brakes, drivers can never exceed the speed limit. And all the Supreme Court and lower court decisions striking down laws as unconstitutional are "the exceptions that prove the rule" that Congress never violates the Constitution.

On a similar note, Rep. Ed Bryant (R-Tenn.) assured everyone: "Neither our constitutional rights nor our fundamental rights of privacy are dismissed. Please keep in mind we are not waiving in any way or voiding the Constitution today."[87] Thus, as long as Congress does not explicitly announce the voiding of the Bill of Rights, citizens have no excuse for fearing that their rights could be violated.

To avoid pointless eye strain, congressmen did not receive copies of the bill before they voted on it. Rep. Ron Paul (R-Tex), the most principled opponent of the bill in the House, complained "the bill wasn't printed before the vote."[88] Rep. Jerrold Nadler (D-N.Y.) said: "We're told we should vote right now before we've had a chance to read the bill. Well, why didn't we take up the committee bill on the House floor earlier this week?"[89] Rep. Pete Stark (D-Cal.) commented: "Most members, in fact, don't even know what the bill contains."[90] Barney Frank (D-Mass.) said: "What we have today is an outrageous procedure: A bill, drafted by a handful of people in secret, comes to us without a committee review and immune to amendment."[91] Frank groused about "the least democratic process for debating questions fundamental to democracy I have ever seen." Rep. David Obey (D-Wis.) scorned the legislation as a "back-room quick fix. . . . Why should we care? It's only the Constitution."[92] Rep. John Dingell (D-Mich), the longest-serving member of the House, strode to the podium and proclaimed: "I find this a distressing process . . . denigrating basic constitutional rights, and I find it to have been done in a sneaky, dishonest fashion."[93]

The Bush administration exploited the rising popular trust in government to greatly increase government's power to spy on and punish the citizenry. Rep. Maxine Waters (D-Cal.) growled: "This Attorney General is using this unfortunate situation to extract extraordinary powers to be used beyond dealing with terrorism, laws that he will place into the regular criminal justice system."[94] Rep. Conyers observed: "It is a bill that provides broad new wiretap authorities that might be used to [investigate] minor drug offenses, to firearm violations to antitrust crimes, to tax violations, to environmental problems, literally to every single criminal offense in the United States code."[95]

To protect America against terrorism, the bill empowered federal agencies to treat almost anyone suspected of violating any law like a terrorist. Rep. Nadler proposed to amend the bill to "give our government the powers. . . . the President and the Attorney General say they need to prevent terrorism and to defeat terrorists, but not grant that power with respect to everything else until we have had proper time to look into the question without the haste that this emergency imposes on us."[96] Rep. Sensenbrenner objected because, "in many cases, what begins as an ordinary criminal investigation will end up leading into material relating to how terrorists finance themselves or how terrorists act and further criminal activity as well."[97] By the same logic, local police should treat every jaywalker like a homicide suspect—since once a person begins a life of crime, no one can know where it will end. Nadler's motion was trounced by a vote of 345 to 73.

Rep. Butch Otter (R-Idaho) captured the historical absurdity of the congressional stampede: "Nationwide warrants and secret courts would have been familiar to the Founding Fathers, because they fought against those very institutions when they fought the British. This bill promises security, but Americans need to be secure with their liberties. This bill promises safety, but Americans are only safe if they are free."[98]

House majority leader Richard Armey closed the "debate," proclaiming that "this Congress knows and the White House knows that a good government makes the people secure while preserving their freedom. And that is what this bill is. That is why we should not only vote for it, but we should thank our lucky stars we are in a democracy where we have that right."[99] Thus, as long as politicians have the opportunity to formally consecrate nearly boundless government power, everyone is still free.

Rep. David Drier (R-Cal.), chairman of the Rules Committee, when asked afterward about complaints that congressmen didn't have a chance to read the bill before voting, replied, "It's not unprecedented."[100] The *New York Times* noted: "Passage of the bill, by a vote of 337 to 79, was the climax of a remarkable 18-hour period in which both the House and the Senate adopted complex, far-reaching antiterrorism legislation with little debate in an atmosphere of edgy alarm, as federal law enforcement officials warned that another attack could be imminent."[101] A *Washington Post* editorial noted that many Democrats opposed the bill but "voted for it anyway, lest there be a further terrorist attack and they be accused of not having provided the government sufficient means to defend against it."[102]

The final enactment of the bill was delayed after an anthrax panic depopulated Capitol Hill. Shortly after experts confirmed that a letter sent to Senate Majority Leader Tom Daschle contained anthrax, House and Senate leaders agreed to temporarily shut down Congress. House Speaker Dennis Hastert announced: "There are people who would like us to fear, there are people in this world that would like us to be afraid."[103] He then asserted that he and his colleagues were not afraid but that they were leaving town anyhow. Rep. Ben Cardin (D-MD) declared: "We're taking the normal precautions that people would want us to take."[104] But few Americans have the option of taking unlimited paid leave from their job when a threat is discovered within a mile radius.

However, senators refused to adjourn, choosing instead to stay in session in a minimal keep-the-lights-on fashion. The Senate decision sparked outrage and a sense of betrayal on the House side. One high-ranking House official complained to Fox News: "It is regrettable and it's embarrassing for the institution as a whole. There is not as much hysteria as there is confusion in the Senate as to what they agreed to this morning."[105] Another House staffer complained to *Roll Call,* a congressional newspaper: "The Senate has stooped to new lows. To me, it's extraordinarily bad form and somewhat embarrassing for Senators to be acting in such a way. It might be more appropriate to respect the Speaker of the House's decision to protect the employees and the Members."[106] Hastert spokesman John Feehery complained that "there was some sort of revolt in the Senate."[107] Wesley Pruden, editor in chief of the *Washington Times,* characterized the House response as "the most humiliating display of congressional courage since Union congressmen fled the battlefield at First Manassas, racing back to Washington with their ladies and their picnic hampers flying off in all directions at once."[108]

One last-minute roadblock popped up before the Patriot Act could be enacted: since the act would greatly increase the power of federal prosecutors, it made sense to remedy their ethics at the same time. One of the few differences between the House and Senate terrorism bills was that the Senate's bill included a provision effectively repealing a 1998 law known as the Citizens Protection Act. That law was passed in response to a 1994 decree by Attorney General Janet Reno that officially exempted federal prosecutors from the ethics guidelines state bar associations imposed on all lawyers.[109] Reno's power grab for federal prosecutors was unanimously condemned by the Conference of Chief Justices, representing all the state supreme courts. Frederick Krebs, of the American Corporate Counsel Association, observed, "There is no evidence of the government's need to ignore the ethical constraints imposed on all other practicing attorneys."[110]

Sen. Leahy, who bitterly opposed the Citizens Protection Act, inserted into the Senate terrorism bill his own legislation, entitled the Professional Standards for Government Attorneys Act of 2001, to reexempt federal lawyers from state ethics guidelines. Sen. Ron Wyden (D-Ore.) supported Leahy's effort, and pointed with alarm at an Oregon Bar Association rule that prohibited lawyers from engaging in "deceit or misrepresentation of any kind." Sen. Wyden claimed that such restrictions on federal prosecutors' conduct "potentially makes Oregon a safe haven for dangerous criminals and terrorists everywhere."[111] Wyden presumed that federal prosecutors would only use their right to deceive to serve the public. Wyden and others threatened to block enactment of the Patriot Act. Wyden received endorsements from Attorney General Ashcroft and White House senior counselor Karl Rove for his effort to nullify the ethics law. Wyden dropped his filibuster threat after the Senate enacted his amendment as an add-on to a foreign aid bill.[112] (The House refused to accept the amendment so the Citizens Protection Act survived.)

## Conclusion

When he signed the Patriot Act into law on October 26, 2001 Bush proclaimed: "Today, we take an essential step in defeating terrorism, while protecting the constitutional rights of all Americans. . . . This bill met with an overwhelming—overwhelming agreement in Congress, because it upholds and respects the civil liberties guaranteed by our Constitution."[113] Bush's assertion was ludicrous:

the vast majority of the Patriot Act's avid supporters never showed any interest in civil liberties. Almost all those members outspoken on civil liberties opposed the bill. Bush's ritual invocation of freedom was merely an attempt to consecrate the new federal powers.

In their campaign for the new act, Bush, Ashcroft, and others implicitly threatened congressmen with political destruction if they did not quickly grant the Bush administration's demands. A *New York Times* editorial chided Ashcroft's "scurrilous remarks" toward Congress.[114] Some of the Patriot Act's provisions are "sunset" provisions that will expire in 2005 unless Congress extends them. But it would be naive to expect future Congresses to show fortitude in the face of executive branch fear-mongering.

The soul of the Patriot Act is blind trust in the arbitrary power of federal agents and federal officials. The Bush-Ashcroft steamroller persuaded the legislative branch of government to largely cede both its own role and that of the judicial branch in the American system of checks and balances. An ACLU report issued just after Bush signed the new law noted that Patriot Act provisions "create the illusion of judicial review while transforming judges into mere rubber stamps. Under many of these provisions the judge exercises no review function whatsoever; the court must issue an order granting access to sensitive information upon mere certification by a government official." The ACLU warned that the Patriot Act "misunderstands the role of the judicial branch of government; it treats the courts as an inconvenient obstacle to executive action rather than an essential instrument of accountability."[115]

The higher Bush's approval ratings rose, the more contempt congressmen showed for their oath of office—their pledge to uphold the Constitution. Curtsies to the Bill of Rights by congressmen were apparently the only protection that Americans' rights deserved. When a congressman votes for a bill, he is signing a contract for the American people. When a Congressman signs a "contract" like the Patriot Act without reading it, he vivifies his contempt for the people's liberties. The fact that congressmen acted so irresponsibly is a warning to Americans not to rely on their representatives to safeguard their rights.

We will examine the details and impact of the Patriot Act in the following chapters.

## CHAPTER FIVE

# Plunder and Proclaim Victory

The attacks of September the 11th required a few hundred thousand dollars in the hands of a few dozen evil and deluded men. All of the chaos and suffering they caused came at much less than the cost of a single tank.

—*President Bush, June 1, 2002*[1]

Federal experts estimated that Mohamed Atta and the other 18 hijackers required only about half a million dollars in total financing to carry out their attacks on September 11.[2] This is a tiny fraction of the trillion of dollars worth of currency transactions that occur daily around the world. Terrorism expert Brian Jenkins observed: "Terrorism tends to be a low-budget item. The real resources are fervent young men who are willing to blow themselves to bits."[3]

Yet the Bush administration invoked the actions of the 9/11 terrorists to greatly expand intrusions into American's financial lives. The terrorist attacks instantly endowed George W. Bush with the right to micro-manage world financial institutions—or so the Bush administration apparently believed. And, while Treasury Department officials portrayed their decrees as first strikes against "money that kills,"[4] in reality it is almost impossible to determine which dollar bills have homicidal intent.

## Vanquishing Terrorism with New Reporting Requirements

On the morning of Monday, September 24, 2001 President Bush strode into the Rose Garden and announced: "At 12:01 A.M. this morning, a major thrust of our war on terrorism began with the stroke of a pen. . . . I've signed an executive order that immediately freezes United States financial assets of and prohibits United States transactions with 27 different entities. . . . If [foreign banks] fail to help us by sharing information or freezing accounts, the Department of the Treasury now has the authority to freeze their bank's assets and transactions in the United States." Bush vowed to "starve terrorists of funding" and promised: "I want to assure the world that we will exercise this power responsibly."[5] The new edict empowered the Secretary of the Treasury to heavily punish any foreign government or financial institution that failed to obey Bush's antiterrorism commands. The only evidence required to strike would be an unsubstantiated assertion from a mid-level Treasury bureaucrat.

While the public saw Bush's grim determination, they were unaware of the last-minute outburst behind the scenes that led to the White House proclamation that morning. As Bob Woodward relates in his book *Bush at War*, Bush called White House counselor Karen Hughes in church the day before the announcement. Bush was angry that the announcement of the financial freezes was going to be handled by the Treasury Secretary, as such announcements were almost always handled in the past. Bush snapped at Hughes, "You all don't get it" and angrily informed her: "This is the first bullet in the war against terrorism. This is the first strike. It's not with guys in uniform. It's guys in pinstripes. This will hone in on the fact that this is a completely different kind of war. I should be making this announcement."[6] The announcement plans were revised accordingly.

The week after the terrorist attacks, the Bush administration released a 50-page plan to create new financial crimes. The *Wall Street Journal* noted that "the administration would like to ease privacy restrictions that limit the Internal Revenue Service's ability to share tax data with outside investigators."[7] The administration also released its "2001 Money Laundering Strategy," which showed far more enthusiasm for confiscating private property than for fighting terrorism. Federal law enforcement task forces were ordered "to submit plans to intensify use of federal asset forfeiture laws" and to establish "a new asset forfeiture reporting system and implement its usage throughout the country by March 2002."[8]

On October 17, 2001, the House of Representatives approved the Bush administration's International Money Laundering Abatement and Antiterrorist Financing Act of 2001 by a vote of 412 to 1. Rep. Ron Paul (R-Tex.), the lone opponent, declared that the act "has more to do with the ongoing war against financial privacy than with the war against international terrorism" and derided it as "a laundry list of dangerous, unconstitutional power grabs. . . . These measures will actually distract from the battle against terrorism by encouraging law enforcement authorities to waste time snooping through the financial records of innocent Americans who simply happen to demonstrate an 'unusual' pattern in their financial dealings."[9]

The money laundering financial crackdown provisions were included, with slight modification, in the final Patriot Act, signed into law on October 26. The act empowers the U.S. government to penalize anyone in the world who allegedly violates U.S. money laundering laws. *Money Laundering Alert,* a pro-government newsletter, hailed the new law: "It is no exaggeration to say that, as a whole, the act has the ability to reach the assets of every financial institution and business in the world and to cripple their ability to function in a world in which the United States is the financial centerpiece."[10] If a foreign bank has a single dollar deposited or held in a U.S. bank, or wires a single dollar through the United States, the Bush administration claims jurisdiction over that bank's operations anywhere in the world. Treasury Department chief counsel David Aufhauser later warned foreign economics ministers that "there will be hell to pay" for any nation that doesn't aid the U.S. war against terrorism.[11]

Congress and the Bush administration exploited the 9/11 attacks to resurrect surveillance schemes previously overwhelmingly rejected by the American people. In December 1998, federal banking agencies proposed "know your customer" (KYC) regulations to require banks to "determine its customers' sources of funds, determine, understand and monitor the normal and expected transactions of its customers, and report appropriately any transactions of its customers that are determined to be unusual or inconsistent."[12] Banks would have been obliged to create "profiles" of each customer—dossiers that law enforcement agents could use if they decided to target that person. Banks would also have been obliged to perform "a risk assessment of the customer and the intended transactions of the customer"[13] and to surrender any financial information on customers within 48 hours after receiving a request from law enforcement—no search warrant required. Plans to impose the 1998 reporting requirements were derailed after more than a quarter million people sent in comments opposing them. But, as the *National Law Journal* noted, "After Sept. 11, Congress reversed course and, in effect, adopted the Fed's earlier KYC proposal."[14]

The *Wall Street Journal* noted, "The full range of anti-terror measures taken by the administration makes it likely that enormous quantities of additional records will be created on the financial lives of Americans."[15] And the information that is stockpiled will be shared far and wide. *Money Laundering Alert* described one financial provision of the Patriot Act as a "dream-come-true information-gathering tool for U.S. agencies,"[16] extending a "welcome mat to the Central Intelligence Agency, National Security Agency and other U.S. counterparts" to look at the new financial information on American citizens and others.[17]

The 9/11 hijackings were preceded by the biggest failure ever by U.S. money cops. The *Financial Times* reported in March 2002: "U.S. Treasury officials have privately told accountants and lawyers who specialize in countering money-laundering that two of the suspected September 11 terrorists (one dead and one indicted) triggered warnings for money-laundering, even under the old rules. Apparently the Treasury received Suspicious Activity Reports but took no action."[18] A May 2002 United Nations report on terrorist financing noted that a "suspicious transaction report" had been filed with the U.S. government over a $69,985 wire transfer that Mohamed Atta, leader of the hijackers, received from the United Arab Emirates. The report noted that "this particular transaction was not noticed quickly enough because the report was just one of a very large number and was not distinguishable from those related to other financial crimes."[19] (The federal government's Financial Crimes Enforcement Network, known as FinCEN, denied receiving a suspicious activity report on Atta.[20]) The *Wall Street Journal* reported that Mohamed Atta was on a Customs Service watchlist and "had been implicated in a 1986 bus bombing in Israel and had traveled in and out of the U.S. on an expired visa," according to a Federal Bureau of Investigations investigator.[21]

The House report on the financial portion of the Patriot Act lamented: "Despite the provisions of the 1970 Bank Secrecy Act and various money laundering laws enacted since, the current money laundering regime appears to have been ineffective in detecting or preventing the terrorist hijackers from operating freely in the United States."[22] The staff report of the Joint House-Senate Intelligence Committee investigation into 9/11 noted: "Prior to September 11, there was no coordinated U.S. Government-wide strategy, and reluctance in some parts of the U.S. Government, to track terrorist funding and close down their financial support networks."[23] According to the federal "2002 National Money Laundering Strategy," tracking terrorist financing is more difficult than tracing drug money: "The financial dealings of a terrorist organization, whose members tend to live modestly and whose funds may be derived from outwardly innocent contributors to apparently legitimate humanitarian, social and political efforts, are considerably more difficult to investigate than those of a drug trafficker."[24] The federal government currently seizes less than 1 percent of all the drug and other illicit money laundered in the United States. Federal money laundering experts expect that the war on terrorist financing will be even less successful than the war on drug money.

Even before the Patriot Act, federal money cops were overwhelmed by too many reports from banks. The Bank Secrecy Act of 1970 made it a federal crime for banks to keep secrets from the government.[25] This law obliged banks and other financial institutions to submit a currency transaction report (CTR) to the federal government for each cash transaction involving more than $10,000. The feds harvested 17 million CTRs in 2000; federal agencies were flooded with tons of paper that bureaucrats often never bothered to examine. Beginning in 1996, banks were also obliged to file a suspicious activity report on any transaction that "has no business or apparent lawful purpose or is not the sort in which the particular customer would normally be expected to engage." The feds received over two hundred thousand suspicious activity reports in 2001.[26]

The number of suspicious activity reports related to terrorists increased by more than twenty-fold in the eight months after 9/11[27]—the vast majority being false positives. Experts compare the search for terrorist funds to "searching for a needle in a haystack the size of Nebraska."[28] Even though the feds failed to analyze the information they possessed on the hijackers before 9/11, vacuuming up more private information is supposedly the cure for all bureaucratic ills.

The Patriot Act made it easy for banks to share confidential information about any customer allegedly suspected of terrorism or money laundering. All that is necessary to authorize such exposures is for a bank to send a formal notice to the Treasury Department announcing its plans to share customer information with other banks.[29] (The form can conveniently be submitted online.) Congress generously provided banks with a "safe harbor" protection that prevents them from being sued for violating their customers' privacy.

The Patriot Act requires hundreds of thousands of businesses—including pawn shops, travel agencies, and car dealers—to designate compliance officers, develop internal policies to control money laundering, and set up an independent audit function. Miami banking lawyer Clemente Vazquez-Bello observed: "Up to 80 percent of the companies that fall under the rules don't know that this is coming."[30] Company officials who fail to comply with all the new reporting requirements could face up to 20 years in prison.[31] The feds have made little or no effort to inform small businesses of their new legal obligations. Such heavy penalties give the feds the power to destroy anyone who does not obey. But multiplying private reporting requirements will not magically engender the brains necessary in federal agencies to read and comprehend all the reports.

## The November 7 Terrorists

Less than two weeks after the Patriot Act was signed, the feds speared their first violators. The Customs Service, the FBI, and the IRS carried out heavily televised raids around the nation, hitting eight storefront operations and busting kingpins of money transmittal services used by Somali immigrants. President Bush, joined by top cabinet officials, went to the Treasury Department's Foreign Terrorist Asset Tracking Center and announced:[32]

> Today we are taking another step in our fight against evil. . . . Acting on *solid and credible evidence,* the Treasury Department of the United States today blocked the U.S. assets of 62 individuals and organizations connected with two terrorist-supporting financial networks, the Al Taqua and the Al-Barakaat. Their offices have been shut down in four U.S. states. . . . The entry point for these networks may be a small storefront operation, but follow the network to its center and you discover wealthy banks and sophisticated technology, all at the service of mass murderers. By shutting these networks down, we disrupt the murderers' work. . . . They skim money from every transaction for the benefit of terrorist organizations.[33]

Bush declared that his action "sends a clear message to global financial institutions: you are with us or you are with the terrorists. And if you're with the terrorists, you will face the consequences."[34] A White House fact sheet declared: "These two financial networks, which are tied to Al Qaeda and Osama bin Laden, raise money for terror, invest it for profit, launder the proceeds of crime and distribute terrorist money around the world to purchase the tools of global terrorism."[35]

Treasury Secretary Paul O'Neill denounced al Barakaat as "a pariah in the civilized world" and "the quartermasters of terror."[36] O'Neill boasted: "Together, the civilized governments of the world have already blocked more than $43 million in terrorist assets."[37] Secretary of State Colin Powell described the money transmittal companies (known as "hawalas") as "the shadowy financial networks that underpin the terrorists' underworld."[38]

Treasury Deputy Assistant Secretary Rob Nichols later declared that Barakaat's founder, Ahmed Nur Ali Jim'Ale, is "a close associate of bin Laden's. We're told they fought together in Afghanistan. Some even say bin Laden co-founded this network."[39] "Some even say" became the U.S. government's standard of proof for the crackdown. While the Bush administration portrayed Barakaat as a secret conspiracy, the Somali company actually had links to "Citibank for money transfers and to AT&T for international calls."[40] Barakaat chairman Jim'Ale declared on the day of Bush's announcement: "Our books are open. We are transparent, we expected someone would come to see for themselves but that did not happen."[41] Jim'Ale derided Bush's charges of an Al Qaeda connection: "This is all lies. We are people who are hard-working and have nothing to do with terrorists."[42] Barakaat Deputy General Manager Abas Adbi Ali announced that the company had been "cooperating with U.S. authorities" prior to the asset freeze.[43]

"Level playing field" is not a term frequently used to characterize federal seizure proceedings. As John Riley deftly explained in *Newsday:*

> Under Bush's order, a target doesn't have to be notified before being listed. No court has to be convinced there is probable cause before a freeze is imposed. No evidence has to be made public. Through related United Nations resolutions, a U.S. listing immediately becomes global. After the fact, the agency that administers financial sanctions—the Treasury Department's Office of Foreign Assets Control—has no time limits for resolving claims from those who dispute the listing. . . . The government doesn't have to prove its case beyond a reasonable doubt, or even by a preponderance of the evidence. Technically, it only has to prove that its action was not "arbitrary and capricious."[44]

In 1994, Congress passed a law requiring all money transmitting businesses to register with the federal government. For seven years, the Treasury Department missed deadline after deadline for issuing regulations to enforce the mandate.[45] The Patriot Act required all money transmitting businesses to have a state license. The feds then rushed to destroy targets out of compliance with a law signed less than two weeks earlier. The government seized all the assets of the individuals and companies named in the Bush administration's November 7 decree and also prohibited anyone else from having any financial dealings with them.

In Seattle, a dozen Customs agents raided a shopping center where a Barakaat service operated. The agents stripped bare other businesses adjacent to the money forwarding service, including a mini-mart and a gift shop. The *Seattle Times* noted: "Authorities removed everything: food, coffee makers, meat freezers, even shelving."[46] Perhaps the feds expected to find hidden terrorist messages in the Twinkies. A few weeks later, the mini-mart owner got a phone call informing him that he would be permitted to retrieve the remnants of his goods from a government warehouse in a neighboring city.[47] All the frozen goat and lamb, as well as all other refrigerated items, had been trashed by the government.

For six months, the feds refused to return the money captured in the cash registers and elsewhere during the mini-mart raid. After the government came under intense pressure from Sen. Patty Murray (D-Wash.) and the ACLU, the feds cut the owner a check for $40,480.80 in May 2002 to cover cash and checks seized on November 7.[48] The feds denied any compensation for the destruction of food products and disruption of business.

The feds raided Barakaat Enterprise U.S.A. in Columbus, Ohio, seizing all its records and the furniture—even the lawn chairs.[49] The feds also grabbed $160,000 in assets, most of which belonged to Somali immigrants.[50] Hassan Hussein, the owner, pleaded: "I ask them to release the funds for the people who are starving. The Somali people, they're waiting. But the government, they don't tell me anything. They don't ever tell me anything."[51] Hussein's lawyer, Kevin O'Brien, complained: "We have asked repeatedly, orally and in writing, that they present evidence that my client or his company is in any way involved in terrorism. They say, 'We don't have to.'"[52]

In Minnesota, the feds raided Aaran Money Wire Service Inc. and Global Services International U.S.A. Jake Tapper, writing on Salon.com, detailed the suffering of Garad Jama, the owner of Aaran Money Wire Service and a Somali native who had proudly become a U.S. citizen. (Federal agents found a red, white, and blue "United We Stand" placard on the wall of his office when they raided it.) The feds froze $166,111 in Jama's business bank account (other people's money that was being transmitted to Africa) and $41,225 in his personal bank account. The federal government never contacted Jama before Bush announced to the world that he was a terrorist supporter. In early December, Jama received a form letter from the Treasury department notifying him that, pursuant to Executive Order No. 13224, he had been formally listed as an SDGT—a "specifically designated global terrorist."[53] Jama had a difficult time getting any help locally because "people feared getting involved with someone whom the president himself had called a terrorist." His lawyer, John Lundquist, asked one Treasury Department lawyer how Jama was expected to survive the paralyzing effect of the government order. The government lawyer responded that if Jama was "breathing," then "he's probably in violation of the blocking notice." Jama's lawyers repeatedly contacted the government to try to provide information to exonerate their client but the government did not respond. On April 12, 2002, Jama's lawyers sued the federal government for violating his rights by labeling him a terrorist and freezing his assets. Lawyer Lundquist observed: "These were actions taken without any notice, without any hearing, without the government presenting whatever evidence they felt they had." Salon's Tapper noted, "After the lawsuit was filed, suddenly the government found Lundquist's phone number and it finally permitted Garad Jama to work and spend up to $3,200 in living expenses a month."[54]

The first person convicted under the Patriot Act was Mohamed Hussein, a 33-year-old Somali native and Canadian citizen who (with his brother) ran a money transmitting service—Barakaat North America—out of the Boston area and Portland, Maine. After Hussein was indicted, the *Boston Herald* characterized him as a "reputed terrorist money man."[55] However, the actual crime for which Hussein was charged was failure to have a state license for his money transmittal service, which the Patriot Act made a federal felony "whether or not the defendant knew that the operation was required to be licensed or that the operation was so punishable."[56] The Husseins were not operating covertly; as the *Portland Press Herald* noted, the brothers "sent an incomplete application for a license to state banking regulators. They even filed incorporation documents with the state, naming themselves as officers in the company and stating the purpose of their business."[57] The FBI had investigated the Husseins the previous year and detected no link to terrorists.[58]

At the trial, federal prosecutors produced no evidence linking Hussein to terrorists, no evidence his money forwarding service provided any benefit to Al Qaeda, and no evidence that he ever bilked any of his countrymen. But, because Hussein failed to complete the process of securing a state license, he was convicted by a jury on two counts. As soon as the jury rendered its verdict, U.S. Attorney Michael Sullivan publicly announced: "The clear message we've received from the president and the attorney general is that we have to essentially dismantle terrorism and thwart potential terrorist activity any way we can. . . . One way is to disrupt the flow of money to terrorist organizations."[59] The link between Hussein and terrorism flourished when the feds first publicized his case, vanished during the entire trial, and then miraculously reappeared moments after the jury verdict. If Sullivan had made the same statement during the trial, the judge might have called a mistrial for the smearing of the defendant with no evidence. (Canada refused to extradite Liban Hussein, Mohamed's brother, to the United States. Canadian Justice Ministry spokesman Patrick Charette commented: "We looked at the evidence" the United States provided on Liban Hussein "and then it became clear there was no evidence.")[60]

When Hussein was sentenced on July 22, 2002, the U.S. attorney's office asked federal judge Robert Keeton to sentence Hussein to five years in prison—far longer than federal sentencing guidelines called for.[61] Judge Keeton exploded: "You're trying to ask me to sentence him as a terrorist. It shocks my conscience that I would even be asked to do that." Keeton denounced the government's behavior as "unfair and unjust"[62] and scowled: "The government issued statements both before and after the case that were not substantiated."[63] Two weeks before the sentencing, the United Nations Security Council removed Liban Hussein from its official list of Al Qaeda financiers. The U.S. government followed suit a week later.[64] But the feds still wanted a harsh sentence for Mohamed Hussein. Keeton sentenced Hussein to 18 months in prison. (Hussein's lawyer is appealing the sentence.)

The U.S. government's targeting of Barakaat—and the UN's endorsement of the action, resulting in crackdowns on Barakaat operations all over the world—devastated Somalia.[65] Ahmed Abdi Hashi, Somalia's ambassador to the United Nations, complained: "Thousands of Somalis had deposits in Al Barakaat. Depositors cannot access their funds. Businessmen cannot do business. Many are going bankrupt."[66] The *Washington Post* observed: "Al-Barakaat is often described as one of the largest and most enterprising companies in Somalia. . . . It has grown into a major telecommunications and construction enterprise that even generates electric power. Hundreds of thousands of Somalis depend on the money the system transfers, thousands work for the company in Somalia, and hundreds of Somali Americans are its shareholders."[67] Somali government officials warned that the sanctions' "impact on the poor has been so devastating—layoffs, lack of access to funds, business disruptions—that it may ultimately be a boon to Islamic radicals who drum up antipathy toward the United States." Barakaat was Somali's largest employer, and it also ran the country's only water-purification plant.[68] The U.S. action shut down the only Internet service provider in Somalia.[69]

U.S. Treasury Department General Counsel David Aufhauser denied that the U.S. government had any responsibility for the devastating impact of the seizures on Somalis: "As a technical legal matter, the money [frozen by U.S. edict] is Al Barakaat's, it is not the people's money. The injury is not done by the [U.S.] Office of Foreign Assets Control, it's done by the people who banked terror."[70] Douglas Cassell of the Northwestern University Law School observed: "A hundred dollars doesn't mean much to a general counsel at the Treasury Department. But $100 can mean a lot to a child in Somalia."[71] A U.S. State Department official named Glenn Warren responded to Somali complaints at a press conference in Mogadishu: "We do not want to harm the economy of Somalia. . . . Last year alone, we gave Somalia 24 million dollars."[72] But this aid was far less than the transfers from Somalia expatriates to their relatives and associates at home—Somalia's largest source of income. Barakaat delivered the majority of the estimated $700 million annual remittances from abroad that Somalis received. The State Department's report "Patterns of Global Terrorism," issued on May 21, 2002, noted: "Civil war, clan conflict, and poverty have combined to turn Somalia into a 'failed state,' with no one group currently able to govern the entire country, poor or nonexistent law enforcement, and an inability to monitor the financial sector."[73] And since it was a "failed state" with insufficient regulation, there was no reason for the U.S. not to stomp its rag-tag financial system.

The dearth of U.S. evidence against Barakaat became clear in the case of the "Somali Swedes."[74] Abdirisak Aden and two other Somalis ran a Barakaat operation out of Stockholm, the assets of which were frozen. Afer the Somalis loudly protested their innocence, the Swedish government requested evidence of their wrongdoing from the U.S. government. The *Wall Street Journal* reported that the U.S. Treasury Department sent Sweden 27 pages of information on the accused but "twenty-three pages were news-release material: a packet of background documents on al Barakaat, including a statement by President Bush on al Qaeda and a transcript of a briefing led by Secretary of State Colin Powell. The Somali Swedes were mentioned only in a flow-chart of al Barakaat's structure. The U.S. also sent four other pages. . . . But a Swedish state-police spokeswoman said that authorities found nothing on the pages that would warrant criminal charges against the men."[75] Anders Kruse, deputy director of Sweden's Foreign Affairs Ministry, observed: "We discovered the sanctions committee didn't have any information whatsoever when they took their action, just a list of names."[76]

Luxembourg's Financial Intelligence Unit, using the U.S. list of terrorist financiers, carried out raids on numerous banks in late 2001, freezing almost $200 million in assets allegedly linked to Barakaat. Seven months later, the investigation collapsed. The *Washington Post* reported that the Luxembourg government froze money in 18 bank accounts "based on a U.S. Treasury list of terrorist-linked groups and persons. Now authorities are on the verge of unfreezing 17 of them, again because they have no legal grounds to do otherwise."[77] The Luxembourg government may be more scrupulous than the U.S. government in part because, under its laws, the government "can be held liable for losses suffered by those whose money was frozen, unless the government can show that it had reasonable cause to block the accounts."[78]

The Barakaat system was the most prominent and largest *hawala* in the world. Hawala—an Arab term for "trust" [79]—developed in areas without formal banking systems. An analysis by Interpol observed that "the components of hawala that distinguish it from other remittance systems are trust and the extensive use of connections such as family relationships." Interpol also noted that "the delivery associated with a hawala transaction is faster and more reliable than in bank transactions."[80] The U.S. Drug Enforcement Agency, in its September 2001 "Drug Situation Report" for Afghanistan, commented that hawalas "provide a confidential, convenient, efficient service at a low cost in areas that are not served by traditional banking facilities."[81] Hawala systems flourish because many Third World governments are kleptocracies—governments of thieves. Hawala allows people to avoid extortionate government exchange-rate controls that are intended to defraud anyone who converts foreign currency. (Pakistan, for instance, is seeking to shut down hawalas to force everyone to use government-licensed exchange services which provide a much worse rupee exchange rate for customers—thereby providing a windfall for the government.)

U.S. government officials have long been intensely hostile towards hawalas. Treasury Secretary O'Neill heaped scorn on "unregulated financial networks constructed to by-pass the civilized world's detection."[82] For government regulators, nothing is more suspicious than a system based on trust. And any financial activity not under government control is now presumed to be linked to terrorism. (While the hawalas spooked U.S. regulators, they impose far less of a burden on Americans than the federal subsidies for U.S. financial institutions. No one guarantees the Barakaat depositor or transmitter that his money will not be pilfered. The U.S. Congress guaranteed depositors in U.S. financial institutions that they would be reimbursed up to $100,000 each. The federal safety net and perverse incentives begot the savings and loan crisis in the late 1980s and early 1990s that cost taxpayers hundreds of billions of dollars. Federal regulations did nothing to prevent pervasive corruption.)

In August 2002, the United States succumbed to European pressure and agreed to revise the rules to permit people the U.S. placed on the international terrorist list to have access to a smattering of their own funds to pay for food, rent, medical care, and legal counsel.[83] The U.S. government also grudgingly acquiesced to the creation of an appeals process by which innocent people's names could be removed from the terrorist list.[84]

On August 21, Undersecretary Jimmy Gurule announced that the United States had notified the UN to remove the names of six people and organizations from the Specifically Designated Global Terrorist list: two Somali Swedes, Garad Jama of Minnesota, and three U.S. companies hit in the November 7 raids.[85] Gurule proudly declared: "In this instance, the individuals and entities have demonstrated that they had no prior knowledge and have taken active steps to cut all ties with those entities funneling funds to terrorism. This is how the process was designed to work."[86] Gurule asserted that the names were removed because the men signed pledges declaring that "they have severed and disassociated themselves in every conceivable way from the Al-Barakaat-related businesses."[87] In reality, the targets had to sign the pledge to get their money and lives back. A U.S. government official explained the ruling to the *Washington Post:* "The United States now *trusts their motives.*"[88] This was most generous, considering that the U.S. government had never presented any evidence linking the de-listed people or companies to terrorist activities.

The Treasury Department was under severe pressure to "do something now" in the war on terrorism. The more people Treasury bureaucrats tarred as Specifically Designated Global Terrorists, the better job they appeared to be doing of protecting America. One U.S. government official explained to the *New York Times* why Barakaat entities were designated as terrorist supporters: "We needed to make a splash. We needed to designate now and sort it out later."[89] No Treasury Department bureaucrat ever lost a day's pay from wrongfully designating someone as a terrorist suspect.

## Grabbing the Green

The Patriot Act effectively overturned a 1998 Supreme Court decision that sought to curb wrongful federal seizures. In 1994, the Customs Service confiscated $357,144 in cash from a Syrian immigrant, Hosep Bajakajian, who was searched at Los Angeles International Airport prior to heading back to Syria. Both a federal district court and an appeals court concluded that the money had been honestly acquired and ordered most of it returned to Bajakajian. The Clinton administration resisted, claiming that the confiscation was justified solely because Bajakajian failed to fill out Customs Form 4790, disclosing that he was taking more than $10,000 in cash out of the country. The Supreme Court decreed that "a punitive forfeiture violates the Excessive Fines Clause [of the Eighth Amendment of the Bill of Rights] if it is grossly disproportional to the gravity of a defendant's offense."[90]

The 9/11 attacks provided the perfect pretext to take a whack at the Eighth Amendment. Congress, at the administration's behest, redefined the possession of cash to make it sound far more insidious. The Patriot Act created a new crime—"bulk cash smuggling"—to punish anyone who doesn't notify the government of how much money they are taking out of or into the United States (if they are carrying more than $10,000). The Patriot Act stated that "if the smuggling of bulk cash were itself an offense, the cash could be confiscated as the *corpus delicti* of the smuggling offense." Congress rewrote the law to pretend that money travels by itself, and money commits the crime. And since a stack of cash has no constitutional rights, the government can do no wrong when it seizes the money. (This is based on a medieval legal doctrine known as an *in rem* proceeding—taking legal action "against the thing.")[91]

Antiterrorism rhetoric bedecked the new confiscatory powers. In the Patriot Act's "Findings," Congress proclaimed that "the movement of large sums of cash is one of the most reliable warning signs of drug trafficking, terrorism, money laundering, racketeering, tax evasion and similar crimes." Congress also ordained: "The intentional transportation into or out of the United States of large amounts of currency. . . . is the equivalent of, and creates the same harm as, the smuggling of goods."[92] Congress did not explain how a person became a smuggler merely by transporting their own money.

The "bulk cash smuggling" provision states that the money cannot be confiscated unless it has been concealed. But this is defined to include "concealment in any article of clothing worn by the individual or in any luggage, backpack, or other container worn or carried by such individual." In other words, anyone with a heap of bills not plumped openly on the airline seat when a G-man walks up to interrogate a traveler is guilty of concealing the money. Violators of the reporting requirement are entitled to five years in prison, as well as loss of all their money.

A Treasury Department September 2002 "progress report" on fighting terrorism warned: "The openness of our modern financial system . . . creates opportunities for *terrorist parasites* to hide in the shadows."[93] Regardless of where these "terrorist parasites" hid, many Americans found themselves plundered instead by federal agents lurking at airports.

Operation Green Quest, the *nom de guerre* of the new Anti-Terrorist Financing Task Force, was launched to "to identify, disrupt, dismantle and ultimately 'bankrupt' terrorist networks and their sources of funding," as Undersecretary Gurule announced at the October 25, 2001 press conference announcing the new initiative.[94] Operation Green Quest included agents from the Customs Service, the IRS, the Secret Service, the Bureau of Alcohol, Tobacco, and Firearms, Treasury's Office of Foreign Assets Control, the FinCEN, the Postal Inspection Service, the FBI, and the Department of Justice.[95]

Operation Green Quest was a marvel of simplicity: any international traveler carrying ample cash who fails to fill out a federal form was automatically a terrorist suspect. In congressional testimony on February 12, 2002, Treasury Deputy Assistant Secretary Juan Zarate bragged that the Customs Service had confiscated $9 million in "bulk cash" from outgoing passengers since October. Zarate crowed: "Law enforcement has always suspected that bulk cash smuggling is used by some terrorist organizations to move large amounts of currency."[96] Zarate offered no evidence that a nickel of the $9 million seized from travelers was linked to terrorism.

On July 17, 2002, Customs Commissioner Robert Bonner announced: "Operation Green Quest has moved aggressively against terrorist funding sources. . . . All the $16 million seized thus far under this initiative constitutes unreported currency being smuggled out of the country, which is a felony. At the same time, these 369 seizures have provided a windfall of intelligence and leads for Operation Green Quest, prompting dozens of new investigations around the country. A portion of the seized funds has been linked to suspected terrorist groups."[97] Four months later, Gurule testified to the Senate: "Bulk cash smuggling has proven to be yet another means of financing adopted by terrorists and their financiers. Customs has executed 650 bulk cash seizures totaling $21 million, including $12.9 million with a Middle East connection."[98] While the "Middle East connection" sounds insidious, Customs does not have a clear definition or standard for this term; it may simply mean that Customs agents nailed some passenger destined for an airline flight to Cairo, Tel Aviv, or Riyadh.[99] The only link to terrorism that Gurule offered in his testimony was the insinuation that anyone who does not fill out a government form is presumptively with Al Qaeda.

Operation Green Quest was the most exhilarating antiterrorist program: *U.S. News and World Report* reported that Customs officials running the operation "seem giddy with their progress."[100] But the fact that the feds have made 650 seizures means that many hits have involved amounts of money not much over $10,000. A Customs spokesman did not have information on how many of the people whose cash was seized were American citizens.[101] Once the money is seized, a person who seeks due process has no alternative except to sue the government in federal court—a process that can easily cost $5,000 or more in legal fees.

Much of what Operation Green Quest did would be considered highway robbery under the standard the Supreme Court established in 1998. In most of the cases, there was no evidence of wrongdoing or bad intent; instead, the program simply clobbered people who failed to report their possessions to the feds before leaving the country.

Prior to the 1998 Supreme Court ruling, high-ranking government officials routinely implied that most of the cash seized from passengers by the Customs Service at airports was linked to narcotics. After 9/11 and the Patriot Act, federal officials now insinuate that most of the seizures are linked to terrorism. Apparently, seizures are automatically linked to the premier hobgoblin of the moment.

It is paradoxical that Customs portrays seizures of outgoing currency as a major victory against terrorism when other reports indicate that the overwhelming majority of money raised for Al Qaeda comes from wealthy donors in Saudi Arabia and other Gulf states. The congressional Joint Inquiry report concluded: "The activities of the September 11 hijackers in the United States appear to have been financed, in large part, from monies sent to them from abroad."[102] At least the plundering of outbound travelers distracts attention from the government's failure to detect possible inflows of money to bona fide terrorist suspects. Cracking down on routine wire transfers to third world countries does nothing to deter terrorism.

In December 2002, Operation Green Quest struck across the nation:

- On December 17, FBI, Customs, and DEA agents, along with local police, carried out raids in Lackawanna, New York (a Buffalo suburb). Three people, including the vice president of the American Muslim Council of Western New York, were busted for running an unlicensed money forwarding service.[103] The feds charged the defendants with illegally wiring $486,548 to Yemen from the United States. Defense lawyer Philip Marshall observed: "There is nothing to suggest the activities were illegal. This appears to be a technical violation of the law."[104] The *Buffalo News* reported that U.S. Attorney Michael Battle said that none of the money was used to fund terrorism.[105]

- On December 17, 60 officers from federal agencies and the Dearborn Police Department raided a gas station, a convenience store, a dollar store, and a restaurant in Detroit and Dearborn, Michigan. The massive raids garnered one handgun and $200,000 confiscated from several private bank accounts.[106] The feds arrested five people, including a 62-year-old man and a 65-year-old man, charging them with operating an unlicensed money transfer business that sent money to people in Yemen. Richard Hoglund, special agent in charge of U.S. Customs investigations in Detroit, said, "I have no reason to believe these individuals arrested today are terrorists. I don't know what they are, other than people who ran an unregistered wire company to transfer money to a country where there are concerns of terrorism."[107] Yemeni immigrants have worked at Ford auto plants almost since Ford was created. As one defense attorney groused: "What is the connection of Yemeni immigrants working at Ford Motor Co., the Rouge plant, to al-Qaida? This is the government's scorched-earth policy to harass people in abject poverty who are trying to send a few dollars home to their families."[108]

- On December 19, the feds scored the biggest hit of them all as G-men carried out raids in Seattle, Nashville, Dallas, Phoenix, and Roanoke, Virginia. Customs Service chief Raymond Bonner proudly announced: "Today we're announcing the dismantling of a global underground wire transfer network that illegally funneled at least $12 million of funds and goods into Iraq, in violation of the U.S. embargo of Iraq."[109] The U.S. government had no evidence that any of the funds transferred to Iraq—which amounted to $400,000 a month during the three-year period of investigation—had been used for terrorist or other nefarious purposes.

One defense attorney noted that his client had been sending money to his family in Iraq because they were "starving to death" thanks to the UN sanctions (maintained primarily at the behest of the U.S. government).[110] When Bonner was asked about American residents sending funds to hard-pressed relatives back in Iraq, he replied: "Let's understand this: It is illegal to send funds to any person in Iraq for any purpose, or to send any materials to any person in Iraq. And the reason that—and the reason is that it's part of the embargo of the United States that prohibits this from happening. So if you're doing that, you're violating the laws of the United States. And so that itself is a—it's a federal crime to do that."[111] This was a pathetic circular analysis: "THE LAW HAS SPOKEN"—therefore Iraqi women and children must perish. No amount of unnecessary Iraqi fatalities could equal the iniquity of violating a U.S. government edict.

Treasury Undersecretary Gurule, appearing at the same press conference, whooped: "This has been a great week for federal law enforcement in the financial war on terror." Bonner stated that federal agents "took action in terrorist financing cases out of Buffalo, New York; Detroit and Seattle."[112] But the Customs Service agents in charge in Buffalo and Detroit stated that there was no evidence of a terrorist link to the money.

Gurule bragged: "We are shining the light of the law on underground money movement that poses a threat to the United States."[113] But the Lackawanna crackdown involved only $486,548 sent from upstate New York to Yemen. Yemen exports more than $1 billion worth of oil and other products a year. Yet Gurule implied that the $486,548 threatened the United States with calamity unless the feds immediately throttled it.

Less than three weeks after the celebratory press conference, the Justice Department dropped all charges against the six defendants in Dearborn and Detroit. While a spokeswoman for the local U.S. attorney's office insisted that "the case is ongoing," Dearborn attorney Nabih Ayad characterized the dismissal of charges as "basically another fumble by the government."[114] A Customs investigator insisted to the Detroit News that the dismissal did not vindicate the arrestees.

Both the Lackawanna and the Detroit-Dearborn busts targeted hawala operations. Ironically, at the same time that some Bush administration officials were punishing American residents using hawalas to send aid to foreign relatives, the U.S. Agency for International Development was using hawalas to distribute foreign aid in Afghanistan. The Wall Street Journal reported: "The World Bank estimates aid agencies have moved at least $200 million through Afghan hawalas since the fall of the Taliban. Not once have CARE's hawalas failed to deliver the money. . . . The aid workers themselves judge a hawala solely by its ability to deliver money reliably and cheaply. U.S. officials see the risk but feel they have no choice but to take it."[115]

On February 26, 2003, the Justice Department indicted four men for allegedly using a charity to send $4 million to Iraq. Attorney General Ashcroft announced: "As President Bush leads an international coalition to end Saddam Hussein's tyranny and support for terror, the Justice Department will see that individuals within our borders cannot undermine these efforts."[116] Yet, federal prosecutors did not charge the four men with any terrorist-related offense and admitted that they did not know where the money ended up after it arrived in Iraq.

On March 21, 2003, Operation Green Quest announced nine more arrests of people around the country. The *New York Daily News* article on the raids was headlined, "Cash for Terror Busts,"[117] while the Associated Press story was headlined, "Feds Launch Raids Against Terror Money."[118] Homeland Security Assistant Secretary Michael Garcia declared: "By dismantling these illegal networks, we are denying avenues for terrorist groups to raise and move funds in this country."[119] (The Customs Service and Operation Green Quest had been transferred to the Homeland Security Department the prior month.) The feds' press release conceded that "agents have no evidence at this time those arrested were terrorists." Among those hit in the raids was a Los Angeles man who was using money orders to ship funds to Beirut and a Newark address that had been used to send numerous checks to Yemen via private express parcels. The Associated Press report noted comments by authorities that Yemen was the "site of the 2000 terrorist attack on the Navy destroyer, the USS *Cole.*"[120] Once again, the fact that none of the arrests or seizures were actually linked to terrorism may have been missed by the majority of people who heard of these cases.

## Victory by the Numbers

Bush administration officials continually portrayed seizure totals as battlefield victories. Deputy Treasury Secretary Kenneth Dam, in Senate testimony on January 29, 2002, declared: "Now one important question—is, how should we measure our success?" The first measure Dam proposed: "Since September 11th, the United States and other countries have frozen more than $80 million in terrorist-related assets." Dam continued, "We also have what I would call a somewhat qualitative measure, and that is how well are we doing in the effort to have international cooperation?" Dam answered his own question: "Foreign governments . . . have blocked a good deal of money . . . over $46 million. . . . A hundred and forty-seven countries in jurisdictions around the world have blocking orders in place."[121]

In the months after Dam's boasting, foreign governments released tens of millions of dollars frozen at U.S. behest after the U.S. government failed to provide evidence justifying the freeze. The *Washington Post* noted in June 2002: "Over the past four months, barely $10 million has been added to the total, while far more than that has been returned to its owners for lack of evidence of terrorist links." Yet, federal officials, as the *Washington Post* reported, declared that "the asset-freezing campaign has largely served its purposes of promoting international cooperation—through both threats and pats on the back—and helping other countries to develop new banking laws and improve intelligence."[122]

In June 2002, Dam explained the lack of fresh seizures of terrorists' assets: "These terrorists are intelligent, adaptable people, and they realize that putting money in bank accounts, particularly in the United States or Western Europe, is not a very good way to make sure it's available when you want it."[123] Though the Treasury Department practically admitted that the new reporting requirements and penalties are unlikely to catch terrorists, the agency remains enthusiastic about tightening the screws on every American's bank account.

Bush administration victory celebrations received a rude jolt from the United Nations in late August 2002. A report by the UN committee monitoring the financial fight against terrorism concluded: "Al Qaeda is by all accounts 'fit and well' and poised to strike again at its leisure." The UN concluded that private contributions to Al Qaeda "continue, largely unabated" and that Al Qaeda "continues to have access to considerable financial and other economic resources." The report noted that tracking down Al Qaeda resources has been "exceedingly difficult."[124]

On the day excerpts from the UN report first surfaced, the Treasury Department issued a rebuttal statement, complaining that the UN report "is limited in scope." The Treasury statement declared: "We are pleased with the success of the terrorist financing efforts, *but dollars seized is the narrowest measure of success.*"[125] After almost a year of Bush administration bragging of seizure totals, "dollars seized" became almost irrelevant. Gurule announced with the passion of a new convert: "This has never been a numbers game. . . . We're not keeping tally here to say what the number of assets blocked today is vis-a-vis a week ago or a month ago."[126] The U.S. government only ceased tracking and publicizing the amounts of money seized after the new seizures dried up.

Gurule bragged that the U.S. financial crackdown on Al Qaeda succeeded in "taking them out of their comfort zone."[127] Treasury general counsel Aufhauser proclaimed that the crackdown was forcing "would-be bankers of terror from 21st century digitized commerce into an awkward, cumbersome, Neanderthal economy of lugging gold bullion across mountain borders under cover

of night."[128] Aufhauser's smugness might be justified if terrorists were as inefficient as the U.S. government—if it took the terrorists a few hundred million
dollars to plan and execute any operation more complex than blowing up the
garbage cans behind some U.S. embassy. But the 9/11 attacks cost the terrorists
only about $500,000 to carry out. A hundred pounds of gold—something one
donkey could carry through a mountain pass—was sufficient to bring down the
World Trade Center and devastate the Pentagon.

## Terrorist Financiers Everywhere

In mid-2002, federal agents struck another death blow against Al Qaeda when
they raided 70 Pakistani-operated mall jewelry kiosks across the nation.[129] A
front-page *Washington Post* article reported, "Authorities are quietly investigating more than 500 Muslim and Arab small businesses across the United States
to determine whether they are dispatching money raised through criminal activity in the United States to terrorist groups overseas."[130]

   As part of the war against terrorists, the federal government also launched a
crackdown on individuals and groups racketeering with grocery discount
coupons. Operation Green Quest put out an advisory to banks and businesses
in October 2002 complaining that terrorists were profiting from "counterfeit
merchandise schemes involving a host of consumer items such as designer clothing, jewelry, fashion accessories and household products."[131] One senior federal
official ominously warned: "These sales produce a steady stream of money, and
we're now trying to reconstruct how the proceeds are laundered back to the
Middle East. We are trying to make the direct link to terror groups."[132] The
specter of terrorism was exploited to instill guilt into anyone buying a name
brand product at a breathtakingly good price: Tim Trainer, chief of the International AntiCounterfeiting Coalition lobby in Washington, declared: "People
who are buying branded products off the street should stop and say to themselves, 'Am I indirectly supporting any type of illegal activity? Is even a dime or
dollar going toward trafficking narcotics or to terrorism?'"[133]

   Yet, while federal press releases continually expand the financial war on terrorism, federal agencies cannot even agree on how to spell the names of the
prime suspects.[134] The *Los Angeles Times,* summarizing a confidential Inspector
General report on the failure of money laundering crackdowns, reported,
"Banking executives complained in interviews that there is widespread confusion over what the Treasury Department expects them to do in the stepped-up
effort to track and seize terrorist-tainted money, and the simplest of tasks—like

how to spell 'Mohammed'—has caused banks no shortage of frustration."[135] The IG report also found that "statistical errors and outdated policies" raised doubts about the "the accuracy of the Treasury Department's data on the thousands of financial transactions blocked each year."[136]

## Conclusion

President Bush, in a November 16, 2002 radio address, declared: "So far we have frozen more than $113 million in terrorist assets, denying them the means to finance their murder."[137] It was ludicrous to assume that every single dollar frozen was somehow equivalent to a terrorist attack stopped in progress—as if every dollar seized would have otherwise been used for plane tickets to attack skyscrapers in U.S. cities. Yet, this has been the core message of the Bush administration on seizures since 9/11.

Because the standard of proof for asset freezes is so low, the raw amount of money frozen—rather than a gauge of victories over terrorism—is simply a measure of government power. Measuring the success of the war on terrorist finances by seizure numbers is like judging a policeman's performance by the number of innocent bystanders he shoots.

The Justice Department is now exploiting powers gained via the Patriot Act to confiscate millions of dollars from foreign banks operating in the United States in cases with no terrorist connections or allegations. Thanks to the Patriot Act, "prosecutors are not even required to trace the money back to the target of an investigation," the *New York Times'* Eric Lichtblau reported. The Justice Department has used the Patriot Act to seize bank accounts in the United States from foreign-based banks in Israel, Oman, Taiwan, India, and Belize, largely on fraud and money laundering charges. One federal investigator with the Bureau of Immigration and Customs Enforcement explained: "Now we can get ahold of money where we couldn't before. But we proceed very cautiously. It's such a powerful tool, you could knock the economy of a country on its head if it were a big enough case." The burden of proof is very low for such seizures; the U.S. State Department is concerned that seizures could spark diplomatic conflicts with foreign countries. A Justice Department spokesman stressed that the department "scrutinizes prosecutors' use of this provision before it is exercised."[138] Yet, in other areas where the feds acquired power to confiscate assets with scant due process, early precedents quickly paved the way for far more aggressive seizures.

After 15 months of nonstop bragging about decisive victories in the war against terrorist financing, the Bush administration in early 2003 announced that it would double the size of its army fighting this menace. The Customs Service planned to create 14 new teams to sniff out illicit money flows around the United States.[139] The *New York Times* noted the grave risks involved, since the anti–money laundering operation in the FBI—a bitter bureaucratic rival—might interpret the expanded Customs crackdown as a major provocation.

On May 13, 2003, after more than 18 months of Customs Service victories against terrorists, the Bush administration effectively ended Operation Green Quest. Bush approved transferring terrorist financing investigations from the Bureau of Immigration and Customs Enforcement to the FBI.[140] One Customs official described the shift as "shocking."[141] The shift was a major victory for the FBI—but, considering that agency's perennial computer illiteracy, it may not bode well for the feds' ability to penetrate complex money machinations by savvy malefactors.

The U.S. government and other governments are justified in going after Al Qaeda money. Al Qaeda leaders have repeatedly announced their plans to attack the United States and wreak havoc. There is no need for the U.S. government to wait passively for the next wave of carnage. But the Bush administration, rather than concentrating on Al Qaeda, enacted a laundry list of proposals to empower government bureaucrats to punish citizens and businesses that pose no threat to national security.

The Patriot Act's financial provisions are a quixotic attempt to control all cash. Treasury Undersecretary Gurule declared on December 19, 2002: "Today's law enforcement actions are an important strike back against the illegal movement of money abroad."[142] The Federal Reserve estimates that $675 billion in U.S. currency is in circulation, most of it overseas.[143] The people at the top of the Treasury Department and Justice Department likely recognize that their stated goal of controlling all the money in the world to prevent any of it from falling into the hands of Specifically Designated Global Terrorists is a pipedream.

Government crackdowns such as Operation Green Quest treat U.S. dollars almost like plutonium—as a pre–Weapon of Mass Destruction. The only reason for the fixation on absolute control is the notion that any money transfer not controlled by the U.S. government can become "magic beans" that cause terrorism to sprout anywhere in the world. This mindset breeds the presumption that the U.S. government is entitled to assume the worst of anything that it does not control.

If the U.S. government cannot catch enough real terrorists, at least it can use the Patriot Act to turn hapless immigrants and cash-heavy travelers into terrorist scarecrows. Congress crafted a law that empowers the government to punish thousands of people for breaking the regs for every terrorist who might get caught laundering money. Treasury and Justice Department lawyers made sure the Patriot Act was written in a way to maximize seizures, regardless of a person's guilt or innocence—and then political appointees have portrayed every seizure as a victory against terrorism. But maximizing political brownie points by making terrorist innuendoes is not the same as protecting the public. The same bureaucrats who failed to notice the suspicious activity report on Mohamed Atta are now empowered to slap million-dollar penalties on bankers who fail to satisfy the government's latest definition of "due diligence" against money laundering. Allowing criminal penalties without criminal intent allows federal prosecutors to grandstand and to inflate their conviction numbers on the wrecked lives of unlucky citizens.

There is no reason to expect the U.S. government to be more successful in tracking wads of cash than it has been in tracking bricks of cocaine or bales of marijuana. The end result will be more federal control, more intrusions, less privacy— and little or no additional protection from terrorists. The issue is not how much money the U.S. government seizes, but how many foreigners are willing to die to punish America. Instead of concentrating scarce law enforcement resources on likely terrorist attackers, the U.S. government is going through a charade of claiming to track every bundle of C-notes that goes into or out of the country. The danger is the homicidal hatred, not the money.

## CHAPTER SIX

# Racking up the Numbers

We're going to protect and honor the Constitution, and I don't have the authority to set it aside. If I had the authority to set it aside, this would be a dangerous government, and I wouldn't respect it.

*—Attorney General John Ashcroft, October 11, 2001*[1]

The requirement that arrest books be open to the public is to prevent any "secret arrests," a concept odious to a democratic society.

*—Morrow v. District of Columbia, 1969*[2]

President Bush, in a June 12, 2002 address to his Homeland Security Advisory Council, bragged that "our coalition has hauled in about 2,400 of these terrorists, these killers."[3] Bush was referring to the total number of "special interest" detainees snared by the Immigration and Naturalization Service (INS) and Justice Department since 9/11, as well as to the roughly 1,200 people arrested by foreign governments. Bush still labeled all the people arrested in the United States as "terrorists" and "killers" long after the Justice Department conceded that most detainees had no link to terrorism.

The Bush administration brought the same mentality to locking up suspects after 9/11 that the Soviet Union used for the potato harvest from collective farms. It didn't matter how many bushels of potatoes were rotten, or how many bushels were lost or pilfered along the way, or how many bushels never really existed except in the mind of the commissars who burnished the official reports. All that mattered was the total number. In the same way, the success of the investigation after 9/11 was gauged largely by the number of people rounded up, regardless of their guilt or innocence.

Bush commendably stressed from the first days after the attack that Americans must not presume that all Muslims were guilty of the carnage wreaked by 19 of their fellow believers. But his comments were mocked by the lengthy incarceration of almost any Muslim or Arab male with a minor immigration violation. Law enforcement was justified in initially focusing suspicions on Muslims and Arab immigrants. But, after conducting mass arrests, top Justice Department officials continually invented new pretexts to deny due process to the detainees while misrepresenting the actual policies being used.

## Hiding the Bodies

Less than three months before the 9/11 attacks, the Supreme Court ruled that immigrants within the United States are protected by the Constitution "whether their presence here is lawful, unlawful, temporary or permanent."[4] Justice Steven Breyer, who wrote the majority opinion, specified that "terrorism" might be one of the "special circumstances where special arguments might be made for forms of preventive detention and for heightened deference to the judgments of the political branches with respect to matters of national security."

The Bush administration responded to the Supreme Court decision by presuming that practically any alien could automatically be considered a terrorist suspect. After 9/11 the Bush administration quickly requested that Congress pass legislation to formally suspend all habeas corpus rights for aliens. A petition for a writ of *habeas corpus*—Latin for "produce the body"—seeks to end unlawful detention of a person by requiring the government to bring the detained person before a judge to be either formally charged or released. Thomas Macaulay, in his *History of England,* proclaimed the Habeas Corpus Act of 1679 "the most stringent curb that ever legislation imposed on tyranny" and hailed it as a law that adds to "the security and happiness of every inhabitant of the realm."[5] The British legislation was part of the common law heritage incorporated into American law at the time of the nation's founding. The Supreme Court declared in 1969 that the writ of habeas corpus is "the fundamental instrument for safeguarding individual freedom against arbitrary and lawless state action."[6]

Ashcroft did not wait for a green light from Congress before making himself Czar of All Aliens. The INS, at Ashcroft's behest, issued a new emergency regulation on September 17 expanding the time from 24 hours to 48 hours that the agency was allowed to detain aliens while deciding whether to formally charge or deport them. The edict also provided for "an exception to the 48-hour general rule for any case arising during or in connection with an emergency or

other extraordinary circumstance, in which case the Service must make the de-
terminations as to custody or release . . . within an additional *reasonable period*
of time."[7] The official announcement of the new regulation repeatedly stressed
that "this 24-hour period is not mandated by constitutional requirements."[8]
And since a 24-hour period is not mandated by the Constitution, the Justice
Department was entitled to suspend habeas corpus for any immigrant it labeled
a terrorist suspect—or a potential material witness—or who was caught with
box-cutters. The INS attested that "this rule does not impose any new reporting
or record-keeping requirements under the Paperwork Reduction Act" and that
"it should have no appreciable economic impact."

The following day, Ashcroft characterized the new rules as "an administrative revision to the current INS regulations regarding the detention of aliens,"
adding that "this rule change will apply to these 75 individuals who are currently
detained by the INS on immigration violations that may also have information
related to this investigation."[9] As immigration lawyer Michael Boyle later testified to Congress: "This exceptionally vague and open-ended provision allows
detention without reason for virtually any period of time that the jailer chooses,
with no recourse or explanation. It, in effect, allows an individual to be held for
long periods for no better reason than that someone in government thinks they
look suspicious." The "reasonable period" edict illustrates how an innocuous
phrase can create a gaping legal sinkhole that threatens to swallow the rights of
ten million people—the number of legal immigrants in the United States.

On September 21, Michael Creppy, the chief immigration judge of the
INS, acting on Ashcroft's command, ordered immigration judges to close all
hearings of "special interest" detainees rounded up after 9/11 and to refuse to
confirm or deny to anyone outside the courts whether such hearings were scheduled. This made it very difficult, if not impossible, for relatives to keep track of
locked-up husbands, sons, or brothers, and also thwarted lawyers' efforts to keep
in touch with clients.[10]

In the days after the attacks, Attorney General Ashcroft told FBI Director
Robert Mueller "that any male from eighteen to forty years old from Middle
Eastern or North African countries who the FBI simply learned about was to be
questioned and questioned hard. And anyone from those countries whose im-
migration papers were out of order—anyone—was to be turned over to the
INS," *Newsweek* columnist Steven Brill reported in his book *After: How Amer-
ica Confronted the September 12 Era.*[11] Brill noted that Ashcroft told FBI and
INS agents that the goal "was to prevent more attacks, not prosecute anyone.
And the best way to do that was to round up, question, and hold as many people as possible." The feds scrambled to follow any and all leads to maximize the

number of people interrogated. Some FBI agents were instructed to look in phone books to find names of Arabs or Muslims who could be targeted.[12] Brill noted that FBI director Mueller "was not comfortable with a dragnet that simply held people on the hope that some might know something simply because they were Muslim men."[13]

While detainees were portrayed as would-be terrorists, most of the actual cases mocked the Bush administration's ominous overtones:

- A Moroccan teenager in Virginia was turned in to the feds by a high school guidance counselor who discovered the boy's tourist visa had expired. (The teenager registered for high school near the time of the terrorist attacks.) The *New York Times* noted on February 3, "The youngster has been detained for four months."[14] No evidence was found linking the boy to terrorist groups.

- Nacer Fathi Mustafa, a 29-year-old American citizen, was traveling back to the United States with his Palestinian father on September 15 after purchasing leather jackets in Mexico for a Florida truck stop he manages. The Mustafas were arrested after a federal official claimed that their passports had "obviously been altered with the introduction of an additional clear sheet on top of the genuine laminate."[15] The Mustafas' lawyer, Dan Gerson, later noted, "The agent attempted to cast the Mustafas in the worst light, stating that, when questioned, 'The Mustafas declined to offer any explanation,' when in fact they denied knowledge of any alterations."[16] His elderly father was jailed briefly and then released on condition that he wear an electronic ankle bracelet. The son was held for 67 days before a government laboratory concluded the passport had not been altered. The Mustafas sued the government to get reimbursement of their legal fees (over $15,000), asserting that the feds had acted in bad faith. Assistant U.S. Attorney Andrew A. Bobb scorned their lawsuit: "Both defendants' passports revealed they had traveled to the Middle East, a factor that could be considered in light of the fact the terrorists who caused the Sept. 11 devastation had traveled from the Middle East into the United States."[17] The Mustafas' lawsuit for compensation was heard and dismissed by the same judge who originally threw them in the slammer; the judge declared that all of the government officials involved had acted "in the utmost good faith."[18]

- On September 19 the FBI nabbed Mohammed Butt, a 55-year-old Pakistani living in a house with other aliens in Queens, New York. A priest had called the FBI to report local suspicions among the house's residents:

they did not cut the grass and failed to say hello. And as one 63-year-old neighbor astutely noted, "They hang their laundry—even their underwear—on the fence. Who does that?"[19] Butt had entered the United States a year earlier and had overstayed a six-month visa. The FBI quickly decided it had no use for Butt and turned him over to the INS. He was being held in the Hudson County jail when he died of a heart attack. Butt repeatedly filled out forms requesting medical assistance in the days before his death but was scorned by the jailers.[20] Hussein Ibish of the Arab-American Anti-Discrimination Committee complained: "There is no reason to believe he did not die of natural causes, but the point is nobody knew he was in jail. His family did not know, nor did the Pakistani consulate. He was never represented by counsel at any stage. He'd been in jail for several weeks. The only reason we know of his existence is that he died in jail and he had to be disposed of."[21] Human Rights Watch filed a Freedom of Information Act request to get information on Butt and his death but the INS refused to provide any information unless Human Rights Watch could provide Butt's "written consent" and "written signature" permitting the INS to release the information.[22]

- Two Moroccan men in their 20s living in Richmond, Virginia, were arrested by police during a September 13 traffic stop and handed over to the INS. The INS locked them up because they were working part-time at a pizza joint, in violation of their student visas.[23] Their lawyer, Syed Hyder, declared: "I've been told no one has any evidence against these boys. But since the F.B.I. had at one time expressed an interest in them, the INS had to hold them."[24]

- Raza Nasir Khan, a pizza cook, got swept up after he asked a state Fish and Wildlife agent for a map while he was hunting with his bow and arrow in Delaware on the morning of September 19.[25] The agent suspected the Pakistani—who possessed a global-positioning-satellite device (as do many hunters) and was within a few miles of a nuclear power plant—and alerted the FBI. FBI agents descended upon his apartment the next night and discovered three firearms. Khan, an avid hunter, had applied to have his visa extended but because it had not yet been renewed, he was guilty of a felony (illegal aliens are prohibited from possessing firearms). A few days later, federal Alcohol, Tobacco, and Firearms agents captured Khan on his way to the pizzeria. He was jailed and held without bond. Federal magistrate Mary Pat Thynge conceded: "There is nothing here to suggest [and] there were no indications that this individual was a terrorist. . . . There is no indication to me that there is a terrorism circumstance here."[26] Richard Andrews, a federal prosecutor in Wilmington, observed, "Mr. Khan was arrested because of Sept. 11 in the sense that they would not have gone out to interview him but for Sept. 11."[27]

Attempting to help the government investigate the terrorists landed at least two people in jail:

- Mustafa Abujdai, a Palestinian living in Texas, was locked up after he voluntarily contacted the FBI after 9/11 to inform them "he had met with two men in Saudi pilots uniforms at a restaurant in Dallas, Texas, and that they had attempted to recruit him for flight training school," according to his lawyer, Karen Pennington.[28] One of the Saudis was one of the 9/11 suicide pilots. Abujdai, who was married to an American, was interrogated for 15 hours and then jailed for over two months for overstaying his visa. Abujdai claimed other jail inmates heavily abused him.
- Eyad Mustafa Alrababah, a Palestinian living in Connecticut, was also locked up after he voluntarily went to the FBI office in Bridgeport to tell them that he recognized pictures of four of the hijackers and had driven them to Virginia in June. He was locked up as a material witness, held in solitary confinement for over 120 days, and kept incommunicado for much of the time.[29]

The Bush administration constantly misrepresented how much power it was seeking over aliens. In his September 25 speech to FBI agents, Bush declared: "We're asking Congress for the authority to hold suspected terrorists who are in the process of being deported until they're deported. . . . We believe it's a necessary tool to make America a safe place. This would, of course, be closely supervised by an immigration judge."[30] But everything that Bush and Ashcroft subsequently did sought to minimize, if not obliterate, judicial supervision of their roundup.

On September 30 Ashcroft announced on CNN: "We've arrested and detained almost 500 people since the Sept. 11 terrorist attacks. . . . We seek to hold them as *suspected terrorists,* while their cases are being processed on other grounds."[31]

On October 8 Ashcroft announced that the count had reached 614 persons[32] and issued new warnings of imminent terrorist attacks.

Ashcroft's call to vigilance brought out the best in law enforcement around the country. Human Rights Watch reported the following cases:

- "Upon arriving at the Newark, New Jersey train station on October 11, 2001, Osama Sewilam asked a policeman for directions to his immigration attorney's office. The policeman asked him where he was from, and he replied, 'Egypt.' The policeman asked him if he had a visa. He said it had expired and that was why he was going to see his lawyer. The policeman took him to the police station and called the FBI. Sewilam was deported on March 15, 2002."[33]

- "Ansar Mahmood, a twenty-four-year-old Pakistani who was a legal permanent resident in the United States, decided to have his picture taken on October 9, 2001, to send to his family, according to a newspaper report. After work, he drove to the highest point in Hudson, New York, a hilltop overlooking the Catskills Mountains, but the view also included the main water treatment plant for the town. Two guards had been posted there that day because of the anthrax scare. While one of the guards took Mahmood's picture, the other called the police. The FBI's investigation of Mahmood uncovered that he had helped an undocumented friend from Pakistan find an apartment and he was charged with harboring an illegal immigrant."[34]

Allegations began popping up of detainees being beaten or prevented from contacting a lawyer. Ashcroft announced on October 16: "I would be happy to hear from individuals if there are any alleged abuses of individuals, because that is not the way we do business."[35] He promised that "we will respect the constitutional rights and we will respect the dignity of individuals."[36] But the fact that many detainees were held incommunicado made it tricky for them to personally contact the attorney general.

The FBI had a form affidavit it presented judges to justify indefinite secret confinement of targeted aliens. In scores, if not hundreds, of cases, the FBI warned: "At the present stage of this vast investigation, the FBI is gathering and culling information that may corroborate or diminish our current suspicions of the individuals that have been detained. . . . In the meantime, the FBI has been unable to rule out the possibility that respondent is somehow linked to, or possesses knowledge of the terrorist attacks on the World Trade Center and the Pentagon. To protect the public, the FBI must exhaust all avenues of investigation while ensuring that critical information does not evaporate pending further investigation."[37] The FBI declared that "the business of counter-terrorism intelligence gathering in the United States is akin to the construction of a *mosaic*. . . . The FBI is gathering and processing thousands of bits and pieces of information that may seem innocuous at first glance. We must analyze all that information, however, to see if it can be fit into a picture that will reveal how the unseen whole operates."[38] The FBI implied that mere mortals could not even hope to grasp the meaning of the details agents were sniffing out: "What may seem trivial to some may appear of great moment to those within the FBI or the intelligence community."[39] The "mosaic" form affidavit pushed the hottest button to intimidate judges—the same tactic Ashcroft successfully used on Congress to railroad through the Patriot Act. The FBI's constant invocation of the need to build "mosaics" is ironic in light of the joint congressional investigation's conclusions about the FBI's analytical incompetence.

Ashcroft portrayed arbitrary power as the key to national survival. On October 25, Ashcroft told the U.S. Conference of Mayors:

> Today's terrorists enjoy the benefits of our free society even as they commit themselves to our destruction. . . . Attorney General Robert Kennedy made no apologies for using all of the available resources in the law to disrupt and dismantle organized crime networks. Very often, prosecutors were aggressive, using obscure statutes to arrest and detain suspected mobsters. . . . Robert Kennedy's Justice Department, it is said, would arrest mobsters for "spitting on the sidewalk" if it would help in the battle against organized crime. Let the terrorists among us be warned. . . . If you violate a local law, you will be put in jail and kept in custody *as long as possible.* We will use every available statute. *We will seek every prosecutorial advantage.*[40]

In Ashcroft's view, any breach of any law or regulation automatically entitles the government to absolute power over the suspected violator. This "maximum-prosecution mentality" is far more dangerous now than it was in the early 1960s. There are far more levers for government to use against those it seeks to destroy. Since 1963 more than 700 new crimes have been added to the federal statute book, the length of the Code of Federal Regulations has quintupled, and the number of federal regulators has increased eightfold. And Robert F. Kennedy never tried to cancel habeas corpus for 10 million people.

The following day, Bush signed the Patriot Act, which gave Bush and Ashcroft almost everything they wanted—except for formally suspending habeas corpus. The law increased the length of time that an alien could be locked up without charges to seven days. If the attorney general certifies that he has "reasonable grounds to believe that the alien is engaged in any activity that endangers the national security of the United States," the detention can be extended almost indefinitely. No evidence is required: the attorney general's rote assertion is sufficient. Georgetown University law professor David Cole observed: "While 'suspected terrorist' might sound like a class that ought to be locked up, the Patriot Act defines that class so broadly that it includes people who have never engaged in or supported a violent act in their lives, but are merely 'associated' with disfavored groups."[41] The Patriot Act included a different definition of terrorism for aliens than for U.S. citizens; aliens are now considered guilty of terrorism if they are convicted of "the use of any explosive, firearm, or other weapon or dangerous device (other than for mere personal monetary gain), with intent to endanger, directly or indirectly, the safety of one or more individuals or to cause substantial damage to property."[42] As Micah Herzog noted in the *Georgetown Immigration Law Journal,* "The parenthetical frees common thieves from classification as a terrorist, but the angry boyfriend who intentionally harms his former girlfriend's car is now in a different class of crime."[43]

The feds became intensely frustrated when the vast majority of detainees would not disclose evidence of terrorist crimes or conspiracies. Some FBI officials suggested that torture might be useful. One senior FBI official told the *Washington Post:* "We're into this thing for 35 days and nobody is talking. Frustration has begun to appear. We are known for humanitarian treatment, so basically we are stuck. Usually there is some incentive, some angle to play, what you can do for them. But it could get to that spot where we could go to pressure . . . where we don't have a choice, and we are probably getting there." The *Post* noted: "Among the alternative strategies under discussion are using drugs or pressure tactics, such as those employed occasionally by Israeli interrogators, to extract information."[44] The FBI's trial balloon generated significant support in the media, led by Harvard law professor Alan Dershowitz.[45]

Boundless hysteria brought out the best in law enforcement. As the *Los Angeles Times* reported, "Sinister interpretations of innocuous details have transformed family vacation film of Niagara Falls and Washington, D.C., into suspicious surveillance footage. A gas station with cots became a suspected 'safe house.'"[46] FBI spokesman Bob Doguim observed: "The only thing a lot of these [suspects] are guilty of is having the Arabic version of Bob Jones for a name."[47] James Ridgeway reported in the *Village Voice:* "The FBI, using the INS as a 'front,' as one attorney puts it, pulled in every Muslim it thought to be suspicious. A police check of a car parked in front of a fire hydrant led to one arrest. Another detainee had renewed his driver's license in a Florida motor-vehicle office shortly after one of the September 11 terrorists renewed his license. An executive was pulled over for a traffic violation and suddenly found half a dozen cops all over him, screaming, 'Terrorist!'"[48]

On October 31 the Justice Department issued a new emergency rule to block immigration judges' orders to release aliens.[49] The *Federal Register* notice stated that the new regulation would help "maintain the status quo while the Immigration and Naturalization Service seeks expedited review of the custody order by the Board of Immigration Appeals or by the Attorney General." "Maintain the status quo" was a euphemism for keeping someone locked up, regardless of a judge's order to release him. The Justice Department promised the new regulation would economize scarce bureaucratic resources: "This provision for an automatic stay will avoid the necessity of having to decide whether to order a stay on extremely short notice with only the most summary presentation of the issues."[50]

The Bush administration exploited an administrative law judge system that, even before 9/11, was heavily politicized.[51] Administrative law judges work for the Justice Department—which also hires the INS lawyers who argue cases before the judges. If an INS lawyer loses before an administrative law judge, he can take the case to the Board of Immigration Appeals. If he loses there, the Attorney General can personally overturn the verdict.[52] The INS judges union—the National Association of Immigration Judges—recently complained: "The taint of inherent conflict of interests caused by housing the Immigration Court within the Justice Department is insidious and pervasive."[53]

Shortly after the president signed the Patriot Act the Justice Department announced that it could henceforth eavesdrop on telephone calls and meetings between anyone detained in a terrorist investigation and their lawyers. A *Federal Register* notice stated that the monitoring would be carried out whenever the attorney general certified "that reasonable suspicion exists to believe that an inmate may use communications with attorneys or their agents to facilitate acts of terrorism."[54] Since it required no evidence for the feds to label someone a terrorist threat, it would presumably require scant suspicion to justify pervasive eavesdropping. Sen. Patrick Leahy, chairman of the Senate Judiciary Committee, complained in a letter to Ashcroft that there are "few safeguards to liberty that are more fundamental than the Sixth Amendment. When the detainee's legal adversary—the government that seeks to deprive him of his liberty—listens in on his communications with his attorney, that fundamental right and the adversary process that depends upon it are profoundly compromised."[55] Irwin Schwartz, president of the National Association of Criminal Defense Lawyers, declared: "The Code of Professional Responsibility is quite clear: a lawyer must maintain confidentiality. If we can't speak with a client confidentially, we may not speak with him at all. And if we can't do that, the client is stripped of his Sixth Amendment right to have a lawyer."[56]

The Bush administration sought to allay rumors of mass roundups of Muslim males. On November 5 White House spokesman Ari Fleischer announced:

"Most of the people, the overwhelming number of the people, were detained, they were questioned, and then they've been released." Fleischer added that President Bush "is fully satisfied that anybody who is continuing to be held is being held for a wise reason."[57] But a Justice Department spokesman contradicted the White House, declaring on the same day that most of people rounded up after 9/11 were still held by the government.[58]

The Justice Department responded to the imbroglio by announcing it would cease disclosing the total number of people locked up in the 9/11 investigation. As *Time* noted, "Ashcroft spokeswoman Mindy Tucker said the department would no longer issue daily or even weekly updates [of the number of detainees], because the task of making and synchronizing lists was too labor intensive."[59] Assistant Attorney General Chertoff later said that the feds ceased giving out updated totals of detainees because it "loses meaning."[60] The media widely reported statements by senior federal officials that 1200 suspects had been detained in the 9/11 investigations.

On November 25 Ayazuddin Sheerazi, age 32, was nabbed by INS agents and local police at a gas station in Torrington, Connecticut, that he was watching briefly for an uncle running an errand. Sheerazi had a valid visa but he was arrested because a local storyteller called the FBI and claimed he heard two Arabs plotting to send anthrax into New York City. Sheerazi was Indian, not Arab, but that was close enough for government work. (Three Pakistanis were locked up in the same roundup.) Sheerazi was jailed for 18 days. INS officials included the gas station on their sweep in Torrington "because they heard it was owned by foreigners," according to Sheerazi.[61] Sheerazi complained: "We are from a family that is respected in India. But to be led away in chains is associated with a great deal of shame."[62] He promptly voluntarily left the United States after his release.

At a November 27 Washington press conference Ashcroft announced: "We're removing suspected terrorists . . . from our streets to prevent further terrorist attacks."[63] Ashcroft declared that, thanks in part to "arrests and detentions, we have avoided further major terrorist attacks, and we've avoided these further major terrorist attacks despite threats and videotape tauntings."[64] Videotape tauntings were, in Ashcroft's mind, almost as dangerous as a hijacked jetliner. Ashcroft did not present any evidence linking any detainee to terrorist attack plans. Referring to the number of detainees, Ashcroft sputtered about "the 540—550—pardon me—I'll get the number exactly right—554, I believe it is, in INS custody."

Ashcroft derided suggestions to release the names of detainees: "I am not interested in providing, when we are at war, a list to Osama bin Laden, the al

Qaeda network, of the people that we have detained that would make in any way easier their effort to kill American citizens—innocent Americans."[65]

Ashcroft denied that any of detainees' rights had been violated: "The Justice Department will not sacrifice the ultimate good to fight the immediate evil." Ashcroft proclaimed that it is "simply not true" that "detainees are not able to be represented by an attorney or to contact their families." Ashcroft sounded deeply hurt by the scurrilous attacks on the Justice Department: "I would hope that those who make allegations about something as serious as a violation of an individual's civil rights would not do so lightly or without specificity or without facts. This does a disservice to our entire justice system. . . ."[66]

A journalist asked Ashcroft's reaction to creating a bipartisan commission to "oversee the conduct of this massive investigation to ensure that there aren't any civil liberty violations." Ashcroft replied: "Now, we already have bipartisan committees whose responsibility it is to oversee the Justice Department. . . . I think it's entirely proper that the United States Senate and House exercise oversight over the Justice Department." Yet, Ashcroft had been stonewalling the committees, refusing to provide almost any information about the post–9/11 investigations. When the journalist again sought a direct response to his question, Ashcroft laughed: "Maybe you ought to make that your platform when you run for president next time!"[67]

Ashcroft bragged at the press conference that 104 people had been charged with crimes as a result of the post-9/11 investigation. One of those honorees was Francois Guagani, a French citizen who was caught as he was crossing the border on a bus into Maine on September 12. Guagani was arrested because he was entering the United States after having been deported for previously violating his immigration status. Because he had box-cutters in his luggage (he worked as a carpenter), he was included on the list of people formally charged by the Justice Department in the terrorism investigation.[68] (He was sentenced to 20 months in prison.)

Another of the "special interest" detainees formally charged with a crime was Arslan Absar Rizvi. As the *Los Angeles Times* reported, Rizvi "was arrested Oct. 31, when local police went to his home in Bloomfield, Colo., on a warrant for domestic violence and assault. The police were accompanied by an INS agent who, according to a federal affidavit, learned that Rizvi's visa from Pakistan was no longer valid and found a .12-gauge shotgun in his basement. Jeff Dorshner of the U.S. attorney's office in Denver acknowledged Tuesday night that, while the charges are serious against Rizvi, he is not a terrorist. 'No, no, no,' Dorshner said. 'This is just that he is in the country illegally and he had a shotgun.'"[69]

None of the other criminal charges that Ashcroft invoked had any link to the 9/11 attacks. The charges were a smorgasbord of credit card fraud, false statements to federal officials, immigration violations, theft, and so on.[70]

On November 28, 2001 Assistant Attorney General Chertoff testified to the Senate Judiciary Committee: "Nobody is held incommunicado. We don't hold people in secret, you know, cut off from lawyers, cut off from the public, cut off from their family and friends. They have the right to communicate with the outside world. We don't stop them from doing that."[71] Under questioning, Chertoff did concede: "It may well be that in the early parts of this investigation, as people were moved around, there was some slippage."[72] Chertoff's choice of the word "slippage" implies that the federal government was cleaning up hazardous roadside slop after a tanker truck overturned.

The right to hire one's own lawyer was sometimes effectively undermined by bureaucratic gaming. As Stephen Brill noted, the INS list of lawyers that detainees received after being arrested "invariably had phone numbers that were not in service. This was discussed at one of the Ashcroft meetings, and, according to one person who says he was there, someone in the room remarked that the government should not try too hard to make sure these people could contact lawyers. 'Let's not make it so they can get Johnnie Cochran on the phone,' another lawyer added."[73] Amnesty International reported in March 2002 that detainees at the Metropolitan Detention Center in New York City "reported being allowed just one phone call a week. They had to choose a number from the list of legal service providers—if no one answered when they called, they had to wait another week before being allowed to try again or seek assistance from another number on the list. There were also reports that detainees were only allowed to make calls after 5.30 P.M. when many offices were closed."[74] Several detainees complained that they were permitted to make only one phone call per month. Lawyers from the Legal Aid Society, who provide free counsel, informed Amnesty International that "they were allowed to visit detainees only if they already had the name or had been retained by the detainee's family—a catch–22 situation" because of the inability of many detainees to successfully contact any lawyer.[75]

Also testifying at the Senate hearing was Ali al-Maqtari, a French teacher and Yemeni citizen who was arrested on September 15 and kept locked away for eight weeks. Three months before his arrest he married an American woman who had converted to Islam. She wanted to join the Army so he had driven her from their home in New England to Fort Campbell, Kentucky, where she was to report for duty. Upon arrival, his car was searched and two box-cutters and postcards of New York City were discovered.[76] Michael Boyle, al-Maqtari's lawyer, noted that his wife's picture "had already been posted at the [Fort Campbell] guardhouse because she had picked up her military orders in Massachusetts on Sept. 13 wearing an Islamic head covering."[77] When controversy arose over al-Maqtari's arrest in late September, Justice Department spokeswoman Mindy Tucker declared: "The president has called this an act of war. This is not a normal terrorism case."[78] After reporting for duty, his wife "was trailed by guards around the base for weeks, while other soldiers openly asked her if she was a spy. She said base officers encouraged her to take an honorable discharge, and she finally did so on Oct. 28," the New York Times noted.[79] Al-Maqtari's case was one of the few in which an immigration judge was not intimidated by an FBI "mosaic" memo: he ordered al-Maqtari released on bond and the INS appeals board also scorned the government's request to hold him indefinitely for "intelligence-gathering" purposes. The feds never offered any evidence linking al-Maqtari to anything aside from box-cutters and postcards. Al-Maqtari testified to the Senate Judiciary Committee: "The investigators said many, many times that our marriage was fake, and that Tiffanay must be married to me because I was abusing her. These accusations were totally false and very painful for me. They also made many negative remarks about Islam, things like Islam being the religion of beating and mistreating women. One acted out a fist hitting his hand, another said my wife had written a letter saying that I beat her, which I knew was false, and another insisted he would beat me all the way to my country because I mistreated my wife. . . . The interrogators were so angry and wild in their accusations that they made me very frightened for what might happen to me."[80] Boyle noted that al-Maqtari "was arrested with an invalid warrant. He wasn't given any rights to counsel; none of these booklets and extensive protections you've heard about. And in virtually every other case we've heard, it's been the same—no warnings, no right to counsel. People are discouraged from getting attorneys. They're told they'll get out quicker or their case will be resolved quicker if they don't."[81]

On December 5, the day before Ashcroft's first testimony on Capitol Hill in more than two months, a coalition of civil liberties groups announced they were suing the government. Kate Martin of the Center for National Security Studies warned: "There is mounting evidence that secrecy is being invoked to shield serious violations of individual rights and not for legitimate investigative purposes."[82]

On December 6 Ashcroft testified under oath to the Senate Judiciary Committee: "We have waged a deliberate campaign of arrest and detention to remove suspected terrorists who violate the law from our streets." Ashcroft again denounced his critics: "Their bold declarations of so-called fact have quickly dissolved, upon inspection, into vague conjecture. Charges of 'kangaroo courts' and 'shredding the Constitution' give new meaning to the term, 'the fog of war.' Since lives and liberties depend upon clarity, not obfuscation, and reason, not hyperbole, let me take this opportunity today to be clear: Each action taken by the Department of Justice . . . is carefully drawn to target a narrow class of individuals—terrorists. Our legal powers are targeted at terrorists. Our investigation is focused on terrorists."[83]

Ashcroft and his subordinates offered an array of reasons for refusing to name the detainees. At a November 26 press conference, Ashcroft declared: "The law properly prevents the department from creating a public blacklist of detainees that would violate their rights."[84] The next day, Ashcroft announced he was not releasing the names of the detainees because it would be "prejudicial" to their "privacy interest."[85] Ashcroft later declared that the names of detainees could not be released because the information is "too sensitive for public scrutiny."[86] In January 2002 Assistant Attorney General Chertoff justified refusing to release the names to avoid tarring "special interest" detainees with an onus like that of "sexual predators."[87] Assistant Attorney General Robert McCallum Jr. later warned that releasing the names could spark attacks on the detainees by "vigilantes."[88] Human Rights Watch pointed out that "the total number of persons detained in connection with the September 11 investigation may never be known" in part because the withholding of the names of the detainees "makes it impossible to check the accuracy of the numbers released by the Department of Justice."[89]

## The Prize Catch that Got Away

Abdallah Higazy, a 30-year-old Egyptian student, arrived in New York City to study engineering at the Polytechnic University in Brooklyn on August 27, 2001. Since he could not find student housing, the Institute of International Education—the U.S. government foreign aid program that was paying his bills—put him up at the Millennium Hilton Hotel, next to the World Trade Center. After the first plane crashed into the World Trade Center, Higazy hot footed it out of the hotel. After the terrorist attack, the hotel was sealed. Three months later, guests were allowed to retrieve their belongings. When Higazy went to the hotel on December 17, he was arrested and accused of possessing an aviation radio. (A hotel security guard reported finding the radio in a safe in Higazy's room.) Higazy denied owning the radio. He was arrested as a material witness and locked up in solitary confinement.

Higazy wanted to clear his name so he agreed to take a polygraph test. An FBI agent wired him up for the test but then proceeded to browbeat him for three hours until he finally admitted owning the radio. Higazy said the FBI agent warned him: "If you don't cooperate with us, the FBI will . . . make sure Egyptian security gives your family hell."[90] The FBI refused to permit Higazy's attorney, Robert Dunn, to be in the room while he was given the polygraph. After the interrogation, Higazy was "trembling and sobbing uncontrollably," according to his lawyer.[91] Dunn observed that Higazy "insisted that he had no connection to the device but felt he had no choice but to make some kind of admission relative to the radio in an effort to remove his family from harm's way."[92] *Newsday* noted: "Prosecutors initially denied any threats were made, but now decline to comment on what happened and on the permissibility of using such threats as an interrogation technique."[93]

On January 11, 2002 Higazy was indicted for perjury. U.S. Attorney Dan Himmelfarb declaimed that "the crime that was being investigated when the false statements [about the radio] were made is perhaps the most serious in the country's history. A radio that can be used for air-to-air and air-to-ground communication is a significant part of that investigation."[94] Higazy was accused of interfering with the 9/11 investigation in "a profound and fundamental way."[95] The *Washington Post* noted that "federal officials paraded [Higazy] before the media as a terrorist."[96] The feds never bothered contacting the Institute for International Education to check out Higazy's story about why he was staying at the hotel next to the World Trade Center.

The prosecutorial celebration wilted three days later when an American pilot showed up at the Millennium Hilton Hotel and asked for the aviation radio he had left in his room when the hotel was evacuated on 9/11. It soon became apparent that the hotel security guard (a former cop who had been fired by the Newark Police Department and who admitted a drug problem)[97] lied about finding the radio in Higazy's room. The case collapsed and, a few days later, Higazy was awarded three dollars for subway fare and released from jail.

The hotel security guard stated that he had lied during a "time of patriotism."[98] After the guard pled guilty to making false statements to the FBI, he received a slap on the wrist: jail time on weekends for six months. *Newsday* columnist Ellis Henican noted that the hotel security guard "was aided and abetted in his recklessness by FBI agents and federal prosecutors—sloppy at best, incompetent or uncaring at worst. And just plain wrong. . . . They were so eager to make a high-profile terror arrest, they didn't only accept the lie of a hotel security guard. They embellished it. They confirmed it. They carried it into court." After Higazy's interrogation, "federal agents were whispering to reporters that

Higazy had confessed. At first, they'd said, he'd tried to weasel. He'd contradicted himself, the way that criminals often do. But then, thanks to the brilliant interrogation tactics of the FBI, the radio man had come clean," Henigan noted.[99]

Federal judge Jed Rakoff demanded that the Justice Department explain how the false confession had been generated. After foot-dragging by the Justice Department, Rakoff summoned the U.S. attorney to his court and groused: "The victim we are here concerned with is not the witness, but the court, which was materially misled."[100] Rakoff ordered the U.S. Attorney's office to investigate the FBI's actions. Higazy's lawyer, Robert Dunn, was disappointed that the judge permitted the Justice Department to investigate its own misconduct.

Justice Department officials fought to prevent the investigation report from becoming public—until they knew the report exonerated the government. When the report was released, U.S. Attorney James Comey announced that he was "very proud of the way our office and the FBI conducted itself in the Higazy case."[101] Robert Dunn, Higazy's lawyer, denounced the report as "a craftily woven cloth of deceit and deception that was essentially a whitewash."[102]

## Judicial Insubordination across the Land

At his November 27, 2001 press conference Ashcroft huffed: "I have yet to be informed of a single lawsuit filed against the government charging a violation of someone's civil rights as a result of this investigation." But by early spring 2002, several court cases were making Justice Department spinmeisters earn their pay.

Rabih Haddad, a Lebanese citizen and chairman of a Muslim charity, was arrested in Michigan on December 14, 2001 on visa violation charges. The court proceedings to deport Haddad were so secretive that, as a British paper noted, "even Haddad has been barred from attending; he has had to watch them on video from his jail cell, without the right of participation."[103] Rep. John Conyers (D-Mich.), the *Detroit News,* the *Detroit Free Press,* and the American Civil Liberties Union sued the Justice Department to open the Haddad proceedings. On April 3, 2002, federal judge Nancy Edmunds announced: "Openness is necessary for the public to maintain confidence in the value and soundness of the government's actions, as secrecy only breeds suspicion." Edmunds ruled that it was unconstitutional to close Haddad's hearings.[104]

The FBI warned that opening the Haddad case file would result in "severe and irreparable harm" to national security. The Justice Department took the case to federal appeals court but got trounced. After that loss, Associate Attorney General Jay Stephens announced that "the release of past transcripts of the immigration proceedings, as required by court order, will not cause irreparable harm to the national security or to the safety of the American people."[105] Herschel Fink, the lawyer who whipped the feds in court, observed that Stephens' comment proves "that the Justice Department has been lying repeatedly about this case. They said over and over again that the release of this information would be a terrible blow to national security, and now they say it's not."[106]

While the feds conceded on the case file, they continued to fight open hearings for Haddad. On September 17 judge Edmunds ordered the feds either to set Haddad free or to give him an open hearing. Edmunds declared that open hearings would "assure the public that the government itself is honoring the very democratic principles that the terrorists who committed the atrocities of 9/11 sought to destroy."[107]

Because of a shortage of federal prison space, the INS dumped many detainees in state and local jails. The ACLU and others sued for a list of the names of INS detainees held in New Jersey jails. On March 26, 2002 New Jersey judge Arthur D'Italia denounced secret detentions as "odious to a democratic society" and declared that New Jersey law required disclosure of detainees' names.[108] D'Italia noted: "Nothing is easier for the government to assert than the disclosure of the arrest of X would jeopardize investigation Y."[109] Justice Department spokesman Mark Corallo announced that the feds would appeal the decision.[110]

But the Justice Department found an easier solution: issuing an emergency regulation banning any state or local government from releasing the detainees' names.[111] The new edict declared that "it would make little sense for the release of potentially sensitive information to be subject to the vagaries of the laws of the various states within which those detainees are housed and maintained."[112] Deborah Jacobs, executive director of the ACLU New Jersey affiliate, denounced the new federal regulation as "basically an attempt to make our state laws null and void."[113]

The Justice Department also appealed the case. At the New Jersey appeals court hearing on the case on May 19, U.S. assistant attorney general Robert McCallum warned that releasing the names could lead to "potentially extraordinarily dangerous" consequences. Judge Howard Kestin fretted: "For a government to say we lost in this case and we're going to cure it by promulgating a regulation, it's troubling."[114]

On June 12 the New Jersey appellate court overturned Judge D'Italia's decision, declaring that, because of the supremacy clause of the U.S. Constitution, the emergency INS regulation trumped New Jersey state law.[115] The court noted: "With regard to the government's national-security argument, there can be no question that the government of the United States has a compelling interest in securing the safety of the nation's citizens against [a] terrorist attack."[116] But the issue was whether merely invoking the threat of future attacks was sufficient to justify closing all proceedings for hundreds of people not linked to terrorism.[117]

On May 29 federal judge John Bissell, ruling in the case of *North Jersey Media Group v. Ashcroft,* prohibited the Justice Department "from closing to the public any immigration proceeding in the absence of case-specific findings demonstrating that closure is narrowly tailored to serve a compelling governmental interest."[118] Bissell scorned the mass secret hearings as "a clear case of irreparable harm to a right protected by the First Amendment."

The Bush administration took the Bissell decision to a federal appeals court, which refused to overturn Bissell's order to immediately open "special interest" hearings.[119] The Bush administration quickly appealed the decision to the Supreme Court. Once again, the issue was a simple choice between total secrecy and national destruction. Bush administration Solicitor General Theodore Olson warned: "It is possible that the disclosure of even a single piece of information concerning the case of a special interest alien that might appear innocuous . . . could be of vital importance to the sophisticated terrorist groups that are monitoring the government's efforts to investigate the Sept. 11 attacks and prevent their recurrence—and thus could have devastating consequences for the nation."[120] The Supreme Court blocked Bissell's order and remanded the case back to the appeals court for a full hearing.[121]

Federal judges continued dogging the Bush administration as other cases snaked through the courts. On August 2 federal judge Gladys Kessler declared: "Secret arrests are 'a concept odious to a democratic society,' and profoundly antithetical to the bedrock values that characterize a free and open one such as ours. . . . The public's interest in learning the identity of those arrested and detained is essential to verifying whether the government is operating within the bounds of law."[122] Kessler declared: "The first priority of the judicial branch must be to ensure that our government always operates within the statutory and constitutional constraints which distinguish a democracy from a dictatorship."[123] Kessler ordered the Justice Department to publish a list of names of all detainees within 15 days, but later extended the deadline to give the Justice Department more time to prepare its appeal.[124]

On August 26, 2002 a federal appeals court in Cincinnati ruled that the blanket closures of hearings of "special interest" detainees violated the First Amendment. The opinion, written by Judge Damon Keith, declared: "The Executive Branch seeks to uproot people's lives, outside the public eye, and behind a closed door. Democracies die behind closed doors. . . . When government begins closing doors, it selectively controls information rightfully belonging to the people. Selective information is misinformation."[125] The Justice Department had previously argued that the release of information about the detainees "would not contribute meaningfully to the public's understanding of the inner workings of the government."[126] The court scorned the Justice Department's arguments as "profoundly undemocratic," declaring: "Open hearings, apart from their value to the community, have long been considered to advance fairness to the parties."[127] The Justice Department, in its briefs in the case, claimed that there was no need for case-by-case decisions on whether to close the hearings because "each special interest detainee has been evaluated and designated on the basis of the government's ongoing investigative interest in him and his relationship to the ongoing anti-terrorism investigation."[128] The judges found this assertion "unpersuasive." The appeals court also noted that "the Government has failed to disclose the actual number of special interest cases it has designated."

None of the advocates who battled the Justice Department in court denied either the government's need to protect national security or the fact that cases could exist in which the government would be justified in closing proceedings. The issue was not whether all hearings and all evidence should be open; instead, the issue was whether all hearings must automatically be closed. The fight was over what standard should be used to close judicial proceedings. According to the Bush administration, a momentary suspicion of a detainee, however baseless, sufficed to perpetually close all hearings on his case.

## Material Witness Malarkey

After 9/11 the Justice Department locked up many people as material witnesses for potential testimony at some future date before a grand jury. On April 30, 2002 federal judge Shira Scheindlin ruled that policy to be unconstitutional: "Since 1789, no Congress has granted the government the authority to imprison an innocent person in order to guarantee that he will testify before a grand jury conducting a criminal investigation."[129] Scheindlin warned that the Bush administration's interpretation of federal law could make "detention the norm and liberty the exception." The Bush administration appealed and ignored the ruling. Federal judge Michael Mukasey later upheld the Bush administration's policy.[130]

The Justice Department refuses to disclose the number of people jailed under the federal witness statute. The *Washington Post* reported in November 2002 that "nearly half" of the 44 people the *Post* confirmed jailed under this provision "have never been called to testify before a grand jury" and that "at least seven of the witnesses were U.S. citizens."[131] Former federal prosecutor Neal

Sonnett noted that the fact that some material witnesses never testified "would tend to indicate that the use of the material witness statute was more of a ruse than an honest desire to record the testimony of that person."[132] The *Post* noted: "The material witness cases have been adjudicated in unusual secrecy. Most, if not all, are subject to judicial sealing orders, and there is confusion among defense attorneys across the nation about what information they can make public. In five cases attorneys confirmed that detainees were material witnesses but refused to release their names, citing judicial orders and privacy concerns. Other lawyers refused even to confirm or deny that they represented material witnesses." A *Loyola of Los Angeles Law Review* analysis concluded: "The government uses these [material witness] laws to round up people because of what it expects them to do, rather than what it can prove they have done."[133]

As author Steven Brill noted, the material witness hook was used in cases in which "not even minor crimes could be established, or where the government was worried that these people were so important that they did not want them to get lawyers quickly (as they would be entitled to if charged with any crime). . . . Ashcroft's team . . . would control when, if ever, that person might be asked to testify—meaning they would seek to hold the person indefinitely so as to coerce him to talk."[134] Detaining people as material witnesses meant that they "could be questioned without lawyers present because they were not being charged with any crime," Brill noted.

Mohamed Kamel Bellahouel was locked up for five months as a material witness largely because he might have served food to two of the 9/11 hijackers at the Delray Beach, Florida restaurant where he worked. An FBI agent also asserted that a movie theater ticket agent claimed to have seen Bellahouel go to the movies in the company of the hijackers. But, as the *Miami Daily Business Review* noted, "The FBI didn't identify the theater employee. Nor did government lawyers produce her for cross-examination at the bond hearing" where Bellahouel was finally set free.[135] Bellahouel denied ever having gone to the movie theater. During his detention Justice Department prosecutors sought "to strip Bellahouel of the court-appointed lawyer to which he became entitled when the material witness warrant was issued at the end of December 2001," according to immigration attorney David Silk, who explained that the feds "quashed the [material witness] warrant to keep him from being represented when the FBI talked to him." Bellahouel, who was a veterinarian in Algeria before coming to America, was released on a $10,000 bond on March 1, 2002. Even though Bellahouel is married to an American citizen, the Justice Department is seeking to deport him because he entered the United States on a student visa in 1996 and only completed one year at Florida Atlantic University.

(Bellahouel's case became public knowledge only because of an error by a clerk at the federal appeals court in Atlanta.)[136]

## Striking Out and Swinging Wider

The Patriot Act requires the Justice Department to report to Congress on how it has used the new power granted over aliens. In late April 2002, the Justice Department sent over a six-line letter stating that no immigrants had been detained as terrorists under the Patriot Act's provisions. The Justice Department ignored the Patriot Act because the feds had far more unchecked power under the new Ashcroft edicts. Rep. John Conyers snarled: "The entire justification for Ashcroft's dragnet approach to detaining Arab and Muslim Americans has collapsed with this admission that he hasn't been able to identify a single terrorist."[137] Professor David Cole observed: "One reason the Patriot Act provision has not yet been invoked may be that it raises a multitude of serious constitutional concerns. The Supreme Court has never permitted preventive detention absent a finding of dangerousness or flight risk, yet this provision would authorize just that."[138]

The Justice Department has been very secretive over the information it received from the "special interest" detainees. Yet, there is scant reason to believe that the heavy-handed interrogations provided much of value to the government. Beginning in late 2001 the Justice Department also launched a program to question 7,600 foreign visitors in the United States who had similar profiles to the hijackers and came from one of the 15 countries in which Al Qaeda has a presence. The General Accounting Office investigated the interview program and reported on May 9, 2003 that "none of the law enforcement officials with whom we spoke could provide examples of investigative leads that resulted from the project. . . . More than half of the law enforcement officers we spoke with expressed concerns about the quality of the questions asked and the value of the responses obtained."[139] Many lawmen involved in the project also believed that it adversely affected community relations with targeted religious and ethnic groups. The feds also did a poor job of finding the people they wanted to question: fewer than half of the people on the list had been questioned as of March 2003. Conyers commented: "The Justice Department cannot provide a shred of evidence that these 7,000 interviews led to a single piece of useful information about terrorist attacks on the United States."[140]

The power that Ashcroft has accumulated after 9/11 could increasingly affect would-be immigrants to America from around the world. On April 23, 2003 the Justice Department released an Ashcroft decision overturning rulings by an immigration judge and the Bureau of Immigration Appeals regarding a 20-year-old Haitian immigrant who had come ashore in Florida the previous October seeking asylum. Ashcroft ruled that asylum seekers could be locked up indefinitely, regardless of the decisions of immigration judges, because releasing them could spur further mass migration attempts from Haiti that would cause "strains on national security and homeland security resources." Ashcroft also justified perpetually incarcerating Haitian asylum seekers because of an increased number of Pakistanis, Palestinians, and other foreign nationals "using Haiti as a staging point for attempted migration to the United States. This increases the national security interest in curbing use of this migration route."[141] Ashcroft's assertion that Palestinians were trying to sneak into the United States via Haiti stunned other federal experts. State Department's Consular Service spokesman Stuart Patt commented: "We all are scratching our heads. We are asking each other, 'Where did they get that?'"[142]

*Miami Herald* columnist Carl Hiaasen commented: "The idea of Islamic militants trying to infiltrate a boatload of Creole-speaking refugees is so ludicrous that even Ashcroft knows better. . . . No matter how much plastic surgery Osama bin Laden has, he will never in a million years blend in on the streets of downtown Port-au-Prince.[143]

## Inspector General vs. Ashcroft et al.

On June 2, 2003, Justice Department Inspector General Glenn Fine issued a long-awaited report on the treatment of the "special interest detainees."[144] The report made mincemeat out of many of the post-9/11 official statements from the Justice Department. The Inspector General concluded that "certain conditions of confinement were unduly harsh," especially at the Metropolitan Detention Center (MDC) in Brooklyn, where 84 detainees were kept in maximum security conditions. In some cases, detainees were kept in small prison cells where the lights were on 24 hours a day for months on end.

The IG looked at the cases of 762 illegal aliens who were classified as "September 11 detainees." The IG did not explain the difference between the 762 number and the 1200-plus that the Justice Department earlier used for the total number of detainees.

Many of the detainees were effectively held incommunicado for weeks after their arrest. Because all the September 11 detainees were put in the highest security classification at the MDC, officials imposed a "blackout" policy and withheld "information about the detainees' status and location. This made it very difficult for attorneys, family members, and, at times, law enforcement officers to visit September 11 detainees or even determine their location."[145] The IG examined written records at the MDC and concluded that "the first legal call made by any September 11 detainee, according to these three sources, was not until October 15, 2001." The report noted: "Five New York–area attorneys told us that they were unable to meet with their September 11 detainee clients for many weeks because MDC staff told them that their clients were not housed at the MDC," when they were there. The detainees' efforts to secure legal representation were also stifled by "the inaccurate pro bono attorney list" provided by the MDC.[146]

In a January 2002 court proceeding, the Justice Department defined the term "September 11 detainees" as "individuals who were originally questioned because there were indications that they might have connections with, or possess information pertaining to, terrorist activity against the United States including particularly the September 11 attacks and/or the individuals and organizations who perpetrated them." Yet, this was a charade. The IG concluded: "Any illegal alien encountered by New York City law enforcement officers following up a PENTTBOM [the Pentagon/Twin Towers Bombings investigation] lead—whether or not the alien turned out to have a connection to the September 11 attacks or any other terrorist activity—was deemed to be a September 11 detainee."[147]

The report offered several examples of dubious classification of aliens as September 11 detainees:

[A] man was arrested on immigration charges and labeled a September 11 detainee when authorities discovered that he had taken a roll of film to be developed and the film had multiple pictures of the World Trade Center on it but no other Manhattan sites. This man's roommates also were arrested when law enforcement authorities found out they were in the United States illegally, and they too were considered September 11 detainees.

Another alien was arrested, detained on immigration charges, and treated as a September 11 detainee because a person called the FBI to report that the [redacted] grocery store in which the alien worked, "is operated by numerous Middle Eastern men, 24 hrs–7 days a week. Each shift daily has 2 or 3 men. . . . Store was closed day after crash, reopened days and evenings. Then later on opened during midnight hours. Too many people to run a small store."

A Muslim man in his 40s, who was a citizen of [redacted] was arrested after an acquaintance wrote a letter to law enforcement officers stating that the man had made anti-American statements. The statements, as reported in the letter, were very general and did not involve threats of violence or suggest any direct connection to terrorism. Nonetheless, the lead was assigned to a special agent . . . and resulted in the man's arrest for overstaying his visa. Because he had been arrested on a PENTTBOM lead, he automatically was placed in the FBI New York's "special interest" category." [The man was detained for more than three months after FBI agents who interviewed him concluded that he was of no interest to the 9/11 investigation and posed no threat.] [148]

The IG noted that the Justice "Department and the FBI did not develop clear criteria for determining who was, in fact, 'of interest' to the FBI's terrorism investigation. From our interviews, we determined that, for the most part, aliens were deemed 'of interest' based on the type of lead the law enforcement officers were pursuing when they encountered the aliens, rather than any evidence that they were terrorists."[149]

Massive delays in the release or deportation of detainees occurred because the Justice Department instituted a policy which prohibited releases until the FBI had cleared the person of any tie to terrorist activity. While officials believed that such clearances could occur within a few days, massive delays occurred. The average September 11 detainee was held for 80 days before being released. The IG noted, "This 'hold until cleared' policy was not memorialized in writing, and our review could not determine the exact origins of the policy. However, this policy was clearly communicated to INS and FBI officials in the field, who understood and applied the policy."

The Inspector General found credible evidence that some detainees at the Metropolitan Detention Center in Brooklyn had been physically and mentally abused. The report noted that one prison guard officer at the MDC who was "interviewed by the OIG told us that he witnessed officers 'slam' inmates against walls and stated this was a common practice before the MDC began videotaping the detainees. . . . He also said he witnessed a supervising officer slam detainees against walls, but when he spoke with the officer about this practice the officer told him it was all part of being in jail and not to worry about it." Several September 11 detainees "stated that when they arrived at the MDC, they were forcefully pulled out of the vehicle and slammed against walls. One detainee further alleged that his handcuffs were painfully tight around his wrists and that MDC officers repeatedly stepped on the chain between his ankle cuffs. Another detainee alleged officers dragged him by his handcuffs and twisted his wrist every time they moved him. All three detainees alleged that officers verbally abused them with racial slurs and threats like 'you will feel pain' and 'someone thinks you have something to do with the World Trade Center so don't expect to be treated well.'"[150]

Security cameras were installed in the prison cells of the September 11 detainees "because the video record could help protect Bureau of Prison staff from unfounded allegations of abuse," according to Bureau of Prison officials. But most of the videotapes were erased after 30 days. The IG noted, "the BOP was concerned that specious allegations of abuse would consume valuable administrative and legal resources." The FBI received the charges against the prison guards but made little or no effort to investigate. In one case, the FBI had not yet interviewed the former detainee and the accused prison guards nine months after the detainee filed the complaint.[151]

The IG noted that September 11 detainees held at two jails in New Jersey were not harshly treated like the detainees in Brooklyn. New Jersey detainees also were not significantly impeded from seeking legal counsel. The Inspector General also found that a number of federal lawyers and officials recognized that the process was bogging down and that detainees' release was being delayed long past legal deadlines. Several of those officials raised concerns with higher-ranking officials but their efforts were largely for naught. INS chief James Ziglar early on became concerned about the long delays for FBI clearances of detainees but the FBI did not heed his comments. [152]

The political appointees reacted with indignation at the Inspector General's criticism. Deputy Attorney General Larry Thompson sent a letter to the IG complaining that it was "unfair to criticize the conduct of my members of staff during this period."[153] Justice Department spokeswoman Barbara Comstock declared: "We make no apologies for finding every legal way possible to protect the American public from further terrorist attacks. The consequences of not doing so could mean life or death."[154]

## Conclusion

Each of the taxi drivers, ex-students, and pizza makers who were rounded up and deported after 9/11 have become additional victories in the Bush war on terrorism. Ashcroft, in Senate testimony on April 1, 2003, bragged that among other antiterrorism successes, there have been "478 deportations linked to the September 11 investigation."[155] If the feds had any reason to believe these individuals were actually terrorists, they almost certainly would have been prosecuted with great fanfare. Ashcroft did not explain how the deportation of people wrongfully suspected of knowledge of or involvement with 9/11 made America safer.

Ashcroft complained in late 2001 that criticism of his antiterrorism policies had been "overblown" and declared: "The more you know about them, the more you support them."[156] This brings to mind the old joke about the boy who murdered his parents and then sought the mercy of the court because he was an orphan. Ashcroft consistently cloaked federal operations in secrecy—and then acted aggrieved when people questioned what the feds were doing behind closed doors.

"Once suspected, forever damned" was the Justice Department's motto for handling "special interest" detainees. Federal agents snared nearly unlimited power via endless unsubstantiated statements, but almost no one outside the government had access to the evidence to rebut them. The "mosaic memo" that the FBI used in hundreds of cases was often little more than institutionalized mass perjury. There was never any penalty for government officials who exaggerated a supposed terrorist threat; they acted as if trying to frighten judges and citizens is simply part of their job description—as if anyone trying to frighten the public automatically must be presumed to be doing the right thing.

On the first anniversary of 9/11 Ashcroft and his subordinates sought to redefine government secrecy to allay any concerns about newly closed doors. During a National Public Radio interview Ashcroft declared: "We believe that in some settings it's important for us to be able to have hearings which are closed. But that should not mean that these are in some way secret. . . . But to the extent that this is some sort of a secret detention, that would certainly be grossly misleading. There are safeguards that are very carefully in place."[157] Deputy Attorney General Larry Thompson revealed: "The only thing that has been secret, if you will, has been the list of the individuals and the actual hearing itself. . . . People do not disappear in this country and we have really not done anything in secret, if you will."[158] This is the Bush version of "pro forma" open government. By this standard, if President Bush publicly announced that all decisions and decrees would henceforth be kept secret, Americans would still have an open government—because the government openly announced its plan to keep secrets.

The more deference the Justice Department received, the more abusive it became. The combination of secrecy and arbitrary power produced more injustices than almost anyone expected when the new policies were first announced. Secrecy breeds injustices because power corrupts: the more secrecy, the more unchecked power—and, eventually, the more abuses. After the federal investigation of "special interest" suspects spun out of control, secrecy became necessary to protect the federal government's reputation—which was equated with national security. New Jersey lawyer Regis Fernandez, who represented two "special interest" Jordanians with visa violations, observed: "What the government really fears is that people will be allowed to attend these hearings for themselves and see that nothing is going on."[159]

The problem was not the Bush administration's attitude toward Muslims but its attitude toward the Constitution. The detainees were not human beings but cannon fodder for speeches about how the government was vigorously protecting the public. As FBI agent Colleen Rowley (who achieved fame based on her testimony about pre-9/11 FBI screw-ups) complained in a February 26, 2003 letter to FBI director Mueller, "After 9/11, [FBI] Headquarters encouraged more and more detentions for what seem to be essentially PR purposes. Field offices were required to report daily the number of detentions in order to supply grist for statements on our progress in fighting terrorism."[160] The detainees' cases illustrate how far the government will go in lying and rewriting the rules of the game to make sure it wins every time.

It makes sense that Ashcroft would treat habeas corpus as a technical nuisance the feds must brush aside. According to Ashcroft's political theology, it is impossible that the federal government could ever wrongfully incarcerate anyone. Habeas corpus is an insurance policy to prevent governments from going berserk. When the government allows itself to violate civil liberties—when the government effectively declares that a class of 10 million people no longer have the right to habeas corpus, the result is not greater public safety but pervasive pointless oppression.

Immunity also corrupts. Abuses abounded after 9/11 in part because no individual federal employee—from Ashcroft on down—expected to be held liable for unjustified detentions. The abuses of the post-9/11 roundup stemmed in part from the Justice Department's success in previous decades in defeating almost every attempt to hold federal agents liable for wrongfully killing, assaulting, or otherwise abusing citizens. Instead, "stuff happened" and all that mattered was the noble intentions of Ashcroft and his minions.

The precedents the Justice Department establishes in abusing aliens will inevitably influence how the federal government treats American citizens. The excesses of the detainees policy provide the clearest warning of how the Justice Department could behave if there is another major terrorist strike within the United States. The precedents established in the wake of 9/11 will be stretched far beyond what complacent Americans expect. The power seized after 9/11 will be the starting line for a sprint toward greater discretionary and punitive power over anyone residing in this nation.

# CHAPTER SEVEN

# Salvation through Surveillance

Why should we grant government the Orwellian capability to listen at will and in real time to our communications across the Web? . . . I believe that moving forward with the president's policy . . . would be an act of folly, creating a cadre of government "peeping toms." . . . This is no reason to hand Big Brother the keys to unlock our e-mail diaries, open our ATM records, read our medical records, or translate our international communications.

—*Sen. John Ashcroft, August 12, 1997*[1]

You should not think you're dealing with a bunch of barbarians. That's not true. . . . We need to be sober about what is a threat to civil liberties.

—*Assistant Attorney General Michael Chertoff, August 11, 2002*[2]

The Bush administration quickly exploited the pervasive fear after 9/11 to decimate restrictions on government surveillance and intrusions. Regardless of the reasons why the Central Intelligence Agency and the Federal Bureau of Investigation failed to stop the hijackers, the solution was far more snooping and the potential creation of hundreds of millions of dossiers on American citizens. Almost overnight, it became widely accepted that the government must have unlimited prerogative to search anywhere and everywhere for enemies of freedom.

## The System Formerly Known As "Carnivore"

The Supreme Court has long recognized that the government has no right to read everyone's mail. In 1878, the Court declared: "The constitutional guaranty of the right of the people to be secure in their papers against unreasonable searches and seizures extends to their papers, thus closed against inspection, wherever they may be. Whilst in the mail, they can only be opened and examined under like warrant . . . as is required when papers are subjected to search in one's own household."[3] Supreme Court Justice Oliver Wendell Holmes, in an opinion recognizing that private letters deserve sanctity from federal prying, declared in 1921: "The use of the mails is almost as much a part of free speech as the right to use our tongues."[4] For most of the twentieth century, federal courts required federal agents to possess search warrants before they could legally open private mail.

However, in the Patriot Act, Congress officially blessed the FBI's use of its Carnivore email wiretapping system. Carnivore is contained in a black box that the FBI compels Internet service providers (ISPs) to attach to their operating system. Though a Carnivore tap might be imposed to target a single person, Carnivore can automatically impound the email of all the customers using that ISP.[5] Technology writer John Guerra noted, "The Carnivore package is designed to scan millions of e-mails per second. By adjusting filters and other parameters, it can be directed to scan only subject lines and headers of incoming or outgoing messages that are linked to a particular suspect or group of suspects. . . . By hitting a single button, the agent can put the software into full mode, and attempt to collect all" email traffic.[6] As the ACLU's Barry Steinhardt told Congress, "Carnivore is roughly equivalent to a wiretap capable of accessing the contents of the conversations of all of the phone company's customers, with the 'assurance' that the FBI will record only conversations of the specified target."

Prior to 9/11, Carnivore was criticized in Congress as an unconstitutional intrusion.[7] In early 2001, the FBI changed the name of Carnivore to DCS 1000 (DSC stands for "digital collection system"). CNET News noted, "A Spokesman for the FBI denied that the name change stemmed from worries that the name Carnivore made the system sound like a predatory device made to invade people's privacy."[8]

After 9/11, the Bush administration was determined to legitimize Carnivore. The Patriot Act amended the federal wiretap statute to include any "device or process" that captures, records, or decodes "dialing, routing, addressing, or signaling information," including Carnivore. Congress and the Bush administration shoehorned Carnivore into the statute book by blatantly misrepresenting its capacities and understating how much information Carnivore captures. A warrantless search is constitutional as long as the government pretends that no one is being searched.[9]

The Patriot Act puts email wiretaps on automatic pilot. An FBI agent or government lawyer need only certify to a judge that the information sought is "relevant to an ongoing criminal investigation" to get permission to install Carnivore. Judges have no discretion: they must approve wiretaps based on government agents' unsubstantiated assertions. It doesn't matter if the target is being investigated for smuggling uranium or for understating his income on his Internal Revenue Service Form 1040. And it doesn't matter if the citizen is guilty or innocent. All a federal agent has to do is pronounce the word "relevant" and he has automatic access not only to a targeted citizen's private life, but to the private lives of all other citizens who happen to use the same Internet service provider. (No one should underestimate the feds' hunger for data. In one 1999 case, the FBI "seized enough computer evidence to nearly fill the Library of Congress twice.")[10]

Once a judge has rubber-stamped the application for a Carnivore wiretap, federal agents have the prerogative to decree which Internet service providers must attach Carnivore to their system. The Patriot Act states that the order "shall apply to any person or entity providing wire or electronic communication service in the United States whose assistance may facilitate the execution of the order." This provision is akin to a general warrant for the roundup of the nation's email.

The Fourth Amendment requires "probable cause" for each search warrant issued.[11] The *Southern California Law Review* noted that Carnivore "conducts a search by reading or filtering through all internet traffic that passes by, which is in essence an unconstitutional general search of individuals who are not subject to a court order. The FBI has asserted that this 'filtering stage' is not a search, as it is the Carnivore program (a machine), and not federal agents, that is processing information of the innocent public. The FBI asserts that, by the time agents attain a copy of the collected data, Carnivore has provided only that information authorized by the court order."[12] But agents have discretion to capture practically as many people's email as they please.

The vacuum-like nature of Carnivore may have bailed out the terrorists who carried out the 9/11 attacks. The Electronic Privacy Information Center (EPIC) hounded the FBI with a Freedom of Information Act lawsuit to find out how Carnivore actually works. After a federal court victory, EPIC received FBI internal memos detailing how a Carnivore glitch led to the destruction in early 2000 of evidence gathered by the Osama bin Laden working group of the FBI's International Terrorism Operations Section. After a Carnivore wiretap snared email from many people unrelated to the investigation, an FBI lawyer ordered all the information gathered to be destroyed. An EPIC press release noted: "Two Bureau documents written one week later discuss Carnivore's tendency to cause 'the improper capture of data,' and note that 'such unauthorized interceptions not only can violate a citizen's privacy but also can seriously "contaminate" ongoing investigations' and that such interceptions are 'unlawful.'"[13] An FBI spokesman denied that the bureau's internal memos were correct.[14]

Though few congressmen fretted about Carnivore's excessive reach, many politicians were gung-ho on spending U.S. tax dollars to protect the privacy of foreign Internet users. On October 2, 2002, Rep. Chris Cox (R-Cal.) proposed a bill entitled the Global Internet Freedom Act. The act's "findings" declared that "the Internet stands to become the most powerful engine for democratization and the free exchange of ideas ever invented. . . . Unrestricted access to news and information on the Internet is a check on repressive rule by authoritarian regimes around the world." The "findings" also noted "the widespread and increasing pattern by authoritarian governments to block, jam, and monitor Internet access and content, using technologies such as firewalls, filters, and 'black boxes.' Such jamming and monitoring of individual activity on the Internet includes surveillance of e-mail messages, message boards, and the use of particular words. . . ." The act called for the U.S. government "to adopt an effective and robust global Internet freedom policy" and "to bring to bear the pressure of the free world on repressive governments guilty of Internet censorship and the intimidation and persecution of their citizens who use the Internet." The proposed Act concluded with a declaration of "a sense of Congress" that the U.S. government should "publicly, prominently, and consistently denounce governments that restrict, censor, ban, and block access to information on the Internet."[15] (Cox voted for the Patriot Act.)

## Watching While You Work: Keystroke Monitoring

In addition to Carnivore, the FBI is inserting software into computers to allow the government to record every keystroke anyone makes. The feds will not need to know a person's passwords because they can see them as they were typed in. This will allow the feds to thwart anyone who uses Pretty Good Privacy or other encryption programs. In the first court case on the new surveillance method, federal judge Nicholas Politan ruled on December 26, 2001 that the FBI could use the keystroke-recording software without a wiretap order—and that the details of the new system could be kept secret because its disclosure "would cause identifiable damage to the national security of the United States."[16] (The case involved illegal gambling.)[17]

As part of its Project Cyber Knight, the FBI is putting the finishing touches on a computer virus, known as "Magic Lantern," that can be inserted via email into targeted computers. The Patriot Act authorizes life sentences in prison for computer hackers who maliciously craft and spread viruses. But this provision will not apply to federal agents. MSNBC reported on November 20, 2001: "The virus can be sent to the suspect via e-mail—perhaps sent for the FBI by a trusted friend or relative. The FBI can also use common vulnerabilities to break into a suspect's computer and insert Magic Lantern."[18] James Dempsey of the Center for Democracy and Technology observed: "In order for the government to seize your diary or read your letters, they have to knock on your door with a search warrant. But [Magic Lantern] would allow them to seize these without notice."[19]

After word leaked out about Magic Lantern, the Associated Press reported that "at least one antivirus software company, McAfee Corp., contacted the FBI . . . to ensure its software wouldn't inadvertently detect the bureau's snooping software and alert a criminal suspect."[20] Sandra England, vice president for Network Associates (which sells McAfee products), declared: "I think the biggest risk is exploitation by hackers."[21] Government spying on citizens seemed like a non-issue for the makers of one of the most popular antivirus programs. Eric Chien, a chief researcher at the company that sells Norton AntiVirus, indicated that his company could leave a hole in their antivirus software to let the feds slip through. Chien declared: "If it was under the control of the FBI, with appropriate technical safeguards in place to prevent possible misuse, and nobody else used it—we wouldn't detect it."[22] After these comments sparked controversy, the companies quickly denied that they had promised to allow the FBI to blindside people who trusted their antivirus software.[23]

## Treating Americans Like Foreign Spies

In 1978, responding to scandals about political spying on Americans in the name of counterespionage, Congress passed the Foreign Intelligence Surveillance Act (FISA). FISA created a different legal standard and a separate court to oversee federal surveillance of foreign agents within the United States. In federal criminal investigations, the government must show probable cause that a person is involved in criminal activity before being permitted to impose a wiretap. Under FISA, the government need only show that a person is a suspected agent of a foreign power or terrorist organization. The standard is different because Americans' rights are protected by the Fourth Amendment, while foreign agents do not receive the same shield from government intrusion. A September 2002 FBI internal document written for FBI agents entitled "What do I have to do to get a FISA?" bluntly "acknowledges that the 'probable cause' standard used in FISA is much less stringent than the 'probable cause' standard that the Fourth Amendment normally requires."[24] FISA created a "wall" between federal prosecutors and intelligence agents conducting FISA-approved surveillance to discourage prosecutors from routinely relying on FISA wiretaps to spy on Americans.

While FISA was intended to be used rarely, it has become the feds' favorite push button for wiretaps. Since 1978, the FISA court has approved over 12,000 wiretap applications—and not rejected a single request from federal agents. As national security expert James Bamford observed, "Like a modern Star Chamber, the F.I.S.A. court meets behind a cipher-locked door in a windowless, bug-proof, vault-like room guarded 24 hours a day on the top floor of the Justice Department building. The eleven judges (increased from seven by the Patriot Act) hear only the government's side."[25] When FISA authorizes surveillance, the feds can switch on all the turbos. In a 2002 decision, the Foreign Intelligence Surveillance Court noted that after it grants a surveillance request, "the FBI will be authorized to conduct, simultaneously, telephone, microphone, cell phone, e-mail and computer surveillance of the U.S. person target's home, workplace and vehicles. Similar breadth is accorded the FBI in physical searches of the target's residence, office, vehicles, computer, safe deposit box and U.S. mails where supported by probable cause."[26] FISA surveillance orders tend to be far more expansive than normal federal criminal surveillance orders. People who are surveilled under a FISA order rarely ever learn the feds have been tracking them or intruding into their lives unless they are arrested as a result.

After 9/11, the Justice Department vigorously lobbied for Congress to revise FISA to permit it to be used for spying on Americans with little or no relations to foreign powers or terrorist plots. Ashcroft claimed that the reform was needed because FISA had impeded efforts to track terrorists. The dispute was not over whether foreign agents should be tracked: no one in Congress was opposed to that. The issue was whether the feds could launch massive surveillance operations against U.S. citizens on the pretext of fighting terrorism even though there was no evidence of their criminal wrongdoing. Congress acquiesced to Ashcroft's demands.

The Patriot Act FISA changes were one of the clearest examples of federal incompetence and misconduct being rewarded with greater power. In September 2000, the Justice Department notified the Foreign Intelligence Surveillance Court (FISC) that the FBI had made at least 75 false representations to the court about wiretaps. The court was so enraged that one senior FBI counterterrorism official was forbidden from ever appearing again before the court.[27] A few months later, the Justice Department notified the court of another bevy of false representations about how closely prosecutors were involved with FISA wiretaps. The Justice Department did not notify any member of Congress of its FISA-related misconduct, even though Congress has a statutory right and duty of oversight.

During the Patriot Act mini-deliberations, the Justice Department claimed that the FISA restrictions fatally delayed its efforts to secure a search warrant for Zacarias Moussaoui, the suspected "twentieth hijacker," who was arrested in Minnesota on August 16, 2001. But, as a 2003 Senate Judiciary Committee report noted, the FBI had sufficient information to get a FISA wiretap before 9/11 but failed to do so because "key FBI personnel responsible for protecting our country against terrorism did not understand the law."[28] FBI headquarters agents believed that, before a FISA wiretap could be requested, Moussaoui must be linked to an organization that the U.S. government formally labeled as terrorists. But that was not the case. The Senate report noted, "In the time leading up to the 9/11 attacks, the FBI and DOJ had not devoted sufficient resources to implementing the FISA, so that long delays both crippled enforcement efforts and demoralized line agents."[29] Eleanor Hill, the staff director for the Joint Intelligence Committee investigation into pre-9/11 failures, observed: "The lesson of Moussaoui was that F.B.I. headquarters was telling the field office the wrong advice. Fixing what happened in this case is not inconsistent with preserving civil liberties."[30]

A few months after the Patriot Act was signed, Ashcroft proposed new regulations to "allow FISA to be used primarily for a law enforcement purpose."[31] The seven FISC judges unanimously rejected Ashcroft's power grab as contrary to federal law. Their May 17, 2002 decision noted that the FISC had approved "many hundreds of surveillances and searches of U.S. persons"—meaning U.S. citizens and permanent residents.[32]

The Justice Department refused to provide senators with a copy of the FISC decision that thrashed the feds' misconduct. Though the decision was a blunt rejection of Ashcroft's attempt to use FISA to unleash federal prosecutors to spy on Americans, the Justice Department believed that no one in Congress was entitled to a copy of the decision of the secret court.

The senators eventually got a copy of the decision directly from the court and released it to the public in August 2002. Ashcroft appealed the decision to the U.S. Foreign Intelligence Surveillance Court of Review—a special court that exists to hear cases in which the government loses in its first swing at a wiretap. The judges of this court (which had never met before) were picked by Supreme Court Chief Justice William Rehnquist, a jurist renowned for his minimalist interpretation of the Fourth Amendment. The FISA appeals court met in secret and only the Justice Department was permitted to argue its side. Steve Aftergood, editor of the Federation of American Scientists' *Secrecy News,* commented that the transcript of the hearing (released months after the fact) showed that "the judges generally assumed a servile posture toward the executive branch, even consulting the Justice Department on how to handle its critics."[33]

The FISA appeals court, in a November 2002 decision, unleashed the Justice Deaprtment and gave Ashcroft everything he wanted. Ashcroft proclaimed that its decision "revolutionizes our ability to investigate terrorists and prosecute terrorist acts."[34] Ashcroft also reminded everyone: "We have no desire whatsoever to in any way erode or undermine constitutional liberties."[35]

The FISA appeals court decision encourages federal agents to seek FISA warrants even in cases with very doubtful links to terrorism or terrorist activity. The Justice Department revealed how far it would stretch the notion of "suspected terrorist" in its roundup of "special interest detainees" after 9/11. Thus, the feds' freedom to wiretap Americans will be limited only by their veracity and/or creativity. American Civil Liberties Union lawyer Ann Beeson observed that the FISA appeals court decision "suggests that this special court exists only to rubber-stamp government applications for intrusive surveillance warrants."[36] Beeson noted: "This is a major constitutional decision that will affect every American's privacy rights, yet there is no way anyone but the government can automatically appeal this ruling to the Supreme Court." The Supreme Court rejected the ACLU's request to consider the FISA ruling.

The number of FISA authorized wiretaps rose by more than 30 percent in 2002, from 934 to 1,228. Every search warrant the FBI requested was granted, although two of the requests did bounce up to the FISA appeals court before being approved.[37]

Miami Attorney Neal Sonnett, chair of an American Bar Association panel on terrorism law, observed that FISA "has now turned into a de facto domestic intelligence act. The line was blurred with FISA for a long time. And when [Congress] passed the Patriot Act, they wiped it out completely."[38] Unfortunately, Americans are unlikely to learn how this domestic intelligence operation actually functions. Sen. Patrick Leahy (D-Vt.) proposed a bill in early 2003 entitled the Domestic Surveillance Oversight Act that would require that the Justice Department report the "aggregate number of FISA wiretaps and other surveillance measures directed specifically against Americans each year."[39] Leahy also sought to compel the Justice Department to reveal to Congress the secret rules by which the secret court operated. Because of staunch Justice Department opposition, Leahy's measure is given little chance of enactment into law.

## Snooping at the Library

A secret court now has jurisdiction over the reading habits of the American people. The Patriot Act empowers FBI agents to go to any library or bookstore and demand a list of what people have borrowed or bought—or even what people have asked about. As part of a terrorist investigation, the FBI need not have any evidence of wrongdoing—only a blanket authorization from a FISA court. Section 215 of the Patriot Act specifies that FBI agents "may make an application for an order requiring the production of any tangible things (including books, records, papers, documents, and other items)" in a terrorism investigation. The Patriot Act specifies that the request must not be justified "solely upon the basis of activities protected by the first amendment to the Constitution." But it will not be difficult for federal agents to cite or gin up other suspicions to authorize intrusions against government critics.

The Patriot Act nullified federal, state, and local laws protecting the privacy of library users and bookstore customers from federal agents. Within a few months after 9/11, federal or local lawmen had already visited almost 10 percent of the nation's public libraries "seeking September 11–related information about patron reading habits," according to a survey conducted by the University of Illinois.[40] The Patriot Act gags librarians and bookstore employees, prohibiting them from disclosing to targets that the FBI is probing into their literary proclivities. Emily Sheketoff of the American Library Association observed that FBI agents "get a search warrant or court order, they come to the library, the librarian cannot appeal to a judge, and they can't tell anybody about it. They can't tell the person whose records are being requested, they can't tell the library director, they can't tell their congressman, they can't tell their senator."[41] The *Tampa Tribune* reported that "FBI Agent Sara Oates of the FBI's Tampa office didn't know whether all Florida libraries will be contacted."[42] Rene Salinas, an FBI spokesman in San Antonio, insisted that people should not worry about the library search provision because "We don't start at the library, we start with the person."[43]

In January 2003, an FBI agent entered a branch of the St. Louis Public Library and requested a list of all the sign-up sheets showing the names of people who used library computers on December 28, 2002. Even though the FBI agent did not have a warrant or subpoena, the library quickly gave him the list of all the users. The *St. Louis Post-Dispatch* noted: "The request was prompted by a tip from a library patron who had used one of the branch's 16 Internet-accessible computers on the same day and at the same time as another patron, who was of

Middle Eastern descent."[44] FBI spokesman Peter Krusing explained that the person who phoned in the tip "thought they smelled something strange; that was part of the description. I don't think from that information we've developed any terrorist information."[45]

Libraries in Santa Cruz, California posted warnings to their patrons informing them that the USA Patriot Act "prohibits library workers from informing you if federal agents have obtained records about you. Questions about this policy should be directed to Attorney General John Ashcroft, Department of Justice, Washington, D.C. 20530."[46] Dale Canelas, library director at the University of Florida at Gainesville, observed: "Just because you read a book about explosives, doesn't mean you're going to blow something up."[47]

The new surveillance powers extend to online purchases—or even browsing. The *San Francisco Chronicle* reported the case of a Stanford-trained scientist who bought some technical books on eBay and then received a visit from FBI agents inquiring whether he intended to commit terrorist acts.[48] The two lawyers hired by the Pakistani native eventually persuaded the FBI that there was no nefarious purpose behind the purchases. An FBI agent said the investigation was launched after eBay reported the purchase; eBay denied reporting the sales to the feds.[49]

Assistant Attorney General Viet Dinh, Ashcroft's top policy mastermind, complained that the feds were getting a bad rap from critics. Dinh observed: "One misunderstanding is that it is specifically targeted at bookstores or libraries. That's not true. This provision is generally applicable to all businesses. And it excepts First Amendment rights. There has to be some criminal activity."[50] From Dinh's perspective, the more intrusive federal agents become, the more comforted Americans should feel. His statement that "there has to be some criminal activity" is false. The only thing necessary for a rubber-stamp search warrant is for a federal agent to assert that he has suspicions. As the *Florida Law Review* noted, "One of the most far-reaching effects of the [Patriot Act] is the removal of the review of a 'neutral and detached magistrate' from the process of citizen surveillance. Many of the provisions that do involve some judicial oversight require that the order be granted if the application is properly filled out."[51]

Justice Department spokesman Mark Corallo continually sought to blunt criticism of the library searches by misrepresenting the law. Corallo told the *Florida Today* newspaper: "This is limited only to foreign intelligence. U.S. citizens cannot be investigated under this act."[52] But when FBI agents get warrants to sweep up all the names of someone who borrowed or bought a specific book, there is no way for libraries or bookstores to segregate the names of American citizens from foreign agents before satisfying the government's demands. Corallo told the *San Francisco Chronicle* that, before an FBI agent gets library or book-store records, he must "convince a judge that the person for whom you're seeking a warrant is a spy or a member of a terrorist organization. The idea that any American citizen can have their records checked by the FBI, that's not true."[53] But the Patriot Act assures that the unsubstantiated assertion by an FBI agent is enough to launch surveillance. Corallo told *USA Today* that a FISA surveillance order "is subject to judicial approval, judicial supervision and congressional oversight. So the checks and balances are there."[54] But the FISA court does zero supervision of the FBI and the Justice Department has made sure that Congress has almost no information with which to perform oversight.

FBI agents are sometimes even omitting the formality of a warrant in their pursuit of library records. The ACLU reported in April 2003 that "the FBI has pressured at least some libraries to 'voluntarily' turn over records relating to their patrons. And if the FBI is pressuring libraries to turn over their records, it is quite likely that the FBI is employing the same practice with respect to book-stores and internet service providers."[55]

Once the principle of government prying into libraries and bookstores is accepted, there will be nothing to prevent expanding the suspect reading list to include books on drugs, radical political philosophy, or even common or garden-variety cynicism.

## Sneak and Peak

Supreme Court Justice Lewis Powell observed in a 1972 opinion that breaking and entering by government agents had long been recognized as "the chief evil against which the wording of the Fourth Amendment is directed."[56] The Supreme Court declared in 1976 that the Fourth Amendment limited government power in order to "prevent arbitrary and oppressive interference by enforcement officials with the privacy and personal security of individuals."[57]

Prior to September 11, it was difficult for law enforcement to persuade a judge to approve a warrant to conduct a secret search in someone's home. After the Patriot Act, such searches could become routine. Section 213 states that searches can now be done in secret if federal agents assert that there is "reasonable cause to believe that providing immediate notification of the execution of the warrant may have an adverse result."[58] All it could take is a simple redundancy: lawmen could claim that a search must be kept secret because otherwise the person will know that they have been searched. *Village Voice* columnist Nat Hentoff deftly described the new search powers: "For up to 90 days, the agents don't have to inform the occupant of their break-ins, and the FBI can delay notice even further by going to a judge and getting extensions of that 90-day provision. Also, if they don't find anything the first and second times, they can keep coming back, hoping they may yet hit pay dirt. Eventually, they will have to give notice."[59]

During traditional searches, someone can usually keep an eye on police to see what they are searching and seizing. As the *New Jersey Law Journal* noted, "It is impossible for a person to assert his or her Fourth Amendment rights if the person does not realize they are being violated. Once given notice, an occupant or owner can . . . object to the warrant as erroneous or overbroad. Without notice and meaningful limitations in what is searched, the searching officer has complete and unsupervised discretion as to what, when and where to search."[60]

Ashcroft personally issued over 170 emergency domestic spying warrants in 2002—permitting agents to carry out wiretaps and search homes and offices for up to 72 hours before the feds needed to request a search warrant from the Foreign Intelligence Surveillance court. Ashcroft is apparently using such powers almost one hundred times as often as attorney generals did before 9/11.[61]

## Tapping We Will Go

The Patriot Act allows feds to get "nationwide roving wiretaps." As the Electronic Frontier Foundation noted, the FBI "can now go from phone to phone, computer to computer without demonstrating that each is even being used by a suspect or target of an order. . . . The government need not make any showing to a court that the particular information or communication to be acquired is relevant to a criminal investigation."[62] Law enforcement will have leeway to wiretap whomever they choose on the outside chance that the suspect might use someone's phone. Boston University law professor Tracey Maclin warns: "If the government suspects that a particular target uses different pay phones at Boston's Logan Airport, then the government would have the power to wire all the public telephones at Logan Airport and the discretion to decide which conversations to monitor."[63]

Ashcroft and others continually portrayed the Patriot Act changes as emergency measures desperately needed to unleash the federal government to protect the American people. But this ignored the fact that, in the years preceding the 9/11 terrorist attack, federal surveillance of the American public was skyrocketing. A 1998 ACLU report observed that the Clinton administration had "engaged in surreptitious surveillance, such as wiretapping, on a far greater scale than ever before."[64] In 1995, the FBI formally demanded that phone companies provide the capacity for simultaneous wiretaps of one out of every hundred phone calls in urban America—"a 1,000-fold increase over previous levels of surveillance," as the ACLU noted.[65] (The FBI backed off slightly from its demand after public criticism.)

The 1990s surge in surveillance had little to do with protecting public safety; instead, most of the new wiretaps were aimed at drug and gambling offenders. Fewer than one-half of 1 percent of all wiretapping requests were in cases involving bombs, guns, or potential terrorist activity.[66] But that did not prevent law enforcement agencies and Congress from exploiting the terrorist attacks to greatly expand government's prying.

Under the Patriot Act, authorized wiretaps are not limited to people suspected of plotting attacks. Georgetown University law professor David Cole warned: "If you're involved in any kind of political activity, you have to fear surveillance by the FBI. We've seen in the past under much more restrictive regimes the FBI engaged in political spying on civil rights activists, on people who are concerned about our policies in Central America, on people concerned about our policies in the Middle East."[67] Morton Halperin, a Nixon White House aide, observed: "Historically, the government has often believed that anyone who is protesting government policy is doing it at the behest of a foreign government and opened counterintelligence investigations of them."[68]

The Patriot Act also opened the floodgates for subpoenas on telephone companies. Michael Altschul of the Cellular Telecommunications and Internet Association observed: "It's not just volume but the scope of the subpoenas we are seeing, where instead of a rifle shot it's more of a shotgun approach. . . . A typical subpoena to a cell phone service provider . . . can be used to identify all calls on a certain date between 10:15 and 10:30 A.M. by everyone in a small town, or within a few square blocks of a big city."[69] In the year after 9/11, the number of subpoenas hitting Internet service providers increased fivefold.[70]

The Patriot Act made it much easier for FBI agents to commandeer private information and to muzzle targets via National Security Letters.[71] These subpoena letters compel individuals, businesses, and other institutions to surrender confidential or proprietary information without a court order—including records on bank accounts, Internet usage, phone calls, email logs, lists of purchases, and so on. Anyone hit with a National Security Letter is obliged to remain forever silent on the FBI's demand; disclosure is punishable by up to five years in prison. There is no judicial oversight of this power, and each FBI field office is entitled to issue its own letters. (The FBI has refused to disclose how often its agents are issuing such orders, or how many Americans' private information has been snared as a result.) There is no requirement that probable cause of law-breaking exist before the FBI forcibly intrudes; instead, the amount of data demanded depends largely on the discretion of the FBI agent. Attorney General Ashcroft notified the House Judiciary Committee in 2003 that FBI agents could be using National Security Letters to seize library records, rather than applying for a FISA search warrant for the same purpose.

National Security Letters turn the Fourth Amendment on its head by creating a presumption that the government is entitled to personal or confidential information unless the citizen or business can prove to a federal judge that the National Security Letter should not be enforced against them. But few Americans can afford the cost of litigating against the Justice Department to preserve their privacy.

Federal agents are arm-twisting many companies to open their books and surrender their records even without a subpoena. Washington lawyer Bill Lawler observed that FBI agents "don't seem to be bothering with [warrants or subpoenas] these days. They just show up and say 'Here we are' and 'Give us your stuff.'"[72] Ohio State University law professor Peter Swire reported that companies are receiving "requests for cooperation from law enforcement agencies with the idea that it is unpatriotic if the companies insist too much on legal subpoenas first."[73] Telecom lawyer Albert Gidari observed: "Investigators have quickly learned that they don't need to leave a paper trail anymore so nobody can judge the lawfulness of a request."[74] Gidari noted that FBI "agents in certain field offices are impatient and view you as unpatriotic [if businesses do not surrender information on demand]. I've had instances where agents have said, 'Give me your Social Security number and your address' to an in-house lawyer who wouldn't produce records without a subpoena."[75]

## More, More, More

Less than a month after Bush signed the Patriot Act, the administration submitted proposals to congressional committees for new federal surveillance powers. The Bush administration proposed "fill-in-the-blank" wiretaps for those times when federal agents do not know the person's name or the location of the suspect's electronic communication. This power, in combination with the new "roving wiretap" authority, could sweep far more innocents into the government's net. The Pentagon also submitted to Congress a 38-item security "wish list," including a "video-powered human tracker and the bomb neutralizer . . . the camera that sees through walls . . . and the software that identifies red-flag retail purchases—any time and anywhere."[76] The *Washington Post* noted in late

2001: "A senior U.S. official said this second wave of anti-terrorism measures reflects the administration's belief that it can harness the political energy of wartime to gain even more power and autonomy for federal law enforcement and intelligence agencies."[77] The senior government official commented: "A lot of this is not being driven by problems that prosecutors or investigators are having. It is just a good time to get everything. It is totally politically and public-perception-driven."[78]

The FBI may seek to convert 9/11 into a veto over technological progress. The FBI pressured telecom providers to redesign how satellite and cell phone calls are transmitted to facilitate FBI real-time monitoring of all phone calls. Some telecom experts fear that the FBI is seeking a Carnivore-type vacuum cleaner for voice calls. The FBI summoned one hundred telecom leaders to Arizona in October 2001 and hinted that "if somebody deployed a new technology and the FBI couldn't intercept it, the FBI would expect the service provider to stop providing the service" until it could be tapped, as one attendee told the *Wall Street Journal*.[79] The FBI also issued telecom providers with "a set of high-level needs . . . considered necessary by law enforcement regardless of the service that is being offered."[80] Nokia Corp.'s Terri Brooks complained: "After Sept. 11, [the FBI is] pushing for anything and everything."[81]

## Unleashing the Feds Near You

In May 2002, after revelations that the FBI missed many warning signs before 9/11, Attorney General John Ashcroft announced that he was effectively abolishing restrictions on FBI surveillance of Americans' everyday life. Those restrictions were first imposed in 1976, after scandals about pervasive FBI abuses. At that time, Attorney General Edward Levi announced guidelines to curtail FBI agents' intrusions into the lives of Americans who were not criminal suspects.

At the May 30 announcement, Ashcroft declared that, after 9/11, "we in the leadership of the FBI and the Department of Justice began a concerted effort to free the field agents—the brave men and women on the front lines—from the bureaucratic, organizational, and operational restrictions and structures that hindered them from doing their jobs effectively." He complained that in the past FBI agents were required "to blind themselves to information that everyone else [was] free to see."[82] However, as the Center for Democracy and Technology noted, "The FBI was never prohibited in the past from going to mosques, political rallies and other public places, to observe and record what was said, but in the past it had to be guided by the criminal nexus—in deciding what mosques to go to and what political meetings to record, it had to have some reason to believe that terrorism might be discussed."[83]

Ashcroft's announcement concluded with the mandatory invocation of freedom consecrating each Bush power grab: "These guidelines will also be a resource to inform the American public and demonstrate that we seek to protect life and liberty from terrorism and other criminal violence with a scrupulous respect for civil rights and personal freedoms. The campaign against terrorism is a campaign to affirm the values of freedom and human dignity. . . . Called to the service of our nation, we are called to the defense of liberty for all men and women."[84] When Bush was asked about the new FBI guidelines at a photo opportunity that same day, he declared that "the initiative that the attorney general will be outlining today will guarantee our Constitution."[85]

Ashcroft talked as if the old guidelines on FBI surveillance were simply the result of a long-ago outbreak of temporary insanity among liberals. Ashcroft declared: "In its 94-year history, the Federal Bureau of Investigation has been . . . the tireless protector of civil rights and civil liberties for all Americans."[86]

It is impossible to grasp the dangers of excessive surveillance without recounting some previous government abuses.[87] The 1976 guidelines were put in place in response to a report by the Senate Select Committee to Study Governmental Operations that detailed many FBI abuses over the preceding decades. For 15 years, from 1956 to 1971, the FBI ran COINTELPRO (Counterintelligence Programs) to actively subvert groups and people that the FBI considered threats to national security or to the established political and social order. Over 2,300 separate operations were carried out to incite street warfare between violent groups, to wreck marriages, to get people fired, to smear innocent people by portraying them as government informants, to sic the IRS on people, and to cripple or destroy left-wing, black, communist, or other organizations. The FBI let no corner of American life escape its vigilance; it even worked to expose and discredit "communists who are secretly operating in legitimate organizations and employments, such as the Young Men's Christian Association and Boy Scouts."[88]

Throughout the COINTELPRO period, presidents, congressmen, and other high-ranking federal officials assured Americans that the federal government was obeying the law and upholding the Constitution. It took a burglary of an FBI office in Media, Pennsylvania, to break the biggest scandal in the history of federal law enforcement. After hundreds of pages of confidential records were commandeered, the "Citizen's Commission to Investigate the FBI" began passing out the incriminating documents to the media.[89] The shocking material sparked congressional and media investigations that eventually temporarily shattered the FBI's legendary ability to control its own image.

The 1976 Senate report noted that COINTELPRO's origins "are rooted in the Bureau's jurisdiction to investigate hostile foreign intelligence activities on American soil" and that the FBI used the "techniques of wartime." William Sullivan, former assistant to the FBI director, declared, "No holds were barred. . . . We have used [these techniques] against Soviet agents. . . . [The same methods were] brought home against any organization against which we were targeted. We did not differentiate."[90]

The FBI sought to subvert many black civil rights organizations, including the Southern Christian Leadership Conference, the Student Nonviolent Coordinating Committee, the Deacons for Defense and Justice, and the Congress of Racial Equality. Federal Bureau of Investigations headquarters ordered field offices to, as the Senate report noted, "exploit conflicts within and between groups; to use news media contacts to disrupt, ridicule, or discredit groups; to preclude 'violence-prone' or 'rabble rouser' leaders of these groups from spreading their philosophy publicly; and to gather information on the 'unsavory backgrounds'—immorality, subversive activity, and criminal activity—of group members." FBI agents were also ordered to develop specific tactics to "prevent these groups from recruiting young people."[91]

Almost any black organization could be targeted for wiretaps. One black leader was targeted for surveillance in large part because he had "recommended the possession of firearms by members for their self-protection." (At that time, some southern police departments and sheriffs were notorious for attacking blacks who stood up for their civil rights.)[92]

The FBI office in San Diego instigated violence between the local Black Panthers and a rival black organization, US (United Slaves Inc.). FBI agents sent forged letters making accusations and threats to the groups purportedly from their rivals, along with crude cartoons and drawings meant to enrage the recipients. Three Black Panthers and one member of the rival group were killed during the time the FBI was fanning the flames. A few days after shootings in which two Panthers were wounded and one killed, and in which the US headquarters was bombed, the FBI office reported to headquarters: "Efforts are being made to determine how this situation can be capitalized upon for the benefit of the Counterintelligence Program." The FBI office bragged shortly thereafter: "Shootings, beatings, and a high degree of unrest continues to prevail in the ghetto area of southeast San Diego. Although no specific counterintelligence action can be credited with contributing to this overall situation, it is felt that a substantial amount of the unrest is directly attributable to this program."[93]

The FBI set up a Ghetto Informant Program that continued after COINTELPRO and had 7,402 informants, including proprietors of candy stores and barbershops, as of September 1972. The informants served as "listening posts" "to identify extremists passing through or locating in the ghetto area, to identify purveyors of extremist literature," and to keep an eye on "Afro-American type bookstores" (including obtaining the names of the bookstores' "clientele").[94] The informants' reports were stockpiled in the FBI's Racial Intelligence Unit.

For most of the last five years of his life, Martin Luther King was "the target of an intensive campaign by the Federal Bureau of Investigation to 'neutralize' him as an effective civil rights leader," the Senate report noted. King's "I Have a Dream" speech in Washington in August 1963 was described by the FBI's Domestic Intelligence Division as evidence that King had become "the most dangerous and effective Negro leader in the country." King's home and office were wiretapped and, on 16 occasions, the FBI placed wiretaps in King's motel rooms, seeking information on the "private activities of King and his advisers" to use to "completely discredit" them. The FBI sent a copy of one tape recording directly to King along with a note "which Dr. King and his advisers interpreted as a threat to release the tape recording unless Dr. King committed suicide," the Senate report noted.[95] The FBI offered to play tapes from the hotel rooms for "friendly" reporters. The FBI sought to block the publication of articles that praised King. An FBI agent intervened with Francis Cardinal Spellman to seek to block a meeting between King and the pope.

FBI informants also "set up a Klan organization intended to attract membership away from the United Klans of America. The Bureau paid the informant's personal expenses in setting up the new organization, which had, at its height, 250 members." During the six years Gary Rowe spent as an FBI informant with the Klan, Rowe, along with other Klansmen, had "beaten people severely, had boarded buses and kicked people off; had went in restaurants and beaten them with blackjacks, chains, pistols." Rowe testified how he and other Klansmen used "baseball bats, clubs, chains, and pistols" to attack Freedom Riders.[96]

The FBI continually expanded its racial surveillance investigations, eventually targeting white people who were "known to sponsor demonstrations against integration and against the busing of Negro students to white schools." The FBI also created a national "Rabble Rouser" Index, a "major intelligence program . . . to identify 'demagogues.'"[97]

From 1967 to 1972, the FBI paid Howard Berry Godfrey to be an informant with a right-wing paramilitary group in the San Diego area known as the Secret Army. The Senate committee discovered that Godfrey or the Secret Army were involved in "firebombing, smashing windows . . . propelling lug nuts through windows with sling shots, and breaking and entering." Godfrey took a Secret Army colleague with him to conduct surveillance of the home of a left-wing San Diego State University professor; the colleague fired several shots into the home, badly wounding a woman inside. The Senate report noted that "even this shooting incident did not immediately terminate Godfrey as an [FBI] informant." Godfrey subsequently sold explosive material to a subordinate in the Secret Army who bombed the Guild Theater in San Diego in 1972.[98]

One FBI informant infiltrated an antiwar group and helped them break into the Camden, New Jersey, Draft Board in 1970. The informant later testified: "Everything they learned about breaking into a building or climbing a wall or cutting glass or destroying lockers, I taught them. I taught them how to cut the glass, how to drill holes in the glass so you cannot hear it and stuff like that, and the FBI supplied me with the equipment needed. The stuff I did not have, the [FBI] got off their own agents."[99] That sting led to a press conference in which J. Edgar Hoover and Attorney General John Mitchell proudly announced the indictment of 20 people on an array of charges. After learning of the FBI's role in the crime, a jury refused to convict any of the defendants.

Some COINTELPRO operations targeted the spouses of political activists, sending them letters asserting that their mate was screwing around. "Anonymous letters were sent to, among others, a Klansman's wife, informing her that her husband had 'taken the flesh of another unto himself,' the other person being a woman named Ruby, with her 'lust filled eyes and smart aleck figure;' and to a 'Black Nationalist's' wife saying that her husband 'been maken it here' with other women in his organization 'and than he gives us this jive bout their better in bed then you.'"[100] One FBI field office bragged that one such letter to a black activist's wife produced the "tangible result" and "certainly contributed very strongly" to the marriage's demise.

The FBI targeted the women's liberation movement, resulting in "intensive reporting on the identities and opinions of women who attended" women's lib meetings. One FBI informant reported to headquarters of a meeting in New York: "Each woman at this meeting stated why she had come to the meeting and how she felt oppressed, sexually or otherwise. . . . They are mostly against marriage, children, and other states of oppression caused by men." Women's lib informants were instructed to "go to meetings, write up reports . . . to try to identify the background of every person there . . . [and] who they were sleeping with."[101] The Senate report noted that "the intensive FBI investigation of the Women's Liberation Movement was predicated on the theory that the activities of women in that Movement might lead to demonstrations and violence."

The Senate report also described

The *"snitch jacket"* technique—neutralizing a target by labeling him a "snitch" or informant, so that he would no longer be trusted—was used in all COINTELPROs. The methods utilized ranged from having an authentic informant start a rumor about the target member, to anonymous letters or phone calls, to faked informants' reports. . . . The "snitch jacket" is a particularly nasty technique even when used in peaceful groups. It gains an added dimension of danger when it is used—as, indeed, it was—in groups known to have murdered informers.[102]

The FBI took a shotgun approach toward protestors partly because of the FBI's "belief that dissident speech and association should be prevented because they were incipient steps toward the possible ultimate commission of an act which might be criminal."[103] Some FBI agents may have viewed dissident speech or protests as a "gateway drug" to blowing up the Washington Monument. The Senate report noted:

> The clearest example of actions directly aimed at the exercise of constitutional rights are those targeting speakers, teachers, writers or publications, and meetings or peaceful demonstrations. Approximately 18 percent of all approved COINTELPRO proposals fell into these categories. The cases include attempts (sometimes successful) to get university and high school teachers fired; to prevent targets from speaking on campus; to stop chapters of target groups from being formed; to prevent the distribution of books, newspapers, or periodicals; to disrupt news conferences; to disrupt peaceful demonstrations, including the SCLC's Washington Spring Project and Poor People's Campaign, and most of the large antiwar marches; and to deny facilities for meetings or conferences.[104]

An FBI memo warned that "the anarchist activities of a few can paralyze institutions of learning, [conscription] induction centers, cripple traffic, and tie the arms of law enforcement officials, all to the detriment of our society." The FBI declared: "The New Left has on many occasions viciously and scurrilously attacked the Director [J. Edgar Hoover] and the Bureau in an attempt to hamper our investigation of it and to drive us off the college campuses." The FBI ordered field offices in 1968 to gather information illustrating the "scurrilous and depraved nature of many of the characters, activities, habits, and living conditions representative of New Left adherents." The headquarters directive informed FBI agents across the land: "Every avenue of possible embarrassment must be vigorously and enthusiastically explored. It cannot be expected that information of this type will be easily obtained, and an imaginative approach by your personnel is imperative to its success."[105] One FBI internal newsletter encouraged FBI agents to conduct more interviews with antiwar activists "for plenty of reasons, chief of which are it will enhance the paranoia endemic in these circles and will further serve to get the point across that there is an FBI agent behind every mailbox."[106]

A major goal of the New Left COINTELPRO operations was to "counter the widespread charges of police brutality that invariably arise following student-police encounters."[107] The FBI was especially incensed at criticisms that Chicago policemen used excessive force when they attacked demonstrators during the 1968 Democratic National Convention. The FBI thus launched an illegal program to smear people the FBI believed had made false assertions of police misconduct.

As COINTELPRO continued, the FBI targeted more and more groups and used increasingly vicious tactics. The Senate report noted: "The White Hate COINTELPRO [that focused primarily on the Klan] used comparatively few techniques which carried a risk of serious physical, emotional, or economic damage to the targets, while the Black Nationalist COINTELPRO used such techniques extensively. The New Left COINTELPRO, on the other hand, had the highest proportion of proposals aimed at preventing the exercise of free speech. Like the progression in targeting, the use of dangerous, degrading, or blatantly unconstitutional techniques also appears to have become less restrained with each subsequent program." The FBI continually discovered new enemies. Nixon aide Tom Charles Huston testified of the program's tendency "to move from the kid with a bomb to the kid with a picket sign, and from the kid with the picket sign to the kid with the bumper sticker of the opposing candidate. And you just keep going down the line."[108]

Other federal agencies also trampled citizens' privacy, rights, and lives during the late 1960s and early 1970s. The IRS used COINTELPRO leads to launch audits against thousands of suspected political enemies of the Nixon administration.[109] The U.S. Army set up its own surveillance program, creating files on one hundred thousand Americans and targeting domestic organizations such as the Young Americans for Freedom, the John Birch Society, and the Anti-Defamation League of B'Nai B'rith.[110]

The Senate report on COINTELPRO concluded: "The American people need to be assured that never again will an agency of the government be permitted to conduct a secret war against those citizens it considers threats to the established order. Only a combination of legislative prohibition and Departmental control can guarantee that COINTELPRO will not happen again." The

Ford administration derailed legislative reforms in 1976 by promising an administrative fix. And, 26 years later, Ashcroft seized the opportunity to throw the restraints out the window and to pretend there was never a valid reason to rein in the FBI.

Ashcroft's unleashing of FBI agents sparked a brief flurry of critical comment. A *New York Times* editorial warned that the new guidelines "could mean that F.B.I. agents will show up at the doors of people who order politically unpopular books on Amazon.com or make phone calls to organizations critical of the government."[111] One of the harshest critics was conservative Rep. James Sensenbrenner, chairman of the House Judiciary Committee: "I don't think we need to throw respect for civil liberties into the trash heap in order to get rid of the problems the FBI has had systematically. I get very, very queasy when federal law enforcement is effectively going back to the bad old days when the FBI was spying on people like Martin Luther King."[112]

Ashcroft's new guidelines liberate FBI agents to pursue far more wild goose chases. A Center for Democracy and Technology analysis noted that the earlier FBI guidelines

> had another purpose: they were intended to make the FBI's security operations more efficient by tying FBI inquiries and investigations to some modest showing that they were focused on suspected criminal or terrorist activity for security reasons as well. . . . During the Hoover years, hundreds of thousands of investigations were opened and files compiled on groups and individuals only engaged in lawful speech, protest, and civil rights activities. Informants were vacuum cleaners of information. This massive surveillance effort proved wholly ineffective and was in fact a barrier in thwarting or preventing terrorism. It was documented by the General Accounting Office that the overbroad investigations of the sixties and seventies prevented not a single serious act of violence. Then, as now, the issue was not information, but analysis.[113]

## TIPSy

In mid-2002, the Justice Department began unveiling plans for Operation TIPS—the Terrorism Information and Prevention System. According to the Justice Department website, TIPS will be "a nationwide program giving millions of American truckers, letter carriers, train conductors, ship captains, utility employees, and others a formal way to report suspicious terrorist activity."[114] TIPSters would be people who, "in the daily course of their work, are in a unique position to serve as extra eyes and ears for law enforcement."[115] The feds aimed to recruit people in jobs that "make them uniquely well positioned to understand the ordinary course of business in the area they serve, and to identify things that are out of the ordinary."[116] Homeland Security director Tom Ridge said that observers in certain occupations "might pick up a break in the certain rhythm or pattern of a community."[117] The feds planned to enlist up to ten million people to watch other people's "rhythms."

The Justice Department provided no guidance to enlistees as to the definition of "suspicious behavior" to guide their vigilance. As the public began to focus on the program's sweep, opposition surfaced; even the U.S. Postal Service briefly balked at participating in the program. Homeland Security Chief Ridge stressed that the program was "voluntary" and asserted that TIPS "is not a government intrusion."[118] Ridge declared: "The last thing we want is Americans spying on Americans. That's just not what the president is all about, and not what the TIPS program is all about."[119] Apparently, as long as the Bush administration did not announce plans to compel people to testify about the peccadilloes of their neighbors and customers, TIPS was a certified "freedom-friendly program."

As controversy swirled around the program, the Justice Department became diffident about releasing more information about how TIPS would work. When Ashcroft was cross-examined by Sen. Leahy on TIPS at a Judiciary Committee hearing on July 25, he insisted that "the TIPS program is something requested by industry to allow them to talk about anomalies that they encounter." But, when President Bush first announced the program earlier in 2002, he portrayed it as an administration initiative. Nor is it credible that thousands of Teamsters Union members petitioned 1600 Pennsylvania Avenue over "anomalies." Sen. Leahy asked if reports to the TIPS hotline would become part of a federal database with millions of unsubstantiated allegations against American citizens. Ashcroft told Leahy: "I have recommended that there would be none, and I've been given assurance that the TIPS program would not maintain a data base." But Ashcroft could not reveal which federal official had given him the assurance.[120]

Rep. Bob Barr (R-Ga.) denounced TIPS as a "snitch system" and warned: "A formal program, organized, paid for and maintained by our own federal government to recruit Americans to spy on fellow Americans, smacks of the very type of fascist or Communist government we fought so hard to eradicate in other countries in decades past."[121] The ACLU's Laura Murphy observed: "This is a program where people's activities, statements, posters in their windows or on their walls, nationality, and religious practices will be reported by untrained individuals without any relationship to criminal activity."[122] San Diego law professor Marjorie Cohn observed, "Operation TIPS . . . will encourage neighbors to snitch on neighbors and won't distinguish between real and fabricated tips. Anyone with a grudge or vendetta against another can provide false information to the government, which will then enter the national database."[123]

On August 9, the Justice Department announced it was fine-tuning TIPS, abandoning any "plan to ask thousands of mail carriers, utility workers and others with access to private homes to report suspected terrorist activity," the *Washington Post* reported.[124] People who had enlisted to be TIPSters received an email notice from Uncle Sam that "only those who work in the trucking, maritime, shipping, and mass transit industries will be eligible to participate in this information referral service."[125] But the Justice Department continued refusing to disclose to the Senate Judiciary Committee who would have access to the TIPS reports and how the charges would be processed and saved.[126]

House Majority leader Richard Armey attached an amendment to homeland security legislation that declared: "Any and all activities of the federal government to implement the proposed component program of the Citizen Corps known as Operation TIPS are hereby prohibited."[127] Though Congress specifically banned TIPS, Ashcroft could still announce some other mass surveillance program with a different name.

If Bush had proposed in August 2001 to recruit 10 million Americans to report any of their neighbors they suspected of acting unusual or being potential troublemakers, the public might have concluded the president had gone berserk. Operation TIPS illustrated how the *momentum of intrusion* is spurring government to propose programs that it never would have attempted before 9/11.

## Total Information Awareness: 300 Million Dossiers

The Patriot Act created a new Information Office in the Pentagon's Defense Advanced Research Projects Agency (DARPA). In January 2002, the White House chose retired admiral John Poindexter to head the new office.[128] White House spokesman Ari Fleischer explained: "Admiral Poindexter is somebody who this administration thinks is an outstanding American, an outstanding citizen, who has done a very good job in what he has done for our country, serving the military."[129] Some cynics quibbled over Poindexter's five felony convictions for false testimony to Congress and destruction of evidence during the investigation of the Iran-Contra arms-for-hostages exchange. (Poindexter's convictions were overturned by a federal appeals court, which cited the immunity Congress granted his testimony.) Poindexter was also the author of a visionary 1980s scheme to give the National Security Agency "control over security for all government computer systems containing 'sensitive but unclassified' information. This was followed by a second directive issued by Poindexter that extended military authority over all computer and communications security for the federal government and private industry," as the Electronic Privacy Information Center reported.[130] Congress rebuked this attempted power grab in 1987.

Poindexter committed the new office to achieving Total Information Awareness (TIA). TIA's mission is "to detect, classify and identify foreign terrorists—and decipher their plans—and thereby enable the U.S. to take timely action to successfully preempt and defeat terrorist acts," according to DARPA.[131] According to Undersecretary of Defense Pete Aldridge, TIA will seek to discover "connections between transactions—such as passports; visas; work permits; driver's licenses; credit cards; airline tickets; rental cars; gun purchases; chemical purchases—and events—such as arrests or suspicious activities and so forth."[132] Aldridge agreed that every phone call a person made or received could be entered into the database.[133] With "voice recognition" software, the actual text of the call could also go onto their permanent record.[134]

TIA is also striving to achieve "Human Identification at a Distance" (HumanID), including "Face Recognition," "Iris Recognition," and "Gait Recognition."[135] The Pentagon issued a request for proposals to develop an "odor recognition" surveillance system that would help the feds identify people by their sweat or urine[136]—potentially creating a wealth of new job opportunities for deviants.

TIA could create a national registry of all gun owners. Aldridge stressed: "If they apply for a gun license, you'd like to have that in the database."[137] Congress, in laws passed in 1986 and 1993, prohibited the federal government from compiling a national registry of gun owners or gun buyers. But laws passed before 9/11 are apparently no longer permitted to impede public safety.

The goal appears to be to stockpile as much information as possible about everyone on Earth—thereby allowing government to protect everyone from everything. *New York Times* columnist William Safire captured the sweep of the new surveillance system:

> Every purchase you make with a credit card, every magazine subscription you buy and medical prescription you fill, every Web site you visit and e-mail you send or receive, every academic grade you receive, every bank deposit you make, every trip you book and every event you attend—all these transactions and communications will go into what the Defense Department describes as "a virtual, centralized grand database." To this computerized dossier on your private life from commercial sources, add every piece of information that government has about

you—passport application, driver's license and bridge toll records, judicial and divorce records, complaints from nosy neighbors to the F.B.I., your lifetime paper trail plus the latest hidden camera surveillance— and you have the supersnoop's dream: a "Total Information Awareness" about every U.S. citizen.[138]

Columnist Ted Rall noted that the feds will even scan "veterinary records. The TIA believes that knowing if and when Fluffy got spayed—and whether your son stopped torturing Fluffy after you put him on Ritalin—will help the military stop terrorists before they strike."[139]

Phil Kent, president of the Southeastern Legal Foundation, an Atlanta-based public interest law firm, warned that TIA was "the most sweeping threat to civil liberties since the Japanese-American internment."[140] The ACLU's Jay Stanley labeled TIA "the mother of all privacy invasions. It would amount to a picture of your life so complete it's equivalent to somebody following you around all day with a video camera."[141] A coalition of civil liberties groups protested to Senate leaders: "There are no systems of oversight or accountability contemplated in the TIA project. DARPA itself has resisted lawful requests for information about the Program pursuant to the Freedom of Information Act."

The Bush administration reacted indignantly to criticisms of TIA. Defense Secretary Donald Rumsfeld declared: "The hype and alarm approach is a disservice to the public. . . . I would recommend people take a nice deep breath. Nothing terrible is going to happen."[142] Poindexter promised that TIA will be designed so as to "preserve rights and protect people's privacy while helping to make us all safer."[143] (Poindexter was not under oath at the time of his statement.) The TIA was defended based on the notion that "nobody has been searched" until the feds decide to have them arrested based on the data the feds snared. Undersecretary of Defense Aldridge declared: "It is absurd to think that DARPA is somehow trying to become another police agency. DARPA's purpose is to demonstrate the feasibility of this technology. If it proves useful, TIA will then be turned over to the intelligence, counterintelligence and law enforcement communities as a tool to help them in their battle against domestic terrorism."[144] In January 2003, Sen. Charles Grassley learned that the FBI was working on a memorandum of understanding with the Pentagon "for possible experimentation" with TIA.[145] Assistant Defense Secretary for Homeland Security Paul McHale confirmed, in March 2003 testimony to Congress, that the Pentagon would turn TIA over to law enforcement agencies once the system was ready to roll.[146]

DARPA also responded to the surge of criticism by removing the Information Awareness Office logo from the website. The logo—a giant eye sitting atop a pyramid, seeing and pulling in the entire world, accompanied by the motto *Scientia est Potentia* (Knowledge is Power)—made some malcontents fear TIA intended to play God. But, though the logo vanished from the DARPA website, it can still be found at www.cryptome.org.

Congress in early 2003 enacted a provision to temporarily rein in TIA.[147] The congressional provision also specifies that if Bush formally certifies that TIA is necessary for national security, then the restrictions are voided. The chances that a majority of members of Congress would stand up to Bush on a national security issue are slim to none.

Regardless of the congressional restraint, DARPA has already awarded 26 contracts for dozens of private research projects to develop components for TIA.[148] Salon.com reported: "According to people with knowledge of the program, TIA has now advanced to the point where it's much more than a mere 'research project.' There is a working prototype of the system, and federal agencies outside the Defense Department have expressed interest in it."[149]

Shortly after DARPA completed a key research benchmark for TIA, Lt. Col. Doug Dyer, a DARPA program manager, publicly announced in April 2003 that Americans are obliged to sacrifice some privacy in the name of security: "When you consider the potential effect of a terrorist attack against the privacy of an entire population, there has to be some trade-off."[150] But nothing in the U.S. Constitution entitles the Defense Department to decide how much privacy or liberty American citizens deserve.

At the same time that controversy erupted over TIA, Americans also learned that the Pentagon was ceasing, at least temporarily, development of "e-DNA," a system to impose an automatic "tag" for every person sending email or browsing the Internet. DARPA explained: "We envisage that all network and client resources will maintain traces of user e-DNA so that the user can be uniquely identified as having visited a Web site, having started a process or having sent a packet. This way, the resources and those who use them form a virtual 'crime scene' that contains evidence about the identity of the users, much the same way as a real crime scene contains DNA traces of people."[151] Every page of every Internet site in existence could suddenly and permanently be turned into a "crime scene"—justifying perpetual government surveillance of everything. DARPA spokeswoman Jan Walker said that the agency was "intrigued" by the challenge of "creating network capabilities that would provide the same level of accountability in cyberspace that we now have in the physical world."[152] But there is no agent or drone from the Defense Department that follows every American every minute of every day. The fact that DARPA currently says that it is not further pursuing this initiative is not reassuring, since many DARPA projects are kept under wraps. The Pentagon may have been floating a "trial balloon" on the idea of mandatory "e-DNA" for all Americans.

In May 2003, the Bush adminstration sought to authorize the Pentagon and the CIA to issue National Security Letters (administrative subpoenas enforced by harsh penalties) to American businesses and citizens. The proposal was rebuffed—at least temporarily—by Democrats on the Senate Intelligence Committee. The proposal stunned many civil liberties experts, since federal law is clear that the Pentagon has no role in domestic law enforcement (except for some drug war activities) and the CIA is also largely banned from such activities. Federal courts would have had little or no oversight of this new surveillance power. According to one senior congressional official, "The Bush administration believes that giving the C.I.A. and the military direct authority to demand the records would . . . give those organizations more flexibility to combat terrorism."[153]

## The Great Stonewall

The Patriot Act required the Justice Department to report to House and Senate Judiciary committees every six months on how often some of the new investigatory powers were being used. After the Justice Department ignored the first semiannual deadline, House Judiciary Chairman James Sensenbrenner sent a letter on June 13, 2002 to Ashcroft formally requesting information on how often federal agents demanded information from libraries and bookstores (as well as from other targets).

The Justice Department ignored Sensenbrenner's letter. After Sensenbrenner threatened to subpoena the information, the Justice Department replied on July 26 that the information requested was "classified" and would not be disclosed to the Judiciary Committees. Instead, Assistant Attorney General Daniel Bryant declared that the information would be provided to the House Intelligence Committee—which has no role in oversight of the Justice Department. (The committee was controlled by Republicans who had shown no interest in possessing or releasing any information that could embarrass the Bush administration.)[154]

The Justice Department provided pro forma responses to several questions. The House Judiciary Committee inquired: "How many times have the records sought been entire databases" of bookstores, public libraries, or newspapers? The Justice Department replied: "Such an order could conceivably be served on a public library, bookstore, or newspaper, although it is unlikely that such entities maintain those types of records"—and then added that the actual number of such demands made by the feds is "classified." The Justice Department also refused to disclose to the Judiciary Committee "how many U.S. citizens or lawful permanent residents have been subject to new FISA surveillance orders since" the Patriot Act's enactment.

Justice Department spokesman Mark Corallo explained the denial: "We are not under any obligation to provide information that could lead to the flight of a suspect or that will ruin a prosecution. We are doing everything we can within the Constitution to stop these guys from killing us again."[155] This is the usual invocation of the specter of mass murder to justify preventing people from learning what the government is doing. Corallo added: "I would say the Patriot Act is effective because we have not had another attack this year."[156] The same argument could have been used to vindicate practically any policy, including public executions of everyone named Mustafa.

Freedom has become so fragile that citizens can no longer be permitted to know how often government invades their privacy. David Sobel of the Electronic Privacy Information Center observed: "Much of the information that the Justice Department claims is classified consists of statistical information whose release could not possibly endanger national security or any other legitimate government interest."[157]

During congressional deliberations on the Patriot Act, Ashcroft repeatedly declared that congressional oversight was key to making sure that the new powers were used appropriately. After the bill became law, however, Ashcroft made sure Congress never had sufficient information to do oversight. Once Congress awarded new powers, its role was finished—except for dutifully appropriating ever-growing budgets.

## Homeland Security Act: More Intrusions, More Threats

In the wake of 9/11, Democrats proposed creating a gargantuan new federal department to fight terrorism. The Bush administration spurned the idea as a bureaucratic boondoggle. However, in June 2002, when Bush was under attack for misstatements by his administration regarding pre-9/11 terrorist attack warnings, he reversed himself and championed the idea of combining 23 federal agencies into the Homeland Security Department. Bush made this proposal his top domestic initiative heading into the 2002 midterm congressional elections. The administration turned the authorization bill for the new department into a

Christmas tree, with all sorts of add-ons to increase federal power. Sen. Robert Byrd (D-W.Va.) fought heroically to block the bill in the Senate, continually warning that the act was a perilous grant of arbitrary power to the president. But, after Republicans picked up control of the Senate in the 2002 election, Byrd lost support from his colleagues and resistance crumbled.

Congress repeated the Patriot Act stampede with the Homeland Security Act. Rep. Ron Paul (R-Tex.) warned that the Bush administration bill for a Homeland Security Department "almost overnight grew from 32 pages to 282 pages. . . . Now we are prepared to vote on a nearly 500-page bill that increases federal expenditures and raises troubling civil liberties questions. Adding insult to injury, this bill was put together late last night and introduced only this morning. Worst of all, the text of the bill has not been made readily available to most members, meaning this Congress is prepared to create a massive new federal agency without even knowing the details. This is a dangerous and irresponsible practice."[158] The House and Senate passed the bill by large margins.

As part of the homeland security legislation, Congress awarded new surveillance powers to government agencies, including the so-called CyberSecurity Enhancement Act, which reduced security for citizens' email. The act empowers almost any government agency to demand copies of citizens' emails without a court warrant. "Public schools, social services departments, the IRS or the local tax assessor" may exploit the new standard to commandeer people's email by claiming an emergency, according to the Electronic Frontier Foundation's Lee Tien.[159] Jennifer Garnick, director of Stanford Law School's Center for Internet and Society, warns that the act's "definition of emergency is so broad, it's a case of the exception swallowing the rule."[160]

The Homeland Security Act eased "the restrictions on law enforcement's ability to install trap-and-trace devices such as the FBI's Carnivore pack-sniffing software without getting a warrant beforehand."[161] Perhaps the Justice Department objected to leaving a "paper trail" of its Carnivore use. This provision will make it more difficult to know how many millions of people's email are being impounded—thereby minimizing supervision of and accountability for law enforcement.

The bill also created a new Homeland Security Advanced Research Projects Agency (HSARPA)—a homeland equivalent of DARPA—slated to collect over $500 million a year to develop new surveillance and other technologies.[162] HSARPA will "promote revolutionary changes in technologies that would promote homeland security, advance the development, and accelerate the prototyping and deployment of technologies that would address homeland vulnerabilities," as ace high-tech journalist Declan McCullagh reported.[163] All sorts of threats to privacy could arise in the coming years from this program.

## Patriot II

Shortly after the Patriot Act passed, rumors swirled that Justice Department lawyers were already working on follow-up legislation to capture more power. Justice Department officials consistently denied that any such bill was in the making. On February 7, 2003, the Center for Public Integrity released an 86-page draft version of the Domestic Security Enhancement Act. Notations on the Justice Department document—stamped "confidential" on every page—showed that it had been sent to Vice President Dick Cheney and House Speaker Dennis Hastert. Rep. John Conyers (D-Mich.) complained to Ashcroft that "the handling of this matter [has] only lent credence to suggestions that . . . the Justice Department is waiting to spring this bill on the Congress when the nation once again has endured a terrorist attack or is in the midst of war."[164]

The Domestic Security Enhancement Act—which quickly became known as Patriot II—aimed to abolish many of the remaining restraints on the power of federal agents and the Justice Department.

Section 101 of the proposed bill is titled "Individual Terrorists as Foreign Powers."[165] It would revise the Foreign Intelligence Surveillance Act to permit the U.S. government to label suspected terrorists—including American citizens—as "foreign powers" for the purpose of conducting total surveillance of their activities. Labeling Americans as "foreign powers" would be sufficient to nullify all their Fourth Amendment rights.

Section 102 of the new bill would authorize wiretaps and other surveillance measures on Americans suspected of gathering information for a foreign power. There is no requirement that the American be involved in illegally gathering information, or in gathering illegal information. The Bush administration's confidential explanation of the bill notes: "Requiring the additional showing that the intelligence gathering violates the laws of the United States is both unnecessary and counterproductive, as such activities threaten the national security regardless of whether they are illegal."[166] But, as the ACLU noted, "This amendment would permit electronic surveillance of a local activist who was preparing a report on human rights for London-based Amnesty International, a 'foreign political organization,' even if the activist was not engaged in any violation of law."[167]

Section 106 would permit federal agents to illegally wiretap and surveil Americans and illegally leak damaging personal information on Americans—as long as the agents were following orders from the president or the attorney general. The ACLU noted: "This section would encourage unlawful intelligence wiretaps and secret searches by immunizing agents from criminal sanctions if they conduct such surveillance, even if a reasonable official would know it is illegal, by claiming they were acting in 'good faith' based on the orders of the President or the Attorney General."[168] This proposal is a further attempt to make federal agents legally untouchable and would bring out the worst in public servants.

Section 201 would make it easier for the federal government to carry out secret mass arrests. The provision, entitled "Prohibition of Disclosure of Terrorism Investigation Detainee Information," notes: "Although existing Freedom of Information Act (FOIA) exemptions . . . permit the government to protect information relating to detainees, defending this interpretation through litigation requires extensive Department of Justice resources, which would be better spent detecting and incapacitate [sic] terrorists."[169] In other words, to save the Justice Department the bother of having to defend secret roundups, the Bush administration seeks to amend the federal statute book to imitate repressive dictatorships around the globe.

Section 312, entitled "Appropriate Remedies with Respect to Law Enforcement Surveillance Activities," would nullify almost all federal, state, and local court "consent decrees" restricting the power of local and state police to spy on Americans. The Bush administration complains that such consent decrees result in police lacking "the ability to use the full range of investigative techniques that are lawful under the Constitution, and that are available to the FBI." But, in almost every case, such consent decrees were imposed after stark abuses of citizens' rights by the police. The Bush administration draft bill declares: "All surviving decrees would have to be necessary to correct a current and ongoing violation of a Federal right, extend no further than necessary to correct the violation of the Federal right, and be narrowly drawn and the least intrusive means to correct the violation."[170] Historically, Supreme Court First Amendment jurisprudence has required the federal government to use the "least intrusive means" necessary to achieve some policy, in order to prevent any unnecessary restriction of freedom of speech. The Bush administration now demands the "least intrusive" restrictions on government intrusions.

Section 402 would permit U.S. attorneys to prosecute Americans for aiding terrorist organizations—even if they made donations to organizations that the U.S. government did not publicly designate as terrorist groups. With the proposed revision, "there would be no requirement to show that the defendants actually had such an intent" to advance terrorist causes or actions before convicting them of being terrorist supporters, according to the Justice Department explanatory text. Robert Higgs of the Independent Institution warns that, with this provision, the feds "can categorize the most innocent action"—such as "signing a petition"—as an act of terrorism.[171]

Section 404 creates "a new, separate crime of using encryption technology that could add five years or more to any sentence for crimes committed with a computer," the ACLU notes.[172] Encryption software is routinely included on new computers and is used far and wide by businesses and others for transactions. The Justice Department thus seeks to treat use of encryption software the same way that the federal government treats gun possession—something sinister enough to routinely justify a doubling or tripling of prison sentences for people who violate other federal statutes.

Section 422 will make it easier for federal prosecutors to target people who rely on hawalas to send money back to their relatives in Third World countries. The section will allow money sent via hawalas is to be treated as illegally "laundered"—even when there is no evidence the money was illegally acquired or used for illicit purposes by recipients. This provision will also assist federal attorneys in achieving their confiscation goals.

Section 501 of the bill was labeled the "citizenship death penalty" by University of Washington law professor Anita Ramasastry.[173] It would empower the Justice Department to strip Americans of their citizenship if the feds accuse them of supporting "terrorism," either domestic or international. And "support" could be something as simple as attending a peaceful rally of an organization that some federal prosecutor subsequently labels terrorist. Yale Law School professor Jack Balkin said, "Give a few dollars to a Muslim charity Ashcroft thinks is a terrorist organization and you could be on the next plane out of this country."[174] Once the U.S. government revokes an American's citizenship, there is nothing to prevent the government from treating that person the same way the feds treated "special interest detainees" after 9/11. The American Immigration Lawyers Association warns that, under this provision, "targeted [U.S. citizens] potentially could find themselves consigned to indefinite detention as undocumented immigrants in their own country."[175]

Shortly after the text of Patriot II surfaced, Ashcroft was asked at a press conference about his plans for expansion of federal power. Ashcroft refused to confirm plans to formally propose Patriot II but did declare: "Every day we are asking each other, what can we do to be more successful in securing the freedoms of America and sustaining the liberty, the tolerance, the human dignity that America represents, and how can we do a better job in defeating the threat of terrorism."[176] But as EPIC director Marc Rotenberg observed: "Apart from the dramatic expansion of government surveillance authority and government secrecy, [Patriot II] transfers enormous power from the Congress and the judiciary to the executive branch and gives the attorney general absolutely unprecedented authority. This is more than an assault on constitutional liberty—it is an attack on the constitutional system of checks and balances."[177]

## Conclusion: Righteous Intruders

The worse the government fails, the less privacy citizens supposedly deserve. Prior to 9/11, the government had all the information it needed to detect and block a conspiracy to hijack four airplanes. The Joint Intelligence Committee concluded: "To much of the Intelligence Community, everything was a priority—the U.S. wanted to know everything about everything all the time."[178] The CIA, the National Security Agency, and the FBI failed to focus on the gravest terrorist threats. Because the government failed to analyze and exploit the information in its possession, it now entitles itself to seize vastly more information and to treat Americans like unindicted co-conspirators with the terrorists. The Bush administration rewarded failure with bigger budgets, more power, and presidential commendations. The investigations after 9/11 failed to hold any government official responsible for failing to use the information they possessed. The incentive for lethargy, risk evasion, and information hoarding were preserved intact.

There is no technological magic bullet that will make the government as smart as it is powerful. The Bush administration is valuing its new intrusive proposals such as Total Information Awareness based not on what they expect to find, but on a mistaken belief that the more information the government captures, the more intelligent it will act. But it is a perennial folly to presume that more information automatically creates better intelligence, as if a person could become a genius simply by buying a bookstore and inscribing his name inside the cover of every book.

The more power the Justice Department acquired, the more bad faith it showed. The Patriot Act was preceded by tall tales by Ashcroft and others about how the federal government had never violated any Americans' rights. The more hostile the Bush administration became towards citizens' privacy, the more secretive it became about the government's own actions. It was as if 9/11 magically transferred the "right to privacy" from private citizens to government agencies. "The Justice Department has erected a one-way mirror between itself and the American people—department officials can look out, but Americans can't look in," observed Charles Levendosky, editorial page editor of the *Casper Star-Tribune*.[179] Perhaps the Bush administration assumes that the less people know about what the government is doing, the more secure they will feel.

The issue of government trustworthiness goes to the heart of the issue of the new surveillance powers. The fact that Ashcroft effectively seized more surveillance powers at the same time that he denied such powers had ever been abused in the past should have obliterated his credibility. Instead, Ashcroft's absurdities have gone largely unchallenged.

COINTELPRO illustrates why federal agents cannot be trusted with reams of personal information on American citizens. People will likely never know how much information the government has gathered on them unless and until the government openly takes some punitive action against them. In the COINTELPRO operation, many victims of government abuse never knew that it was FBI agents who turned the screws and wrecked their marriages, destroyed their jobs, or poisoned their hometown reputations. The more information the government gathers, the greater the temptation to exploit that information for political or personal gain. While Ashcroft portrayed government collection of personal information on millions of citizens as innocuous, the 1976 Senate report warned: "The mere existence of the additional information gained through the investigative programs inevitably demonstrated those particular organizational or personal weaknesses which were vulnerable to disruption."[180]

There is power in information: the more information government gathers on people, the more power it will have over them. The more power the government has to surveil, the more intimidated Americans will become. And the further the government intrudes, the more difficult it becomes to leash the government. House Majority Leader Hale Boggs explained in 1971 that congressmen failed to check FBI abuses because of pervasive fear on Capitol Hill: "Freedom of speech, freedom of thought, freedom of action for men in public life can be compromised quite as effectively by the fear of surveillance as by the fact of surveillance. Our apathy in this Congress, our silence in this House, our very fear of speaking out in other forums has watered the roots and hastened the growth of a vine of tyranny . . . which is ensnaring that Constitution and Bill of Rights which we are each sworn to uphold." Boggs, speaking five years before a Senate Committee finally revealed the extent of federal abuses, warned: "Our society can survive many challenges and many threats. It cannot survive a planned and programmed fear of its own government bureaus and agencies."[181]

The Bush administration's surveillance policies scorn fundamental principles that long restrained government forays into Americans' lives. The Supreme

Court declared in a 1934 decision: "A general, roving . . . investigation, conducted by a commission without any allegations . . . is unknown to our constitution and laws; and such an inquisition would be destructive of the rights of the citizen, and an intolerable tyranny."[182] Federal judge Gerhard Gesell, in a 1974 ruling on illegal Nixon administration searches, observed: "The American Revolution was sparked in part by the complaints of the colonists against the issuance of writs of assistance, pursuant to which the King's revenue officers conducted unrestricted, indiscriminate searches of persons and homes to uncover contraband."[183] Unfortunately, the revolutionary spirit now animating Washington is fighting to replace the right to privacy with the right to intrude.

## CHAPTER EIGHT

# Groping to Safety

We will not surrender our freedom to travel.

—*George W. Bush, September 27, 2001*[1]

If we get impatient, the terrorists win.

—*George W. Bush, January 22, 2002*[2]

In the wake of the hijacking and crashing of four airliners and the subsequent shutdown of the nation's airports, many Americans were hesitant to return to fly the friendly skies. Speaking on September 27, 2001 at Chicago's O'Hare International Airport, President Bush decried the "atmosphere of fear" created by the terrorist attack. Bush declared that "one of the great goals of this Nation's war is to restore public confidence in the airline industry, to tell the traveling public, get onboard."[3] Bush proudly announced: "Tomorrow, nine Cabinet members will board U.S. airlines to fly around the country to do their jobs."[4] The secretaries' courage aimed to rally all Americans and prove that there was no need for Americans to "live in fear," Bush said.[5]

Only five cabinet secretaries made it to the airport and up and away the next day. Labor Secretary Elaine Chao flew to Louisville, Kentucky, on the morning of September 28. Chao declared: "I am flying today to encourage all Americans to get back to work, to visit family, to resume our way of life. We need to all do our part in getting America back to work, and defeating terrorism. Each person who steps onto a plane is sending a message to the world that we will not live in fear."[6] Arriving in Louisville, Chao told reporters that there was no additional security on her flight that morning.[7]

Commerce Secretary Don Evans bragged that morning on CBS's *Early Show:* "I'm also traveling commercial, as you know, sending another signal to Americans all across this country that it's safe to fly."[8]

Housing and Urban Development Secretary Mel Martinez arrived at Minneapolis-St. Paul International Airport and announced: "I'm traveling without bodyguards, just like anyone else would travel. . . . America is back, flying is safe."[9]

A few days later, news leaked out that the Federal Aviation Administration (FAA) had placed armed undercover federal air marshals on each of the cabinet secretaries' flights. FAA security director Michael Canavan, a former Army lieutenant general, was fired after he balked at placing marshals on the politicians' flights, since he believed other flights that day were at higher risk of hijacking.[10] (He was overruled.)

The heroic cabinet secretaries hoax received little or no mention in the vast majority of the American media. There were too many other confidence-building news events to cover in those exciting times. Transportation Secretary Norm Mineta justified the ruse: "In the case of the Cabinet members flying on commercial airlines, those flights had been previously announced by the president and were highly publicized, potentially raising the threat for every passenger on each of those flights. . . . Clearly, if air marshals were added to those flights this action would have been taken to ensure the safety of all of the passengers."[11] Except for the passengers on other flights the FAA security director concluded were at greater risks. Mineta never explained why the Bush administration deceived the public by claiming the cabinet secretaries were flying without additional protection.

Bush's public praise and endorsements of the Transportation Department would have swayed fewer Americans if the public had known more about how FAA bureaucratic negligence contributed to 9/11. On the morning of September 12 airlines received a fax from the FAA with a list of 300 people classified as dangerous by federal agencies and who were henceforth prohibited from boarding any flight. Steven Brill, in his book *After: How America Confronted the September 12 Era,* noted that the FAA had not previously bothered compiling and forwarding to airlines a list of "flight risks" it received from the FBI, CIA, and its own experts. Brill learned from FAA and Justice Department officials that "two of the [9/11] hijackers were on those September 10 lists—something that Ashcroft would later say he could not confirm or deny. In fact, says the FAA official, his agency had crossed those names off on September 12 to avoid embarrassment." The FAA official explained: "We just never got around to setting up a protocol for who would control the list and how we would get the airlines to implement it." Brill noted that "this failure of the FAA to circulate that no-fly list . . . seems clearly to have resulted in, or contributed to, at least two of the hijackings."[12]

From the start, the Bush administration seemed far more concerned with restoring public confidence than with making air travel secure. Two days after the attack, President Bush practically announced that the problem of airline safety had been solved, telling reporters: "We have taken every precaution to make sure that it is safe to fly in America. There are beefed up security at our airports. There is increased presence on the airplanes."[13] But the old crew in Washington was left completely in charge.

Immediately after details of the hijackers' strategy became public, airline pilots pleaded with the federal government to be allowed to carry firearms to stop hijackings. Instead, Secretary Mineta announced a ban on all nonplastic knives on airplanes and in the restaurants in secure areas of airports.[14] Mineta even banned steak knives in first class. He also demanded that airport security screeners become far more vigilant. Within days, the number of fingernail clippers and cigar cutters seized at airports broke all previous records.

It took less than a week for Washington politicians to transform the FAA's greatest debacle into its finest hour. Secretary Mineta announced on September 16: "Let me take this opportunity to thank all of the employees of the Federal Aviation Administration under the great leadership of Jane Garvey and Monty Belger for the heroic work that they have done in response to this national crisis. And everyone from the screeners at the airports to the pilots to cabin crews, the additional law enforcement personnel, everyone is working at a high level of dedication and teamwork, and all I would like to say to everyone is, Thanks a million."[15] Yet the FAA had been repeatedly warned by its own agents and Inspector General that the federally mandated security system was full of holes and completely unreliable. Former Transportation Department Inspector General Mary Schiavo observed that FAA officials "absolutely don't like this job function. They don't want to do security. They're very, very poor at it."[16] Schiavo noted: "What we have done over the past is pay ticket taxes and facility charges that went into the aviation trust fund which was supposed to be for aviation safety and security but we use it for things like the nice concourses and the airport and the stores."[17]

FAA chief Jane Garvey commented a few days after the attack: "I don't think any system that we put in place, any system that we've had in place, has contemplated people's willingness to commit suicide."[18] Yet hundreds of suicide bombing attacks had occurred worldwide, stretching back to Beirut in the early 1980s. Less than three months before the hijackings, an FAA advisory committee decided to upgrade the training manuals and official guidance for responding to hijacking attempts. FAA official Mike Morse said the new "scenario will be one involving a team of hijackers with a higher degree of sophistication and training. And that scenario will more replicate what we've faced in some of the international hijackings abroad in recent years."[19] Morse told the advisory committee that "we hope to have some new training materials out in the Fall" of 2001 to replace the preemptive surrender approach FAA urged in response to hijacking attempts. But the hijackers moved faster than the bureaucrats.

With each passing week, the actions of bureaucrats on 9/11 became more heroic. In an appearance before the National Press Club on October 17, Garvey even asserted that the immediate grounding of aircraft on 9/11 "thwarted" other hijackings: "I think the acts that the controllers took, the calmness with which they approached the landing of all the aircraft, the calmness and professionalism of the pilots as well, I think really did avert some other potential tragedies that day."[20] Garvey never offered any evidence that other hijackings were prevented. Former FAA Security chief Billie Vincent noted that Garvey's own "security service has been giving strident warnings of a possible terrorist attack on U.S. aviation for the past 2 to 3 years."[21]

Bush and Mineta sought to reassure the public by placing National Guard troops in airports. However, some states, such as New York and Pennsylvania, prohibited the guardsmen from carrying loaded weapons in airports. A spokesman for Pennsylvania Governor Mark Schweiker justified posting guards with unloaded guns in airports because it "reassured the traveling public during an uneasy time."[22] In most airports, the guards did little more than take up space and consume oxygen. At San Francisco International Airport, a Guardsman shot himself in the butt while he was extracting his pistol from his holster.[23]

The initial revving-up of airport security may have boosted the employment rate of village idiots. Twenty-two-year-old Neil Godfrey was randomly selected for a baggage search before his October 10 flight from Philadelphia to Phoenix. A screener discovered the book *Hayduke Lives!*, a novel about a fanatic environmentalist, in Godfrey's carry-on bag, as the *Philadelphia City Paper* reported.[24] The book cover showed a drawing "of a man's hand holding several sticks of dynamite." Ten minutes later, a guardsman summoned Godfrey to step aside and proceeded to cross-examine him about why he was reading the book. *City Paper* noted: "Within minutes, Godfrey says, Philadelphia Police officers, Pennsylvania State Troopers and airport security officials joined the National Guardsman. About 10 to 12 people examined the novel for 45 minutes, scratching out notes the entire time. They also questioned Godfrey about the purpose of his trip to Phoenix. . . . Eventually, one of the law enforcement officials told Godfrey his book was 'innocuous' and he would be allowed to board the plane."[25] But Godfrey was informed by a United Airlines employee that he was being prohibited from flying in part because he was "reading a book with an illustration of a bomb on the cover."

Godfrey went home and then, after making various calls, got rebooked on another flight to Phoenix later that day. He left *Heyduke Lives!* at home and instead took *Harry Potter and the Prisoner of Azkaban* to read on the flight. After a police officer recognized Godfrey from his trouble making earlier that day, he was pulled aside and a guardsman and three other people spent 20 minutes studying the Harry Potter novel. He was eventually cleared by airport officials to make the flight—but once again, United prohibited him from getting on board.

New security policies created more hassles than safety. Just under a month after 9/11, two *New York Daily News* reporters easily slipped knives, razor blades, and scissors past checkpoints at ten airports in a test of the new, improved airport security. FAA spokesman Jim Peters assured the paper: "We will look into the things that got through. We will talk to the appropriate people at the screening."[26]

New federal policies quickly created gridlock at airports, forcing people to wait hours to pass through checkpoints. One result was a 30-fold increase in the number of laptop computers accidentally left behind by harried travelers at some airports.[27] Rather than amending the procedures to end pointless delays, Mineta preached that "patience is the new form of patriotism."[28] Baltimore-Washington International Airport—renown for the longest lines in the nation after 9/11—hired clowns and entertainers dressed up as Uncle Sam and Groucho Marx to divert people while they waited up to four hours in line. Airport spokesman John White explained: "We decided anything to make the environment more friendly and comfortable would help—anything that would be distracting would be good."[29] Government officials acted as if they had a right to squander unlimited amounts of time of any person who chose to fly.

On October 30 Mineta, responding to reports of continued airport security flaws, publicly conceded that "an unacceptable number of deficiencies continue to occur. And the result is a growing lack of confidence and increasing criticism of the actions that are being taken by the Federal Aviation Administration. And I want to reverse that trend."[30] There was nothing more perilous than criticizing the FAA.[31] Mineta declared: "Every time the system is not followed it breaks down the confidence of the traveling public, and it reduces the confidence they have in the federal government."[32] For an old politician like Mineta, maintaining faith in government is the ultimate public service. (The Norman Y. Mineta San Jose International Airport and the Mineta Transportation Research Institute, established by act of Congress in 1991, are testament to Mineta's clout from his long service in Congress.)

Six days later, Subash Gurung, a 27-year-old Nepali, was arrested at Chicago's O'Hare International Airport after he successfully passed through airport security with seven knives, a can of Mace, and a stun gun. A checkpoint security screener confiscated two knives from Gurung but did not detect all the other potential weapons, which were discovered when he was selected for a random baggage search before boarding the plane.[33] Mineta responded to the debacle by swearing he would have "zero tolerance" for airport security failures and vowing: "When I say zero tolerance, that means zero tolerance."[34]

In mid-November, Congress passed a law creating the Transportation Security Administration and requiring all airport security checkers to be federal employees. *Government Executive* magazine crowed: "It had, stunningly, become politically incorrect to oppose the biggest single expansion of the federal government in decades."[35] The *Washington Post*'s E. J. Dionne hailed the seismic shift: "The rhetoric of free market omnipotence, so dominant for so long, became a bit less believable when Republicans and Democrats in Congress agreed that the marketplace couldn't keep the airlines flying; only the government, however clumsily, could do that."[36] Senate Majority Leader Tom Daschle proclaimed: "I am extremely pleased. Our skies and our airports are going to be a lot safer."[37] Sen. John McCain (R-Ariz.) said: "As soon as the President signs it, we can restore confidence in air safety"[38] Airport security consultant Michael Boyd, a former Braniff Airlines executive, offered a different perspective: "This legislation institutionalizes the cover-up of the massive negligence of the FAA/DOT before 9/11 and since. It's like putting Bonnie & Clyde in charge of bank security."[39] The federal government had long been in charge of setting standards and auditing the quality of airport security. But because the screeners would now be federal employees, all previous problems would supposedly vanish.

The ink on the bill was barely dry before the nation's air traffic system was thrown into chaos after a frustrated football fan at Atlanta's Hartsfield International Airport bypassed a security checkpoint to run down an up escalator to retrieve a camera bag.[40] Government officials panicked, shut down the entire airport for four hours, herded 10,000 people outside the terminal, and sealed all the roads around the airport. Hundreds of flights were delayed.

## Biggest Antihijacking Success: Shoe Defused

The Bush administration relied on creating a bevy of new hoops and battalions of federal agents to deter any hijackers. But in the one confirmed Muslim terrorist attack on a U.S. flight after 9/11, it was private citizens who saved the day. On December 22, 2001 Richard Reid, a Muslim from Britain, sought to ignite a bomb in his shoe during an American Airlines flight from Paris to Miami.[41] A stewardess noticed the smell from his matches and she, along with several passengers, wrestled Reid to the floor and stopped his attempt to destroy the airplane.

The vigorous crew and passenger response to Reid was an indication of what might have happened on all the hijacked flights on 9/11 if airlines and citizens had not been kept blindfolded from warnings the feds were receiving—and if people had not been encouraged to acquiesce to aggression and trust government to rescue them.

## Equal Opportunity Harassment

Secretary Mineta, who as a child was locked for years in U.S. detention camps during World War II solely because of his Japanese ancestry, was determined that no ethnic or national origin profiling should be used at airports. Mineta declared that "surrendering to . . . discrimination makes us no different than the despicable terrorists who rained such hatred on our people."[42] Transportation Department regulations decreed: "Ask yourself, 'But for this person's perceived race, ethnic heritage, or religious orientation, would I have subjected this individual to additional safety or security scrutiny?'" If the answer is no, then it is a crime for screeners to further investigate the person who aroused their suspicions.

Mineta's exercise in piety ignored the fact that all the hijackers were foreign-born Arabs. Stuart Taylor argued in *Legal Times*: "If you make the plausible assumptions that al Qaeda terrorists are at least 100 times as likely to be from the Middle East as to be native-born Americans, and that fewer than 5 percent of all passengers on domestic flights are Middle Eastern men, it would follow that a randomly chosen Middle Eastern male passenger is roughly 2,000 times as likely to be an al Qaeda terrorist as a randomly chosen native-born American. It is crazy to ignore such odds."[43] Heightened attention to groups most likely to be hijackers could have been done in a way that respected their dignity and protected public safety.

On the other hand, relying on profiling alone as a panacea would be disastrous. Richard Reid, the shoe bomber, had a Jamaican father and a British mother and would not have been noticed by airport screeners looking solely for men from the Mideast.

The result of Mineta's "no profiling" edict was endless harassment for old folks, mothers with young babies, and people in wheelchairs. At Reagan Washington National Airport, 75-year-old congressman John Dingell was taken to a side room and required to drop his pants to prove he wasn't a hijacker. (His steel hip joint, knee brace, and ankle pins kept setting off the metal detector.)[44] At the Phoenix airport, an 86-year-old World War II fighter ace faced repeated intensive searches and cross-examination after screeners became suspicious of his Medal of Honor—fearing he could scratch somebody with it.[45]

Breasts cropped up as major threats to airline security. Flight attendant Sylvia Paisley-Gee complained of receiving "a pat-down that was more than a pat-down. Her hands lingered on my breasts. I was in uniform. I tried to make light about it and told her, 'Oh, they're real.' She just said, 'keep your arms up.'" *Denver Post* columnist Patty Calhoun complained: "Dare to wear an underwire [bra] through security, and you're likely to get a patdown more intimate than anything you experienced on prom night. . . . It's just major-league groping."[46] The Association of Flight Attendants formally complained to Mineta about sexual harassment by security screeners.[47] Some government officials portrayed screeners as victims of a gruesome duty. Patrick Orlandella, spokesman for the Massachusetts Port Authority, which oversees Boston's Logan International Airport, asserted: "Most screeners don't want to do it, either." Orlandella explained that the screeners are "not trying to touch the breast. They're trying to go around it. Maybe the pinky slips a little." Jessica Neal, spokeswoman for a company that provided security at 35 airports, explained: "We have to resolve the source of an alarm. If the source of an alarm is in the bra area, you have to feel it up." But Ms. Neal added: "You can't grope it full on. You can't put your whole hand on it." The *Los Angeles Times* noted, "Rare is the flier who dares to challenge those with the power to keep her or him off a flight. . . . Others also want to get the touching over quickly, so they can keep an eye on their purses or computers, which typically sit unattended on the metal detector's conveyor belt during the search." At least 35 women contacted Arizona attorney general Janet Napolitano about being improperly touched during pat-down searches in Phoenix and Tucson. The *Los Angeles Times* reported that "Transportation Department officials worry that horror stories of passenger harassment will create a political backlash."[48]

Federal policies which were prone to panic turned airports into crapshoots for travelers who aspired to leave on schedule:

- On February 20, 2002 two concourses of New Orleans International Airport were evacuated after someone discovered a suspicious package in a bathroom. The bomb squad arrived, examined the suspect item, and determined it contained several packages of non-toxic gumbo. The airport concourses were closed for five hours.[49]
- On February 25 Los Angeles International airport concourses were evacuated and flights delayed after an incoming passenger left a tin cookie

can in the Customs Service inspection area. Security personnel removed the can and successfully blew it up.[50]

- On March 5 the discovery of one pair of scissors in a trash can in a "secured" area of the Bradley International Airport in Hartford, Connecticut sparked an emergency evacuation and delayed ten flights. Vigilant airport security managers ordered an American Airlines flight to Puerto Rico to reverse flight and return 400 miles to Hartford so passengers could be re-herded through airport metal detectors.[51]

High technology and laggardly airport clerks did not always perfectly harmonize. On January 30, 2002 the shoes of a passenger chosen for a random check at San Francisco International Airport tested positive for explosives.[52] The screener put the loafers back on the table after the test and shuffled off to find a supervisor. The passenger was not informed his loafers flunked, so he slipped them back on and wandered off to his flight. An hour later, airport officials ordered the evacuation of the terminal. Flights were delayed and disrupted across the nation as a result. Two flights en route to the East Coast were diverted to Chicago, where government canines gave everyone a sniff.[53] (The tests that were used on the shoe are renowned for giving false positives.) Airport spokesman Ron Wilson explained: "Security did not use proper procedures. They are supposed to hold the shoes and the passenger. Obviously there may be a problem with our security screening."

San Francisco airport officials subsequently displayed the highest footwear vigilance. On April 11, part of a terminal was evacuated after security personnel discovered a pair of battery-powered, self-heating shoes in a carry-on bag of a Chinese passenger connecting to a flight to New York.[54] Guo Yongqiiang was taking his homemade feet-warming shoes to a trade show in New York, hoping to persuade an American company to mass produce his cure for cold feet.[55] Even after security personnel concluded the shoes posed no threat, the bomb squad blew them up to insure the shoes did not "cause further confusion," according to a security spokesman.[56] Airport spokesman Ron Wilson boasted of the incident: "The screener did everything correctly this time."[57]

After 9/11, it can now be a federal crime to embarrass airport authorities. Robert Hedrick was flying from North Carolina to Columbus, Ohio, when he stopped in Pittsburgh to change flights. After landing in Pittsburgh, he realized screeners failed to notice that his belt buckle had a knife with a three-inch blade hidden in it. After a few drinks in an airport bar, Hedrick called up his favorite radio talk show host in Columbus to tell him of the screw-up: "I'm just more concerned that it happened and you guys are in my cell phone and I thought I got someone to tell this to and that's great."[58] When his flight landed in Columbus, police ordered all male passengers into a screening room, where Hedrick told him he was the man they were looking for. He was arrested and charged with having a concealed dangerous weapon accessible to him on board an aircraft in flight. Bail was set at half a million dollars, and later lowered to $20,000. Hedrick faced up to ten years in prison. Assistant U.S. attorney Gary Spartis explained: "The statute doesn't really talk about criminal intent. It deals with knowledge of having the weapon."[59] The charge against Hedrick was eventually reduced to a misdemeanor—breaching airport security—and he was sentenced to 108 hours of community service and one year probation.[60]

While Mineta insisted that the feds were doing all they could to protect travelers, the FAA grounded its Red Team—an elite squad that travels the nation to covertly test airport security. The Red Team was created in the wake of the Pan Am 103 disaster in 1988, in response to widespread recognition of the poor quality of airport security. In February 2002, John Dzakovic, a Red Team leader, publicly revealed that the FAA had perennially ignored his reports in earlier years about the gross failures of airport security. Dzakovic's team breached security in 85 percent of their attempts at one large U.S. airport; he observed, "No action was taken to remedy this security problem and we have never been back to this airport, or any other airport, to test security in this manner."[61] Dzakovic complained: "The more severe the security problem we identified, the more the FAA tried to bury the information. . . . There is not one single instance that I am aware of in which action was taken to correct these security loopholes." Dzakovic concluded: "The manner in which the Federal Aviation Administration failed to execute its mission to protect the flying public made it inevitable that terrorists could attack in this particularly heinous manner." After Dzakovic went public with his complaints, the Transportation Department required the Red Team's top inspectors to devote their time replying to letters from congressional offices rather than policing airport safety.[62]

The federal Office of Special Counsel, which exists to probe whistleblower complaints, investigated Dzakovic's charges and concluded in early 2003 that "the Red Team Program was grossly mismanaged and that the result was . . . a substantial danger to public safety."[63] James Loy, the chief of the new Transportation Security Administration, responded to the report by effectively blaming the members of the Red Team itself—though there was no evidence of Red Team malfeasance.[64] Special Counsel Elaine Kaplan's report noted that the Transportation Department's response to Dzakovic's charges "does not appear reasonable because it does not identify the individuals responsible for the management failures identified in the [DOT Inspector General] report, nor does it explain what measures have been taken to hold them accountable."[65] Dzakovic complained: "Not one manager within FAA is being held accountable for supporting the dysfunctional and dangerous way FAA conducted security and for ignoring intelligence warnings leading up to 9/11."[66] The Red Team was abolished after 9/11 to be replaced, Dzakovic groused, "by a Pink Team that now concentrates on paper audits handicapped to novice-screener skill levels, instead of mock terrorist raids."[67]

Former Inspector General Schiavo also noted that airport security tests had long been a farce: "For a time, the inspector general was forced to use official FAA test weapons, which were easily recognized by screeners. It was the same stupid Samsonite briefcase every time. They all recognized it—it might as well have had the FAA seal on it." The IG was only allowed to use a fake bomb that "looked like sticks of dynamite attached to an alarm clock by long, curly wires." Schiavo sneered: "It was like the bomb from Acme Supply on the Road Runner cartoons."[68] The tests were designed "with an eye toward 'fairness' to the airline industry," the Office of Special Counsel reported, noting that "simulated explosive devices would be placed in uncluttered bags, in a way that would be readily visible to x-ray machine operators."[69]

On February 17, 2002 the federal government took over direct control of airport security nationwide. The number of snafus quickly skyrocketed.

- On February 25 dozens of flights were delayed in Louisville and 1,500 passengers rescreened after a National Guardsman noticed a security checkpoint screener sound asleep.[70]
- In Chicago, Buffalo, Boston, Salt Lake City, and Los Angeles, an epidemic of unplugged checkpoint metal detectors threw air travel into chaos. More than 400 flights were delayed from a single unplugged machine in Los Angeles. Even Mineta admitted that the new problem was "embarrassing." One airline executive bought a gizmo to lock in electric plugs from a hardware store for $29.95 and presented the magic solution to a Transportation Security Administration (TSA) official. As *Time* magazine noted, "Rather than buy the devices for all the airports that need them, however, the Transportation Security Administration simply suggested that its employees purchase the device and get reimbursed later."[71]

Almost every day after the federal takeover brought another airline terminal evacuation.[72] Jim Mitchell, a TSA spokesman, declared: "There are bound to be things that happen . . . but they're happening because somebody realized something was wrong and rang the bell."[73]

On March 6, Mineta, citing Gallup Poll results, boasted that Americans were starting again to "have trust and confidence in our national transportation system."[74] Unfortunately, the poll likely failed to survey potential hijackers. From November 2001 through early February 2002 the Transportation Department Inspector General ran almost 800 tests and found that the new, improved airport security failed to detect 70 percent of the knives, 60 percent of the fake explosives, and 30 percent of the fake guns put through the system. Undercover agents were also able to penetrate through secured airport areas, such as tarmacs, half the time. The failure rate of airport security after 9/11 was actually higher than tests in previous years.[75]

Such historic trivia did not deter White House spokesman Ari Fleischer from praising "renewed vigilance" by the feds: "As a result of the legislation enacted by the Congress last year, and its implementation throughout the course of this year, security gets better at the airports every day."[76]

## 24-Karat Frankenstein: The TSA

The Bush administration and Congress responded to the 9/11 hijackers with the usual Washington panacea—creating a new federal agency. The Federal Aviation Administration was widely perceived as inept, if not incorrigible. Instead of razing the failed bureaucracy and remedying the profound flaws in the federal approach to aviation,[77] Congress and Bush solved the problem of airport/airline safety by creating a new federal agency and vesting it with sweeping power and near-zero responsibility.

Within six months of its founding, it was clear that the Transportation Security Administration had "become a monster," as the chairman of the House Aviation subcommittee, John Mica (R-Fla.) observed[78] A Senate Appropriations Committee report declared that the TSA's behavior "has been characterized by arrogance and disregard of the public's views."[79] The House Appropriations Committee noted that TSA was "seemingly unable to make crisp decisions . . . unable to work cooperatively with the nation's airports; and unable to take advantage of the multitude of security-improving and labor-saving technologies available."[80]

To head the new agency, George Bush chose John Magaw, who had served his father as chief of the Secret Service and served Clinton as chief of the Bureau of Alcohol, Tobacco, and Firearms from 1993 to 1999. Magaw brought a hard-nosed law enforcement mentality to the job, which bred a contempt for the rights and convenience of airline passengers.

In Orlando, Florida, the *Los Angeles Times* reported, "a TSA advance team recently showed up unannounced at the airport and set up a hiring center for screeners. When the airport director went to investigate—and introduce himself—he was threatened with arrest for trespassing in a federal area. The agency apologized."[81] The airport was plagued with delays of up to two hours for passengers to clear security checkpoints. Airport managers pleaded with the TSA to permit doubling the number of metal detectors to handle the crowds, but the TSA said the issue must first be studied.[82]

Mineta announced on March 15, 2002 that the TSA's motto would be "no weapons, no waiting."[83] Mineta also frequently reminded people that the feds had set a goal that no one would have to wait more than ten minutes to clear airport security.[84] But disgruntled airline employees groused that TSA stood for "Thousands Standing Around"[85] as lines in airports continued to drain patience and airline profits. Others disparaged the new agency as "the DMV from hell" or an "army of occupation."[86]

TSA blamed passengers for airport delays. TSA spokeswoman Deirdre O'-Sullivan declared that if passengers "would leave items like scissors at home or in checked-in luggage, we would have fewer delays and shutdowns."[87] But there is nothing intrinsic in a pair of scissors to cause rational people to shut down an airport terminal.

The TSA notified Congress that the new federal agents at airport checkpoints would be paid salaries of $70,000 plus overtime. Rep. David Obey (D-Wis.) complained: "Try telling the County Board in Rhinelander [Wisconsin] that you're going to be paying the guard who is just standing there watching twice as much as most areas are going to be paying their chiefs of police and their airport managers."[88] Obey demanded to know: "Does the TSA take this committee to be a bunch of chumps?" After the howling from Capitol Hill, a TSA spokesman announced that the salary information the agency sent Congress was "outdated."[89] (TSA chief Magaw later whined that congressmen "became frustrated and it was very difficult for them to give us the time to come up with accurate numbers."[90])

The TSA will be "larger than the Departments of Energy, Labor, State, HUD, and Education combined," *National Review*'s Kate O'Beirne reported.[91] At a June 20, 2002 congressional hearing, House Appropriations Committee chairman Harold Rogers declared that the TSA "is running out of money like a young child whose money burns a hole in the pocket. We will not hire a standing army of 70,000 people to screen your bags, take off your shoes and check your briefcases three times."[92] Rogers was especially irate about the TSA's plan to hire 3,407 "shoe bin runners." Lawmakers learned that the TSA is providing federal air marshals with double the starting pay of other federal lawmen.

Congress passed a law prohibiting the TSA from hiring more than 45,000 employees. TSA ignored the law and signed up over 28,000 temporary employees—many with five-year contracts and full benefits. (Only in the federal government is a five-year job considered a temp position.) The agency had 66,000 employees as of early 2003.[93] The tens of thousands of additional employees guaranteed that the TSA would spend billions of dollars more than Congress appropriated for the agency.

The TSA quickly became a world-class spendthrift. The Transportation Department Inspector General revealed that "half of the TSA's employees who don't screen passengers make more than $100,000, including criminal investigators and general inspection, investigation and compliance employees who are paid $101,000 to $136,000."[94] TSA paid its lawyers almost 50 percent more ($111,000 on average) than other lawyers in the Transportation Department received.[95] The average salary at TSA headquarters exceeded the average salary paid at the White House or the Supreme Court.[96]

TSA originally estimated that it would cost $107 million to hire new federal airport screeners; the contract cost ballooned to $700 million.[97] Recruiters for TSA seeking airport screeners in the northwestern New Mexico/southwestern Colorado area checked into the luxurious "Wyndham Peaks Resort and Golden Door Spa near Telluride, a ski resort town, with an 18-hole golf course, indoor and outdoor pools, fluffy robes and oversized bathrooms—at $147 a night. They stayed for seven weeks to fill 50 airport-screener jobs. While at the resort, they also paid $29,000 for extra security to the local Mountain Village police department, whose chief said that on some days, only one or two job candidates showed up," the *Wall Street Journal* reported.[98] The resort was more than an hour drive from the nearest airport.

Congress fully funded the Bush administration's initial request for the TSA. In mid-2002, the Bush administration rattled the tin cup for another $4.4 billion. Congress filled the cup most of the way with $3.85 billion. Secretary Mineta indignantly warned: "Less money with no flexibility means fewer TSA employees, less equipment, longer lines, delay in reducing the hassle factor and/or diminished security at our nation's airports."[99] Mineta whined that, because of the reduced funding, "we are confronted with a load TSA cannot lift."[100]

In late June, 2002, news leaked out that TSA airport screeners missed 24 percent of weapons and imitation bombs in the latest government undercover tests. At some major airports screeners failed to detect potentially dangerous objects in at least half the tests.[101] The results were worse than they first appeared since the testers were ordered not to "artfully conceal" the deadly contraband and instead pack their luggage "consistent with how a typical passenger in air transportation might pack a bag."[102] The test seemed designed to see if screeners could catch terrorists with single-digit IQs. But airport security continued to be a sieve. One TSA official complained: "The testing was so simple, it is not really accurate if you want to establish a baseline for terrorists using trickery. It's still the same flawed security—it's just costing a lot more money."[103] Shortly afterward, Transportation Secretary Mineta fired TSA chief Magaw—just before a congressional hearing at which the TSA was expected to receive another four-star lambasting.

## Therapeutic Busts

Among the PR efforts the Bush administration conducted to restore confidence were mass arrests of airport workers. "Operation Tarmac" and similarly named crackdowns spawned press conferences around the nation at which federal attorneys proudly announced roundups of Hispanic immigrants who were portrayed as would-be terrorists. Over a thousand airport employees were arrested and indicted nationwide.

Salt Lake City was the first airport hit by federal sweeps. Sixty-nine people were indicted on December 11, 2001 for false statements on employment applications or bogus Social Security numbers. Though U.S. Attorney Paul Warner declared that "there is no evidence that anyone indicted as part of Operation Safe Travel has attempted any kind of terrorist activity at the airport," he still characterized the crackdown as a "joint anti-terrorism effort."[104] However, Salt Lake City mayor Rocky Anderson denounced the investigation as "grandstanding"[105] and complained: "At the end of the investigation, state and federal officers arrested and imprisoned dozens of workers. These arrests left many families in turmoil, with children waiting at home for their parents to return from work."[106] Authorities were chagrined at the negative publicity over the three-day lockup of a food service worker who was also a breast-feeding mother. While federal officials portrayed the crackdown as a triumph, the *Salt Lake Tribune* later reported that "nearly two-thirds of the original 69 indicted workers either had their cases dismissed or were sentenced to probation, for terms that ranged from 36 months down to a single day."[107] Most of the arrestees were married, under 35, and had young children—not the usual terrorist profile.[108] The *Tribune* noted: "Most had valid Social Security numbers, which were intended only for drivers licenses. They allegedly broke the law when they illegally used those Social Security cards to gain employment."[109] Half a dozen of the people who were busted no longer worked at the airport.

In Charlotte, North Carolina, in March, 2002, 66 people were indicted in Operation Access Denied. Almost all of the current or former airport workers busted were Hispanics charged with abusing Social Security numbers or immigration violations. U.S. Attorney Bob Conrad declared: "In the wake of 9/11, our mandate has changed. Our efforts now include terrorism—rooting it out and preventing it—especially at the airport."[110] Conrad warned: "Terrorists could use the fact that workers are illegal aliens to blackmail them into assisting the effort to sabotage a plane. That's the concern that motivated this investigation. This is a preventative effort."[111] The Charlotte investigation involved 70 federal agents. At a time when the Bush administration was continually portraying the nation at risk of additional terrorist attacks, the feds concentrated their resource on janitors who wrote the wrong number on a job application.[112] The U.S. attorney puffed up his resume by also charging each arrestee with "entering an aircraft or airport area in violation of government security requirements." The Transactional Records Access Clearinghouse (TRAC) at Syracuse University reported, "In previous years, these 66 cases almost certainly would have been classified as simple immigration matters. But in the post 9/11 world, the choice was obvious and each one was officially placed in the 'domestic terrorism' category."[113] TRAC noted that this categorization allowed the mass arrests in Charlotte to be portrayed as "an outstanding example of the government's successful 'war on terrorism.'" The arrestees were given a choice of going to trial—and getting a sentence of up to 20 years if they lost—or pleading guilty to a misdemeanor and getting out of jail after only a few weeks.[114] U.S. Attorney Conrad bragged: "It's probably the first time in the court's history that 50 defendants have been indicted, convicted and deported all in the span of one month."[115] Conrad talked as if deporting a busload of janitors was the same as vanquishing Al Qaeda.

On April 23, 2002 Operation Fly Trap arrested 94 workers employed at Dulles International Airport and Reagan Washington National Airport. U.S. Attorney Paul McNulty characterized the raids on employees as an "anti-terrorism initiative" but admitted that there was "no evidence at this point of any connection of these individuals to any terrorist organizations."[116] Attorney General John Ashcroft appeared at the victory press conference and proclaimed: "Our response has been to weave a web of terrorism prevention that brings together all agencies of justice and every level of law enforcement" and said the sweep was "the result of the unprecedented interagency, multijurisdictional cooperation among law enforcement that defines our effort to prevent terrorist attacks."[117] Ashcroft added: "What this investigation uncovered should be a wake-up call for every airport in America."[118] Ashcroft did not explain why it should take airports seven months to "wake-up" after 9/11. Ashcroft warned that many defendants faced maximum penalties of up to ten years in prison and a $250,000 fine.[119]

A *Chicago Tribune* analysis of Operation Fly Trap noted: "Among those swept up were two nursing mothers, a 54-year-old Bolivian grandmother with rheumatoid arthritis, a National Guardsman, a man who operates a shoe shine business in one of the office buildings for the House of Representatives, and a student who made $6.35 an hour by taking notes for a deaf classmate."[120] Ashcroft's bragging about potential ten-year prison sentences was all smoke: "None of those arrested served sentences beyond the time they served in jail waiting for plea agreements to be approved. Only one case went to trial, resulting in a not guilty verdict on one count and a hung jury on the other."[121] The *Tribune* concluded: "Rather than striking a major blow against terrorism, the arrests ended up turning people's lives inside out, causing tremendous embarrassment, anger and despair."[122]

In Hampton Roads, Virginia, Operation Plane View erupted on June 6, 2002 with feds ordering many of the targets to "report to a secure basement area for a fictitious training program."[123] The targets soon learned that only federal officials have the right to make false statements in the vicinity of airports. Federal agents also zipped through the Hampton Roads area "rousting former workers from their beds at dawn," the *Virginian Pilot* reported.[124] The arrestees were cuffed and marched before the television cameras. At the celebratory press conference, U.S. Attorney Paul McNulty, after conceding that none of the suspects were linked to terrorism, proclaimed: "I think there should be considerable concern that individuals who could be a threat to safety have been employed at the airport."[125] McNulty stressed: "All of these individuals present a risk. We don't have information as to exactly what risks have occurred. We just know that the potential for harm is there."[126]

A total of 21 people were arrested or indicted. The U.S. Attorney's Office proposed to expedite and simplify the administration of justice by having group trials for the defendants, finding them innocent or guilty in groups of up to six people.[127] Defense lawyers squealed to high heaven over the proposal.

Most Operation Plane View cases quickly collapsed as a result of false charges, government paperwork snafus, and other problems. Two weeks after the initial raids, a *Virginian Pilot* editorial observed: "In contrast with the government's loud trumpeting of its 'very successful' roundup, it is remarkably silent on its embarrassing and possibly illegal goof-up. In the government's hasty retreat, suddenly nothing is in plain view."[128] The paper denounced the operation as a "dangerous flop"[129] and declared: "The only thing the government succeeded with in these pre-dawn raids on innocent citizens was to further shatter the public's confidence in its ability to catch the right bad guys."[130] By September 2002 charges had been dismissed against 15 of the 21 people arrested for lying about criminal records. The harshest penalty levied on any of the remaining defendants who had gone to trial was a $100 fine.[131]

Operation Tarmac crackdowns at five southern California airports scored 80 arrests and over 100 indictments. Angelica Barrera, a janitor at John Wayne Airport in Orange County, was nine months pregnant when she was busted. The *Orange County Register* reported that two days after her arrest, "while in detention at the Santa Ana County Jail, the Mexican immigrant said she went into labor and was transported to Western Medical Center. Barrera delivered her daughter, saw her for a few minutes and then was whisked back to jail where she spent a week apart from her newborn."[132] Barrera later commented: "I was so scared. I didn't know if I would ever see my daughter again. I was going crazy."[133]

Houston proudly conducted the biggest roundup in the country, bagging 143 people on September 9, 2002 for having bogus Social Security numbers, making false statements on job applications, having fake identification, or other offenses. U.S. Attorney Michael Shelby proclaimed: "Our goal is to make the airports secure for every man, woman and child in the southern district of Texas so when they look up into the sky and see that airplane overhead, they can have some assurance that it is not being used as a manned missile."[134] But many of the people arrested had quit their jobs months or weeks before and were no longer in a position to aid Muslim fanatics. The crackdown was based on a list that the INS received of airport employees in February; it took the feds more than six months to get around to dropping the hammer.[135]

On September 17, 2002, 110 workers at Denver International Airport (DIA) were indicted as part of Operation Safe Sky. The vast majority were accused of using false Social Security numbers to get their airport security badges. U.S. Attorney John Suthers announced: "If you were a terrorist, you could do a lot of damage." Suthers conceded that none of the arrestees were terrorist suspects but stressed: "We have every reason to believe a person who has terrorist motives could come into secure areas of the airport through the means we've described."[136] The cases were classified as "internal security—terrorism."[137] Six months later, the *Rocky Mountain News* reported that two-thirds of the people indicted had never been arrested. Very few of the indictees who were not nabbed during the heavily publicized federal raid at DIA were ever caught. Many of the cases were dismissed and none of the arrestees were sentenced to additional jail time (aside from time already served). U.S. Attorney Suthers explained away federal lethargy: "We have no reason to believe that these people were, in fact, attempting to infiltrate."[138]

The airport mass arrests are, according to Attorney General Ashcroft, one of the greatest achievements in the war on terrorism. In an October 1, 2002 speech to a conference of U.S. Attorneys, Ashcroft bragged: "We have conducted the largest investigation in history; disrupting and punishing possible terrorist related activity throughout the United States. It's working. Let me note just a few instances. . . ."[139] After invoking the arrests of Zacarias Moussaoui and John Walker Lindh, Ashcroft mentioned "Charlotte: 67 undocumented aliens indicted for identification document fraud. Dulles and Reagan National Airports: 94 workers arrested and charged with falsifying Social Security applications and immigration violations. At close to a dozen other airports: cracking down on fraudulent document scams that allow access to secure areas."

Secretary Mineta hailed Operation Tarmac's busts: "We will not stop until we are satisfied we have a work force that the traveling public can trust."[140] But what of the far more dangerous whoppers told by high-ranking government officials—such as their lies to the public that flying was safe before 9/11? American travelers are at far greater risk from gutless cabinet secretaries than from undocumented fast food workers. Operation Tarmac illustrated how "retail" lying is dangerous and can result in a prison sentence—while "wholesale" lying is a stepping stone to fame and greater power.

None of the people arrested in any of the airport crackdowns had any links to terrorist organizations or were suspected of plotting violence against planes or passengers. The crackdowns did little more than turn hapless janitors into political trophies for aspiring federal prosecutors. No matter how long it took the feds to make arrests—even more than a full year after 9/11—people were still supposed to feel comforted. There was no reason to believe that certified members of terrorist groups would kindly delay absconding until their arrests were convenient for ambitious prosecutors. The Justice Department may have concluded that the American people are so vacuous that, regardless of the circumstances, mass arrests would be good for public morale and reassure people that the government is winning the war on terrorism.

## The Feds' Airport Bombs

The Aviation and Transportation Security Act enacted in late 2001 required that all baggage be run through bomb-detection machinery or checked with hand-held bomb detectors by December 31, 2002. While some congressmen portrayed the machines as superb defenses against terrorist threats, Rep. John Mica, chairman of the House Aviation Subcommittee, aptly characterized the bomb-detection machines as "crap." Former FAA special agent Steven Elson said that the machines are so unreliable that they "can't tell the difference between a bomb and a bowel movement."[141] Mineta conceded that the large bomb detectors have a false positive rate of over 30 percent.[142] This does not mean that one out of three bags the machines identify as having a bomb do not have a bomb. Instead, the machines identify a third of all baggage as containing bombs.[143] After a machine signals an alert, the bag has to be thoroughly and slowly searched by hand. James O'Bryon, the Pentagon official who oversaw the tests on the FAA bomb detectors, testified to Congress: "I can state unequivocally . . . that the current levels that have been established for . . . permissible false alarm rates . . . have been driven by the inability of the current equipment to perform any better. If the thresholds were tightened by only a couple of percentage points, there would currently be few, if any [explosives detection] equipment certified at all."[144]

The 17,000-pound devices—as big as a minivan—are far heavier than the floors of many airports can support. Their deployment requires a massive reconfiguration of airport terminals, as well as new conveyor belts to run through airports to deliver luggage to them. A study by the Reason Foundation estimated that the total cost of buying and installing the machines could exceed $12 billion.[145] Though it costs roughly $1 million to install each new machine, TSA will reimburse only $175,000 of that cost—despite new federal ticket fees to finance airport security.[146] Dallas–Fort Worth International Airport expects to spend almost $200 million on installing the machines.[147] The process of installing the new systems in airports around the country could cause major disruptions and flight delays. The Senate Appropriations Committee complained that the TSA was making a mess of airport terminals with its bomb-detection-machine mandate and noted that the TSA is "prepared to allow this less-than-satisfactory situation to persist for a number of years."[148]

The 2001 laws, mandates, and deadlines were especially wasteful because industry experts predict that, within the next year or 18 months, new bomb detecting machines will be available that are far smaller, cheaper, and more reliable. Christopher Yates, airport security editor for *Jane's Transport* magazine, observed: "The U.S. is spending an absolute fortune on equipment that is only marginally effective. The net result will be only marginally improved security, if there's any improvement at all. What is happening is more of a public-relations exercise than anything else."[149]

Taxpayers could receive another opportunity to enrich the two companies that produced the bomb detection machines with stratospheric error rates. In early 2003 the companies launched an effort to persuade the federal government to spend $200,000 per machine to buy new technology to purportedly fix some of the worst flaws. This could add $200 million to the cost of making air travel appear safe.[150]

TSA's bogus bomb detectors are revolutionizing how Americans travel. Shortly before Christmas 2002 the TSA warned passengers that bars of chocolate, books, fruitcakes, and wheels of cheese could be mistaken for bombs.[151] The TSA website advises: "Avoid packing food and drink items in checked baggage. Avoid over-packing your bag. This will make it easier for the screener to reseal your bag if it is opened for inspection. If possible, spread your contents over several bags. Check with your airline or travel agent for maximum weight limitations and any fees that may apply. Spread out books and documents within your baggage; do not stack them on top of each other."

Thanks to the unreliable machines, far more baggage will be opened and inspected after triggering false alarms. TSA strongly recommends that no one lock their baggage any more. The TSA website helpfully notes that "you help prevent the need to break your locks by keeping your bag unlocked. . . . You may keep your bag locked if you choose, but TSA is not liable for damage caused to locked bags that must be opened for security purposes." For people who must travel with thousands of dollars worth of electronic, photographic, or other high tech equipment, the "no locks" mandate is a nightmare. Collecting compensation from the TSA for items stolen after the TSA broke baggage locks could be as easy as finding an honest politician. An article in the *Chicago Daily Law Bulletin*, entitled "Sovereign Immunity, Pilfered Luggage," recommended that frequent flyers "itemize and insure expensive items carried in their luggage under their homeowner policies, take a photo of the items and leave the pictures in their safe deposit box. Keep the sales slips to establish costs and list the serial numbers of electronic equipment such as computers, cell phones and the like."[152] Such precautions do wonders to boost the transaction costs of flying.

Because TSA employees spend their days pawing through passengers' private goods, TSA suggested in a March 4, 2003, press release that "travelers put personal items like a toothbrush in a clear plastic bag so screeners do not have to handle them."[153] Since the government gave fair warning, Americans who unpack their bags after a flight and discover that their toothbrush is wet will have no one to blame except themselves.

TSA provided abysmal training to many of the new bomb catchers. The *San Francisco Chronicle* reported on August 25, 2002 that "dozens of members of an elite team of federal airport screeners received as little as 15 minutes' training before starting to inspect baggage for bombs."[154] The screeners were members of the TSA's Mobile Screening Force, which moves around the country to lead the way in federalizing airport security. One disgruntled new "expert" screener complained: "They handed us a swab and told us to wipe the bags this way and put us to work. The whole thing took 10, 15 minutes tops."[155] The law Congress enacted in late 2001 required "security screeners" to receive at least 100 hours of training. The *Chronicle* noted that the new screeners said their "requests for proper training have been ignored."[156]

In late January 2003 *Newsday* reporter Thomas Frank reported pervasive cheating on TSA tests by screeners hired at LaGuardia Airport and elsewhere across the nation. Class instructors read the tests to students beforehand, made sure students understood the correct answers, and then gave the tests. One screener commented: "They knew that they would need us to fill these positions, so we were not allowed to fail."[157] One St. Louis screener said she received "only about 40 minutes of hands-on training on two explosives-detection machines, instead of the day-and-a-half prescribed by the TSA. One machine, which produces computer images of each bag's interior, was not working, so instructors 'just said if it was running, this is what would happen.'"[158] Several people hired to teach airport screeners also reported having been given test answers before taking the tests to become certified instructors.[159] *Newsday* noted that one instructor "spent a week certifying baggage screeners in Orlando, Fla., who were learning how to operate a bomb-detection machine that he himself was not certified to use."[160]

Despite how badly the bomb detectors and screeners functioned, they remained a valuable symbol of how much Bush and Congress care about the safety of the American people. As long as Bush and congressmen could pirouette as saviors, the billions of dollars' cost was not wasteful spending—regardless of how many holes the new comfort blanket contained.

## Gun Nuts at 30,000 Feet?

After the pervasive failure of airport security on 9/11 the Air Line Pilots Association sought federal permission for pilots to carry handguns to defeat hijackers. Capt. Steve Luckey, chairman of the association's flight security committee, explained: "The only reason we want lethal force in the cockpit is to provide an opportunity to get the aircraft on the ground. We don't have 911. We can't pull over."[161] The Bush administration rejected the request, preferring instead to rely on jet fighters to shoot down hijacked civilian planes. Secretary Mineta declared on March 4, 2002, "I don't feel we should have lethal weapons in the cockpit"—

as if airplanes themselves were not among the most deadly lethal weapons.[162] Congress eventually trumped the administration, passing a law in September 2002 to create a program to train pilots to use firearms to defend their planes. (The TSA effectively buried the program with red tape, ensuring that only 48 would be permitted to carry guns in early 2003.)[163]

TSA chief Magaw was the administration's point person in the fight against permitting pilots to be armed. Magaw announced: "The use of firearms aboard a U.S. aircraft must be limited to those thoroughly trained members of law enforcement."[164] The federal air marshal program was touted as a silver bullet against hijacking threats. A White House statement on aviation safety in the wake of 9/11 declared: "The requirements and qualifications of Federal Air Marshals are among the most stringent of any U.S. federal law enforcement agency."[165]

The TSA was determined to quickly expand the number of marshals from a few hundred to more than six thousand. However, most of the applicants failed the marksmanship test. The TSA solved that problem by dropping the marksmanship test for new applicants—even though the ability to shoot accurately in a plane cabin is widely considered a crucial part of a marshal's job.[166] Some would-be marshals were hired even after they repeatedly shot flight attendants in mock hijack-response training exercises.[167] One marshal groused that the training for new marshals was "like security-guard training for the mall." *USA Today*'s Blake Morrison noted a report that "one marshal was suspended after he left his gun in a lavatory aboard a United Airlines flight from Washington to Las Vegas in December. A passenger discovered the weapon." An air marshal left his pistol on a Northwest flight from Detroit to Indianapolis; a cleaning crew discovered the weapon.[168] Morrison noted: "At least 250 federal air marshals have left the top-secret program, and documents obtained by *USA Today* suggest officials are struggling to handle what two managers call a flood of resignations."[169] One bitter marshal declared: "We were promised the Garden of Eden. We were given hell." An internal August 29, 2002 TSA memo noted that 1,250 air marshals "reported sick during a recent 18-day period" and warned that "sick leave abuse has become a serious issue" for air marshals.[170]

TSA director James Loy (who was hired after Magaw was fired) insisted that the "traveling public should rest assured that the Federal Air Marshal Service is providing the largest, highest caliber, best trained and most professional protective force in American aviation history."[171] The Transportation Department responded to the *USA Today* expose by sending Secretary Mineta to an air marshal training facility where he witnessed a training exercise in which marshals shot a would-be hijacker. Mineta commented: "I not only saw a remarkable demonstration of skill, professionalism and marksmanship, but a degree of professionalism we are instilling throughout our aviation security system."[172]

Eight days later, on August 31, 2002, Delta Flight 442 with 183 people on board was proceeding from Atlanta to Philadelphia on a Saturday afternoon when a passenger got up and began rummaging in the overhead bin. The *Philadelphia Inquirer* reported that the trouble began when the man described as "fortyish and disheveled made inappropriate comments to a female passenger a few rows behind him."[173] Two plainclothes air marshals jumped up and tackled the guy, shoving him first to the back of the plane and then dragging him to the first class area.

Then the trip got interesting. One of the marshals returned to the front of the coach section, drew his Glock semiautomatic pistol, and started screaming and pointing his gun at passengers. Philadelphia judge James Lineberger, a passenger on the flight, commented, "I assumed at that moment that there was going to be some sort of gun battle. . . . There were individuals looking to see what they were pointing at and [the air marshals] were yelling, 'Get down, get out—get your head out of the aisle.'"[174] In a formal complaint to the TSA, Lineberger declared that "there was no apparent reason for holding all the passengers of the plane at gunpoint, and no explanation was given. . . . It appeared a gun battle was imminent, causing great distress."[175]

Lineberger was sitting diagonally across from the initial target of the marshals; he did not notice any problem on the flight until the marshals went ballistic.[176] Susan Johnson, a social worker from Mobile, Alabama, was also unaware of any disturbance until the air marshals seized the man. She said: "It never made sense. This guy was not any physical threat that we could see. Maybe he said some things to them that made them concerned. He just appeared to us unstable, emotionally."[177] Becky Johnson, a reporter who wrote a column about the episode for her Waynesville, North Carolina, newspaper, observed: "They never, ever said who they were, that they were air marshals or whoever."[178]

After the flight landed, the marshals nailed another terrorist suspect— Robert "Bob" Rajcoomar. He was handcuffed and taken into custody because, as TSA spokesman David Steigman later explained, Rajcoomar, "to the best of our knowledge, had been observing too closely."[179] Rajcoomar had been sitting in first class quietly reading and drinking a beer until the marshals dumped the allegedly unruly passenger from coach class into the adjacent seat. Rajcoomar recalled: "One [marshal] sat on the guy. . . . he was groaning, and the more he groaned, the more they twisted the handcuffs."[180] Rajcoomar asked the stewardess for permission to move to another seat in first class; she told him to take one of the seats the marshals vacated.

When the plane landed, Rajcoomar recalled, "One of these marshals came down to me and said, 'Head down, hands over your head!' They pushed my head down, told me to bend down." Rajcoomar said one of the marshals told him "We didn't like the way you looked" and "We didn't like the way you looked at us."[181] Some air marshals apparently think of themselves as minor league deities whom no mortal should be permitted to directly observe. He was locked up in a filthy cell for three hours before being released without charges. His wife was left to roam the Philadelphia airport, not knowing what had happened to her husband.

Rajcoomar was born in India and became a U.S. citizen in 1985. He was a retired U.S. Army major and a practicing physician in Florida. He filed notice that he could sue the TSA for violating his civil rights via "blatant racial profiling."[182] Rajcoomar complained that the marshals "were behaving like terrorists themselves."[183] After the plane landed, the first person the marshals had handcuffed was questioned but a U.S. attorney decided not to file charges.

TSA spokesman David Steigman told the *Palm Beach Post:* "If the air marshals say, 'Sit down, keep eyes straight forward,' well, don't even think about moving around."[184] (The TSA has not yet formally proposed that Congress legislate a death penalty for getting out of one's seat in violation of a TSA command.) TSA spokeswoman Heather Rosenker justified the response to the Associated Press because marshals are trained to "do what they believe is the right thing to do to get control of the airplane."[185] TSA spokesman Steigman told the *Philadelphia Inquirer:* "There was a passenger who was being obstreperous, who was subdued by sky marshals and has since been released."[186] "Obstreperous" could simply mean the guy made some noise. Does this mean that air marshals feel entitled to threaten people with imminent death any time someone raises his voice during a flight? TSA spokesman Robert Johnson, speaking to the Associated Press a few days later, blamed the passengers for being held at gunpoint: "If people would have stayed in their seats and heeded those warnings, that would not have happened. It's our opinion that it was done by the book."[187] Johnson explained: "It's a highly charged situation. It's about keeping the plane secure."[188] But it wasn't a highly charged situation until the marshals panicked.[189]

The air marshal who brandished his weapon had twice applied to a be a cop in Philadelphia but failed the police department's psychological tests; the marshal was also rejected in his attempt to get a job as a prison guard.[190] The marshal had received only two weeks of training at the time he threatened scores of coach passengers. TSA spokesman Steigman, responding to the *Philadelphia Inquirer* scoop about the air marshal's psych test strikeouts, declared, "Federal air marshals are highly trained law enforcement professionals, each of whom can be called upon to make, at any moment, a split-second decision while traveling hundreds of miles per hour 30,000 feet above the ground with no backup."[191] Steigman's comment implied that the marshals were miraculously piloting the plane and maintaining altitude at the same time they wave their guns in the air.

What escalates this episode beyond a mere bizarre anecdote is the fact that the TSA hailed its marshals as models. Several days after the incident, Thomas Quinn, the national director of the air marshal program, asserted: "The federal air marshals did a very good job. They did exactly as they're trained to do."[192] This makes stark that all the onus will be placed on airline passengers when TSA employees lose control of themselves and threaten to kill people. Problems are caused only by people who disobey the commands of federal agents.

## Jumpy, Jumpy, Jumpy

On May 3, 2002 the main concourse of Cleveland's Hopkins International Airport was evacuated after a screener failed to notice a positive alert from an explosive-detection check on a young girl's bag. Checkpoint screeners did confiscate a pair of scissors from the child, but allowed the girl and her mother to proceed on their way. Cleveland airport spokeswoman Shelley Shockley explained: "A second screener came to the area and said, 'Hey, you have a positive.'"[193] It took more than an hour from the time the girl passed through the checkpoint until the evacuation order was given. More than 50 flights were delayed or canceled. The young hooligan was never apprehended.

On May 29, screeners at San Francisco International Airport scored another PR home run when they seized a tiny pair of wire cutters from Army Lt. Greg Miller. Miller, a Purple Heart recipient and Special Forces veteran, had been shot in the jaw in Afghanistan. Army doctors had wired his jaw shut and ordered Miller to keep the cutters with him at all times so that in case he began choking, someone could "snip his jaw open."[194] Airport screeners decreed that the cutters could endanger flight safety. Miller later observed: "The blade is less than one inch long. Actually, less than my thumbnail long."[195] Miller was later told by flight attendants that "there was nothing on board to open his jaw if he became sick."[196] After Miller contacted national media, San Francisco airport spokesman Mike McCarron shrugged off the incident: "I think it's just a matter of miscommunication."[197]

Though Washington Reagan National Airport had not been used by the hijackers, the FAA decreed special rules for all flights using that airport. The FAA effectively created a 100-mile "urination-free zone" in the skies above the nation's capital: Passengers were not allowed to get out of their seats for the first half-hour out of, or the last half hour of a flight into Washington. On June 13, 2002, Rep. Sanford Bishop (D-Ga.) took things in hand after his Delta flight to Atlanta from Reagan Washington National Airport was delayed an hour on the ground before takeoff. Once the pilot finally allowed passengers to get out of their seats, a long line formed outside the toilet. Bishop got a paper cup from the stewardess, stepped into a corner, and whizzed to his heart's content. The *Washington Post* noted that "the flight attendant was distressed and related the incident to other attendants, who in turn alerted the cockpit, which then called ahead to Atlanta police. . . . Bishop was briefly detained and questioned at the airport after the 90-minute flight. . . . Atlanta police concluded no laws covered urinating publicly on an airline."[198] The *Atlanta Journal and Constitution* reported that one of the flight attendants saw what Bishop did and was "distracted from her duties," which "constituted a breach of security she was required to report."[199] Bishop surrendered to nature's call after the man in line in front of him was taking forever in the toilet. The *Journal and Constitution* noted, "Delta security officials told Bishop the man in the lavatory ahead of the congressman was in fact a sky marshal."[200]

On July 1, screeners at San Jose International Airport tested a bag for explosives and, after 20 or 30 seconds, got a positive reaction. However, by that time, the passenger had retrieved his bag and headed off to his flight. The *San Jose Mercury News* noted, "Security officials searched desperately for an hour but, without knowing what the person looked like, they were forced . . . to shut down one of the airport's terminals."[201] Thirteen flights were delayed and thousands of passengers rescreened. The *Mercury News* noted: "San Jose airport spokesman Fernando Pena said the airport now has cameras trained on each security checkpoint, but, for security reasons, he would not say whether they are all fully operational yet."[202]

On July 15 a terminal at Los Angeles International Airport was evacuated for an hour after security agents became alarmed about an object in a bag sent through the x-ray machine. The bomb squad was summoned and after a brief investigation, concluded the culprit was tubs of jam.[203] Los Angeles Police Department officer Jason Lee explained: "It's routine that we check these things out. When we do that, we evacuate the immediate areas all the time."[204]

Six days later, a terminal at the same airport was evacuated for 40 minutes because checkpoint screeners spotted a belt buckle with an image of an explosive device. The screeners called in the bomb squad, who concluded that the belt buckle would not hurt anyone. Six flights were delayed.[205]

On July 16 two F-16 fighter jets were scrambled to target, trail, and escort a flight from Chicago to New York after a passenger became alarmed at the behavior of a 20-year-old Indian movie star and her traveling troupe.[206] Alan Hicks, a spokesman for the Port Authority of New York, explained: "At least one passenger perceived the seven to be engaged in suspicious actions. According to passengers they were constantly passing notes and switching seats. A passenger reported this to a flight attendant, who notified the pilot, who notified ground control."[207] The actress and her associates were detained and questioned for four hours after the plane landed. The incident caused a major uproar in India. But from another perspective, the U.S. security system worked well, since the fighter jets did not shoot down the passenger jet.

On October 4, 2002 several concourses at Lambert St. Louis International Airport were evacuated for up to 90 minutes after a federal security screener spotted what appeared to a "cutting tool" in a carry-on bag that passed through his checkpoint. After detecting the suspicious object, the screener followed proper procedure: He fetched his supervisor to take a look at the frozen image on the video screen at the checkpoint. A few minutes later, the supervisor concluded that the bag was indeed suspicious and needed to be manually searched. However, the passenger had long since retrieved it and headed off to his or her flight. Hundreds of passengers were evacuated and up to 60 flights were delayed; despite many re-searches, the suspicious item was never found. The federal security director at the airport, Bill Switzer, declared that the federal screeners "did everything according to the book, but we probably should have done it maybe a little bit more efficient."[208]

On January 15, 2003 the Tampa airport was evacuated after airport screeners discovered an abandoned briefcase near a Southwest Airlines ticket counter that appeared to be packed with bombs.[209] The ticketing level of the terminal was cleared, the roads outside were closed, and the bomb squad arrived. An hour later, the all-clear was given after it was determined that the briefcase was a TSA dummy designed to test airport security. TSA security director Dario Compain explained: "We use these bags repeatedly, so the fact that the bag was in that area was not surprising. That it was unattended, that there was no one with it who knew its true nature and could stop the escalation of our action before it reached the evacuation stage, is what's troubling."[210]

## The New Gestapo?

Over a thousand people have been arrested at airport checkpoints since the February 2002 federal takeover.[211] The TSA assumed that the more arbitrary power airport screeners received, the safer air travel would become. A new regulation—CFR 49.1504.109, promulgated on February 17, 2002—made it a federal crime to interfere with airport screening personnel, declaring:

> No person may interfere with, assault, threaten, or intimidate screening personnel in the performance of their screening duties. . . . The rule prohibits interference that might distract or inhibit a screener from effectively performing his or her duties. . . . Previous instances of such distractions have included verbal abuse of screeners by passengers and certain air carrier employees. . . . A screener encountering such a situation must turn away from his or her normal duties to deal with the disruptive individual, which may affect the screening of other individuals. . . . Checkpoint disruptions potentially can be dangerous in these situations.

Thanks to the new regulation, a single word is sufficient to get arrested at airports. Betsylew Miale-Gix, a 43-year-old personal injury lawyer and former world boomerang record holder,[212] was stopped at a security checkpoint at Hartford's Bradley International Airport on June 30, 2002, and informed that she could not carry her boomerangs into the plane with her.[213] The boomerangs weighed less than three ounces each and were fragile—the type of item that is routinely crushed if sent as checked luggage. One of her fellow boomerang enthusiasts commented that throwing a competitive boomerang at someone is "like throwing a first-class letter."[214] Miale-Gix had flown many times after 9/11 and had never gotten any guff about carrying on her boomerangs. The state trooper who banned the boomerangs from the flight refused to listen to Miale-Gix's explanation and she swore at him as she was departing the screening area. Miale-Gix was quickly arrested, handcuffed, charged with breach of the peace and compelled to pay $500 bail. TSA spokeswoman Deirdre O'Sullivan commented that, although boomerangs are not on the official list of prohibited carry-on items, "the screeners have the discretion to decide whether or not that item could be used as a weapon."[215]

Judith Kleinfeld, a University of Alaska psychology professor, was almost banned from a flight from Seattle to Fairbanks after she insulted a checkpoint screener. The screener summoned a security supervisor who, according to Kleinfeld, "told me he could bar me from flying for life. He said he had just barred from flying home a man who had called him a 'jerk.'"[216] He also told Kleinfeld that "calling a screener an idiot is unacceptable and is a violation of federal law."[217] Kleinfeld was told by a Seattle security agent that "raising your voice to a screener" is "intimidation"—and thus a federal crime.[218]

Travelers who assert their legal rights can find themselves bounced. Della Maricich was banned from flying from Portland to Seattle on May 1, 2002, after she asked airport screeners to keep her purse where she could see it while they searched it. (The new search procedures have sparked a surge in accusations of thefts by airport screeners.) The screener refused and Maricich demanded to speak to his supervisor. A National Guardsman arrived on the scene a few minutes later and, according to Maricich, "He told me that because I had disrupted the line by calling for a supervisor, I would not be allowed to fly out of PDX that day. He told me that I was a troublemaker and I was the only one who had ever complained."[219]

"What do you expect to find in there, a rifle?" Fred Hubbell, an 80-year-old World War II combat veteran, asked a screener at Hartford's Bradley International Airport who was poking into his wallet. Hubbell was exasperated after he and his wife had already endured two full searches at the airport on the morning of August 2, 2002. Hubbell was arrested for "causing a public disturbance" and fined $78. Dana Cosgrove, the TSA airport security chief, later justified the arrest because "all that the people around him in the waiting room heard was the word 'rifle.'"[220] But no one alleged Hubbell had shouted out the comment. State Police Sgt. Paul Vance explained that Hubbell was not hit with a more costly charge because "it wasn't a situation where a person became obnoxious or irate."[221] But there was no explanation of what right a screener had to rummage in an old man's wallet.

Even casual comments made in an airport can spark an arrest. *USA Today* reported the following from the TSA's "daily incident report" for busts on February 22, 2002:

4:27 p.m.: Birmingham International Airport, Birmingham, Ala.: A security official reports that, earlier that afternoon, a screener "overheard two (American Airlines) passengers speaking about security and one passenger stated that security was so lousy that he would be able to get through with a bomb in his pants." The screener notified police, who arrested the passengers "under state charges for disorderly conduct." The FBI interviewed the passengers, who might be subpoenaed to return to Birmingham "to face federal charges for utterances of a threat." Even so, they boarded their American flight to Dallas.[222]

Some airports are very aggressive in arresting passengers for dangerous contraband. Chuck Strouse, writing in *Miami New Times,* reported the case of Gregory Sulava, a Russian-born Brooklyn limousine-company owner, who was arrested after a search disclosed "a tiny lighter with a one-inch folding knife that he had bought on the street in Brazil for fifty cents. He had passed through security multiple times with it and had stowed it during the flight from Rio to Miami. 'This thing couldn't clip your fingernails,' he says. 'You can bend it with a thumbnail.' Still Sulava was held for five hours in the Miami-Dade County Jail before he raised bail. Then he spent $2500 on legal bills before settling with authorities for ten hours of community service."[223] Swedish executive Peter Tsounis was arrested and held in a lockup pen with hardcore felons for ten hours after a random search at a departure gate at Miami International Airport found a Swiss Army knife with a 1.5-inch blade in his carry-on bag.[224]

The TSA also flaunts its power to bar people from flights—often based on little or no evidence. A group of 20 high school students and Catholic priests and nuns—members of Peace Action Milwaukee—were detained at Milwaukee airport on April 19, 2002, after some of their names turned up on a "No Fly Watch List" issued by the federal government.[225] The group was heading to Washington, D.C. to protest U.S. policies in Latin America and elsewhere. One member of the group said she was told by a sheriff's deputy: "You're probably being stopped because you are a peace group and you're protesting against your country."[226] A spokeswoman for Midwest Express stated: "The TSA made the decision that since this was a group, we should re-screen all of them." Sister Virginia Lawinger complained to *Progressive* magazine: "What caused the computer to flag those names? I did feel it was profiling a particular group without a basis—a peace group. The abuse of power was so obvious."[227] Many of the travelers missed their flights and had to fly the following day. Yet Sergeant Chuck Coughlin of the Milwaukee sheriff's department insisted: "Although it was time-consuming, and although they were flight-delayed, the system actually worked."[228]

The "no-fly" lists the TSA now provides to airlines are often poor sources of information. The *Wall Street Journal* noted: "Many entries on the list lack details that could make it easy to know if a traveler is really the person named. And the TSA gives airlines little guidance on just when a passenger's name is close enough to one on the list to warrant flagging the person for a law enforcement check."[229] At San Francisco International Airport, 339 travelers' names set off alarms in the official database as they sought to travel between September 2001 and early 2003. Many travelers are erroneously stopped time and again, and taken aside for intensive questioning, regardless of how many times they have previously proved that they are not a threat to national security. David Sobel, general counsel of the Electronic Privacy Information Center (EPIC), observed: "Nobody wants to accept responsibility for the maintenance of the [no-fly] list and nobody wants to claim the authority to remove a name."[230]

The TSA, at Congress's behest, is creating the Computer Assisted Passenger Prescreening System in order to assign a "threat level" to every person who flies within the United States. This is the second version of the system—which is why it is known as CAPPS II. The ACLU warns that CAPPS II "would secretly rate every American as a potential terrorist," assigning a color code—green, yellow, or red—indicating a person's risk level.[231] TSA has provided almost no information on how the system would operate, though the government has indicated that it could sweep up a vast amount of personal information on each traveler—including credit history, "financial and transaction records" (i.e., data on what a person may have purchased in previous months or years), Internet usage, legal record (including any speeding or parking tickets), and so on. EPIC notes that "CAPPS II shares many of the same elements of the Defense Department's Total Information Awareness program."[232]

In January 2003 the TSA revealed a new regulation empowering the agency to suspend pilot licenses based on unproven suspicions that the pilot might pose a security risk. Pilots who lose their livelihoods as a result of TSA edicts may not even be permitted to see the evidence against them. The Air Line Pilots Association complained that "this rule is rooted more in '1984' than in Sept. 11, 2001."[233] The airline industry was angered because the TSA permitted no advance comments from the public before announcing its new trump card. The new regulation fails to define "security risk" and the TSA refused to provide any insight into how the term would be interpreted.[234] Phil Boyer, president of the Aircraft Owners and Pilots Association, protested: "TSA is the cop, prosecutor, judge, jury and appeals court. . . . Clearly, this is a violation of basic constitutional rights."[235] TSA spokesman Brian Turmail dismissed the concerns: "The bottom line is: If you're not a terrorist, you don't need to worry about this."[236]

## The TSA's Last Confessed Foul-up?

Dallas-Fort Worth International Airport is home to 1,800 of TSA's best screeners. At 1:50 P.M. on January 9, 2003 a screener swabbed the outside of a passenger's laptop bag to check for explosives. The screener returned the bag to the passenger, who proceeded to his plane. Three minutes later, the screener noticed that the explosive trace-detection-machine indicated a positive alert for Semtex, a plastic explosive, from the laptop.[237] The screeners then spent three more minutes checking the machine to confirm the accuracy of the positive alert before they informed a TSA supervisor of the problem. The supervisor and screeners then left the checkpoint to walk around and see if they could find the man suspected of having plastic explosives in his laptop. (The explosive detection test is notorious for false positives.)

The TSA screeners and supervisors searched four airport departure gates and after they could not find the man, returned to the checkpoint to retest the machine.[238] More than half an hour after the positive alert for plastic explosives occurred, the TSA notified an airport policeman standing 15 feet from their checkpoint of the problem. Orders were quickly given to empty the terminal. It was almost an hour after the suspected laptop owner passed through the checkpoint before his description was circulated through the airport.

Three terminals at the nation's third-largest airport were closed for almost two hours. Thousands of people were evacuated from the airport and at least 200 flights delayed. Hundreds of passengers already on planes waiting for take-off were obliged to deplane. Forty other airports were affected.

Because the Dallas-Forth Worth airport was not blown up that afternoon, the TSA declared victory. TSA spokesman Ed Martelle declared of the suspected laptop owner: "We caught him, but we lost him. But what he couldn't do was harm anyone. The system worked."[239] The TSA refused to identify either the manufacturer of the machine that gave the alert or the name of the TSA screener; TSA spokesman Brian Doyle declared, "There are privacy issues involved here."[240] After TSA screeners had pried into tens of millions of American's bags, the agency suddenly developed respect for privacy—at least for itself and its corporate suppliers.

Though the TSA promised to issue a full report, it reneged, announcing a few weeks later that national security prevented releasing any more details of the debacle.[241] Martelle announced: "We're not going to be issuing any kind of report because anything beyond the most general of comments would lead us into areas which concern sensitive security information. And we are prohibited by federal regulation in discussing sensitive security information."[242] The TSA also announced that "details about future breaches also would be kept secret because of national security," the *Dallas Morning News* reported.[243] The *Fort Worth Star Telegram* noted: "Too much information was made public about the breach, local TSA officials have been told. Further disclosures by airport officials or anyone else privy to the final report could result in fines and/or jail time."[244]

While some people may retain hope that the preceding TSA debacles are merely the birth pangs of a pending paragon of public service, contrary evidence continues to cascade in:

- On February 6, 2003 San Francisco International Airport was disrupted after a Taiwanese woman "with two carry-on bags sprinted through an unmanned security checkpoint at 10:46 A.M. It wasn't until 1 P.M. that TSA officials evacuated the terminal," according to Airport Security Report.[245] TSA agents first looked for the woman—concluded she was "lost in the crowd"—and then spent time reviewing the videotape of the security checkpoint before ordering the evacuation and re-screening.

- On February 7 Honolulu International Airport was disrupted for three hours after a baggage explosive test indicated a positive alert—after the passenger retrieved the bag and went to his flight. Despite the best efforts of devoted canines, "neither the person nor the bag was found."[246]

- On March 8 one terminal at the Hartford, Connecticut International Airport was evacuated after a TSA screener was caught taking a late afternoon nap by an x-ray machine.[247]

- On March 11 the Birmingham, Alabama International Airport was shut down by TSA officials after "four people were discovered lurking on the airport tarmac. They fled on foot when officers questioned them about their badges identifying them as airport security workers," Airport Security Report noted.[248] Dozens of flights were delayed and hundreds of people were evacuated before it was learned that the four suspicious individuals were TSA officials testing airport security.

- On March 16 the Cincinnati International Airport was closed for almost two hours after one passenger left a checkpoint before TSA agents finished giving him a "secondary screening" after he passed through the magnetometer. Four thousand passengers had to be re-screened, Airport Security Report noted.[249]

- On March 21 Cleveland Hopkins International Airport was placed under a 40 minute lockdown—prohibiting all passenger entries or exits and all plane departures. TSA agents hit the alarm when they spotted a little toy gun on a child's belt buckle in a carry-on bag. TSA confiscated the child's belt buckle. TSA spokesman Rick DeChant announced: "Had Mom or Dad helped this kid pack, this [airport lockdown] could have been avoided."[250]

- On March 24 a Detroit Metropolitan Airport terminal was evacuated for almost two hours after TSA screeners suspected they saw a pair of scissors in a carry-on bag. The passenger retrieved the bag and went off to his plane before the TSA agents went for his bag.[251] The Associated Press reported that TSA spokesman Ed Martelle "would not describe the object and said he could not confirm broadcast reports that it was a pair of scissors."[252]

- On April 3 a female passenger at Baltimore-Washington International airport refused to be re-screened after the metal detector signaled an alarm from her first pass. Instead, she walked on to her flight.[253] Though two concourses were closed for an hour, the culprit was never apprehended.[254]

- On April 16 one wing of Washington Reagan National Airport was evacuated and shut down for an hour after a screener became suspicious about an x-ray image of a carry-on bag. Before the TSA agent manually searched the bag, the passenger picked up his bag and went on to his plane. Ten flights were delayed.[255]

## Conclusion: Security as Political Theater

On March 10, 2003 a TSA press release proudly announced: "The Transportation Security Administration has intercepted more than 4.8 million prohibited items at passenger security checkpoints in its first year, contributing to the security of the traveling public and the nation's 429 commercial airports."[256] TSA chief James Loy bragged: "Those statistics are strong testimony to the professionalism and attention to detail of our highly trained security screeners."[257] A few weeks later, Loy upped the ante, informing the House Appropriations Committee: "We have identified, intercepted, and therefore kept off aircraft more than 4.8 million dangerous items."[258] All the fingernail clippers and cigar cutters seized since 9/11 transmogrified into proof the federal government is protecting people better than ever. The press release did not mention that the checkpoint seizures including frying pans, sets of dumbbells, horseshoes, toy robots, and an unknown but gargantuan number of petty pointed objects.

When the federal government launched its hiring binge for airport screeners, Transportation Secretary Norman Mineta stressed his "commitment to hire the best and the brightest" for the new jobs.[259] The federal takeover of airport security was sparked in part because of the incompetence of private companies in hiring people of dubious character and trustworthiness as airport screeners. Yet, in May 2003 Americans learned that the TSA had fired scores of TSA screeners in Los Angeles and New York after finding that they had criminal records—after the screeners had been on the job for several months. The *Los Angeles Times,* in an article headlined, "U.S. Agency Bungled Airport Hiring," reported that the TSA "lost background questionnaires, failed to run some employee fingerprints through a national crime database and was unable to complete background checks."[260] The *Times* noted that congressmen began investigating the TSA's "background check process after reports that a screener at Kennedy airport was arrested earlier this year for allegedly stealing $6,000 from a passenger." At Dulles International Airport in Washington, the TSA failed to complete background checks on more than a third of the 600 screeners. One TSA employee complained: "It defeats the purpose of what you are here for. It's a 200-[person] plus security breach."[261] Nationwide, more than twenty thousand TSA screeners were on the job even though the TSA had not completed background checks on them.

Many of the absurdities in airport security after 9/11 were the result of a fixation on little objects—as if any item could suddenly have absolute power to topple tall skyscrapers. What made box-cutters so dangerous before 9/11 was that the American people were encouraged to acquiesce to hijackers—to submit and trust the government to rescue them. Once people realized that the government was not going to save them (as on Flight 93), their behavior radically changed. After 9/11, nail clippers, knitting needles, and other common items would have been much less helpful to hijackers than before 9/11. Yet, because the government was determined to remind people every step of the way that Washington would protect them—and because the federal government wanted to assert its authority over airline passengers—federal policies sparked millions of pointless seizures.

The Transportation Security Administration is the archetype of new government agencies after 9/11. The TSA blatantly scorned Congress on its budget and staffing levels and suffered no retribution. And, once TSA snafus became sufficiently blatant to make a mockery of the entire agency, the TSA suddenly announced that "national security" requires the cover-up of the details of its airport disruptions.

While the TSA has appeared as a multibillion-dollar Keystone Kops operation in its first year, the agency is increasingly showing contempt for due process and constitutional rights. At a June 3, 2003 House Appropriations subcommittee hearing, TSA revealed that 1200 screeners had been fired because of "suitability issues"—in many cases, felony convictions discovered after they had been on the job for months. The TSA scrambled to clean house, firing 250 screeners on the Friday before the hearing. Rep. Martin Sabo (D-Minn.) complained: "It appears to me that the management of TSA is virtually a misnomer. It does not exist from what I can tell. . . . Over and over again we hear from the inspector general and others of contracts that have not been properly overseen and costs that have spiraled out of control."[262] Congressmen were outraged at both the agency's screw-ups—its abysmal failure to screen its screeners—and its secrecy. Rep. John Sweeney (R-N.Y.) groused: "One of the most frustrating experiences you have as a member of Congress is trying to deal with your agency and get answers and provide oversight. One of the things that confounds me is I have been told by my local airport authority that they can't talk to me about how they are spending money because they have been ordered by you, and your staff, not to talk to me." Despite the debacles, TSA chief "Loy and the [TSA] contractors remained relatively self-congratulatory" during the hearing, the *Los Angeles Times* noted.[263]

The *New York Daily News* celebrated the first anniversary of 9/11 by sending two reporters traipsing around the country, taking 14 flights on six airlines and passing through eleven major airports over Labor Day weekend 2002. The reporters carried box cutters, razors, knives, and pepper spray in their luggage. The *News* reported: "Not a single airport security checkpoint spotted or confiscated any of the dangerous items, all of which have been banned from airports and planes by federal authorities."[264] The reporters took their contraband through the checkpoints at all four of the airports used by the hijackers on 9/11. The reporters were selected for hand searches several times but nothing was found. There were more security personnel and searches than a year before "but it amounted to nothing more than a big show."[265] The Transportation Security Agency blamed the failures on its prehistory, commenting that the *Daily News'* findings "underscore the failures of an aviation security system inherited by the federal government last fall."[266] Mineta spokesman Leonard Alcivar, on the other hand, greeted the findings with a spout of positive thinking: "The reality is Americans have never had a higher level of security in the history of aviation."[267]

CBS News also celebrated the anniversary of 9/11 by testing airport security. CBS employees, in a test codesigned by former FAA special agent Steve Elson, took X ray–blocking film bags through the checkpoints.[268] The bags cannot be penetrated by the X ray systems used at airport checkpoints and must be manually opened and searched by screeners. Seventy percent of the airport checkpoints failed to detect or examine the film bags—roughly the same failure rate that occurred six months earlier when CBS first used this method to test airport security. Screeners at Reagan National, Los Angeles International, and New York's LaGuardia Airport failed to check any of the opaque bags.

In the wake of 9/11 the federal mentality toward airports and airline customers is best summarized by the motto posted at the headquarters of the TSA air marshal training center: "Dominate. Intimidate. Control."[269] But it takes more than browbeating average Americans to make air travel safe. Airline expert Michael Boyd observed: "The TSA is a poorly focused, unaccountable Washington political bureaucracy geared to screen for objects, not for security threats."[270] *Air Transport World* magazine noted, "Security processing at U.S. airports one year after the Sept. 11 attacks has the sophistication of a sledgehammer and the selectivity of a tsunami sweeping all before its irresistible force."[271] *Airport Security Report* newsletter judged: "One year after the most deadly day in aviation history, there is a growing consensus that the U.S. government and industry have failed to build a stronger aviation security system."[272]

There is no series of tricks or reforms that will guarantee the safety of airports and airplanes. But a first step toward better security is to recognize the facades the feds have created. The Transportation Security Administration should no longer be permitted to burden travelers or taxpayers. The armies of federal agents occupying American airports should be disbanded. Airports and airlines must not be shielded from liability if their negligence results in carnage. The specter of devastating liability lawsuits could produce more innovations and sounder security policies than the incentives produced by Washington political circuses. Federal intelligence agencies should do a much better job of notifying airports and airlines of current specific threats. Resources should be focused on determining actual threats—rather than treating every grandmother and toddler as a potential hijacker. Pilots should not be effectively banned by the federal government from carrying firearms or other means to defend their cockpits against deadly threats. It would also be helpful to amend U.S. foreign policy to reduce the number of foreigners willing to kill themselves to slaughter Americans.

# CHAPTER NINE

# License for Tyranny

There's a vast coalition of other countries that love freedom like we do.

—*President Bush, March 27, 2002*[1]

I view this as a struggle of tyranny versus freedom, of evil versus good.

—*President Bush, February 5, 2002*[2]

In a December 11, 2001 speech at the Citadel Military Academy, President Bush proclaimed: "They love only one thing—they love power. And when they have it, they use it without mercy."[3] While Bush was denouncing terrorists at that particular moment, his description fits many of the governments in the world. Unfortunately, the war on terrorism is proving more effective at unleashing governments than at eradicating terrorists.

## Carnage for a Good Cause

On June 27, 2002 Bush declared that Russian President Vladimir Putin understands "that there won't be peace if terrorists are allowed to kill and take innocent life. And therefore, I view President Putin as an ally, strong ally, in the war against terror."[4] The Russian government welcomed the U.S. call for a worldwide crackdown on terrorism. After 9/11 Western governments hushed their criticism of Russian conduct in the breakaway republic of Chechnya and the Russian military capitalized on the silence to wreak new carnage. *Newsweek* columnist Fareed Zakaria noted that since the early 1990s the Russian government "has killed an estimated 100,000 civilians—almost 10 percent of the prewar population" of Chechnya.[5] Oleg Mironov, Russia's human rights commissioner for Chechnya, stated in June that there were "systemic and massive violations of human rights."[6] In May and June 2002, Russian troops conducted a "cleansing operation" in the village of Mesker Yurt, near Grozny. The *Washington Post* reported statements from survivors who said that after the soldiers were done, relatives went to retrieve victims who included a "man whose eye was gouged out; another whose fingers were cut off; a third whose back had been sliced in rows with the sharp edge of broken glass, then doused with alcohol and set afire."[7] In July 2002 the International Helsinki Federation (IHF), a human rights monitoring organization created during the Soviet era, issued a report warning that "the numbers of disappeared Chechens in recent months indicate a continuing assault against the Chechen people that borders on genocide. . . . The Russian forces are often beheading, burning, mutilating, and otherwise destroying bodies in an effort to conceal this process, which is claiming more lives than the bombings during the two military campaigns."[8] The IHF characterized Russian policy as "a process of thinning out a population of young men" in Chechnya.[9]

In the wake of the October 2002 Russian slaughter of Chechen hostage takers at a Moscow theater (as well as the negligent killing of 130 Russians in the botched rescue), Bush gushed over Putin's handling of the hostage crisis: "Eight hundred people were going to lose their lives. These people were killers, just like the killers that came to America."[10] When White House press spokesman Ari Fleischer was asked if Russia was to blame for the bloodbath, Fleischer protested: "The people who shoulder the burden and the blame are the terrorists. And there is no excuse around the world in any region for people resorting to terror against innocent civilians."[11] But, as *Newsweek*'s Zakaria wrote, "Russia has destroyed Chechnya as a place, as a polity and as a society. Chechnya is now a wasteland, populated by marauding gangs. No leader can control the increasingly radicalized and lawless youth, such as those who took over the Moscow theater."[12] Anna Politkovskaya, a correspondent with *Novaya Gazeta*, observed: "It's now quite clear that the methods our military is using during the so-called antiterrorism operation in Chechnya have been transformed into methods for reproducing terrorism."[13] Politkovskaya also noted that "as far as the main task—the prevention of terrorist acts—is concerned, our special forces are impotent and the bold rhetoric of President Vladimir Putin about the rebirth of the mighty security service has proved a myth."[14]

Russia launched its second war on Chechnya within days of three apartment bombings in September 1999 that killed hundreds of people. The government acted as if it was self-evident that Chechens were the attackers. The terrorist attacks and the war produced a surge in popularity for the Russian government and paved the way for Vladimir Putin to be elected as president. However, on April 30, 2003 Russia's prosecutor general announced it was closing its investigation into the 1999 bombings without charging any Chechens for the attacks.[15] Some Russians suspected that the apartment bombings were the work of the Russian security service, the F.S.B.

Uzbekistan also seized on 9/11 to sanctify and intensify its oppression. On October 9, 2001 Uzbek president Islam Karimov announced: "Indifference to, and tolerance of, those with evil intentions who are spreading various fabrications, handing out leaflets, committing theft and sedition in some neighborhoods and who are spreading propaganda on behalf of religion should be recognized as being supportive of these evil-doers"—that is, terrorists. Anyone who participates in private Muslim prayer groups or distributes literature not previously approved by the government can be prosecuted for "anti-state activity" or "attempted subversion of the constitutional order" and sentenced to 20 years in prison.[16] An Uzbek dissident leader wrote in the *New York Times:* "If militiamen kill citizens, they can simply fill out documents claiming the victim was a terrorist, or even a follower of Osama bin Laden. No civilian has any ability to question this characterization."[17] As the International Helsinki Federation noted, "In the name of combating terrorism . . . Islamic believers have been tortured and even murdered by authorities; large numbers have been imprisoned with no legal basis. The IHF has drawn attention to the deportation from their homes of thousands of the inhabitants of the Sukhandaria region because of their alleged sympathies with the Islamist extremists."[18] Such policies did not prevent President Bush from sending Uzbek President Karimov a letter on the first 9/11 anniversary expressing his readiness to work with Karimov "to work together to create a world which values people and promises them a future of freedom and hope."[19] The head of the largest independent human rights group in Uzbekistan complained in September 2002 that the Uzbek government "decided to liquidate the Human Rights Society of Uzbekistan" after receiving "private approbation" from Washington for its "repressive political regime."[20]

India was one of the nations that most enthusiastically endorsed the U.S. war on terrorism. In March 2002 the Indian Parliament used extraordinary procedures to enact the Prevention of Terrorism Ordinance (POTO), which gave the government sweeping arbitrary power over terrorist suspects, including the right to detain suspects for up to a year without bail.[21] Since previous terrorist legislation in India had sparked pervasive torture and wrongful arrests, many people feared a new wave of oppression from the new law. Opposition Congress Party leader Sonia Gandhi complained that "POTO has been selectively used and misused . . . to ban organizations in a partisan manner. It poses a larger threat to the freedom of ordinary people than to terrorists."[22] The Indian government previously was harshly criticized for using antiterrorism laws to repress Muslims while ignoring Hindus who committed the same crimes. Gandhi asserted that the recent bloodshed between Muslims and Hindus in Gujarat proved that the government wanted to "arm itself with the menacing power of [the POTO] to promote its divisive ideology."[23] The Indian government conceded that more than 850 people were killed—mostly Muslims—while private sources estimated that two thousand people died in Gujarat violence in late February and early March 2002, after an attack on a train carrying Hindu religious activists resulted in 58 deaths. A Human Rights Watch analysis concluded that "the attacks on Muslims throughout the state were planned . . . and organized with extensive police participation and in close cooperation with officials of the Bharatiya Janata Party (Indian People's Party) state government." The analysis noted that "the attackers descended with militia-like precision . . . guided by computer printouts [obtained from the local government] listing the addresses of Muslim families and their properties." The police were "directly implicated' in almost all the attacks: "In many cases, under the guise of offering assistance, the police led the victims directly into the hands of their killers." Panicky Muslims who called police for assistance were told: "We don't have any orders to save you." Human Rights Watch also noted that "scores of Muslim girls and women were brutally raped in Gujarat before being mutilated and burnt to death."[24]

## China: From Oppressor to Victim

Bush, commenting in Shanghai on October 19, 2001, hailed the government for China's effort to fight terrorism: "We have a common understanding of the magnitude of the threat posed by international terrorism. . . . President Jiang and the government stand side by side with the American people as we fight this evil force."[25]

At the time of Bush's tribute, China was exploiting the war on terrorism to crush Uighur Muslims in its western provinces (where the Silk Road passed through), arbitrarily arresting and sentencing thousands of people guilty of nothing more than practicing their religion.[26] Uighurs are Turkic-speaking Muslims (roughly eight million people) who were conquered by the Chinese communist government in 1949. A month after 9/11 Chinese government security forces razed a mosque and arrested 180 people who protested the destruction.[27] Amnesty International reported that the government has "subjected the Islamic clergy to intensive scrutiny and 'political education' . . . campaigns which are reminiscent of those held during the Cultural Revolution [and] aim both to force participants to follow closely the party's dictates and to identify potential opponents and dissenters."[28] Chinese government agents have burned Uighur books and closed down Uighur magazines. One Western expatriate living in the area observed: "Uighur literature is defined as distorted history and accused of inciting national separatism."[29]

The U.S. government had long harshly criticized Chinese brutality toward the Uighurs. Francis X. Taylor, the State Department's chief counterterrorism official, declared in December 2001: "The legitimate economic and social issues that confront the people of western China are not necessarily terrorist issues and should be resolved politically rather than using counter-terrorism methods."[30]

But, as the Bush administration strove to build international support for its plan to attack Iraq, Undersecretary of State Richard Armitage stunned the international community when he announced that the U.S. government had added the East Turkestan Islamic Movement [ETIM] to its official list of terrorist organizations. After a meeting with Chinese officials in Beijing, Armitage revealed on August 26, 2002: "After careful study we judged that [ETIM] was a terrorist group, that it committed acts of violence against unarmed civilians without any regard for who was hurt."[31] The U.S. government did not present any evidence at the time to support the designation.[32] The *New York Times* noted: "The American condemnation of the group was a propaganda coup for China, which had sought to blunt criticism of its repressive tactics in Xinjiang [in western China], saying that it faces an organized, global terrorist threat."[33]

A few days later, the State Department issued a background paper blaming ETIM for all of the alleged terrorist incidents that occurred in Xinjiang in the previous decade.[34] But the Chinese government did not even publicly mention the group's existence until a year before the State Department announcement. The Chinese government long attributed most of the violence in Xinjiang to other so-called terrorist organizations. The State Department's August 2002 assertions also starkly contradicted its own *Patterns of Global Terrorism* report, issued four months earlier, which blamed other groups for violence in that area. At that time, the State Department commented on the situation in western China: "Two groups in particular are cause for concern: the East Turkestan Islamic Party (ETIP) and the East Turkestan Liberation Organization (or Sharki Turkestan Azatlik Tashkilati, known by the acronym SHAT). ETIP was founded in the early 1980s with the goal of establishing an independent state of Eastern Turkestan and advocates armed struggle. SHAT's members have reportedly been involved in various bomb plots and shootouts."[35]

After the designation of ETIM as terrorists sparked skepticism far and wide, the U.S. Embassy in Beijing announced that ETIM was planning attacks on the U.S. embassy in Bishek, Kyrgyzstan.[36] No evidence was supplied to support the charge, and no attack occurred.

Two weeks later the United States and China announced that the United Nations had added ETIM's name to the official UN list of terrorist organizations. A Chinese foreign ministry spokesman hailed the formal UN condemnation of ETIM as "an encouraging result from China's cooperation with the United States and other countries in fighting terrorism."[37] No evidence is required to add an alleged terrorist group to the UN list. Instead, it is an "honor" program: each member government of the United Nations effectively takes another government's "word" that some group is actually terrorist.

Erkin Dolat of the exiled Uighur Information Agency complained that the Bush administration's terrorist designation is "disastrous to the Uighur freedom movement" and "opened the floodgates of Chinese persecution."[38] Another Uighur Muslim commented: "We are fighting for our freedom, not for the overthrow of Western governments. Our anger is not directed against the U.S. and the international community, but against the Chinese government."[39] A *Washington Times* analysis noted, "Xinjiang specialists consider the Uighurs among the most liberal and pro-U.S. Muslims in the world, and in Kashgar women interact freely with men, run businesses and hold political office."[40]

China did not need the U.S. government's permission to repress its own subjects. But the U.S. terrorist designation of ETIM shielded China against international criticism. Wang Yong, a specialist in international relations at Beijing University, observed: "The U.S. action on ETIM was probably a posture of exchange for China's support on Iraq."[41] (China is a member of the UN Security Council and could veto a UN resolution endorsing military action against Iraq.)

When Attorney General John Ashcroft visited China in late October 2002 he declared that the ETIM terrorist designation was "not based on political negotiations or a sense of timing. It is based on the availability of evidence that supports the designation."[42] However, the U.S. government still did not release any of the evidence. Ashcroft happily announced that the Chinese government had finally given permission for the FBI to open a liaison office in Beijing.

## Repressing Everything in the Name of Antiterrorism

Immediately after the 9/11 attacks the U.S. government campaigned for a United Nations antiterrorism resolution. On September 28, 2001, the UN unanimously adopted Resolution 1373, calling on all "States to work together urgently to prevent and suppress terrorist acts" and commanding all governments to "refrain from providing any form of support, active or passive, to entities or persons involved in terrorist acts, including by suppressing recruitment of members of terrorist groups and eliminating the supply of weapons to terrorists."

The UN received reports from more than 150 governments on how they were fighting terrorism. Many governments bragged about antiterrorism policies that went above and beyond the UN's appeal. Bacre Waly Ndiaye of the UN High Commissioner for Human Rights' Office complained: "In some countries, nonviolent activities have been considered as terrorism, and excessive measures have been taken to suppress or restrict individual rights, including the presumption of innocence, the right to a fair trial, freedom from torture, privacy rights, freedom of expression and assembly, and the right to seek asylum."[43]

Algeria informed the UN that its legal code allows for two years of pretrial detention for terrorist suspects, or four years of pretrial detention if the crime was "transnational." Algeria keeps clerics in line: "Use of a place of worship to preach without authorization from the competent public authorities is punishable by 1 to 3 years' non-rigorous imprisonment."[44] Any private "fund-raising activity" not pre-authorized by the government "exactly as described in Ordinance No. 77.03 of 19 February 1977" is punishable by up to two years in prison. The Algerian government has long been notorious for torture and "extrajudicial killings" and its security services led the world in the 1990s in the number of people they made "disappear"—at least seven thousand people.[45] Assistant Secretary of State William Burns, visiting Algiers in late 2002 to announce that the United States would resume selling arms to the country after a ten-year embargo (after a military coup), proclaimed: "Washington has much to learn from Algeria on ways to fight terrorism."[46]

Syria bragged to the UN that "financial support for terrorists is effectively curtailed by the absence of any private banking system or independent charities."[47] A government that totally destroys freedom expects to be applauded as an antiterrorist superstar. Botswana boasted that its "Banking Act of 1995 provides for, among other things, unfettered access of the law enforcement agencies to information on bank accounts."[48] Gabon reported that it had increased monitoring of "groups belonging to foreign communities likely to breach Gabonese internal security."[49] Belarus informed the UN that, as part of its response to terrorism, "[t]he subdivisions of the Ministry of Internal Affairs of Belarus are taking steps to detect and suppress the activities of criminal individuals belonging to criminal ethnic groups. Twenty-four ethnic groups with a total of more than 300 members are listed in the automated databank of the Ministry's Committee on

Combating Organized Crime and Corruption."[50] The notion of ethnic groups as criminals was probably not what Bush was thinking of when he called for a terrorism crackdown.

Belarus also enacted a law three months after 9/11 to exempt government antiterrorist agents, including anyone "temporarily or permanently cooperating with state agencies involved in combating terrorism" from any liability for "inflicting damage" on civilians. The new law entitles the agents to "cause harm to the lives, health, and property of terrorists."[51] (The Belarus judicial system is wonderfully adept at designating terrorists.) The new law also severely restricts the news media "in the zone of the conduct of an antiterrorist operation."

Dictators around the globe cheered the U.S. call for a crackdown on terrorists. Egyptian prime minister Atef Abeid suggested that "Western countries should begin to think of Egypt's own fight against terror as their new model."[52] Egyptian president-for-life Hosni Mubarak announced: "There is no doubt that the events of September 11 created a new concept of democracy that differs from the concept that Western states defended before these events, especially in regard to the freedom of the individual." Secretary of State Colin Powell announced that the United States has "much to learn from" Egypt in dealing with the "scourge of terrorism."[53] But the State Department had perennially criticized Egypt for relying on torture, repression, detention without trials, and military court martials for terrorist suspects.[54]

Similarly, Prime Minister Mahathir Mohamad of Malaysia declared: "Events in the United States have shown that there are instances where certain special powers need to be used in order to protect the public for the general good."[55] The U.S. government had previously harshly criticized Mohamad for destroying freedom of the press and abusing the Internal Security Act (ISA) to crush all opposition. As Human Rights Watch noted, "the ISA allows for indefinite detention without trial and allows for arrest without a warrant of anyone any police officer has 'reason to believe' has acted or is likely to act 'in any manner prejudicial to the security of Malaysia.'" People arrested can be detained for years without being charged. After a White House meeting in May 2002 Mohamad crowed that Bush "did not raise anything about democracy or human rights in Malaysia."[56] Malaysian Minister Datuk Seri Rais Yatim bragged that he had explained the benefits of the ISA to Attorney General John Ashcroft and declared: "After today's talks, there's no basis to criticize each other's systems. If they do that, they could jeopardize the credibility of the Patriot's Act."[57]

In Indonesia, the government proposed legislation to define terrorism so broadly that it would allow "the potential labeling of any political activity considered a threat by the state as terrorism," the *Jakarta Post* reported.[58] The bill would permit the government to hold terrorist suspects for one year incommunicado, with no access to a lawyer or family members. Minister for Political and Security Affairs Susilo Bambang Yudhoyono warned: "We must be careful not to place human rights in the context of drafting this bill, as an absolute . . . and therefore allow the nation to be reduced to chaos or instability."[59] The Indonesian government has never been accused of letting human rights impede its progress. The Indonesian parliament balked at the sweeping bill. After terrorist bombers killed more than two hundred people at a Bali night club in October 2002, Indonesian president Megawati Soekarnoputri issued two decrees that included many provisions of the stalled antiterrorism legislation.

The Cuban government, as part of its war on terrorism, added a new law mandating the death penalty for anyone who uses the Internet to incite political violence. Cuban dictator Fidel Castro decreed: "I have not the slightest doubt about the death penalty as an appropriate punishment in terrorism cases."[60]

The Zimbabwe government announced that journalists "who wrote stories on attacks on whites and political violence in Zimbabwe would be treated as terrorists," as Human Rights Watch reported.[61] A Mugabe spokesman warned: "As for the correspondents, we would like them to know that we agree with U.S. President Bush that anyone who in any way finances, harbors or defends terrorists is himself a terrorist. We, too, will not make any difference between terrorists and their friends and supporters." In early 2002 a senior government official denounced a proposal to allow the media to freely cover an upcoming national election as a "mad request especially in this age of terrorism when governments are coming together to fight terrorism."[62] At the time, Zimbabwe was on the verge of mass starvation as a result of the government's slaughter of white farmers, confiscation of private farmland, and disruption of the agricultural economy.

Liberian President Charles Taylor informed the Liberian parliament in 2002: "September 11th ushered in a new threat to our national security. That threat is terrorism, and it is manifested in many forms, including political, social and military."[63] Taylor started labeling critical journalists and human rights workers as "unlawful combatants" in 2002—after which the designees were arrested and, in some cases, tortured. When Liberian Minister of Information Reginald Goodridge was asked about this practice by an American journalist, he replied: "It was you guys [the U.S. government] who coined the phrase. We are using the phrase you coined."[64]

Similarly, the government of Uganda denounced the nation's largest independent paper as terrorist supporters in October 2002 and arrested three editors and charged them with "publishing articles that are contrary to national security and that give comfort to the enemy." As a report by the Lawyers Committee on

Human Rights noted, the government justified the arrests based on "a new antiterrorism law that came into effect in May 2002. . . . Under this law, publishing news 'likely to promote terrorism' is punishable by death."[65]

The *Far Eastern Economic Review* noted in April 2002 that the U.S. government, as part of its war on terrorism, was endorsing repression throughout Asia: "In Indonesia it may be helping the government hound opposition politicians; and in the Philippines it has given a licence to overzealous law-enforcement officials to make false accusations. . . . Critics describe the U.S. approach as a witch-hunt."[66] Amitav Acharya, the deputy director of the Institute of Defense and Strategic Studies in Singapore, warned in April 2002 that since 9/11, "any internal security problems are seen as terrorism," and the distinction between "external security threats and internal security disappears."[67]

As evidence accumulated of governments exploiting the terrorist threat to intensify oppression, human rights activists and some UN officials sought to take action—or at least to pass a resolution. During the spring 2002 meeting of the UN Commission on Human Rights, the United States helped torpedo a resolution by Mexico that urged that antiterrorism measures respect international humanitarian standards.[68] After UN High Commissioner for Human Rights Mary Robinson urged the commission to proclaim that "human rights should not be sacrificed in the fight against terrorism,"[69] U.S. Ambassador Kevin Moley sniped that "Mary Robinson has a totally backward vision of human rights."[70] In a formal statement to the UN commission, Moley complained that Robinson's analysis of the campaign against terrorism "does not focus on Al Qaeda's aims, essence and ideology. Indeed, it has more to do with counter-terrorism than with terrorism itself."[71] Any public utterance not devoted solely to castigating terrorism apparently threatened to annul the war on terrorism. Moley warned that focusing on human rights could help the terrorists: "Let us be under no illusion that our necessary commitment to human rights will be a compelling argument with the terrorists themselves."[72] But the purpose of respecting human rights was not to assuage terrorists but to protect nonterrorists. (The UN Commission on Human Rights is often a farce—dominated of late by some of the worst regimes in the world. However, despite its flaws, the U.S. government for decades sought to use the Commission as a podium to build international support for better human rights policies.)

## Arms for All

On December 7, 2001 Bush announced that the federal government was seizing the assets of and shutting down several Muslim charities operating in America.

Bush proclaimed: "Those who do business with terror will do no business with the United States or anywhere else the United States can reach."[73] President Bush declared that "one dime of money into a terrorist activity is one dime too much." Treasury Undersecretary Jimmy Gurule later explained that although some of the Muslim charities "may be offering humanitarian services here or abroad, funds raised by certain charities have been diverted to terrorist causes. This scheme is particularly troubling because these funds are earmarked for good and they are being grossly perverted to fund acts of evil against innocent civilians."[74]

But the U.S. government is apparently exempt from the "one dime" test. The United States gives more than $14 billion in foreign aid each year to foreign governments and international organizations. Foreign aid has been aptly described as handouts "from governments, to governments, for governments."[75] Every dollop in foreign aid frees up an equivalent amount of a recipient government's own funds to be spent for other purposes. As a Justice Department court brief noted, "[m]oney is fungible; giving support intended to aid an organization's peaceful activities frees up resources that can be used for terrorist acts."[76]

Bush, speaking on the six-month anniversary of the 9/11 attacks, offered U.S. military aid and training to "governments everywhere" and announced that he "expects governments everywhere to help remove the terrorist parasites that threaten the world and the peace of the world." Bush promised: "If governments need training or resources to meet this commitment, America will help."[77] After 9/11, almost every regime in the world is considered worthy of receiving U.S. tax dollars or military arms. Pentagon spokeswoman Navy Lt. Cmdr. Barbara Burfeind observed: "It is easier to list what countries do not receive American military assistance than those that do. Virtually every country but Cuba, Iraq, Iran and the other countries on the terrorist list receive some military training or aid from us."[78] As the Federation of American Scientists noted in an August 2002 report, "[s]ince September 11th, the administration has requested nearly $3.8 billion in security assistance and related aid for 67 countries allegedly linked in some way to the struggle against terrorism. Many of these countries are of dubious relevance to the 'war on terror,' and some are even waging their own campaigns of terror against their citizens."[79] Frida Berrigan of the World Policy Institute noted that the State Department's 2002 *Country Reports on Human Rights Practices* "lists 52 countries that are currently receiving U.S. military training or weapons as having 'poor' or 'very poor' human-rights records."[80]

The U.S. government gave $160 million in 2002 to the government of Uzbekistan. Nitpickers at Human Rights Watch complain that Uzbek government officials seek to enlighten dissidents with methods such as "beatings, electric shock, temporary suffocation, hanging by the ankles or wrists, removal of fingernails, and punctures with sharp objects." On the occasion of Uzbek leader Islam Karimov's visit to the White House in March, a Human Rights Watch press release noted: "Local officials stage Stalin-style 'hate rallies,' at which communities gather to upbraid perceived religious 'extremists' and their families."[81] An Uzbek human rights association complained: "The use of torture helps law-enforcement and security agencies carry out the 'special government order' of keeping society in constant fear of the authorities, suppressing dissent, and undermining the will of opposition-minded people."[82]

The government of Georgia received $64 million in U.S. aid after 9/11. Amnesty International noted that the Georgian government was guilty of "widespread and continuing" torture. Amnesty International also quibbled with "a series of fatalities suffered by detainees after allegedly falling or jumping out of the upper floor windows of police stations."[83] On March 11, 2002 Bush announced that "terrorists working closely with al Qaeda operate in the Pankisi Gorge"[84] area along the Georgia-Chechen border. In April 2002 U.S. Special Forces arrived, purportedly to train the local army on how to fight insurgents sneaking in from Chechnya. Many observers suspected that the aid was actually intended to bolster the regime of Eduard Shevardnadze, tottering as a result of civil wars in two breakaway regions of his country. At a May 7 Pentagon press conference, Georgian Defense Minister David Tevzadze was asked if he agreed with the U.S. government that Al Qaeda had infiltrated his country. Tevzadze replied: "You know, actually, for me personally, it is very difficult to believe in that, because to come from Afghanistan to that part of Georgia, they need to [cross] at least six or seven countries, [and the] Caspian Sea." He insisted that "al Qaeda influence can't be" in Georgia.[85] The U.S. program hit a major snag when only 100 Georgians applied to be part of the 500-member U.S.-trained battalion.[86]

Pakistan received a windfall of more than $600 million in U.S. aid after the government of military commander Pervez Musharraf, who seized power in a 1999 coup, promised to support the war against the Taliban and Al Qaeda. Yet, as *New York Times* columnist Nicholas Kristof noted, "Pakistan's intelligence agency is responsible for more terrorist killings than Al Qaeda."[87] The State Department's 2002 human rights report on Pakistan observed: "The Government's human rights record remained poor. . . . Police committed numerous extrajudicial killings. . . . Police abused and raped citizens."[88]

The United States provided more than $47 million in 2002 to the government of Kazakhstan. According to the State Department's 2002 report on human rights practices in Kazakhstan: "The Government's human rights record was poor. . . . Members of the security forces committed a small number of extrajudicial killings. . . . Police tortured detainees. . . ."[89] Otherwise, there was no reason not to expect a good return for the Kazak people from the U.S. tax dollars Bush delivered to their rulers. The Kazak government became far more repressive in mid-2002 after press reports that Nursultan Nazarbayev, the country's ruler, had shuffled a billion dollars of government funds into his Swiss bank account. The *Washington Post* noted: "As the scandal blossomed, opposition leaders were suddenly arrested, newspapers and television stations shut down, and critical journalists beaten in what foes of the government consider a new wave of repression."[90] Twenty newspapers ceased publication and more than a dozen television stations were either knocked off the air or faced closure. Assylbeck Kozhakhmetov, a prominent opposition candidate and a leader of Democratic Choice for Kazakhstan, complained: "All this is happening with the silent consent of the West. The ostrich party of Western democracies actually unties the hands of dictators."[91] The government's grisly record did not inhibit Bush from issuing a joint statement with President Nazarbayev pledging to "reiterate our mutual commitment to advance the rule of law and promote freedom of religion and other universal human rights."[92] Nor did the crackdown deter the U.S. government from formally pledging to provide far more financial assistance and military equipment to the Kazak government in mid-July.[93]

The United States delivered $72 million in 2002 to Kyrgyzstan which recently renamed itself the Kyrgyz Republic. The State Department noted in March 2002 that the Kyrgyz "government's human rights record remained poor. . . . Members of the security forces at times tortured, beat, and otherwise mistreated persons."[94] Kyrgyz strongman and president Askar Akayev vindicated himself in a September 24, 2002 speech in Washington: "In the post-Soviet era a strong presidential government is a condition for democratic development."[95]

The government of Tajikistan harvested $125 million from the U.S. government in 2002.[96] According to the State Department, "[s]ome members of the security forces were responsible for killings and beatings, and often abused detainees. These forces were also responsible for threats, extortion, looting, and abuse of civilians."

Turkmenistan received more than $11 million from the U.S. government in 2002. A March 2002 report by the State Department Bureau of Political-Military Affairs noted that U.S. military aid helps pay for sending Turkmen "military personnel to the U.S. for English language training, professional military education and other courses. . . . The goal of the program is to further Turkmenistan's military professionalization and to enhance the ability of Turkmen forces to participate in . . . any future coalition contingencies."[97] The U.S. government is bankrolling one of the most oppressive regimes in the world. A June

10, 2002 joint press release, issued in Vienna, Austria, by Turkmenistan independent groups and human rights advocates, declared: "The National Security Committee and police strictly monitor all aspects of life, seeking to hold citizens in a constant state of fear. The Turkmen government tolerates no opposition, represses all critical thinking, imprisons or deports religious figures, and has crushed the most elementary trappings of democratic institutions. Torture is widespread. . . . The government banned opera, ballet, the circus, and the philharmonic, and closed the Academy of Sciences. The government is seeking to replace the traditional body of national and cultural values with Rukhnama, a book of the thoughts of [President] Niazov, which Turkmen citizens are forced to learn and to which they must swear allegiance. In 1999, President Niazov had himself declared president for life, and the cult of personality around him has reached grotesque proportions."[98] A U.S. State Department report on Turkmenistan conceded: "There is still a great deal that needs to be done in Turkmenistan on both democratic and economic reform."[99]

The U.S. military provided training to the Nigerian army in 2001 and 2002. (Nigeria received $66 million in U.S. aid in 2002.) The benevolent impulses imparted in the training were not sufficient to deter Nigerian soldiers from slaughtering hundreds of civilians in October 2001, as well as destroying thousands of homes and shops. The Associated Press, citing reports from human rights groups, reported that troops assembled villagers "as if for a meeting" before "separating the men from the women and children. Commanders then gave orders to fire on those assembled, by voice command or blasts on whistles."[100] In some cases, villagers were burned alive. The Nigerian government shrugged off the incident and the soldiers were not punished. In its 2002 *Patterns of Global Terrorism* report, the State Department praised Nigeria: "Nigeria has strongly supported U.S. antiterrorism efforts around the world as well as the military action in Afghanistan. Nigeria led diplomatic efforts in the UN and the Economic Community of West African States and in the battle against terrorism."

The Indonesian army has long been one of the most brutal and murderous entities in Asia. The State Department reported in March 2002 that Indonesian "security forces were responsible for numerous instances of, at times indiscriminate, shooting of civilians, torture, rape, beatings and other abuse."[101] The State Department's verdict did not deter a senior Pentagon official from telling *USA Today* a few weeks later: "We would certainly like the handcuffs removed"—the handcuffs that prevent the U.S. military from training the Indonesian army.[102] The "handcuffs" were imposed by Congress after the Indonesian army's tally in its invasion of East Timor reached a quarter million dead. The city of Dili, East Timor, was described as an "unimaginable apocalyptic ruin" by UN peacekeepers in late 1999 after the Indonesian army and its militia proxies looted and burned down almost every building in the city.[103] After the Indonesian National Commission on Human Rights issued a report linking 50 military and police officers to the slaughter of civilians, officers simply refused to testify to the panel investigating the killings.[104] The Indonesian army has likely been involved in the deaths of a hundred times as many innocent civilians as Hamas. Yet, private donations by Americans to Hamas are a federal crime while U.S. government aid to the Indonesian army is a triumph of good intentions.

The Bush administration delivered more than $20 million to the government of Nepal to fight Maoist guerillas. After Nepali Prime Minister Sher Bahadur Deuba met in the White House with President Bush on May 7, 2002, he announced: "I am very glad, I am very happy, President Bush is very much supportive to our campaign against terrorism and he has assured us he will help in many ways."[105] The guerillas have brutalized many Nepalese but, with U.S. aid, the Nepal government may be able to match the guerrillas corpse for corpse. The *Christian Science Monitor* described a 4 A.M. raid by government troops dressed as Maoists in a village. Any villager who returned the pumped-fist "red salute"—the guerillas' trademark—was taken out and shot. The *Monitor* noted that "the current state of emergency has largely kept the stories of civilian atrocities out of the newspapers and away from the scrutiny of human-rights groups. With nearly 100 local journalists arrested thus far, and 30 still in jail without charge, few reporters and editors are able to delve into the stories behind the death counts and to monitor human-rights atrocities by either the Maoists or the government."[106] Amnesty International questioned a May 2002 clash which, according to the Nepal government, resulted in the deaths of three soldiers, one policeman, and 548 Maoists. The organization noted, "So far, no figures have been released with the number of Maoists wounded or arrested. That could be an indication that the security forces went out to deliberately kill rather than arrest, a common practice in Nepal."[107] The mother of one Nepali victim explained: "Terrorists are [in Nepal], but the Army can't kill them, so they kill us."[108] The U.S. government aid is expected to make the Nepali army more efficient. U.S. military advisors reportedly recommended increasing the size of the Nepali army fivefold, from forty thousand to two hundred thousand.[109]

The Bush administration's determination to glorify its antiterrorism allies inspired the whitewashing of the first genocide of the twentieth century. Turkey is a vital ally for Bush, thanks to its U.S. military bases and its border with Iraq. The United States provided Turkey with more than $200 million in foreign aid in 2002. In an interview on CNN's Turkey affiliate on July 14, 2002 Deputy Defense Secretary Paul Wolfowitz praised Turkey: "I think a real test of whether a country is a democracy is how it treats its minorities. And actually it's one of the things that impress me about Turkish history—the way Turkey treats its own minorities."[110] Between 1915 and 1918, the Turks exterminated a million and a half Armenians—marching them into the desert to starve or die of thirst, rounding up the men for mass executions, and butchering people in their homes—in a concerted effort to solve what the Turkish government labeled "the Armenian problem."[111] Wolfowitz saluted the Turks' exemplary humanitarian record in order to contrast them with Saddam Hussein: "I think it is one of the things that are so appalling about this tyrant in Baghdad is that he treats even the majority pretty badly. The minorities' situations are terrible."[112] Nothing in Hussein's brutal record matches the Armenian genocide.

President Bush, in a speech on his vision of "compassionate conservatism," declared, "America has always had a special mission to defend justice and advance freedom around the world."[113] However, not only does U.S. aid help foreign militaries kill their own people—it now also provides American soldiers with a license to kill. The latest obligation of U.S. aid recipients is to publicly proclaim that American soldiers are exempt from international law. In August 2002, the Bush administration threatened to cut off all U.S. military aid to foreign nations that refused to promise they would not extradite U.S. soldiers accused of war crimes to the International Criminal Court in The Hague in the Netherlands. The *New York Times* characterized the new policy as the Bush administration's "broadest and most coercive tool to keep American peacekeepers out of the hands of the new court."[114] Congress enacted the Serviceman Protection Act which created the hammer on foreign governments and authorized the president to use U.S. military force to rescue any American soldiers being held for trial or prosecution by the International Criminal Court.[115] State Department spokesman Philip Reeker responded to the uproar about the new law, derided by some as "The Hague Invasion Act," by stressing that the U.S. record on human rights and punishing crimes against humanity "remains unmatched."[116] The Bush administration had sound reasons to distrust the International Criminal Court. The likelihood of trials becoming political circuses, among other problems, are very high. Yet, at the same time he announced that U.S. soldiers must be exempt, Bush continued proclaiming his intent to arrest foreign leaders for war crime trials.

The Bush administration also sought absolute freedom to scorn every law in the federal statute book about distributing U.S. tax dollars abroad. A supplemental Pentagon appropriation bill passed by Congress in 2002 provided, at the administration's behest, $120 million "for certain classified activities," including the distribution of U.S. tax dollars overseas, "notwithstanding any other provision of the law" for "projects not otherwise authorized by law."[117] Tamar Gabel-nick of the Federation of American Scientists characterized this as "a virtual blank check to send aid regardless of legal restrictions."[118]

## Conclusion

In the wake of the destruction of the World Trade Center, the United States suddenly was praising the same laws and procedures that it had previously condemned—as if the 9/11 attacks completely reversed all the principles of political morality—as if 9/11 automatically expunged all the previous sins of almost every government in the world (or at least every government not part of an "axis of evil").

In speeches after 9/11 Bush assured audiences: "I believe that out of the evil of September the 11th will come incredible good . . . because Americans are such a compassionate and kind people."[119] But, though Bush loves to remind people how wonderful they have become, in reality Bush has conscripted every American taxpayer to underwrite many of the most oppressive regimes in the world. Many of these regimes were receiving U.S. aid before 9/11. But the amount received by many of the worst governments has soared. And U.S. government officials have raced to abolish any restrictions previously established to prevent the United States from directly bankrolling tyranny.

The result of putting governments on a pedestal around the world is that it is more likely that average people will be ground into the dirt beneath some government agent's boot. The precedents that have been established around the globe since 9/11 will continue to haunt hundreds of millions of people long after Osama bin Laden has gone to hell.

It is absurd to assume that any government which is anti-terror is automatically pro-freedom. The fact that a government objects to outsiders killing its taxpayers provides no assurance that it will not molest its subjects. The fact that politicians seek to maintain a monopoly on the violence within their geographical domain does not make them benefactors of humanity.

The international war against terrorism has made the world a less free place. Over a billion people have seen at least some of their rights and liberties sacrificed on the antiterrorism altar—or face greater risks of unjustified arrest and detention in their daily lives—or face greater likelihood of government surveillance and government intrusion in their personal lives. Most of the people in the world had little to fear from international terrorists before 9/11—but now many of them have more reason to fear their own government.

## CHAPTER TEN

# State Terrorism and Moral Clarity

Our mission is to make the world free from terror.

*—President George Bush, January 30, 2002*[1]

A single death is a tragedy, a million deaths is a statistic.

*—Josef Stalin*[2]

Since 9/11, President George W. Bush has continually portrayed terrorism as the worst evil the world faces. On December 20, 2001 Bush declared, "With the help of freedom-loving countries around the world, we will do much more to rid the world of evil and of terrorists."[3] Bush's concept of terrorism is key to understanding his promise to "rout out terror wherever it exists."[4]

## The Loophole That Swallowed the War

The United States has long insisted that government agents cannot be terrorists. Federal agencies have an array of definitions for "terrorism":[5]

- Defense Department: "the unlawful use or threatened use of force or violence by a revolutionary organization against individuals or property, with the intention of coercing or intimidating governments or societies, often for political or ideological purposes."[6]

- Federal Bureau of Investigation: "the unlawful use of force or violence against persons or property to intimidate or coerce a government, the civilian population, or any segment thereof, in furtherance of political or social objectives."[7]
- The State Department, 1981: "the use or threat of the use of force for political purposes in violation of domestic or international law."[8] With this definition, a government could never terrorize its own people as long as the government issued an edict authorizing the oppression.

Drug Enforcement Administration chief Asa Hutchinson relied on the U.S. definition of terrorism when he declared: "In the first few months of 2002, 13 law enforcement officers have been murdered in Mexico. You say, 'this may not be terrorism.' When you're going after government officials, judicial officials, to impact the stability of a government, in my judgment, it is terrorism."[9] Nine months after Hutchinson's declaration, Mexico disbanded its elite seven-hundred-member national narcotics police because of pervasive corruption, including suspected kidnapping and extortion.[10] (Some elements of the Mexican police have a long history of killing innocent Mexicans and terrorizing anyone who falls under their sway.)

The common theme to the U.S. government definitions is that only private citizens and private groups can be guilty of terrorism. George Moose, U.S. ambassador to the UN Commission on Human Rights, explained on April 23, 2001 why the U.S. government was opposing a resolution on terrorism: "Our reason is that the sponsors have included language that grants terrorists and terrorist organizations a measure of legitimacy by equating their conduct with that of states. . . . Terrorists are not state actors, but criminals who bear individual criminal responsibility for their actions. The perpetuation of this unfortunate confusion adds nothing to the ability, or the obligation, of member states to cooperate in the effort to combat terrorism."[11]

When the UN General Assembly tried to enact a convention to advance the international war on terrorism in 2002, the effort was paralyzed by conflicts over how to define terrorism. "The United States, backed by most European nations, says the convention should not apply to any acts of violence against civilians committed by the military forces of recognized states—a provision fought by Arab states and others that insist that 'state terrorism' should also be penalized," the *Los Angeles Times* reported on April 16, 2002.[12]

The notion that "states cannot be terrorists" is not a Bush innovation; it extends back at least to the early twentieth century. The League of Nations in 1937 defined terrorism as "criminal acts directed against a State and intended or calculated to create a state of terror in the minds of particular persons or the general public."[13] The league's efforts to build an international consensus against private terrorists ended after Hitler's seizure of Czechoslovakia and invasion of Poland.

The U.S. definitions of terrorism focus far more on the perpetrator than on the act. The same act is either public service or terrorism, depending on whether the killer is wearing a uniform.

## What Terrorism Is and Isn't

The U.S. government's selective definition of terrorism is exemplified in the list of "significant terrorist incidents" the State Department includes in its annual *Patterns of Global Terrorism* report. The 2002 report notes: "The incidents listed have met the U.S. Government's Incident Review Panel criteria. An International Terrorist Incident is judged significant if it results in loss of life or serious injury to persons, abduction or kidnapping of persons, major property damage, and/or is an act or attempted act that could reasonably be expected to create the conditions noted."[14]

Among the 346 international terrorist incidents recognized by the State Department in 2001 were the following attacks:

- January 6, Greece: In Athens press reported an incendiary bomb placed under the vehicle of a Turkish commercial attaché exploded, resulting in no injuries but causing major damage to the car. A group calling themselves the "Crazy Gas Cannisters" claimed responsibility.
- January 29, Indonesia: In Lombok a bomb exploded causing no injuries but damaging the subsidiary office of the U.S. firm Newmont Mining Corporation, according to press reports. No one claimed responsibility.
- February 17, Turkey: In Istanbul press reported a bomb was found at a McDonald's restaurant and safely defused by police. No one claimed responsibility.
- April 17, Greece: In Athens, according to press reports, two diplomatic vehicles were set on fire—one belonging to the Israeli Embassy and the other to the Thai Embassy. No one claimed responsibility.
- May 16, India: In Kashmir a grenade thrown at the private residence of the Forest Minister fell short of its target, landing outside the main gate, resulting in no injuries or damage, according to press reports. No one claimed responsibility.
- October 11, Saudi Arabia: In Riyadh unidentified assailants threw a Molotov cocktail at a car carrying two Germans, but no injuries resulted, according to press reports. No one claimed responsibility.

- October 16, Spain: In Catalonia, a letter bomb sent to the Catalan Prison Employees' Union Chatac failed to explode, according to press reports. The Italian Anarchist Black Cross claimed responsibility.

Elsewhere in the *Patterns of Global Terrorism* report, the State Department noted: "In Brazil, one incident occurred during 2001 that could be characterized as a terrorist incident—an after-hours bombing of a McDonald's restaurant in Rio de Janeiro in October. The incident resulted in property damage but no injuries, and while Brazilian police suspect antiglobalization extremists perpetrated the attack, no arrests were made."[15] The section on terrorist incidents in Ecuador noted that "two McDonald's restaurants were firebombed in April."

The State Department report stated: "The Abu Sayyaf Group (ASG) in the Philippines . . . kidnapped three U.S. citizens and 17 others from a resort in the southern Philippines. Among many others, one U.S. citizen was brutally murdered, and two U.S. citizens and one Filipino remained hostages at year's end." President Bush mentioned this terrorist incident in an August 26, 2002, speech in which he personally thanked Philippine President Gloria Arroyo: "She heard the message, 'Either you're with us, or you're with the enemy,' and she responded. She asked for help. We provided help, but her troops were the ones that got this guy that was running what they call Abu Sayyaf, the person who killed—kidnapped two brave Americans, the Burnhams."[16] The Bush administration invoked the kidnapping of Martin and Gracia Burnham, Christian missionaries, to help justify sending twelve hundred U.S. troops to the Philippines to provide "training" for the Philippine army to fight "Islamic extremists." Martin Burnham was killed (possibly by Filipino troops) in a botched rescue in June 2002; Gracia Burnham was shot in the leg but survived the rescue.[17]

But there was no mention in the State Department terrorist report about the April 16, 2001 incident in which U.S.–financed Peruvian fighter jets shot down a small plane carrying five American civilians, including several Baptist missionaries. Veronica Bowers, a 35-year-old missionary, and her infant daughter, Charity, were killed; her husband, Jim, was badly wounded. Shortly before the killings, a CIA surveillance plane notified Peruvian jets that the Bowerses' plane might be smuggling narcotics.[18] Scores of other unidentified civilian planes had previously been shot down after being suspected of drug offenses under the joint U.S.–Peru program, but none of the other incidents involved Baptist missionaries with contacts in the United States capable of publicizing the killings.[19] The United States provides $100 million a year to bankroll the Peruvian fighter jet intercepts of civilian planes and other antidrug policies.

After the Cessna was blasted out of the sky and crashed in flames, "hundreds of villagers watched as at least one of the air force planes fired at the disabled Cessna and the survivors as they floated in the Amazon River,"[20] the *Orlando Sentinel* noted. When Nazi U-boats rose to the surface in 1943 and machine-gunned the survivors of a merchant marine ship they had torpedoed, Americans rightly considered such conduct a war crime. But when U.S.–funded Peruvian jets commit similar atrocities, it is only another stepping stone to a drug-free America.

The U.S. embassy in Peru initially denied that the U.S. government tracking plane had any role in the shoot-down of the Americans' plane.[21] President Bush quickly labeled the incident a "terrible tragedy" but insisted the U.S. government was blameless: "Our role was to . . . provide information as to tail numbers. Our role was to help countries identify planes that failed to file flight plans. . . . Our role was simply to pass on information."[22] Bush reassured the world: "I want everybody in my country to understand that we weep for the families whose lives have been affected."[23]

The U.S. government busied itself with covering up the killing and blaming the victims (falsely accusing the pilot of failing to file a flight plan with nearby airport authorities).[24] The CIA contract employees—flying in a Pentagon-owned plane—may have failed in last-moment efforts to dissuade the Peruvian jet from shooting down the Cessna because they did not speak Spanish.[25] The automatic shoot-down policy was temporarily suspended but resumed after the war on terrorism distracted public attention from the earlier fiasco. After the killings, the U.S. government strong-armed the Association of Baptists for World Evangelism (ABWE), for whom the Bowers were on their mission. When the ABWE sought compensation for the loss of its plane and for the survivors' medical bills, the government warned them that "nothing would be done for our missionaries unless we agreed to release the U.S. government from responsibility for any payment for losses to our organization," the association reported.[26] The ABWE signed a release, and shortly before Bush traveled to Peru, the government agreed to compensate Jim Bowers. (The White House wanted to settle the issue to avoid bothersome questions about the killings during the official visit.) The Bush administration also issued a statement on the shoot-down in March 2002 with careful wording "stopping just short of an apology," the Associated Press noted.[27] The U.S. government never apologized to Jim Bowers for its role in killing his wife and daughter.[28]

The *Patterns of Global Terrorism* report makes frequent derogatory references to "rebels" or "armed rebels" or "militants." The State Department report listed several cases of rebel attacks on oppressive governments as terrorist incidents:

- On January 29, 2001 "in southern Nigeria, armed militants stormed oil flow stations causing the loss of 40,000 barrels per day, according to press reports. The Ijaw Youths are probably responsible."[29] But the Nigerian army's massacre of hundreds of civilians in October 2001 did not make the list of terrorist incidents.

- On March 8, 2001 in Sudan "armed rebels attacked a village, abducting four NGO relief workers—two Kenyan and two Sudanese—and killing two persons, according to U.S. Embassy and press reports. The Sudanese Government obtained their release after initiating negotiations. The Sudan Peoples Liberation Army (SPLA) is probably responsible." The report does not mention that the Sudanese government is causing a famine, that it is brutally persecuting Christians, that its army is running the largest slave-trading system in the world, and that it is responsible for 2 million fatalities since 1983.

- Several "rebel" attacks occurred in Angola, including a February 18 incident in Cassanguidi in which "rebels ambushed and burned a vehicle, killing two persons and wounding two others. The National Union for the Total Independence of Angola (UNITA) claimed responsibility." At the same time, the Angolan government was carrying out a "scorched Earth" policy in which it burned all the villages in a large part of the country, destroying all the crops, and intentionally drove people into uninhabited regions in order to undermine support for the UNITA forces.[30] The government's policy threatened hundreds of thousands of Angolans with starvation but it did not make the official U.S. list of "significant terrorist incidents." (UNITA forces deserve to be on the terrorist list: They are among the most brutal organizations in the world. President Reagan praised UNITA leader Jonas Savimbi as a "freedom fighter"[31]—even after Savimbi bragged about shooting down a civilian airliner, killing all passengers onboard.)

According to the State Department report, most of the international terrorist attacks that occurred in the world in 2001 (178 out of 346) involved leftist guerrilla attacks on one oil pipeline in Colombia operated jointly by the Occidental Petroleum Corp., a U.S. company based in Los Angeles, and the Colombian government oil company. The report noted that two left-wing terrorist groups "struggled with one another for dominance in the bombing of the Cano-Limon-Covenas oil pipeline—combining for an unprecedented 178 attacks."[32]

But not all pipelines were created equal, and not all pipeline-related violence qualifies as a terrorist incident. In 2001, the International Labor Rights Fund (ILRF), a Washington activist organization, sued Exxon Mobil for its alleged role in atrocities committed along a pipeline it operated in northern Sumatra (co-owned by the Indonesian government oil company). The ILRF, representing 11 local residents who claimed to have been physically abused or had kinfolk killed, sued under the Alien Tort Claims Act and Torture Victims Protection Act. Exxon Mobil bankrolled the Indonesian military forces brought in to "protect" the pipeline. Entire villages were burned to the ground. *Time* reported that local residents "literally line up to tell stories of abuse and murders committed by the troops they call 'Exxon's Army.'"[33] Some plaintiffs alleged that they were tortured by soldiers inside the Exxon Mobil compound. An Indonesian human rights group accused Exxon Mobil of providing bulldozers for digging giant graves for the army's victims.[34] (Exxon Mobil denies all the charges.) Human Rights Watch estimated that more than a thousand locals had been killed or tortured in the long-running conflict with the Indonesian government.[35]

The U.S. government sought to have the lawsuit thrown out of court. State Department chief legal advisor William Taft IV warned the judge that permitting Exxon Mobil to be sued for alleged involvement in slaughtering Indonesians could "risk a potentially serious adverse impact on significant interests of the United States, including interests related directly to the ongoing struggle against international terrorism."[36] The State Department also fretted that a large award against Exxon Mobile "could have decidedly negative consequences for the Indonesian economy" by discouraging foreign investment. (No mention was made of how foreign investment is discouraged by the Indonesian government's genocidal proclivities.) Besides, as the State Department letter noted, a high-ranking Indonesian official formally labeled the lawsuit an "unacceptable act." *Nation* magazine noted that Exxon Mobil was the second largest campaign contributor to Bush and the Republican Party.[37] (Enron took first prize.)

## Private Terrorism vs. Government Killings

Few people dispute that terrorist attacks that kill innocent women, children, and men are an evil. But how does terrorism compare to other evils people face?

According to the State Department *Patterns of Global Terrorism,* 576 Americans were killed by international terrorists between 1980 and 1989, a period during which 4,833 people were killed by international terrorists worldwide.[38] U.S. fatalities from international terrorist attacks in the 1990–2000 period are shown in table 10.1.[39]

Many of the U.S. fatalities from terrorist attacks since 1980 have been military personnel on active duty. The State Department *Patterns of Global Terrorism* noted: "We also consider as acts of terrorism attacks on military installations or on armed military personnel when a state of military hostilities does not exist at the site, such as bombings against U.S. bases."[40] Many foreigners perceive the U.S. military as shoring up oppressive regimes or threatening their security. But as long as the U.S. government has not formally declared that a state of violent hostilities or war exists, attacks on U.S. forces are classified as terrorist actions—regardless of how many local residents the U.S. military may have previously killed.

From 1990 to 2000, a total of 69 American civilians were killed in international terrorist attacks, according to the U.S. State Department.

In most years of the 1990s, Americans were at far greater risk of being gunned down by local, state, and federal law enforcement agents than of being killed by international terrorists. The Prince George's County, Maryland, Police Department killed more Americans in the 1990s than did any terrorist organization in the world. The *Washington Post* noted in 2001: "Since 1990, Prince George's police have shot 122 persons, killing 47. Almost half of those shot were unarmed; many had committed no crime."[41] Prince George's police kill citizens more often than do any other major police department in the country. The Prince George's Police Department ruled that all the shootings were justified, including the following cases: "An unarmed construction worker was shot in the back after he was detained in a fast-food restaurant. An unarmed suspect died in a fusillade of 66 bullets as he tried

Table 10.1

| Year | Total U.S. Dead | U.S. Military | U.S. Civilians | World Dead |
|---|---|---|---|---|
| 1990 | 9 | 0 | 9 | 218 |
| 1991 | 7 | 4 | 3 | 102 |
| 1992 | 2 | 2 | 0 | 93 |
| 1993 | 6 | 0 | 6 | 109 |
| 1994 | 4 | 0 | 4 | 314 |
| 1995 | 12 | 0 | 12 | 165 |
| 1996 | 24 | 19 | 5 | 311 |
| 1997 | 7 | 0 | 7 | 221 |
| 1998 | 12 | 3 | 9 | 741 |
| 1999 | 5 | 0 | 5 | 233 |
| 2000 | 19 | 17 | 2 | 405 |
| TOTAL | 107 | 45 | 62 | 2,912 |

to flee from police in a car. A homeless man was shot when police mistook his portable radio for a gun. And an unarmed man was killed after he pulled off the road to relieve himself."[42] Deaths in police custody are also a problem in Prince George's County. The *Post* noted, "No one knows how many people have died while in the custody of Prince George's officers. Police said they don't keep track of such deaths. By examining autopsy reports and other documents, however, the *Post* was able to identify 12 people who have died in police custody since 1990."[43]

From 1990 through 2000, police in the nation's 50 largest county and police departments shot and killed more than twenty-one hundred people.[44] Many of those killed were in the process of robbing a bank, or a liquor store, or a 7–11, and many others may have been stopped in the process of attacking innocent parties. However, it is likely that many of the shootings might have been considered homicide or manslaughter if the killer had been a private citizen. A 1998 Human Rights Watch report observed, "Police officers engage in unjustified shootings, severe beatings, fatal chokings, and unnecessarily rough physical treatment in cities throughout the United States, while their police superiors, city officials, and even the Justice Department fail to act decisively to restrain or penalize such acts or even to record the full magnitude of the problem."[45] In 1994 Congress passed a law requiring national record-keeping on police shootings. However, neither the Justice Department nor most local police departments have bothered to track such trifles. The *Washington Post* noted: "Law enforcement experts say many of the more than 17,000 [law enforcement] agencies are reluctant to cooperate for fear of drawing outside scrutiny."[46] University of South Carolina professor Geoffrey Alpert observed: "This is a decision in which cop becomes judge, jury and executioner, and we don't know who these officers are, what their decisions entail or the rates, or anything else on a national level."[47]

The number of people killed during the final FBI assault at Waco on April 19, 1993—80—exceeded the total number of American civilians killed in all the international terrorist attacks during the 1990s. Attorney General Janet Reno became a national hero after ordering an attack that began with FBI tanks dousing a private residence with toxic, flammable gas for six hours. After the building burst into flames, the FBI on-scene commander stopped fire trucks from approaching to douse the inferno.[48] If the same attack had been carried out by a group of Muslims fanatics, Waco would have been classified as one of the worst terrorist incidents in American history.

According to the U.S. State Department, between 1980 and 2000, 7,745 people were killed in international terrorist incidents. During the same period, governments around the globe killed more than 10 million people. Some of the worst carnage occurred in the following cases:

- Indonesia, 1975–present: More than a quarter million people on East Timor perished after the Indonesian army invaded to seize the territory.
- Afghanistan, 1979–1989: Up to two million Afghans died in the Soviet invasion of Afghanistan and the subsequent struggle, thanks in part to the Soviets' indiscriminate bombing and massacres of villages.[49]
- Ethiopia, 1980s: More than 1.5 million Ethiopians died as a result of government attacks and the systematic destruction of the agricultural system, including a brutal resettlement program financed in part by the World Bank. According to the French relief group Doctors without Borders, the government's forced resettlement program in 1985 caused the death of 100,000 Ethiopians—more than the number of people who died from the famine that year.[50] One dissident World Bank official described the resettlement program as "genocide with a human face."[51] And the government simultaneously carried out a "villagization" program—seeking to force Ethiopia's 33 million rural citizens (75 percent of the total population) to abandon their private land and move to a government-controlled village, complete with armed guards and watchtowers.
- Mozambique, 1975–1992: Between 350,000 and 600,000 people were killed by the Marxist government and a rebel group during a long-running civil war.[52]
- Rwanda-Burundi, 1994–present: More than one million people were killed by government forces and rampaging paramilitaries carrying out ethnic cleansing campaigns.[53]
- North Korea, 1992–present: The communist government effectively destroyed the agriculture system, prohibiting private farming and blocking the import of sufficient food to compensate for the failure of state farms. An estimated 3 million Koreans have died as a result of such policies. The North Korean government received ample foreign aid in this period but devoted the windfall to building nuclear bombs rather than preserving the populace.
- Sudan, 1983–present: the government's brutal civil war and forced starvation policies have cost more than two million people their lives in the past two decades.
- The Congo, 1998–2003: Between 3 million and 4.7 million people have been killed in the Congo, by seven foreign armies and their local paramilitary allies, according to an April 2003 estimate by the International Rescue Committee. Most of the fatalities have been the result of starvation and the proliferation of disease that has followed the war's chaos.[54]

The carnage in recent decades is typical of government atrocities in the modern era. Professor R. J. Rummel, in his book *Death by Government,* declared: "Almost 170 million men, women, and children have been shot, beaten, tortured, knifed, burned, starved, frozen, crushed, or worked to death; buried alive, drowned, hung, bombed, or killed in any other of the myriad ways governments have inflicted death on unarmed, helpless citizens and foreigners" during the twentieth century.[55] Professor Irving Horowitz, in a 1989 essay titled "Counting Bodies: The Dismal Science of Authorized Terror," observed, "In raw numerical terms, the source of the killing in this century tells the story: governments have been directly responsible for the deaths of roughly 120 million people, while war (both international and civil) accounts for thirty-five million deaths. In other words, in this century, really in the last forty-five years, over three-and-a-half times more people have been killed by their own governments than by opposing states."[56]

Year in and year out, governments kill at least a hundred times as many people as do international terrorists. The attacks on 9/11 were probably the only time that the number of people killed by international terrorists even approached 1 percent of the number of people killed by governments. The killing ratio of international terrorists versus governments indicates the relative level of danger citizens face. The fact that governments kill more people than terrorists does not make terrorist killers any less loathsome. The question is whether the evil of the terrorists should eclipse the far greater danger of government carnage.

While the U.S. government trumpets individual terrorist incidents and hypes its annual report on global terrorism, it makes far less effort to track or report the number of government atrocities that occur around the globe. Consider how the State Department *Country Reports on Human Rights Practices,* the annual compilation of thumbnail sketches of misdeeds of nations, would look if it had the same level of detail of "significant incidents" that the *Patterns of Global Terrorism* report contained. The *Country Reports* would be thousands of pages long—and instead of a list of pipe bomb explosions, there would be endless details of senseless murders, torture, and floggings, punctuated by occasional massacres, politically caused famines, and "extra-judicial" killings.

## Intentions *Über Alles:* Blameless Killings

At a Washington prayer breakfast on February 7, 2002 President Bush declared: "Some acts and choices in this world have eternal consequences. It is always and everywhere wrong to target and kill the innocent."[57] In a White House dinner speech on June 10, 2002 Bush declared, "We believe targeting innocent civilians for murder is always and everywhere wrong."[58] In a radio address on November 10, 2001, Bush announced: "No political cause can justify the deliberate murder of civilians. There is no such thing as a good terrorist."[59] President Reagan offered a similar concept of terrorism in 1986: "Terrorists intentionally kill or maim unarmed civilians, often women and children, often third parties who are not in any way part of a dictatorial regime."[60]

By the Bush standard, however, as long as a government does not intentionally, deliberately target civilians, its killings are practically blameless. This notion has long guided the actions of the U.S. government. For instance, the U.S. military, with a little help from NATO allies, killed 500 civilians in Serbia during the 78-day bombing campaign in 1999, according to Human Rights Watch.[61] (The Serbian government stated that 2000 civilians were killed.) The U.S. government insisted that it was blameless in all fatalities because, as it repeatedly declared, it was not U.S. policy to target civilians.

The *Los Angeles Times* detailed some of the "glitches" that occurred during attacks by U.S. and British war planes:

- April 5 [1999]—An attack on a residential area in the mining town of Aleksinac kills 17 people.
- April 12—NATO missiles striking a railroad bridge near the Serbian town of Grdelica hit a passenger train, killing 17.
- April 14—75 ethnic Albanian refugees die in an attack on a convoy near Djakovica.
- April 27—A missile strike in the Serbian town of Surdulica kills at least 20 civilians.
- May 1—A missile hits a bus crossing a bridge north of Pristina, killing 47.
- May 7—A cluster bomb attack damages a marketplace and the grounds of a hospital in Nis, killing at least 15.
- May 8—Fighter pilots using outdated maps attack the Chinese Embassy in Belgrade, killing three journalists and injuring 20 other people.
- May 13—87 ethnic Albanian refugees are killed and more than 100 injured in a late-night NATO bombing of a Kosovo village, Korisa.
- May 21—NATO bombs a Kosovo jail, killing at least 19 people and injuring scores.
- May 31—NATO missiles slam into a bridge crowded with market-goers and cars in central Serbia, killing at least nine people and wounding 28.[62]

NATO dropped more than three hundred thousand cluster bomblets on Serbia.[63] Cluster bombs are antipersonnel devices designed to be scattered across enemy troop formations. Cluster bombs have a high percentage of duds; up to twenty-six thousand unexploded bombs were left scattered across the cities and countryside of Serbia at the war's end.[64] As a 2002 *Arizona Law Review* article noted, "Tragically, dud cluster bombs appear to have a special allure for children. The BLU-97B, for example, bright yellow, the size of a soda can, with a small parachute on the top, looks like a high tech toy. A high percentage of civilians killed or maimed by dud cluster bombs are boys and girls who pick the duds up to play with."[65] Bombs can be detonated simply by walking near them.

If Serbian terrorists had blown up hospitals, bridges, and old folks' homes in the United States at the same rate that NATO hit such sites in Yugoslavia, Americans would have considered the Serbs the worst terrorists in American history (prior to 9/11). While Slobodan Milosevic was a corrupt, brutal ruler, that did not entitle the U.S. government to kill hundreds of randomly selected Serbs. Barbara Ehrenreich, author of *Blood Rites: Origins and History of the Passions of War,* observed: "The NATO assault has been conducted as though we're attacking just one individual, not an entire population. It's the one-man theory of the nation-state. And its effect is to eliminate both the psychological impact of nationalism and the guilt produced by civilian casualities since civilians don't fully exist under this theory."[66] Rather than dead Serbian human beings, there were simply collateral babies, collateral mothers, and collateral geezers who met an unfortunate but morally irrelevant fate.

## The Great Exemption

How many people is a government allowed to accidentally kill?

In the same way that politicians are rarely held responsible for their lies, governments are rarely held responsible for their killings. In order to compare the actions of terrorists and governments, it is important to understand how governments avoid blame for their own killings.

Government is the only institution that has the privilege of investigating and judging its own killings. It is routine for governments to block external or independent investigations of its actions. Government killings are almost never considered to be murders because government officials have the final word in labeling a shooting as accidental or justified. Even when a government "self-investigation" report is openly derided as a "whitewash"—as the *New York Times* characterized the first Justice Department report on Waco[67]—the report's conclusions about the government's innocence are still repeated far and wide.

Intentions are the great exonerator of government action. Governments almost always conclude that the motives of its own agents are exculpatory, regardless of how many people they killed. But a focus on motive as the prime determinant of the morality of action is inherently flawed when judging State actions because politicians and governments routinely misrepresent their motives. It is far easier to count the dead than to determine the thoughts in the minds of the killers.

The U.S. government rarely holds foreign governments culpable for their wrongful killings. This explains the perpetuation of U.S. foreign and military aid to governments the State Department labels as torturers or mass killers. The paragraphs of watered-down prose in the State Department's annual *Country Reports on Human Rights* are vastly outweighed by the guns, rocket launchers, and money the U.S. government delivers to oppressive regimes. And the more strategic value a foreign nation has to the United States, the higher percentage of its subjects it is entitled to kill without effective U.S. protest.

What a government says is far more important than how many people it kills. "Under color of law" is a phrase that magically transforms senseless violence into public service. All that is necessary for a government killing to become blameless is for the government to announce—preferably before the funeral or memorial service—is that the killing was accidental. For many Statists, the only "wrongful government killing" is when a government agent shoots someone different than who he was aiming at.

The only governments that do not possess an automatic license to kill are those that the United States formally labels as part of an Axis of Evil. Once a government is designated a member of the Axis of Evil, it automatically forfeits all the privileges and immunities to which governments are naturally entitled.

There are honest mistakes by government agents seeking to protect public safety. Every killing by a government agent is not the equivalent of murder or a terrorist act. But if there is a long pattern of such killings—if the pretexts for the killings become more implausible over the years, and the government almost never punishes any of its own agents for killing innocent people—then government killings become no better than terrorist attacks.

*Any action done by private citizens that would be considered terrorism should also be considered terrorism if done by government agents.* If a government persistently slaughters innocent civilians, then it is morally equivalent to evil gangs that blow up buses and airplanes. This simple standard invalidates much of the current thinking on terrorism. A consistent definition of terrorism will not end the terrorist threat or suddenly make Al Qaeda operatives around the world turn themselves in and plead for mercy. Nor will it lessen the grief of the survivors and relatives of those slain by senseless violence. But it will help citizens better understand the danger of unleashing government agents to scourge terrorists—and anyone else politicians or bureaucrats decide needs whacking.

## Conclusion

Having a "State action" exemption to the concept of terrorism is like having a "mass murder exemption" in the homicide statute. The U.S. definition of terrorism is pure political expediency, masquerading as a lofty statement of principle. President Bush offers a parody of political morality at the same time that the United States claims to be pristine.

The denunciation of terrorism is often an exercise in demonology—converting a semantic distinction into a pretext for denying the nature of government or the reality of oppression. Bush first insists that this war on terrorism is a battle of good versus evil—and then defines evil in a way that ignores much of the worst depravity. One grave danger in letting politicians define evil is that they will exempt their own crimes from any onus. Good intentions do not trump body counts.

Terrorists cannot compete with governments when it comes to persistently wreaking mass carnage. By raising terrorist attacks to the pinnacle of political evil, the war on terrorism implicitly sanctifies whatever tactics governments use in the name of repressing terrorism. Exaggerating the risk from terrorists puts people at greater risk of destruction from their political overlords. Unleashing governments to fight terrorists is like opening the lion cages at the zoo in hopes that the lions will devour some pesky squirrels. If the squirrels have rabies, they need to be exterminated. But there are better ways to suppress such threats.

By treating terrorism as the supreme evil, and insisting that governments can never be guilty of terrorism, the Bush administration effectively makes the crimes of most governments morally negligible. Not only does the Bush administration put government on a pedestal—it effectively says that any corpses beneath the pedestal don't exist—or are at least unworthy of notice. Killings by governments are statistics, not tragedies—and governments are entitled to manipulate the statistics to minimize the outrage.

The official U.S. doctrine that governments cannot be terrorists has fueled the righteousness of American foreign policy. The notion that "governments cannot terrorize" has perhaps done more than anything else to prevent Americans from understanding how their government is perceived in many parts of the world.

The U.S. government terrorism definition is also the key to the Bush administration notion that the war on terrorism is automatically a war for freedom. Without the "State-exempt" concept of terrorism, fighting terrorism would, in most parts of the world, have little or nothing to do with defending freedom. If an honest, even-handed definition of terrorism is accepted, many governments in the Bush "freedom-loving coalition" will become guilty of inflicting more terrorism than they have prevented.

## CHAPTER ELEVEN

# The Drugs-Terrorism Charade

When we fight drugs, we fight the war on terror.

—*President George W. Bush, February 12, 2002*[1]

Terrorism and drugs go together like rats and the plague. . . . They thrive in the same conditions, and they feed off of each other.

—*Attorney General John Ashcroft, March 19, 2002*[2]

While President Bush insisted that no CIA or FBI agent or chieftain was to blame for the hijackers' success on 9/11, the president did find 28 million culprits: any American who used any illicit drug. It did not matter whether it was homegrown marijuana or an extra codeine pill pocketed from a spouse's prescription. Every American drug law violator was, by presidential fiat, personally culpable not only for Al Qaeda but also for the actions of every other terrorist group on Earth.

The Bush administration invoked the 9/11 attacks to sanctify the war on drugs. Drug Czar John Walters openly declared that the war against terrorism could revitalize the war on drugs.[3] Yet, at the same time that Bush and his appointees invoke terrorist threats to justify new drug crackdowns on Americans, the administration's actions helped spark an explosion in opium production. And while the United States was vigorously denouncing Saddam Hussein on suspicion of possessing weapons of mass destruction, it was conducting a chemical warfare campaign that is wreaking havoc in Colombia.

# The Bush Opium Boom?

The single biggest one-year increase in opium production in world history probably occurred in 2002. After the Bush administration toppled the Taliban regime, opium production in Afghanistan soared from 185 tons in 2001 to 3,700 tons in 2002. Afghanistan has historically produced more than two-thirds of the world's opium supply.

In the late 1990s the Taliban regime profited from a 10 percent tax on the opium (a lower tax rate than cigarettes face in America). The U.S. government and other governments heavily pressured the Taliban to suppress opium production. On July 28, 2000 Taliban leader Mullah Muhammad Omar banned any poppy growing in Afghanistan because it was henceforth to be considered un-Islamic.[4]

The Taliban were far more effective drug warriors than their American counterparts. The Taliban achieved the end of opium production "without the usual multimillion-dollar aid packages that finance police raids, aerial surveillance and crop subsidies for farmers," the *New York Times* noted.[5] The opium ban was enforced by the Department for the Promotion of Virtue and Prevention of Vice. Abdul Hamid Akhundzada, the director of the opium ban, explained: "We used a soft approach. When there were violations, we plowed the fields. At most, violators spent a few days in jail, until they paid for the plowing."[6] One farmer explained: "No one dared disobey. If they catch you, they blacken your face and march you through the bazaars with a string of poppies around your neck."[7] The Taliban regime was notorious for public executions and inflicting death sentences as casually as other governments wrote parking tickets.

On May 17, 2001 Powell announced a package of $43 million in humanitarian assistance for Afghanistan to be delivered through the United Nations agencies and nongovernmental organizations. Powell said: "We will continue to look for ways to provide more assistance for Afghans including those farmers who have felt the impact of the ban on poppy cultivation, a decision by the Taliban we welcome."[8]

Five days later *Los Angeles Times* columnist Robert Scheer bashed the Bush administration for its "recent gift of $43 million to the Taliban rulers of Afghanistan, the most virulent anti-American violators of human rights in the world today." Scheer declared that the aid made the United States "the main sponsor of the Taliban" and that "the Bush administration is cozying up to the Taliban regime."[9] Scheer's denunciation of the aid echoed widely throughout American editorial pages.

A week later, the *Los Angeles Times* published an indignant response from Alan Eastham, acting Assistant Secretary of State: "We do not support the Taliban and never have. . . . Scheer apparently bases his claim on the fact that the U.S. is providing humanitarian assistance to Afghans. U.S. aid goes to all parts of Afghanistan and is distributed through the World Food Program and other reputable organizations directly to needy Afghans. The Taliban is not involved in any stage of this process, which cannot be seen in any way as support for this group."[10] At the time of Powell's announcement, the Taliban government was under a UN arms embargo and other sanctions for its failure to deliver Osama bin Laden for prosecution for his role in numerous bombings, including the attacks on the U.S. embassies in Africa in 1998.

Reasonable people would probably agree that sending food aid via a third party to a nation with millions facing starvation was worth the risk that some aid might fall into devious hands. However, by the Bush administration's own standards, it was guilty of aiding the Taliban. Customs Service chief Robert Bonner in December 2002 justified federal felony charges against people who sent money back to their starving relatives in Iraq because "any funds that go to Iraq help support that regime."[11] If the U.S. government applied to itself the standard it uses to prosecute Americans in the money transfer cases, it would be obliged to indict every U.S. government official involved with the decision to commit $43 million in aid to Afghanistan when the Taliban was still in power.

The opium ban devastated Afghan farmers who were already struggling from a multiyear drought. (Poppy is one of the few crops that thrives despite minimal rainfall.) Steven Casteel of the Drug Enforcement Administration admitted, "The bad side of the ban is that it's bringing their country—or certain regions of their country—to economic ruin."[12] The Associated Press noted in June 2001: "The lack of foreign help for desperate former poppy farmers has strained relations between the Taliban and the international aid community. It may also help explain some of the militia's recent mischief, including the destruction of ancient Buddha statues and an order to force Hindus to wear yellow labels on their shirts to distinguish them from Muslims."[13]

On August 1, 2001 UN Secretary-General Kofi Annan announced that Afghanistan had achieved "most impressive" results—"the almost total disappearance of the opium poppy in areas controlled by the Taliban."[14] Bernard Frahi, director of the UN Drug Control Program, commented: "If this had happened in Colombia, where the U.S. is spending billions of dollars and reducing drug cultivation by maybe five per cent, this would have gotten the Nobel Prize. But because it's the Taliban, there's a different reaction."[15] U.S. Assistant Secretary of State Christina Rocca announced that the United States would donate

$1.5 million to UN efforts to aid former poppy growers and declared: "We wel-
come the Taliban's enforcement of the ban and hope it will be sustained."[16] On
September 2, 2001 Mullah Omar announced that Afghan farmers would be
prohibited from growing poppy for a second straight year—proving that the
previous year ban was not a one time fluke.[17] (Some American officials suspected the Taliban had banned poppy growing solely to boost the value of the
surplus opium stocks being held in Afghanistan.)

Nine days later, Al Qaeda terrorists struck. The Taliban had been sheltering Al
Qaeda for several years and the U.S. government quickly made it clear the Taliban
regime would be held accountable for the actions of its guest, Osama bin Laden.

As American forces surged into Afghanistan, President Bush made it stark
that suppressing heroin trafficking was a top priority. Bush proclaimed on November 15, 2001: "The Taliban Government and Al Qaida—the evil ones—use
heroin trafficking in order to fund their murder. And one of our objectives is to
make sure that Afghanistan is never used for that purpose again."[18]

By the end of 2001 the Taliban regime was shattered, with its top officials
either captured, dead, or on the run. The United States installed Hamid Karzai
as the head of an interim government. After Karzai announced in early 2002
that poppy growing would continue to be banned, the United Nations Office
of Drug Control and Crime Prevention issued a press release praising him and
stressing the need for more foreign aid to help the new Afghan government "establish effective law enforcement capacities and specifically a drug control commission in Kabul with drug control units in key provinces."[19]

In April 2002 the Karzai government offered farmers up to $600 an acre not
to plant poppy. Many farmers who accepted the government proposal were de-
frauded. Instead of cash, they were given a government voucher that was often
very difficult to redeem.[20] In other cases, farmers acceded to government demands to destroy their crops but were never paid anything—not even a
voucher.[21] One farmer in the southern Helmand province swore: "We will never
believe the government again."[22]

The Karzai government also promoted the poppy ban by shooting farmers.
Reuters reported that "several dozen opium farmers were killed in a battle with
government forces in the southern province of Helmand."[23] The British
*Guardian* reported that "security forces fired on a rally of 2,000 farmers that was
allegedly turning into a riot. Eight farmers were killed and 16 injured."[24] The
Karzai government sent out a few agents to destroy opium fields but desisted
after receiving heavy gunfire from tribesmen.[25]

U.S. Drug Czar John Walters announced on February 26, 2002: "As
Afghanistan's interim government rebuilds the country, the United States will

work to ensure that the drug trade will never again finance regional instability or international terrorism."[26] As signs grew that Afghan farmers would have a bumper opium harvest, Bush administration officials scrambled to reassure Congress that a solution was imminent. Undersecretary of State Alan Larson, testifying to Congress on March 14, 2002, revealed that the U.S. government had provided the Afghan government with a shipment of textbooks with "two cartoons" on the book covers "and what it says on it is one guy's eating fruits, he's healthy, the other guy is hooked on heroin, on the back, and he looks in pretty terrible condition. That will be on 9.7 million textbooks for every school child." Larson did concede: "I'm not suggesting that's going to end the opium trade." Larson added: "Recognizing that this is a crop that's going to be harvested within a couple of months, we're going to want to move very, very quickly." At the same hearing, Agency for International Development chief Andrew Natsios revealed: "We'll be doing a $3 million crop substitution program beginning next week in the Helman Valley in the south, which is one of the principal poppy growing areas."[27]

The new Afghan government and international agencies were grossly incompetent at even attempting to fill the void they sought to create by outlawing the drug trade. Drug dealers are the Afghan equivalent of the Farmers Home Administration. Tom Brown, an American agricultural expert with the Central Asia Development Group, observed: "The opium buyers are the only people encouraging these farmers to grow anything."[28] Lakhdar Brahimi, the UN special representative to Afghanistan, noted that for Afghan farmers "the poppy offers a return on investment that is 38 times that of wheat."[29]

Strife occurred within the Pentagon over whether U.S. military forces should launch a poppy eradication campaign, perhaps by using heavily armored airplanes to douse thousands of acres with herbicides.[30] Fumigation advocates warned that the poppy harvest would provide windfalls to Al Qaeda or Taliban remnants. But the U.S. military prudently decided not to go into the poppy-stomping business. Yet, if a DEA agent came across some California hippie growing acres of poppy for opium production, the agency would hold a four star press conference, seek to send the farmer to prison for life, and award bonuses and promotions both to the DEA agent and his supervisor.

At the same time Afghan opium output jumped 2,000%, President Bush proudly announced a goal of reducing Americans' consumption of illicit drugs by 25% over the next five years.[31] The rout of the Taliban may have smitten any hope of permanently reducing Afghan opium output. By late 2002 United Nations officials were warning that it would take a decade to eradicate Afghan opium production.

The resurgence of opium production in 2002 may have done more than for-eign aid to prevent starvation in Afghanistan. Many foreign countries, including the United States, effectively defaulted on their pledges to provide prompt, mas-sive aid to Afghanistan after the fall of the Taliban. The United Nations estimated that opium generated $1.2 billion for Afghans in 2002—more than the total in-ternational aid Afghans received that year.[32] The vast majority of the opium money ends up in private pockets, while much of the international aid goes for setting up new government bureaucracies, fattening American consultants, and hiring enforcement agents to take the place of the Taliban's God Squad.

Bush administration officials scrambled to explain away the Great Poppy Revival. In January 2003 Drug Enforcement Agency chief Asa Hutchinson tes-tified: "We are seeing poppy production grow, to our regret, to the same levels prior to the dismantling of the Taliban."[33] In reality, production was astronom-ically higher than it was before the United States ousted the Taliban. Hutchin-son also asserted that "eradication has been moderately successful."[34] Afghan farmers told Western journalists that the eradication efforts were little more than a make-work project that resulted in destroying a minuscule percentage of plants. If Hutchinson considers the 2002 crackdown "moderately successful," what would it take for DEA to concede failure—the planting of every acre in Afghanistan with poppy? Hutchinson explained: "Enforcement is where the gap is."[35] At a time when Karzai's grip appeared to be limited to the city limits of Kabul, U.S. drug warriors wanted to send the puppet government on an anti-poppy suicide mission—simply to provide themselves with political cover when they discuss the Afghan drug debacle.

Since the U.S. invasion in late 2001, the production of opium may have in-creased faster than anything else in Afghanistan. (The 2003 opium harvest was forecast to exceed 6,000 tons.)[36] If only the same incentives could be created for "order" and "justice" that exist for poppy growing, many of Afghanistan's prob-lems would be solved.

## Colombia Capers

Colombia has long been a top target for U.S. drug warriors. The United States greatly expanded its campaign to spray herbicides on coca plants in Colombia in the years before Bush took office. Coca production surged despite the spray-ing—which proved that even more spraying would solve the problem. The Bush administration adopted the Clinton administration strategy and also began pro-viding military aid to the Colombian government specifically to fight leftist guerillas. The Bush administration effectively relabeled the Colombian civil war as an international terrorist problem.

The U.S. blanket spraying of herbicides has harmed the health of many people. Colombians complained to the United Nations Commission of Human Rights that U.S. spraying was causing "gastrointestinal disorders (e.g., severe bleeding, nausea and vomiting), testicular inflammation, high fevers, dizziness, respiratory ailments, skin rashes and severe eye irritation."[37] Eduardo Cifuentes, the chief human rights official in the Colombian government, urged in October 2002 that the spraying be stopped because it was destroying legal crops, leaving peasants sick with skin and respiratory problems, and polluting rivers and other water supplies.[38] Hundreds of farmers claimed that their legal crops have been ruined by the spraying, but no government official bothered to come out and investigate their claims.[39] The head of one Colombian farmers association complained: "The animals have died from the poison. The government of the United States has to put its hand over its heart. They are fumigating us like rats."[40] A spokesman for a group of Colombian governors who visited the United States in 2002 to plead for an end to spraying commented that the program "doesn't really take into account the human being. All it cares about are satellite pictures."[41]

Some congressmen are pushing to intensify the war by using a new mycoherbicide (a plant-killing fungus also known as Agent Green) that would destroy almost all plants in a targeted area for a long period. U.S. Ambassador to Colombia Anne Patterson informed Congress on December 12, 2002: "My understanding is that [the mycoherbicide] was tested some years back, a couple of years ago and proven to be effective in Colombia."[42] Author Jeffrey St. Clair, in a December 2002 article entitled "How Dr. Mengele Might Wage the Drug War Biowarfare in the Andes,"[43] noted:

Agent Green is a genetically engineered pathogenic fungi, conjured up by the U.S. Department of Agriculture's experiment station in Beltsville, Maryland. It is now being produced with U.S. funds by Ag/Bio Company, a private lab in Bozeman, Montana and at a former Soviet bioweapons factory in Tashkent, Uzbekistan. The labs are brewing up two types of killer fungi. . . . The problem is that both fungi are indiscriminate killers, posing threats to human health and to non-target species. Add to this the fact that when sprayed from airplanes and helicopters, Agent Green will be carried by winds and inevitably drift over coffee plantations, fields, farms, villages, and water supplies. Agent Green also threatens the ecology of the Colombian rainforest, one of the most biologically diverse on the planet.[44]

Congress decreed that the U.S. government could not disburse antidrug aid to Colombia unless the U.S. State Department first annually certified that the government of Colombia was making human rights progress. On September 10, 2001 Secretary of State Powell formally designated the right-wing paramilitary United Self-Defense Forces of Colombia, commonly known as the AUC, as a terrorist organization, declaring: "Last year, AUC members reportedly committed at least 75 massacres that resulted in the deaths of hundreds of civilians."[45] Even though the Colombian military and the AUC routinely work in cahoots, the State Department officially certified Colombia's human rights progress in May 2002.[46] Human Rights Watch's Jose Miguel Vivanco observed: "The administration is proposing millions of dollars in counter-terrorism aid to Colombia even as the Colombian military refuses to break ties with a designated terrorist group."[47]

(The Bush administration's nonchalance over the U.S. bankrolling of Colombian abuses continues a venerable tradition. In 1997, Rep. Dennis Hastert [R-Ill.], who was then chairman of Speaker Newt Gingrich's Task Force for a Drug-Free America, visited Colombia and assured Colombian military leaders that he would try to "remove conditions on [U.S. foreign] assistance" to the military. Hastert whined to the generals that "leftist-dominated" U.S. Congresses had "used human rights as an excuse to aid the left in other countries."[48] A 1997 Amnesty International report on Colombia noted: "More than 1,000 civilians were extrajudicially executed by the security forces and paramilitary groups operating with [Colombian officials'] support or acquiescence. . . . More than 120 people 'disappeared' after detention by the armed forces or paramilitary groups."[49])

The Bush administration flogged the link between drugs and terrorism in a series of 2002 indictments of Colombian drug traffickers. When Attorney General John Ashcroft announced drug charges against two AUC leaders on September 24, 2002, he declared: "Today we see more clearly than ever the interdependence between terrorists that threaten American lives and the illegal drugs that threaten America's potential. As today's indictment reminds us, the lawlessness that breeds terrorism is also a fertile ground for the drug-trafficking that supports terrorism. To surrender to either of these threats is to surrender to both of them. We will not surrender."[50]

When Ashcroft announced indictments of three leaders of the Revolutionary Armed Forces of Colombia, known by its Spanish language acronym, FARC, on drug trafficking and other charges on November 13, 2002, he declared: "The war on terrorism has been joined with the war on illegal drug use. . . . Today marks another significant milestone in the war against terrorism and drug trafficking in the Americas."[51] FBI chief Robert Mueller announced that the indictments "represent the continuing commitment of the FBI to fully investigate and to bring to justice terrorists throughout the world who harm citizens of the United States."[52] DEA chief Hutchinson proclaimed: "We have learned, and we have demonstrated, that drug traffickers and terrorists work out of the same jungle; they plan in the same cave and they train in the same desert."[53]

The Colombian organizations account for the majority of "terrorism" supposedly financed by American drug users, according to the U.S. government estimates. But the Colombian groups are not international terrorist groups of the same ilk as Al Qaeda. They are simply factions in a grisly 40-year-old civil war. Some of the Colombian organizations wreak havoc in Medellin or Bogota but they pose no threat to Fargo, Boise, or Yazoo, Mississippi. A *Philadelphia Inquirer* analysis noted: "Washington is going after these groups under its new policy of opposing anybody it considers 'terrorists,' even though Colombian outlaws attack only inside their country, have no known ties to outside terrorists, and rarely single out Americans in their bombings and extortion rackets."[54]

Yet, the Bush administration was never at a loss for reasons why Americans should dread the Colombian terrorist groups. Administration officials fretted in early 2002 that Colombian guerillas were using crude homemade mortars "to bombard targets with unconventional materials, including excrement. Used that way, they can spread contagion, and become a kind of cheap and frightening biological weapon," the *Los Angeles Times* reported.[55] Bush administration officials invoked the "poop shoots" to escalate U.S. military involvement in the conflict. This could set a precedent to justify sending in U.S. Marines any time some group of hooligans splatters crap on the walls of some Third World government building.

Some Bush administration statements linking drugs and terrorists are creative to a fault. In 2001, the International Labor Rights Fund filed a lawsuit in federal court claiming that U.S. government drug spraying had destroyed the crops and harmed the health of up to ten thousand Ecuadorans living near the border with Colombia. (The government of Ecuador in April 2003 formally requested that Colombia cease spraying within six miles of the border because of the damage to Ecuadorian food crops.)[56] The United States sought to have the lawsuit dismissed because it could undermine the war on terrorism. Assistant Secretary of State Rand Beers, the chief of the Bureau of International Narcotics and Law Enforcement, submitted a sworn statement to a federal court in late 2001 asserting a link between FARC and Osama bin Laden: "It is believed that FARC terrorists have received training in Al Qaida terrorist camps in Afghanistan."[57] Beers warned: "Any disruption through this litigation of the aerial eradication of illicit drug crops in Colombia will undermine national security by depriving the United States of a key weapon in its arsenal for stemming the flow of illicit narcotics into this country and by allowing international terrorist organizations in

Colombia to continue to reap huge profits from drug trafficking with which they will target U.S. interests and American lives."[58]

However, as the court case progressed, a glitch arose: The State Department could not find a shred of evidence to support the link. A top federal law enforcement official told United Press International: "That statement is totally from left field. I don't know where Beers is getting that. We have never had any indication that FARC guys have ever gone to Afghanistan."[59] In August 2002 Beers notified the federal judge that he was revoking his assertion: "At the time it [the statement which he swore] was put before me in November, I had received some indications that it was possible."[60] This is the "standard of proof" the Bush administration uses before making sworn assertions of links between terrorist groups: merely that some high-ranking officials "receive[d] some indications that it was possible." Beers's renunciation indicates he felt no personal responsibility for his statement; instead, it was merely something that "was put before me" which he perchance happened to sign. Beers's declaration could have prevented thousands of foreigners from achieving recompense from damage they claimed to have suffered from the actions of the U.S. government. Terry Collingsworth, a lawyer for the International Labor Rights Fund, commented: "They are so desperate to keep this suit away from a jury that they'll say anything to convince the judge it's related to terrorism."[61]

## Joint-and-Several Liability for All Potheads

Is it fair to hold George W. Bush personally responsible for perhaps the biggest annual increase in opium output in history? Probably not.

Unless one chooses to reason like the Bush administration.

Three months after the terrorist attacks, in a speech to antidrug groups in Washington, President Bush announced: "It's so important for Americans to know that the traffic in drugs finances the work of terror, sustaining terrorists, that terrorists use drug profits to fund their cells to commit acts of murder. If you quit drugs, you join the fight against terror in America."[62]

Seven weeks later, the White House Office of National Drug Control Policy spent three million dollars for two television ads to appear during the Super Bowl. One ad asked viewers: "Where do terrorists get their money?" The answer: "If you buy drugs, some of it might come from you." Drug users were portrayed as terrorist financiers—practically the moral equivalent of the hijackers who destroyed the World Trade Center towers. Cameos showed young people confessing what their illicit drug purchases had accomplished:

Teen #1: I helped murder families in Colombia.
Teen #2: I helped the bomber get a fake passport.
Teen #3: I helped kill a judge.
Teen #4: I helped blow up buildings.

The ad purported to show the different costs that go into a drug smugglers' operation. One item that flashed briefly on the screen was $3,000 for bribes. The ad did not mention who was being bribed—whether it was the U.S. Coast Guard, or the Customs Service, or perhaps foreign government officials. The Drug Czar's office condemned drug users for financing bribes—but said nothing about the G-men who collect the hush money. The ad also flashed an item "boxcutters: $2"—encouraging viewers to wrongly presume that the 9/11 hijackers relied on drug financing.

Drug czar Walters responded to criticism about the ads' accuracy: "There's really one outcome that matters. Do the ads contribute to a drop in drug use? That's all I care about and all the president cares about."[63] Yet, an Office of Management of Budget analysis released in early 2003 observed that "there is no evidence of direct effect on youth behavior" from the antidrug ads.[64] On April 1, 2003 the drug czar's office canceled the terrorist ad campaign after research proved the ads failed to deter youth drug abuse.[65]

On February 12, 2002 President Bush announced: "If you're buying illegal drugs in America, it is *likely* that money is going to end up in the hands of terrorist organizations. . . . When we fight drugs, we fight the war on terror."[66] Walters, appearing at a White House press briefing the same day as Bush's declaration, was badgered about the president's assertion:

Reporter: But in terms of a percentage of overall drug trade, what percentage of the money goes to terrorists, to put it in perspective? . . . I mean, is it a penny on a dollar, is it a penny on $1,000, or is it a dime on a dollar?

Mr. Walters: I think the truth is, since we don't know exactly the budgets of all the terrorist organizations, and we don't know the—they don't have to submit their budget to the White House press corps. But of the— the Americans spend, we estimate, $66 billion on drugs. We know that hundreds of millions of those dollars go to organizations that have been identified as terrorist and drug-related. I can't tell you what percentage because that would require a level of knowledge we don't have.[67]

Walters revealed the magic wand with which the Bush administration linked every narcotics violation in the nation to terrorism: "So while there certainly [is] some drug production that takes place only in the United States, all drug production has the component of criminal activity with it."[68] And since every criminal is a potential terrorist, every drug user is a terrorist financier.

The White House drug czar's website, www.theantidrug.com, announced plans to capitalize on 9/11: "From this tragedy we must re-energize efforts to prevent drug use. . . . The September 11 terrorist attack deeply touched the emotions of Americans. Connecting terrorism to drug trafficking also is a subject that has great emotional impact."

The website declared: "We must recognize that when money goes from the pocket of an American to buy drugs it could end up financing unspeakable crimes around the world." But, as the "License for Tyranny" chapter of this book shows, the same is true when money goes from the pocket of an American to pay federal taxes, since the U.S. government bankrolls some of the world's most oppressive regimes.

The DEA opened a new exhibit at its headquarters museum titled "Target America" just before the first anniversary of the attacks. A large hunk of twisted metal wreckage recovered from Ground Zero at the World Trade Center is the exhibit's centerpiece. Attorney General Ashcroft declared at the opening of the exhibit: "Law enforcement has long known about the strong linkages between terrorism and drug trafficking. And September 11th made that awareness available to a wider audience of Americans to see that the drug threat and the terrorist threat are largely one and the same."[69] But the feds never provided any evidence showing that even 1 cent of the $500,000 that Al Qaeda used to pull off the 9/11 attacks came from drug trafficking.

The Bush administration relied on the slightest tangential connections to make its case linking drugs and terrorism. Ashcroft declared on September 3, 2002: "Earlier this year, I asked federal law enforcement agencies to identify for the first time on a single list the major trafficking organizations that are responsible for the U.S. drug supply. . . . This list has now been developed, and what it reveals is nothing short of shocking. Nearly one-third of the organizations on the State Department's list of foreign terrorist organizations also appear on our list of targeted U.S. drug suppliers."[70] But aside from the Colombian organizations, none of the other terrorist groups on the list had a major impact on the U.S. narcotics market.

There is no evidence that any U.S. drug purchase ever helped finance an international terrorist attack on the United States. Instead, political appointees repeatedly lunge at doubtful linkages. On September 1, 2002 DEA chief Hutchinson announced: "There is increasing intelligence information from the investigation that for the first time alleged drug sales in the United States are going in part to support terrorist organizations in the Middle East."[71] However, the hot case turned out to be little more than a cabal of people who were buying popular cold and allergy medications in Canada and using them to extract ingredients to produce methamphetamine, known as "crystal meth."[72] Some of the proceeds of their sales were sent to the Middle East. The DEA used the same logic used by the Justice Department in unlicensed money transfer cases: Since the U.S. government was not sure where the money ended up, it assumed terrorists got the loot. Assistant Attorney General Michael Chertoff stated in April 2003 that no terrorism charges had been filed against the people involved in the case.[73]

The Bush administration's efforts to tar all drug users as terrorist financiers is belied by federal data on Americans' drug habits. According to the National Household Survey on Drug Abuse, 28 million Americans used illegal drugs in 2001 (based on the number of people astute enough to tell government-hired survey takers that they were committing crimes).[74] There were 21 million marijuana users, almost 5 million cocaine and crack users, and 450,000 heroin users. The report noted that almost 5 million Americans were illicit "users of psychotherapeutic drugs. . . . 3.5 million [illegally] used pain relievers, 1.4 million [illegally] used tranquilizers, 1.0 million [illegally] used stimulants, and 0.3 million [illegally] used sedatives."[75]

According to the DEA, much of the marijuana smoked in the United States is domestically produced, with the remainder reportedly being grown in Mexico or Central America.[76] There is no terrorist link to the marijuana operations in Mexico or Guatemala, or in Humboldt County, California, or in the mountains of eastern Kentucky. Nor is there any evidence that a painkiller such as Oxy-Contin is linked to terrorists.

The United Nations estimates that the illicit drug trade worldwide generates $500 billion a year.[77] The Bush administration has not made a public estimate of the total amount of drug revenue that ends up in terrorist coffers, but it is unlikely that all international terrorist organizations combined receive even 1 percent of the total revenue from the world drug trade. Terrorist organizations that actually pose an international threat probably snare less than one-tenth of 1 percent of the global drug market.

Yet, a single dollar of drug money in the coffer of any terrorist group in the world automatically turns every American drug user into a terrorist financier, according to the Bush administration. Because some terrorist groups traffic in drugs, any American who purchases any banned substance automatically becomes fully responsible for the abuses of any terrorist in the world.

## 18 Percent Protection for the American People

While Bush and his appointees loudly hype the drugs-terrorism connection, they are diffident about admitting the federal government's abysmal failure to shut down the narcotics trade. When DEA chief Asa Hutchinson testified to the House Subcommittee on Coast Guard and Maritime Transportation on October 17, 2001, he was asked about the DEA's goals. Hutchinson replied: "Well, in reference to interdiction of assets, the national drug strategy provides that we should have an 18 percent rate of interdiction. And if you look back in 2000, the seizure rate was 10.6 percent. . . . In 2002, the goal was 18 percent and unless we devote the necessary assets to assist the interdiction, it's going to be difficult to achieve the goals of the national strategy."[78]

The U.S. government's goal for drug interdiction mocks any claim to protect America from the scourge of illicit drugs. A confidential 1993 National Security Council review of military efforts to detect and prevent drug smuggling found that they had virtually no effect on the price or supply of cocaine imports.[79] The General Accounting Office informed Congress in 1994 that "the supply of illegal drugs reaching the United States via Central America continues virtually uninterrupted despite years of U.S. drug interdiction efforts."[80] Janet Reno, attorney general at the time, said that federal experts estimate that "to have any impact on drugs in America you would have to interdict 75 percent of the stuff and that would be economically prohibitive."[81] In February 2003 the Office of Management and Budget thumped the DEA for being "unable to demonstrate progress in reducing the availability of illegal drugs in the United States"[82] despite the doubling of the agency's budget since 1995.

Drug prohibition is a price support program for criminals. The black-market prices of heroin and cocaine are as much as a hundred times higher than the cost of producing the drugs.[83] Because narcotics are illicit, they tend to attract violent, ruthless people and organizations to carry out their production and marketing. Groups that specialize in violence—such as terrorists—take to drug trafficking like ducks to water. Even though the Bush administration greatly overstates the link between drugs and terrorists, illicit drugs do provide an easy avenue of cash for some terrorists.

Some federal experts expect terrorist groups to rely more on drug financing after the government shuts down all other terrorist funding avenues. Acting DEA chief John Brown warned on April 1, 2003: "State-sponsored terrorism is disappearing and as a result terrorists are seeking other funding . . . from drug traffickers."[84] Or, in the more lurid words of U.S. attorney Michael

Shelby: "Drugs are the currency of terrorists. This is the medium of terrorism in the 21st century."[85]

Drug laws are far more effective at inserting profits into narcotics than law enforcement is at extracting profits. U.S. government officials are knowingly perpetuating policies that they admit could provide financial aid to terrorist groups. Instead of admitting the futility of the drug bans, the politicians promise that new waves of crackdowns will somehow repeal the laws of economics. Efforts to persuade Third-World farmers to cease growing illicit crops will be about as successful as a program to persuade stockbrokers and law firm partners to abandon their high-paid jobs, move to Mexico, and make a living assembling toilet brushes for sale at Wal-Mart.

Politicians ritually invoke 9/11 to sanctify both the war on terrorism and the war on drugs. But if we have to count on victory in the drug war to prevent new terrorist attacks, Americans are doomed. Would the government dare announce an official goal of stopping only 10 percent or 18 percent of would-be terrorists from entering the United States?

## Conclusion

When Bush signed the Patriot Act on October 26, 2001, he said: "Current statutes deal more severely with drug-traffickers than with terrorists."[86] Prior to 9/11, there were more political profits in waging war against drugs than in protecting Americans against terrorists. The U.S. government devoted massive resources to having a marginal impact on the price and availability of narcotics, rather than protecting the American people from aspiring mass murderers.

Are politicians more interested in controlling people or in protecting them? The issue is not whether illicit drugs are harmful—but what other damage can be caused in a futile effort to ban them. Current drug laws offer easy profits to terrorists and other malefactors. While drugs can leave a person in the gutter, they do not destroy 110-story buildings. While drugs can blur people's vision, they do not cause airliners to crash. While drugs can perforate a person's sense of responsibility, they do not leave large holes in the side of the Pentagon.

# CHAPTER TWELVE

# The Israeli Model for Fighting Terrorism

How should the United States respond to terrorist acts? There is the Israeli way: when attacked, attack—each and every time. It is Israel's way because of Israel's circumstances."
— *New Republic*, 1984[1]

In the aftermath of 9/11 "We are all Israelis now" was the chorus of Americans ranging from *New Republic* editor in chief Martin Peretz[2] to *Washington Times* columnist Larry Kudlow,[3] to *USA Today* commentator Samuel Freedman,[4] to *Arkansas Democrat-Gazette* editorial page editor Paul Greenberg,[5] to former drug czar and conservative moral eminence Bill Bennett.[6] Many Americans believed that the attack by Arab terrorists proved once and for all that the destinies of the United States and Israel are intertwined.

Prominent Israelis also promptly linked the attacks to their country's plight. Former Israeli Prime Minister Benjamin Netanyahu, speaking of the terrorist attacks, told Israeli radio on September 12, 2001: "This was a very good thing for Israel's relationship to the United States."[7] Israel's deputy UN ambassador Aharon Ya'acov declared that the lesson of the 9/11 attacks is that "those who close their eyes to Palestinian terrorism will eventually find it on their doorstep."[8] Israel Prime Minister Ariel Sharon continually preached after 9/11: "There is no good terror and bad terror; there is only terror."

The Israeli war on terrorism is, in many ways, a more advanced form of the American war on terrorism. Israel is also relevant to the U.S. war on terrorism because, more than any other nation in the world, Israel is seen as a U.S.

proxy—possessing an entitlement from the U.S. government to use its American-made weapons and aid however it pleases.

The United States official definition of terrorism—that terrorism is a private, not a governmental, crime—drives the U.S. government's perception of the Middle East conflict. The *New York Times* noted on April 7, 2002: "Israel, as American officials often note, is a democracy accountable to the norms of international law. The practical effect is that only the Palestinians, who lack a state, are generally labeled terrorists."[9] Most of the American media and the vast majority of congressmen presume that Israeli actions against Palestinians are inherently more legitimate than almost any action taken by Palestinians against Israelis.

Palestinian suicide bombers who intentionally kill Israeli civilians are terrorists. People who intentionally slaughter men, women and children on buses, in cafes, and on street corners are not freedom fighters. Mass murder is mass murder, regardless of political intent or religious fatwa. Some Palestinian organizations—including Islamic Jihad and Hamas—have been ruthless in their statements and actions, seeking to whip up hatred toward Israel at the same time that they kill as many Jews as possible.

Israel's policies are analyzed at length in this chapter because many Americans hold up Israel as a model for the United States to follow. The Russians have been far more brutal in Chechnya than the Israelis in the West Bank. The Chinese and Uzbek governments deal far more harshly with Islamic activists than do the Israelis. Israel's human rights policies are superior to the policies of Egypt, Syria, Iraq, and Iran. Yet to uncritically accept Israel as a model—at the same time that all the failures and abuses of Israeli policies are swept under the rug—is a recipe for disaster.

## The Early Stages of Israel's War Against Terrorism

Israel was born in the shadow of the Holocaust. In the years before the nation's modern founding, the Nazis slaughtered millions of Jews in an orchestrated campaign to exterminate the Jewish people. Jews also felt betrayed by the refusal of Western nations, including the United States, to permit the emigration of many Jews seeking to escape the Nazi death machine. Considering the surge of anti-Semitism around the Western world in the early twentieth century, many Jews decided that their best hope was to return to the Holy Land and start their own nation.

But the homeland was not empty.[10] As the Zionist movement gathered steam, Jewish immigration to Palestine surged. Conflicts erupted with the native Arab population, sometimes with catastrophic results. As the British government—which received Palestine as a Protectorate from the League of Nations after the breakup of the Ottoman Empire—struggled to maintain order, Jewish terrorist organizations increasingly targeted British soldiers and civilians as well as Arabs, and Arabs brutally attacked Jewish émigrés.

SUNY political science professor Jerome Slater noted in *Tikkun:* "Even before the Arab invasion in the spring of 1948, and continuing well after Israel won the war, some 600,000–700,000 Palestinians were deliberately driven out of their country, their homes, and their villages, in what prominent Israeli and American Jewish historians are beginning to acknowledge was nothing less than 'ethnic cleansing.' Emotionally loaded as that term is, it accurately describes the Israeli psychological warfare, economic pressures, artillery bombardments, political assassinations, terrorist attacks, and even massacres that forced the Palestinians to flee."[11] Such tactics sparked harsh criticism from some early Zionists. Albert Einstein, scholar Hannah Arendt, philosopher Sidney Hook, and 13 other prominent Jews signed a letter that the *New York Times* published on December 4, 1948, denouncing Menachem Begin and his "Freedom Party" as "closely akin in its organization, methods, political philosophy and social appeal to the Nazi and Fascist parties . . . for whom terrorism (against Jews, Arabs, and British alike), and misrepresentation are means, and a 'Leader State' is the goal."[12]

Israel defeated the armies of five Arab nations and seized far more territory for itself than authorized under the 1947 United Nations partition of Palestine between Arabs and Jews. Sporadic violence occurred along the new borders in the following years. In early October 1953 Arab infiltrators killed a Jewish mother and her two children near the West Bank border. The Israeli government responded by sending Lt. Col. Ariel Sharon and his commando Unit 101 on October 14, 1953 to the village of Qibya, on the West Bank. The Israeli government had no evidence that the perpetrators of the attack on its citizens came from Qibya. The IDF ordered the commandos to "carry out maximum destruction and killing," in order to drive the inhabitants of the village from their homes.[13] Israeli historian Benny Morris noted that Sharon's "order was to kill as many Arabs as possible, it did not distinguish between civilians, National Guardsmen, and legionnaires."[14] The soldiers ravaged the village, blowing up homes and tossing hand grenades through doors and windows. Seventy Arabs were killed, mostly women and children. Not a single Israeli soldier was killed or wounded. A subsequent United Nations report noted: "Bullet-riddled bodies near the doorways and multiple bullet hits on the doors of the demolished houses indicated that the inhabitants had been forced to remain inside until their homes were blown up over them."[15]

In October 1956, Israel, attacking in coordination with the French and British armies, seized the Sinai Peninsula and rolled its tanks all the way to the Suez Canal. President Eisenhower demanded that Israel withdraw—which was the last time an American president successfully issued an ultimatum to an Israeli leader, according to *Haaretz,* one of Israel's most respected newspapers.[16] After the 1956 war Israel enjoyed a decade of relative peace. Martin van Crevald, Israel's best-known military historian, observed: "Between 1957 and 1967 the number of Israelis who lost their lives as a result of enemy action was just thirty-five."[17]

Intermittent saber rattling by Israel, Syria, and Egypt occurred throughout the spring of 1967. On June 5, 1967 Israel launched a first strike and promptly devastated the Syrian and Egyptian armies. While Israeli politicians subsequently sought to portray the Six Day War as strictly defensive, Prime Minister Begin, in an August 8, 1982 speech to the Israeli National Defense College, conceded: "The Egyptian army concentrations in the Sinai approaches do not prove that Nasser was really about to attack us. We must be honest with ourselves. We decided to attack him. . . . The Government of National Unity then established decided unanimously: we will take the initiative and attack the enemy, drive him back, and thus assure the security of Israel and the future of the nation."[18]

Israel seized the West Bank and the Gaza Strip during the war. The United Nations passed Resolution 242, ordering Israel to withdraw from the territories it seized in the war, but Israel (with U.S. support) ignored the resolution. Historian van Crevald observed: "During the first months after the Six Day War, the Israelis sought to rid themselves of as many Arabs as possible, pressuring them to migrate across the River Jordan and refusing reentry when they tried to return."[19]

The Palestinians at first offered little resistance to the Israelis, but brutal occupation policies eradicated their docility. The 1967 land seizures helped spark more than 35 years of terrorist attacks. Though the Palestinian Liberation Organization had been formed in 1964, it was little more than a paper entity until Israel seized direct control over Palestinians in Gaza and the West Bank. Shortly after the 1967 war the PLO began attacking Israelis.

On Yom Kippur 1973, Syria and Egypt launched surprised attacks on Israel. With massive U.S. military aid rushing to help the reeling Israeli armies, the battlefield tide eventually turned. The Arabs responded to the U.S. support of Israel with an Arab embargo that helped throw the United States and western Europe into the deepest recession since World War II.

Since the 1970s, Israel has claimed a right to inflict massive retaliation for attacks originating from Lebanon. In 1982, as discussed in chapter 2, Israel invaded Lebanon to eliminate the Palestinian Liberation Organization once and for all. A would-be whirlwind campaign turned into an 18-year quagmire that cost the lives of more than 1,500 Israeli soldiers. Israel maintained control over a swath of land in South Lebanon to protect itself from terrorist attacks by Hezbollah and others. Israel also trained, equipped, and paid the South Lebanon Army (SLA). From 1993 to 1999, the Israeli Defense Forces (IDF) and its SLA proxies killed at least 355 Lebanese civilians while Muslim guerrillas in Lebanon killed 9 Israeli civilians, according to B'Tselem, Israel's premier human rights organization. In 1993 and 1996 Israel launched massive shelling campaigns on Lebanese villages in order to stampede hundreds of thousands of people north toward Beirut. Israeli prime minister Yitzhak Rabin stated the goal of the 1993 attack: "We want to cause a wave of flight and damage to everyone involved in Hezbollah activity."[20]

On April 18, 1996 the IDF artillery shelled a United Nations compound near Qana that was overflowing with 800 Lebanese civilians "who had fled from their villages on IDF orders."[21] The barrage killed 102 refugees and wounded hundreds of others. Hezbollah guerillas had fired Katyusha rockets a few hundred yards from the compound. A spokesman for United Nations forces in Lebanon quickly denounced the attack as a "massacre."[22] Maj. Gen. Dan Harel, the commander of the Israeli offensive, insisted that the shelling of the camp could not possibly have been deliberate because "that thing cannot happen in a democratic country like Israel."[23] Israeli Prime Minister Shimon Peres declared that "the sole guilty party, still on the ground, is Hezbollah. . . . We are dealing here with a horrible, cynical and irresponsible organization. Hezbollah's grand strategy all along has been to hide behind the backs of civilians."[24] A United Nations investigation concluded that "it is unlikely that the shelling of the United Nations compound was the result of gross technical and/or procedural errors." The IDF insisted that it was unaware that the camp was chock full of refugees; the UN report retorted: "Contrary to repeated denials, two Israeli helicopters and a remotely piloted vehicle [drone] were present in the Qana area at the time of the shelling."[25] An Amnesty International report concluded that the IDF "intentionally attacked the UN compound."[26] A few weeks after the attack, two of the Israeli gunners involved in the shelling were interviewed by a Jerusalem newsweekly. One of the gunners commented: "In a war, these things happen. . . . It's just a bunch of Arabs."[27] A second gunner said that, after bombarding the refugee camp, a commander told the gunners that "we were shooting well and to continue this way and that Arabs, you know, there are millions of them."[28] *Haaretz* columnist Ari Shavit, who had fought at Qana 18 years earlier while serving in the IDF, observed: "An Israeli massacre can be distinguished in most respects from an Arab massacre in that it is not malicious, not carried out on orders from High Above and does not serve any strategic purpose. . . . An Israeli massacre usually occurs after we sanction an unjustifiable degree of violence so that at some point we lose the ability to control that violence. Thus, in most cases, an Israeli massacre is a kind of work accident."[29]

Israel sometimes acted as if its war on terrorism entitled it to absolute power over Lebanese living in Israeli-declared war zones. Several Israeli jets were shot down over Lebanon; Ron Arad, the pilot of one of the downed planes, came to symbolize for the Israeli public the plight of Israeli servicemen who were either missing in action or held as prisoners in Lebanon. The Israeli government and its proxies rounded up 21 Lebanese civilians and held them many years in Israeli prisons, seeking to use them as leverage to gain the release of or information on Arad. Hasan Hijazi was 16 years old when he was seized in his village of Mays al-Jabal in 1986 by Israel soldiers; he was taken to Israel and held in prison for 14 years.[30] The Israeli High Court of Justice (the nation's Supreme Court), in a 1997 case, ruled that the Israeli government could legitimately hold innocent people as bargaining chips to achieve the release of Israelis held captive outside of Israel.[31] The court reversed its position two years later, declaring that 13 Lebanese must be released. Moshe Negbi, a prominent Israeli commentator, observed: "The Supreme Court is finally, after a long time, starting to mark out the red lines that Israel cannot cross, even when fighting terrorism. In this case, what they are saying is, no longer will they be able to kidnap people and keep them hostage." B'Tselem noted: "Taking hostages for any purpose, no matter how worthy, is the method used by terrorist organizations, not by modern democracies."

Though the Israeli army initially justified the incursion as seeking to "rout out terrorist nests" in southern Lebanon[32] the subsequent occupation by the IDF would spur terrorist attacks on Israeli forces far beyond what Israel suffered before the invasion. The clearest legacy of Israel's Operation Peace for Galilee, launched in 1982, is Hezbollah. Muslim guerrillas rallied to fight the IDF throughout the Lebanon occupation zone. Aided by Iran and later by Syria, Hezbollah developed into a fighting force that could hold its own against the IDF.

Perhaps the single largest mistake in the history of the Israeli government's long war on terrorism was its covert financing, cosseting, and arming of Hamas, the Islamic resistance movement. Israeli Prime Minister Ariel Sharon denounced Hamas as "the deadliest terrorist group that we have ever had to face."[33] But the Israeli government is reticent about admitting its role in creating this Frankenstein. Beginning in the 1970s Israel began pouring money into Islamic organizations—especially the Moslem Brotherhood—hoping that religion would distract the Palestinians from political activism and the radical left-wing Palestinian Liberation Organization. Hamas was a late offspring of the Moslem Brotherhood. Prior to 1988 Moslem Brotherhood activists "had refrained from openly anti-Israel activities."[34] But with the outbreak of the first Intifada (uprising) in late 1987, the Israeli government was stunned to see how fast Hamas became the primary source of deadly attacks against Israelis.

Anthony Cordesman, a former State Department and Defense Department intelligence officer and currently a scholar at the Center for Strategic and International Studies in Washington, stated that the Israeli government "aided Hamas directly—the Israelis wanted to use it as a counterbalance to the PLO."[35] A United Press International analysis reported, "According to several current and former U.S. intelligence officials, beginning in the late 1970s, Tel Aviv gave direct and indirect financial aid to Hamas over a period of years." UPI noted that, according to documents provided by Israeli terrorism experts, "Hamas was legally registered in Israel in 1978 by Sheikh Ahmed Yassin, the movement's spiritual leader, as an Islamic Association by the name Al-Mujamma al Islami."[36] The *Jerusalem Post* reported on May 29, 1989, that, until the late 1980s, the Moslem Brotherhood "organizations in Gaza and the Islamic University received much encouragement from the [Israeli] military government. . . . The military government believed that their activity would undermine the power of the PLO and of leftist organizations in Gaza. They even supplied some of their activists with weapons, for their protection."[37] During the first Intifada (uprising), the PLO and Hamas openly clashed over how to resist the Israeli occupation. The *Jerusalem Post* noted: "The [Israeli] security forces greeted this tension [between Palestinian groups] with satisfaction, in line with the principle of divide and conquer. In several cases, Palestinians noticed that troops stood by quietly during Hamas street activity, but did interfere when PLO activists engaged in the same activity."[38] The Israeli government assumed that if the PLO could be thwarted, the Palestinian problem would be solved. But Hamas was far more bloodthirsty and radical than the PLO. The PLO effectively recognized Israel's right to exist in 1988, while Hamas devoted itself to seizing all of Palestine for an Islamic state. After the Oslo agreement in 1993, Hamas persistently used violence to undermine relations between the Israeli government and the Palestinian Authority.

## Settlers & Terrorists

It is impossible to understand the Israeli war on terrorism without considering its settlement policy. Settlements were justified in part as a means of keeping an eye on the Palestinians, thereby helping deter terrorist attacks. After Israel seized the West Bank and Gaza Strip in 1967, the Israeli government began confiscating much of the land for military and other purposes. A small number of Israeli settlements were established on seized land, mostly in areas that were sparsely inhabited. In 1977 the right-wing Likud party took power, and settlements were placed in or near Palestinian cities or towns and expanded rapidly. The settlements became a key flank in Likud's "Greater Israel" campaign to permanently claim land seized in 1967.

Army chief of staff Rafael Eitan explained the goal of settlement policy to a Knesset parliamentary committee in 1983: "When we have settled the land, all the Arabs will be able to do about it will be to scurry around like *drugged cockroaches in a bottle.*"[39] (Eitan was elected to the Knesset the following year.) The settlers intensified the pressure on Arabs. The *New York Times* reported on March 14, 1983: "After years of tolerating political violence by Jewish settlers in the occupied West Bank, the Israeli authorities are considering whether to crack down. . . . Some officials are reported to have become alarmed at the growing specter of Jewish terrorism. Some are also worried that a fringe of Jewish militants are discrediting the settlement program, both here and abroad. Bombs have been planted at mosques. . . . Most of the clashes in the last few years in which settlers have shot and killed Arabs have produced no arrests, and none have resulted in a conviction."[40]

Ten years later, in December 1993, a television cameramen captured Jewish settlers firing machine guns into a group of unarmed Arabs in Hebron while Israeli soldiers fled the scene. Two months later, on February 25, 1994, Baruch Goldstein, wearing his Army reserve uniform and carrying an Army-issued automatic weapon, passed two Israeli soldiers[41] stationed outside and entered a Hebron mosque at the site of the Cave of the Patriarchs. Goldstein emptied three ammo clips into Arabs praying in the mosque, killing 29 and wounding more than 130 before he was overwhelmed and killed by survivors of his rampage.[42] (Palestinians stated that Goldstein killed 40 people.)[43] Goldstein was a former political campaign manager for Rabbi Meir Kahane, who became famous for preaching hatred toward Arabs and advocating their violent expulsion from both Israel and the Occupied Territories.[44]

Israeli Prime Minister Rabin denounced Goldstein, an émigré from Brooklyn: "You are a foreign implant. . . . A single, straight line connects the lunatics and racists of the entire world."[45] But Goldstein instantly became a hero to many settlers. At Goldstein's funeral service, Rabbi Yaacov Perrin declaimed: "One million Arabs are not worth a Jewish fingernail."[46] Mourners shouted "We are all Goldstein!"[47] The *Baltimore Sun* noted: "Mourners shouted 'Slaughter the journalists' and stoned reporters trying to cover the ceremony."[48] Rabbi Moshe Zemer of the Tel Aviv Institute of Progressive Halacha commented: "You have these rabbis over a period of time indicating . . . every non-Jew can be thought of as one who is trying to kill you."[49]

A subsequent Israeli inquiry commission learned that Israeli soldiers had orders to never fire upon Israeli settlers—even if the settlers were busily gunning down innocent Arabs. Meir Tayar, commander of the Border Police in Hebron, testified: "Instructions are to take cover, wait until the clip is empty or the gun jams and then overpower him. Even if I had been there [in the mosque], I could not have done anything—there were special orders."[50] Maj. Gen. Shaul Mofaz, the IDF commander in Hebron, disclosed that "the instructions are not to shoot at Jews because Jews are not the enemy."[51] The *Toronto Star* noted that "the army let heavily armed settlers do almost anything in the West Bank and Gaza, while Palestinians were gunned down for throwing stones."[52]

Goldstein's attack sparked violent protests across the Occupied Territories. In the following weeks, the IDF killed dozens of Palestinians and wounded hundreds. The Israeli government also imposed a severe lockdown on all Palestinians. Goldstein's attack and the subsequent crackdowns were followed by the first major suicide bombing in Israel, an attack launched by Hamas that killed five Israelis on a bus in Hadera.

Hebron continued to be a cauldron of hatred and violence. In 2001, three Palestinians were killed and six wounded when their car—which was headed for a wedding in Hebron—was stopped and shot up by a settler group calling itself the Committee for Road Safety.[53] David Wilder, the spokesman for Jewish settlers in Hebron, said: "When it comes to the Arabs, everything that happens to them today is their own fault. . . . A lot of people today look back on what Kahane said, and they say Kahane was right."[54]

On July 28, 2002 Jewish settlers carried out a "pogrom" against Arabs in Hebron, according to Col. Moshe Givati, an advisor on settlement security for Public Security Minister Uzi Landau. Givati was witnessing a Jewish funeral service when 20 or 30 people "all carrying army-issue weapons . . . charged into the Palestinian houses. . . . There were long bursts of fire by the Israelis—into the air and at the houses." A 14-year-old Palestinian girl was shot and killed and 15 Palestinians wounded. Givati observed: "Dozens of thugs, including youths from Hebron, burst into Arab houses for no reason. They broke windows, destroyed property and threw stones. These people were there for the purpose of making a pogrom."[55] The settlers also injured 15 Israeli police officers. Israel's former deputy chief of intelligence, Eran Lerman, characterized the situation in Hebron as "shocking": "These [settlers] are deliberately provoking confrontation and crisis while they shelter behind an army whose mission they refuse to facilitate."[56]

On January 23, 2003 *Haaretz* published a photo of graffiti proclaiming "Arabs to the crematoria" next to a Star of David painted on the wall in the Jewish settlement in Hebron.[57] Jewish settlers in Hebron wear T-shirts proclaiming

"Goldstein, King of Israel" and "Goldstein, Our Hero."[58] Young settler boys dress up as Goldstein and strut through the streets.[59] The *Boston Globe* noted: "In the center of Hebron, where 500 to 700 Jews—protected by large contingents of Israeli soldiers and police—live in the midst of 150,000 Palestinians, the Star of David and graffiti vowing 'Death to the Arabs' and 'No Arabs in Our City' are painted on Arab-owned shops. Mosques and holy books are desecrated. Jewish children insult, push, and throw stones at Arabs in the street with relative impunity, according to Palestinian, Israeli, and foreign witnesses."[60]

There is no illusion of "equal justice" in the Occupied Territories. In January 2001 Nahum Korman, a 32-year-old West Bank settler, was sentenced to six months of public service after he kicked a 12-year-old Palestinian boy to death.[61] A judge concluded that Korman did not intend to kill the boy he repeatedly kicked on the ground. B'Tselem declared that, "In this verdict, the court has delivered a message that the lives of Palestinians in the territories are unprotected, and that Israeli citizens in the territories can continue to relate to Palestinians as punching bags."[62]

Many settlers exploit their legal immunity to tyrannize Palestinians. In October 2002, settler violence forced the total evacuation of the Palestinian village of Khirbat Yanun. The *New York Times* noted: "The last families living here left on Friday, broken by what they said was a year of steadily mounting violence by Jewish settlers living in neighboring outposts on the hills. The gunfire, stone-throwing, physical assaults and vandalism had become unbearable."[63] Khirbat Yanun was a peaceful village until a Jewish settlement was erected on a hilltop a few miles away in 1997. The settlers wrecked the village's infrastructure: "A blackened building held the rusting remains of a generator, which residents said had been burned by settlers in April, leaving the village with no electricity. Three water tanks that had supplied the village lay empty. Residents said they had been toppled by settlers." The *Times* observed that the fate of Khirbat Yanun is "an example of how militant young settlers are shaping the conflict in the West Bank."[64]

Palestinians are often forced to live like captives on their own land. Uri Savir, the chief Israeli negotiator for the Oslo accords between the Palestinians and the Israeli government, noted that before the 1993 agreement "a West Bank Palestinian could not build, work, study, purchase land, grow produce, start a business, take a walk at night, enter Israel, go abroad, or visit his family in Gaza or Jordan without a permit from us."[65] Though Palestinians expected restraints to decline and new settlement activity to slow or cease after Oslo, punitive restrictions greatly increased. And while Palestinians believed the Oslo agreement meant a curtailment of new settlements, the total number of Israelis living in the Occupied Territories almost doubled—from 110,000 in 1992 to more than 200,000 in 2000. (Most of the settlers are not violent extremists; many of them are immigrants who were sent directly to the Occupied Territories upon arrival from the former Soviet Union.)

As settlements proliferated, the IDF clamped down ever tighter on nearby Palestinians. A 2002 B'Tselem study titled "Land Grab" noted: "The areas of jurisdiction of the Jewish local authorities, most of which extend far beyond the built-up area, are defined as 'closed military zones . . . ' Palestinians are forbidden to enter these areas without authorization from the Israeli military commander. Israeli citizens, Jews from throughout the world and tourists are all permitted to enter these areas without the need for special permits."[66] The Israeli government has commandeered more than half the land in the West Bank.[67]

The Occupied Territories have been splintered to maximize the number of Israeli chokepoints on Palestinian life. Dr. Sara Roy, of the Harvard University Center for Middle Eastern Studies, observed in a 2002 study entitled "Ending the Palestinian Economy":

> Israeli closure (and work-permit) policy remains largely unknown and misunderstood in the West. Yet it proved to be the primary measure affecting the Palestinian economy and society during the Oslo period and beyond. Closure refers to Israeli-imposed restrictions on the free movement of Palestinian goods, labor and people across internal and external borders and within WB/G Given Palestine's deep economic integration into Israel—e.g., for every dollar earned by Palestinians, approximately 75 cents returns in some form to the Israeli economy—closure's effects have been devastating. Because of this integration, the Palestinian economy remained extremely vulnerable to Israeli policy and other external shocks even during periods of economic growth.
>
> Closure is (and always has been) the primary factor underlying Palestinian economic demise. . . . Closure proved to be the single most damaging measure affecting the Palestinian economy during the Oslo period. It was during the years of the peace process and not during the current crisis that the inextricable connection between closure and economic growth was established and demonstrated. Indeed, long before September 2000, closure had already done considerable damage to the Palestinian economy. This is one reason economic conditions deteriorated so quickly afterward.[68]

Roy points out how the closure policy has had far greater impact than most casual observers assume:

> By December 1999, the Gaza Strip had been divided into three cantons and the West Bank into 227, the majority of which were no larger than

two square kilometers in size. While Palestinians maintained control over many of the cantons and were promised authority over more if not most, Israel maintained jurisdiction over the land areas in between the cantons, which in effect gave Israel control over all the land and its disposition. Hence, the actual amount of land under Palestinian authority proved far less important than the way that land was arranged and administered.[69]

Roy notes that the closures are a continuation of policies that began after Israel seized the West Bank and Gaza strip in 1967:

> In this regard, Israeli policy toward West Bank/Gaza has not changed fundamentally throughout the occupation despite various modifications to that policy, both benign (e.g., allowing the free movement of Palestinians in the early years of the occupation) and malignant (e.g., closure). Israeli policy has always aimed to prevent the emergence of a viable Palestinian economy and state and has consistently used economic measures to insure continued Palestinian dependence and de-development.[70]

Many Israelis recognized the paralyzing impact of the current policy. As Danny Rubinstein noted in *Haaretz:* "The West Bank is a land of roadblocks. . . . Palestinians are banned from most roads. To prevent Palestinian traffic, most West Bank towns and villages have been surrounded by hundreds of roadblocks and are under permanent siege and closure. . . . Movement restrictions . . . automatically turn most of the Palestinian public into law breakers. Almost every Palestinian who leaves home for work, school, shopping, medical treatment or family visits must bypass a barrier and, as a result, violate Israeli security regulations."[71]

Palestinians are often forced to live in perpetual lockdowns, with capital punishment awaiting violators. B'Tselem, in an October 2002 report titled "Lethal Curfew," noted, "The IDF has turned curfew, the most extreme method of restriction on movement into a routine, daily measure, thus harming hundreds of thousands of people."[72] B'Tselem condemned "the frequent use of live ammunition to enforce the curfew. Sometimes, the soldiers fire without warning. Fifteen Palestinians, twelve of them children under age 16, have been killed by soldiers enforcing the curfew. Dozens of others have been wounded. None of those killed endangered the lives of soldiers. . . . Shooting a person simply because he left home during curfew constitutes an excessive use of force. Curfew is no longer a tool to meet specific security needs, but a sweeping means of collective punishment."[73]

Curfew killings have resulted from "the lack of clarity of the procedures for imposing curfew and of the hours of curfew. . . . Contrary to IDF claims, the IDF does not provide information in an orderly manner to the residents regarding the hours of curfew; as a result, the residents are often uncertain if the curfew is in force," B'Tselem reported. One curfew confusion case occurred in Jenin, a West Bank city, on June 21, 2002, after residents had been confined to their homes for three days. Word spread that there was a one-hour break in the curfew. When people gathered on the streets and in the marketplace, Israeli tanks opened fire without warning. One tank opened fire on young boys on bicycles, killing two brothers and badly wounding a third. An amateur cameraman on a Jenin roof captured the scene, showing that the tank crew had a clear view down the street before firing at the boys.[74] Another tank fired shells into a crowded marketplace, killing a 5-year-old girl and a 50-year-old teacher and wounding 19 other people.[75] No one was attacking Israelis at the time of the killings. The tank fire reportedly destroyed 20 cars and 30 shops.[76] The initial Israeli military statement claimed that an IDF force searching houses in Jenin "identified a group of Palestinians who broke the curfew over the city and approached the forces. The force fired two tank shells in order to deter the crowd from approaching."[77] The IDF later issued a statement conceding: "An initial inquiry indicates that the force erred in its action."

The Israeli government uses the law and legalisms to give itself prerogative to destroy whatever any Palestinian builds in some areas of the West Bank and Jerusalem. As a B'Tselem study noted, "While facilitating Jewish settlement, the planning system works vigorously to restrict the development of Palestinian communities. The main tool used to this end is to reject requests for building permits filed by Palestinians."[78] In some areas of the West Bank, the Israeli government almost never approves an application from Palestinians to build a home or other building on their own land. If someone builds anyway, the IDF can come in and raze the home or marketplace because it is illegal.

From September 2000 through April 2003 Israel demolished the homes of more than 12,000 Palestinians.[79] The rate of destruction increased sharply in early 2003, despite a lull at that time in Palestinian suicide attacks on Israelis. The UN Relief and Works Agency for Palestine Refugees noted in May 2003: "Demolitions often occur late at night with little or no warning. Israeli military units—supported by tanks, APCs [armored personnel carriers], and helicopters—enter Palestinian areas to destroy a variety of targeted houses. . . . Houses close to settlements are often also destroyed. . . . Increasingly, explosives rather than bulldozers are used to destroy property creating widespread collateral damage."[80] Many Palestinian civilians have been killed in house detonations. Jeff

Halper, the chief of the Israeli Committee against Home Demolition, observed that the IDF will "use any excuse to demolish as many houses as possible. The idea is to deter Palestinian building and keep as much area as possible free for Israeli building and the military."[81] Rachel Corrie, a 23-year-old college student from Olympia, Washington, was crushed to death by an IDF bulldozer on March 15, 2003 while she was protesting Israeli demolitions in Gaza.

Even when the Israeli government does not totally thwart Palestinian efforts, the Palestinians have to deal with militant settlers. In recent years, settlers have routinely shot or attacked Palestinians who sought to harvest olives on Palestinian-owned land. Peace activists who have come to the West Bank to aid and protect the Palestinians have also been assaulted. The *Los Angeles Times* noted of one olive conflict: "The Jewish residents have decided that no Palestinian may pick olives within a clear view of the settlement [Tappuah], whose red-roofed homes are perched high on a hill that can be seen from more than two miles."[82]

Israeli policies have also made it far more difficult for Palestinian families to feed their children. A 2002 study funded by the U.S. Agency for International Development found that "22.5 percent of Palestinian children suffer from acute or chronic malnutrition . . . equivalent to levels found in Chad and Nigeria and higher than rates in Bangladesh and Somalia." The AID study concluded: "Market disruptions from curfews, closures, military incursions, border closures, and checkpoints affected key high protein foods, especially meat and poultry and dairy products, and in particular, infant formula and powdered milk."[83] A much larger survey conducted for UNICEF by the Palestinian Central Bureau of Statistics found much higher rates of chronic and acute malnutrition among Palestinian children age six months to five years.[84] Almost half the children in the Occupied Territories suffered from anemia.[85] A few months earlier, Maj. Gen. Amos Gilad, the coordinator of Israeli government activities in the Occupied Territories, "stressed there is no famine in the territories," the BBC reported.[86]

## Democratic Torture against Terrorism

Shortly after the 9/11 attacks former prime minister Benjamin Netanyahu praised Israel as "the Middle East's only democracy and its purest manifestation of Western progress and freedom."[87] But Israel's war on terrorism has spurred departures from that lofty standard.

After Israel took possession of the West Bank and Gaza Strip, Palestinians frequently alleged that they had been tortured by Israeli troops or agents. The government of Israel adamantly denied using coercion in interrogations.[88] But, in 1987 an official commission (known as the Landau Commission) was created to examine interrogation procedures. As Barak Cohen noted in the *Indiana International and Comparative Law Review,* "The Commission's appointment was motivated by two notorious incidents. The first incident involved the fabrication of evidence by GSS [General Security Service, commonly known as Shin Bet] officials to hide the fact that agents had beaten to death two Palestinian bus hijackers. The second incident concerned a Turkic Muslim Israeli Defense Forces officer falsely imprisoned for espionage on the basis of a false confession coerced from him by GSS agents. The agents later lied in court as to how they had forced the confession from the officer."[89] The president of Israel pardoned the Shin Bet agents who killed the Palestinians during interrogation, declaring that "in the special conditions of the State of Israel we cannot allow ourselves any relaxation of effort, nor permit any damage to be caused to the defense establishment and to those loyal men who guard our people."[90]

The Landau Commission concluded that Shin Bet had systematically used "physical pressure" on Palestinian suspects after 1971 and that Shin Bet interrogators had routinely lied about the use of such methods when testifying in court.[91] The commission stopped short of condemning such practices. Shin Bet's interrogation methods were "largely to be defended, both morally and legally," the commission said, and it recommended that none of the officials who committed perjury in court—denying torture—be prosecuted.[92] The commission concluded that the Israeli "government should acknowledge that some measure of coercion is permissible, and then codify and carefully monitor the allowable techniques."[93] Michael L. Gross of the University of Haifa observed that the Landau Commission "formulated a new 'Jewish-democratic' approach; in defiance of all international norms, they suggested that Israel could set standards and establish a regulatory mechanism to oversee the use of 'moderate physical pressure.'"[94]

While "moderate physical pressure" sounded akin to an overly firm handshake, the reality was sometimes deadly. The U.S. State Department estimated that ten Palestinians were killed during interrogations in 1988 and 1989.[95] At the same time that Shin Bet interrogators were instructed to use "moderate" pressure, Defense Minister Yitzhak Rabin told IDF soldiers to break the bones of Palestinian protesters.[96] It would be naïve to expect Shin Bet to treat Palestinians better behind closed doors than Israeli troops treated Palestinians in open view.

After a surge in suicide bombings in 1994, the Israeli government formally authorized Shin Bet to use "increased physical pressure."[97] No clear definition was given: The government instead granted vast discretion to all interrogators. The interrogations proved far more effective at punishing detainees than preventing suicide bombings.

Many Palestinian detainees filed complaints alleging abuses with Israeli courts. Beginning in 1996 the Israeli High Court of Justice issued several rulings authorizing physical force during interrogations of people accused of security offenses.[98] Prime Minister Benjamin Netanyahu applauded the rulings: "We're a democratic country, respectful of human rights, that is threatened by wild people who have no respect for human rights."[99]

In 1998 B'Tselem reported that some Palestinians detained by the Israelis "must eat with their hands in toilet stalls" and that Shin Bet agents use "painful stretching" and "threaten to murder the interrogee, mentioning detainees who died during interrogation or detention, and to harm his relatives."[100] The report noted that the Israeli government "admits to using violent shaking as an interrogation method. In April 1995, Abd a-Samad Harizat died as a result of being violently shaken by GSS interrogators. Even though the state acknowledged this, and though it could not guarantee unequivocally that violent shaking would not cause deaths in the future, or even less severe injuries, it has continued to use this method." Prime Minister Yitzhak Rabin admitted in 1995 that Israeli interrogators had given eight thousand detainees the "shaking" treatment.[101] B'Tselem noted that interrogators used "slapping, beating, and kicking" on detainees, as well as pulled them across the floor by their shackles.

Israel came under intense criticism from international organizations because of its interrogation practices. As the *Iowa Law Review* noted, "Instead of retreating under international scrutiny, Israel adopted the rhetoric of human rights by repeating that Israeli law banned torture and by distinguishing GSS techniques from the outlawed practice."[102] But as the *Berkeley Journal of International Law* observed in 2001, "Numerous independent studies, conducted by international and local human rights organizations, revealed that Israel employed numerous methods of torture while interrogating Palestinians, including: electric shock; beatings (with truncheons, rifle butts, rubber mallets, wrenches, whips, boots and fists) to all areas of the body including bottoms of feet, the torso and genitals; sexual assault, including sodomy and prolonged squeezing and beating of the testicles; application of burning cigarettes. . . ."[103] Palestinians were also forced to spend hours in awkward, uncomfortable positions, squatting on their toes with a hood over their heads while deafening music filled the room, or being handcuffed or shackled in positions that became increasingly painful. Sleep deprivation and exposure to temperature extremes were other common punishments for detainees.

The Israeli government insisted that coercive methods were, as B'Tselem's Jessica Montell explained, "reserved for 'ticking bomb' cases, where torture might extract information vital to prevent an imminent tragedy. It is doubtful there has been a genuine ticking-bomb case in the past decade, yet physical force was a standard part of security service interrogations."[104] Montell noted, "During the 1990s, Israel slid far down a frightening slope. The Israeli government justified the use of 'intense pressure' when 'moderate' pressure proved ineffective. When torturing a suspect didn't yield the necessary information, they tortured the suspect's friends and relatives. . . . In some cases, individuals suspected of no offenses were tortured in order to pressure them to collaborate with Israel."[105] Shin Bet also "routinely tortured political activists, students suspected of Islamic tendencies, and people whose professions theoretically made them capable of manufacturing bombs."[106]

Torture is addictive. Once the Israeli High Court authorized using force, Shin Bet and the IDF proceeded to physically abuse the vast majority of Palestinians they interrogated. Eitan Fellner of B'Tselem said that "torture became a bureaucratic routine in all Shin Bet interrogation centers. We estimate that 85 percent of Palestinian detainees were tortured, though many were later released without a charge."[107] The *Berkeley Journal of International Law* noted, "Even when prisoners are charged, the 'crime' is usually one that poses no real threat to state security, for example stone-throwing, possession of banned books and participation in non-violent political demonstrations . . . the GSS tortured thousands of Palestinians for so-called 'security violations' that had nothing to do with 'hostile terrorist activity.'"[108]

The precedents established in treating Palestinians spread to the treatment of Israelis. According to the activist group the Public Committee Against Torture in Israel, "Degradation and torture is not limited to Palestinian detainees but have also been the lot of soldiers and left wing and right wing political activists who had undergone interrogation by the GSS, the police and the investigative military police."[109] Former Shin Bet director Ya'acov Perry explained: "If you arrest someone, you can't just sit with them and have a nice talk over coffee and a cigarette. You can't fight terrorism that way."[110]

In 1999, the Israeli High Court of Justice acknowledged that the GSS and IDF were using several abusive interrogation methods that were not authorized by Israeli law. The Court did not ban torture as a human rights violation. Instead, it ruled that the government could enact a new law to allow Shin Bet to use "physical means" as long as the interrogation methods were "befitting the values of the State of Israel, 'designed' for a proper purpose, and [employed] to an extent no greater than is required."[111]

After the High Court decision, a majority of the members of the Knesset cosponsored "a bill authorizing [Shin Bet] to use physical pressure during interrogations," the *Iowa Law Review* noted. The bill's author explicitly acknowledged that his bill would be "introducing torture into the law of the State of Israel."[112] (The bill was not enacted, largely as a result of vigorous lobbying by nongovernmental organizations.)

Even though the Knesset did not enact torture legislation, Palestinians continued to be roughed up. B'Tselem reported in July 2001 the experiences of ten youths, ages 14 to 17, who had been arrested on suspicion of throwing stones in late 2000 and early 2001. B'Tselem noted, "In most of the cases, the police arrested them at their homes in the middle of the late night and took them to the Police station in Gush Etzion, where police interrogators tortured them until morning," using methods that included "beating the minors severely for many hours, at times with the use of various objects" and "pushing the minor's head into the toilet bowl and flushing the toilet."[113]

In late 2001 the United Nations Committee Against Torture heard testimony on Israel's interrogation methods. Amnesty International and the World Organization Against Torture testified that torture continued to occur in Israel. But the Israeli government representative, Ya'akov Levy, testified that a "careful reading" of the UN Convention against Torture "clearly suggests that pain and suffering, in themselves, do not necessarily constitute torture."[114]

Israeli torture policy illustrates what happens after a government grants itself almost absolute power over millions of people in order to stop terrorists. The "ticking time bomb" justification mushrooms until almost everything is considered a ticking time bomb. Once the security forces were unleashed, it was almost inevitable that their power would be grossly abused. Even when Shin Bet killed Palestinians while torturing them, the deaths in custody were often treated as the equivalent of bureaucratic paperwork errors. And torture failed to make Israel safer. The number of deadly terrorist attacks against Israelis was far higher after the Landau Commission sanctioned torture than before.

## IDF: Accidentally Shooting to Kill

The Israeli Defense Force's Doctrine on Purity of Arms proclaims: "IDF soldiers will not use their weapons and force to harm human beings who are not combatants or prisoners of war, and will do all in their power to avoid causing harm to their lives, bodies, dignity and property."[115] The longer Israel's war on terrorism continues, the more hollow this doctrine appears.

Violent conflicts between the Israelis and Palestinians subsided in the late 1990s, partly because the Oslo peace agreement generated hope on both sides for a peaceful resolution to the long conflict. The breakdown of negotiations between Israeli prime minister Ehud Barak and Yassar Arafat in August 2000 produced great disappointment among both Israelis and Palestinians.[116] Ariel Sharon took the opportunity to announce that he would visit the Temple Mount in Jerusalem—an area sacred to both Jews and Muslims. Sharon's visit predictably panicked Muslims into fearing Israel was planning to commandeer the entire area (as it had commandeered most of Jerusalem in the preceding decades). The Israeli government sent one thousand guards and police with Sharon to protect him during his visit. On the day following Sharon's visit, Arabs began throwing rocks at Israeli police after their Friday afternoon prayers at the mosque on the site. Israeli police opened fire with rubber-coated metal bullets, wounding over 200 Palestinians and killing 4. There was no gunfire from the Palestinian side. B'Tselem observed: "The harsh and violent response of the police significantly contributed to the violent nature of the events and the high number of casualties."[117] (Seventy Israeli policemen were injured, none fatally.)

In the following months the Israeli government chose to crush demonstrators by opening fire with live ammo and rubber-coated bullets (which are frequently fatal)—rather than relying on tear gas and water cannons. B'Tselem noted in early December 2000: "From 29 September to December 2, 2000, Israeli security forces killed 204 Palestinian civilians and 24 Palestinian security forces, and wounded approximately 10,000 Palestinians."[118] Twenty-nine Israelis were killed by Palestinians during the same period. Three-quarters of the clashes at which the IDF killed or wounded Palestinians involved no Palestinian gunfire.[119] A senior IDF officer told *Haaretz* in December 2000: "Nobody can convince me we didn't needlessly kill dozens of children."[120]

The surge in violence undermined the Barak government, and after elections in January 2001, Ariel Sharon became Israeli prime minister—largely as a result of the cycle of violence his visit to the Temple Mount helped launch. Over the following year, attacks and counterattacks between Israelis and Palestinians increased and the death toll continually escalated.

In late March 2002 an Arab suicide bomber detonated himself in the middle of a Passover dinner at a Haifa hotel, killing 28 Israelis and wounding 140. Sharon responded with "Operation Defensive Shield." He announced that the IDF must hit Palestinians harder: "They must be beaten. We have to cause them heavy casualties, and then they will know that they cannot keep using terror and win political achievements."[121]

IDF attacks were especially fierce in the refugee camp in Jenin, where fourteen thousand people lived in densely packed concrete block housing. Sharon described Jenin and other places the IDF attacked as "terror towns."[122] The Israeli government declared the entire area a closed military zone and prohibited any journalists, human rights officials, or Palestinian ambulances from entering. On April 12 IDF spokesman Brig. Gen. Ron Kitrey told Israeli Army Radio that "there were apparently hundreds of people killed in the Jenin refugee camp."[123] The IDF issued a correction the same day, insisting that Kitrey was referring to both killed and wounded. *Haaretz* reported on April 9 that Foreign Minister Shimon Peres said the Jenin siege was a "massacre."[124] One Israeli officer commented: "When the world sees the pictures of what we have done there, it will do us immense damage."[125] Fears that a massacre had occurred—and would be covered up—were further inflamed when the IDF announced plans to bury the corpses of Palestinian fighters in unmarked graves in a cemetery in the Jordan Valley. Kitrey announced: "The terrorists we found with guns we are going to bury in what we call the enemy cemetery site. The civilians we will try to give back to the Palestinians."[126] (The IDF abandoned this policy after the Israeli High Court issued an injunction.[127])

The Israeli military responded to criticisms by invoking its moral superiority. Maj. Gen. Dan Halutz declared on April 6: "The IDF is keeping the highest combat ethics comparing to any force in the world."[128] Brig. Gen. Eyal Shlein, head of army operations in the Jenin camp, proclaimed: "The IDF is one of the most humanitarian armies in the world."[129] Brig. Gen. Kitrey stressed on April 9: "We have given strict orders not to shoot, to hold back fire, the moment you see or feel civilian families, apart from that, we evacuated the area before we went in, or during the first stages of our operation there."[130] Col. Gal Hirsh, head of operations in the Central Command, announced: "We asked the Palestinian civilians to evacuate their homes so they would not get hurt; some chose not to."[131]

But the top brass were contradicted by front-line soldiers. Army reservist Moshe Nissim, the driver of one of the 50-ton Caterpillar D-9 bulldozers used to raze large parts of the Jenin refugee camp, told *Yedioth Ahronoth,* Israel's largest daily newspaper: "Over the loudspeaker, they were told to leave their houses before I destroyed them. But I did not give a chance to anyone. I did not wait. . . . I would simply give the house a massive blow so that it would collapse as quickly as possible. I wanted to do it as quickly as possible in order to get to other houses. To do a lot."[132] Nissim admitted: "I'm certain that people died inside these houses but it was difficult to see. . . . I got a great deal of pleasure from every house that came down, because I knew that they do not care about dying, and that losing their house hurts them more. . . . Other [bulldozer drivers] may have been more restrained. Or they say they have. Don't believe their stories." Nissim drank whiskey throughout his 70-hour rampage.

An Israeli army sergeant who fought at Jenin later confided to a *Washington Post* reporter: "The orders were to shoot at each house. The words on the radio were to 'Put a bullet in each window.'"[133] The sergeant told the *Post* that Israeli soldiers "pounded a group of cinder-block homes—the apparent source of Palestinian sniper fire—with .50-caliber machine guns, M-24 sniper rifles, Barrett sniper rifles and Mod3 grenade launchers." The sergeant said: "It's not true there was a massacre, because guys did not shoot at civilians just like this. However— and this is terrible—it is true that we shot at houses, and God knows how many innocent people got killed." The *Post* said that the sergeant was also troubled by "insufficient efforts by the army to allow civilians to leave their homes in safety. He also questioned the decision to use bulldozers to knock down houses at a time when he said the fighting had mostly subsided." The sergeant observed: "The civilians . . . never got a real chance to get out."[134] A Human Rights Watch investigation concluded that some "civilians who attempted to flee were expressly told by IDF soldiers that they should return to their homes."[135]

Despite the razing of a large swath of Jenin, despite the attacks by helicopter gunships on apartment houses, despite the tank shells crashing into living rooms of innocent Palestinians, the IDF portrayed itself as a nonaggressor. When Maj. Gen. Halutz was asked by a journalist about calls for a cease fire, Halutz replied: "It is not a fire between two forces. It's under terror, not under fire. . . . And it's not a cease fire, it's to cease terror which is a unilateral action that should be taken by only one side, because we are not taking any terror actions."[136]

A few days after the fighting was finished, the IDF opened up Jenin to outsiders, and no evidence of a massacre was discovered. Palestinian spokesmen apparently sharply overstated the number of fatalities. The accusations of a Jenin massacre sparked great bitterness in Israel and among Israeli supporters worldwide. However, as Uri Avnery, a combat veteran of Israel's 1948 war and the leader of Gush Shalom, a peace organization, noted, "An objective person could only draw the conclusion that the army wanted to prevent the entrance of eyewitnesses into the camp at any price. The army knew that this would give rise to rumors about a terrible massacre, but preferred this to the disclosure of the truth. What is the height of cynicism? When one blocks free access to a place, and then argues that no one has the right to say what happened there, because he has not seen it with his own eyes."[137]

During Operation Defensive Shield, the IDF deliberately destroyed much of the infrastructure of Palestinian life. A United Nations report noted, "Fifty Palestinian schools were damaged by Israeli military action, of which 11 were totally destroyed, 9 were vandalized, 15 used as military outposts and another 15 as mass arrest and detention centers."[138] *Haaretz's* Amira Hass reported that in hundreds of Palestinian offices occupied by IDF troops during the operation, the aftermath found "smashed, burned and broken computer terminals heaped in piles and thrown into yards; server cabling cut, hard disks missing, disks and diskettes scattered and broken, printers and scanners broken or missing, laptops gone, telephone exchanges that disappeared or were vandalized, and paper files burned, torn, scattered, or defaced—if not taken."[139]

The killings by Israelis and Palestinians did not stop after Sharon proclaimed Operation Defensive Shield a success. On May 5, 2002 an Israeli tank was driving on a road near Jenin when a tank tread snapped. The soldiers inside thought a bomb had detonated under them and turned their heavy guns on a Palestinian family who were picking grape leaves across open fields 70 yards away. A 30-year-old woman and three of her children were killed. An IDF spokesman quickly announced: "A large bomb was activated against an IDF tank near Camp Bezek. One soldier was lightly injured and taken to the hospital. The soldiers identified several figures escaping through the nearby grove. The tank crew and the soldiers on the armored personnel carrier that was traveling next to it opened fire with light weapons. As a result, a Palestinian woman and two of her children were killed."[140] In the following days, the IDF admitted that there had been no bomb. *Haaretz*'s Gideon Levy interviewed the husband and father of the victims—a tenant farmer named Mohammed Abu Samra Zakarna. After the heavy firing stopped, seven soldiers came up to him, handcuffed his hands behind his back and took his pants away. Zakarna said: "I told the soldier—You killed my children and I am a farmer. He told me to be quiet and not say another word." While he was handcuffed on the ground for three hours, he watched his wounded son bleeding to death. Eventually, an IDF officer who spoke Arabic arrived on the scene and informed Zakarna: "I'm sorry for your loss." Levy noted of Zakarna: "He isn't crying or angry or thirsty for vengeance; he only hopes that his loved ones will be the last victims, for both peoples."[141]

While the IDF insists that it does not intentionally kill innocent civilians, the "rules of engagement" allow soldiers to preemptively kill any Palestinian seen in the wrong place at the wrong time. B'Tselem noted in a March 2002 report that "new regulations were issued that permit opening fire, automatically, on any Palestinian who approaches certain areas in the Gaza Strip, termed 'danger zones.'"[142] A reserve soldier who served in the Gaza Strip informed B'Tselem that "there were special open-fire regulations regarding particular roads. According to these regulations, at night one must shoot to kill with no warning towards any figure approaching the road. This is despite the fact that near the road were many houses belonging to Palestinians as well as children's playing fields." Another soldier commented, "If an unarmed person in civilian dress, but who is carrying a load that may be an explosive, is walking near the fence [dividing Israel and Gaza]—the directive is to shoot him. If an adult is walking near the fence—the directive is to shoot him." B'Tselem noted, "The new regulations allow . . . sniper fire from ambush. In some areas . . . soldiers are allowed to fire without warning at Palestinian suspects."[143] Palestinians are prohibited from carrying weapons and can be shot on sight if an IDF soldier suspects they are armed; settlers, on the other hand, are issued automatic weapons by the government.

B'Tselem observed: "The directive to kill anyone who approaches 'danger zones' . . . constitutes a death sentence for every person who approaches, whether deliberately or by mistake, a settlement's fence, certain roads, or the fence along the border. The order is particularly grave because of the reality in the Gaza Strip, where IDF posts and settlements are located in the heart of a densely packed civilian population, and the IDF does not mark the areas in which the directive applies to warn those who come into the area." The order also "completely ignores the attempts of many Palestinians to sneak into Israel to go to work and not to injure Israeli soldiers or civilians." B'Tselem offered many cases of innocent people being killed as a result of the policies, including the following case: "On 2 March 2001, Mustafa Rimlawi, 42, who was mentally retarded, was shot on the Karni-Netzarim Road. The IDF Spokesperson's statement immediately following the incident contended that, 'IDF soldiers tonight thwarted a terrorist attack against civilians and IDF soldiers moving along the Karni-Netzarim Road. IDF Forces in the midst of an operation identified a terrorist plac[ing] a charge on the road, and opened fire at him.' The IDF later admitted that no terrorist charge was found at the site in which Rimlawi was killed, but it justified his killing on the grounds that, 'by wandering around the area at night, he turned himself into a suspect.'"[144]

The IDF's efforts to cultivate a benign image have been hobbled by occasional outbursts of sincerity. In August 2002, Lt. Gen. Moshe Yaalon, IDF Chief of Staff, announced: "The Palestinian threat harbors cancer-like attributes that have to be severed and fought to the bitter end."[145] He explained to *Haaretz:* "There are all kinds of solutions to cancerous manifestations. Some will say it is necessary to amputate organs. But at the moment, I am applying chemotherapy, yes."[146] Yaalon's comments outraged many Israelis.

Even when the Palestinian suicide bombings temporarily ceased, the IDF killings continued. A *Washington Post* editorial on New Year's Day 2003 noted:

There has been a lull recently in Palestinian attacks against Israelis. . . . But almost every day, Palestinian civilians, including many children, are being killed by the Israeli army and police. An 18-year-old high school student named Amran Abu Hamediye was found beaten to death in the West Bank town of Hebron on Monday; family and neighbors say he had been detained by Israeli forces a few minutes before. On Sunday, an 11-year-old boy was shot and killed by troops in the town of

Tulkarm. The day before, a 9-year-old girl was killed as she played out-side her home in the Gaza Strip. At least four other Palestinian children under the age of 16 were killed by Israeli fire in Gaza during the past month. In one case, an 11-year-old girl was shot in the chest and killed as she leaned out her bedroom window to watch the funeral of a teenage boy who had been gunned down the previous day.[147]

Between the start of the second Intifada in September 2000 and April 2003, more than 2400 Palestinians and more than 700 Israelis were killed, according to the *St. Louis Post-Dispatch*.[148]

After an incident in March 2003 in which the IDF vigorously tracked and brutally killed two Israeli security guards (under the mistaken impression that they were Palestinian suspects), a *Haaretz* editorial remonstrated: "The IDF, which brought up generations of soldiers on the myth of purity of arms . . . is turning into a killing machine whose efficiency is awe-inspiring, yet shock-ing."[149] *Haaretz* observed: "The reality in the territories shows that innocent people stand very little chance of proving their innocence."[150]

## Routine Whitewashes and Cover-ups

As the civilian casualties mounted after late 2000 the Israeli government perenni-ally insisted that its forces were following the law. However, *Haaretz* noted in De-cember 2000: "In practice, legal oversight of low-level military field operations simply does not exist."[151] Knesset member Ran Cohen complained in 2001 that when the IDF provided information to the Knesset's Foreign Affairs and Defense Committee on cases of Palestinians killed, "all the de-briefings were shallow and attempted cover ups, although they were conducted by senior officers."[152]

B'Tselem continually requested that the army investigate questionable killings of Palestinian civilians. The army routinely replied with a perfunctory letter effectively exonerating any and all soldiers involved. In one case, however, the usual letter stating that nobody had done anything wrong was accompanied by internal documents indicating otherwise. On July 7, 2001, 11-year-old Khalil al-Mughrabi was killed by a bullet from a tank's heavy machine gun as he rested on a pile of dirt after playing soccer at the Yubneh refugee camp in the Gaza Strip; two young friends of his were also wounded. Though Israeli regula-tions prohibit soldiers from firing warning shots with long-range weapons, an Israeli tank passing near the Egyptian border apparently did exactly that when some Palestinians sought to obstruct the road with debris and barbed wire. Col.

Einat Ron, the chief military prosecutor, concluded in an internal report that "it is likely that the shots [fired by Israeli soldiers] did not hit the children who were identified as rioters, but rather children who were some distance from the place of the event." Though Col. Ron recognized the facts, her official letter to B'Tselem declared: "Live gunfire was not aimed at the rioters, and no hits were detected as a result of this gunfire." The internal documents showed that Col. Ron formally considered three different explanations for the event, then knowingly chose a false version that completely exonerated the IDF. B'Tselem complained that Col. Ron's letter "raises a serious concern that lying is considered legitimate practice in the office of the Judge Advocate General."[153]

## "Pinpoint Preventive Operations"

For decades Israel has relied on special troop units or intelligence agents to assassinate suspected terrorists or enemies. Former CIA deputy director George Carver commented in 1988 that Israel is the only government in the world that makes "the assertion that they have a right to be judge, jury and executioner and carry out sentences anywhere in the world."[154] The IDF label such actions as "focused prevention" or "pinpoint preventive operations."[155] Israeli undercover units killed 162 Palestinians between 1988 and 1998, according to B'Tselem.[156] The assassination pace picked up after the start of the second Intifada. Between September 2000 and the end of 2002, Israeli forces assassinated at least 82 Palestinian suspects and killed at least 52 bystanders in the planned killings.

Though Israeli hit teams initially sought to kill specific terrorists, the attacks have evolved to include premeditated killings of large numbers of innocent people. On May 18, 2001 the IDF sent an F-16 fighter jet to try to kill a Hamas leader by bombing the Palestinian jail in Nablus where he was held. This was the first time a U.S.-made fighter jet had been used to bomb the Occupied Territories since 1967.[157] The attack killed nine Palestinian policemen but only wounded the Hamas leader. Maj. Gen. Giora Eiland, head of strategic planning for the Israeli army, said: "We decided to target that building, hoping to kill [the Hamas leader]. He was only lightly wounded and in this sense the operation was not a complete success."[158] Eiland justified the attack: "The F-16 is a heavy weapon and it has the image of excessive use of force. But the reality is [that] it is an accurate weapon, and we made an accurate attack on a legitimate military target."[159] Though the policemen were not specific targets, "the damage that was caused to the other side was just the anticipated damage."[160] Eiland said the bombing sent the message to Palestinians that "there is a cost not only on the Israeli side of the line but on their lives."[161] At that point, five times as many Palestinians as Israelis had been killed since hostilities erupted the previous September.[162]

On July 23, 2002, on Sharon's specific approval, an Israeli F-16 dropped a 2,000-pound "smart bomb" in a densely populated shantytown in the Gaza Strip. The attack killed Salah Shehadeh, a senior Hamas leader, and 14 others (including 11 children); 140 other people were wounded. Sharon hailed the destruction of the undefended apartment building as "one of the most successful operations ever in the war against terror."[163] Two other apartment buildings were also destroyed. Maj. Gen. Dan Halutz, commander in chief of the air force, told the pilots: "You are not responsible for the contents of the target. Your execution was perfect. Wonderful."[164]

Many Israelis were aghast. Opposition leader and Meretz Party head Yossi Sarid denounced the attack as "state terrorism."[165] Knesset member Zahava Galon declared: "We made a horrendous mistake. A country can't behave like a terrorist group."[166] After several days' international backlash from the bombing, Sharon asserted that the civilian carnage was the result of mistaken intelligence: "Israel did not know that there were civilians in Shehadeh's house. Had it known this, it would have found another way to hit him."[167] Deputy Prime Minister Silvan Shalom conceded: "There's no question there was a glitch. No one gets 100 percent results."[168] Israeli President Moshe Katsav declared: "It truly pains our heart to see children that were killed and seriously injured. That was not our intention. That is not us. That is not our policy. Mistakes happen and this was a mistake."[169] Dropping a 2000-pound "smart bomb" in the middle of a shantytown—and then professing surprise at casualties—strains credulity. The *Sydney Morning Herald* noted: "Only four of those killed were in Shehadeh's home. Most of the victims were in neighboring buildings. This fact has called into question the advice allegedly given to the Government that the attack would only have a 'minor effect' on other dwellings."[170]

Air Force chief Halutz, however, was unable to stick to the new script. A month after the attack, Halutz vented his anger at media criticisms and declared that the bombing was both "militarily and morally" proper.[171] Halutz declared: "The decision-making process was correct, balanced and careful. The problem was with the information, the information changed," regarding the number of people living in the neighborhood.[172] But the Gaza Strip is one of the most densely populated areas in the world, and the IDF had no reason to expect that its target would be surrounded by vacant lots.

The attacks by assassination teams also intimidate Palestinians en masse. One high-ranking Israeli security official told the Knesset Foreign Affairs and Defense Committee in late 2000: "The liquidation of wanted persons is proving itself useful. . . . This activity paralyzes and frightens entire villages and as a result there are areas where people are afraid to carry out hostile activities."[173]

Israel's assassination campaign has been widely criticized on moral and tactical grounds. Former CIA counterterrorism director Vincent Cannistraro observed in 2001 that the assassination campaign "replaces known Palestinian activists with new militants who are less known and more determined to escalate violence. . . . Targeted killings may satisfy a blood lust and a perceived need for revenge, but they are ineffective in achieving their stated objective of deterring terrorism."[174] Cannistraro noted that Israeli assassinations of Hezbollah and Islamic Jihad chieftains were followed by the ascension of ruthless leaders who wreaked greater havoc on Israelis.

"Pinpoint preventive operations" are a good example of a policy that provides more gratification than protection. A 2002 poll by *Yedioth Ahronoth* found that 74 percent of Israelis support the assassination policy. Yet, as political scientist Neve Gordon, who teaches at Ben Gurion University, pointed out, "when asked if they thought the assassinations were effective, 45 percent claimed that they actually increase Palestinian terrorism, 31 percent stated that they have no effect on terrorism and only 22 percent averred that assassinations help deter terrorism." Gordon concluded that the poll "indicates that many Israelis have lost the ability to think clearly, suggesting also that a visceral instinct has taken over the national psyche, marginalizing and repressing all forms of political reasoning."[175] British Chief Rabbi Jonathan Sacks observed that "there is no question that this kind of prolonged conflict, together with the absence of hope, generates hatreds and insensitivities that in the long run are corrupting to a culture."[176]

The Bush administration appears intent on imitating Israel's assassination policy. U.S. government legal experts have been conferring with Israeli experts to benefit from their operational expertise. The *Forward*, a New York–based Jewish newspaper, reported on February 7, 2003 that "American representatives were anxious to learn details of the legal work that Israeli government jurists have done during the last two years to tackle possible challenges—both domestic and international—to its policy of 'targeted killings' of terrorist suspects."[177]

## Fighting Terrorism with Mass Expulsion

Some Israelis have concluded that the solution to their terrorism problem is to forcibly expel all Arabs. A 2002 poll showed that 44 percent of Israelis favored expelling millions of Palestinians from the Occupied Territories—this is known as the "transfer" option. Rehavam Zeevi, Sharon's tourism minister, was the most prominent advocate of transfer. Zeevi denounced Arabs as "lice" and proposed mass expulsion to "cure a demographic ailment."[178] (The Palestinian birth rate is extremely high, creating fears in Israel that the Arabs could outnumber Jews in the coming decades.) After Zeevi was assassinated by gunmen from the Palestinian Liberation Front in 2001 (several weeks after the IDF assassinated their leader), the Likud government made him a national hero, issuing a postage stamp with his portrait and commanding all Israeli schools to teach students about Zeevi's love of the land.

In February 2002 Benny Elon, who replaced Zeevi as Israel's tourism minister, launched a high-profile campaign to generate support for expelling all Arabs from the Occupied Territories. Billboards from his Moledet (Homeland) Party proclaimed "Only transfer will bring peace."[179] Elon took his cleansing proposal to Washington. At an October 2002 Washington convention of the Christian Coalition, Elon's call to "resettle" and "relocate" the Palestinians brought cheers from thousands of people in the audience.[180] Elon quoted from chapter 33 of Numbers, in which God commands the Israelis: "Ye shall drive out all the inhabitants of the land from before you. . . . But if ye will not drive out the inhabitants of the land from before you, then shall those that ye let remain of them be as pricks in your eyes, and as thorns in your sides, and they shall vex you in the land wherein ye dwell." A senior official with the Christian Coalition told the *Forward* that Elon was invited to speak specifically because of his ideology.[181] House Majority Leader Richard Armey endorsed expelling Palestinians in a CNBC interview on May 1, 2002, declaring, "I am content to . . . have those people who have been aggressors against Israel retired to some other arena."[182]

When a *Christian Science Monitor* reporter asked Sharon's spokesman, Raanan Gissin, for a reaction to Elon's proposal, Gissin replied: "There is a difference between wishful thinking and realpolitik. If the Palestinians would have a change of heart and move elsewhere, OK, but Sharon realizes transfer cannot be done because of the stance of the Israeli public. What Elon is saying is not something that today seems possible."[183]

Gamla, a self-described "ideological watchdog" organization consisting of former Israeli military officers, settlers, and others, published a study in July 2002 titled "The Logistics of Transfer." The study urged the forcible expulsion of all Arabs (including Israeli citizens of Arab descent) as a means to "drastically" reduce "the threat to world peace."[184] Gamla promised that, after the expulsion, "Both the Jews and Arabs can start recovering their lives and establishing real neighborly relations no longer marred by constant conflict."[185] Alternatively, Gamla declared, "Israeli Arabs can be given one more option—to convert to Judaism if they prefer to stay put." (This was the same incentive plan the Spanish Inquisition offered Jews five hundred years earlier.)

Israeli historian Benny Morris stated: "The idea of transfer is as old as modern Zionism and has accompanied its evolution and praxis during the past century."[186] Historian Martin van Crevald, a professor at Hebrew University in Jerusalem, observed in 2002 that Sharon "has always harbored a very clear plan—nothing less than to rid Israel of the Palestinians."[187] Van Creveld predicted that Sharon could use some pretext to launch a massive military strike to empty the Occupied Territories of Arabs.[188] A 2002 letter signed by more than a hundred Israeli academics warned: "We are deeply worried by indications that the 'fog of war' could be exploited by the Israeli government to commit further crimes against the Palestinian people, up to full-fledged ethnic cleansing."[189]

Many comments on the "transfer" option seem to presume that it would be almost bloodless—the equivalent of a cop telling some drifter to move along. Ori Banks of the Moledet Party's executive committee told National Public Radio: "We will have to dismantle the refugee camps. That's a problem that has to be dealt with by physically removing them and dispersing them into their world. But we are not for bringing in trucks and loading all the Palestinians on the trucks and getting them out of here."[190] There is no mention that forcibly expelling millions of people could easily involve killing tens of thousands of men, women, and children.

## Conclusion

Israeli National Security Council chairman Maj. Gen. Uzi Dayan, in a speech in December 2001, defined terrorism as "any organization that systematically harms civilians, irrespective of its motives."[191] By this standard, many IDF operations, actions, and policies would be properly classified as terrorism. Yet, many members of Congress seem to presume that IDF killings of innocents are always accidental—and thus that the IDF is and always will be morally superior to the Palestinians. Apparently, as long as the Israeli government did not intend to get blamed for killing civilians, the killings are not intentional.

The Israeli government seems to use "terrorism" as a blanket term to cover everything except its own actions. An Associated Press analysis noted that "the Israelis employ [the word 'terrorist'] liberally, expanding it on occasion to cover low-level activists with no clear involvement in violence. The army has on several occasions announced the killing of a 'terrorist,' only to retract that later and acknowledge it was an unarmed civilian killed unintentionally."[192] The expansive

Israeli definition of terrorist was evident during Operation Defensive Shield. Maj. Gen. Dan Halutz, in a Jerusalem briefing on April 6, 2002, explained that Israel's actions in Jenin and elsewhere in the West Bank were attacks on terrorists, not civilians. He added: "By saying terrorists—we are shooting at those who are shooting at us."[193] Thus, anyone who shoots back at an IDF sniper is automatically a terrorist. Anyone who returns fire during an IDF ambush is a terrorist. Anyone who forcibly resists is a terrorist. Leah Harris of the Washington-based Jews for Peace in Palestine and Israel, observed: "All people who denounce the Israeli occupation are accused of supporting terrorism. According to this twisted logic, if you oppose Israeli state terrorism, then you of course support other forms of terrorism."[194]

The misdefinition of terrorism is the key to the "good versus evil" nature of the Middle East conflict. Both Palestinians and Israelis have committed vicious attacks on one another. But the U.S. government—especially the Bush administration—presumes that all of the attacks by one side are illegitimate, and almost all the attacks by the other side are justified. U.S. policy, by siding blindly and completely with Sharon, presumes that all Palestinians deserve punishment because of the actions of a single suicide bomber, while no Israeli deserves any blame for any of the wrongful killings by the IDF.

Unless the Israeli war on terrorism is measured simply by the number of Palestinians killed, homes razed, and lives thwarted, it is a miserable failure. The Israelis have relied on continually escalating oppression. The more violence the IDF used, the more violence Israeli civilians suffered. More Israelis have been killed in terrorist attacks since Sharon became prime minister than the total number of soldiers who died in the Six Day War in 1967.

Israel has created more terrorists than it has vanquished. Israeli attacks helped spawn Hamas and Hezbollah, as well as busloads of suicide bombers. A senior Israeli government security officer told reporters in Tel Aviv in late 2001: "All of the anti-terror measures which we've implemented during the past year can be compared figuratively to trying to empty the sea by using a spoon. . . . It is clear to all of us that there is no military solution to terror. Nowhere in the world have such situations been solved via military action."[195] Former State Department counter-terrorism official Larry Johnson observed, "The Israelis are their own worst enemies when it comes to fighting terrorism. They do more to incite and sustain terrorism than curb it."[196]

The Israeli government appears more interested in maximizing the amount of land seized than in minimizing Israeli casualties. This is made stark with the situating of settlements in areas that are almost impossible to defend. At least 66 new fledgling Jewish settlements cropped up in the two years after the start of the second Intifada.[197] Instead of admitting the futility of protecting the settlers, the Israeli government further dehumanizes the lives of Palestinians for miles around. Nahum Barnea, chief columnist of *Yedioth Ahronoth*, sees the toll the settlements take on hopes for peace: "Anyone who says that there is no connection between our presence, settlement-wise and militarily, in the territories and the insane dimensions to which Palestinian hatred has grown, is lying to his people."[198]

The Bush administration has accepted Sharon's notion that the Palestinians are responsible for all the violence they suffer from Israeli "retaliations." Yet, as *Washington Post* columnist Jackson Diehl noted, "Each period of Palestinian restraint was greeted with Israeli assassinations, home demolitions or incursions into Palestinian territory. Each terrorist attack launched by Arafat's extremist rivals was answered by devastating Israeli assaults on Arafat's own security forces."[199] Lev Grinberg, a political sociologist at Ben Gurion University, observed: "Every Israeli terror attack is always justified in terms of the last Palestinian terror attack, ignoring the fact that each attack is part of an unfinished circle of mutual violence and futile retaliation."[200] Neve Gordon wrote in the *Jerusalem Post:* "Insofar as terrorism is determined by the nature of the act and not by the identity of the perpetrator or the methods used, Israel's F-16 attacks are no different from Hamas's suicide bombers in terms of the effect they have on the Palestinian population. If anything, Israel's actions are much worse, both because they are state sanctioned and because the force used is much greater and therefore more destructive."[201]

The Bush administration has hitched its war on terrorism to Ariel Sharon. On April 18, 2002, as the world viewed pictures of wrecked and ravaged Jenin, Bush was asked by a journalist: "Do you believe that Ariel Sharon is a man of peace, and are you satisfied with his and his Government's assurances that there was no massacre in Jenin?" Bush replied: "I do believe Ariel Sharon is a man of peace."[202] Yet Sharon shows no intention of seeking peace. In an off-the-record speech to the U.S. Senate Foreign Relations Committee in June 2002, "Sharon pointed to no Israeli-Palestinian deal for at least 10 years. . . . Sharon claimed the ancient boundaries of the 'Land of Israel' are guaranteed to the Jewish people by Holy Scripture. . . . Committing himself to a hundred years' war against Arabs, Sharon warned the senators not to trust his adversaries—including moderate states closely aligned with the U.S.," columnist Robert Novak reported in the *Washington Post.*[203] Israeli writer Gideon Samet complained, "Instead of calming things down and balancing the pressure on Arafat with demands on Sharon to start talking with the Palestinians seriously, Uncle Sam is writing a script for a horrifying Western of the good guys against the bad guys, to death."[204]

While some critics portray Israel as supremely oppressive, far more Arabs were killed by the sanctions on Iraq in the 1990s than were killed by Israel in the Occupied Territories. Turkey has killed more Kurdish civilians since 1985 than Israel has killed Palestinians. The U.S. government accepts the same rationales for Israeli killings of innocent civilians that the United States used for its own killings of civilians in Panama (1989), Iraq (1991 and 2003), Somalia (1993), Serbia (1999), and Afghanistan (2001-the present).

To recognize Israeli abuses is not to condone similar abuses of the Palestinian Authority. Palestinians have been badly served by their own government at the same time they have been oppressed by the Israelis. The PA has routinely used torture. Arafat's intelligence operatives routinely murder Palestinians suspected of collaborating with Israel.[205] B'Tselem condemned the PA's human rights record as "appalling."[206] Almost two hundred Palestinian lawyers and human rights and law institutions signed a petition in late 2002 and early 2003 condemning the Palestinian Authority's "abuses against the judicial system," subversion of due process, and contempt for the constitution.[207] Many Palestinians believe that the PA, at least in the late 1990s, was more interested in collecting foreign aid for itself than in standing up for the rights and interests of the Palestinian people against the expanding settlements and mutliplying curfews.

The Israeli government operates to a far higher moral standard behind the Green Line—the 1967 borders—than in the Occupied Territories. Israel has one of the most vibrant, brave-hearted human rights movements in the world, as well as media outlets that consistently and courageously expose the follies of government policy. But, as Gila Svirsky of the Coalition of Women for a Just Peace, observed, "'Occupation corrupts,' we say in Israel, with reference to the moral deterioration of our society as a result of being the oppressor of others."[208]

# CHAPTER THIRTEEN

# Iraq and the War on Terrorism

Free societies do not intimidate through cruelty and conquest and open societies do not threaten the world with mass murder.

*—President Bush, United Nations, September 12, 2002*[1]

Whatever the duration of this struggle and whatever the difficulties, we will not permit the triumph of violence in the affairs of men; free people will set the course of history.

*—President Bush, January 28, 2003*[2]

Nowhere is Bush's antiterror opportunism starker than in his war against Iraq. Nothing symbolizes Bush's exploitation of 9/11 better than his campaign to cajole Americans into acquiescing to a preemptive attack against a nation that posed no threat to the United States.

From January 2003 onward, Bush constantly portrayed the United States as an innocent victim of Saddam's imminent aggression:

- On January 28, 2003, in his State of the Union address, Bush vowed: "If *war is forced upon us,* we will fight in a just cause and by just means, sparing, in every way we can, the innocent. And if war is forced upon us, we will fight with the full force and might of the United States military, and we will prevail."[3]
- On February 10, 2003, in a speech to the National Religious Broadcasters Convention in Nashville, Bush orated: "If war is forced upon us—and

I say 'forced upon us' because use of the military is not my first choice. I hug the mothers and the widows of those who may have lost their life in the name of peace and freedom."[4]

- On February 20, in remarks at a high school in Kennesaw, Georgia, Bush declared: "If war is forced upon us, we will liberate the people of Iraq from a cruel and violent dictator."[5]

- On February 26, in a speech at a Washington think tank dinner, Bush announced: "If war is forced upon us by Iraq's refusal to disarm, we will meet an enemy who . . . is capable of any crime."[6]

There was never any evidence that a war was forced upon the American people—at least not by a foreign government. The U.S. war with Iraq sprang from a fatal mixture of political mendacity and public ignorance.

Saddam Hussein was a brutal ruler who relied on violent suppression of the Kurds in the north of Iraq, the Shiite Muslims in the south, and anyone else suspected as a threat to his power. Saddam rose to power partly because of his skill in torture. However, brutal dictators were a dime a dozen in his neck of the woods. During the Iraq-Iran war, from 1980 to 1988 the United States provided Saddam with military intelligence as well as stores of materials that could be used to develop biological and chemical weapons.[7]

But after Saddam invaded Kuwait in August 1990 he quickly became a mortal enemy to the United States. President George Herbert Walker Bush denounced Saddam as a "Hitler" and committed the United States to leading a coalition to restore democracy to Kuwait, an Arabic monarchy. The United States and its allies promptly expelled Saddam from Kuwait and, after encouraging Kurds and Shiite Muslims to rebel, stood passively by while Saddam crushed their revolts.

## Sanctions and American Intentions

President Bush, in the months before attacking Iraq, continually stressed his affection for the Iraqi people. In his State of the Union address on January 28, 2003 Bush promised that, after the United States invaded Iraq, "we will bring to the Iraqi people food and medicines and supplies and freedom."[8] Bush made the same promise in his March 17, 2003 "48-hour ultimatum" speech: "Many Iraqis can hear me tonight in a translated radio broadcast, and I have a message for them. . . . As our coalition takes away their power, we will deliver the food and medicine you need."[9]

Bush portrayed the sufferings and deprivation of the Iraqi people as result-ing solely from the evil of Saddam Hussein. Bush's comments were intended as an antidote to the charge by Osama bin Laden a month after 9/11 that "a mil-lion innocent children are dying at this time as we speak, killed in Iraq without any guilt."[10] Bin Laden listed the economic sanctions against Iraq as one of the three main reasons for his holy war against the United States.

Most Western experts believe that bin Laden sharply overstated the death toll.[11] A United Nations Children Fund (UNICEF) report in 1999 concluded that half a million Iraqi children had died in the previous eight years because of the sanctions.[12] Colombia University Professor Richard Garfield, an epidemiolo-gist and an expert on the effects of sanctions, estimated in 2003 that the sanctions had resulted in between 343,900 and 529,000 infant and young child fatalities.[13]

Regardless of the precise number of fatalities (which will never be known), the sanctions were a key factor in inflaming Arab anger against the United States. The sanctions were initially imposed to punish Iraq for invading Kuwait and then were kept in place after the Gulf War purportedly in order to pressure Saddam to disarm.

Sanctions wreaked havoc on the Iraqi people in part because the Pentagon in-tentionally destroyed Iraq's water treatment systems during the first U.S.-Iraq war:

- A January 22, 1991, Defense Intelligence Agency report titled "Iraq Water Treatment Vulnerabilities" noted: "Iraq depends on importing specialized equipment and some chemicals to purify its water supply, most of which is heavily mineralized and frequently brackish to saline. . . . Failing to se-cure supplies will result in a shortage of pure drinking water for much of the population. This could lead to increased incidences, if not epidemics, of disease. . . . Unless the water is purified with chlorine, epidemics of such diseases as cholera, hepatitis, and typhoid could occur."[14]
- The U.S. Defense Intelligence Agency estimated in early 1991 that "it probably will take at least six months (to June 1991) before the [Iraqi water treatment] system is fully degraded" from the bombing during the Gulf War and the UN sanctions.[15]
- A May 1991 Pentagon analysis entitled "Status of Disease at Refugee Camps," noted: "Cholera and measles have emerged at refugee camps. Further infectious diseases will spread due to inadequate water treatment and poor sanitation."[16]
- A June 1991 Pentagon analysis noted that infectious disease rates had in-creased since the Gulf War and warned: "The Iraqi regime will continue to exploit disease incidence data for its own political purposes."[17]

George Washington University professor Thomas Nagy, who marshaled the preceding reports in an analysis in the September 2001 issue of *The Progressive,* concluded: "The United States knew it had the capacity to devastate the water treatment system of Iraq. It knew what the consequences would be: increased outbreaks of disease and high rates of child mortality. And it was more concerned about the public relations nightmare for Washington than the actual nightmare that the sanctions created for innocent Iraqis."[18]

A *Washington Post* analysis published on June 23, 1991 noted that Pentagon officials admitted that, rather than concentrating solely on military targets, the U.S. bombing campaign "sought to achieve some of their military objectives in the Persian Gulf War by disabling Iraqi society at large" and "deliberately did great harm to Iraq's ability to support itself as an industrial society."[19] The bombing campaign targeted Iraq's electrical power system, thereby destroying the country's ability to operate its water treatment plants. One Pentagon official who helped plan the bombing campaign observed: "People say, 'You didn't recognize that it was going to have an effect on water or sewage.' Well, what were we trying to do with sanctions—help out the Iraqi people? No. What we were doing with the attacks on infrastructure was to accelerate the effect of the sanctions."[20] Col. John Warden III, deputy director of strategy for the Air Force, observed: "Saddam Hussein cannot restore his own electricity. He needs help. If there are political objectives that the U.N. coalition has, it can say, 'Saddam, when you agree to do these things, we will allow people to come in and fix your electricity.' It gives us long-term leverage." Another Air Force planner observed: "We wanted to let people know, 'Get rid of this guy and we'll be more than happy to assist in rebuilding. We're not going to tolerate Saddam Hussein or his regime. Fix that, and we'll fix your electricity.'" The *Post* explained the Pentagon's rationale for punishing the Iraqi people: "Among the justifications offered now, particularly by the Air Force in recent briefings, is that Iraqi civilians were not blameless for Saddam's invasion of Kuwait. 'The definition of innocents gets to be a little bit unclear,' said a senior Air Force officer, noting that many Iraqis supported the invasion of Kuwait. 'They do live there, and ultimately the people have some control over what goes on in their country.'"[21]

A Harvard School of Public Health team visited Iraq in the months after the war and found epidemic levels of typhoid and cholera, as well as pervasive acute malnutrition. The *Post* noted, "In an estimate not substantively disputed by the Pentagon, the [Harvard] team projected that 'at least 170,000 children under five years of age will die in the coming year from the delayed effects' of the bombing."[22]

The U.S. military understood the havoc the 1991 bombing unleashed. A 1995 article entitled "The Enemy as a System" by Air Force Col. John Warden

III, published in the Air Force's *Airpower Journal,* discussed the benefits of bombing "dual-use targets" and noted: "A key example of such dual-use targeting was the destruction of Iraqi electrical power facilities in Desert Storm. . . . [D]estruction of these facilities shut down water purification and sewage treatment plants. As a result, epidemics of gastroenteritis, cholera, and typhoid broke out, leading to perhaps as many as 100,000 civilian deaths and a doubling of the infant mortality rate." The article concluded that the U.S. Air Force has a "vested interest in attacking dual-use targets" that undermine "civilian morale."[23]

In 1995, a team of doctors (including a representative of the Harvard School of Public Health) visited Iraq under the auspices of the UN Food and Agricultural Organization to examine the nutritional status and mortality rates of young children in Baghdad. They concluded that the sanctions had resulted in the deaths of 567,000 children in the previous five years.[24] (Most subsequent studies implicitly concluded that this study sharply overestimated the mortality toll in the first years of the sanctions.) CBS correspondent Lesley Stahl relied on this estimate in 1996 when she asked U.S. ambassador to the United Nations Madeline Albright: "We have heard that a half million children have died. That's more children than died in Hiroshima. And—and you know, is the price worth it?" Albright answered: "I think this is a very hard choice, but the price—we think the price is worth it."[25] Albright's words echoed like thunder through the Arab world in the following years.

At the behest of the United States and Britain, the United Nations maintained a de facto embargo on Iraq through 1996, when an oil-for-food program was approved. Saddam and the UN had wrangled for five years over the conditions under which Iraq would be permitted to resume oil exports. The oil-for-food program gave the UN Security Council veto power over how every cent of Iraqi oil revenues would be spent.

The de facto blockade on the Iraqi people made many common illnesses far more lethal. The *Detroit News* noted, "Many diseases—including cancer—cannot be treated in Iraq."[26] The *Washington Post* noted in December 2002, shortly after the Bush administration proposed new restrictions on antibiotic imports by Iraq: "As a practical matter, the most modern and effective medicines already are hard to come by here, even some of those used to treat routine illness." One Baghdad pharmacist groused that he "cannot get atropine or inhalers for asthmatics or insulin for diabetics."[27]

The infant/young child mortality rate in Iraq rose from 50 per 1,000 live births in 1990 to 133 per 1,000 in 2001 (meaning that more than 13 percent of Iraqi children die before the age of five). Iraq had by far the sharpest rise in infant/young child mortality of any nation in the world during that period, according to UNICEF.[28] Professor Richard Garfield declared: "It is the only instance of a sustained increase in mortality in a stable population of more than 2 million in the last 200 years."[29]

Sanctions advocates claimed that the punitive policy would spur discontent and eventually undermine Saddam's rule. However, a *Harvard International Review* analysis noted that "sanctions seem to have bolstered Saddam's domestic popularity. He uses the sanctions to demonize the West and to rally support for his leadership; they have been a convenient scapegoat for internal problems. The rations system he has established in response to the sanctions has tightened his control of Iraqi citizens' everyday lives, making them totally dependent on the government for mere survival and less likely to challenge his authority for fear of starvation."[30]

While Pentagon officials bluntly admitted in 1991 that sanctions aimed to punish the Iraqi people, candor evaporated as the death toll rose. The State Department web page announced in June 1999: "Sanctions are not intended to harm the people of Iraq. That is why the sanctions regime has always specifically exempted food and medicine."[31] This was false. Banning exports of oil effectively also banned imports of food, medicine, and other humanitarian goods. Some of the worst impacts of the sanctions dissipated after the oil-for-food program was launched, but by that point, hundreds of thousands of Iraqis may have already perished.

Denis Halliday, the UN administrator of the oil-for-food program, resigned in 1998 to protest the ravages the sanctions were continuing to inflict on Iraqis. Halliday complained: "We are in the process of destroying an entire country" and denounced the sanctions as "nothing less than genocide."[32] Hans von Sponeck, his replacement, served two years before resigning in protest in early 2000, denouncing the sanctions as a "criminal policy."[33] The International Committee of the Red Cross warned in a report in December 1999 that the oil-for-food program "has not halted the collapse of the health system and the deterioration of water supplies, which together pose one of the gravest threats to the health and well-being of the civilian population."[34] Seventy members of Congress sent a letter to President Clinton in early 2000 denouncing the sanctions as "infanticide masquerading as policy."[35]

While sanctions were maintained after the Gulf War purportedly to compel Iraq to disarm, the U.S. government long pursued a different goal. Secretary of State James Baker declared in May 1991: "We are not interested in seeking a relaxation of sanctions as long as Saddam Hussein is in power."[36] President Clinton decreed in November 1997 that "sanctions will be there until the end of time, or as long as he [Saddam Hussein] lasts."[37] At the end of the Clinton era, Defense Secretary William Cohen bragged: "We have been successful, through the sanctions regime, to really shut off most of the revenue that will be going to rebuild [Saddam Hussein's] military."[38]

Joy Gordon, a lawyer and professor at Fairfield University, spent three years researching the effects of the UN sanctions programs on Iraq. Gordon obtained many confidential UN documents that showed that "the United States has fought aggressively throughout the last decade to purposefully minimize the humanitarian goods that enter the country," as she reported in a November 2002 *Harper's* article (an extract from a book by Gordon forthcoming from Harvard University Press).[39] After the first Gulf War, the UN Security Council set up a committee to administer sanctions on Iraq. The U.S. government vigorously exploited its veto power on the committee by placing holds on contracts.

The *Economist* declared in early 2000 that Americans and British on the sanctions committee are "abusing their power to block suspicious imports."[40] The United States blocked the import of ambulances, tires, and soap. Imports of children's pencils were restricted "because lead could have a military use."[41] The U.S. vetoed allowing car batteries and fork lifts to be included on a list of humanitarian goods that could automatically be sent into Iraq. The Associated Press summarized controversies around U.S. vetoes of imports: "Most of the disputed contracts are for equipment to improve Iraq's dilapidated oil industry, power grid and water sanitation infrastructure."[42]

The U.S. government routinely and perennially vetoed delivery of goods that UN weapons inspectors had certified as posing no military benefit to Saddam. As of September 2001, the United States was blocking "nearly one third of water and sanitation and one quarter of electricity and educational—supply contracts were on hold." Gordon noted: "As of September 2001, nearly a billion dollars' worth of medical-equipment contracts—for which all the information sought had been provided—was still on hold." In early 2002, the U.S. blocked contracts for the delivery of "dialysis, dental, and fire-fighting equipment, water tankers, milk and yogurt production equipment, printing equipment for schools." Gordon reported: "Since August 1991 the United States has blocked most purchases of materials necessary for Iraq to generate electricity. . . . Often restrictions have hinged on the withholding of a single essential element, rendering many approved items useless. For example, Iraq was allowed to purchase a sewage-treatment plant but was blocked from buying the generator necessary to run it; this in a country that has been pouring 300,000 tons of raw sewage daily into its rivers.[43]

Gordon observed that the U.S. government "has sometimes given a reason for its refusal to approve humanitarian goods, sometimes given no reason at all, and sometimes changed its reason three or four times, in each instance causing a delay of months." Gordon noted: "The United States found many ways to slow approval of contracts. Although it insisted on reviewing every contract carefully, for years it didn't assign enough staff to do this without causing enormous delays." Large shipments of humanitarian aid were delayed "simply because of U.S. disinterest in spending the money necessary to review them."[44]

The U.S. government played politics with its holds, turning Iraq into a pork barrel for wheeling and dealing on the UN Security Council. In 2001, the United States proposed a reform called "smart sanctions" that would have automatically slowed down many more imports into Iraq—while removing the United States from culpability for blocking the relief. Secretary of State Colin Powell said that the U.S. government was confident that the revised sanctions system would be "able to keep the box as tightly closed as we have the last 10 years, without receiving on our shoulders all the baggage that goes with it."[45]

When Russia refused to support "smart sanctions," the United States responded by slapping holds on almost all the contracts that Russian companies had to deliver goods to Iraq. After Russia agreed to support a revised sanctions reform in April 2002, U.S. government holds on three-quarters of a billion dollars in Russian contracts for Iraq suddenly vanished in what one diplomat told the *Financial Times* was "the boldest move yet by the U.S. to use the holds to buy political agreement."[46]

Gordon concluded that "U.S. policy consistently opposed any form of economic development within Iraq."[47] As of mid-2002, the importation of almost $5 billion in humanitarian goods was blocked—almost entirely because of holds imposed by the U.S. and British governments.

President Bush sought to blame all the Iraqi people's suffering on Saddam's weapons lust. In an October 7, 2002 speech Bush declared: "The world has also tried economic sanctions and watched Iraq use billions of dollars in illegal oil revenues to fund more weapons purchases, rather than providing for the needs of the Iraqi people."[48] While Saddam did use some of the revenue from "illegal" (i.e., unauthorized by the UN) oil sales to Syria and elsewhere to purchase weapons, the United States never presented any evidence that such purchases amounted to "billions of dollars." The United States position appeared to be that, as long as Saddam spent a single cent on weapons, the United States was blameless for the devastation from its "siege warfare" tactics.

After human rights advocates had harshly condemned sanctions on Iraq for almost a decade, the sanctions suddenly morphed into a *causa belli*. At a March 27, 2003 joint press conference for Bush and British prime minister Tony Blair, Blair declared: "Over the past five years, 400,000 Iraqi children under the age of five died of malnutrition and disease, preventively, but died because of the nature of the regime under which they are living. Now, that is why we're acting."[49] *Progressive* editor Matthew Rothschild observed that Bush and Blair "refuse to acknowledge any responsibility for those deaths and instead seize upon them simply to justify their war of aggression."[50]

After the war started, the suffering caused by sanctions became further proof of Saddam's depravity. In a March 25, 2003 press conference announcing plans for humanitarian aid after the Iraq War, Agency for International Development administrator Andrew Natsios declared: "There has been a water issue, and I am not sure everybody entirely understands this. It predates the war. Water and sanitation are the principal reasons children have died at higher rates than they should have for a middle-income country. . . . It is a function of a deliberate decision by the regime not to repair the water system or replace old equipment with new equipment, so in many cases people are basically drinking untreated sewer water in their homes and have been for some years."[51] In reality, the United States government perennially blocked the importation of the necessary equipment and supplies to repair the water system—as if it were a "dual use" because of the possibility that Iraqi soldiers would get glasses of water from the repaired systems.

From 1991 through the end of 2002, 8,924 people were killed in attacks by international terrorists, according to the U.S. State Department.[52] The sanctions on Iraq may have killed more than 50 times as many civilians as did terrorists during a time when terrorism was supposedly one of the gravest threats to humanity.

During the 2000 election campaign, Bush criticized the Clinton administration for failing to keep sanctions as tight as possible.[53] In the lead-up to the war, Bush frequently relished recounting the details of Saddam's brutality, especially the alleged gas attacks against Kurdish villages that, according to Bush, "killed or injured at least 20,000 people, more than 6 times the number of people who died in the attacks of September the 11th."[54] (It is unclear whether it was the Iraqis or the Iranians who actually carried out the gas attacks.[55]) But far more Iraqi children were killed by sanctions after Bush's inauguration on January 20, 2001 than Saddam killed in his alleged gas attacks on the Kurds.

If the estimate of 500,000 dead as a result of sanctions is correct, that would be the equivalent of snuffing out the lives of all the babies and young children in Montana, Wyoming, South Dakota, and North Dakota.

The fact that bin Laden greatly exaggerated the sanctions death toll does not absolve the U.S. government. Within a year or two after the end of the Gulf War, it should have been obvious that sanctions would neither turn Saddam into a Boy Scout nor bring him to his knees. The U.S. government knew the sanctions were scourging the Iraqi people. Three U.S. Presidents escaped any liability for the

Iraqi deaths caused by U.S. policy. The people who worked in the World Trade Center may not have been so lucky.

## Origins of an Unnecessary War

Deputy Secretary of Defense Paul Wolfowitz was obsessively pushing to attack Iraq long before 9/11. At a Pentagon press briefing on September 13, 2001, Wolfowitz announced: "It's not just simply a matter of capturing people and holding them accountable, but removing the sanctuaries, removing the support systems, ending states who sponsor terrorism. It will be a campaign, not a single action."[56] Wolfowitz's "ending states" threat sent shudders through America's allies as it was the first hint that the United States might exploit 9/11 to go on an international rampage against its suspected enemies.

At a September 15, 2001 meeting of top administration officials, Wolfowitz pushed to attack Iraq. Bob Woodward, in his book *Bush at War,* summarized the arguments Wolfowitz made to the inner sanctum: "Attacking Afghanistan would be uncertain. He worried about 100,000 American troops bogged down in mountain fighting in Afghanistan six months from then. In contrast, Iraq was a brittle, oppressive regime that might break easily. It was doable. He estimated that there was a 10 to 50 percent chance Saddam was involved in the September 11 terrorist attacks. The U.S. would have to go after Saddam at some time if the war on terrorism was to be taken seriously."[57] Thus, a hypothetical 10 percent chance that Saddam was linked to the 9/11 hijackers was, according to Wolfowitz, sufficient justification to invade Iraq and crush its government.

At a White House meeting on September 17, 2001 Bush announced: "I believe Iraq was involved, but I'm not going to strike them now. I don't have the evidence at this point."[58] Bush did not permit the lack of evidence to impede the path of righteousness. Bush issued an order to the Pentagon to "begin planning military options for an invasion of Iraq," according to senior administration officials.[59]

Wolfowitz is one of the most prominent and influential neoconservatives in the Bush administration. In January 1998, Wolfowitz and 17 other neoconservatives sent a letter to President Clinton urging him to launch a military attack to overthrow Saddam Hussein.[60] David Wurmser, the top aide to Undersecretary of State John Bolton, proposed shortly before Bush took office that Israel and the United States should "strike fatally, not merely disarm, the centers of radicalism in the region—the regimes of Damascus, Baghdad, Tripoli, Tehran, and Gaza. That would establish the recognition that fighting either the United

States or Israel is suicidal."[61] Richard Perle, the chairman of the Defense Policy Board who became known as the "father of the Iraq war,"[62] orchestrated a high-level Pentagon briefing by a former top aide of Lyndon LaRouche who denounced Saudi Arabia as an enemy of the United States and urged giving the Saudis an ultimatum to stop their anti-Israel propaganda, among other steps, or else the United States would seize their oil fields.[63]

The Israeli newspaper *Haaretz* reported on April 5, 2003: "The war in Iraq was conceived by 25 neoconservative intellectuals, most of them Jewish, who are pushing President Bush to change the course of history."[64] (Many neoconservatives are not Jewish, and most Jews are not neoconservatives.) A week before Bush started the war, the *Wall Street Journal* noted: "The U.S. is soon likely to go to war in Iraq in no small part because of the arguments of thinkers who have graced the pages of *Commentary* magazine over the years."[65] (*Commentary* is the magazine of the American Jewish Committee.) A separate article, "A Pro-U.S. Democratic Area Is a Goal That Has Israeli, Neoconservative Roots," noted that "if Mr. Bush emerges with a quick victory in Iraq, it could embolden Mr. Sharon's policy of pre-emptive action, not just against Palestinian militants but also in places such as the northern border with Lebanon."[66]

*Washington Post* columnist Michael Kinsley observed in October 2002 that, in the U.S. debate about war with Iraq, Israel "is the proverbial elephant in the room: Everybody sees it, no one mentions it."[67] While mentioning Israel's interests as one motive for the war was often considered taboo, smearing the motives of war opponents was not. Former Bush speechwriter David Frum labeled all the antiwar protestors who marched in the United States in January 2003 as presumptively anti-Semitic: "Why do we call them peace marchers? . . . What you see there is not opposition to war. They are all for war, when it is waged against Israel."[68] Frum's verdict would have been news to the many Jewish individuals and groups that participated in antiwar demonstrations across the land. The neoconservative *New York Sun* suggested in February 2003 that the New York Police Department "send two witnesses along for each participant [in an antiwar demonstration], with an eye toward preserving at least the possibility of an eventual treason prosecution" since all the demonstrators were guilty of "giving, at the very least, comfort to Saddam Hussein."[69]

Most neoconservatives believe that the United States must vigorously dominate the Middle East in order to protect Israel from all possible threats. The Likud Party panted at the prospect of the United States razing Saddam. The *Guardian* reported on August 17, 2002 that "Israel signalled its decision yesterday to put public pressure on President George Bush to go ahead with a military attack on Iraq" via alarmist statements by senior Sharon advisor Ranaan

Gissin.[70] Former Israeli prime minister Benjamin Netanyahu told a congressional committee on September 12, 2002, "I speak for the overwhelming majority of Israelis in supporting a preemptive strike against Saddam's regime."[71] Columnist Robert Novak noted in the *Washington Post* in late 2002: "In private conversation with [Sen. Chuck] Hagel and many other members of Congress, [Sharon] leaves no doubt that the greatest U.S. assistance to Israel would be to overthrow Saddam Hussein's Iraqi regime."[72]

*Washington Post* editor Robert Kaiser noted in February 2003: "For the first time a U.S. administration and a Likud government are pursuing nearly identical policies."[73] Rep. Tom Lantos, one of the most powerful Democrats in the House of Representatives, told an Israeli parliament member in September 2002 that, after the U.S. deposed Saddam, "we'll install a pro-Western dictator, who will be good for us and for you."[74] Lantos estimated that the U.S.-chosen dictator would rule for at least five years.

In a speech to the neoconservative American Enterprise Institute on February 26, 2003 Bush portrayed his pending war against Iraq as the solution to the Israel-Palestinian conflict. Bush declared: "The passing of Saddam Hussein's regime will deprive terrorist networks of a wealthy patron that pays for terrorist training and offers rewards to families of suicide bombers. And other regimes will be given a clear warning that support for terror will not be tolerated."[75] Israeli prime minister Sharon hoped that Palestinians would be daunted—and more submissive—after the United States toppled the Iraqi government. On April 10, 2003, Israeli defense minister Shaul Mofaz declared: "I hope that in the era after the toppling of Saddam Hussein's regime, the Palestinians will understand that the world has changed."[76]

Though the neoconservatives had profound influence on Bush policy and on the mainstream media, many rabbis in the Reform movement strongly opposed the war with Iraq, as did Rabbi Ismar Schorsch, the chancellor of the Jewish Theological Seminary and the leader of Conservative Judaism in America, who declared that Bush's foreign policy suffered from "hubris."[77] Many libertarian and leftist Jewish writers were in the forefront of the opposition to the war, including Sheldon Richman, Richard Ebeling, Joe Klein, Norman Solomon, Robert Scheer, and a bevy of fiery American and Israeli contributors at Counterpunch.org. But the opponents to the war had nothing to match the clout of the pro-war American Israel Political Action Committee, renowned as Washington's most powerful interest group.[78]

Bush would not have been easily swayed by neoconservative arguments if he had not lusted to be a war president. After 9/11, Bush was exalted far more than ever before in his life. It was unlikely that shifting his primary energy to the faith-based initiative would sustain his poll ratings in the same way that foreign conflicts would. On December 21, 2001, Bush announced to reporters that "next year will be a war year as well because we're going to continue to hunt down these al Qaeda people."[79] James Moore, co-author of *Bush's Brain: How Karl Rove Made George W. Bush Presidential,* declared: "Karl Rove led the nation to war to improve the political prospects of George W. Bush."[80] Revelations after the fighting stopped that the president's reelection campaign would be based on a war theme are further evidence of the political calculations that may have influenced the decision to invade.[81]

Another major factor in the rush to war was explained by the common quip of the time: "How did our oil get under their sand?" Some Bush appointees may have been anxious to stake a claim for U.S. control of the second-largest proven oil reserve in the world. Iraqi oil has been a spur of Western imperial ambitions since the 1920s. The role of oil appeared to loom larger after the war, when the administration rushed to award a lucrative noncompetitive contract for oil field repair to Halliburton, a company formerly headed by Dick Cheney. The Bush administration's initial post-war proposal to the United Nations would have given the United States control and vast discretion over the use of Iraqi oil revenues and left "open the prospect of the United States tapping into Iraq's oil revenue to finance its own costly efforts to disarm Iraq."[82]

Bush took great pains to convince Americans and the world that he was sincerely interested in a peaceful resolution of any dispute with Iraq. In reality, he decided to go to war at least a year before he announced his final decision. In March 2002, National Security Advisor Condy Rice was having a White House meeting with three U.S. senators on Iraq when Bush stuck his head in the door and announced "Fuck Saddam! We're taking him out!"[83] Rice and the senators had been discussing whether to deal with Saddam via the United Nations or with military action. *Time* magazine said that Bush "waved his hand dismissively, recalls a participant, and neatly summed up his Iraq policy in that short phrase. The Senators laughed uncomfortably; Rice flashed a knowing smile. The President left the room."[84] Bush's declaration meant that all his subsequent posturing, all his concerns about inspections, all his pretended devotion to the UN Security Council process was a ruse to convince people he was making a good-faith effort to avoid war—and to help provide cover for British Prime Minister Blair to bring his country into the war as well. (*Newsweek,* in a cover article titled "Bush and God," declared that Bush "just decided that Saddam was evil, and everything flowed from that."[85])

## Saddam as the Twentieth Hijacker

In a memo Bush sent on March 18, 2003, notifying Congress that he was launching the war against Iraq, Bush declared that he was acting "to take the necessary actions against international terrorists and terrorist organizations, including those nations, organizations, or persons who planned, authorized, committed, or aided the terrorist attacks that occurred on September 11, 2001.[86]

Bush invoked this justification even though his administration had never offered a shred of evidence tying Saddam to 9/11. But the Saddam–al Qaeda link was the key to the administration's exploitation of the ignorance of the American people. Bush and team continually threw out new accusations and then backed off, knowing that few people were paying close enough attention to recognize that previous charges had collapsed like a row of houses of cards. The Los Angeles Times noted in late January 2003: "After pressing the case last year that it suspected Iraq–Al Qaeda links, the administration seemed to drop the matter in recent months. But in a campaign to regain momentum in the diplomatic push for confronting Iraq, the White House has revived those claims of ties to Al Qaeda this week."[87]

As much as Bush may have personally disliked Saddam, he still needed pretexts to rally public support to attack a nation six thousand miles away that appeared to pose no threat to America.

In the first months after 9/11, there was little mention of Iraq in the public pronouncements by Bush and his top officials. But in his State of the Union address on January 29, 2002, Bush stunned many people by announcing that Iraq, along with Iran and North Korea, were part of an "axis of evil."[88]

Since the war on terrorism had stratospheric support levels in the polls from the American people, the best way to sanctify a war against Iraq was to redefine it as part of the war on terrorism. Bush, commenting to the press on September 25, 2002, compared Al Qaeda and Saddam: "Al Qaeda hides, Saddam doesn't, but the danger is, is that they work in concert. The danger is that al Qaeda becomes an extension of Saddam's madness and his hatred and his capacity to extend weapons of mass destruction around the world. . . . You can't distinguish between al Qaeda and Saddam when you talk about the war on terror. . . . They're both equally as bad, and equally as evil, and equally as destructive."[89] Bush had barely made the accusation before the White House began spinning his comments. White House press secretary Ari Fleischer "tried to play down the specificity of Bush's charge, saying the president was talking about what he feared could occur," the Washington Post reported the following day.[90]

The next day, National Security Advisor Rice announced during a TV interview: "We clearly know that there were in the past and have been contacts between senior Iraqi officials and members of al Qaeda going back for actually quite a long time."[91] After dangling the two villains together in front of the TV audience's eyes, Rice added: "No one is trying to make an argument at this point that Saddam Hussein somehow had operational control of what happened on September 11, so we don't want to push this too far, but this is a story that is unfolding, and it is getting clearer, and we're learning more."[92]

On the same day, Defense Secretary Donald Rumsfeld announced that the United States possessed "bulletproof" evidence linking Saddam and Al Qaeda. But it was apparently a bullet that could never be exposed to sunlight. (An earlier alleged link between Iraqi agents and hijacker Mohamed Atta meeting in Prague had long since collapsed, with the story disavowed by both the Central Intelligence Agency and the Czech government.)

On October 7, 2002, Bush, speaking to a selective audience of Republican donors and others in Cincinnati, laid out his logic: "We know that Iraq and the Al Qaida terrorist network share a common enemy—the United States of America. We know that Iraq and Al Qaida have had high-level contacts that go back a decade. Some Al Qaida leaders who fled Afghanistan went to Iraq. These include one very senior Al Qaida leader who received medical treatment in Baghdad this year, and who has been associated with planning for chemical and biological attacks. . . . And we know that after September the 11th, Saddam Hussein's regime gleefully celebrated the terrorist attacks on America."[93] The fact that some Iraqis cheered the carnage on September 11 was offered as evidence that Saddam could team up with Al Qaeda for a second 9/11.

On November 1, 2002, at a Republican campaign rally in New Hampshire, Bush denounced Saddam: "We know he's got ties with Al Qaida. A nightmare scenario, of course, is that he becomes the arsenal for a terrorist network, where they could attack America, and he'd leave no fingerprints behind."[94]

The link between Saddam and Al Qaeda then took a three-month recess, returning in the 2003 State of the Union address, when Bush declared that "Saddam Hussein aids and protects terrorists, including members of Al Qaeda." Bush reached for the ultimate hot button: "Imagine those 19 hijackers with other weapons and other plans, this time armed by Saddam Hussein. It would take one vial, one canister, one crate slipped into this country to bring a day of horror like none we have ever known."[95]

Three days later, when Bush was directly asked by a journalist at a White House press conference, "Do you believe that there is a link between Saddam Hussein, a direct link, and the men who attacked on September the 11th?" Bush replied: "I can't make that claim."[96] Yet, that did not stop him from continually making the inference.

The bevy of new allegations were based on nothing more than guesses and hunches. The *Los Angeles Times* revealed: "The Bush administration's renewed assertions of links between Iraq and Al Qaeda are based largely on the murky case of a one-legged Al Qaeda suspect who was treated in Baghdad after being wounded in the war in Afghanistan."[97] Abu Musab Zarqawi, an Al Qaeda leader, spent time in Baghdad after the U.S. forces attacked Afghanistan but there was no evidence that he conspired with Saddam's regime while there. *Time* noted of Bush's message on Saddam and Al Qaeda: "If there was no visible evidence to link the two, he just used that fact to argue his point: the danger is everywhere, even if we can't see it; the threat is growing, even if we can't prove it. The Administration's argument for war is based not on the strength of America's Intelligence but on its weakness."[98]

The *New York Times* reported in February 2003: "Some analysts at the Central Intelligence Agency have complained that senior administration officials have exaggerated the significance of some intelligence reports about Iraq, particularly about its possible links to terrorism, in order to strengthen their political argument for war. . . . At the FBI, some investigators said they were baffled by the Bush administration's insistence on a solid link between Iraq and Osama bin Laden's network."[99] Elizabeth Drew, writing in the *New York Review of Books,* noted, "When [Secretary of State] Colin Powell was preparing his presentation to the UN Security Council on February 6, he resisted citing the alleged links between Iraq and al-Qaeda; he was forced to do so at the White House's insistence."[100]

Unless someone followed Bush's rhetoric on a full-time basis, they would miss the switching off and on of the Saddam–Al Qaeda connection. But it was not necessary for administration officials to continually assert the link—as long as they mentioned it often enough to plant the seeds and fan the fears in Americans' minds.

In the first weeks after 9/11, less than ten percent of Americans suggested to poll takers that Saddam was the source of the terrorist attacks.[101] However, after the constant accusations and insinuations by the Bush administration, the number soared. A February 2003 poll found that 72 percent of Americans believed that Hussein was "personally involved in the September 11 attacks."[102] A January 2003 poll found that almost half of Americans believed that one or more of the 9/11 hijackers were Iraqi—even though not a single hijacker hailed from that country.[103] Seventy-three percent believed that Saddam "is currently helping al-Qaeda."[104]

Bush played the Saddam–9/11 link like a master violinist. A *Christian Science Monitor* analysis published on March 14, 2003, noted: "In his prime-time press conference last week, which focused almost solely on Iraq, President Bush mentioned Sept. 11 eight times. He referred to Saddam Hussein many more times than that, often in the same breath with Sept. 11. Bush never pinned blame for the attacks directly on the Iraqi president. Still, the overall effect was to reinforce an impression that persists among much of the American public: that the Iraqi dictator did play a direct role in the attacks. . . . The White House appears to be encouraging this false impression, as it seeks to maintain American support for a possible war against Iraq."[105]

Bush revved the rhetoric to frighten people into supporting his war, including the obligatory comparisons to the Third Reich. In a speech to Czech teenagers on November 22, 2002, Bush warned that the threat from evil leaders such as Saddam was as bad or worse than the threat from Hitler: "We face perils we've never thought about, perils we've never seen before. They're just as dangerous as those perils that your fathers and mothers and grandfathers and grandmothers faced."[106] White House chief of staff Andrew Card warned that Saddam could threaten the world "with a holocaust."[107] Pentagon spokeswoman Victoria Clarke hyped Saddam as the worst dictator in history: "The Iraqi people will be free of decades and decades and decades of torture and oppression the likes of which I think the world has not ever seen before."[108]

## Weapons of Mass Deception

In the lead-up to war, Bush continually sought to frighten Americans with the specter of an attack by Iraq. In his January 28, 2003, State of the Union address, Bush denounced Saddam as "the dictator who is assembling the world's most dangerous weapons" and listed vast quantities of biological and chemical weapons that few independent experts believed Saddam possessed. Bush concluded: "A future lived at the mercy of terrible threats is no peace at all."[109] In his March 19 "ultimatum address," after listing Saddam's alleged WMDs, Bush declaimed: "And this very fact underscores the reason we cannot live under the threat of blackmail."[110] In his March 20, 2003 announcement of the start of the war, Bush declared: "The people of the United States and our friends and allies will not live at the mercy of an outlaw regime that threatens the peace with weapons of mass murder.[111]

In his March 17, 2003, speech on his 48-hour ultimatum to Saddam, Bush declared that "the Iraq regime continues to possess and conceal some of the most lethal weapons ever devised. . . . Under [UN] Resolutions 678 and 687—both still in effect—the United States and our allies are authorized to use force in ridding Iraq of weapons of mass destruction."[112] Bush warned: "In one year, or five years, the power of Iraq to inflict harm on all free nations would be multiplied many times over."[113] There was no evidence that the Iraq "threat" had increased in recent years and no reason to expect it to "multiply many times over" in the following 12 months—especially since UN weapons inspectors were busily ferreting in Iraq at that moment.

The Bush team waved nuke after alleged Iraqi nuke over Americans' heads in the run-up to the war. On August 26, 2002, Vice President Dick Cheney, speaking to the Veterans of Foreign Wars, warned that Saddam could have nuclear weapons "fairly soon."[114] Two weeks later, President Bush told reporters: "I would remind you that when the inspectors first went into Iraq and were denied, finally denied access, a report came out of the Atomic—the IAEA—that they were six months away from developing a weapon. I don't know what more evidence we need."[115] On March 16, 2003, Cheney announced on NBC's "Meet the Press" that "we believe [Saddam] has, in fact, reconstituted nuclear weapons."[116] But the Bush administration never presented any evidence to support these assertions. The International Atomic Energy Agency (IAEA), the UN organization that was conducting inspections for nuclear weapons in Iraq, never produced the report Bush "reminded" reporters of in September. Mohamed El-Baradei, IAEA's director general, informed the UN Security Council that "there is no indication of resumed nuclear activities" in Iraq.[117] Although Cheney and Bush repeatedly invoked some aluminum tubes that Iraq sought to purchase as key steps toward making a nuke, UN experts investigated and concluded that the tubes were not intended for use in nuclear weapon production.

Perhaps the most decisive evidence offered by the Bush administration was the fact that Iraq sought to buy 500 tons of uranium oxide for use in nuclear weapons from uranium mines in Niger. CIA chief George Tenet gave a classified briefing to congressmen on this and other charges in September 2002, a few weeks before Congress voted to endorse war with Iraq.[118] Secretary of State Colin Powell also informed a closed hearing of the Senate Foreign Relations Committee two days later of the Iraq attempt to secure the key ingredient for a nuclear weapon. The revelation sent shock waves through Capitol Hill and helped squelch resistance to going to war.

In his January 28 State of the Union Address, Bush declared: "The British government has learned that Saddam Hussein recently sought significant quantities of uranium from Africa." But in early March, the IAEA announced that the documents detailing the attempted purchases of uranium were frauds. One senior IAEA official told the *New Yorker*'s Seymour Hersh: "These documents are so bad that I cannot imagine that they came from a serious intelligence agency. It depresses me, given the low quality of the documents, that it was not stopped."[119] The British government had long refused to give the documents to the IAEA; when the Brits finally passed along the "smoking gun," it took IAEA inspectors "only a few hours to determine that the documents were fake," Hersh reported. The letters appeared to be a crude cut-and-paste operation with Niger government letterhead; however, the names of officials in power did not match the dates on the letter and the signature of Niger president Tandja Mamadou was an obvious forgery. A senior IAEA official observed that the flaws in the letters could have been "spotted by someone using Google on the Internet."[120] Hersh, who wrote a superb exposé on the scam, noted: "Forged documents and false accusations have been an element in U.S. and British policy toward Iraq at least since the fall of 1997, after an impasse over U.N. inspections."[121] Sen. Jay Rockefeller (D-W.V.) requested that Federal Bureau of Investigations Chief Robert Mueller investigate the document fraud because "there is a possibility that the fabrication of these documents may be part of a larger deception campaign aimed at manipulating public opinion and foreign policy regarding Iraq."[122] The FBI effectively brushed off Rockefeller's request.[123]

Six weeks after Hersh's piece appeared, *New York Times* columnist Nicholas Kristof reported that, much earlier, the vice president's office had made an investigation into the Iraq-Niger nuclear documents, sending a former U.S. ambassador to Niger. In February 2002, "that envoy reported to the C.I.A. and State Department that the information was unequivocally wrong and that the documents had been forged. . . . The envoy's debunking of the forgery was passed around the administration and seemed to be accepted—except that President Bush and the State Department kept citing it anyway," Kristof reported.[124]

Both Bush and Cheney invoked the testimony of Gen. Hussein Kamel, an Iraqi defector who was chief of Saddam's secret weapons development before he exited to Jordan in August 1995. Cheney declared on August 26, 2002 that the defection of Kamel "should serve as a reminder to all that we often learn more as the result of defections than we learned from the inspection regime itself." While Bush and Cheney invoked Kamel as a shining example of an Iraqi truth teller, they chose to ignore—or, more accurately, bury—the most important information Kamel revealed: that "Iraq had halted the production of VX nerve agent in the late 1980s and destroyed its banned missiles, stocks of anthrax and other chemical agents and poison gases soon after the Persian Gulf War."[125] Kamel told the UN: "I ordered destruction of all chemical weapons. All weapons—biological, chemical, missile, nuclear were destroyed."[126] If Bush had publicly recited the preceding quote from Kamel, his case for war would have collapsed like a bad soufflé. If U.S. officials trusted Kamel as much as Bush and Cheney implied, then Kamel's revelation also meant that the U.S. government acted in bad faith in perpetrating sanctions on Iraq long after the weapons were destroyed.

The Bush administration scorned any evidence that did not support a rush to war. When Defense Secretary Rumsfeld was asked in February 2002 about evidence of Iraq supply of weapons of mass destruction to terrorists, Rumsfeld replied that " the absence of evidence is not evidence of absence."[127] After the United Nations weapons inspectors returned to Iraq in late 2002, they followed scores of leads from U.S. intelligence agencies to suspected sites of Iraqi weapons and found nothing—but that was irrelevant to the case for war. Deputy Defense Secretary Wolfowitz, commenting in San Francisco on the eve of the Iraqi government's release of a twelve-thousand-page report on its weapons, made it clear the Iraqi presentation was irrelevant: "If [Saddam] flatly denies that he has weapons of mass destruction, that's good evidence [of his guilt]. If he comes forth with new programs that we didn't know about, that's good evidence." Wolfowitz asserted that Saddam was guilty "until proven otherwise."[128] In another forum, Wolfowitz explained the "standard" which Saddam must satisfy: "It's like the judge said about pornography. I can't define it, but I will know it when I see it."[129] When the news media continued requesting evidence of Iraqi perfidy, Rumsfeld groused to the press corps on February 4, 2003: "The fixation on a smoking gun is fascinating to me. You all . . . have been watching 'L.A. Law' or something too much."[130] Rumsfeld earlier declared that there was almost nothing worse than a smoking gun: "The last thing we want to see is a smoking gun. A gun smokes after it has been fired. The goal must be to stop such an action before it happens."[131]

Though the budget for U.S. intelligence agencies jumped in the wake of 9/11 (the precise increases are kept secret on grounds of "national security"), the Bush administration often avoided tainting its decisions and proclamations on Iraq with credible information. U.S. diplomat John Brady Kiesling, the political counselor at the U.S. embassy in Athens, resigned in protest over what he considered the Bush administration's foul play. Kiesling declared: "We have not seen such systematic distortion of intelligence, such systematic manipulation of American opinion, since the war in Vietnam. We spread disproportionate terror and confusion in the public mind, arbitrarily linking the unrelated problems of terrorism and Iraq."[132] Former CIA counterterrorism chief Vince Cannistraro observed: "Basically, cooked information is working its way into high-level pronouncements, and there's a lot of unhappiness about it in intelligence, especially among analysts at the CIA."[133] The *Philadelphia Inquirer* reported on October

8, 2002: "A growing number of military officers, intelligence professionals and diplomats . . . charge that the administration squelches dissenting views and that intelligence analysts are under intense pressure to produce reports supporting the White House's argument that Saddam poses such an immediate threat to the United States that pre-emptive military action is necessary."[134] Richard J. Durbin (D., Ill.), a member of the Senate Intelligence Committee, received classified briefings from top administration officials on the extent of the Iraqi threat. Durbin publicly complained: "It's troubling to have classified information that contradicts statements made by the administration."[135]

## Miscounting the World

After snubbing the United Nations after the Security Council did not endorse going to war, the Bush administration strove to portray its efforts against Iraq as a true international coalition. Administration officials jiggered together a long list of countries that they labeled "the coalition of the willing." When he announced on March 19 that he was launching the war, Bush declared: "More than 35 countries are giving crucial support, from the use of naval and air bases, to help with intelligence and logistics, to the deployment of combat units. Every nation in this coalition has chosen to bear the duty and share the honor of serving in our common defense."[136] Defense Secretary Rumsfeld announced on March 20: "The coalition against Iraq . . . is large and growing. This is not a unilateral action, as is being characterized in the media. Indeed, the coalition in this activity is larger than the coalition that existed during the Gulf War in 1991."[137] White House press secretary Ari Fleischer bragged: "All told, the population of coalition of the willing is approximately 1.18 billion people around the world. The coalition countries have a combined GDP of approximately $21.7 trillion. Every major race, religion and ethnic group in the world is represented. The coalition includes nations from every continent on the globe."[138]

The pretensions were sufficient to mislead anyone who was catching the television news with one eye on the tube and the other on their freedom fries. While the 1991 anti-Iraq coalition consisted of 30-plus nations that committed their military forces, the 2003 version was more a list of foreign government officials who signed on a dotted line. After Palau joined the coalition, Hersey Kyota, Palau's ambassador to Washington, explained that his country's president "thought it was a good idea to write a letter of support, so he did."[139] That was sufficient to get Palau enrolled—even though the tiny nation has no military to send to the Gulf. The Marshall Islands and Micronesia also joined the coalition.[140] The government of the Solomon Islands was shocked when informed it had enlisted in the coalition. Solomon Islands Prime Minister Allan Kemakeza quickly announced: "The Government is completely unaware of such statements being made, therefore wishes to disassociate itself from the report."[141] Dana Milbank noted in the *Washington Post:* "After initially including Angola in the coalition of the willing last week, the White House removed the country without explanation. . . . Angolan Embassy officials didn't respond yesterday to phone calls. With luck, Angola can be replaced by Morocco. . . . Morocco's weekly *al Usbu' al-Siyassi* claimed that Morocco has offered 2,000 monkeys to help detonate land mines. An official at the Moroccan Embassy could not confirm the presence of monkeys in the coalition of the willing."[142]

## Liberating to Death

White House press spokesman Ari Fleischer declared on April 10, 2003 that weapons of mass destruction "is what this war was about and it is about."[143] Yet, some foreigners may have wondered if the Bush administration may have been hypocritical on this issue. The war against Iraq began with a massive "shock and awe" cruise missile and aerial bombardment of Baghdad and other primary targets, attempting to almost instantly shatter the Iraqi will to resist. Though "shock and awe" failed to bring the Iraqi government to its knees, the pictures of mushroom clouds rising from Baghdad after bomb explosions mesmerized viewers around the world and enraged millions of Arabs.

The doctrine of "shock and awe" was developed by Harlan Ullman, a National War College professor, along with James Wade. In a 1996 study financed by the National Defense University, Ullman and Wade wrote: "Theoretically, the magnitude of Shock and Awe . . . seeks to impose (in extreme cases) is the nonnuclear equivalent of the impact that atomic weapons dropped on Hiroshima and Nagasaki had on the Japanese."[144] Shortly before the war started, Ullman reiterated the goal of "shock and awe": "You have this simultaneous effect, rather like the nuclear weapons at Hiroshima, not taking days or weeks but minutes."[145]

During the war and its aftermath, President Bush continually bragged about the accuracy of American weapons. In his victory speech on the USS *Abraham Lincoln* on May 1, Bush declared, "With new tactics and precision weapons, we can achieve military objectives without directing violence against civilians."[146] In a speech a few weeks earlier at a Boeing plant in St. Louis, Bush said: "The overwhelming majority of the munitions dropped in the Iraqi campaign were precision-guided. In this new era of warfare, we can target a regime, not a nation."[147]

While the U.S. military may not have specifically targeted civilians, it often seemed to largely ignore civilian casualties. Brig. Gen. Vince Brooks, the spokesman at U.S. central command in Qatar was asked about tracking civilian casualties on April 6; Brooks replied, "It just is not worth trying to characterize by numbers. And, frankly, if we are going to be honorable about our warfare, we are not out there trying to count up bodies. This is not the appropriate way for us to go."[148]

Evidence accumulated after the war showing that civilian casualties were far higher than previously indicated:

- The *Christian Science Monitor* reported on May 22, 2003 that independent surveys in Iraq were finding evidence "to suggest that between 5,000 and 10,000 Iraqi civilians may have died during the recent war."[149]
- The Associated Press reported in early June that at least 3,240 Iraqi civilians were killed during the war. The AP noted that its count was "fragmentary" and that the "complete toll" is "sure to be significantly higher."[150]
- The *Los Angeles Times* surveyed hospitals in and around the capital and concluded in mid-May 2003 that between 1,700 and 2,700 Iraqi civilians were killed in the battle of Baghdad; more than 8,000 Iraqi civilians were wounded. The *Times* noted, "Those victims included in the toll died as a direct result of the conflict, but not necessarily at American hands."[151]
- Iraqbodycount.net, a website run by professors and human rights activists who compiled and analyzed online media reports on civilian casualties, estimated that between 5,334 and 6,942 Iraqi civilians were killed as "as a result of coalition military action, both during and after the war."[152]

Many civilians were likely killed by American and British forces as they sought to escape fighting. Shortly after the war started, one U.S. officer warned journalists against driving on Iraq highways because U.S. weapons systems "aren't line-of-sight. . . . If they've got word that Iraqis are fleeing in a couple of vehicles, and target acquisition spots your two vehicles over the horizon, you may well get targeted."[153] Maj. Gen. Victor Renuart warned: "The battlefield extends across the country now and it's really not safe for the Iraqi people to try to leave the cities and drive away to avoid danger."[154] But it was not surprising that Iraqis fled when their towns were being bombed. Haidar Tari of the Iraqi Red Crescent observed: "On one stretch of highway alone, there were more than

50 civilian cars, each with four or five people incinerated inside, that sat in the sun for 10 or 15 days before they were buried nearby by volunteers."[155]

One Marine sharpshooter told a *New York Times* reporter after a series of clashes on the road to Baghdad: "We had a great day. We killed a lot of people." The sergeant conceded: "We dropped a few civilians, but what do you do?" The sergeant, who blamed the Saddam Feydayeen militia for mixing in among Iraqi civilians, mentioned one case in which marines shot a woman who was among two or three Iraqi civilians standing near an Iraqi soldier: "I'm sorry but the chick was in the way." He added that, in a case of "one Iraqi soldier, and 25 women and children," he didn't take the shot.[156]

Cluster bombs were a major cause of civilian fatalities during and after the war. Human Rights Watch researchers discovered evidence of "massive use of cluster bombs in densely populated areas."[157] Gen. Richard Myers, chairman of the Joint Chief of Staffs, stated on April 25 that 1,500 cluster bombs had been dropped from planes (with each bomb containing hundreds of bomblets) but that "there's been only one recorded case of collateral damage from cluster munitions noted so far." Myers declared that "only 26 of those approximately 1,500 hit targets within 1,500 feet of civilian neighborhoods."[158] Myers's assertion on the small number of cluster bombs dropped near civilian neighborhoods specifically ignored cluster bombs launched via artillery shells or rockets.[159] Up to fifteen percent of bomblets fail to explode on impact and can continue to pose a threat long after a war is finished. *Time's* Michael Weisskopf found pervasive leftover cluster bombs in towns and cities outside of Baghdad: "I visited the town of Karbala about 90 miles south of Baghdad and found thousands and thousands of these cluster bombs. . . . They were found in schools, found in homes, hospitals grounds, and other places civilians frequently occupy."[160] In the weeks after the war, reports of children being killed and maimed by initially unexploded cluster bombs became an almost daily occurrence.

As with the war in Afghanistan, the U.S. military heavily publicized the food aid that U.S. troops intended to deliver to Iraqi civilians. The theme of the message campaign was "Iraq: From Fear to Freedom."[161] But the PR campaign was subverted by the civilian casualties. Khaled Abdelkariem of the Middle East News Agency commented on the administration's strategy: "The Arabs or Muslims are not 4-year-old kids who don't know what's happening around them. . . . This feed-and-kill policy—throwing bombs in Baghdad and throwing food at the people—is not winning hearts and minds."[162]

The congressional report on the Iraq War Supplemental Appropriations Act, passed in April 2003, specified that it was Congress's intent that the Pentagon "seek to identify families of non-combatant Iraqis who were killed or injured or whose homes were damaged during recent military operations, and to provide appropriate assistance."[163] Sen. Patrick Leahy (D-Vt.), who wrote the provision, commented that "we should do what we can to assist the innocent, to show that we were not at war against them and that the United States does not walk away. It is the right thing to do, and it is in our own national interest."[164] However, the Pentagon indicated that it would ignore the provision and would make no effort to estimate how many Iraqi civilians were killed during the war. The *Washington Post* reported: "One Air Force general, asked why the military has not done such postwar accounting in the past, said it has been more cost-effective to pour resources into increasingly sophisticated weaponry and in-telligence-gathering equipment."[165]

## No Weapons, No Bother

In the wake of the war, the Bush administration failed to find the masses of weapons of mass destruction that it had promised the world Saddam Hussein possessed. On May 11, the 75th Exploitation Task Force—the main U.S. military group searching for WMDs—began "winding down operations" in preparation for leaving Iraq without finding any WMDs.[166] The *Washington Post* noted that, among other achievements, the members of one of the Army's crack WMD-discovery teams "have dug up a playground, raided a distillery, seized a research paper from a failing graduate student and laid bare a swimming pool where an underground chemical weapons stash was supposed to be."[167] All of their digging was for naught.

As frustrations and criticisms grew over the failure to find WMDs, Bush administration officials continually re-defined success. On May 14, Reuters reported that the Bush administration has "changed its tune" on Iraqi WMDs: "Instead of looking for vast stocks of banned materials, it is now pinning its hopes on finding documentary evidence."[168] But, considering the abundance of forgeries prior to the war, the discovery of incriminating documents after the war may not satisfy skeptics.

Undersecretary of State for Arms Control and International Security Affairs John Bolton, in a May 24, 2003 speech sponsored by the National Defense University Foundation, revealed that the war was justified because of Iraqi "intellectual capacity." Bolton said that IAEA officials "could have inspected for years and years and years and probably never would have found weapons-grade plutonium or weapons-grade uranium. But right in front of them was the continued existence of what Saddam Hussein called the 'nuclear mujahadeen,' the thousand or so scientists, technicians, people who have in their own heads and in their files the intellectual property necessary at an appropriate time ... to recreate a nuclear weapons program."[169] With this standard, the U.S. government is now justified in attacking any potentially hostile nation that has a university with a good physics department.

In late May 2003, the House Intelligence Committee requested that CIA director George Tenet conduct an evaluation of the intelligence information the Bush administration used on Iraqi WMDs and ties to Al Qaeda. Rep. Jane Harman (D-Cal.), the senior Democrat on the committee, observed, "This could conceivably be the greatest intelligence hoax of all time."[170] It is unlikely that any internal self-investigation will rock the Bush administration's boat.

Part of the failure of intelligence may have been due to the Pentagon's dismissal of much of the evidence accumulated by other parts of the intelligence community. The Pentagon created the Office of Special Plans in order to produce arguments, if not evidence, to support going to war with Iraq. The office was staffed by fewer than a dozen policy advisers and analysts who referred to themselves as "the Cabal," as Seymour Hersh reported.[171] Abram Shulsky, the director of the office, is very familiar with Soviet disinformation techniques and a former student and devotee of Leo Strauss, a philosopher who taught that the masses must sometimes be deceived.[172] W. Patrick Lang, a former top analyst with the Defense Intelligence Agency, observed that Pentagon officials "started picking out things that supported their thesis and stringing them into arguments that they could use with the president. It's not intel. It's political propaganda."[173] One critic described the Bush administration's method as "faith-based intelligence."[174]

The United States failure to find evidence that Saddam posed any threat made little or no impact within the United States. The *Washington Post* reported on May 17, 2003, that "Bush appears to be in no political danger from the failure to find chemical, biological and nuclear weapons in Iraq, with Democrats reluctant to challenge Bush on any aspect of the war and polls showing Americans unconcerned about weapons discoveries."[175]

## Fomenting Terrorism?

In his victory speech on the USS *Abraham Lincoln,* Bush continually portrayed the defeat of Saddam as a devastating blow against Al Qaeda: "The liberation of Iraq is a crucial advance in the campaign against terror. We have removed an ally of Al Qaida and cut off a source of terrorist funding. . . . No terrorist network will gain weapons of mass destruction from the Iraqi regime, because the regime is no more."[176] Bush invoked the Al Qaeda threat even though no evidence had surfaced before, during, or after the war to justify any link between Saddam and bin Laden.

Yet many experts believed that the war against Iraq increased the likelihood of terror strikes. The CIA warned in a September 2002 report that it was unlikely that Saddam would launch any chemical or biological attack against the United States.[177] FBI agent Coleen Rowley, who achieved fame after her testimony regarding FBI headquarters snafus before 9/11, sent a letter to FBI director Robert Mueller warning that the "plan to invade Iraq . . . will, in all likelihood, bring an exponential increase in the terrorist threat to the U.S., both at home and abroad."[178] Richard Lugar (R-Ind.), the chairman of the Senate Foreign Relations committee, surveying the chaos of the post-war scene, warned of the danger of Iraq becoming "an incubator for terrorist cells and activity."[179]

The Bush administration sought to allay concerns of post-war chaos with a rosy picture of Iraq becoming a model democracy that would radically change the culture of the Middle East. Yet, a pre-war confidential State Department report should have dashed such talk, warning that "liberal democracy would be difficult to achieve" in Iraq and "could well be subject to exploitation by anti-American elements."[180] Besides, as Joshua Micah Marshall noted in the *Washington Monthly:* "Every time a Western or non-Muslim country has put troops into Arab lands to stamp out violence and terror, it has awakened entire new terrorist organizations and a generation of recruits."[181]

Terrorist attacks in Riyadh, Saudi Arabia on May 13—which killed 34 people, including 9 Americans—were widely seen as evidence that Al Qaeda continued to be a danger. Jonathan Stevenson, senior fellow for counter-terrorism at London's International Institute for Strategic Studies, declared that the Iraq war "clearly increased the terrorist impulse."[182] Paul Wilkinson, head of the Centre for the Study of Terrorism and Political Violence at St. Andrew's University in Scotland, observed: "The political masters in the U.S. and Europe underestimated the extent to which bin Laden would use the war in Iraq as a propaganda weapon to rejuvenate the movement and attract more funds."[183]

## Conclusion: Defrauding the Nation to War

From early 2002 through mid-April 2003, President Bush referred to Iraq and war dozens of times. Suddenly, during his May 1 victory speech on the USS *Abraham Lincoln,* Bush revealed: "The battle of Iraq is one victory in a war on terror that began on September the 11th, 2001 and still goes on." After tens of billions of dollars of U.S. spending, after more than a hundred U.S. soldiers had died and after thousands of Iraqis had been killed, Bush revealed that Iraq was a mere battle—and of course the war must continue. And Bush, equating Al Qaeda and Saddam and others yet to be named, invoked 9/11: "That terrible morning, 19 evil men, the shock troops of a hateful ideology, gave America and the civilized world a glimpse of their ambitions."[184]

The longer Bush continues warring, the more vital it is for Americans to learn the lessons of the Iraq war. Simply because Saddam was evil did not purify George Bush's war against Iraq. A military victory does not automatically absolve the Bush administration of all the falsehoods it told prior to launching an unprovoked and unnecessary war. If victory is the only measure of justice, then the U.S. government could lie about almost any government in the world and—after the U.S. military bombed and bludgeoned the country into submission—it would be another triumph for "the American way."

The U.S. war against Iraq could not have occurred unless the American people and members of Congress had blindly trusted Bush. According to Rep. Thomas G. Tancredo (R-Col.), the key question upon which support for a congressional resolution in favor of war was: "Do you believe in the veracity of the President of the United States?"[185] The evidence that Bush and his top appointees offered of Iraq's crimes continually fell apart. Yet no number of false charges against Iraq could undermine the support of the American people for a president fixated on attacking a foreign nation that posed no threat to the United States.

The fact that Bush went to war against Iraq based on a deceptive strategy is core to knowing what to expect from the remainder of the Bush presidency. There is no reason to presume that Bush was more deceptive and manipulative about the war on Iraq than he is about the war on terrorism or other subjects. The main difference is that the evidence of false claims on Iraq became much clearer, especially after the U.S. invasion. As long as terrorist groups do not succeed in launching high-profile attacks on America or Americans, Bush can represent the war on terrorism however he pleases.

# CHAPTER FOURTEEN

# Bastardizing Freedom

Freedom needs America.

*—President George W. Bush, June 19, 2002*[1]

It's as simple as that. It's good versus evil, and freedom is under attack.

*—President George W. Bush, February 16, 2002*[2]

Perhaps no American president has praised freedom as often as George W. Bush. From his declarations that the United States was attacked because of freedom, to the names "Operation Enduring Freedom" and "Operation Iraqi Freedom," to his proclamations of a "calling" from history to defend freedom, *freedom* quickly became the cloak draping all of Bush's actions after 9/11. It is impossible to understand the long-term political consequences of 9/11 without examining Bush's freedom rhetoric.

## The First Day

Bush quickly mastered the art of invoking freedom to sanctify power.

In a 2:30 P.M. address on September 11, 2001 from Barksdale Air Force Base in Louisiana, where he was taken after the initial attacks, Bush declared: "Freedom, itself, was attacked this morning by a faceless coward, and freedom will be defended."[3] At 8:30 P.M. Bush, ensconced in the Oval Office, opened his televised speech: "Today our fellow citizens, our way of life, our very freedom came under attack in a series of deliberate and deadly terrorist acts. . . . America was targeted for attack because we're the brightest beacon for freedom and opportunity in the world."[4] Bush pronounced authoritatively on the motives of the attackers even before the FBI and CIA knew their identities. Bush concluded: "We go forward to defend freedom and all that is good and just in our world."

Three days later, in a rousing speech at the National Cathedral in Washington, Bush declared, "In every generation, the world has produced enemies of human freedom. They have attacked America because we are freedom's home and defender."[5]

In his speech to Congress and the American people on September 20, 2001, Bush invoked freedom in almost every paragraph:

- Tonight we are a country awakened to danger and called to defend freedom.
- On September the eleventh, enemies of freedom committed an act of war against our country.
- All of this was brought upon us in a single day, and night fell on a different world, a world where freedom itself is under attack.
- Freedom and fear are at war. The advance of human freedom—the great achievement of our time, and the great hope of every time—now depends on us. . . . I will not yield, I will not rest, I will not relent in waging this struggle for the freedom and security of the American people.[6]

## Values Victimology

Bush has a simple explanation for Al Qaeda's animosity:

- In a November 29, 2001 speech to federal attorneys, Bush said: "Our enemies . . . can't stand what America stands for. It must bother them greatly to know we're such a free and wonderful place. . . . It must grate on them greatly."[7]
- At a July 11, 2002 political fundraiser in Minneapolis Bush put his war on terrorism into a handy syllogism: "What we stand for is freedom, and they hate freedom. And therefore, they hate us."[8]
- In a September 5, 2002 speech in Louisville, Kentucky Bush declared: "The more we value freedom, the more they hate us. That's why. That's why the enemy still exists."[9]

At a time when people were most prone to rally around the president, Bush defined the clash between the terrorists and the United States government in a way to maximize sympathy and support for the United States. With the attacks defined in these terms, the more evil the terrorists appear, the more glorious and virtuous the U.S. government automatically becomes. Bush constantly framed the response to Al Qaeda in a way to make any criticism of America politically incorrect. He also seized the opportunity to define the attacks in a way that would sanctify his demands for greater power for the federal government.

In a March 4, 2002 speech at a Minnesota high school, Bush scorned the terrorists: "And when they find a nation that's willing to defend freedom, they try to attack it."[10] Bush implied that everyone who hates freedom automatically feels compelled to go out and attack enemies seven thousand miles away—as if the hatred of freedom magically overcomes all geographical obstacles, so that the hater will sacrifice his own life to annoy a distant regime instead of staying home and tormenting local government officials.

Bush's characterization of terrorists' antifreedom inspiration is rebutted by the U.S. government's own reports. The Heritage Foundation and the *Wall Street Journal* editorial page issue an annual "economic freedom index" ranking of the different nations of the world. In 2002 the four nations with the most economic freedom were Hong Kong, Singapore, Luxembourg, and New Zealand, according to this index. None of these nations have suffered extensive "international terrorist" incidents in recent years, according to the U.S. State Department annual *Patterns of Global Terrorism* reports.

Reporters without Frontiers, an international journalism organization based in France, issued an index of worldwide press freedom in 2002.[11] The five nations with the most press freedom were Finland, Iceland, Norway, the Netherlands, and Canada. The first three nations have suffered zero "international terrorist" incidents in recent years, and the Netherlands and Canada come in very low on the list of nations hit by terrorists, according to the U.S. State Department. (The reporters organization ranked the United States sixteenth in press freedom, lower than Costa Rica, Slovenia, and Portugal.)

According to a United Nations Freedom Index compiled in the early 1990s, twelve nations have more freedom than the United States, including Sweden, Denmark, the Netherlands, Austria, Finland, Germany, Canada, Switzerland, and Australia.[12] Most of these nations have suffered few recent international terrorist attacks, and none of them has suffered nearly as many attacks upon its citizens as has the United States. Terrorism poses little or no threat to the vast majority of nations considered to have governments that respect freedom.

In his public utterances, Osama bin Laden never cited the Bill of Rights as a reason for his attacks on America. As *Washington Post* editor Robert Kaiser noted, "Bin Laden's own statements and the personal histories of participants in the Sept. 11 plot suggest there are more specific reasons for the terrorists' hatred. They include American support for regimes that they detest in the Arab world; American bases on Arab territory, especially in Saudi Arabia; and American support for Israel's occupation of Palestinian territory and for Israel's military campaign against the Palestinians."[13]

Nor is hostility towards freedom a primary source of opposition to America in the nations from which the 19 hijackers originated. A late 2002 poll of opinion in the Arab world, conducted by pollster James Zogby of the Arab American Institute, found that while most Arabs have a negative opinion of the U.S. government, most have a positive opinion of freedom. Most Arabs had a positive view of France and Canada, two Western nations with a large amount of personal freedom (compared to the rest of the world). Zogby reported: "Between 90 percent and 96 percent of the respondents rated personal and civil rights as their first or second priority, choosing from 10 issues that included health care, moral standards and personal economic conditions."[14] The poll showed an intense, widespread focus by Arabs on the Israeli-Palestinian conflict. Zogby observed: "It is not a foreign policy issue for Arabs. It defines almost existentially their sense of who they are."[15]

Some terrorists may hate freedom but most probably simply hate the government they are trying to terrorize. By insisting on a false dogma, Bush blighted any serious discussion of terrorist motives. A *Washington Post* analysis noted: "'Roots' was a taboo word in the Bush administration for a time, with 'evil' the only acceptable explanation for the attacks of Sept. 11."[16] Once Bush's characterization of the conflict is accepted, the only prudent conclusion is that terrorists as a species are completely immune to human reason. Fighting terrorism becomes a simple task of exterminating bad guys. But this assumes that nothing the U.S. government does can influence the number of people who decide to throw away their lives trying to kill Americans. In reality, the supply of foreign terrorists is related to the perceived output of U.S. abuses.

## Freedom to Be "With Us"—Or Else

President Bush loves either/or commands:

- "Every nation, in every region, now has a decision to make. Either you are with us, or you are with the terrorists." (Speech to Congress, September 20, 2001)
- "Either you're with us, or you're against us; either you stand for freedom, or you stand with tyranny.[17] (Speech at Elmendorf Air Force Base in Anchorage, Alaska, February 16, 2002)
- "Either you love freedom, or you stand against the United States of America."[18] (Speech at Kansas City Republican fundraiser, June 11, 2002)
- "Either you're with the United States of America and freedom-loving countries, or you're with the terrorists."[19] (Speech at Minnesota Republican campaign rally, July 11, 2002)
- "Either you're with us, or you're with the enemy; either you're with those who love freedom, or you're with those who hate innocent life."[20] (Speech at Fort Hood, Killeen, Texas, January 3, 2003)

One government in the world became not just the personification of freedom, but freedom itself. "Standing for freedom" now requires kowtowing to the U.S. government. This is almost a Stalinesque concept of freedom: The only way that people can know that they are free is when they submit their wills to a distant foreign government which claims to know what is best for humanity—and also claims the right to destroy anyone it labels an enemy. Anyone who does not "love freedom" (according to Bush's latest definition) can be treated as the equivalent of a suicide bomber on the way to blow up American civilians. In the name of freedom, one government practically proclaimed a right to attack every other nation on Earth.

Because America is the freest nation in the world, the Bush administration has the right to draw the line in the sand wherever it chooses—and to destroy anyone who does not hop to the right side. Because Bush is now freedom personified, anyone who opposes Bush is by definition an enemy of freedom. The preservation of freedom requires that one person in the world be exempt from all restraints and that he be entitled to attack whoever he chooses based on secret evidence.

Bush's either/or dictate was not mere throwaway political rhetoric. Bush believed that 9/11 gave him the right to demand submission from every other government on earth. *Washington Post* senior editor Bob Woodward interviewed Bush extensively for his book *Bush at War.* Woodward concluded: "When it came to fighting terrorism, the president also wanted world leaders to equate their national interests with American interests.

Some would go along with him when their interests and goals coincided roughly with his, but go their own way when they did not. Bush didn't like that when it happened, and at times he took it personally."[21] This attitude partly explains Bush's rage toward the governments of France, Germany, and Russia over the Iraq war.

There are many people who despise both terrorists and the U.S. government. The vast majority of people in Europe who disdain Bush have no hankering to cosy up to Muslim fanatics. Similarly, few of the American critics of Bush's policies favor laws obliging all women to wear *burkas*.

Asserting that anyone who does not stand with the U.S. government is a friend of tyranny is a slap in the face to all of those people in the world who are resisting the oppressions of governments in the Bush "freedom-loving coalition." From the Uighurs in western China to peaceful Muslims in Uzbekistan to ethnic and religious minorities in other former Soviet republics, people are struggling against governments for the right to live their own lives. And yet, all a government has to do is to publicly recite the Bush catechism on terrorism and all its victims become invisible.

Bush's rhetoric on America as a force for freedom is impossible to understand without considering his assertions on America as the greatest force for goodness in the world. Bush loves accolades for America; he reminded a Chicago audience shortly after 9/11 that "We're a nation based upon fabulous values."[22] In a February 28, 2003 speech to the employees of the Department of Homeland Security, Bush declared: "There is no doubt in my mind that this nation will prevail in this war against terror, because we're the greatest nation, full of the finest people, on the face of this earth."[23]

Bush's argument hinges not only on the notion that the United States is an absolute force for good and freedom in world affairs—but that this truth is so undeniable that only "evil" people would deny it. Thus, the denial of U.S. goodness by itself becomes evidence of malicious intent.

The more Bush repeated his "either /or" dictate, the more an absurdity became accepted as a triumph of idealism. Bush's either/or dogma is an example of how a Big Lie becomes accepted as a Great Truth by endless repetition. This is a dictate that, once the smoke cleared from Ground Zero in New York, should have failed the laugh test. Yet it is respected and, worse, it provides the sanction for using or threatening deadly force against tens of millions of people. Once people accept the either/or imperative, it becomes far more difficult to understand either how Bush's actions subvert their own freedom or how U.S. policies threaten the peace of the world.

## War Freedom

In remarks at the National Republican Senatorial Committee fundraising dinner in Washington on September 24, 2002 Bush declared: "We believe in freeing people while we free ourselves from threats. . . . We will do whatever it takes to make the homeland secure and to make freedom reign across the world."[24]

But a desire to spread freedom does not automatically confer a license to kill.

Going to war is, for Bush, perhaps the highest proof of devotion to freedom. Speaking at an August 5, 2002 Republican fundraiser in Pittsburgh, Bush proclaimed: "We're fighting the first war of the 21st century. I say 'the first war'—there's no telling how many wars it will take to secure freedom in the homeland."[25] In a saber-rattling speech at West Point on June 1, 2002 Bush announced that "all Americans" must "be ready for preemptive action when necessary to defend our liberty."[26]

For Bush, the Pentagon budget is one of the clearest measures of America's devotion to freedom. At an April 9, 2002 Republican fund raiser in Connecticut, Bush observed, "That's why my defense budget is the largest increase in 20 years. You know, the price of freedom is high, but for me it's never too high because we fight for freedom."[27] And if the government seized all of every citizen's paycheck—instead of only 38 percent of it—and used all the revenue to bankroll foreign military conquests, Americans would have absolute freedom.

Bush glorifies American military power probably as much as any U.S. president ever did. On June 18, 2002 Bush informed Congress that the "Department of Defense has become the most powerful force for freedom the world has ever seen."[28] For Bush, military power is practically freedom incarnate. In his speech to West Point graduates, Bush declared, "Wherever we carry it the American flag will stand not only for our power but for freedom." The more militarily aggressive the United States becomes, the greater a champion of freedom it will be. In his 2002 State of the Union address, after bragging about victories in Afghanistan, Bush proclaimed: "We have shown freedom's power."[29] Every B-52 bomber and every 15,000-pound daisycutter bomb is now as much a symbol of American freedom as the Bill of Rights. In an April 2003 speech to workers at the Army Tank Plant in Lima, Ohio, Bush declared: "You build the weapons you build here because we love freedom in this country."[30]

For Bush, the idealism of liberty is all that matters. In his October 7, 2001 speech announcing the beginning of the bombing of Afghanistan, Bush declared: "The name of today's military operation is Enduring Freedom. We

defend not only our precious freedoms but also the freedom of people everywhere to live and raise their children *free from fear.*"[31] And regardless of how
many bombs must be dropped, Bush is determined to inflict freedom from
fear everywhere. Bush feels entitled to have U.S. foreign interventions judged
solely by Bush's proclaimed goals, not by any carnage the United States
wreaks.

Bush declared in February 2002 that "we're not going to give up until [bin
Laden] and every other potential killer and every other body who hates freedom
will be brought to justice."[32] Bush talks as if a threat to freedom anywhere in the
world is a threat to American freedom. Thus, the U.S. government must have the
power to crush any alleged enemy of freedom on Earth in order to make freedom
safe in Pea Ridge, Arkansas. Bush is trying to persuade people that freedom in the
world must survive everywhere or nowhere. But the Taliban, for instance, posed
no threat to "world freedom." They were an obnoxious and oppressive government but they had neither the means nor the will to impose their system on
Ecuador, Luxembourg, and the Fiji Islands. And while Bush claims that the loss
of freedom anywhere is a threat to American freedom, he blithely bankrolls
dozens of governments that are harshly repressing their subjects. Perhaps Bush
believes that Americans' freedom is threatened only when private entities subvert
freedom.

Listening to Bush's speeches, one might think that it was only recently that
foreign governments and foreign groups were hostile to freedom. Yet, throughout American history, from 1776 onward, the world has been full of enemies of
freedom. At the time that the United States was founded, very few nations in
the world had even a semblance of freedom. Somehow, the threat to freedom
has become much greater now, at a time when far fewer governments are openly
hostile to freedom than in earlier times. Has America become so fragile that it
cannot tolerate the existence of any government in the world that openly dis-
dains American values or the American way? Bush's views on forcibly spreading
freedom and democracy resemble a religious crusade. Unless the United States
forcibly converts all the governments in the world, then America's own political
soul will be at risk of damnation.

Bush declared on 9/11/2002 that "there is a line in our time . . . between
the defenders of human liberty, and those who seek to master the minds and
souls of others."[33] But if the United States attacks the people of any foreign
regime that refuses to swear allegiance to the latest U.S. definition of liberty, the
world will see America as the aggressor shackling the minds and wills of people
around the world. The more nations that America attacks in the name of liberty,

the more foreigners will perceive America as the greatest threat both to their peace and self-rule.

And while Bush portrays U.S. foreign interventions as near-automatic triumphs for freedom, the record in recent years provides scant reason for optimism:

- The 1991 "Operation Desert Storm" pulverized Iraq but did nothing to free the Iraqi people. At the end of the war, the first Bush administration effectively blessed Saddam Hussein's savage crushing of Kurdish revolts in the north and Shi'ite Muslim revolts in the south of the country.
- The 1992–93 "Operation Restore Hope" resulted in U.S. troops battling the forces of a Somali warlord—killing hundreds of Somalis but suffering 18 high-profile casualties that devastated the Clinton administration's image. After the United States withdrew, Somali reverted to chaos.
- The 1994 "Operation Restore Democracy" invasion of Haiti sent 20,000 U.S. troops to wave a magic wand in one of the most repressive countries in this hemisphere. After American troops left, political violence resumed and Jean-Bertrand Aristide, whom the U.S. government put back in power, is now being compared to "Papa Doc" Duvalier by Haitians bitter about the oppression and corruption.
- The 1995 "Operation Deliberate Force" featured heavy U.S. and NATO bombing of Serb forces in Bosnia. After the bombing ended, a fragile peace agreement was crafted and U.S. troops remained in the area. But the situation remains a powderkeg and, once foreign troops leave, the locals will likely begin butchering each other with all the enthusiasm they showed in the early 1990s.
- The 1999 "Operation Allied Force" bombed Belgrade into submission purportedly to liberate Kosovo. Though Slobodan Milosevic raised the white flag, ethnic cleansing continued—with the minority Serbs being slaughtered and their churches burnt to the ground in the same way that the Serbs previously oppressed ethnic Albanians.

Freedom cannot be forcibly exported without being subverted at home. Perpetual war will inevitably beget perpetual repression. It is impossible to destroy all the alleged enemies of freedom in the world without also destroying freedom in the United States. The amount of military power the United States would have to acquire and use—the number of preemptive attacks—the likelihood of terrorist counterattacks which would be exploited by American politicians for domestic crackdowns—the perpetual fear that would engulf the

American public—all these would overwhelm the parchment barriers bequeathed by the Founding Fathers. James Madison, the father of the Constitution, warned in 1795:

> Of all enemies to public liberty war is, perhaps, the most to be dreaded because it comprises and develops the germ of every other. War is the parent of armies; from these proceed debt and taxes. And armies, and debts, and taxes are the known instruments for bringing the many under the domination of the few. In war, too, the discretionary power of the Executive is extended. Its influence in dealing out offices, honors, and emoluments is multiplied; and all the means of seducing the minds are added to those of subduing the force of the people. . . . No nation could preserve its freedom in the midst of continual warfare.[34]

## 9/11 and the Bush
## Redefinition of American Freedom

Since *freedom* is the mantra for Bush's war on terrorism, a few words are in order on the traditional American understanding of freedom. "The Restraint of Government is the True Liberty and Freedom of the People" was a common American saying in the eighteenth century.[35] Thomas Jefferson wrote in 1799: "Free government is founded in jealousy, not confidence. It is jealousy and not confidence which prescribes limited constitutions, to bind those we are obliged to trust with power. . . . In questions of power, then, let no more be heard of confidence in men, but bind him down from mischief by the chains of the Constitutions."[36] The Bill of Rights sought to secure Americans' freedom by imposing binding limits in perpetuity on government power.

The Founding Fathers were not prone to the delusion that government is inherently benevolent. They had experienced the ravages of British colonial rulers—seeing government agents seize their property, pilfer their homes, seize men on the streets for the British navy, subvert the independence of judges, and deport Americans to England for show trials. The Founders were determined to create a system of government with safeguards to protect citizens. As James Madison warned, "The essence of Government is power; and power, lodged as it must be in human hands, will ever be liable to abuse."

For President Bush, freedom has little or nothing to do with limits on government power. On May 8, 2002, Bush told a high school audience: "I will not let—*your Government's not going to let people destroy the freedoms* that we love in America."[37] In a February 14, 2003 speech at the Bonaparte Auditorium at FBI headquarters in Washington, Bush declared: "For years the freedom of our people were really never in doubt because no one ever thought that the terrorists or anybody could come and hurt America. But that changed."[38] Homeland Security Director Tom Ridge reflected the attitude of the Bush administration when he announced: "Liberty is the most precious gift we offer our citizens."[39] If freedom is a gift from the government to the people, then government can take freedom away at its pleasure.

In a *New York Times* op-ed published on 9/11/02, Bush declared: "Today, humanity holds in its hands the opportunity to further freedom's triumph over all its age-old foes. . . . Poverty, corruption and repression are a toxic combination in many societies, leading to *weak governments* that are unable to enforce order or patrol their borders and are vulnerable to terrorist networks and drug cartels."[40] Government is not one of freedom's "age-old foes" in the Bush lexicon. Instead, "weak governments" are a primary threat. And, as the late Yugoslav Marshal Tito promised, "The more powerful the State, the more freedom."[41]

In his West Point speech, Bush said that "the greatest danger to freedom lies at the perilous crossroads of radicalism and technology."[42] But historically, *governments* have been by far the greatest enemies of freedom. The repressive potential of either technology or theology is rarely fully exploited except by bureaucrats and enforcement agents.

Bush's vision of freedom is practically the mirror image of that of the Founding Fathers. For Bush, the survival of freedom requires unleashing government power to preemptively destroy any potential enemy of freedom or America. As the chapters on the Patriot Act and post-9/11 policies showed, *Bush freedom* requires that neither Congress nor federal courts be able to curb the power of the executive branch. James Madison's carefully crafted checks and balances are as anachronistic and subversive as taking a flight while carrying a pocket screwdriver. Bush's concept of freedom is similar to that of many authoritarian rulers throughout history who promised future bounties of liberty after the latest emergency crackdown.

*Bush freedom* is based on trust in almost all governments. Bush's "world freedom" campaign does not aim to make governments less oppressive: instead, it provides U.S. military aid and tax dollars to support almost every government's effort to crush opposition. In Bush's view, freedom is something that can occur only after governments seize enough power to crush all terrorists, or would-be terrorists, or potential terrorists, or suspected terrorist sympathizers.

The war on terrorism is a war for freedom, regardless of how much additional power governments around the world seize, because, for Bush, the threats to freedom come largely from the private sector—from private citizens, from malcontents, from rebels. Bush sometimes resembles Britain's Stuart kings in his horror of resistance. He thinks of government as the protector of freedom the same way that seventeenth-century princes thought of government as the protector of the One True Faith—whatever that faith happened to be at the moment (depending largely on the prince's latest political calculations). And in the same way that some Reformation princes rushed to burn at the stake anyone priests or preachers labeled a heretic, this administration seems ready to target anyone they feel is an enemy of freedom.

## Conclusion:
## The Mirage of Bush Freedom

Bush is encouraging Americans to judge actions of the federal government solely by his proclaimed goal—freedom—and not by what the government does. But the issue is not whether Bush personally loves or hates freedom. The issue is that he constantly invokes freedom in order to unleash government.

Bush's message on freedom implies that only self-proclaimed and officially designated tyrants pose a threat to people's rights and liberties. But the actual process of destruction of liberty is rarely brazen, with trumpets blaring and neon warning signs flashing. Instead, freedom is destroyed piecemeal, one emergency edict at a time—and with continual public assurances that the government does not intend to go any further—unless absolutely forced to by events beyond its control.

Freedom will only be permanently secured when people cease craving power over other people. In other words, as long as human beings are human, freedom will be in peril. The notion that a one-time buildup of government and military power can save freedom long-term is a childlike delusion.

Invoking freedom may simply be a charade for Bush. He may care as little about freedom as he does veracity (as shown in his statements on the Iraq war). If Bush was able to get the same amount of support by invoking motherhood instead of freedom, perhaps his speeches would be full of allusions to motherhood and of the vital need to fight preemptive wars for motherhood and to defeat all enemies of motherhood around the world. (Many of his supporters and likely even some of his appointees sincerely believe Bush is championing freedom.)

Bush is a champion of freedom only if, as German philosopher G. W. F. Hegel asserted, the State is "the actualization of freedom."[44] Bush's concept of freedom hinges upon the presumption of absolute benevolence both of himself and the entire U.S. government. In other words, it requires assuming that Bush is unlike any previous president, and that the U.S. government in the future will behave unlike the U.S. government acted in the past. This notion of freedom-via-benevolent-power requires the nullification of all historical memory. The principles and precedents that Bush is establishing will pose grave threats to freedom long after the war on terrorism cools down, and long after Saddam Hussein and other contemporary despots are on the junk heap of history.

# CHAPTER FIFTEEN

# A Few Steps
# to Protect America

And you know what's going to happen: Good will overcome evil with the leadership
of the United States, and we're going to provide that leadership.

—President George W. Bush, June 19, 2002[1]

Nothing happened on September 11 or since which fundamentally changed the
nature of American government. In considering how to defend America against
terrorists in the future, the limits of existing governmental machinery must be
kept constantly in mind.

Some of the reforms made after 9/11—such as new restrictions and better
background checks on dubious foreigners seeking to enter the United States or
to claim asylum and revisions of wiretap statutes to adjust for new technologies—make good sense and do not threaten Americans' rights and liberties. The
government is justified in using a lower standard to deport suspicious aliens now
than it did before 9/11. However, it is difficult to craft policies to guarantee that
the deportations are done in good faith—to protect national security—and not
simply to run up numbers to generate political bragging points. The government is justified in freezing assets clearly linked to terrorist organizations. It is
good that airport security is now no longer a zombie zone—though it would be
dangerously naive to believe that the new system provides protection against
savvy, motivated attackers. Federal intelligence agencies are eminently justified
in hiring more employees who speak and read Arabic and other languages used
by organizations that have launched terrorist attacks against the United States.

It is good that federal law enforcement and intelligence agencies are devoting far more resources and attention to terrorist threats than in the past. But that will not be enough.

## Eternally Slipshod

There is no reason to expect the federal government to be significantly more competent in the future than it was in the past. The key lesson of previous U.S. government antiterrorism efforts is that government will too often do a slipshod job of protecting citizens.

After 9/11, there was no bureaucratic accountability. As Sen. Charles Grassley (R-Iowa) observed, "The lesson at the FBI still is if you mess up, do something wrong, you get promoted, you get an award."[2] Grassley complained: "I can't think of a single person being held accountable anywhere in government for what went on and what went wrong prior to Sept. 11."[3] Sen. Arlen Specter (R-Pa.) observed: "There is a real question as to whether the Federal Bureau of Investigation is capable of carrying out counter-intelligence to protect the citizens of the United States."[4] As a Senate Judiciary Committee report noted in February 2003, "A deep-rooted culture of ignoring problems and discouraging employees from criticizing the FBI contributes to the FBI's repetition of its past mistakes in the foreign intelligence field. There has been little or no progress at the FBI in addressing this culture."[5]

The FBI's institutional culture still prevents many FBI agents from doing their best work. A Minneapolis-based FBI agent who was on a team investigating theft from the World Trade Center ruins was notified early in 2003 that she would be fired because she "tarnished the image" of the FBI after she reported that an FBI evidence response team had stolen a crystal globe worth $5,000 from the Trade Center site.[6]

One of the clearest tests of the ability of the new, "improved" law enforcement to respond to a perceived terrorist attack occurred during the sniper rampage in the Washington, D.C. area in October 2002. Bush announced on October 14, 2002: "I weep for those who've lost their loved ones. . . . We're lending all the resources of the Federal Government, all that have been required, to do everything we can to assist the local law authorities to find this—whoever it is." Bush declared that the attacks were "a form of terrorism."[7] The *Washington Post* reported that "several law enforcement and government officials said federal agencies are making all the important decisions" in the pursuit of the killers.[8] More than seven hundred FBI agents were involved in the case.[9]

After panic erupted over the first shootings, FBI trainees were brought in to staff the telephone tip lines at the Montgomery County, Maryland police head-quarters. The FBI, scorning the technological revolutions of the last half cen-tury, relied on the same tried-and-true methods the bureau used to catch targets like John Dillinger in the 1930s. The *Washington Post* reported: "Authorities said information is taken down by hand on forms that make multiple carbon copies. Copies are sorted and marked 'immediate,' 'priority' or 'routine.' Tips that con-cern Montgomery County are put in one pile, Fairfax in another, Richmond in a third. FBI employees then drive the paperwork out to police in those loca-tions. The system handling the huge volume of leads, dubbed 'Rapid Start' in the days after Sept. 11, is anything but that, say some police and FBI sources who have called it 'Rapid Stop.'"[10] The *Post* noted complaints by numerous law-men that "the FBI's problems handling thousands of phone tips are slowing and hampering the probe."[11]

When the FBI trainees were not laboriously scrawling down the latest tip, they were busy hanging up on the snipers. In a note attached to a tree after the ninth shooting, the snipers complained that operators at the tip line had hung up on them five times. The note denounced police "incompitence" [sic] and de-clared: "We have tried to contact you to start negotiation. These people took [our] calls for a hoax or a joke, so your failure to respond has cost you five lives."[12]

Shortly after the arrest of the two suspects, Washington, D.C. Police Chief Charles Ramsey publicly confessed: "We were looking for a white van with white people, and we ended up with a blue car with black people."[13] The only "evidence" that the killers were white was the dogma of FBI and other serial killer profilers. The fixation on white killers spurred police to disregard several witness reports about darker-skinned murder suspects.

Several eyewitnesses reported to police that they had seen an old Chevrolet Caprice at the scenes of shootings, but police scorned their reports. Police spot-ted the snipers' ratty blue car and recorded its out-of-state license plates at least ten different times during the month of the killings; the vehicle was reportedly stopped or seen five times at roadblocks established immediately after shoot-ings.[14] But because they were searching for a white van or truck, police disre-garded the suspects again and again. One federal investigator later complained: "The car was screaming: 'Stop me.' It's dilapidated. It's got Jersey tags. It's got a homemade window tint."[15]

John Poindexter, Bush's Total Information Awareness czar, declared that the sniper case illustrated how the Total Information Awareness surveillance could have helped the police more quickly narrow the search to the suspect's car.[16] Poindexter's attempt to invoke the sniper rampage to justify far greater surveillance is ludicrous considering that the killers could have easily been caught earlier with relatively ancient technology. The computer system already existed 40 years ago that could have easily put out the list of the most suspicious vehicles in the wake of the shootings and roadblocks: an IBM mainframe computer that relied on punch cards. It would have been a simple operation to key in the data and run the cards through the machine to get a list of the most frequent vehicles at shooting sites—and then to question each of a few dozen vehicle owners.

Months before the sniper rampage began, five different people in Washington state contacted the FBI to report their suspicions about alleged sniper John Allen Muhammad's comments about killing police, his interest in buying silencers for his rifle, and his visit to a gunsmith to inquire about modifying the rifle to make it more easily concealed. The federal Bureau of Alcohol, Tobacco and Firearms was also contacted repeatedly. The FBI and ATF disregarded all the warnings.[17]

The feds and local police, instead of using common sense and analyzing excellent leads, brought in Pentagon spy planes to canvas the entire Washington area. The use of the RC-7 planes may have been a breach of the Posse Comitatus Act (which prohibits using the military for domestic law enforcement) but all that mattered was assuring frightened people that the government cared and was taking action.[18] The planes provided no information that aided the apprehension of the suspects.

Federal agents and Montgomery County Police chief Charles Moose sought to keep a tight grip on key information regarding the case. But it was a leak that led directly to the apprehension of the snipers. News media had been listening to police scanners and, on October 23, heard the renewed suspicions about the Caprice. Both MSNBC and CNN broadcast the license plate and car description hours before Chief Moose went public with the information. Within six hours of the media "leaking" the license plate number, an alert citizen phoned in a tip that the suspects' car was at an interstate rest stop in Frederick County, Maryland. Neither of the two sniper suspects would likely have qualified for admission to med school to become brain surgeons. The ineptness of the government response indicates how much harm could be done by a clique of savvy, well-trained foreigner snipers.

One of the most dramatic failures before 9/11 occurred when the Central Intelligence Agency neglected to add the names of two Al Qaeda members to the terrorist watch lists until after they had entered the United States. Yet, a General Accounting Office report in late April 2003 concluded that the federal government's terrorist watch lists continue to be "overly complex, unnecessarily inefficient and potentially ineffective."[19] The nine agencies that compile such lists use different software and different criteria, making it difficult for agencies to share crucial terrorist information with other agencies. "Information hoard-ing" also continues to be a major problem, with feds unwilling to share what they know with local and state police as well.

Many of the government's assertions since 9/11 seem crafted to spur mind-less panic and maximum appropriations. In July 2002, the FBI warned Con-gress that Al Qaeda could have five thousand operatives inside the United States. Most experts doubt that Al Qaeda has that many operatives in the entire world. The "five thousand operatives" caused a stir when publicly revealed by Rep. Saxby Chambliss (R-GA) during a CNN interview. A *New York Times* analysis noted: "The F.B.I.'s final number was more or less a wild guess based loosely on a small number of actual suspects, the number of graduates of Qaeda training camps (current estimates top out at about 15,000, though many didn't actually join Al Qaeda) and maybe some immigration statistics." The *Times* explained the FBI's number as "bureaucratic politics. The greater the threat, the larger the budget that can be justified."[20]

While the feds have not been able to put Al Qaeda out of business, Ashcroft and others have provided entertaining press conferences in which they sought to frighten Americans with the specter of imminent doom, miraculously avoided thanks to the efforts of federal agents. On June 10, 2002, Ashcroft appeared on national television to breathlessly announce—via satellite while he was visiting Moscow—that "we have disrupted an unfolding terrorist plot to attack the United States by exploding a radioactive 'dirty bomb'" which could have caused "mass death and injury."[21] Ashcroft repeatedly mentioned radiation or "dirty bombs," giving the impression that the United States had narrowly averted a major disaster in its arrest of Abdullah Al Muhajir—formerly known as Jose Padilla, an American citizen of Puerto Rican origin. Ashcroft gushed praise for the FBI and other federal agencies. Homeland Security Director Tom Ridge an-nounced in Washington: "It was very important for America to witness the col-laboration between or among the respective agencies that ultimately resulted in the apprehension of this individual" and that the "public revelation gives the country greater confidence."[22]

Nerves had not stopped rattling from Ashcroft's announcement before the Bush administration was backtracking. Deputy Defense Secretary Paul Wolfowitz conceded the following day that "I don't think there was actually a plot beyond some fairly loose talk."[23] Ashcroft declared on June 10: "While in Afghanistan and Pakistan, Al Muhajir trained with the enemy, including studying how to wire ex-plosive devices and researching radiological dispersion devices." The *Washington Post* noted a week later that Padilla's "research on radiological weapons, U.S. offi-cials said, consisted largely of surfing the Internet."[24]

Ashcroft had greatly exaggerated Padilla's capacity as a high-tech bomb maker. Ashcroft's statements earned him the nickname "Minister of Fear." Former State Department counterterrorism director Larry Johnson said that Padilla "couldn't make a dirty burrito, let alone a dirty bomb."[25] Padilla, a high school dropout who had a long rap sheet for firearms and other offenses, was a former gang member who became a Muslim during an extended visit to a penitentiary. USA Today reported: "Administration sources say the White House emphatically told Ashcroft that it was dissatisfied with his description of the alleged plot."[26]

After congressional Democrats and media commentators raised questions about the timing of the announcement (which occurred at a high tide of criticisms of the FBI's pre-9/11 botches), White House spokesman Ari Fleischer declared: "These very few people who want to make such an outlandish political accusation represent the most cynical among the most partisan. And they're not to be taken seriously."[27]

The reason for Ashcroft's sudden announcement was the fear that a federal judge might rule that Padilla had constitutional rights. Padilla had been arrested on May 8, but Ashcroft did not announce his arrest until the Bush administration decided to strip him of all rights. The Bush administration scrambled to ensure that Padilla would be the first American citizen arrested on American soil cast into the netherworld of "enemy combatant." U.S. law enforcement officials conceded two months later that "the FBI's investigation has produced no evidence that Jose Padilla had begun preparations for an attack and little reason to believe he had any support from Al Qaeda to direct such a plot."[28] But the Bush administration continued holding Padilla in a military brig in South Carolina and denying him all access to federal courts. Federal judge Michael Mukasey in March 2003 rebuked the Bush administration, warning that if Padilla continues to be denied all legal rights, "a dictatorship will be upon us, the tanks will have rolled."[29]

Similarly, there is little reason for confidence in the new Homeland Security Department. On February 10, 2003, three days after the federal government had raised the terrorist warning to "orange" as a result of "the most serious and credible warnings of additional attacks since 9/11," Homeland Security Director Tom Ridge held a press conference at which he urged Americans to buy duct tape and plastic sheeting in order to make a room in their home secure after a biological or chemical weapons attack by terrorists.

Ridge's warning did wonders for Home Depot's business. Panic buying ensued. Sen. Robert C. Byrd (D-W.Va.) complained: "We did not create a new Department of Homeland Security just to be told 'Buy duct tape and plastic.'"[30] Jay Leno quipped: "This means the only people who are going to survive an attack are serial killers. Who else has duct tape and plastic sheeting in their car?"[31] The

*New York Times* noted that the Homeland Security Department's "preparedness guidelines sounded a bit like those TV weathermen who mark every cold snap by earnestly instructing their viewers to wear more layers of clothing."[32]

Some experts quibbled that Ridge's advice could prove inopportune to people who successfully made a room air-proof and then suffocated. New York City mayor Michael Bloomberg denounced the recommendation as "preposterous" and warned Big Apple residents that sealing their apartments could result in deaths from asphyxiation.[33] Ridge reacted angrily to what he termed "the political belittling of duct tape."[34] Though sheeting and duct tape could be useful in some situations, the federal government made no effort to explain or coach people how to safely use the materials against chemical attacks. Instead, the mere possession of duct tape—like Linus's blanket—would somehow make people safer. (Ridge defended the proposal by stressing that the homeland security recommendations had been tested on focus groups for eight months before being publicly released.[35])

Nor is there evidence that federal law enforcement has learned to concentrate resources on actual dangers to public safety. In January 2003, the FBI ordered all its 56 field offices to go out and count the number of mosques in their areas. *Newsweek* reported that the mosque counts would be one factor used by the FBI "to set specific numerical goals for counter terrorism investigations and secret national-security wiretaps in each region."[36] One FBI official explained: "This is not politically correct. . . . but it would be stupid not to look at this, given the number of criminal mosques that may be out there."[37] In Frederick, Maryland, FBI agents sought a list of all the members of a local mosque from mosque leaders. Nihad Awad, executive director of the Council on American-Islamic Relations, declared: "That the FBI is seeking lists of ordinary, law-abiding American Muslims only serves to confirm the Islamic community's worst fears of religious and ethnic profiling. . . . One has to wonder how many mosques have already been intimidated into turning over this kind of information."[38] Human Rights Watch director Jamie Fellner said: "This is as offensive as counting Christian churches on the assumption they may harbor abortion clinic bombers."[39] After a ruckus erupted, the FBI asserted that it was counting the mosques in order to prevent hate crimes against them. FBI spokeswoman Charlene Sloan insisted: "All the ideas out there that we're going to launch an investigation—and that we are profiling based on religion—all that is inaccurate. The FBI is opposed to racial and ethnic profiling of any kind."[40]

Once the FBI begins evaluating its agents based on whether they counted the mosques, it is a small step to evaluating them on whether they infiltrated the mosques and on how many confidential undercover informants they signed up.

This could spur more entrapment schemes to gin up conspiracies that will permit more indictments and more Ashcroft victory press conferences—regardless of whether any threat existed.

Though the Great Mosque Count is a boondoggle, neither the FBI nor any other law enforcement agency should permit a mosque to be a sanctuary for criminal activity. As has been the policy for decades: if there is probable cause to believe people are engaging in criminal activity such as terrorist plots, the government need not turn a blind eye. After 9/11, law enforcement is justified in having heightened concerns about Muslim males with similar traits, records, and profiles of the 19 hijackers. The FBI is justified in being warier about mosques than about churches or synagogues. But it is absurd to assume that all mosques are "criminal" and potential targets for wiretaps.

The natural tendency of government work is to measure success by raw numbers rather than by real achievements. Attorney General Ashcroft, testifying to the Senate Judiciary Committee on March 4, 2003, bragged that thousands of FBI agents "have covered more than 337,400 leads, and produced more than 165,000 FBI 302 reports of investigation. . . . The FBI Laboratory has received more than 585 submissions of evidence from the crash sites and related searches, representing approximately 6,332 items of potential evidence. . . . The 9/11 investigation has resulted in criminal charges against 211 individuals, 108 convictions, and the deportation of 478 individuals."[41] But few of the 211 individuals were convicted of crimes related to terrorism, and few or none of the 478 deportees had anything to do with terrorist plots. The Justice Department continues misleading the American public about the number of terrorism charges it files. The *Philadelphia Inquirer* reported in May 2003 that most of the 56 federal terrorism charges reported by the Justice Department in early 2003 were mislabeled, including "28 Latinos charged with working illegally at the airport in Austin, Texas, eight Puerto Ricans charged with trespassing on Navy property on the island of Vieques, and a Middle Eastern college student charged in Trenton [New Jersey] with paying a stand-in to take his college English-proficiency tests."[42]

At the same time that Ashcroft exaggerates antiterrorism successes, he is encouraging Americans to be content with whatever morsels of freedom they are permitted to retain. In a National Public Radio interview on September 11, 2002, Ashcroft declared: "We're not sacrificing civil liberties. We're securing civil liberties. That's what our defense is. The assault on civil liberties is one by the terrorists. They are the ones who don't believe in freedom."[43] Ashcroft offered the ultimate proof of the Bush administration's championing of freedom: "I believe when you go out to walk the dog—and I wish I had a dog to walk; that's one of the things in Washington I haven't been able to keep is a dog—you're safer, more secure and your liberties are intact, and we'll fight to make sure that that's so."[44]

There are many excellent federal agents and intelligence analysts—people who are competent, hard working, and dedicated to their jobs and to protecting the American people. However, the administrative systems in which they are immersed consistently produce less than the sum of their parts. There will be cases in which individuals triumph over the system and score major victories for public safety. But to bet against the perennial triumph of the bureaucracy would be unwise.

## 9/11 and the Right to Rule the World

In his book *Bush at War*, Bob Woodward relates a solemn gathering in Afghanistan on February 5, 2002, by 25 men from several Special Forces units and CIA paramilitary teams. After a prayer and the invocation of 9/11, one of the men, speaking for the group, pledged: "We will export death and violence to the four corners of the earth in defense of our great nation."[45]

The intellectual version of this blood vow was the "The National Security Strategy of the United States," released by the Bush administration in September 2002. The strategy report warned the world: "We will not hesitate to act alone, if necessary, to exercise our right of self-defense by acting preemptively."[46] After 9/11, the clearest increase in government power was the right to attack any foreign nation, group, or individual that the U.S. government labeled as a threat to freedom—regardless of whether the feds supplied any evidence, and regardless of whether publicly proffered evidence was quickly shot full of holes.

The National Security Strategy declared: "In the 1990s we witnessed the emergence of a small number of rogue states that . . . hate the United States and everything for which it stands."[47] It is telling that the Bush administration's most important policy document mimics a line from the Pledge of Allegiance. On the other hand, since Bush seems convinced that he is entitled to unquestioning obedience, perhaps the wording is apt. It is false to imply that only in recent years have some governments despised what the United States stands for; many foreign governments have despised the United States ever since 1789. The ideals upon which America was founded are naturally threatening to tyrants—regardless of whether the current U.S. government honors those ideals.

The Bush "Security Strategy" announced its commitment to "maintain a balance of power that favors freedom."[48] But other Bush administration statements make clear that, when the Bush administration says "balance of power," it means U.S. hegemony. The report declared that the U.S. military must "dissuade future military competition" from foreign nations: "Our forces will be strong enough to dissuade potential adversaries from pursuing a military buildup in hopes of surpassing or equaling the power of the United States."[49] Military spending by some other countries can apparently now be viewed as an act of aggression against the United States.

Bush's first-strike doctrine is premised on the Absolute Righteousness of the U.S. Government—as if this government is so far morally superior to every other government on Earth that it is entitled to powers that would have ensured endless wars and devastation if claimed by any other government that ever existed. The Bush administration should formally renounce its hegemony doctrine and issue a revised National Security Strategy less likely to maximize paranoia around the globe.

## Finish Off Al Qaeda, End War on Terrorism

The U.S. government and its allies must finish off Al Qaeda—track down its leaders, disrupt its operations, and prevent it from launching another wave of devastating strikes. It is difficult to tell how well the battle against Al Qaeda has gone because some U.S. government pronouncements have likely vastly overstated successes.

While the U.S. government continues pursuing Al Qaeda, it is time to abandon foolish notions about exterminating all terrorists everywhere. Bush, speaking on February 16, 2002, to U.S. troops in Alaska, declared: "This is about fighting terror wherever it hides. . . . The world must understand that this nation won't rest until we have destroyed terrorism."[50] But, as former National Security Advisor Zbigniew Brzezinski observed, "Terrorism is a technique, a tactic. You can't wage war on a technique."[51]

A concentrated targeted campaign against a terrorist group that has attacked the United States is sound defense strategy. An endless campaign against anyone who attacks established governments anywhere on earth is damn foolery. To claim to conduct a world war on terrorism makes as much sense as conducting a world war on political bad attitudes.

The United States must cease viewing terrorism as a moral abstraction—a simple question of good versus evil. Bush administration comments at times portray terrorism as the modern equivalent of heresy—something which must be stomped out everywhere in order to have true peace anywhere. But this is a moral crusade based on a semi-ludicrous definition of the targeted evil. The U.S. government should cease going after terrorist groups that are not threatening the United States.

## Exiting the Middle East Quagmire

The U.S. government must cease attempting to micro-manage the Middle East. None of the U.S. government efforts in the Middle East have fundamentally advanced peace since President Jimmy Carter hosted Menachem Begin and Anwar Sadat at Camp David in 1978 (and that breakthrough owed far more to Sadat and Begin than to the U.S. government).

It is an illusion that America will be able to permanently crush or quell any and all potential enemies of Israel. The war with Iraq was launched in part to remove a threat to Israel. The war had barely begun before members of the American Israel Political Action Committee launched a major lobbying campaign on Capitol Hill to pressure the U.S. government to also take action against Syria. The *Forward* reported on April 4, 2003: "Openly pleased with the Bush administration's recent warnings to Syria not to aid Iraq, Israel and its supporters here have begun ratcheting up their accusations against its radical neighbor in apparent hopes of widening the rift between Damascus and Washington."[52] Shortly after the lobbying campaign began, the Bush administration issued ominous warnings that Syria could be next on the hit list.

But even toppling the Syrian government would not be enough to satisfy the neoconservatives who appear to be driving Bush administration foreign policy. Some neoconservatives espouse a "clash of civilization" viewpoint that will make perpetual war almost inevitable. Daniel Pipes, a *New York Post* columnist and author, bluntly equates "Islamism with fascism" and warns: "An Islamist is a danger in the same way a fascist is a danger."[53] Norman Podhoretz, editor emeritus of *Commentary,* urged that the United States have "the will to fight World War IV— the war against militant Islam—to a successful conclusion, and. . . . then have the stomach to impose a new political culture on the defeated parties."[54] *Haaretz* reported that William Kristol, the *Weekly Standard* editor who helped persuade the Bush administration to attack Iraq, believes of the Iraq war that "at a deeper level it is a greater war, for the shaping of a new Middle East. It is a war that is intended to change the political culture of the entire region."[55]

The irony is that the largest grievance that Arabs have against the United States is its backing and bankrolling of Israeli government policies that abuse the Palestinians. Because Arabs continue to be outraged about Israeli policies, the United States is supposedly obliged to invade Arab nations, to overthrow Arab governments, and to forcibly change their societies so that they will have a friendlier attitude toward Israel. Because Arabs as a group cannot recognize the humanitarianism of Ariel Sharon's latest crackdown, the U.S. military must install pro-Israeli regimes to govern them until the backward Arab masses see the light.

It is hypocritical for the U.S. government to help prop up Arab dictators while condemning the Arab people for failing to develop democracies. It is also disingenuous to say that the United States is primarily concerned with the lack of civil liberties in Arab countries.

The Bush administration's boundless support for Ariel Sharon severely undercuts less hawkish Israeli political parties. The Labor Party candidate for prime minister in the January 2003 election, retired Gen. Amran Mitzna, offered a plan that could have better protected Israelis while reducing provocations to Palestinians. Sharon won a landslide victory in part because he exploited his close ties to President Bush. While the Sharon government appears fixated on maximizing the amount of land seized in the Occupied Territories, many Israelis would willingly trade land for peace. A 2002 poll by *Yedioth Ahronoth* found that "47% of the [Israeli] public think all the settlements in Gaza Strip and in the West Bank should be dismantled for a peace agreement with the Palestinians. . . . 66% think all the settlements in Gaza Strip should be dismantled, and a majority of 70% support evacuating settlements in regions densely populated by Arabs," as columnist Ran HaCohen noted.[56] U.S. policies have impeded the peace process by giving Israel a blank check to pay for its policies and military machine, including a $9 billion aid package (direct aid and loan guarantees) in early 2003 in part to compensate Israel for the cost of its "war on terrorism" against the Palestinians.

The United States has no right to dictate peace terms to the Israelis and Palestinians. But the United States should immediately end all foreign aid to all governments in the Middle East. Since 1973, the United States has given Israel $240 billion in aid (in 2001 dollars), as well as $117 billion to Egypt and $22 billion to Jordan, according to an analysis prepared for the U.S. Army War College by economist Thomas Stauffer.[57] The Palestinian Authority has also received a smattering in aid from the U.S. government. If Americans want to donate to or invest their own money in any of the countries in the Middle East, that is their right. But the profusion of U.S. aid has failed to bring lasting peace, prosperity, or justice to the region.

Israel, like every other nation, has legitimate security concerns. Arabs need to make concessions on issues such as the right of return for all 1948 Palestinian refugees. Finland's status during the Cold War could provide a model for the first years of an independent Palestinian state. Finland was independent after World War II but avoided aligning itself with the West in order not to spark a military reaction from the neighboring Soviet Union. As Palestinians have more hope for a viable future, the popularity of groups advocating suicide bombing will likely plummet. Unfortunately, there has been ample bad faith on both the Palestinian and Israeli sides, and achieving even a provisional peace settlement will not be easy.

President Bush enunciated a standard on April 26, 2002, that could provide a far better guide for U.S. policy than Bush's own actions: "One thing that the world can count on is that we will not allow Israel to be crushed."[58] But preventing Israel from being crushed and empowering Israel to crush any potential opponent to its dominance and aggressive policies—are two different standards. Israel has a large nuclear weapons stockpile that guarantees security against all the foreign armies within hundreds of miles.[59] The United States has no vested interest in the continued repression of Palestinians in the Occupied Territories.

## Acting Honorably toward Afghans

The Bush administration should come clean on Afghanistan. Bush, in a September 5, 2002 speech in Louisville, Kentucky, boasted: "We went in to liberate people from the clutches of the most barbaric regime in history."[60] That statement may have conned a few slow-witted folks whose idea of history is last week's issue of *TV Guide*. The Taliban were oppressive but were no worse than many other Asian governments of recent decades.

Bush's bragging about "liberating Afghanistan" is, at best, premature. The *New York Times* reported in April 2003: "In a very real sense the war here has not ended. . . . Nearly every day, there are killings, explosions, shootings and targeted attacks on foreign aid workers, Afghan officials and American forces, as well as continuing feuding between warlords."[61] The Afghan puppet government is one assassin's bullet away from collapsing.

Torture may also be an ongoing practice by U.S. forces in Afghanistan. In December 2002, U.S. government agents killed two Afghans while interrogating them. (The medical report listed the cause of one of the deaths as homicide by blunt impact.)[62] The U.S. government refused to disclose whether any action was taken against the Americans who killed the Afghans. Some Afghans may doubt that the U.S. troops are liberators if Americans appear to have carte blanche to kill Afghans.

Some U.S. policies in the post-Taliban Afghanistan have been profoundly dishonorable. Though U.S. bombing killed hundreds of innocent Afghans, the U.S. government refuses to pay any compensation to survivors or to people who were maimed by U.S. attacks. Lt. Col. Roger King explained after an

April 2003 incident in which a thousand-pound laser-guided U.S. bomb destroyed a house and killed seven Afghan women and four men: "It has been the policy in the past of the U.S. government that there are no compensation or reparations for losses due to combat."[63] But the people in the house were not involved in the combat and were guilty only of living near an area that the U.S. military was bombing that day. Though Congress appropriated funds for the U.S. government to provide "appropriate assistance" to Afghan victims of U.S. bombing, the Bush administration has refused to spend a cent. The *Washington Post* reported on April 28, 2003, that AID had $1.25 million in its 2002 budget "to help Afghan civilians who suffered losses as a result of U.S. military action. . . . But the agency has not spent any of that money helping Afghans who had their relatives killed, their children maimed, their homes leveled or their livestock and livelihoods destroyed by American bombing, several U.S. officials in Afghanistan conceded this week."[64] The U.S. government is concerned about setting a precedent that could vindicate the claims of future victims of U.S. bombing and U.S. government officials are also apprehensive about a profusion of false claims.

This is the paradigm for the justice of the Bush war on terrorism: billions for bombs, and not a cent for innocent bombing victims. The U.S. government appears to have more fear of false claims than of wrongfully killing innocent people. The fact that some Afghans would lie nullifies the fact that the U.S. government unjustifiably killed Afghan civilians.

The suspected enemy fighters captured in Afghanistan and taken to Guantanamo Naval Base in Cuba were labeled "enemy combatants." Yet, no evidence has been publicly presented showing that the bulk of the detainees are linked to Al Qaeda. The Bush administration has played games with the courts to ensure that the people locked up on the U.S. military base in Cuba never have access to American justice—or even to any semblance of American fair play.

Some of the detainees appear to have been barbarized at least at times during their captivity. The persistent reports of abusive interrogation techniques—torture—should have ignited major controversies in the United States but most Americans have shrugged them off. And the Bush administration's proposals for military tribunals for some or many of the Guantanamo detainees is an American precedent that is being eagerly applauded by the world's dictators.

The U.S. government should immediately end all foreign aid to any foreign government that violates its own citizens' rights, according to the State Department's annual Country Reports on Human Rights. The federal government has no right to force Americans to bankroll foreign atrocities. At the same time, the U.S. government should continue and accelerate its program to purchase nuclear weapons material from nations that were part of the former Soviet Union, regardless of the records of such governments.

It is unlikely that fundamental reform will occur in the war on terrorism as long as President Bush sees this war as his political salvation. Bush believes that America found its "calling" in fighting terrorism—and the war certainly gave direction and momentum to an administration that was otherwise accomplishing little. Bush is exploiting the war on terrorism to help snare a second four year term in the presidency. A confidential White House paper, leaked in December 2002, listed the "War on terrorism" as the first agenda item for Bush's reelection strategy.[65] The White House donated a photo of Bush talking on the phone on Air Force One on 9/11 to the Republican National Party, which proceeded to give free copies of the photo to anyone who donated $150.[66] In a May 2003 fundraising appeal sent to one million potential donors, Bush declared: "I'll depend on friends and supporters like you to get my campaign organized and operating across our country. We have no more urgent and important duty than to wage and win the war on terrorism."[67] The Republicans will be holding their national convention in New York City in early September 2004. *New York Times* columnist Maureen Dowd observed that Bush advisor Karl Rove "envisions merging the Madison Square Garden party with the 9/11 anniversary commemorations into one big national security lollapalooza. Perhaps President Bush should just skip the pretense of the Garden and give his acceptance speech at ground zero."[68] Manhattan officials intend to lay the cornerstone for the 1,776 memorial tower at Ground Zero during the Republican National Convention.

---

There will always be ways for conniving terrorists to skate around the edges of government security and wreak havoc. The key variable is how hard are terrorists trying and how many terrorists are willing to give their lives to settle what they believe is a blood debt.

The fewer rights a government violates, the fewer attacks it tends to suffer. Respecting human rights is not an antiterrorist panacea. But it is a good tactic to stack the odds in favor of domestic tranquility.

Killing foreigners is no substitute for protecting Americans. The best defense against terrorism is to make fewer enemies. Unless there are profound and sweeping changes in American foreign policy, it is only a question of time until new terrorist attacks occur in America. The best way to block suicide bombers is to defuse them before they launch themselves. The vast majority of international terrorist attacks against the United States in the last 20 years occurred after the United States got involved in squabbles that it had no need to get involved in—after the United States blundered into foreign conflicts which it was unable to solve. In the name of antiterrorism, the U.S. government should cease meddling in the affairs of almost every foreign nation on earth.

Yet, even if the United States treats every person and every government in the world honorably, there will still be perils. A call to respect human rights is not an appeal for pacifism or disarmament. The United States, like many other nations, will continue to have enemies. Regardless of whether the U.S. government has wronged foreign peoples and nations in the past, the United States cannot prostrate itself now. The United States must actively protect the American people at the same time that it abandons unjust or abusive policies that inflame foreign hatred and homicidal lust for vengeance.

The best way to export American political values is by showing how freedom and a representative, limited government breed peace and prosperity. At a time when many Americans are questioning the best role for the United States in the world, the sage words of John Quincy Adams' Fourth of July 1821 oration are more apt than ever before:

> Wherever the standard of freedom and Independence has been or shall be unfurled, there will her heart, her benedictions and her prayers be. But she goes not abroad, in search of monsters to destroy. She is the well-wisher to the freedom and independence of all. She is the champion and vindicator only of her own.[70]

## CHAPTER SIXTEEN

# Conclusion

These are good days in the history of freedom.

—*President Bush, April 15, 2003*[1]

There is no crueler tyranny than that which is exercised under cover of law, and with the colors of justice . . .

—*United States v. Jannottie, 1982*[2]

In the long run, people have more to fear from governments than from terrorists. Terrorists will come and go, but power-hungry politicians will always be with us. We must ensure that each new debacle caused by government incompetence is not converted into another coffin nail for individual liberty.

The war on terrorism has profoundly changed how the government can exploit challenges to its authority or policies. If there were another Boston Tea Party in this country, Bush might be the first to accuse the protestors of being terrorists. Attorney General John Ashcroft might leap at the chance to round up everyone suspected of being involved in dumping tea, or of uttering seditious thoughts in the vicinity of teapots. Bush could issue an executive order to immediately activate the Total Information Awareness surveillance system, thereby allowing the feds to vacuum up enough information to craft a profile for suspected "tea politico-psychopaths." The FBI could use the profile to carry out hundreds of "black bag job" secret searches to determine which Americans were stockpiling tea for nefarious purposes. Just to be on the safe side, the FBI could also arrest anyone who, based on confidential informants' reports, might become involved in future tea protests. FBI agents could race to federal judges and proclaim that the detainees must be held in secret without bail for as long as the government chooses because their interrogation could reveal a grand mosaic of plots among coffee, soda, and even traitorous Perrier drinkers. FBI agents could also scramble to infiltrate any groups or organizations suspected of having an inordinate interest in either tea or dumping. Justice Department officials could anonymously leak to the media that the tea dumpers were linked to Al Qaeda, or at least to Hezbollah. The Justice Department could also launch a special TIPS program to encourage people to report anyone who buys more than 100 bags of tea at one time, or more than 50 bags of tea from a foreign company (except for Red Rose of Canada). Homeland Security chief Tom Ridge could raise the national alert one color level and hint that the tea dumping may be only the first step to a concerted effort to disrupt the American food supply and thereby starve millions of Americans. Republican congressmen could rush to the floor of the House to praise the administration for its prompt and vigorous action to prevent the destruction of all civil order in the United States. And after the smoke began to clear, President Bush could give a televised speech to reassure the American people that the federal government's prompt action once again saved their freedom.

## Bush, Terror, and Freedom

President Bush has invoked freedom in more than two hundred speeches and declarations since 9/11. Yet the immediate threat to Americans' freedom does not stem from a depraved interpretation of the Koran, but from a perverse reading of the Constitution. The Bush administration "defends freedom" by destroying the power of judges to release people who have been jailed without charges, by refusing to inform Congress of how new federal powers are being used, by giving itself the right to impound millions of people's email, by carrying out thousands of secret searches, and by seeking to lower an iron curtain of secrecy around all federal agencies. The failures of the federal government to stop the terrorists on 9/11 sanctified almost unlimited government surveillance. The worse the government failed, the further it entitled itself to intrude.

The more loudly Bush praises freedom, the more carefully Americans should count their remaining constitutional rights. For Bush, freedom appears to be simply a word to invoke to sanctify himself and his commands. For Bush, "freedom" seems to be whatever extends his own political power. Whatever razes any barriers to executive power—that is "freedom." Whatever prevents Americans from learning of their government's actions—that is "freedom."

The more freedoms Americans lose, the more dangerous government becomes. The de facto suspension of habeas corpus means the government could conduct another, even larger mass roundup of people deemed dangerous—including American citizens labeled "material witnesses." The less freedom of speech, freedom of association, and freedom of information that Americans have, the less ability they will have to rein in the government and the greater the risk that government policies will spur new terrorist attacks on the United States. A government that has sufficient power to destroy a foreign regime based on brazen false accusations will not hesitate to also damage Americans' freedoms and rights based on bogus charges.

The sacrifice of freedom, per se, is as likely to produce security as the sacrifice of virgins is to produce good rains and bountiful harvests. There is no god of terrorism whom the United States can appease by putting the Bill of Rights on the sacrificial altar. There was nothing in the Constitution or federal statute book that prevented federal agencies from detecting and thwarting the 9/11 attacks. And there is nothing in the gutting of Americans' rights that will stop the next terrorist attack. In many areas where Americans' freedom has been sacrificed, the main benefit is to make it easier for the government to hide its mistakes and abuses.

## Moralizing to Death

Since 9/11, Bush often seems blinded by the glare from his own halo. The moral self-adulation at the heart of the war on terrorism is a danger both to America and the world.

Moral power also corrupts. After 9/11, America was the premier Designated Victim of the World. But the more sympathy politicians receive, the more damage they can inflict. Bush and his top advisors sensed that the U.S. government could push further than it ever had because of the 9/11-related deference from other nations. The result was an unnecessary war and the potential wrecking of both the United Nations and NATO.

U.S. aggression and unnecessary interventions have been the major sources of terrorist attacks against the U.S. government and U.S. citizens around the world. Yet American politicians continue to disdain any serious consideration of the role that U.S. government policy may have played in sparking foreign attacks. Americans cannot understand the terrorist threat without recognizing how much hatred some U.S. foreign policies produce abroad. It takes more than presidential assertions of American good intentions to absolve this nation in the eyes of the world.

The United States has no right to forcibly remake the world in its own image. This nation has no right to impose its system of government on foreign nations—any more than it has the right to forcibly impose Christianity or any other religion on foreign peoples. The more the U.S. government seeks to inflict "American values" overseas, the more that it betrays this country's original ideals. The United States may have done more to reduce freedom around the world via its bad example and its aid to oppressive regimes than anything the U.S. military could do to increase freedom abroad.

The U.S. government is far more efficient at making enemies than at defending Americans. There are better ways to fight terrorism than by attacking everyone in the world with a bomb and a bad attitude toward America. It is not possible to kill or imprison every person in the world who might develop homicidal hatred as a result of U.S. policies. The U.S. government is far more able to reduce its foreign provocations than to perpetually increase its competence.

## Bush's Wars and the
## Future of American Democracy

A federal appeals court, ruling on August 26, 2002, on the case of secret arrests and detentions of suspected terrorists, concluded: "A true democracy is one that operates on faith—faith that government officials are forthcoming and honest, and faith that informed citizens will arrive at logical conclusions. This is a vital reciprocity that America should not discard in these troubling times."[3]

Unfortunately, American democracy is failing this simple standard. The 9/11 attacks increased the credulity of much of the American public. Politicians exploited that gullibility to seize more power, spend more money, and violate more rights.

The Patriot Act and other anti-terrorism measures will be Pandora's Boxes from which scandal after scandal arise in coming years. Americans have likely not yet learned of even the tip of the iceberg of federal abuses that have occurred since 9/11.

Most of the homeland successes in the war on terrorism have been farces or frauds. From the busting of a thousand Hispanic janitors, food service workers, and other airport employees in bogus "antiterrorism" crackdowns, to Ashcroft's ludicrous misrepresentations of high-school dropout Jose Padilla, to the hiring of an army of overpaid TSA employees to rummage through Americans' baggage and have them arrested for saying a single harsh word, to the secret arrests of twelve hundred "suspected terrorist" taxi drivers et al with expired visas, the war on terrorism has never had a shortage of scams. But the U.S. government has failed to shut down Al Qaeda.

Excessive trust of government can be subversive of democracy. People trusted Bush—and Bush launched an unprovoked war against Iraq. People trusted Ashcroft—and Ashcroft unleashed the FBI to vacuum up the nation's email and send undercover agents almost anywhere they choose to go. People trusted Tom Ridge—and his Homeland Security Department notified local police departments that critics of government policies should be viewed as suspected terrorists.

A lie that is accepted by a sufficient number of ignorant voters automatically becomes a political truth. Shortly after his inauguration, Bush joked to a crowd of Washington insiders: "You can fool some of the people all of the time, and those are the ones you need to concentrate on."[4] It would be naive to assume that all of Bush's false statements are accidents or oversights. White House senior policy advisor Karl Rove explained how the war on terrorism would be judged by the American public: "Everything will be measured by results. The victor is always right. History ascribes to the victor qualities that may or may not actually have been there. And similarly to the defeated."[5]

None of the false statements by Bush or his appointees or other federal officials documented in this book were necessary for national security. Bush's assertion that most American illicit drug buyers were probably terrorist financiers did nothing to defund Al Qaeda. Ashcroft's hokum about the FBI's 94-year history as champions of freedom did nothing to expose sleeper cells that might be scattered across this land. Transportation Secretary Norm Mineta's claim that the feds were hiring the "best and the brightest" to be airport screeners did nothing to prevent endless disruptions of airports and airline travel by boneheaded government clerks.

Lies regarding the use of government power are almost never harmless errors. The more lies government officials are allowed to tell, the less chance citizens have of controlling the government. And the more power a politician seeks, the more dangerous his lies become.

If freedom is to be revived, citizens must stop presuming that politicians are more honest than they seem—or presuming that politicians' lies are irrelevant to their intentions toward the governed. For the future of the American Republic, Americans must realize that government does not know best, that there is no superhuman wisdom lurking in the bowels of the White House or the National Security Council or the State Department or CIA.

The final verdict is not yet in on how American democracy responded to 9/11. The longer time passes with scant effective oversight by Congress, the greater the blemish on the American Republic. The vast majority of congressmen brazenly defaulted on their oath of office and appear to be far more fearful of being criticized by the Bush administration than of letting federal agents violate the rights and privacy of American citizens.

The United States will not have politically recovered from 9/11 until the government ends all the unjustified intrusions into Americans' lives, until the government abandons its prerogative of mass secret arrests, until the government obeys the Freedom of Information Act and opens its files, and until the government ceases seeking to fearmonger and demagogue Americans into submission. As of this time, there is no indication that the Bush administration is veering toward any of these steps.

Citizens should distrust politicians who distrust freedom. Americans must be vigilant to prevent politicians from exploiting the terrorist attacks which their own policies helped provoke.

No one should understate the evil of terrorists who explode bombs or crash planes or otherwise butcher innocent men, women, and children. None of the criticisms of governments in this book are intended to excuse or diminish the guilt of those who murder innocent people for political ends. There is no motive that can justify the wrongful taking of innocent life. And there is no reason not to harshly punish those who seek to slay others for their creed or ideology.

Yet, it is a mistake to myopically focus on terrorists as a supreme evil on the contemporary landscape. The evil of private terrorists must not be permitted to expunge the guilt of state terrorism. The failure to have a clear view of the frequently oppressive nature of government action is the root source of many of the worst abuses of the war on terrorism.

It would be naive to presume that terrorism is the only thing preventing the birth of a Golden Age for humanity. Terrorism will not be totally eradicated until oppression is exterminated from the globe. But as long as humans are human, misgovernment will continue to occur almost as often as bad weather.

It is possible to crush the Al Qaeda terrorist network without permanently placing the federal government on a pedestal. Most of the post-9/11 laws and federal policies provide an illusion of public safety while doing little or nothing to remedy grave flaws in U.S. security and foreign policy. It will take more than multibillion dollar safety placebos to protect the American people.

The word "terrorism" must not become an incantation that miraculously razes all limits on government power. It is time to end the aura of righteousness that has enshrouded government for the last two years. American politicians who invoke the evil of terrorism must not be permitted to slip the leash the Founding Fathers crafted to bind the rulers of America in perpetuity.

# Acknowledgments

Many individuals have contributed or inspired ideas that went into this book. I want to especially thank Greg Rushford, Jacob Hornberger, Jim Petersen, and Nancy Dunne for their feedback and their comments on various chunks of the manuscript.

At Palgrave Macmillan, Senior Editor Michael Flamini's enthusiasm and encouragement was much appreciated. I greatly appreciate having an editor and a publisher with no shortage of spine. Production Director Alan Bradshaw did fine work shepherding the manuscript into book form, expediting the project into print, and infusing a tight deadline with patient calm. Copyeditors Norma McLemore, Amanda Fernandez, and Sonia Wilson were a joy to work with and I appreciated their catching flaws and their suggestions for improving the text.

# Notes

## Chapter 1—Introduction

1. Remarks by the President upon Arrival on the South Lawn," White House Office of the Press Secretary, September 16, 2001.
2. Richard Morin and Claudia Deane, "Poll: Americans' Trust in Government Grows," *Washington Post*, September 28, 2001.
3. Ronald Brownstein, "The Government, Once Scorned, Becomes Savior," *Los Angeles Times*, September 19, 2001; Al Hunt, "Government to the Rescue," *Wall Street Journal*, September 27, 2001; Jim Hoagland, "Government's Comeback," *Washington Post*, September 26, 2001.
4. "Attorney General John Ashcroft Testimony before the Commerce, Justice, State and Judiciary Subcommittee of the Senate Appropriations Committee April 1, 2003," Justice Department Office of Public Affairs, April 1, 2003.
5. Uniting and Strengthening America by Providing Appropriate Tools Required to Intercept and Obstruct Terrorism (USA PATRIOT) Act of 2001, October 26, 2001.
6. Steve Fainaru, "U.S. Bans the Release of Detainees' Names; INS Order Issued to counter N.J. Ruling," *Washington Post*, April 19, 2002.
7. David Cole, "National Security State," *Nation*, December 17, 2001.
8. "Remarks at a Meeting of the President's Homeland Security Advisory Council," *Public Papers of the Presidents*, June 12, 2002.
9. Jane Kirtley, "Hiding Behind National Security," *American Journalism Review*, January-February, 2002.
10. Deb Reichman, "Critics Blast Bush Order on Papers," Associated Press, November 2, 2001.
11. Ron Hutcheson, "White House Takes Media War to Newspapers," *Knight Ridder newspapers*, October 12, 2001.
12. Jim Hoagland, "The Limits of Lying," *Washington Post*, March 21, 2002.
13. Federal News Service, "Senate Judiciary Committee Hearing on War on Terrorism," December 6, 2001.
14. Jack Douglas, "U.S. Security Memos Warn of Little Things," *Fort Worth Star-Telegram*, May 25, 2003. (Italics added.)
15. Ibid.
16. "Remarks by the President in Roundtable Interview with Asian Editors," White House Office of the Press Secretary, October 17, 2001. (The interview occurred on October 16, 2001.)
17. "President Bush Holds Press Conference," White House Office of the Press Secretary, March 13, 2002.
18. "Remarks by the President to the Chamber of Commerce, Charlotte, North Carolina," White House Office of the Press Secretary, February 27, 2002.

19.  Ibid.
20.  "Bush Remarks at Booker T. Washington High School, Atlanta Georgia," White House Office of the Press Secretary, January 31, 2002.
21.  M. Robespierre, "Report upon the Principles of Political Morality which Are To Form the Basis of the Administration of the Interior Concerns of the Republic" (Philadelphia, 1794). Posted                                                                                     at http://www.arts.adelaide.edu.au/personal/DHart/ETexts/FrenchRevolution/Robespierre-PolMorality.html.
22.  Todd S. Purdum, "What Do You Mean, 'Terrorist'?" *New York Times,* April 7, 2002.
23.  Craig Whitney, "What's Left Behind, "*New York Times,* April 1, 1973.
24.  Barton Gellman, "Though Terrorism May Be Hard to Define, This Administration Takes It Seriously," *National Journal,* September 12, 1981.
25.  Ibid.
26.  For the years 1980 to 1989, the source is a fax from State Department spokesman Joe Reap to author, May 16, 2003. For subsequent years, statistics are taken from annual reports ("Patterns of Global Terrorism," U.S. State Department, 1990–2000).
27.  Associated Press, "U.S. Denies Report that Al-Qaida Funds Are Flowing," *New York Times,* August 30, 2002.
28.  David Johnston, " CIA Chief Warns of New Terror from Al Qaeda," *New York Times,* October 18, 2002.
29.  Paul Krugman," Paths of Glory," *New York Times,* May 16, 2003.

## Chapter 2

1.  "Domestic and Foreign Issues—Interview with the Washington Times," *Public Papers of the Presidents,* November 27, 1984.
2.  Richard Harwood, Bob Woodward and Christian Williams, "U.S. Ponders Morality of Striking Back," *Washington Post,* February 12, 1984.
3.  Lawrence Knutson, "Haig Sounds Anti-Terrorism Foreign Policy Emphasis," Associated Press, January 29, 1981.
4.  Charles Mohr, "Data on Terrorism under U.S. Revision," *New York Times,* April 24, 1981.
5.  Ibid.
6.  Robert Pear, "F.B.I. Director Sees No Evidence Soviet Fosters Terrorism in U.S.," *New York Times,* April 27, 1981.
7.  "Text of Haig's Speech on American Foreign Policy," *New York Times,* April 25, 1981.
8.  Barton Gellman, "Though Terrorism May be Hard to Define, This Administration Takes It Seriously," *National Journal,* September 12, 1981.
9.  Thomas Friedman, *From Beirut to Jerusalem* (New York: Doubleday, 1990), p. 130.
10.  "Eitan Says Invasion Planned a Year Ago," United Press International, July 2, 1982.
11.  William Claiborne, "Tanks, Troops Seek to Push PLO North," *Washington Post,* June 7, 1982.
12.  David Martin and John Walcott, *Best Laid Plans: The Inside Story of America's War against Terrorism* (New York: Harper & Row, 1988), p. 88.
13.  Mel Laytner, "Israel Calls for PLO Cease Fire," United Press International, June 28, 1982.
14.  Charles Kaiser with Theodore Stanger, "The Battle Israel Lost," *Newsweek,* September 13, 1982. "New York Times correspondent Thomas L. Friedman provided some of the most balanced and comprehensive coverage of the siege from Beirut. But even he became enraged when he wrote that the Israelis had carried out 'indiscriminate' bombing of Beirut on Aug. 4—and his editors dropped the adjective without informing him. 'I found your decision to excise the word 'indiscriminate' from my lead a most disturbing and appalling

news judgment,' Friedman telexed his editors in New York. The fact that the published version of his story still reported that 'Israeli planes, gunboats and artillery rained shellfire all across West Beirut today' apparently failed to placate the correspondent."

15. Martin and Walcott, *Best Laid Plans,* p. 96.
16. William Smith, "The New Lebanon Crisis," *Time,* September 27, 1982.
17. Ibid.
18. Thomas Friedman, "The Beirut Massacre: The Four Days," *New York Times,* September 26, 1982.
19. Ibid.
20. "Palestinians Slain in Lebanese Refugee Camps," Facts on File *World News Digest,* September 24, 1982.
21. Tim Llewellyn, "The Bitter Legacy of Sharon's Unfinished Business," *Scotsman,* September 16, 2002.
22. Martin and Walcott, *Best Laid Plans,* p. 95.
23. Quoted in James MacManus, "The Complicity in a Massacre," *Manchester Guardian Weekly,* October 3, 1982.
24. "Palestinians Slain in Lebanese Refugee Camps," Facts on File *World News Digest,* September 24, 1982.
25. Ibid.
26. William Smith, "Crisis of Conscience; Israel Anguishes over the Question of Its Guilt for the Palestinian Massacre," *Time,* October 4, 1982.
27. Ibid.
28. "Address to the Nation Announcing the Formation of a New Multinational Force in Lebanon," *Public Papers of the Presidents,* September 20, 1982.
29. Martin and Walcott, *Best Laid Plans,* p. 102.
30. Bernard Gwertzman, "Reagan Calls Bombing Cowardly," New York Times, April 19, 1983.
31. "U.S. Embassy in Lebanon Devastated by Bomb Blast; Dozens Killed, Pro-Iran Group Named," Facts on File *World News Digest,* April 22, 1983.
32. Angus Deming with Holger Jensen and James Pringle, "Blood and Terror in Beirut," *Newsweek,* May 2, 1983.
33. Ibid.
34. Larry Margasak, "U.S. Relied on PLO for Embassy Security, Congress Told," Associated Press, May 15, 1982.
35. "Transcript of President's News Conference on Foreign and Domestic Matters," *New York Times,* April 23, 1983.
36. Charles Mohr, "Marines' Security Raises Questions," *New York Times,* October 24, 1983.
37. Ibid.
38. "Events in Lebanon and Grenada," *Public Papers of the Presidents,* October 27, 1983.
39. Michael Getler, "The Beirut Massacre; Security Questioned at Marines' Bombed Building," *Washington Post,* October 27, 1983.
40. "The Marine Tragedy; Experts List Ways to Avert Attacks," *New York Times,* December 11, 1983.
41. Joel Brinkley, "President Doubts Marines' Leader Misled Congress," *New York Times,* December 21, 1983.
42. Joel Brinkley, "Questions by House Panel Anger Marine General," *New York Times,* November 3, 1983.
43. Ibid.
44. Philip Taubman, "Major Questions Raised on C.I.A.'s Performance," *New York Times,* November 3, 1983.
45. Ibid.
46. "The U.S. Marine Tragedy: Causes and Responsibility," *New York Times,* December 11, 1983.

47. Philip Taubman and Joel Brinkley, "The Marine Tragedy; Chain of Command: Lack of Guidance for Officers in Beirut," *New York Times,* December 11, 1983.

48. "The U.S. Marine Tragedy: Causes and Responsibility," *New York Times,* December 11, 1983.

49. Philip Taubman and Joel Brinkley, "The Marine Tragedy; Security: As Threats Grew, Defenses Were Improvised," *New York Times,* December 11, 1983.

50. Ibid.

51. Philip Taubman and Joel Brinkley, "The Marine Tragedy; Policy: Shifting Diplomacy Made Troops 'Sitting Ducks,'" *New York Times,* December 11, 1983.

52. Ibid.

53. Thomas L. Friedman, "Marines Seemingly Did Little to Deter a Car-Bomb Attack," *New York Times,* October 25, 1983.

54. "The Marine Tragedy; Experts List Ways to Avert Attacks," *New York Times,* December 11, 1983.

55. Ibid.

56. "'83 Terror Warning at Marine Barracks Ignored, Expert Says," *Chicago Tribune,* September 24, 1986.

57. Margaret Shapiro, "Security; Intelligence in Beirut Reported Still Faulty," *Washington Post,* December 22, 1983.

58. "Texts of Summary of Investigation into Attack on Marines and of Dissent," *New York Times,* December 21, 1983.

59. Fred Hiatt, "Report Hits U.S. Reliance on Force in Lebanon," *Washington Post,* December 29, 1983.

60. Philip Taubman, "Pentagon's Inquiry Blames Major Marine Commanders and Faulty Policy in Beirut," *New York Times,* December 29, 1983.

61. Quoted in William Arkin, "War Plays into Terrorists' Hands," *Los Angeles Times,* December 29, 2002.

62. Fred Hiatt, "Report Hits U.S. Reliance on Force in Lebanon."

63. Philip Taubman, "Reagan's Timing and Reasons: Protecting Corps," *New York Times,* December 28, 1983.

64. "Pentagon Report on the Security of U.S. Marines in Lebanon," *Public Papers of the Presidents,* December 27, 1983.

65. "Remarks and a Question-and-Answer Session with Reporters on the Pentagon Report on the Security of United States Marines in Lebanon," *Public Papers of the Presidents,* December 27, 1983.

66. "Pentagon Report on the Security of U.S. Marines in Lebanon," *Public Papers of the Presidents,* December 27, 1983.

67. Lou Cannon, "President Accepts Blame in Attack on Marine Base," *Washington Post,* December 28, 1983.

68. Ibid.

69. Patrick Sloyan, "The Warnings Reagan Ignored; Marine Barracks Bombing," *Nation,* October 27, 1984.

70. James Gerstenzang, "White House Blames Carter for Intelligence Deficiencies," Associated Press, December 28, 1983.

71. James Gerstenzang, "President Orders Investigation of Leak of Lebanon Recommendations," Associated Press, November 22, 1983.

72. Lou Cannon, "Justice Probe Fails to Disclose Source of Leaks on Mideast," *Washington Post,* December 16, 1983.

73. Martin and Walcott, *Best Laid Plans,* p. 159.

74. John Kifner, "Flaws Seen at West Beirut Embassy," *New York Times,* September 25, 1984.

75. Philip Taubman, "House Committee Says U.S. Embassy Ignored Warnings," *New York Times,* October 4, 1984.

76. Editorial, "Yet Again in Beirut," *New York Times,* September 22, 1984.

77. Bernard Gwertzman, "Reagan Concedes Embassy Security Was Not Complete," *New York Times,* September 24, 1984.

78. Ibid.

79. Cliff Haas, "Speaker Blast Reagan's "Lame Excuses" in Embassy Bombing," Associated Press, September 24, 1984.

80. Mark Whitaker with Kim Willenson, "Beirut: Who's to Blame?" *Newsweek,* October 8, 1984.

81. Elizabeth Wharton, "Carter Angered by Reagan's Remark," United Press International, September 27, 1984.

82. John M. Goshko, "Shultz Hits Security Criticism; Embassy Bombing Issue Still Dogging Administration," *Washington Post,* October 1, 1984.

83. "Dozens Had Roles in Security Measures for Beirut," *New York Times,* September 27, 1984.

84. "Foreign and Domestic Issues," *Public Papers of the Presidents,* October 2, 1984.

85. Philip Taubman, "House Committee Says U.S. Embassy Ignored Warnings," *New York Times,* October 4, 1984.

86. Bob Woodward, "U.S. Had Reliable Warnings Diplomats Were Bomb Target," *Washington Post,* October 18, 1984.

87. Philip Taubman, "House Committee Says U.S. Embassy Ignored Warnings."

88. Joel Brinkley, "Senate Panel Report Faults State Dept. Aides in Lebanon Bombing," *New York Times,* November 3, 1984.

89. Bernard Weinraub, "Mondale Seeks Apology from Bush on Lebanon," *New York Times,* October 13, 1984.

90. Juan Williams, "Vice President Criticizes Mondale for 'Tearing Down the President,'" *Washington Post,* October 3, 1984.

91. "International Terrorism," *Public Papers of the Presidents,* May 31, 1986.

92. "International Terrorism," *Public Papers of the Presidents,* May 31, 1986.

93. "International Terrorism," *Public Papers of the Presidents,* May 31, 1986.

94. "Law Day U.S.A.," *Public Papers of the Presidents,* April 16, 1986.

95. John M. Goshko and Margaret Shapiro, "CIA Manual for Guerrillas Denounced by Rep. Boland; Contras Instructed in Assassination," *Washington Post,* October 18, 1984.

96. Joanne Omang, "CIA Manual Based on Vietnam; Wording in Nicaragua Booklet Similar to '68 'Lesson Plans,'" *Washington Post,* October 30, 1984.

97. "C.I.A. Said to Produce Manual for Anti-Sandinistas," *New York Times,* October 15, 1984.

98. Joanne Omang, "CIA Manual Based on Vietnam; Wording in Nicaragua Booklet Similar to '68 'Lesson Plans.'"

99. Robert Parry, "CIA Manual Exhorts Nicaraguans to Sabotage," Associated Press, June 29, 1984.

100. Ibid.

101. Dan Williams, "Assassinations by Contras in Honduras Told," *Los Angeles Times,* January 15, 1985.

102. "Contra Atrocities Reported," Facts on File *World News Digest,* March 8, 1985.

103. Doyle McManus, "Rights Groups Accuse Contras; Atrocities in Nicaragua against Civilians Charged," *Los Angeles Times,* March 8, 1985.

104. On the abuses by the Nicaraguan government, see, for instance, James LeMoyne, "Peasants Tell of Rights Abuses by Sandinistas," *New York Times,* June 28, 1987.

105. Joanne Omang and Lou Cannon, "Reagan Orders Investigation of Controversial CIA Manual; Aides Say Writer Was 'Overzealous,'" *Washington Post,* October 19, 1984.

106. Neil Roland, "Casey Spared Top Officials of Discipline for Contra Manual," United Press International, February 8, 1987.

107. "Reagan Now Says Manual Was Mistranslated," *New York Times,* November 4, 1984.

108. Alessandra Stanley, "Letter to Capitol Hill; CIA Director Casey Defends His Agency's Controversial Primer," *Time*, November 12, 1984.

109. "CIA Mid-Level Personnel Punished on Terror Manual; Said to View Themselves 'Scapegoats,'" Facts on File *World News Digest*, November 16, 1984.

110. J. Patrice McSherry, "Operation Condor: Clandestine Inter-American System," *Social Justice*, December 22, 1999. The 1954 manual was declassified in 1997.

111. David Hoffman, "President Agrees to Punishment in CIA Manual Case," *Washington Post*, November 11, 1984.

112. Neil Roland, "Casey Spared Top Officials of Discipline for Contra Manual."

113. "Dallas, Texas," *Public Papers of the Presidents*, June 21, 1985.

114. Gary Cohn, Ginger Thompson, and Mark Matthews, "Torture Was Taught by CIA; Declassified Manual Details the Methods Used in Honduras," *Baltimore Sun*, January 27, 1997.

115. Bob Woodward and Walter Pincus, "1984 Order Gave CIA Latitude; Reagan's Secret Move To Counter Terrorists Called 'License to Kill,'" *Washington Post*, October 5, 1988.

116. Joe Pichirallo and Edward Cody, "U.S. Trains Antiterrorists; CIA, Military Aid Foreign Squads," *Washington Post*, March 25, 1985.

117. Bob Woodward and Charles R. Babcock, "Anti-terrorist Plan Rescinded After Unauthorized Bombing," *Washington Post*, May 12, 1985.

118. Bob Woodward and Charles R. Babcock, "Anti-terrorist Plan Rescinded After Unauthorized Bombing." Also, Stuart Taylor, "Lebanese Group Linked to C.I.A. Is Tied to Car Bombing Fatal to 80," *New York Times*, May 13, 1985.

119. Bob Woodward, "Exclusive Excerpts from *Veil: The Secret Wars of the CIA*," *Newsweek*, October 5, 1987.

120. "Hijackers Claiming Revenge for Bombing," United Press International, June 14, 1985.

121. Martin and Walcott, *Best Laid Plans*, p. 152.

122. "Reagan Accuses 5 'Outlaw States' of Backing Terrorism; Warns U.S. Will Defend Itself," Facts on File *World News Digest*, July 12, 1985.

123. Seymour M. Hersh, "The U.S. Plot to Kill Gadhafi," *New York Times Magazine*, February 22, 1987.

124. William Claiborne, "Rabin Cites Abu Nidal in Airport Terror Raids; Austrians, Italians Also Suspect Foe of Arafat," *Washington Post*, December 30, 1985.

125. Martin and Walcott, *Best Laid Plans*, p. 268.

126. "The President's News Conference—Economic Sanctions against Libya," *Public Papers of the Presidents*, January 7, 1986.

127. Noel Koch, "The Hostage Labryrinth . . . But Our 'No Negotiations' Policy May Not Have Helped," *Washington Post*, March 18, 1990.

128. "United States Air Strike against Libya," *Public Papers of the Presidents*, April 14, 1986.

129. Martin and Walcott, *Best Laid Plans*, p. 310.

130. Ibid.

131. Ibid.

132. "United States Air Strike against Libya," *Public Papers of the Presidents*, April 14, 1986.

133. Martin and Walcott, *Best Laid Plans*, pp. 312–13.

134. Lou Cannon and David Hoffman, "U.S. Officials Claim Unrest in Libya; Targets Said Chosen to Raise Discontent," *Washington Post*, April 17, 1986.

135. Seymour M. Hersh, "The U.S. Plot to Kill Gadhafi," New York Times Magazine, February 22, 1987.

136. "American Business Conference," *Public Papers of the Presidents*, April 15, 1986.

137. Robert Oakley, "International Terrorism," *Foreign Affairs: America and the World 1986*, 1987.

138. "United States Chamber of Commerce," *Public Papers of the Presidents*, April 23, 1986.

139. "Poll: Reagan Approval Improves," ABCNews.com, August 6, 2001.

140. Martin and Walcott, *Best Laid Plans*, p. 82.

141. "President's Trip to the Far East," *Public Papers of the Presidents,* May 4, 1986.
142. "Iran-United States Relations," *Public Papers of the Presidents,* November 13, 1986.
143. "Iran Arms and Contra Aid Controversy," *Public Papers of the Presidents,* December 6, 1986.
144. "Iran Arms and Contra Aid Controversy," *Public Papers of the Presidents,* January 30, 1987.
145. Michael Kinsley, "Pardon Them?" *Washington Post,* July 23, 1987.
146. "The Iran Deception; Reagan's Greatest Crisis; The Unfolding of The Iran Deception; A Chronology," *Los Angeles Times,* December 28, 1986.
147. Nicholas M. Horrock, "Tower Report Stirs Doubts about Reagan's Forgetfulness," *Chicago Tribune,* March 1, 1987.
148. George Lardner, "Meese Details White House Crisis; Fear of Impeachment Gripped Staff in Late '86, North Trial Told," *Washington Post,* March 29, 1989.
149. Jack Nelson, "Implication of Being Above Law Held to Hurt President," *Los Angeles Times,* May 22, 1987.
150. Jack Nelson, "Aide's '87 Memo Raised Question of Removing Reagan From Office," *Washington Post,* September 15, 1988. Nelson noted: "Most high-level White House aides believed that President Reagan was so depressed, inept and inattentive early last year in the wake of disclosures in November 1986 about the Iran-contra scandal that the possibility of invoking the 25th Amendment to remove him from office was raised in a memo to Howard H. Baker Jr., who was just taking office as Reagan's chief of staff."
151. "Embarrassment May Have Caused Suicide," Cable News Network, May 17, 1996.
152. "The White House Crisis; Excerpts from the Tower Commission's Report," *New York Times,* February 27, 1987.
153. Martin and Walcott, *Best Laid Plans,* p. 329.
154. Seymour M. Hersh, "The Iran-Contra Committees: Did They Protect Reagan?" *New York Times Magazine,* April 29, 1990.
155. "Foreign and Domestic Issues," *Public Papers of the Presidents,* May 27, 1987.
156. John Barry and Roger Charles, "Sea of Lies," *Newsweek,* July 13, 1992.
157. Ibid.
158. George C. Wilson, "Navy Missile Downs Iranian Jetliner," *Washington Post,* July 4, 1988.
159. Michael Kinsley, "Rally Round the Flag, Boys," *Time,* September 12, 1988.
160. Elaine Sciolino, "Persian Gulf Journal: Muting Anguish in Iran over '88 Air Disaster," *New York Times,* July 4, 1998.
161. Ibid.
162. "Remarks at a Republican Party Fundraising Brunch in Boca Raton, Florida," *Public Papers of the Presidents,* September 23, 1988.
163. "Remarks at a Republican Party Rally in Raleigh, North Carolina," *Public Papers of the Presidents,* October 21, 1988.
164. "Remarks and a Question-and-Answer Session with Students and Guests of the University of Virginia in Charlottesville, Virginia," *Public Papers of the Presidents,* December 16, 1988.
165. Norman Kempster, " Pan Am Tip Was Hoax, FBI Asserts; Call in Helsinki Citing Bomb Threat Fully Discredited," *Los Angeles Times,* December 26, 1988.
166. Gerard Henderson, "Terrorism Will Dog Us Forever," *Sydney Morning Herald,* January 4, 2000.
167. Noel Koch, "The Hostage Labryrinth . . . But Our 'No Negotiations' Policy May Not Have Helped."
168. Ibid.

## Chapter 3

1. Laurie Goodstein, "Carrying On Kahane Goals," *Washington Post,* March 6, 1994.
2. Bill Berkeley, "Murder Trial Draws Passion of Middle East," *National Law Journal,* December 30, 1991.

3.  "ADL Research Report: 'Extremism in the Name of Religion: The Violent Legacy of Meir Kahane,'" U.S. Newswire, February 16, 1995.

4.  Ibid.

5.  Ibid.

6.  Ibid.

7.  Joint Intelligence Committee, "Joint Inquiry Staff Statement: Hearing on the Intelligence Community's Response to Past Terrorist Attacks Against the United States from February 1993 to September 2001," October 8, 2002.

8.  Joint Intelligence Committee, "Joint Inquiry Staff Statement," October 8, 2002.

9.  Bill Berkeley, "Murder Trial Draws Passion of Middle East," *National Law Journal*, December 30, 1991.

10. William C. Rempel, "N.Y. Trial in Rabbi's Death Planted an Explosive Seed," *Los Angeles Times*, July 4, 1993.

11. Ibid. Others share this conclusion. Authors John Miller and Michael Stone noted in their 2002 book, *The Cell: Inside the 9/11 Plot, and Why the FBI and CIA Failed to Stop It*, that the assassination of Kahane is "where the law enforcement aspect of the Sept. 11 story began and where American law enforcement agencies first revealed themselves to be institutionally ill equipped for the war this new enemy had brought to U.S. shores." Quoted in a review by Jeff Stein, "Cops and Plotters," *New York Times*, September 8, 2002.

12. Robert Friedman, "The CIA and the Sheik," *Village Voice*, March 30, 1993.

13. Bill Berkeley, "Murder Trial Draws Passion of Middle East," *National Law Journal*, December 30, 1991.

14. "N.Y. Acquittal Ignites Emotions; Jewish Leaders Urge Federal Action in Kahane Murder Case," *Houston Chronicle*, December 23, 1991.

15. James C. McKinley, "Key Witness in Bomb-Plot Trial Admits Lying about His Exploits," *New York Times*, March 8, 1995.

16. Patricia Cohen, "Did FBI Blow It? Informer, on Tape, Tells Feds They Could've Stopped Blast," *Newsday*, October 27, 1993.

17. David Pugliese, "A Matter of Culpable Ignorance," *Ottawa Citizen*, November 3, 2002.

18. "His Vow: To Kill Americans," ABC News, June 10, 1998.

19. William A. Henry III, "Biting His Handlers," *Time*, November 8, 1993.

20. Larry Neumeister, "FBI, Prosecutors Await Own Verdicts; Experts Saw Missteps in Terror Trial," Associated Press, September 25, 1995.

21. Ralph Blumenthal, "The Twin Towers: FBI Inquiry Failed to Detect Any Sign of Attack," *New York Times*, March 6, 1993.

22. Carolyn Skorneck, "Freeh Suspends Top FBI Agent in New York," Associated Press, December 21, 1993.

23. Kevin McCoy, "Bomb Spy Worked More Than 1 Year," *Newsday*, July 15, 1993.

24. Alison Mitchell, "Official Recalls Delay in Using Informer," *New York Times*, July 16, 1993.

25. David Kocieniewski and William K. Rashbaum, "Tale of the Tape: FBI Informant Recorded Agents," *Newsday*, August 3, 1993.

26. Patricia Cohen, "Defense: Spy Was Bomber," *Newsday*, December 15, 1993.

27. Ralph Blumenthal, "Tapes in Bombing Plot Show Informer and F.B.I. at Odds," *New York Times*, October 27, 1993.

28. Ibid.

29. David Kocieniewski, "Whitman Defends State Police Finalist Criticized for Role in Terrorist Inquiry," *New York Times*, July 21, 1999.

30. William A, Henry III, "Biting His Handlers," *Time*, November 8, 1993.

31. Ralph Blumenthal, "Tapes Depict Proposal to Thwart Bomb Used in Trade Center Blast." A correction published on the following day noted that the FBI stated that it was not aware of which building the terrorist cabal was planning to blow up. "Transcripts of tapes made

secretly by an informant, Emad A. Salem, quote him as saying he warned the Government that a bomb was being built. But the transcripts do not make clear the extent to which the Federal authorities knew that the target was the World Trade Center."

32. Ibid.
33. Patricia Cohen, David Kocieniewski, and Kevin McCoy, "Tapes Reveal What Feds Knew," *Newsday*, October 29, 1993.
34. 60 Minutes, "The Notebook," CBS News Transcripts, November 13, 1994.
35. Douglas Frantz, "Terrorism Signs Went Unheeded, Sources Say," *Los Angeles Times*, June 30, 1993.
36. Ariel Cohen, "Analysis: Intelligence Disaster, Bureaucratic Sclerosis," United Press International, September 16, 2001. Cohen was summarizing research by Judge Abraham Sofaer of the Hoover Institution.
37. Joint Intelligence Committee, "Joint Inquiry Staff Statement, Part I: Statement of Eleanor Hill," September 18, 2002.
38. James Bovard, "Louis Freeh: The New J. Edgar Hoover," *American Spectator*, August 1995.
39. Joint Intelligence Committee, "Joint Inquiry Staff Statement—Hearing on the Intelligence Community's Response to Past Terrorist Attacks Against the United States from February 1993 to September 2001."
40. Ibid.
41. *Time* noted during just after the trial: "It was Salem, after all, who consulted Abdel Rahman on possible bombing targets; rented the 'safe house' in Queens, New York, where the conspirators gathered (and in which the FBI installed the video cameras); and had the only key to the garage where the explosives were prepared. Moreover, he even bragged to Barbara Rogers, his wife at the time, that he was the leader of the group. 'I am the shepherd,' Rogers recalls him saying. 'They are the sheep.' Kevin Fedarko, "The Imaginary Apocalypse," *Time*, October 16, 1995.
42. James C. McKinley, "Lawyer Forces Bomb-Trial Witness to Admit Trail of Lies," *New York Times*, March 23, 1995.
43. Keven Fedarko, "The Imaginary Apocalypse," *Time*, October 16, 1995.
44. "HPSCI-SSCI Joint Inquiry Staff Statement, Part I: Statement of Eleanor Hill," Federal News Service, September 18, 2002.
45. Ibid.
46. Brian Jenkins, "Terrorism trial begins in New York; 3 men accused of plotting to bomb U.S. planes," CNN News, May 13, 1996.
47. Joint Intelligence Committee, "Joint Inquiry Staff Statement, Part I: Statement of Eleanor Hill," September 18, 2002.
48. Doug Struck, Howard Schneider, Karl Vick, and Peter Baker, "Borderless Network of Terror," *Washington Post*, September 23, 2001.
49. John W. Whitehead, "Religious Profiling Potential," *Washington Times*, November 26, 1999.
50. Michael Hedges, "U.S. Hate Groups Most Likely to Strike at Y2K, FBI Concludes," Scripps Howard News Service, December 23, 1999.
51. Dave Boyer, "Conservatives Want Probe of FBI Terrorism Report," *Washington Times*, November 19, 1999.
52. John W. Whitehead, "Religious Profiling Potential," *Washington Times*, November 26, 1999.
53. Patrick E. Tyler, "U.S. and Bahrain Near Pact on Permanent Military Base," *New York Times*, March 25, 1991.
54. Stephen Clarkson, "After the Catastrophe: Canada's Position in North America," Canadian Business and Current Affairs, March 2002. (The article is adapted from a speech Clarkson gave on October 25, 2001.)
55. Department of Defense, "Personal Accountability for Force Protection at Khobar Towers," July 31, 1997.

56. Joint Intelligence Committee, "Joint Inquiry Staff Statement," October 8, 2002.
57. Linda D. Kozaryn, "Perry Accepts Blame for Force Protection Lapses," American Forces Press Service, September 18, 1996.
58. Eric Schmitt, "Exoneration Shows New Military Ethos," *New York Times,* December 17, 1996.
59. Ibid.
60. Department of Defense, "Personal Accountability for Force Protection at Khobar Towers," July 31, 1997.
61. Barton Gellman, "Sudan's Offer to Arrest Militant Fell Through after Saudis Said No," *Washington Post,* October 3, 2001.
62. Ibid.
63. Ibid.
64. Timothy Carney and Mansoor Ijaz, "Intelligence Failure? Let's Go Back to Sudan," *Washington Post,* June 30, 2002.
65. Ibid.
66. Joint Intelligence Committee, "Joint Inquiry Staff Statement, Part I: Statement of Eleanor Hill."
67. Ibid.
68. "Ambassador Warned State Department of Nairobi Embassy Security Problems," CNN, August 13, 1998.
69. "U.S. Lax on Embassy Security," CBS News, January 8, 1999.
70. Ibid.
71. "The President's Radio Address," *Public Papers of the Presidents,* August 22, 1998.
72. Otis Bilodeau, "When Bombs Miss the Mark," *Legal Times,* November 26, 2001.
73. The "senior administration official" was unnamed—even though the entire briefing was ON the record and printed up and disseminated around the world. But since the name of the briefer was not revealed, some grave national security interest was thereby protected. "Back Ground Briefings with Senior Administration Intelligence Officials—Subject: U.S. Air Strikes against Terrorist Targets in Afghanistan and Suspected Chemical Weapons Facility in Libya," Federal News Service, August 20, 1998.
74. "USIA Foreign Press Center Briefing—Subject: U.S. Strikes of Terrorist Sites in Sudan and Afghanistan—Briefer: Thomas Pickering, Under Secretary of State for Political Affairs," Federal News Service, August 25, 1998.
75. Anthony Shadid, "Questions Remain, but Some Sudanese Claims on Factory Prove True," Associated Press, August 24, 1998.
76. Ibid.
77. Michael Barletta, "Chemical Weapons in the Sudan: Allegations and Evidence," *Nonproliferation Review,* Fall 1998.
78. "Press Availability with Secretary of Defense William Cohen and General Hugh Shelton, Chairman, Joint Chiefs of Staff—Subject: U.S. Attacks on Terrorist Sites in Afghanistan and Sudan," Federal News Service, August, 1998.
79. Vernon Loeb, "A Dirty Business," *Washington Post,* July 25, 1999.
80. "DoD News Briefing," DefenseLINK News, August 20, 1998.
81. Jules Lobel, "The Use of Force to Respond to Terrorist Attacks: The Bombing of Sudan and Afghanistan," *Yale Journal of International Law,* Summer 1999.
82. "Soil Sample Key to U.S. Missile Strike in Sudan," *Chemical and Engineering News,* August 31, 1998.
83. James Risen, "Question of Evidence: To Bomb Sudan Plant, or Not: A Year Later, Debates Rankle," *New York Times,* October 27, 1999
84. Michael Barletta, "Chemical Weapons in the Sudan: Allegations and Evidence
85. Vernon Loeb, "A Dirty Business."
86. "Soil Sample Key to U.S. Missile Strike in Sudan."

87. "Press Availability with Michael McCurry, White House Spokesman Aboard Press Plane Returning from Martha's Vineyard following Announcement of U.S. Attacks on Terrorist Sites in Afghanistan and Sudan," *Federal News Service,* August 20, 1998.

88. Seymour Hersh, "Annals of National Security: The Missiles of August," *New Yorker,* October 12, 1998.

89. James Risen, "Question of Evidence: To Bomb Sudan Plant, or Not: A Year Later, Debates Rankle," *New York Times,* October 27, 1999.

90. "Address to the Nation on Military Action against Terrorist Sites in Afghanistan and Sudan," *Public Papers of the Presidents,* August 20, 1998.

91. "News Conference with Mahdi Ibrahim Mahammad, Sudanese Ambassador," *Federal News Service,* September 2, 1998.

92. "USIA Foreign Press Center Briefing—Subject: U.S. Strikes of Terrorist Sites in Sudan and Afghanistan," *Federal News Service,* August 25, 1998.

93. Quoted in Hugo Young, "Britain Should Not Act as a Puppet of the US over Iraq," *Guardian* (U.K.), January 28, 1999.

94. "Remarks on the 35th Anniversary of the March on Washington in Oak Bluffs, Massachusetts," *Public Papers of the Presidents,* August 28, 1998.

95. "Sudan Blames U.S. Missile Attack for Malaria Epidemic," Associated Press, February 20, 1999.

96. Tim Weiner and Steven Lee Myers, "U.S. Notes Gaps in Data about Drug Plant but Defends Attack," *New York Times,* September 3, 1998.

97. Ibid.

98. For a review of Clinton tall tales in that war, see "Moralizing with Cluster Bombs," in James Bovard, *"Feeling Your Pain: The Explosion and Abuse of Government Power in the Clinton-Gore Years"* (New York: St. Martin's Press, 2000), pp. 325–340.

99. Address to the Nation on Military Action against Terrorist Sites in Afghanistan and Sudan," *Public Papers of the Presidents,* August 20, 1998.

100. Alan Cullison and Andrew Higgins, "Terror Pact Forged by Cruise Missiles," *Wall Street Journal,* August 2, 2002.

101. Tim Weiner, "Missile Strikes against bin Laden Won Him Esteem in Muslim Lands, U.S. Officials Say," *New York Times,* February 8, 1999.

102. Joint Intelligence Committee, "Joint Inquiry Staff Statement, Part I: Statement of Eleanor Hill," September 18, 2002.

103. Ibid.

104. "Early Warnings: The Surprise Was More When Than Whether or How," *New York Times,* May 19, 2002.

105. Hal Bernton, Mike Carter, David Heath, and James Neff, "The Terrorist Within," *Seattle Times,* June 23, 2002.

106. Joint Intelligence Committee, "Joint Inquiry Staff Statement," October 8, 2002.

107. Steven Lee Myers, "Navy Inquiry on *Cole* Urges No Punishment of Captain or Crew," *New York Times,* January 8, 2001.

108. Patrick J. Sloyan, "A Lack of Security: Cracks in *Cole's* Defenses Allowed Bombers' Approach," *Newsday,* March 4, 2001.

109. Steven Lee Myers, "Navy Inquiry on *Cole* Urges No Punishment of Captain or Crew," *New York Times,* January 8, 2001.

110. Thomas E. Ricks, "*Cole* Lapses May Go Unpunished," *Washington Post,* January 07, 2001.

111. Roberto Suro, "Military Personnel Not at Fault in *Cole* Attack, Cohen Says," *Contra Costa (Calif.) Times,* January 20, 2001.

112. "*Cole* Panel Calls for More Funds, Better Anti-terror Training," Agence France Presse, January 9, 2001.

113. Thomas E. Ricks, "*Cole* Lapses May Go Unpunished."

114. Pauline Jelinek, "Pentagon Sees 'Collective Responsibility' for *Cole* Bombing," Associated Press, January 20, 2001.

115. Steven Lee Myers, "Cohen Says the Blame for the *Cole* Is Collective," *New York Times,* January 20, 2001.

116. Pauline Jelinek, "Pentagon Sees 'Collective Responsibility' for *Cole* Bombing."

117. Pauline Jelinek, "Pentagon Sees 'Collective Responsibility' for *Cole* Bombing."

118. Steven Lee Myers, "Navy Inquiry on *Cole* Urges No Punishment of Captain or Crew."

119. "September 11 and the Imperative of Reform in the U.S. Intelligence Community Additional Views of Senator Richard C. Shelby, Vice Chairman, Senate Select Committee on Intelligence," December 10, 2002.

120. Joint Intelligence Committee, "Joint Inquiry Staff Statement," October 17, 2002.

121. Michael Isikoff, "The Informant Who Lived with the Hijackers," *Newsweek,* September 16, 2002.

122. Greg Miller, "More 9/11 Clues Were Overlooked," *Los Angeles Times,* December 12, 2002.

123. Joint Intelligence Committee, "The Intelligence Community's Knowledge of the Sept. 11 Hijackers Prior to September 11, 2001: Statement of Eleanor Hill," September 20, 2002.

124. Joint Intelligence Committee, "Final Report: Part 1: The Context: Findings and Conclusions," December 10, 2002.

125. Joint Intelligence Committee, "Joint Inquiry Staff Statement, Part I: Statement of Eleanor Hill."

126. Joint Intelligence Committee, "Joint Inquiry Staff Statement, Part I: Statement of Eleanor Hill."

127. Ibid.

128. Joint Intelligence Committee, "The FBI's Handling of the Phoenix Electronic Communication and Investigation of Zacarias Moussaoui prior to September 11, 2001: Statement of Eleanor Hill," September 24, 2002.

129. Joint Intelligence Committee, "Joint Inquiry Staff Statement, Part I: Statement of Eleanor Hill."

130. Ibid.

131. Ibid.

132. Ibid.

133. Ibid.

134. Jim Yardley and Jo Thomas, "For Agent in Phoenix, the Cause of Many Frustrations Extended to His Own Office," *New York Times,* June 19, 2002.

135. John Solomon, "FAA Alerted by Flight School in Early 2001 about Eventual Hijacker," Associated Press, May 10, 2002.

136. Greg Gordon, "FAA Security Took No Action against Moussaoui," *Minneapolis Star Tribune,* January 13, 2002.

137. Greg Gordon, "At Flight School, Suspect Raised Eyebrows Quickly," *Milwaukee Journal Sentinel,* December 26, 2001.

138. James Risen, " F.B.I. Told of Worry Over Flight Lessons Before Sept. 11," *New York Times,* May 4, 2002.

139. Joint Intelligence Committee, "FBI's Handling of the Phoenix Electronic Communication."

140. Joint Intelligence Committee, "Final Report," December 10, 2002.

141. Barton Gellman, "Before Sept. 11, Unshared Clues and Unshaped Policy," *Washington Post,* May 17, 2002.

142. Ibid.

143. Philip Shenon, "Early Warnings on Moussaoui Are Detailed," *New York Times,* October 18, 2002.

144. Greg Gordon, "A Persistent Suspicion: Eagan Flight Trainer Wouldn't Let Unease about Suspect Rest," *Minneapolis Star Tribune,* December 21, 2001.

145. Philip Shenon, "Flight School Warned F.B.I. of Suspicions," *New York Times*, December 22, 2001.

146. Brian Ross, "U.S. Targets Overlooked," ABCNews.com, February 20, 2002.

147. Philip Shenon, "Early Warnings on Moussaoui Are Detailed," *New York Times*, October 18, 2002.

148. Ibid.

149. Philip Shenon, "Congress Criticizes F.B.I. and Justice Department over Actions before Secret Wiretap Court," *New York Times*, September 11, 2002.

150. Joint Intelligence Committee, "FBI's Handling of the Phoenix Electronic Communication," September 24, 2002.

151. Senate Judiciary Committee, "FISA Implementation Failures," February 2003.

152. David Johnston, "F.B.I. Says Pre-Sept. 11 Note Got Little Notice," *New York Times*, May 9, 2002.

153. n.a. "Coleen Rowley's Memo to FBI Director Robert Mueller," *Time*, May 21, 2002.

154. Senate Judiciary Committee, "FISA Implementation Failures," February 2003.

155. Senate Judiciary Committee, "FISA Implementation Failures."

156. "Coleen Rowley's Memo to FBI Director Robert Mueller."

157. "Afternoon Session of a Hearing of the Joint House/Senate Select Intelligence Committee— Subject: Events Surrounding September 11th," Federal News Service, September 24, 2002.

158. Brian Blomquist, "Feds Admit They Blew Chance to Stop 9/11 Terror," *New York Post*, December 13, 2001.

159. Daniel Franklin, "Freeh's Reign," *American Prospect*, January 1, 2002.

160. See Transactional Records Access Clearinghouse data at http://trac.syr.edu/tracfbi/findings/national/intellStaff.html

161. Daniel Franklin, "Freeh's Reign."

162. Ibid.

163. "CIA Analysts Will Aid FBI Intelligence Analysis," *CNN Live Today*, CNN, May 29, 2002.

164. Eric Lichtblau and Charles Piller, "War on Terrorism Highlights FBI's Computer Woes," *Los Angeles Times*, July 28, 2002.

165. Ibid.

166. "Afternoon Session of a Hearing of the Joint House/Senate Select Intelligence Committee—Subject: Events Surrounding September 11th."

167. Senate Select Committee on Intelligence, "September 11 and the Imperative of Reform in the U.S. Intelligence Community: Additional Views of Senator Richard C. Shelby, Vice Chairman," December 10, 2002.

168. Senate Select Committee on Intelligence, "September 11 and the Imperative of Reform."

169. Senate Judiciary Committee, "FISA Implementation Failures," February 2003.

170. Joint Intelligence Committee"Joint Inquiry Staff Statement," October 8, 2002.

171. Senate Select Committee on Intelligence, "September 11 and the Imperative of Reform."

172. Senate Judiciary Committee, "FISA Implementation Failures," February 2003.

173. Joint Intelligence Committee, "Joint Inquiry Staff Statement." Italics mine.

174. Ibid.

175. Ibid.

176. "Criminal Enforcement against Terrorists, Transactional Records Access Clearinghouse, " December 3, 2001 and June 17, 2002 (Special Supplement). The Justice Department responded to criticism over its paucity of terrorist cases by slashing the amount of information it provided TRAC researchers for their analyses.

177. Eric Lichtblau, "F.B.I., under Outside Pressure, Gets Inside Push," *New York Times*, December 2, 2002.

178. Mark Fazlollah and Peter Nicholas, "U.S. Overstates Arrests in Terrorism," *Philadelphia Inquirer*, December 16, 2001.

179. Adam Nossiter, "New Orleans Brothel Made a Federal Case," *Washington Post*, June 3, 2002.

180. Joint Intelligence Committee, "FBI's Handling of the Phoenix Electronic Communication," September 24, 2002.
181. Jim Yardley and Jo Thomas, "For Agent in Phoenix, the Cause of Many Frustrations Extended to His Own Office."
181. Arrianna Huffington, "Did the Drug War Claim Another 3,056 Casualties on 9/11?" Arrianna Online, June 3, 2002.
182. Joint Intelligence Committee, "Joint Inquiry Staff Statement, Part I: Statement of Eleanor Hill."
184. Senate Select Committee on Intelligence, "September 11 and the Imperative of Reform."
185. Ibid.
186. Joint Intelligence Committee, "Final Report," December 10, 2002.
187. Philip Shenon, "Lawmakers Say Misstatements Cloud F.B.I. Chief's Credibility," *New York Times,* May 31, 2002.
188. Ibid.
189. Don Van Natta, Jr., "Democrats Raise Questions over Remarks on Warnings," *New York Times,* May 18, 2002.
190. Bill Gertz, "For Years, Signs Suggested 'That Something Was Up,'" *Washington Times,* May 17, 2002.
191. Bob Woodward and Dan Eggen, "Aug. Memo Warned of Attacks within U.S.," *Washington Post,* May 19, 2002.
192. Michael Elliott, "How The U.S. Missed the Clues."
193. Joseph Curl and Dave Boyer, "Bush Rebukes 'Second-Guessers," *Washington Times,* May 18, 2002.
194. "Cheney Warns Democrats," Associated Press, May 17, 2002.
195. Michael Elliott, "How The U.S. Missed the Clues."
196. Greg Miller, "Bush Team on Defensive in Threat Inquiry," *Los Angeles Times,* May 17, 2002.
197. Kathy Gambrell and Mark Benjamin, "Bushes Push Back on September 11," United Press International, May 17, 2002.
198. Steve Fainaru, "Clues Pointed to Changing Terrorist Tactics," *Washington Post,* May 19, 2002.
199. Robert Schlesinger and Wayne Washington, "The Administration's Account: Series of Warnings Detailed," *Boston Globe,* May 17, 2002.
200. Dan Eggen and Dana Priest, "Bush Aides Seek to Contain Furor," *Washington Post,* May 17, 2002.
201. Bob Woodward and Dan Eggen, "Aug. Memo Warned of Attacks within U.S."
202. Joint Intelligence Committee, "Joint Inquiry Staff Statement, Part I: Statement of Eleanor Hill."
203. Steve Fainaru, "Clues Pointed to Changing Terrorist Tactics," *Washington Post,* May 19, 2002.
204. Joel Bleifuss, "Fear and Loathing," *In These Times,* May 24, 2002.
205. "Sen. Graham Seeks to Declassify Key 9/11 Data," Reuters News Service, October 20, 2002.
206. "Statement by the President," White House Office of the Press Secretary, December 13, 2002.
207. Michael Isikoff and Mark Hosenball, "Secrets of 9/11," Newsweek.com, April 30, 2003.
208. "Graham: Bam! Bob Kicks It Up a Notch," Hotline, May 14, 2003.
209. "Panel 1 of a Hearing of the Senate/House Joint Select Intelligence Committee," Federal News Service, September 18, 2002.
210. Joint Intelligence Committee, "Joint Inquiry Staff Statement," October 17, 2002.
211. Ibid. Italics mine.

## Chapter 4

1. "Stakeout Media Availability with Attorney General John Ashcroft," News Service, October 2, 2001.
2. "Address before a Joint Session of the Congress on the United States Response to the Terrorist Attacks of September 11," *Public Papers of the Presidents,* September 20, 2001.
3. Robin Toner, "Some Foresee a Sea Change in Attitudes on Freedoms," *New York Times,* September 15, 2001.
4. "Opposition to FBI Computer Surveillance Emerges after Vote," *National Journal's Technology Daily,* September 14, 2001.
5. Steven Brill, *After: How American Confronted the September 12 Era* (New York: Simon & Schuster, 2003), p. 73.
6. Jonathan Ringel, "Anti-Terrorism Bill's Grueling Rite of Passage," *Legal Times,* October 15, 2001.
7. Roland Watson, "Bush Law Chief Tried to Drop Habeas Corpus," *Times* (U.K.), December 3, 2001.
8. Philip Shenon and Alison Mitchell, "Lawmakers Hear Ashcroft Outline Antiterror Plans," *New York Times,* September 17, 2001.
9. "John Ashcroft Holds Justice Department Briefing," Federal Document Clearing House, September 17, 2001.
10. Brill, *After: How American Confronted the September 12 Era,* p. 73.
11. Sharon Lerner, "Slowing the Ashcroft Act," *Village Voice,* October 2, 2001.
12. Ibid.
13. Eric Slater, "Boston Unnerved by Ashcroft's Warning of Possible Threat," *Los Angeles Times,* September 22, 2001.
14. Nikki Tait, "Warning of New Attacks Spurs FBI to Alert Cities," *Financial Times,* September 22, 2001.
15. Ted Bridis and Gary Fields, "Bush's New Surveillance Proposals Could Bring Information Overload," *Wall Street Journal,* September 26, 2001.
16. Bob Woodward, *Bush at War* (New York: Simon & Schuster, 2002), p. 106.
17. "Hearing of the House Judiciary Committee," Federal News Service, September 24, 2001.
18. Ibid.
19. Sanford J. Ungar, *FBI* (Boston: Little, Brown, 1976), p. 405.
20. "Hearing of the House Judiciary Committee," Federal News Service, September 24, 2001.
21. Krysten Crawford, "Home Front: Fighting Financial War on Terror," *Recorder,* January 18, 2002.
22. "Hearing of the House Judiciary Committee," Federal News Service, September 24, 2001.
23. Ibid.
24. Ibid.
25. Author call to Justice Department Office of Public Affairs, May 2, 2003.
26. "Hearing of the House Judiciary Committee," Federal News Service, September 24, 2001.
27. Ibid.
28. "Remarks by President George W. Bush to Employees of the Federal Bureau of Investigation," Federal News Service, September 25, 2001.
29. "Homeland Security: Ashcroft Willing to Back Off a Bit," *Hotline,* September 26, 2001.
30. "Remarks by President George W. Bush to Employees of the Federal Bureau of Investigation," Federal News Service, September 25, 2001.
31. Brill, *After: How America Confronted the September 12 Era,* p. 123.
32. "Hearing of the Senate Judiciary Committee," Federal News Service, September 25, 2001.
33. Greg B. Smith and Corky Siemaszko, "New Threat Causes Gridlock Nightmare," *New York Daily News,* September 26, 2001.

34. "Hearing of the Senate Judiciary Committee," Federal News Service, September 25, 2001.

35. Ibid.

36. Ibid.

37. Ibid.

38. "Prepared Remarks of Attorney General John Ashcroft—Press Briefing with FBI Director Mueller, FBI Headquarters," U.S. Department of Justice, September 27, 2001.

39. Eric Lichtblau, "Ashcroft Says Our Danger Level Is Up," *Orlando Sentinel,* October 1, 2001.

40. "Homeland Security: Not Exactly a Calming Presence?" *Hotline,* October 1, 2001.

41. Forum on the Bush Administration's Antiterrorism Legislation, Cato Institute (Washington, D.C.), October 2, 2001.

42. "Media Availability with Attorney General John Ashcroft; Senator Orrin Hatch (R-UT); Senator Trent Lott (R-MS), Senate Minority Leader; Senator Richard Shelby (R-AL)," Federal News Service, October 2, 2001.

43. John Lancaster, "Anti-Terrorism Bill Hits Snag on the Hill," *Washington Post,* October 3, 2001.

44. Raymond Bonner with John Tagliabue, "Eavesdropping, U.S. Allies See New Terror Attack," *New York Times,* October 21, 2001.

45. Susan Crabtree, 'Hatch's Comments Lead to Crackdown," *Roll Call,* September 17, 2001.

46. Dana Milbank and Peter Slevin, "Bush Edict on Briefings Irks Hill; White House Stems Information Flow," *Washington Post,* October 10, 2001.

47. Ibid.

48. John Lancaster, "Hill Puts Brakes on Expanding Police Powers," *Washington Post,* September 30, 2001.

49. Naftali Bendavid, "Ashcroft Performing a Unique Juggling Act," *Chicago Tribune,* October 7, 2001.

50. Robert Pear and Neil A. Lewis, "House Panel Approves Bill Expanding Surveillance," *New York Times,* October 4, 2001.

51. "John Ashcroft Holds Justice Department Briefing," Federal Document Clearing House, October 4, 2001.

52. Ibid.

53. See James Bovard, *Lost Rights: The Destruction of American Liberty* (New York: St. Martin's Press, 1994) and James Bovard, *Feeling Your Pain: The Explosion and Abuse of Government Power in the Clinton-Gore Years* (New York: St. Martin's Press, 2000).

54. The Bush administration vigorously sought to cover up the FBI's role in the Boston mob murders. See Glen Johnson, " Bush Halts Inquiry of FBI and Stirs Up a Firestorm," *Boston Globe,* December 14, 2001.

55. Jeff Zeleny, "Reprisal Fears Put U.S. on High Alert," *Chicago Tribune,* October 8, 2001.

56. Bennett Roth, "U.S. Launches Second Round; Missiles Strike Taliban Targets," *Houston Chronicle,* October 9, 2001.

57. Sean Mussenden, "Nation on 'Highest State of Alert,'" *Orlando Sentinel,* October 9, 2001.

58. *Congressional Record,* October 9, 2001, p. S10363.

59. Ibid., p. S10364.

60. Ibid., p. S10364.

61. Michael Beach, "New Terror Warnings: Attacks Likely in Days—FBI," *Herald Sun* (Melbourne), October 13, 2001.

62. Paul Bedard, "Oops—The Sky Isn't Falling," U.S. News and World Report Online, October 12, 2001, and at http://www.usnews.com/usnews/politics/whispers/october2001.htm

63. Maurice Tamman and Rebecca Carr, "FBI Warns Americans We May Be Hit Again," *Atlanta Journal and Constitution,* October 12, 2001.

64. Woodward, *Bush at War,* p. 235.

65. *Congressional Record,* October 11, 2001, p. S10548.

66. Ibid., p. S10548.
67. Ibid., p. S10577.
68. Ibid., p. S10560. Italics mine.
69. Steven A. Osher, "Privacy, Computers and the Patriot Act," *Florida Law Review,* July 2002, p. 521.
70. *Congressional Record,* October 11, 2001, p. S10578.
71. Ibid., p. S10570.
72. Ibid., p. S 11021.
73. Ibid., p. S10570.
74. Ibid., p. S10572.
75. Ibid., p. S10574.
76. Ibid., p. S10575.
77. Ibid., p. S10577.
78. Ibid., p. S10577.
79. Ibid., p. S10571.
80. Robert Scheer, "With Powers Like These, Can Repression Be Far Behind?" *Los Angeles Times,* October 30, 2001.
81. Matthew Rothschild, "Russ Feingold: The Progressive Interview," *Progressive,* May 2002.
82. Ibid.
83. Rachel King, "Is Congress Giving Too Much Surveillance Power to Federal Law Enforcement?" *Insight on the News,* January 14, 2002.
84. Dan Eggen and Bob Woodward, "Terrorist Attacks Imminent, FBI Warns," *Washington Post,* October 12, 2001.
85. Edward Walsh, "Cheney Echoes Warnings of New Terrorist Attacks," *Washington Post,* October 13, 2001.
86. *Congressional Record,* October 12, 2001, p. H6759.
87. Ibid., p. H6762.
88. Kelly Patricia O'Meara, "Police State," *Insight on the News,* December 3, 2001.
89. Declan McCullagh, "House Endorses Snoop Bill," Wired.com, October 13, 2001.
90. *Congressional Record,* October 12, 2001, p. H6771.
91. Declan McCullagh, "House Endorses Snoop Bill," Wired.com, October 13, 2001.
92. *Congressional Record,* October 12 2001, p. H6766.
93. Ibid., p. H6765.
94. Ibid., p. H6763.
95. Ibid., p. H6767.
96. Ibid., p. H6774.
97. Ibid., p. H6774.
98. Ibid., p. H6762.
99. Ibid., p. H6768.
100. Robin Toner and Neil A. Lewis, "House Passes Terrorism Bill Much Like Senate's, but with 5-Year Limit," *New York Times,* October 13, 2001.
101. Ibid.
102. Editorial, "Stampeded in the House," *Washington Post,* October 16, 2001.
103. Neely Tucker and Helen Dewar, "Tough Talk, Tears, Confusion and Concern," *Washington Post,* October 18, 2001.
104. Kelley Beaucar Vlahos, "Scurrying Away or Soldiering On," Fox.com, October 18, 2001.
105. Ibid.
106. Susan Crabtree and Mark Preston, "Leaders Split over Closing," *Roll Call,* October 18, 2001.
107. Ibid.
108. Wesley Pruden, "They Also Serve Who Head for the Hills," *Washington Times,* October 19, 2001.

109. Rory Little, "Who Should Regulate the Ethics of Federal Prosecutors?" *Fordham Law Review,* October 1996, vol. 65, p. 355.

110. "Prepared Statement by Frederick Krebs, American Corporate Counsel Association, before the House Judiciary Committee, on H.R. 3386, the Ethical Standards for Federal Prosecutors Act," Federal News Service, September 12, 1996.

*111. Congressional Record,* October 15, 2001, p. S 10676.

112. Jim Barnett, "Senate Passes Bill Relating to Oregon Undercover Work," *Oregonian,* October 25, 2001.

113. "Bush Remarks at Signing of USA Patriot Act," U.S. Newswire, October 26, 2001.

114. Editorial, "Toward a Balanced Terrorism Bill," *New York Times,* October 4, 2001.

115. Ronald Weich, "Upsetting Checks and Balances," American Civil Liberties Union, October 2001.

# Chapter 5

1. "Text of Bush's Speech at West Point," *New York Times,* June 1, 2002.

2. John Mintz and Douglas Farah, "Small Scams Probed for Terror Ties," *Washington Post,* August 12, 2002.

3. Stephen Franklin and Terry Atlas, "U.S. Vows to Halt Cash Benefiting Terrorists: $800,000 in Assets Seized in Past Year from 3 Hamas Backers," *Chicago Tribune,* March 7, 1996.

4. "Deputy Secretary Dam: Remarks at the Launch of 'Operation Green Quest,'" Treasury Department Office of Public Affairs, October 25, 2001.

5. "Remarks by the President, Secretary of the Treasury O'Neill and Secretary of State Powell on Executive Order," White House Office of the Press Secretary, September 24, 2001.

6. Bob Woodward, *Bush at War* (New York: Simon & Schuster, 2002), p. 120.

7. Michael M. Phillips, "Bush to Set Up Enforcement Teams to Combat Money-Laundering Fight," *Wall Street Journal,* September 19, 2001.

8. "New U.S. Laundering Strategy Eyes 'High Risks,' Seeks SAR Reforms," *Money Laundering Alert,* October 2001.

9. *Congressional Record,* October 17, 2001, p. H6943.

10. "Patriot Act Has Many Laundering Traps Even in Unexpected Places," *Money Laundering Alert,* April 2002.

11. Scott Bernard Nelson, "US Demands Seizing of Terror Funds," *Boston Globe,* September 10, 2002.

12. *Federal Register,* December 7, 1998, pp. 67515–67424.

13. *Federal Register,* December 7, 1998, pp. 67515–67424.

14. Michael Zeldin and Edward Rial, "USA Patriot Act," *National Law Journal,* May 6, 2002.

15. Glenn R. Simpson and Jathon Sapsford, "New Money-Laundering Rules to Cut Broad Swath in Finance," *Wall Street Journal,* April 23, 2002.

16. "Bold U.S. Regulations Open Information-Sharing," *Money Laundering Alert,* March 2002.

17. "BSA Gets Great Expansion in Coverage, Reach and Strength," *Money Laundering Alert,* November 2001.

18. Patti Waldmeir, "Unaccustomed Warriors: A New Law in the US Will Draft Thousands of Businesses into the Fight against Terrorism," *Financial Times,* March 21, 2002.

19. Edith M. Lederer, "U.N. Experts Investigating Allegations That al-Qaida Has Moved Assets into Gold, Diamonds and Other Precious Stones," Associated Press, May 22, 2002.

20. "U.S. Treasury Department Denies U.N. Report Saying Bank Flagged Money Transfer to Sept. 11 Suicide Hijacker," Associated Press, May 23, 2002.

21. David Armstrong and Joseph Pereira, "FBI Gives Carriers Access to Watchlists," *Wall Street Journal,* October 23, 2001.

22. House, "Financial Anti-Terrorism Act of 2001," Report 107–250, October 17, 2001.

23. Joint Intelligence Committee, "Final Report: Part 1: The Context: Findings and Conclusions," December 10, 2002.

24. Treasury Department and Justice Department, "2002 National Money Laundering Strategy," July 2002.

25. As Sen. Paul Sarbanes explained, "The statute is called the 'bank secrecy act,' because it bars bank secrecy in America, by preventing financial institutions from maintaining opaque records, or discarding their records altogether. Secrecy is the hiding place for crime, and Congress has barred our institutions from allowing those hiding places." *Congressional Record,* October 11, 2001, p. S10562.

26. Michael M. Phillips, "Treasury to Order Wall Street to Report Suspicious Dealings," *Wall Street Journal,* June 28 or 29 2002.

27. "FinCEN Gives First Look at Money Flows and Activity of Terrorists," *Money Laundering Alert,* October 2002.

28. Josh Meyer and Eric Lichtblau, "Crackdown on Terror Funding Is Questioned," *Los Angeles Times,* April 7, 2002.

29. "How Institutions, Trade Groups Can Now Share Data 'with One Another,'" *Money Laundering Alert,* November 2002.

30. Richard W. Stevenson and Leslie Wayne, "More Regulations to Thwart Money Laundering Are Imposed," *New York Times,* April 24, 2002.

31. Ron Scherer and Abraham McLaughlin, "Boutique to Wall Street: Feds Monitor Books," *Christian Science Monitor,* April 25, 2002.

32. In hindsight, the location of the announcement was ironic, since the Tracking Center apparently found nothing on many of the people that Bush publicly tarred as terrorists.

33. "Remarks by the President in Announcement on Financial Aspects of Terrorism," White House Office of the Press Secretary, November 7, 2001.

34. Antonio Fins, "U.S. Zeroes in on Terror Funds," Fort Lauderdale (Fla.) *Sun-Sentinel,* November 8, 2001.

35. "Fact Sheet: Shutting Down the Terrorist Financial Network," White House Office of the Press Secretary, November 7, 2001.

36. "Statement by Secretary Paul O'Neill at Fin Cen," Treasury Department Office of Public Affairs, November 7, 2001.

37. "Statement by Secretary Paul O'Neill at Fin Cen," Treasury Department Office of Public Affairs, November 7, 2001.

38. "Attorney General Transcript—Department of Justice Shuts Down Several Financial Networks Exploited by Terrorist Groups," Justice Department Office of Public Affairs, November 7, 2001.

39. David Olinger, "Terror-Linked Money System Provided Somali Lifeline," *Denver Post,* February 24, 2002.

40. Donald G. McNeil, "How Blocking Assets Erased a Wisp of Prosperity," *New York Times,* April 13, 2002.

41. Osman Hassan, "Chairman of al-Barakaat Group Says Charges They Were Involved in Terrorism Are Untrue and Unfounded," Associated Press, November 7, 2001.

42. Joseph Guinto, "Raids Focus on Terrorist Funding," *Investor's Business Daily,* November 8, 2001.

43. Josh Meyer and Sebastian Rotella, "U.S. Coalition Freezes Assets in Terror War," *Los Angeles Times,* November 8, 2001.

44. John Riley, "A Powerful Weapon," *Newsday,* September 17, 2002.

45. "FinCEN Delays Registration of MSBs Despite 28-Month Lead Time," *Money Laundering Alert,* October 2001.

46. Florangela Davila, "Somalian Shop Owners Return with Merchandise Seized in Raid," *Seattle Times,* November 29, 2001.

47. Ginny NiCarthy, "'Things Like That Don't Happen Here': Customs Agents Crack Down on Wire Transfer Services," *Progressive,* January 2002.

48. Editorial, "Seeking What Is Owed to a Somali Grocer," *Seattle Times,* May 9, 2002.

49. T. C. Brown, "Somali Man Accused of Funneling Money to al-Qaida Can Reopen Business," *Cleveland Plain Dealer,* August 23, 2002.

50. Mark Niquette, "Lawyer Says Client Must Start Over: No Connection Found between al-Qaida, Somali Businessman," *Columbus Dispatch,* August 23, 2002.

51. Liz Sidoti, "Somali Whose Business Was Raided by Federal Agents Wants Answers," Associated Press, April 26, 2002.

52. John Riley, "A Powerful Weapon," *Newsday,* September 17, 2002.

53. Jake Tapper, "A Post-9/11 American Nightmare," Salon.com, September 5, 2002. The letter was as follows:

U.S. Department of Treasury
Nov. 30, 2001

Dear Mr. Jama:

This letter is to inform you that pursuant to Executive Order No. 13224 (66FR49079), issued by President Bush on September 23, 2001 (the "Order"), and under the authority granted by the International Emergency Economic Powers Act, 50 U.S.C. SS 1701–06 ("IEERA"), the Office of Foreign Assets Control ("OFAC"), U.S. Department of the Treasury, added your name to the list of persons who commit, threaten to commit, or support terrorism (specifically designated global terrorist ("SDGT")). . . .

R. Richard Newcomb
Director
Office of Foreign Assets Control

54. All quotes in this paragraph not otherwise cited are taken from Jake Tapper, "A Post-9/11 American Nightmare," Salon.com, September 5, 2002.

55. J. M. Lawrence and Dave Wedge, "Alleged Hub Terrorism $ Man May Surrender," *Boston Herald,* November 10, 2001.

56. "Strengthened U.S. Laundering Law Helps Convict Transmitter," *Money Laundering Alert,* June 2002.

57. Gregory D. Kesich, "Federal Trial Begins for 'Hawala' Operator," *Portland Press Herald,* April 24, 2002.

58. J. M. Lawrence and Dave Wedge, "Alleged Hub Terrorism $ Man May Surrender," *Boston Herald,* November 10, 2001.

59. Cosmo Macero, "Anti-terror Inc. Sets Up Shop in Boston," *Boston Herald,* May 6, 2002.

60. John Riley, "A Powerful Weapon," *Newsday,* September 17, 2002.

61. "Money Transfers Land Canadian in U.S. Jail," *Ottawa Citizen,* July 23, 2002.

62. "Money Transfers Land Canadian in U.S. Jail," *Ottawa Citizen,* July 23, 2002.

63. "US Court Jails Somali Businessman but Rules Out al-Qaeda Link," Agence France Presse, July 23, 2002.

64. "Money Transfers Land Canadian in U.S. Jail," *Ottawa Citizen,* July 23, 2002.

65. Donald G. McNeil, "How Blocking Assets Erased a Wisp of Prosperity," *New York Times,* April 13, 2002.

66. Tim Golden, "5 Months after Sanctions against Somali Company, Scant Proof of Qaeda Tie," *New York Times,* April 13, 2002.

67. Marc Kaufman, "Somalis Said to Feel Impact of U.S. Freeze of al-Barakaat," *Washington Post,* November 30, 2001.

68. Tim Golden, "5 Months After Sanctions Against Somali Company, Scant Proof of Qaeda Tie," New York Times, April 13, 2002; Donald G. McNeil, "How Blocking Assets Erased a Wisp of Prosperity," New York Times, April 13, 2002.

69. Osman Hassan, "Somali Internet Company Forced to Close Two Weeks after Being Put on Terrorism Suspect List," Associated Press, November 22, 2001.

70. John Riley, "A Powerful Weapon," Newsday, September 17, 2002.

71. John Riley, "A Powerful Weapon," Newsday, September 17, 2002.

72. "US Intelligence Services Have Credible Evidence on al-Barakaat: US Diplomat," BBC Worldwide Monitoring, December 20, 2001.

73. U.S. State Department, Office of the Coordinator for Counterterrorism, "Patterns of Global Terrorism: 2001," May 21, 2002.

74. Christopher Cooper, "Crackdown on Terrorism Financing Ties Hands of Businessman in Sweden," Wall Street Journal, May 6, 2002.

75. Christopher Cooper, "Crackdown on Terrorism Financing Ties Hands of Businessman in Sweden," Wall Street Journal, May 6, 2002.

76. Christopher Cooper, "Crackdown on Terrorism Financing Ties Hands of Businessman in Sweden," Wall Street Journal, May 6, 2002.

77. Peter Finn, "Terrorism Probes Falter in Europe," Washington Post, June 1, 2002.

78. Peter Finn, "Terrorism Probes Falter in Europe," Washington Post, June 1, 2002.

79. U.S. Treasury Department, "Contributions by the Department of the Treasury to the Financial War on Terrorism Fact Sheet," September 2002. Hawala is also sometimes equated with the Arab word for "transfer." See Mohammed el-Qorchi, "Hawala," Finance and Development, International Monetary Fund, December 2002.

80. Patrick M. Jost, "The Hawala Alternative Remittance System and Its Role in Money Laundering," Interpol General Secretariat, Lyon, France, January 2000.

81. "Afghanistan Country Brief: Drug Situation Report," Drug Enforcement Agency, September 2001.

82. "Statement by Secretary Paul O'Neill at Fin Cen," Treasury Department Office of Public Affairs, November 7, 2001.

83. Colum Lynch, "Easing Sanctions on Bin Laden Associates Urged," Washington Post, August 16, 2002.

84. Carola Hoyos, "US Backs Down over 'Terror' Assets: Washington Yields to European Pressure on Sanctions," Financial Times, August 16, 2002.

85. Colum Lynch, "U.S. Seeks to Take 6 Names Off U.N. Sanctions List," Washington Post, August 22, 2002.

86. T. C. Brown, "Somali Man Accused of Funneling Money to al-Qaida Can Reopen business," Cleveland Plain Dealer, August 23, 2002.

87. "US Requests 6 Be Removed from UN's Sanctions List," Associated Press, August 22, 2002.

88. Colum Lynch, "U.S. Seeks to Take 6 Names Off U.N. Sanctions List," Washington Post, August 22, 2002.

89. Tim Golden, "5 Months after Sanctions against Somali Company, Scant Proof of Qaeda Tie," New York Times, April 13, 2002.

90. U.S. v. Bajakajian, 524 U.S. 321 (1998).

91. For a good analysis of the in rem doctrine, see Terrance Reed, "American Forfeiture Law: Property Owners Meet the Prosecutors," Cato Institute Policy Analysis no. 179, September 29, 1992.

92. USA Patriot Act Of 2001, October 26, 2001, sec. 371.

93. U.S. Treasury Department, "Contributions by the Department of the Treasury to the Financial War on Terrorism: Fact Sheet," September 2002.

94. "Remarks by Undersecretary Gurule at the Launch of 'Operation Green Quest,'" Treasury News, October 25, 2001.

95. "Senate Finance: The Financial War on Terrorism: Testimony by Jimmy Gurule, Under Secretary for Enforcement," Federal Document Clearing House Congressional Testimony, October 9, 2002.

96. "Investigating Patterns of Terrorism Financing: Testimony by Juan C. Zarate, Deputy Assistant Secretary," Federal Document Clearing House, February 12, 2002.

97. "Operation Green Quest Seizes More Than $22 Million in Ongoing Efforts to Dismantle Terror Finance Networks," Customs Service Office of Public Affairs, July 17, 2002.

98. "Testimony of Jimmy Gurule before the U.S. Senate Judiciary Committee," U.S. Treasury Department Office of Public Affairs, November 20, 2002.

99. U.S. Treasury Department, "Contributions by the Department of the Treasury to the Financial War on Terrorism: Fact Sheet," September 2002; and interview with Customs spokesman Ronald Dean Boyd, May 30, 2003.

100. David E. Kaplan, "Run and Gun," *U.S. News & World Report,* September 30, 2002.

101. Interview with Customs spokesman Ronald Dean Boyd, May 30, 2003.

102. Joint Intelligence Committee, "Final Report," December 10, 2002.

103. Michael Beebe, Phil Fairbanks, and Henry L. Davis, "Three Make Bail after Raids Tied to Yemen Money Trail," *Buffalo News,* December 18, 2002.

104. Michael Beebe, Phil Fairbanks, and Henry L. Davis, "Three Make Bail after Raids Tied to Yemen Money Trail," *Buffalo News,* December 18, 2002.

105. Michael Beebe, Phil Fairbanks, and Henry L. Davis, "Three Make Bail after Raids Tied to Yemen Money Trail," *Buffalo News,* December 18, 2002.

106. David Shepardson, "Fed Raids Target Money to Yemen," *Detroit News,* December 19, 2002.

107. Tamara Audi and Jim Schaefer, "Money Transfers Targeted: Federal Agents Raid Metro Area Homes, Businesses," *Detroit Free Press,* December 19, 2002.

108. David Shepardson, "Fed Raids Target Money to Yemen," *Detroit News,* December 19, 2002.

109. "U.S. Customs Service Press Conference re 'Operation Green Quest': Global Financial Investigation Involving Iraq," Federal News Service, December 19, 2002.

110. Jeannine Aversa, "A Dozen Indicted in Alleged Schemes to Send Money Illegally to Iraq," Associated Press, December 19, 2002.

111. "U.S. Customs Service Press Conference re 'Operation Green Quest': Global Financial Investigation Involving Iraq," Federal News Service, December 19, 2002.

112. Ibid.

113. "U.S. Customs Service Press Conference re 'Operation Green Quest': Global Financial Investigation Involving Iraq," Federal News Service, December 19, 2002.

114. David Shepardson, "Feds Drop Charges against Yemenis," *Detroit News,* January 8, 2003.

115. Michael M. Phillips, "Afghanistan Aid Flows through Dark Channels, *Wall Street Journal,* November 12, 2002.

116. Thomas J. Lueck, "4 Accused of Illegally Sending Money to Iraq," *New York Times,* February 27, 2003.

117. Greg B. Smith, "Cash for Terror Busts," *New York Daily News,* March 22, 2003.

118. John Solomon, "Feds Launch Raids against Terror Money," Associated Press, March 22, 2003.

119. U.S. Department of Homeland Security—Bureau of Immigration and Customs (ICE), "Operation Green Quest Conducts Separate Enforcement Actions in Five States," March 21, 2003.

120. Press release: "Operation Green Quest Conducts Separate Enforcement Actions In Five States," U.S. Department of Homeland Security—Bureau of Immigration and Customs Enforcement, March 21, 2003; AP: John Solomon, "Feds Launch Raids against Terror Money," Associated Press, March 22, 2003.

121. "Panel II of a Hearing of the Senate Banking, Housing and Urban Affairs Committee—Subject: Financial War on Terrorism and Implementation of Money-Laundering Provisions in the USA Patriot Act," Federal News Service, January 29, 2002.

122. Karen DeYoung and Douglas Farah, "Infighting Slows Hunt for Hidden al Qaeda Assets, *Washington Post,* June 18, 2002.

123. Karen DeYoung and Douglas Farah, "Infighting Slows Hunt for Hidden al Qaeda Assets, *Washington Post,* June 18, 2002.

124. Colum Lynch, "War on al Qaeda Funds Stalled, *Washington Post,* August 29, 2002.

125. "Treasury Statement on UN Terrorism Report," Treasury Department Press Release PO-3382, August 29, 2002.

126. Cam Simpson and John Crewdson, "U.S., Italy Target al. Qaeda Cash: But Finding Assets Not Easy, UN Says," *Chicago Tribune,* August 30, 2002.

127. "State Department, Washington, Foreign Press Center Briefing—Update on Tracking Financial Assets of Terrorists," Federal News Service, September 9, 2002.

128. Scott Bernard Nelson, "US Demands Seizing of Terror Funds,," *Boston Globe,* September 10, 2002.

129. John Mintz and Douglas Farah, "Small Scams Probed for Terror Ties: Muslim, Arab Stores Monitored as Part of Post-Sept. 11 Inquiry," *Washington Post,* August 12, 2002.

130. John Mintz and Douglas Farah, "Small Scams Probed for Terror Ties; Muslim, Arab Stores Monitored as Part of Post-Sept. 11 Inquiry," *Washington Post,* August 12, 2002.

131. John Solomon and Ted Bridis, "Feds Track Sales of Counterfeit Goods, Money to Terror Groups," Associated Press, October 25, 2002.

132. John Solomon and Ted Bridis, "Feds Track Sales of Counterfeit Goods, Money to Terror Groups," Associated Press, October 25, 2002.

133. John Solomon and Ted Bridis, "Feds Track Sales of Counterfeit Goods, Money to Terror Groups," Associated Press, October 25, 2002.

134. John Diamond, "Arab Spelling Slows Inquiries in Terror War," *USA Today,* July 1, 2002.

135. Eric Lichtblau, "Money-Laundering Rules Awash in the Bureaucracy," *Los Angeles Times,* June 27, 2002.

136. Eric Lichtblau, "Money-Laundering Rules Awash in the Bureaucracy," *Los Angeles Times,* June 27, 2002.

137. "The President's Radio Address," *Public Papers of the Presidents,* November 16, 2002.

138. Eric Lichtblau, "U.S. Cautiously Begins to Seize Millions in Foreign Banks," *New York Times,* May 30, 2003.

139. Eric Lichtblau, "Agency to Expand Units Tracing Terrorist Finances," *New York Times,* January 10, 2003.

140. Gary Fields and Glenn R. Simpson, "FBI Prevails in Turf Battle Over Terror-Money Probes," Wall Street Journal, May 22, 2003.

141. CurtAnderson, "FBI Prevails in Turf Fight over Lead on Terror Finance Probes," Associated Press, May 23, 2003.]

142. "U.S. Customs Service Press Conference re: 'Operation Green Quest': Global Financial Investigation Involving Iraq," Federal News Service, December 19, 2002.

143. "Fed Point 1: How Currency Gets Into Circulation," Federal Reserve Bank of New York, 2002.

## Chapter 6

1. "Nightline," ABC News, October 11, 2001.

2. *Morrow v. District of Columbia,* 417 F.2d 728, 741–42 (D.C. Cir. 1969).

3. "Remarks at a Meeting of the President's Homeland Security Advisory Council," *Public Papers of the Presidents,* June 12, 2002.

4. Henry Weinstein, Daren Briscoe, and Mitchell Landsberg, "Civil Liberties Take Back Seat to Safety," *Los Angeles Times,* March 10, 2002.

5.   Thomas Macaulay, *History of England*, vol. 2, (Philadelphia: Porter & Coates, 1860), p. 15. [pirated edition]
6.   *Harris v. Nelson*, 394 U.S. 286, 290–91 (1969).
7.   *Federal Register*, September 20, 2001, p. 48334. Italics mine.
8.   Ibid.
9.   "John Ashcroft Holds Justice Department Briefing," Federal Document Clearing House Transcripts, September 18, 2001.
10.  "Panel II of a Hearing of the Senate Judiciary Committee Subject: Suspects Detained since September 11th," Federal News Service, December 4, 2001.
11.  Steven Brill, *After: How America Confronted the September 12 Era* (New York: Simon and Schuster, 2003), p. 38.
12.  Brill, *After*, p. 46.
13.  Brill, *After*, p. 149.
14.  Tamar Lewin, "As Authorities Keep Up Immigration Arrests, Detainees Ask Why They Are Targets," *New York Times*, February 3, 2002.
15.  Tamar Lewin, "The Detainees: Cleared after Terror Sweep, Trying to Get His Life Back," *New York Times*, December 28, 2001.
16.  Dan B. Gerson, "Tale of the Mustafas," www.Vancouver.Indymedia.org, October 18, 2002.
17.  "U.S. Government Denies Blame for Legal Bills of Two Palestinian-Americans," Associated Press, January 8, 2002.
18.  Dan B. Gerson, "Tale of the Mustafas."
19.  Ann Davis, Maureen Tkacik, and Andrea Petersen, "Ashcroft's Call to Report Suspicious Activity Pits Neighbor vs. Neighbor in War on Terror," *Wall Street Journal*, November 21, 2001.
20.  Anne-Marie Cusac, "Ill-treatment on Our Shores," *Progressive*, March 2002.
21.  Robert Hennelly, "Justice Delayed?: For Post-9/11 Detainees, Questions of Fairness and Punishment," *Bergen County, N.J. Record*, January 27, 2002.
22.  Human Rights Watch, "Presumption of Guilt: Human Rights Abuses of Post—September 11 Detainees," August 2002.
23.  William Glaberson, "Detainees' Accounts are at Odds with Official Reports of an Orderly Investigation," *New York Times*, September 29, 2001.
24.  Glaberson, "Detainees' Accounts Are at Odds With Official Reports of an Orderly Investigation."
25.  Richard A. Serrano, "Detainee Caught in Backwash of Sept. 11," *Los Angeles Times*, November 19, 2001.
26.  Ibid.
27.  Ibid.
28.  "Lawyers Speak Out about Immigration Charges Brought against Foreigners in the US," National Public Radio, December 5, 2001.
29.  Human Rights Watch, "Presumption of Guilt: Human Rights Abuses of Post–September 11 Detainees," August 2002.
30.  "Remarks by President George W. Bush to Employees of the Federal Bureau of Investigation," Federal News Service, September 25, 2001.
31.  Joyce Howard Price, "Ashcroft Urges Stricter Laws to Jail Alien Suspects Longer," *Washington Times*, October 1, 2001. Italics mine.
32.  "John Ashcroft Holds Justice Department Briefing," Federal Document Clearing House Political Transcripts, October 8, 2001.
33.  Human Rights Watch, "Presumption of Guilt: Human Rights Abuses of Post—September 11 Detainees."
34.  Ibid.
35.  Richard A. Serrano, "Ashcroft Denies Wide Detainee Abuse," *Los Angeles Times*, October 17, 2001.

36. Neil A. Lewis, "Detentions after Attacks Pass 1,000, U.S. Says," *New York Times,* October 30, 2001.

37. "Prepared Statement of Kate Martin, Director, Center for National Security Studies before the Senate Committee on the Judiciary—Subject: DoJ Oversight: Preserving Our Freedoms while Defending against Terrorism," Federal News Service, November 28, 2001.

38. Richard A. Serrano, "Isolation, Secrecy Veil Most Jailed in Roundup," *Los Angeles Times,* November 4, 2001. Italics mine.

39. Human Rights Watch, "Presumption of Guilt: Human Rights Abuses of Post—September 11 Detainees."

40. "Attorney General John Ashcroft: Prepared Remarks for the U.S. Mayors Conference," Justice Department Office of Public Affairs, October 25, 2001. Italics mine.

41. David Cole, "The Ashcroft Raids," Amnesty International USA, posted at www.amnestyusa.org/usacrisis/ashcroftraids.html.

42. Cited in Micah Herzig, "Is Korematsu Good Law in the Face of Terrorism? Procedural Due Process in the Security versus Liberty Debate," *Georgetown Immigration Law Journal,* Spring, 2002, p. 685.

43. Micah Herzig, "Is Korematsu Good Law in the Face of Terrorism? Procedural Due Process in the Security versus Liberty Debate," *Georgetown Immigration Law Journal,* Spring, 2002, p. 685.

44. Walter Pincus, "Silence of 4 Terror Probe Suspects Poses Dilemma for FBI," *Washington Post,* October 21, 2001.

45. Quoted in Jed Babbin, "The Silence of the Lambs," *Washington Times,* March 21, 2002.

46. Patrick J. McDonnell, "Nation's Frantic Dragnet Entangles Many Lives," *Los Angeles Times,* November 7, 2001.

47. Ibid.

48. James Ridgeway, "After 9–11, Official Terror Kicks In: Victims of the Dragnet," *Village Voice,* April 17, 2002.

49. *Federal Register,* October 31, 2001, p. 54909.

50. Ibid.

51. Lisa Getter, "Judges Fighting Justice Dept. Sway," *Los Angeles Times,* January 31, 2002.

52. Lynn Waddell, "Court of No Return," *Broward Daily Business Review,* April 1, 2002.

53. Lisa Getter, "Judges Fighting Justice Dept. Sway."

54. Pete Yost, "Government Proposes to Eavesdrop on Phone Calls between Lawyers and Clients in Terrorist Probe," Associated Press, November 8, 2001.

55. Ann McFeatters, "White House Watch: Sliding Down the Slippery Slope," *Pittsburgh Post-Gazette,* November 18, 2001.

56. George Lardner, "U.S. Will Monitor Calls to Lawyers," *Washington Post,* November 9, 2001.

57. Dan Eggen and Susan Schmidt, "Count of Released Detainees Is Hard to Pin Down," *Washington Post,* November 6, 2001.

58. Ibid.

59. Michele Orecklin, "Why Hide the Numbers?" *Time,* December 3, 2001.

60. Jim Edwards, "Chertoff Warns of Future Terrorism, Lays Out Broad Responsive Strategy," *New Jersey Law Journal,* May 27, 2002.

61. Rinker Buck, "Detainee Has Had Enough of U.S.; Indian Man Eager to Leave after INS Holds Him 18 Days," *Hartford Courant,* December 14, 2001.

62. Ibid.

63. Elisabeth Frater, "Studying Terrorists' Lessons," *National Journal,* December 1, 2001.

64. "News Conference with Attorney General Ashcroft," Justice Department Office of Public Affairs, November 27, 2001.

65. Ibid.

66. Ibid.

67. Ibid.

68. John Richardson, "Man Jailed in Maine on U.S. List of Detainees," *Portland Press Herald,* November 29, 2001.

69. Richard A. Serrano, " Detainees: Innocuous Make List, but Notables Don't," *Los Angeles Times,* November 28, 2001.

70. Josh Meyer, "Dragnet Produces Few Terrorist Ties," *Los Angeles Times,* November 28, 2001.

71. Michelle Mittelstadt, "Civil Liberties Groups Sue Justice over Detainees," *Dallas Morning News,* December 6, 2001.

72. Chris Mondics, "Immigration Noose Snags Minor Violators," *Saint Paul Pioneer Press,* December 1, 2001.

73. Brill, *After,* p. 147.

74. "Amnesty International's Concerns Regarding Post—September 11 Detentions in the USA," Amnesty International, March 14, 2002.

75. Ibid.

76. David Firestone, "The Detainees: Ali al-Maqtari," *New York Times,* November 25, 2001.

77. Ibid.

78. Ana Radelat, "FBI Manhunt Uses Unusual Tactics," Gannett News Service, September 28, 2001.

79. David Firestone, "The Detainees; Ali al-Maqtari."

80. Human Rights Watch, "Presumption of Guilt: Human Rights Abuses of Post—September 11 Detainees."

81. "Testimony of Michael Boyle, American Immigration Lawyers Association, before the Committee on the Judiciary, United States Senate Regarding Current U.S. Policies and Practices Related to the Detention of Noncitizens," December 4, 2001; available at the American Immigration Lawyers Association website at http://www.aila.org.

82. Michelle Mittelstadt, "Civil Liberties Groups Sue Justice over Detainees," *Dallas Morning News,* December 6, 2001.

83. "Hearing of the Senate Judiciary Committee—Subject: The Department of Justice and Terrorism," Federal News Service, December 6, 2001. Italics mine.

84. Karen Gullo, "Ashcroft Says Naming Detainees Would Create Illegal 'Public Blacklist'," Associated Press, November 26, 2001.

85. "News Conference with Attorney General Ashcroft," Justice Department Office of Public Affairs, November 27, 2001.

86. Alan Elsner, "Hundreds of Arabs Still Detained in U.S. Jails," Reuters News Service, March 13, 2002.

87. Dan Eggen, "Delays Cited in Charging Detainees: With Legal Latitude, INS Sometimes Took Weeks," *Washington Post,* January 15, 2002.

88. Alan Elsner, "Hundreds of Arabs Still Detained in U.S. Jails," Reuters News Service, March 13, 2002.

89. Human Rights Watch, "Presumption of Guilt: Human Rights Abuses of Post—September 11 Detainees," August 2002.

90. John Riley, "Held without Charge: Material Witness Law Puts Detainees in Legal Limbo," *Newsday,* September 18, 2002.

91. Joanne Mariner, "The Cautionary Tale of a Post—September 11 Detainee," www.CNN.com-FindLaw Forum, August 20, 2002.

92. Ibid.

93. John Riley, "Held without Charge: Material Witness Law Puts Detainees in Legal Limbo."

94. Jane Rosenberg, "Student Charged with Lying to FBI about Radio," Associated Press, January 12, 2002.

95. Robert Gearty and Greg B. Smith, "Bust Egyptian over Lies to FBI had Pilot Radio in Hotel across from Trade Center," *New York Daily News,* January 12, 2002.

96. Christine Haughney, "Judge Orders Inquiry into Detainment of Egyptian," *Washington Post,* August 17, 2002.

97. Chisun Lee, "Spooky Goofs: Indications of Serious Flaws in a 9–11 FBI Flop," *Village Voice,* August 28, 2002.

98. Quoted in Human Rights Watch, "Presumption of Guilt: Human Rights Abuses of Post—September 11 Detainees," August 2002.

99. Ellis Henican, "Prisoner of His Own Lie," *Newsday,* June 2, 2002.

100. Mark Hamblett, "Government Ordered to Complete Inquiry into False Sept. 11 Charges," *New York Law Journal,* August 6, 2002.

101. "Agents Cleared in 9/11 Hotel Probe," Associated Press, November 25, 2002.

102. John J. Goldman, "Man Not Coerced in 9/11 Confession, Report Says," *Baltimore Sun,* November 26, 2002.

103. Andrew Gumbel, "The Disappeared," *Independent* (UK), February 26, 2002.

104. Siobhan Roth, "Judiciary Pushes Back over Anti-Terror Tactics," *Recorder,* May 31, 2002.

105. Dan Eggen, "Court Papers on Detainee Released: Justice Dept. Says It Will Still Withhold Information about Others," *Washington Post,* April 20, 2002.

106. Ibid.

107. Steve Fainaru, "Detainee to Get Open Immigration Hearing," *Washington Post,* September 26, 2002.

108. Steve Fainaru, "U.S. Bans the Release of Detainees' Names: INS Order Issued to Counter N.J. Ruling," *Washington Post,* April 19, 2002.

109. Siobhan Roth, "Judiciary Pushes Back over Anti-Terror Tactics."

110. Elizabeth Neuffer, "Judge Says N.J. Can't Hide ID's of People in Custody," *Boston Globe,* March 27, 2002.

111. "DOJ Directive Bars Release of Information on Detainees," *Bulletin's Frontrunner,* April 19, 2002.

112. Ibid.

113. Elise Young, "Despite State Judge's Order for Release, U.S. Tells Jails to Withhold Detainee IDs," *Bergen County, NJ, Record,* April 19, 2002.

114. Amy Westfeldt, "Justice Department Says Releasing Detainees' Names Could Be 'Dangerous,'" Associated Press, May 20, 2002.

115. Jim Edwards, "Detainees' Names Secret," *New Jersey Law Journal,* June 17, 2002.

116. Elizabeth Llorente, "U.S. May Hide Identity of Detainees, Court Rules," *Bergen County, NJ, Record,* June 13, 2002.

117. Ibid.

118. Jim Edwards, "As Judge Enjoins Blanket Secrecy, U.S. Adopts Rules for Closed Deport Hearings," *New Jersey Law Journal,* June 3, 2002.

119. Dan Eggen, "U.S. Must Keep Terror Hearings Open, Court Says," *Washington Post,* June 18, 2002.

120. Steve Fainaru, "Immigration Hearings Case Goes to High Court," *Washington Post,* June 22, 2002.

121. Steve Fainaru, "Court Allows Closed Immigration Hearings to Continue," *Washington Post,* June 29, 2002.

122. Josh Meyer, "U.S. Ordered to Disclose Names of Detainees in Sept. 11 Inquiry," *Los Angeles Times,* August 3 2002.

123. Neil A. Lewis, "Judge Orders U.S. to Release Names of 9/11 Detainees," *New York Times,* August 3, 2002.

124. Josh Meyer, "Judge Delays Her Order to Reveal Names of Detainees," *Los Angeles Times,* August 16, 2002.

125. *Detroit Free Press, et al., v. John Ashcroft,* no. 02–1437, 2002 Fed. App. 0291P, August 26, 2002.

126. Quoted in Human Rights Watch, "Presumption of Guilt: Human Rights Abuses of Post–September 11 Detainees," August 2002.

127. *Detroit Free Press, et al., v. John Ashcroft,* no. 02–1437, 2002 Fed. App. 0291P, August 26, 2002.

128. Ibid.
129. Siobhan Roth, "Judiciary Pushes Back Over Anti-Terror Tactics."
130. Steve Fainaru and Margot Williams, "Material Witness Law has Many in Limbo," *Washington Post*, November 24, 2002.
131. Ibid.
132. Ibid.
133. Laurie L. Levenson, "Detention, Material Witnesses & the War on Terrorism," *Loyola of Los Angeles Law Review*, June, 2002, pp. 1217+.
134. Brill, *After*, p. 148.
135. Dan Christensen, "Low Burden of Proof," *Miami Daily Business Review*, March 14, 2003.
136. Ibid.
137. Tom Brune, "U.S. Evades Curbs in Terror Law," *Newsday*, April 26, 2002.
138. David Cole, "The Ashcroft Raids," Amnesty International USA, posted at http://www.amnestyusa.org/usacrisis/ashcroftraids.html.
139. Dan Eggen, "Report Criticizes Post—Sept. 11 Interviews," *Washington Post*, May 10, 2003.
140. Ibid.
141. 23 I&N Dec. 572 (A.G. 2003) Interim Decision #3488. (April 17, 2003)
142. Jacqueline Charles, "Diplomats Puzzled by Claim Migrants Use Haiti to Enter U.S.," *Miami Herald*, April 25, 2003.
143. Carl Hiaasen, "A Homeland Security Charade," *Miami Herald*, May 11, 2003.
144. "The September 11 Detainees: A Review of the Treatment of Aliens Held on Immigration Charges in Connection with the Investigation of the September 11 Attacks," Justice Department Office of Inspector General, June 2003.
145. Ibid.
146. Ibid.
147. Ibid.
148. Ibid.
149. Ibid.
150. Ibid.
151. Ibid.
152. Ibid.
153. Ibid.
154. Jess Bravin and Gary Fields, "Report Criticizes U.S. Detentions of Illegal Aliens after Sept. 11," *Wall Street Journal*, June 3, 2003.
155. "Attorney General John Ashcroft Testimony before the Commerce, Justice, State and Judiciary Subcommittee of the Senate Appropriations Committee April 1, 2003," Justice Department Office of Public Affairs, April 1, 2003.
156. Dan Eggen, "Ashcroft Undaunted as Criticism Grows," *Washington Post*, November 29, 2001.
157. "Attorney General John Ashcroft Speaks about the Challenges since September 11th, 2001," National Public Radio—Morning Edition, September 11, 2002.
158. "Liberty vs. Security," The NewsHour with Jim Lehrer, Transcript #7452, September 10, 2002.
159. Steve Fainaru, "Court Allows Closed Immigration Hearings to Continue," *Washington Post*, June 29, 2002.
160. "Rowley Letter to FBI Director," *Minneapolis Star Tribune*, March 26, 2003.

## Chapter 7

1. John Ashcroft, "Welcoming Big Brother," *Washington Times*, August 12, 1997.

2. Gina Holland, "Justice Dept Lawyer Defends Program," Associated Press, August 11, 2002.
3. *Ex Parte Jackson,* 96 U.S. 733 (1878).
4. *Milwaukee Social Democratic Publishing Co. v. Burleson,* 255 US 407 (1921). As a 1976 Senate report noted, Holmes wrote the opinion "in a dissent now embraced by prevailing legal opinion." "Intelligence Activities and the Rights of Americans," Senate Select Committee to Study Governmental Operations with Respect to Intelligence Activities, April 14, 1976.
5. David McGuire, "House To Pass Legislation Requiring Carnivore Report," Newsbytes, July 23, 2001.
6. John L. Guerra, "Carnivore: FBI's Packet Sniffer May Have Loose Fangs," Billing World and OSS Today, April, 2002. Along the same lines—The *New York Times* noted that, "depending on the size of the Internet service provider using it, [Carnivore] may look at messages from every one of the company's customers as part of the [search] process." John Schwartz, "Privacy Debate Focuses on F.B.I. Use of an Internet Wiretap," *New York Times,* October 13, 2001.
7. Ed Sutherland, "U.S. House Votes for Carnivore Accountability," NewsFactor Network, July 24, 2001.
8. Erich Luening, " FBI Takes the Teeth out of Carnivore's Name," CNET News.com, February 9, 2001.
9. Gina Tufaro, "Will Carnivore Devour The Fourth? An Exploration of the Constitutionality of The FBI Created Software," *New York Law School Journal of Human Rights,* Spring 2002, p. 305.
10. "Carnivore's Challenge to Privacy and Security Online—Testimony of Alan B. Davidson Center for Democracy and Technology before the Subcommittee on the Constitution of the House Judiciary Committee," July 24, 2000.
11. Gina Tufaro, "Will Carnivore Devour The Fourth? An Exploration of the Constitutionality of The FBI Created Software," *New York Law School Journal of Human Rights,* Spring 2002, p. 305.
12. Maricela Segura, "Is Carnivore Devouring Your Privacy?" *Southern California Law Review,* November 2001, p. 231.
13. Press Release, " FBI's Carnivore System Disrupted Anti-Terror Investigation—Internal Memo Calls Over-Collection of Data Part of 'Pattern'," Electronic Privacy Information Center, May 28, 2002.
14. Dan Eggen, "'Carnivore' Glitches Blamed for FBI Woes," *Washington Post,* May 29, 2002.
15. H.R. 5524, "Global Internet Freedom Act," (Introduced in House by Rep. Chris Cox), October 2, 2002.
16. Mary P. Gallagher, " FBI May Use Keystroke-Recording Device without Wiretap Order," *New Jersey Law Journal,* January 3, 2002.
17. Bob Port, " FBI's New Weapon a lot like a Virus," *San Diego Union-Tribune,* December 25, 2001.
18. Bob Sullivan, "FBI Software Cracks Encryption Wall," MSNBC, November 20, 2001
19. Kim Zetter, " New Technologies, Laws Threaten Privacy," *PC World,* March 1, 2002.
20. Ted Bridis (Associated Press), "FBI Is Building a 'Magic Lantern' (washingtonpost.com), November 23, 2001. Also, Declan McCullagh, "'Lantern' Backdoor Flap Rages," Wired.com, November 27, 2001.
21. William Jackson, "Antivirus Vendors Wary of FBI's Magic Lantern," *Government Computer News,* December 9, 2001.
22. John Leyden, "AV Vendors Split over FBI Trojan Snoops," *The Register* (UK), November 27, 2001.
23. Declan McCullagh, "'Lantern' Backdoor Flap Rages," Wired.com, November 27, 2001.

24. "Patriot FOIA: The Government's Response," American Civil Liberties Union, April 2003. At http://www.aclu.org/patriot_foia/foia3.html
25. James Bamford, "Washington Bends the Rules," *New York Times,* August 27, 2002.
26. "In re: All Matters Submitted to the Foreign Intelligence Surveillance Court," U.S. Foreign Intelligence Surveillance Court, May 17, 2002.
27. Ibid.
28. FISA Implementation Failures," Interim Report on FBI Oversight in the 107th Congress by the Senate Judiciary Committee: Senator Patrick Leahy, Senator Charles Grassley, and Senator Arlen Specter, February 2003.
29. Ibid.
30. Michael Moss and Ford Fessenden, "America under Surveillance: New Tools for Domestic Spying, and Qualms," *New York Times,* December 10, 2002.
31. "In re: All Matters Submitted to the Foreign Intelligence Surveillance Court," U.S. Foreign Intelligence Surveillance Court, May 17, 2002.
32. Ibid.
33. Steve Aftergood, "Transcript Shines Light on FISA Review Court," Secrecy News, February 6, 2003.
34. Curt Anderson, "Special Review Court Upholds Surveillance Expansion under Patriot Act," Associated Press, November 18, 2002.
35. Ibid.
36. Ibid.
37. Julia Scheeres, "Feds Doing More Secret Searches," Wired News, May 9, 2003.
38. Larry Lebowitz, "Federal Case against Florida Professor Treads New Ground under Patriot Act," *Miami Herald,* February 26, 2003.
39. Congressional Record, February 25, 2003, p. S 2703.
40. Carolina Bolado, "FBI Probes Librarygoers' Records," *The State* (Columbia, S.C.), June 29, 2002.
41. "Many Librarians Fear Federal Law Requires They Violate Their Commitment to Protect Patrons' Privacy," National Public Radio, January 21, 2003.
42. Brad Smith, "FBI Can Check Out Reading Habits," *Tampa Tribune,* July 5, 2002.
43. Amy Dorsett and Megan Middleton, "Library Records Easier to Access," *San Antonio Express-News,* July 5, 2002.
44. Karen Branch-Brioso, "Agents' Post-9-11 Inquiries at Libraries Raise Privacy Questions," *St. Louis Post-Dispatch,* January 23, 2003.
45. Ibid.
46. Bob Egelko and Maria Alicia Gaura, "Libraries Post Patriot Act Warnings," *San Francisco Chronicle,* March 10, 2003.
47. Zenaida A. Gonzalez, "FBI Can Request Library Logs," *Florida Today,* September 23, 2002.
48. Seth Rosenfeld, "9-11-01; Looking Back, Looking Ahead," *San Francisco Chronicle,* September 8, 2002.
49. Ibid.
50. Bill Marvel, "Is the FBI Watching What You're Reading?" *The Record* (Bergen County, N.J.), August 25, 2002.
51. Steven A. Osher, "Privacy, Computers and the Patriot Act," *Florida Law Review,* July, 2002: p. 521.
52. Zenaida A. Gonzalez, "FBI Can Request Library Logs," *Florida Today,* September 23, 2002.
53. Bob Egelko and Maria Alicia Gaura, "Libraries Post Patriot Act Warnings," *San Francisco Chronicle,* March 10, 2003.
54. Martin Kasindorf, "FBI's Reading List Worries Librarians," *USA TODAY,* December 17, 2002.

55. "Patriot FOIA: The Government's Response," American Civil Liberties Union, April 2003. At http://www.aclu.org/patriot_foia/foia3.html

56. *United States v. United States District Court*, 407 US 297, 313 (1972).

57. *United States v. Martinez-Fuerte*, 428 U.S. 543, 554 (1976).

58. Uniting and Strengthening America by Providing Appropriate Tools Required to Intercept and Obstruct Terrorism (USA PATRIOT Act) Act Of 2001, October 26, 2001, Sec. 213.

59. Nat Hentoff, "The End of Privacy," *Washington Times*, June 3, 2002.

60. Editorial, "The New Normalcy," *New Jersey Law Journal*, October 29, 2001.

61. "Attorney General John Ashcroft Testimony before the Commerce, Justice, State and Judiciary Subcommittee of the Senate Appropriations Committee April 1, 2003," Justice Department Office of Public Affairs, April 1, 2003.

62. "EFF Analysis Of The Provisions Of The USA PATRIOT Act that Relate to Online Activities," Electronic Frontier Foundation, October 31, 2001.

63. Tracey Maclin, "On Amending the Fourth: Another Grave Threat to Liberty," *National Law Journal*, November 12, 2001

64. "Big Brother in the Wires Wiretapping in the Digital Age," American Civil Liberties Union, March 1998.

65. Ibid.

66. Ibid.

67. "Talk of the Nation," National Public Radio, October 30, 2001.

68. Patricia Williams, "By Any Means Necessary," *Nation*, November 26, 2001.

69. Miles Benson, "In the Name of Homeland Security, Telecom Firms Are Deluged with Subpoenas," *Newhouse News*, April 18, 2002.

70. Sarah Lai Stirland, "Reluctant Snoops: For Internet Services, War against Terror Means Flood of Subpoenas," *Seattle Times*, September 30, 2002.

71. "Patriot FOIA: The Government's Response," American Civil Liberties Union, April 2003. At http://www.aclu.org/patriot_foia/foia3.html

72. Daniela Deane, "Legal Niceties Aside . . . Federal Agents without Subpoenas Asking Firms for Records," *Washington Post*, November 7, 2001.

73. Miles Benson, "In The Name of Homeland Security, Telecom Firms Are Deluged with Subpoenas," *Newhouse News*, April 18, 2002.

74. Ibid.

75. Karen Branch-Brioso, "Many Firms Voluntarily Hand Over Data on Customers in Name of National Security," *St. Louis Post-Dispatch*, December 23, 2002.

76. Elise Young, "Snooping and Surveillance Get a Boost," *The Record* (Bergen Co., N.J.), November 12, 2001.

77. Jim McGee, "Bush Team Seeks Broader Surveillance Powers," *Washington Post*, December 2, 2001.

78. Jim McGee, "Bush Team Seeks Broader Surveillance Powers," *Washington Post*, December 2, 2001.

79. Jess Bravin And Dennis K. Berman, "FBI Pushes Telecoms for Network Changes to Ease Surveillance of Criminal Suspects," *Wall Street Journal*, November 21, 2001.

80. Ibid.

81. Ibid.

82. "Remarks of Attorney General John Ashcroft," Justice Department Office of Public Affairs, May 30, 2002.

83. Jerry Berman and James X. Dempsey, "CDT's Guide to the FBI Guidelines: Impact on Civil Liberties and Security—The Need For Congressional Oversight," Center for Democracy and Technology, June 26, 2002.

84. "Remarks of Attorney General John Ashcroft," Justice Department Office of Public Affairs, May 30, 2002.

85.  "Remarks by President George W. Bush during Photo Opportunity at Cabinet Meeting,"
     Federal News Service, May 30, 2002.
86.  "Remarks of Attorney General John Ashcroft," Justice Department Office of Public Affairs,
     May 30, 2002.
87.  For federal abuses in the 1980s and 1990s, see James Bovard, *Lost Rights: The Destruction
     of American Liberty* (St. Martin's Press, 1994), and James Bovard, *Feeling Your Pain: The Ex-
     plosion and Abuse of Government Power in the Clinton-Gore Years* (St. Martin's Press, 2000).
88.  "Intelligence Activities and the Rights of Americans," Senate Select Committee to Study
     Governmental Operations with Respect to Intelligence Activities, April 14, 1976.
89.  Mark Wagenveld, "25 Years Ago, before Watergate, a Burglary Changed History," *Philadel-
     phia Inquirer,* March 10, 1996.
90.  Both quotes taken from "COINTELPRO: The FBI's Covert Action Programs against
     American Citizens," Final Report of the Senate Committee to Study Governmental Oper-
     ations with Respect to Intelligence Activities, Book III, April 23, 1976. Online at
     http://www.icdc.com/~paulwolf/cointelpro/churchfinalreportIIcc.htm
91.  Ibid.
92.  Robert J. Cottrol and Raymond T. Diamond, "The Second Amendment: Toward an Afro-
     Americanist Reconsideration," *Georgetown Law Journal,* December 1991, p. 309.
93.  "The FBI'S Covert Action Program to Destroy the Black Panther Party," Supplementary
     Detailed Staff Reports on Intelligence Activities and the Rights of Americans, Final Report
     Of The Select Committee to Study Governmental Operations with Respect to Intelligence
     Activities United States Senate, Book III, April 23, 1976.
94.  All quotes taken from "The Use of Informants in FBI Domestic Intelligence Investiga-
     tions—Supplementary Detailed Staff Reports on Intelligence Activities and the Rights of
     Americans—Final Report of the Select Committee to Study Governmental Operations
     with Respect to Intelligence Activities, United States Senate, April 23, 1976.
95.  All quotes from "Intelligence Activities and the Rights Of Americans: Dr. Martin Luther
     King, Jr., Case Study," Book III of the "Final Report of the Select Committee to Study
     Governmental Operations with Respect to Intelligence Activities United States Senate,"
     April 23, 1976.
96.  All quotes taken from "The Use of Informants in FBI Domestic Intelligence Investiga-
     tions—Supplementary Detailed Staff Reports on Intelligence Activities and the Rights of
     Americans—Final Report of the Select Committee to Study Governmental Operations
     with Respect to Intelligence Activities, United States Senate, April 23, 1976.
97.  "Intelligence Activities and the Rights of Americans," Senate Select Committee to Study
     Governmental Operations with Respect to Intelligence Activities, April 14, 1976.
98.  All quotes taken from "The Use of Informants in FBI Domestic Intelligence Investigations—
     Supplementary Detailed Staff Reports on Intelligence Activities and the Rights of Americans—
     Final Report of the Select Committee to Study Governmental Operations with Respect to
     Intelligence Activities, United States Senate, April 23, 1976.
99.  Ibid.
100. "Intelligence Activities and the Rights of Americans," Senate Select Committee to Study
     Governmental Operations with Respect to Intelligence Activities, April 14, 1976.
101. Ibid.
102. COINTELPRO: The FBI's Covert Action Programs against American Citizens, Final Re-
     port of the Senate Committee to Study Governmental Operations with respect to Intelli-
     gence Activities, Book III +, April 23 (under authority of the order of April 14), 1976.
103. Ibid.
104. Ibid.
105. For sources of all quotes in this paragraph see ibid.
106. Mark Wagenveld, "25 Years Ago, before Watergate, a Burglary Changed History," *Philadel-
     phia Inquirer,* March 10, 1996.

107. COINTELPRO: The FBI's Covert Action Programs against American Citizens, Final Report of the Senate Committee to Study Governmental Operations with respect to Intelligence Activities, Book III +, April 23 (under authority of the order of April 14), 1976.

108. Ibid.

109. "The Internal Revenue Service: An Intelligence Resource and Collector," Intelligence Activities and the Rights of Americans, Final Report of the Select Committee to Study Governmental Operations with Respect to Intelligence Activities United States Senate," Book II, April 26, 1976.

110. Intelligence Activities and the Rights of Americans, Senate Select Committee to Study Governmental Operations with Respect to Intelligence Activities, April 14, 1976.

111. Editorial, "An Erosion of Civil Liberties," *New York Times,* May 31, 2002.

112. Joyce Howard Price, "Scrapping Domestic-Spying Restrictions 'Goes too Far'," *Washington Times,* June 2, 2002.

113. Jerry Berman and James X. Dempsey, "CDT's Guide to the FBI Guidelines: Impact on Civil Liberties and Security—The Need for Congressional Oversight," Center for Democracy and Technology, June 26, 2002.

114. Editorial, "What Is Operation TIPS?" *Washington Post,* July 14, 2002.

115. Ibid.

116. "Statement of Barbara Comstock, Director of Public Affairs, Regarding the Tips Program," Justice Department Office Of Public Affairs, July 16, 2002.

117. "Safety Or Stasi?" Associated Press, July 17, 2002. (Posted at http://www.cbsnews.com/stories/2002/07/17/national/main515404.shtml.)

118. Randolph E. Schmid, "Postal Service Won't Join Tips Program," Associated Press, July 17, 2002.

119. "Safety Or Stasi?" Associated Press, July 17, 2002. (Posted at http://www.cbsnews.com/stories/2002/07/17/national/main515404.shtml.)

120. All of the statements in this paragraph—from both Ashcroft and Leahy—are from "Hearing of the Senate Judiciary Committee—Subject: Oversight of the Department of Justice," Federal News Service, July 25, 2002.

121. Adam Clymer, "Worker Corps To Be Formed To Report Odd Activity," *New York Times,* July 26, 2002

122. Ibid.

123. Marjorie Cohn, "Urging Americans to Snitch on each other," *San Diego Union Tribune,* July 18, 2002.

124. Dan Eggen, Under Fire, Justice Shrinks TIPS Program," *Washington Post,* August 10, 2002.

125. Dave Lindorff, ": New life for Operation TIPS," Salon.com, August 30, 2002.

126. Ibid.

127. Dave Lindorff, "Lieberman Support for Domestic Terror-Tips Program," Salon.com, September 6, 2002.

128. John Markoff, "Agency Weighed, but Discarded, Plan Reconfiguring the Internet," *New York Times,* November 22, 2002.

129. "Press Briefing by Ari Fleischer," White House Office of Public Affairs, February 25, 2002.

130. Total Information Awareness web page, Electronic Privacy Information Center, at http://www.epic.org/privacy/profiling/tia/.

131. http://www.darpa.mil/iao/TIASystems.htm.

132. "Transcript of Pentagon briefing on Poindexter's 'TIA' program," Declan McCullagh's Politech, November 24, 2002.

133. Ibid.

134. Ibid.

135. Hendrik Hertzberg, "Too Much Information," *New Yorker,* December 9, 2002.

136. " Pentagon Seeks to Detect People by Odor," Associated Press, December 19, 2002.

137.  "Transcript of Pentagon briefing on Poindexter's 'TIA' program," Declan McCullagh's Po-
      litech, November 24, 2002.
138.  William Safire, "You Are a Suspect," *New York Times,* November 14, 2002.
139.  Ted Rall, "The Right to Privacy Dies with a Whimper," Yahoo.com, November 28, 2002.
140.  Helen Thomas, "White House Steps over the Line," *Heart Newspapers,* December 11,
      2002.
141.  Susan Baer, "Broader U.S. Spy Initiative Debated," *Baltimore Sun,* January 5, 2003.
142.  John Barry, "Big Brother Is Back," *Newsweek,* December 2, 2002.
143.  Editorial, "A Snooper's Dream," *New York Times,* November 18, 2002.
144.  "Transcript of Pentagon briefing on Poindexter's 'TIA' program," Declan McCullagh's Po-
      litech, November 24, 2002.
145.  "FBI May Have Aided Pentagon Data Project," Associated Press, January 21, 2003.
146.  "Pentagon Will Not Use TIA, Defense Official Says," *Periscope Daily Defense News Cap-
      sules,* March 14, 2003.
147.  Public Law 108–7, Total Information Awareness Spending Limitation, February 20, 2003.
148.  Declan McCullagh, "Pentagon Spy Database Moves Dorward," CNET News.com, Febru-
      ary 28, 2003.
149.  Farhad Manjoo, "Total Information Awareness: Down, but not Out," Salon.com, January
      29, 2003.
150.  Aaron Ricadela, "Total Information Awareness Project Gets First Test," *Information Week,*
      April 11, 2003.
151.  John Markoff, "Agency Weighed, but Discarded, Plan Reconfiguring the Internet," *New
      York Times,* November 22, 2002.
152.  Declan McCullagh, "Pentagon Drops Plan to Curb Net Anonymity," CNET News.com,
      November 22, 2002.
153.  Eric Lichtblau and James Risen, "Broad Domestic Role Asked for C.I.A. and the Penta-
      gon," *New York Times,* May 2, 2003.
154.  Mary Minow, "The USA PATRIOT Act," *Library Journal,* October 01, 2002.
155.  Julia Scheeres, "How Changed Laws Changed U.S.," *Wired News,* September 11, 2002.
156.  Ibid.
157.  Press Release, "ACLU Seeks Information on Government's Use of Vast New Surveillance
      Powers," American Civil Liberties Union, August 21, 2002.
158.  Press Release, "Oppose the New Homeland Security Bureaucracy!" Office of Rep. Ron
      Paul, U.S. House of Representatives, November 13, 2002.
159.  Ryan Singel, "Stage Set for Homeland Act," *Wired News,* November 6, 2002.
160.  Ibid.
161.  Ibid.
162.  Declan McCullagh, "Homeland Security's tech effects," CNET News.com, November 20,
      2002.
163.  Ibid.
164.  Naureen Shah, "Secrets and Lies: Leaked Documents Describe Patriot Act II," *In These
      Times,* March 17, 2003.
165.  "Domestic Security Enhancement Act Of 2003—Section-By-Section Analysis," Justice
      Department, January 9, 2003.
166.  Ibid.
167.  Timothy Edgar, "Interested Persons Memo: Section-by-Section Analysis of Justice Depart-
      ment draft 'Domestic Security Enhancement Act of 2003,' also known as PATRIOT Act
      II," American Civil Liberties Union, February 14, 2003.
168.  Ibid.
169.  "Domestic Security Enhancement Act Of 2003—Section-By-Section Analysis," Justice
      Department, January 9, 2003.
170.  Ibid.

171. Christian Bourge, "Analysts Worry About Patriot II," *United Press International,* March 10, 2003.

172. Timothy Edgar, "Interested Persons Memo: Section-by-Section Analysis of Justice Department Draft 'Domestic Security Enhancement Act of 2003,' also known as PATRIOT Act II," American Civil Liberties Union, February 14, 2003.

173. Anita Ramasastry, "Patriot II," FindLaw.com, February 17, 2003.

174. Editorial, "Patriot Act II Features Security Measures of Totalitarian Regimes," *San Jose Mercury News,* February 22, 2003.

175. Suzanne Seltzer, "Proposed Legislation May Strip U.S. Citizens of Rights," *Legal Intelligencer,* March 19, 2003.

176. "Transcript of Attorney General John Ashcroft Regarding Guilty Plea by Enaam Arnaout—Media Availability Following Speech to Council on Foreign Relations," Justice Department Office of Public Affairs, February 10, 2003.

177. Declan McCullagh, "Perspective: Ashcroft's Worrisome Spy Plans," CNET News.com, February 10, 2003.

178. Eleanor Hill, Joint Inquiry Staff Statement," Hearing on the Intelligence Community's Response to Past Terrorist Attacks against the United States from February 1993 to September 2001, October 8, 2002.

179. Charles Levendosky, "Patriot Act Chills First Amendment Freedoms," *Casper Star-Tribune,* January 22, 2003.

180. "Intelligence Activities and the Rights of Americans," Senate Select Committee to Study Governmental Operations with Respect to Intelligence Activities, April 14, 1976.

181. *Congressional Record,* April 27, 1971, p. 11562.

182. *Jones v. SEC,* 298, US 1, 27 (1934).

183. *United States v. Ehrlichman,* 376 F. Supp. 29, 32 (D.D.C. 1964).

## Chapter 8

1. Christopher Newton, "Government Putting Security Blankets on Airports; Releases Photos of Alleged Terrorists," Associated Press, September 27, 2001.

2. "Remarks by the President to the Employees of Cecil I. Walker Machinery Company, Charleston, West Virginia," White House Office of the Press Secretary, January 22, 2002.

3. "Bush Outlines New Airline Security Measures, Urges Public to Fly," *Bulletin's Frontrunner,* September 28, 2001.

4. "Heightened Security Measures Announced to Reassure Flying Public," *Air Safety Week,* October 1, 2001.

5. "Bush Outlines New Airline Security Measures, Urges Public to Fly

6. "Chao Encourages Americans to Fly, Get Back to Business; U.S. Secretary of Labor Flies to Louisville Tonight," U.S. Newswire, September 28, 2001.

7. Dylan T. Lovan, "Labor Secretary Says Airlines Safe," Associated Press, September 28, 2001.

8. "Secretary of Transportation Norman Mineta and Secretary of Commerce Don Evans Talk about Safety in Flying," CBS News Transcripts: The Early Show, September 28, 2001.

9. "HUD Secretary Tells Minnesotans Skies are Safe," Associated Press, September 28, 2001.

10. Tim Lemke, "Security Chief for FAA Out of a Job," *Washington Times,* October 6, 2001. Also, Don Phillips, "Internal Clashes Led to Ouster of FAA Security Chief," *Washington Post,* October 12, 2001.

11. Norman Y. Mineta, "Fliers Can Have Confidence," *USA Today,* October 17, 2001.

12. Steven Brill, *After: How America Confronted the September 12 Era* (New York: Simon & Schuster, 2003), p. 30.

13. "Security Breakdown: Tenet on the Hot Seat," *Hotline,* September 13, 2001.

14. "New Security Precautions Being Taken at U.S. Airports Now," National Public Radio "All Things Considered," September 12, 2001.

15. "Briefing by Secretary of Transportation Norman Mineta," Federal News Service, September 16, 2001.

16. Matt Slagle, "Analysis Shows FAA Levied Few Fines for Airport Security Lapses," Associated Press, September 26, 2001.

17. Cable News Network, Transcript no. 09171503.V54, September 16, 2001.

18. Glen Johnson, "US Air Security Not Ready for Suicide Mission, FAA Head Says," *Boston Globe,* September 14, 2001.

19. Burt Hubbard, "FAA Change Anticipated Hijack Scenario," *Rocky Mountain News,* October 6, 2001.

20. "National Press Club Luncheon with Jane Garvey, Administrator, Federal Aviation Administration," Federal News Service, October 17, 2001.

21. Billie Vincent, "Events Cast Blame on U.S. Air Security," *USA Today,* October 23, 2001.

22. Marcia Gelbart, "Airport Soldiers' Guns were Unloaded," *Philadelphia Inquirer,* May 26, 2002.

23. "SFO Guardsman Shoots Self When Gun Misfires," KRON, January 7, 2002.

24. Gwen Shafer, "Novel Security Measures," *Philadelphia City Paper,* October 18, 2001.

25. Ibid.

26. Alison Gendar and Robert Ingrassia, "Weapons Easily Slip by Airport Security," *New York Daily News,* October 7, 2001.

27. Jeffrey Selingo, "At Airport X-Ray Machines, a Mountain of Forgotten Laptops," *New York Times,* July 25, 2002.

28. "Transportation Secretary Norm Mineta Speaks to American Public Transportation Union," CNN Live, October 30, 2001.

29. Fern Shen, "At BWI, Cleared for Takeoffs," *Washington Post,* November 10, 2001.

30. "Remarks by Secretary of Transportation Norman Mineta to the National Transportation Security Summit," Federal News Service, October 30, 2001.

31. This connection was first noted by Michael Boyd, "Mineta Feeling The Heat," Boyd Group/ASRC, Inc., November 1, 2001. Available at http://www.aviationplanning.com.

32. "Remarks by Secretary of Transportation Norman Mineta to the National Transportation Security Summit."

33. "Man Arrested with Knives, Stun Gun at O'Hare," Cable News Network, November 5, 2001.

34. "U.S. Transportation Secretary Pledges a Tightening of Airport Security in the Wake of the O'Hare Incident," Fox News, November 6, 2001.

35. Tom Shoop, "Bold Government: America Has Regained Its Love of Big Government. But Can the Romance Last?" *Government Executive,* February 2002.

36. E. J. Dionne, "Seriously, a Political Turn for the Better," *Washington Post,* October 7, 2001.

37. "Airline Security: Deal Finally Cut; Bush to Sign Monday," *Hotline,* November 16, 2001.

38. Ibid.

39. Michael Boyd, "Security Legislation: An Outline," Boyd Group/ASRC, Inc., November 16, 2001.

40. "Security Breach Closes Atlanta Airport," AirDisaster.Com News, November 17, 2001.

41. "Government, Industry Face Logistics Nightmare in Meeting Screening Deadline," Airport Security Report, April 10, 2002.

42. Rich Lowry, "Mineta's Folly," *National Review,* January 10, 2002.

43. Stuart Taylor, "Blind to Terror: Politically Correct Concerns Make Air Travel Dangerous," *Legal Times,* March 18, 2002.

44. Nancy Benac, "Everyone Gets Checked at the Airport," Associated Press, January 8, 2002.

45. Ricardo Alonso-Zaldivar, "Public's Anger Simmers over Airport Searches," *Los Angeles Times,* March 11, 2002.

46. Dick Kreck, "Patdowns 'Intimate' at DIA," *Denver Post,* December 1, 2001.

47. Sara Rimer, "Underwireless, but Wishing for Wings," *New York Times,* February 19, 2002.

48. Ricardo Alonso Zaldivar, "Public's Anger Simmers Over Airport Searches," *Los Angeles Times,* March 11, 2002.

49. "Gumbo Forces N.O. Airport Evacuation," Associated Press, February 20, 2002.

50. Nick Madigan, "Seventh Evacuation in 8 Days Snarls Air Traffic," *Los Angeles Times,* March 5, 2002.

51. "Scissors Found in Conn. Airport," Associated Press, March 5, 2002.

52. Evelyn Nieves, "Suspect Walks Off as Explosive Is Detected," *New York Times,* January 31, 2002.

53. Jennifer Oldham, "Suspicious Shoes Shut Down Part of San Francisco Airport," *Los Angeles Times,* January 31, 2002.

54. "War on Terrorism Claims Shoe," *Townsville Bulletin,* April 13, 2002.

55. Aaron Davis, "Unusual Shoes Force Security Lockdown at San Francisco Airport," *San Jose Mercury News,* April 11, 2002.

56. "War On Terrorism Claims Shoe."

57. "Passenger's Warming Shoes Blown Up by Police at Airport," Agence France Presse, April 11, 2002.

58. Dennis B. Roddy, "Homefront: Passenger with Belt-Knife Defended as Well-Meaning," *Pittsburgh Post-Gazette,* January 30, 2002.

59. Ibid.

60. Kevin Mayhood, "Knife Belt Results in Probation," *Columbus Dispatch,* October 12, 2002.

61. "Project On Government Oversight (POGO): Statement of Bogdan John Dzakovic," Paul Revere Forum: National Security Whistleblowers Speak, February 27, 2002.

62. Paul Sperry, "Covert Airport-Security Inspectors 'Grounded': Elite Red Team Answering Congressional Mail," WorldNetDaily, April 4, 2002.

63. Blake Morrison, "FAA Whistle-Blower Supported," *USA Today,* March 19, 2003.

64. Elaine Kaplan, Letter to the White House, Report on OSC File No. DI-02–0207, U.S. Office of Special Counsel, March 18, 2003.

65. Ibid.

66. Ibid.

67. Tom Devine and Martin Edwin Andersen, "Reprisals Make for Terrorist Targets," *Washington Times,* April 23, 2003.

68. Michael A. Hiltzik and David Willman, "How Did Hijackers Get Past Airport Security?" *Los Angeles Times,* September 23, 2001.

69. Elaine Kaplan, Letter to the White House.

70. "Dozing Screener Shuts Louisville Airport," Reuters, February 19, 2002.

71. Sally B. Donnelly, "Airport Security Unplugged," *Time,* April 1, 2002.

72. Mac Daniel, "Logan's Security Breaches at Issue," *Boston Globe,* April 7, 2002.

73. "As U.S. Runs Screening, Airports' Woes Go On," *Philadelphia Inquirer,* March 2, 2002.

74. "Remarks by the Honorable Norman Y. Mineta, Secretary of Transportation, Travel and Tourism Industry Unity Dinner," Federal Document Clearing House, March 6, 2002.

75. Blake Morrison, "Tests Show No Screening Improvements Post-Sept. 11," *USA Today,* March 25, 2002.

76. "Press Briefing by Ari Fleischer," White House Office of the Press Secretary, March 25, 2002.

77. The Competitive Enterprise Institute and the Reason Foundation have done many excellent studies over the past 15 years on the failure and follies of federal policies regarding air travel.

78. Seth Borenstein, "Airline-Safety System is Called 'a Monster,'" *San Jose Mercury News,* July 21, 2002.

79. Senate Appropriations Committee, "Department of Transportation and Related Agencies Appropriations Bill, 2003," Senate Report 107–224, July 26, 2002.

80. House Appropriations Committee, "Department of Transportation and Related Agencies Appropriations Bill, 2003," House Report 107–722, October 7, 2002.

81. Ricardo Alonso Zaldivar, "Airport Security Stakes Rising," *Los Angeles Times,* July 7, 2002.

82. Editorial, "The New Transportation Security Agency Isn't Meeting Airport Needs," *Orlando Sentinel,* April 19, 2002.

83. Alan Gathright, "Fast, Safe Airport Checks Pledged," *San Francisco Chronicle,* March 16, 2002.

84. Tom Shoop, "Bold Government."

85. Editorial, "Another Airline Bailout," *Wall Street Journal,* September 30, 2002.

86. Michael Boyd, "Forget the Fluff Stories," Boyd Group/ASRC, Inc., October 7, 2002.

87. Lisa Cornwell, "Government: Some Security Breaches Inevitable, Others Disagree," Associated Press, May 29, 2002.

88. Adam Clymer, "Salaries for Airport Guards Set Off Complaints in Congress," *New York Times,* May 1, 2002.

89. Ibid.

90. Greg Schneider and Sara Kehaulani Goo, "Twin Missions Overwhelmed TSA," *Washington Post,* September 3, 2002.

91. Kate O'Beirne, "Encountering Turbulence: So How Goes the Federal Takeover of Airline Security?" *National Review,* June 17, 2002.

92. Sara Kehaulani Goo, "House Panel Criticizes Request for Airport Security Spending," *Washington Post,* June 21, 2002.

93. "Senate Commerce, Science, and Transportation Committee; Subject: Aviation-Security; Testimony by: Honorable Kenneth M. Mead, Inspector General," Federal Document Clearing House Congressional Testimony, February 5, 2003.

94. Sara Kehaulani Goo, "House Panel Criticizes Request for Airport Security Spending."

95. Dan Morgan and Greg Schneider, "$410,000 Fix-Up of TSA Offices Raises Eyebrows," *Washington Post,* June 20, 2002.

96. David Obey, "A 'Security' Power Grab," *Madison, WI, Capital Times,* August 3, 2002.

97. "Senate Commerce, Science, and Transportation Committee; Subject: Aviation-Security; Testimony by: Honorable Kenneth M. Mead, Inspector General."

98. Stephen Power, "Airport-Security Agency Draws Ire with Spending," *Wall Street Journal,* October 30, 2002.

99. "Mineta: U.S. Congress Hinders Airport Security Improvements," Associated Press, July 23, 2002.

100. Matthew L. Wald, "Lack of Money Is Called a Bar to Air Security," *New York Times,* July 24, 2002.

101. Blake Morrison, "Airport Security Failures Persist," *USA Today,* July 1, 2002.

102. Ibid.

103. Ricardo Alonso Zaldivar, "Airport Security Flaws Bring Criticism," *Los Angeles Times,* July 2 2002.

104. "Salt Lake City Airport Employees Arrested," Cable News Network, December 12, 2001.

105. Michael Vigh and Greg Burton, "Leavitt Defends Airport Sweep," *Salt Lake Tribune,* December 27, 2001.

106. Rocky Anderson, "Compassion, Security Not Mutually Exclusive," *Salt Lake City Deseret News,* December 23, 2001.

107. Michael Vigh, "Did Airport Raid Turn into a Bust?" *Salt Lake Tribune,* April 21, 2002.

108. Michael Vigh and Kevin Cantera, "No Hardened Criminals Found in Airport Sweep," *Salt Lake Tribune,* December 23, 2001

109. Ibid.

110. Eric Frazier, Gary L. Wright and Ted Reed, "66 Indicted at Charlotte's Airport," *Charlotte Observer,* March 7, 2002.

111.  Eric Frazier, Gary L. Wright, and Ted Reed, "Airport Workers Arrested," *Charlotte Observer,* March 9, 2002.

112.  Ibid.

113.  "Federal Criminal Enforcement on Terrorism: What Do These Counts Mean?," The Transactional Records Access Clearinghouse, 2002.

114.  Tim Funk and Gary L. Wright, "Airport Worker Pleads Guilty in False ID Case," *Charlotte Observer,* April 20, 2002.

115.  Ibid.

116.  Ted Bridis, "Nearly 100 Arrested in Security Raids at Washington-Area Airports," Associated Press, April 24, 2002.

117.  "Department Of Justice Press Conference Re: Arrests Of Workers At Washington-Area Airports," Federal News Service, April 23, 2002.

118.  John Solomon, "Ashcroft Announces Arrests of 94 Workers at Virginia Airports," Associated Press, April 23, 2002.

119.  "Department of Justice Press Conference Re: Arrests of Workers at Washington-Area Airports."

120.  Michael Tackett, "Sting Designed to Root Out Terrorists Falls Short," *Chicago Tribune,* October 6, 2002.

121.  Ibid.

122.  Ibid.

123.  Tim McGlone and Debbie Messina, "Federal Agents Arrest Dozens of Norfolk, Va., International Airport Employees," *Virginian-Pilot,* June 7, 2002.

124.  Ibid.

125.  Tim McGlone and Debbie Messina, "In Norfolk: 30 Named in Airport Sweep," *Virginian-Pilot,* June 7, 2002.

126.  Jonathan D. Salant, "Terrorism 'Zero Tolerance' Policy Leads to Hundreds of Airport Worker Arrests," Associated Press, April 24, 2002.

127.  Tim McGlone, "Many Nabbed in Airport Sweep to be Tried in Groups," *Virginian-Pilot,* June 13, 2002.

128.  Editorial, "Airport Arrests Don't Inspire Confidence," *Virginian-Pilot,* June 21, 2002.

129.  Editorial, "Innocent Airport Fireman Deserves His Job Back," *Virginian-Pilot,* September 6, 2002.

130.  Editorial, "Airport Arrests Don't Inspire Confidence."

131.  Tim McGlone, "Operation Came Up Short," *Virginian-Pilot,* September 4, 2002.

132.  Valeria Godines, "Charges Against Most Workers Arrested during 'Operation Tarmac' Reduced," *Orange County Register,* October 8, 2002.

133.  Ibid.

134.  "Dozens Arrested in Airport Worker Sweep," News 2 Houston, September 9, 2002.

135.  Edward Hegstrom, "'Tarmac' Crackdown Under Fire," *Houston Chronicle,* September 13, 2002.

136.  Judith Graham, "110 Denver Airport Workers Indicted in ID Fraud," *Chicago Tribune,* September 18, 2002.

137.  Burt Hubbard, "Immigration Raid at DIA Netted Few," *Rocky Mountain News,* March 6, 2003.

138.  Ibid.

139.  "Attorney General Ashcroft Addresses U.S. Attorneys Conference New York City," Justice Department Office of Public Affairs, October 1, 2002.

140.  Jonathan D. Salant, "Hundreds Arrested in Airport Sweeps," Associated Press, April 28, 2002.

141.  Paul Sperry, "Agents to Mineta: Rethink Airport-Security Plan," WorldNetDaily, April 26, 2002.

142.  "Senate Grills Mineta on Security, Airport Reimbursement Funds," *Aviation Daily,* May 3, 2002.

143. Marc Caputo, "Scanners Can Mistake Chocolate for Bombs," *The Miami Herald,* July 7, 2002.
144. Ricardo Alonso Zaldivar, "Undercover Teams Fake Out Bomb Screeners," *Orlando Sentinel,* February 28, 2002.
145. Robert Poole, "A Very High Price for Airport Security," *San Diego Union-Tribune,* July 26, 2002.
146. Ricardo Alonso Zaldivar, "New Federal Security Mandates Mean Financial Crunch for Major Airports,"*Los Angeles Times,* April 13, 2002.
147. Ibid.
148. Senate Appropriations Committee, "Department of Transportation and Related Agencies Appropriations Bill, 2003," Senate Report 107–224, July 26, 2002.
149. Bob Curley, "Sense of Security: U.S. Airports Have Random Baggage and Passenger Screening in Place," *Business Traveler,* February 1, 2003.
150. Sara Kehaulani Goo, "U.S. Weighs Air Security Upgrades," *Washington Post,* January 24, 2003.
151. Richard Roeper, "Nipple Rings Aren't All that Alert Airport Security," *Chicago Sun-Times,* December 24, 2002.
152. Garland Watt, "Sovereign Immunity, Pilfered Luggage," *Chicago Daily Law Bulletin,* March 12, 2003.
153. "TSA Urges Spring Break Travelers to Prepare for Trips," Transportation Security Administration Office of Public Affairs, March 4, 2003.
154. Alan Gathright, "Screeners Got Scant Training," *San Francisco Chronicle,* August 25, 2002.
155. Ibid.
156. Ibid.
157. Thomas Frank, "Cheating Security: LaGuardia Screeners Say They Were Given Answers to Tests," *Newsday,* January 26, 2003.
158. Thomas Frank, "Feds to Probe Screener Tests," *Newsday,* January 30, 2003.
159. Thomas Frank, "Instructors: Our Test Was Rigged," *Newsday,* January 28, 2003.
160. Ibid.
161. Alan Levin, "Lawmakers Add Pressure to Let Pilots Have Guns," *USA Today,* May 3, 2002.
162. "Mineta Opposes Guns in Plane Cockpits," Associated Press, March 4, 2002.
163. Leslie Miller, "48 Pilots Will Be Armed during Flights," Associated Press, February 26, 2003.
164. Editorial, "Arm the Pilots," *Washington Times,* September 7, 2002
165. "Enhancing Aviation Safety & Security," White House Office of the Press Secretary, September 27, 2001.
166. Blake Morrison, "Air Marshal Program in Disarray, Insiders Say," *USA Today,* August 15, 2002.
167. Greg Schneider and Sara Kehaulani Goo, "For Air Marshals, a Steep Takeoff," *Washington Post,* January 2, 2003.
168. Blake Morrison, "Air Marshals Charge New Policies Could Endanger Passengers," *USA Today,* December 19, 2002.
169. Blake Morrison, "Air Marshals' Resignations Flood TSA, Managers Say," *USA Today,* August 29, 2002.
170. Blake Morrison, "Air Marshals' Low Morale Spelled Out," *USA Today,* October 24, 2002.
171. James Loy, "Give Air Marshal Program Its Due Credit," *USA Today,* August 28, 2002.
172. John Curran, "Transportation Secretary Tours Sky Marshal Program," Associated Press, August 23, 2002.
173. Sam Wood, "Disturbance on Delta Scares Travelers," *Philadelphia Inquirer,* September 1, 2002.
174. Patrick Walters, "Authorities Defend Actions of Air Marshals Who Drew Guns Aboard Airliner," Associated Press, September 2, 2002.

175. Thomas Ginsberg, "Agency Defends Its Air Marshals," *Philadelphia Inquirer,* September 20, 2002.
176. Patrick Walters, "Authorities Defend Actions of Air Marshals."
177. Patrick Walters, "Authorities Defend Actions of Air Marshals."
178. John Pacenti and Scott Mccabe, "Air Marshals' Behavior Jeopardizes Passengers' Civil Liberties," Cox News Service, September 21, 2002.
179. Thomas Ginsberg, "Profiling Charged on 'Nightmare' Flight," *Philadelphia Inquirer,* September 19, 2002.
180. Ibid.
181. Ibid.
182. Ibid.
183. Scott McCabe, "Arrest by Sky Marshals Angers Lake Worth Man," *Palm Beach Post,* September 4, 2002.
184. Ibid.
185. Patrick Walters, "Air Marshals' Response Questioned," Associated Press, September 4, 2002.
186. Sam Wood, "Disturbance on Delta Scares Passengers."
187. Patrick Walters, "Authorities Defend Actions of Air Marshals."
188. Ibid.
189. Sam Wood, "Disturbance on Delta Scares Travelers."
190. Thomas Ginsberg, "Federal Air Marshal Failed Police Psychological Exam," *Philadelphia Inquirer,* October 3, 2002.
191. Ibid.
192. "Scattered Criticism Over the Nation's Sky Marshal Program," CNBC News Transcripts, September 4, 2002.
193. Carol Biliczky, Katie Byard, and Carl Chancellor, "Incidents Trigger Security Concerns at Cleveland Airport," *Akron Beacon Journal,* May 4, 2002.
194. Matthew B. Stannard, "Wounded Soldier Loses SFO Battle," *San Francisco Chronicle,* May 30, 2002.
195. Ibid.
196. "Wounded Soldier with Wired Jaw Prevented from Boarding Plane with Wire Clippers," Associated Press, May 31, 2002.
197. Matthew B. Stannard, "Wounded Soldier Loses SFO Battle."
198. "Ga. Lawmaker May Face Penalty in Flight Incident," *Washington Post,* June 15, 2002.
199. Chris Reinolds, " Lawmaker Answers Untimely Call," *Atlanta Journal and Constitution,* June 16, 2002.
200. Ibid.
201. Aron Davis, "S. J. Screeners Failed to Detain Bag's Owner," *San Jose Mercury News,* July 2, 2002.
202. Ibid.
203. "Suspicious Bag Prompts Partial Evacuation of LA Airport Terminal," Associated Press, July 15, 2002.
204. Ibid.
205. "LAX Terminal Evacuated Over Buckle," Associated Press, July 21, 2002.
206. Lydia Polgreen, "Actress's Detainment Upsets Indians in U.S. and Abroad," *New York Times,* July 19, 2002.
207. Lydia Polgreen, "Bollywood Farce: Indian Actress and Family are Detained," *New York Times,* July 18, 2002.
208. Ken Leiser and Sarah Trotto, "Report of Knifelike Object Delays Lambert Flights for Hours," *St. Louis Post-Dispatch,* October 5, 2002.
209. Mike Brassfield, "Security at TIA Alarmed by Fake Bombs—Its Own," *St. Petersburg Times,* January 15, 2003.

210. Jean Heller, "Security Has New Fake Bag Rules," *St. Petersburg Times,* January 16, 2003.
211. Leslie Miller, "More Than 4.8 Million Items Seized by Federal Airport Screeners," Associated Press, March 10, 2003.
212. "Boomerang Brings Strife," *Cairns Post,* July 8, 2002.
213. Scott Sunde, "Boomerangs Result in Airport Arrest," *Seattle Post-Intelligencer,* July 2, 2002.
214. Joe Sharkey, "The Case of the Banned Boomerangs," *New York Times,* July 9, 2002.
215. Ibid.
216. Judith Kleinfeld, "Don't Get Mad, Get Airborne," *Christian Science Monitor,* May 20, 2002.
217. Judith Kleinfeld, "Airport Security Holds All the Cards," *Anchorage Daily News,* April 19, 2002.
218. Judith Kleinfeld, "Don't Get Mad, Get Airborne."
219. Jane Costello, "Airport Screening: Fickle Sticklers," *Wall Street Journal,* May 14, 2002.
220. Paul Marks, "80 Year Old Texan Arrested at Airport for Rifle Remark," *Hartford Courant,* August 5, 2002.
221. Ibid.
222. Blake Morrison, "Frequent Hassles Confront Today's Fliers," *USA Today,* April 10, 2002.
223. Chuck Strouse, "Dumb Passengers: 50, Caught Terrorists: 0," *Miami New Times,* July 18, 2002.
224. Ibid
225. Matthew Rothschild, "McCarthyism Watch," *Progressive,* April 27, 2002
226. Ibid.
227. Ibid.
228. Ibid.
229. Ann Davis, "Why a 'No Fly List' Aimed at Terrorists Delays Others," *Wall Street Journal,* April 22, 2003.
230. Edward Alden, "US to Tackle Flaws in Airline Watch List," *Financial Times,* April 15, 2003.
231. Michael Miklofsky, "New Rules On Air Security Stir Up Civil Rights Groups," *Investor's Business Daily,* April 7, 2003.
232. http://www.epic.org/privacy/airtravel/profiling.html
233. Jean Heller, "FAA Rule Robs Aviators of Rights, Pilots Say," *St. Petersburg Times,* February 12, 2003.
234. Ibid.
235. Ron Laurenzo, "Pilots Denounce TSA's Under-Public-Radar Rule," *White House Weekly,* March 11, 2003.
236. Ron Laurenzo, "U.S. Rule On Revoking Pilot Licenses Stirs Fight," *Defense Week,* March 10, 2003.
237. Terri Langford, "Security Error Snarls D/FW Travel," *Dallas Morning News,* January 10, 2003.
238. Ellen Schroeder, "Delays Reported in D/FW Security Scare," *Fort Worth Star-Telegram,* January 11, 2003.
239. Ben Tinsley, "D/FW Grinds to a Halt after Security Scare," *Fort Worth Star Telegram,* January 10, 2003.
240. Terri Langford, "Delay in D/FW Alert is Criticized," *Dallas Morning News,* January 11, 2003.
241. Terri Langford, "Report on Incident at D/FW is Sealed," *Dallas Morning News,* January 24, 2003.
242. Ibid.
243. Ibid.
244. Bryon Okada, "Public Will Not Be Told Details of D/FW Breach," *Fort Worth Star Telegram,* January 24, 2003.

245. "ASR's Breach Report," Airport Security Report, February 26, 2003.
246. "ASR's Breach Report," Airport Security Report, March 12, 2003.
247. "ASR's Breach Report," Airport Security Report, April 9, 2003.
248. Ibid.
249. Ibid.
250. "Toy Gun Causes 40-Minute Delay at Cleveland Airport," Associated Press, March 21, 2003.
251. "ASR's Breach Report," Airport Security Report, April 9, 2003.
252. "Teminal Temporarily Shut Down at Detroit Metropolitan Airport," Associated Press, March 24, 2003.
253. "Woman Causes Evacuation of Two Concourse at Baltimore-Washington Airport," Airline Industry Information, April 4, 2003.
254. "ASR's Breach Report," Airport Security Report, April 23, 2003.
255. "ASR's Breach Report," Airport Security Report, May 7, 2003.
256. "Air Travelers' Security Enhanced as TSA Intercepts Over 4.8 Million Prohibited Items in First Year, Including 1,101 Firearms," Transportation Security Administration, March 10, 2003.
257. Ibid.
258. "Statement of Admiral James M. Loy, Under Secretary of Homeland Security Transportation Security Administrator, to the Committee on House Appropriations, Subcommittee on Homeland Security," Federal Document Clearing House Congressional Testimony, March 27, 2003.
259. "Uncle Sam Wants You," CBS News, March 4, 2002.
260. Jennifer Oldham, "U.S. Agency Bungled Airport Hiring," Los Angeles Times, May 16, 2003.
261. Sara Kehaulani Goo, "Dulles Screening Force not Completely Vetter," Washington Post, May 17, 2003.
262. David Hughes, "TSA Hiring Jumble," Aviation Week & Space Technology, June 9, 2003.
263. Justin Gest, "Agency Defends Efforts to Screen Its Screeners," Los Angeles Times, June 4, 2003.
264. Maki Becker and Greg Gittrich, "Weapons Still Fly at Airports," New York Daily News, September 4, 2002.
265. Ibid.
266. Maki Becker and Greg Gittrich, "Pols, Fliers Rip Airport Security," New York Daily News, September 5, 2002.
267. Ibid.
268. "Airport Security Investigation Compares Last Year's Results to This Year's," CBS News Transcripts: CBS Evening News, September 3, 2002.
269. Leslie Miller, "Marshal Mantra: Dominate, Intimidate, Control," Associated Press, September 21, 2002.
270. Michael Boyd, "The TSA PR Blitz," The Boyd Group/ASRC, Inc., November 18, 2002.
271. J. A. Donoghue, "Waiting for the Government," Air Transport World, September 1, 2002.
272. "Industry Sees Massive Security Failures, But Divided over Remedies," Airport Security Report, September 11, 2002.

## Chapter 9

1. "Remarks at a Fundraiser for Senatorial Candidate Lindsey Graham in Greenville," Public Papers of the Presidents, March 27, 2002.

2. "Remarks at the University of Pittsburgh in Pittsburgh," *Public Papers of the Presidents,* February 5, 2002.

3. "President Speaks on War Effort to Citadel Cadets," White House Office of the Press Secretary, December 11, 2001.

4. "Remarks by President Bush and Russian President Putin in Photo Opportunity Kananaskis, Canada," White House Office of the Press Secretary, June 27, 2002.

5. Fareed Zakaria, "This Is Moral Clarity?" *Washington Post,* November 5, 2002.

6. Sharon LaFraniere, "Chechen Refugees Describe Atrocities by Russian Troops," *Washington Post,* June 29, 2002.

7. Ibid.

8. "Adequate Security Conditions Do Not Exist in Chechnya to Allow the Return of Displaced Citizens," International Helsinki Federation, July 23, 2002.

9. Steven Eke, "Russia 'Thinning Out' Chechens," BBC, July 23, 2002.

10. Mike Allen, "Bush Defends Putin in Handling of Siege," *Washington Post,* November 19, 2002.

11. Fareed Zakaria, "This Is Moral Clarity?" *Washington Post,* November 5, 2002.

12. Ibid.

13. Anna Politkovskaya, "Russia and the Wages of Terror," *New York Times,* November 8, 2002.

14. Ibid.

15. Steven Lee Myers, "Russia Closes File on Bombings Linked to Chechnya War," *New York Times,* May 1, 2003.

16. "Opportunism in the Face of Tragedy, Repression in the Name of Anti-Terrorism," Human Rights Watch, 2002, at http://www.hrw.org/campaigns/september11/opportunismwatch.htm.

17. Muhammad Salih, "America's Shady Ally Against Terror, *New York Times,* March 11, 2002.

18. "Human Rights are Endangered in the Context of Efforts to Combat Terrorism," International Helsinki Federation, September 23, 2001.

19. "U.S. President Thanks Uzbekistan for Support to Fight Terrorism," BBC Monitoring Central Asia Unit, September 18, 2002. [Text of report by Uzbek National News Agency website]

20. Marina Kozlova, "Uzbek Activist Blames U.S. Government," United Press International, September 23, 2002.

21. Ranjit Devraj, "India: Misuse Alleged of Anti-Terrorist Law in Gujarat," Inter Press Service, March 25, 2002.

22. Elizabeth Roche, "Controversial Anti-Terrorism Law Adopted by Indian Parliament," Agence France Presse, March 26, 2002.

23. Rama Lakshmi, "India Passes Tough Anti-Terror Law," *Washington Post,* March 27, 2002.

24. "'We Have No Orders to Save You': State Participation and Complicity in Communal Violence in Gujarat," Human Rights Watch, April 30, 2002.

25. "Remarks by President Bush and President Jiang Zemin in Press Availability," White House Office of the Press Secretary, October 19, 2001.

26. "China 'Cracks Down on Muslims,'" BBC News Online, March 22, 2002.

27. "Authorities in West China Demolish Mosque, Arrest 180 Protesters," Agence France Presse, October 12, 2001.

28. "Rights at Risk: Amnesty International's Concerns Regarding Security Legislation and Law Enforcement Measures," Amnesty International On-line, January 18, 2002.

29. "China Intensifies Actions against Moslem Uighurs," Deutsche Presse-Agentur, September 3, 2002.

30. Jonathan Manthorpe, "Terror War Throws a Curve Ball: China's Handling of Its 'Internal Affairs' Crops Up in a Game Already Charged with Suspicion and Mistrust," *Vancouver Sun,* September 10, 2002.

31. Erik Eckholm, "American Gives Beijing Good News: Rebels on Terror List," *New York Times,* August 27, 2002.

32. William Foreman, "U.S. Embassy Says Muslim Group in China's Northwest Plotted Attacks on Embassies," Associated Press, August 30, 2002.

33. Erik Eckholm, "China Muslim Group Planned Terror, U.S. Says," *New York Times,* August 31, 2002.

34. Philip P. Pan, "U.S. Warns of Plot by Group in W. China," *Washington Post,* August 29, 2002.

35. Office of the Coordinator for Counterterrorism, "Patterns of global Terrorism—2001," U.S. State Department, May 21, 2002.

36. Jason Leow, "China Terrorist Group Planning to Attack a U.S.Embassy," *Straits Times* (Singapore), August 31, 2002.

37. "China Hails UN Move to List Xinjiang Group as Linked to al-Qaeda," Agence France Presse, September 12, 2002.

38. Erik Eckholm, "U.S. Labeling of Group in China as Terrorist Is Criticized," *New York Times,* September 13, 2002.

39. Christian M. Wade, "Sept. 11: Chinese Muslims Face Backlash," United Press International, September 6, 2002.

40. Joshua Kurlantzick, "Xinjiang 'Terror' Crackdown Called Ploy to Foil Ethnic Group," *Washington Times,* October 23, 2002.

41. "Texas Ranch Summit Rewards Jiang's 'Perfect' Diplomacy," Deutsche Presse-Agentur, October 21, 2002.

42. Elisabeth Rosenthal, "Ashcroft Says U.S. Will Place Agents in China," *New York Times,* October 25, 2002.

43. Serge Schmemann, "U.N. Gets a Litany of Antiterror Plans," *New York Times,* January 12, 2002.

44. "Letter dated 24 December 2001 from the Permanent Representative of Algeria to the United Nations addressed to the Chairman of the Security Council Committee established pursuant to resolution 1373 (2001)." Letter available at http://www.un.org/docs/sc/committees/1373/.

45. "Algeria Led World in Forced Disappearances," Human Rights Watch, February 27, 2003.

46. Keith Somerville, "U.S. Military Aid for Algeria," BBC News Online, December 10, 2002.

47. William Orme, "UN Fears Abuses of Terror Mandate," *Los Angeles Times,* January 2, 2002.

48. Letter dated 22 December 2001 from the Permanent Mission of Botswana to the United Nations addressed to the Chairman of the Committee established pursuant to resolution 1373 (2001) concerning counter-terrorism. Letter available at http://www.un.org/docs/sc/committees/1373/.

49. Serge Schmemann, "U.N. Gets a Litany of Antiterror Plans," *New York Times,* January 12, 2002.

50. Letter dated 21 December 2001 from the Permanent Representative of Belarus to the United Nations addressed to the Chairman of the Security Council Committee established pursuant to resolution 1373 (2001) concerning counter-terrorism. Letter available at http://www.un.org/docs/sc/committees/1373/.

51. "Opportunism in the Face of Tragedy, Repression in the Name of Anti-Terrorism," Human Rights Watch, 2002, at http://www.hrw.org/campaigns/september11/opportunismwatch.htm.

52. Ibid.

53. "Remarks by Secretary of State Colin L. Powell and Egyptian Minister of Foreign Affairs Ahmed Maher after Their Meeting," U.S. Department of State Office of the Spokesman, September 26, 2001.

54. "Opportunism in the Face of Tragedy, Repression in the Name of Anti-Terrorism," Human Rights Watch, 2002. At http://www.hrw.org/campaigns/september11/opportunismwatch.htm.

55. Rohan Sullivan, "Malaysian Leader Likens His Country's Detention Law to U.S. Treatment of Terror Suspects," Associated Press, March 28, 2002.

56. Arshad Mohammed, "Bush Welcomes Mahathir as Anti-Terrorism Ally," Reuters News Service, May 15, 2002.

57. Salmy Hashim, "U.S.Understands Reason for Isa, Says Rais," Bernama the Malaysian National News Agency, May 11, 2002.

58. Yogita Tahilramani, "Definition of terrorism opens to abuse," *Jakarta Post,* April 2, 2002.

59. Ibid.

60. "Cuba Toughens Anti-Terrorism Law," Associated Press, December 21, 2001.

61. "Opportunism in the Face of Tragedy, Repression in the Name of Anti-Terrorism," Human Rights Watch, 2002, at http://www.hrw.org/campaigns/september11/opportunismwatch.htm.

62. Chris McGreal, and Andrew Meldrum, "Mugabe Launches New Salvo at Britain," *Guardian* (UK), January 14, 2002.

63. *Human Rights: A Year of Loss,* Lawyers Committee for Human Rights, September 2002.

64. "Imbalance of Powers," Lawyers Committee on Human Rights, March 2003.

54. Ibid.

66. Barry Wain, "Wrong Target," *Far Eastern Economic Review,* April 18, 2002.

67. Tim Shorrock, "Aftershock of Sep. 11 Felt Most in Domestic Politics," Inter Press Service, April 9, 2002.

68. Gustavo Capdevila, "Rights: NGOs Disenchanted with U.N. Commission's Results," Inter Press Service, April 26, 2002.

69. Elizabeth Olson, "U.N. Fears 'Bloc' Voters are Abetting Rights Abuses," *New York Times,* April 28, 2002.

70. Gustavo Capdevila, "Rights: NGOs Disenchanted with U.N. Commission's Results," Inter Press Service, April 26, 2002.

71. "Statement by Ambassador Moley, Commission on Human Rights," Session of the United Nations Commission on Human Rights, March 20, 2002.

72. "Statement by Ambassador Moley, Commission on Human Rights."

73. "Financial Fight against Terror," Public Papers of the Presidents, December 4, 2001.

74. "Remarks of Under Secretary Jimmy Gurule—2002 National Money Laundering Strategy Roll Out," Treasury Department Office of Public Affairs, July 25, 2002.

75. For an excellent analysis of the frauds of foreign aid, see P. T. Bauer, *Equality, the Third World, and Economic Delusion* (Cambridge, MA: Harvard University Press, 1981).

76. Quoted in Marilyn Karfeld, "Charities that Fund Terror May be Liable for Damages," *Cleveland Jewish News,* November 30, 2001.

77. "Bush Remarks on Sept. 11 Six-Month Anniversary," White House Press Office, March 11, 2002.

78. Elizabeth Becker, "U.S. Ties Military Aid to Peacekeepers' Immunity," *New York Times,* August 10, 2002.

79. Federation of American Scientists, *Arms Sales Monitor* 48, August 2002.

80. Frida Berrigan, "U.S. Aid Going to the Wrong People," *Charleston, W.V. Sunday Gazette Mail,* April 14, 2002.

81. Press Release, "Repressive Uzbek Leader to Visit White House," Human Rights Watch, March 8, 2002.

82. "Police Torture Is Part of Uzbek Government Policy—Rights Activist," BBC Monitoring International Reports, April 23, 2002.

83. "Georgia: Immediate Action Needed on Persistent Human Rights Violations," Amnesty International On-line, April 8, 2002.

84. Sharon LaFraniere, "Pressed by U.S., Georgia Gets Tough with Outsiders," *Washington Post,* April 28, 2002.

85. Christopher Deliso, "A Georgian Gaffe and the War on Terror," Antiwar.com, June 18, 2002.

86. "Georgia Short on Troops for U.S.," Associated Press, July 5, 2002.

87. Nicholas Kristof, "What Is Democracy Anyway?" *New York Times,* May 3, 2002.

88. "Pakistan," Country Reports on Human Rights Practices—2001, U.S. State Department Bureau of Democracy, Human Rights, and Labor, March 4, 2002.

89. "Kazakhstan," Country Reports on Human Rights Practices—2001, U.S. State Department Bureau of Democracy, Human Rights, and Labor, March 4, 2002.

90. Peter Baker, "New Repression in Kazakhstan," *Washington Post,* June 10, 2002.

91. Ibid.

92. "Amnesty International News Conference—2002 Annual Report on Global Human Rights," Federal News Service, May 28, 2002.

93. "Kazakhstan Holds Out Hope for Closer Military Ties with United States," Associated Press, July 16, 2002.

94. "Kyrgyzstan," Country Reports on Human Rights Practices—2001, U.S. State Department Bureau of Democracy, Human Rights, and Labor, March 4, 2002.

95. "Kyrgyz Leader Highlights Democracy Credentials," Agence France Presse, September 24, 2002.

96. Ahmed Rashid, "Aftermath Of Terror—To Boost Military Campaign, U.S.Blinks at Repression in Central Asia," *Wall Street Journal,* May 13, 2002.

97. "Foreign Military Training and DoD Engagement Activities of Interest: Joint Report to Congress," U.S. State Department Bureau of Political-Military Affairs, March 2002.

98. "Appeals and Statements for Human Rights and Civil Society in Turkmenistan," International Helsinki Federation, June 10, 2002.

99. "Foreign Military Training and DoD Engagement Activities of Interest: Joint Report to Congress," U.S. State Department Bureau of Political-Military Affairs, March 2002.

100. Glenn Mckenzie, "Nigeria Criticized in Army Massacre," Associated Press, April 1, 2002.

101. Frida Berrigan, "U.S. Aid Going to the Wrong People," Charleston, *W.V. Sunday Gazette Mail,* April 14, 2002.

102. Jonathan Weisman, "Pentagon Wants to Send Troops to Indonesia," *USA Today,* March 19, 2002.

103. Rajiv Chandrasekaran, "Saved from Ruin: The Reincarnation of East Timor," *Washington Post,* May 19, 2002.

104. Ian Timberlake, "Activists See Clout of Army Growing; Fear Civilian Rule Could be Undone," *Washington Times,* April 1, 2002.

105. Akhilesh Upadhyay, "Deuba Secures U.S. Support," Institute of Foreign Affairs (the Nepal Ministry of Foreign Affairs), May 7, 2002.

106. Scott Baldauf, "In Nepal's Maoist Hunt, Villagers are Hit Hardest," *Christian Science Monitor,* May 8, 2002.

107. Press Release, "Nepal—Unlawful Killings Must be Prevented," Amnesty International, July 5, 2002.

108. Scott Baldauf, "In Nepal's Maoist Hunt, Villagers are Hit Hardest," *Christian Science Monitor,* May 8, 2002.

109. Akhilesh Upadhyay, "Deuba Secures U.S. Support," Institute of Foreign Affairs (the Nepal Ministry of Foreign Affairs), May 7, 2002.

110. "DoD News: Transcript of Deputy Secretary Wolfowitz Interview with CNN Turkey," Department of Defense, July 14, 2002.

111. John Shamsey, "80 Years Too Late: The International Criminal Court and the 20th Century's First Genocide," *Journal of Transnational Law and Policy,* Summer 2002.

112. "DoD News: Transcript of Deputy Secretary Wolfowitz Interview with CNN Turkey," Department of Defense, July 14, 2002.

113. "Remarks on Compassionate Conservatism in San Jose, California," *Public Papers of the Presidents,* April 30, 2002.
114. Elizabeth Becker, "U.S. Ties Military Aid to Peacekeepers' Immunity," *New York Times,* August 10, 2002.
115. Ibid.
116. Barry Schweid, "State Department Urges Foreign Diplomats to Protect Americans from Reach of New International War Crimes Court," Associated Press, August 10, 2002.
117. Federation of American Scientists, *Arms Sales Monitor* 48, August 2002.
118. Tamar Gabelnick, "Security Assistance after September 11," Federation of American Scientists, May 2002.
119. "Remarks at Logan High School in La Crosse, Wisconsin," *Public Papers of the Presidents,* May 8, 2002.

## Chapter 10

1. "Remarks by the President on Citizen Preparedness," White House Office of the Press Secretary, January 30, 2002.
2. Angus Roxburgh, "How Russia Faced Its Dark Past," BBC Online, March 5, 2003.
3. "Remarks on Financial Aspects of Terrorism," White House Office of the Press Secretary, December 20, 2001.
4. "Remarks by the President on Citizen Preparedness."
5. A July 2002 report by the report by the House Permanent Select Committee on Intelligence subcommittee on terrorism complained: "The subcommittee has found that practically every agency of the United States government with a counterterrorism mission uses a different definition of terrorism. Without a standard definition, terrorism might be treated no differently than other crimes." Quoted in "Report: U.S. Agencies Cannot Define Terrorism: U.S. Agencies Can't Agree on a Definition for Terrorism," Worldtribune.com, July 23 2002.
6. "Key Sections of Pentagon's Report on Attack on the Marines," *New York Times,* December 29, 1983.
7. Quoted at the FBI Denver Terrorism page, http://denver.fbi.gov/inteterr.htm
8. Barton Gellman, "Though Terrorism May Be Hard to Define, This Administration Takes It Seriously," *National Journal,* September 12, 1981.
9. Asa Hutchinson, "Narco-Terror: The International Connection between Drugs and Terror," speech at Heritage Foundation, Washington, D.C., Drug Enforcement Agency Office of Public Affairs, April 2, 2002.
10. "Mexico Anti-Drug Force to be Sscrapped," BBC News, January 17, 2003.
11. Statement by Ambassador George Moose, U.S. delegate to the fifty-ninth session of the United Nations Commission on Human Rights, "Human Rights and Terrorism," April 23, 2001. Available at http://www.humanrights-usa.net/statements/0423terrorism.htm
12. William Orme, "Anti-Terrorism Drive Idling," *Los Angeles Times,* April 16, 2002.
13. Neve Gordon, "The Word on Terrorism; Human Rights Watch," *Humanist,* July 17, 1997.
14. Office of the Coordinator for Counterterrorism, "Patterns of Global Terrorism—2001," U.S. State Department, May 21, 2002.
15. Ibid.
16. "Remarks to the Community in Central Point, Oregon," *Public Papers of the Presidents,* August 22, 2002.
17. Jim Gomez, "American Hostages Survived Gunfights, Harsh Jungle Life for a Year before Bloody Rescue," Associated Press, June 14, 2002.
18. Anthony Faiola, Karen DeYoung and Ellen Nakashima, "U.S. Notified Peru of Suspect Plane," *Washington Post,* April 22, 2001.

19. Sebastian Rotella and Natalia Tarnawiecki, "U.S. Role in Peru Plane Downing Adds to Mystery," *Los Angeles Times,* April 22, 2001.
20. "U.S. Guided Peru in Shoot-Down of Missionary Plane," *Orlando Sentinel,* April 22, 2001.
21. Sebastian Rotella and Natalia Tarnawiecki, "U.S. Role in Peru Plane Downing Adds to Mystery," *Los Angeles Times,* April 22, 2001.
22. "Bush Calls Missionary Plane Incident 'Terrible Tragedy'," www.cnn.com, April 22, 2001.
23. Robert Burns, "Bush Says U.S. Role in Downing of Plane Was to Provide Information," Associated Press, April 22, 2001.
24. Dave Kopel, "License to Kill," *National Review Online,* August 16, 2001.
25. Ken Guggenheim, "State Department Inquiry Finds U.S., Peru Share Blame in Shooting Down of Private Airplane," Associated Press, July 31, 2001.
26. "Missionary Agency Decides to End Settlement Discussions with the USA and Peru," PR Newswire, March 21, 2002.
27. Ron Fournier, "Government Prepares to Offer Compensation in Shoot Down of Plane over Peru," Associated Press, March 21, 2002.
28. "Missionary Awaits Apology for Errors That Ripped Family," (Memphis, Tenn.) *Commercial Appeal,* (Memphis, Tenn.) July 6, 2002.
29. Office of the Coordinator for Counterterrorism, "Patterns of Global Terrorism—2001."
30. Hans Pienaar, "Savimbi's Death Brings Hope of End to Angola's Scorched-Earth Disaster," *Independent* (UK), February 25, 2002.
31. "Savimbi Death: What Next for Angola?" BBC News, March 11, 2002.
32. Office of the Coordinator for Counterterrorism, "Patterns of Global Terrorism—2001."
33. David Corn, "ExxonMobil-Sponsored Terrorism?" *Nation,* June 14, 2002.
34. Ibid.
35. "Indonesia: Accountability for Human Rights Violations in Aceh," Human Rights Watch, March 2002.
36. Elaine Monaghan, " U.S. Says Interests Hurt by Suit against Exxon," Reuters, August 6, 2002.
37. David Corn, "ExxonMobil-Sponsored Terrorism?."
38. Fax from State Department spokesman Joe Reap to author, May 16, 2003.
39. Statistics from "Patterns of Global Terrorism," U.S. State Department, 1990–2000.
40. Office of the Coordinator for Counterterrorism, "Patterns of Global Terrorism—2001."
41. Editorial, "Brutality in Blue," *Washington Post,* July 4, 2001.
42. Craig Whitlock and David S. Fallis, "County Officers Kill More Often Than Any in U.S.; Officials Ruled Shootings Justified in Every Case—Even of Unarmed Citizens," *Washington Post,* July 1, 2001.
43. Craig Whitlock and David S. Fallis, "Official Secrecy Shrouds Fatal Arrests; Prince George's Police Hamper Prosecutors," *Washington Post,* July 4, 2001.
44. David S. Fallis and Craig Whitlock, "How Reporting for This Series Was Done," *Washington Post,* July 1, 2001.
45. Roberto Suro and Cheryl Thompson, "Group Says Police Abuses Persist Because of Lack of Prosecution," *Washington Post,* July 8, 1998.
46. David S. Fallis and Craig Whitlock, "How Reporting for This Series Was Done."
47. Ibid.
48. James Bovard, *Feeling Your Pain: The Explosion and Abuse of Government Power in the Clinton-Gore Years* (New York: St. Martin's Press, 2000), pp. 269–289.
49. Lee Michael Katz, "Afghanistan's President Is Ousted," *USA Today,* April 17, 1992.
50. Blaine Harden, "Ethiopia Bars Relief Team," *Washington Post,* December 3, 1985.
51. Author interview with World Bank official who requested anonymity, August 6, 1987. James Bovard, "The World Bank vs. the World's Poor," Cato Institute, September 28, 1987.
52. Jan Van Criekinge, "Transforming Arms into Art," *Peace News,* September 2000.

53. Holger Jensen, "The Forgotten Wars—Conflicts Rage across Other Continents While NATO Bombs Balkans," *Denver Rocky Mountain News,* May 23, 1999.

54. James Astill and Isabelle Chevallot, "Conflict in Congo Has Killed 4.7 Million People, Charity Says," *Guardian* (UK), April 8, 2003.

55. R. J. Rummel, *Death by Government* (New Brunswick, N.J.: Transaction, 1994), p. 9.

56. Irving Louis Horowitz, "Counting Bodies: The Dismal Science of Authorized Terror," in *State Crime,* Vol. 1, ed. David O. Friedrichs, (Dartmouth, Mass.: Ashgate, 1998), p. 19.

57. "Remarks at the National Prayer Breakfast," *Public Papers of the Presidents,* February 7, 2002.

58. "Remarks by the President to International Democratic Union Leaders Dinner," White House Office of the Press Secretary, June 10, 2002.

59. "Radio Address by the President to the Nation," White House Office of the Press Secretary, November 10, 2001.

60. "Radio Address to the Nation," *Public Papers of the Presidents,* May 31, 1986.

61. "Civilian Deaths in the NATO Air Campaign," Human Rights Watch, February 7, 2000.

62. Richard Boudreaux, "Civilian Deaths in Airstrikes Erode NATO Credibility," *Los Angeles Times,* May 31, 1999.

63. Richard Norton-Taylor, "NATO Cluster Bombs Kill 15 in Hospital and Crowded Market and Hospital," *Guardian* (Manchester, UK), May 8, 1999.

64. Thomas Michael McDonnell, "Cluster Bombs over Kosovo: A Violation of International Law?" *Arizona Law Review,* spring 2002.

65. Ibid.

66. Arianna Huffington, "Clinton Plays into Milosevic's Hand," *Chicago Sun-Times,* April 11, 1999.

67. Editorial, "The Waco Whitewash," *New York Times,* October 12, 1993.

## Chapter 11

1. "Remarks on the 2002 National Drug Control Strategy," Public Papers of the Presidents, February 12, 2002.

2. "Prepared Remarks of Attorney General John Ashcroft—DEA/Drug Enforcement Rollout," Justice Department Office of Public Affairs, March 19, 2002.

3. Will Weissert, "Homeland Security Renews Drug War," Associated Press, December 5, 2002.

4. "Drugs: Member States Welcome Afghan Ban on Opium Growing," *European Report,* July 11, 2001.

5. Barry Bearak, "At Heroin's Source, Taliban Do What 'Just Say No' Could Not," *New York Times,* May 24, 2001.

6. Ibid.

7. Ibid.

8. "U.S. Department of State—Statement on Afghanistan's Humanitarian Crisis," Federal Document Clearing House, May 17, 2001. The value of the U.S. aid was less than its cost, since it was in food commodities—primarily wheat—and the program is designed to benefit American farmers and U.S. merchant ships more than foreign recipients. See James Bovard, "Free Food Bankrupts Foreign Farmer," *Wall Street Journal,* July 2, 1984.

9. Robert Scheer, "Bush's Faustian Deal with the Taliban," *Los Angeles Times,* May 22, 2001.

10. Alan Eastham (Letter to the Editor), "Aid for Afghanistan, Not the Taliban," *Los Angeles Times,* May 29, 2001.

11. "U.S. Customs Service Press Conference Re: 'Operation Green Quest'—Global Financial Investigation Involving Iraq," Federal News Service, December 19, 2002.

12. Barbara Crossette, "Afghanistan: Taliban's Ban on Growing Opium Poppies Is Called a Success," *New York Times,* May 20, 2001.

13. Steven Gutkin, "Former Poppy Growers in Afghanistan Facing Growing Hardship," Associated Press, June 15, 2001.

14. Thalif Deen, "Drugs: U.N. Pays Rare Compliment to Taliban over Opium Ban," Inter Press Service, August 9, 2001.

15. Scott Baldauf, "Life Under Taliban a Mixed Blessing," *Christian Science Monitor,* September 22, 2001.

16. "Taliban Chief Renews Ban on Poppy Growing in Afghanistan," Agence France Presse, September 2, 2001.

17. Ibid.

18. "Remarks with President Putin and a Question-and-Answer Session with Crawford High School Students in Crawford," Public Papers of the Presidents, November 15, 2001.

19. "Opium Ban in Afghanistan: Important Step in Global Drug Control Efforts, Says UN Office for Drug Control and Crime Prevention," United Nations Information Service, January 17, 2002.

20. Kathy Gannon, "Ban on Poppy Growing Worries Afghan Farmers," Associated Press, November 29, 2002.

21. Pamela Constable, "Afghan Farmers Threatening to Replant Opium Poppies," *Washington Post,* August 17, 2002.

22. Kathy Gannon, "Ban on Poppy Growing Worries Afghan Farmers."

23. "Tribesmen Take Up Arms to Resist Afghan Drug War," Reuters News Service, December 29, 2002.

24. Rory Carroll, "Dozens Dead as Opium Protests End in Violence," *Guardian* (United Kingdom), April 10, 2002.

25. "Tribesmen Take Up Arms to Resist Afghan Drug War."

26. "Testimony of John Walters before the House Government Reform and Oversight Committee, Subcommittee on Criminal Justice, Drug Policy, and Human Resources," February 26, 2002. Available at http://www.useu.be/Terrorism/USResponse/Feb2602DrugControl-Cooperation.html.

27. Ibid.

28. "Kansas Native at Crossroads of Drug War, Terrorism," *Lawrence (Kans.) Journal-World,* September 30, 2002.

29. Todd Pitman, "Karzai: Opium Growers Need Livelihood," Associated Press, October 18, 2002.

30. Bill Gertz, "Military Opposes Spraying Poppies," *Washington Times,* March 25, 2002.

31. "Bush Unveils Drug Strategy, Vows to Cut Usage by 25% in Five Years," *Bulletin's Frontrunner,* February 13, 2002.

32. Mark Berniker, "Back to Bad Opium Habits," *Asia Times,* December 25, 2002.

33. Jerry Seper, "Afghan Drug Crops Up Despite Crubs," *Washington Times,* January 9, 2003.

34. Ibid.

35. Jonathan D. Salant, "DEA Chief: Afghanistan Unable to Enforce Poppy-Growing Ban," *Myrtle Beach, S.C. Sun News,* January 9, 2003.

36. Sergei Artemyev, "Opium Yield in Afghanistan to Exceed 6,000 Tonnes," *Tass* (Moscow), April 17, 2003.

37. Christopher Marquis, "U.S. Law Imperils Colombia Coca Spraying," *New York Times,* July 11, 2002.

38. "Official: Eradiction Hurts Colombia," Associated Press, October 10, 2002.

39. Rachel Van Dongen, "Legal Crops' Damage," *Washington Times,* October 15, 2002.

40. Ibid.

41. Christopher Marquis, "U.S. Law Imperils Colombia Coca Spraying."

42. "Hearing of the House Government Reform Committee—Subject: America's Heroin Crisis, Colombian Heroin, and How We Can Improve Plan Colombia," Federal News Service, December 12, 2002.

43. Jeffrey St. Clair, "How Dr. Mengele Might Wage the Drug War: Biowarfare in Colombia," *Counterpunch,* December 24, 2002.

44. Ibid.

45. "Designation of the AUC as a Foreign Terrorist Organization," State Department Office of Public Affairs, September 10, 2001.

46. Jim Lobe, "Politics—U.S.: U.S. Ruling on Colombia Angers Rights Groups," Inter Press Service, May 2, 2002.

47. Ibid.

48. "U.S. Embassy Colombia Cable CODEL [Congressional Delegation] Hastert's May 24–27 Visit to Colombia May 28, 1997, [Secret]," reprinted in *War in Colombia—Volume III—Guerrillas, Drugs and Human Rights in U.S. Colombia Policy, 1988–2002,* National Security Archive Electronic Briefing Book No. 69, National Security Archive, Washington, D.C., 2002.

49. Amnesty International 1997 Annual Report, available at http://www.amnesty.org/ailib/aireport/ar97/.

50. "Press Conference Re: Indictment of Colombians on Drug Trafficking Charges," Federal News Service, September 24, 2002.

51. "Justice Department News Conference—Subject: War on Drugs and Terrorism in Americas," Federal News Service, November 13, 2002.

52. Ibid.

53. Robyn Blumner, "Terror Connection Puts Drug War into Parallel Legal Universe," *Salt Lake Tribune,* November 29, 2002. (Originally published in *St. Petersburg Times.*)

54. Thomas Ginsberg, "Latin Battleground: U.S. Takes on Two Wars in One Country," *Philadelphia Inquirer,* December 1, 2002.

55. Paul Richter, "U.S. Debating Wider Assault on Colombia Rebels," *Los Angeles Times,* February 23, 2002.

56. "Ecuador: Foreign Ministry Asks Colombia to Suspend Spraying on, Near Border," BBC Monitoring International Reports, April 2, 2003.

57. P. Mitchell Prothero, "Claim of FARC—al Qaida Link Rescinded," United Press International, February 9, 2002.

58. Ibid.

59. Ibid.

60. Ibid.

61. Ibid.

62. "Remarks by President George W. Bush to the Community Anti-Drug Coalitions of America Leadership Forum," Federal News Service, December 14, 2001.

63. Frank Davies, "White House's In-Your-Face Antidrug Ads Fuel Debate," *Miami Herald,* March 17, 2002.

64. Sylvia A. Smith, "Drug War's Finances Probed," *Fort Wayne, Ind. Journal Gazette,* February 16, 2003.

65. Ira Teinowitz, "White House to End Drugs and Terror Ads," AdAge.com, April 1, 2003.

66. "Remarks on the 2002 National Drug Control Strategy," *Public Papers of the Presidents,* February 12, 2002. Italics mine.

67. "Press Briefing by Director of the Office of National Drug Control Policy John Walters," Office of National Drug Control Policy, February 12, 2002.

68. Ibid.

69. "John Ashcroft Participates in Opening of Exhibit on Connections between Drug Trafficking and Terrorism," Federal Document Clearing House, September 3, 2002.

70. Ibid.

71. "Drug Money Funds Terror Group," Associated Press, September 1, 2002.
72. "Canadian Drug Being Used to Fund Terrorist Activity, U.S. Official Says," *Canadian Press*, August 13, 2002.
73. "Major Meth Ring Disrupted, Officials Say," *Los Angeles Times*, April 16, 2003.
74. http://www.samhsa.gov/oas/nhsda/2k1nhsda/vol3/Sect1v1_PDF_W_31–35.pdf.
75. "Chapter 2: Illicit Drug Use—2001 Summary of Findings," *2001 National Household Survey on Drug Abuse*, Substance Abuse and Mental Health Services Administration, U.S. Department of Health and Human Services, 2002.
76. "National Drug Threat Assessment 2003," National Drug Intelligence Center, online at http://www.usdoj.gov/ndic/pubs3/3300/marijuan.htm#Availability.
77. "The United Nations Drug Control Program—The United Nations Office of Drug Control and Crime Prevention (ODCCP) Programs," at http://www.usun-vienna.rpo.at/undcp.htm.
78. "House Transportation and Infrastructure—U.S. Representative Frank Lobiondo (R-NJ) Holds Hearing on Drug Interdiction," Federal Document Clearing House, October 17, 2001.
79. Michael Isikoff, "U.S. Considers Shift in Drug War," *Washington Post*, September 16, 1993.
80. "Drug Control: Interdiction Efforts in Central America have had Little Impact on the Flow of Drugs," General Accounting Office, August 2, 1994.
81. "Attorney General Janet Reno and Office of National Drug Control Policy Director-Designate Lee Brown Address to the 1993 National Summit on U.S. Drug Policy," Reuters Transcript Report, May 7, 1993.
82. Eric Lichtblau, "White House Report Stings Drug Agency on Abilities," *New York Times*, February 5, 2003.
83. Sam Staley, *Drug Policy and the Decline of American Cities* (New Brunswick, NJ: Transaction, 1992), p. 110.
84. Juan Zamorano, "U.S. Drug Chief: Terrorism Increasingly Funded by Drug Trafficking," Associated Press, April 1, 2003.
85. "DEA Ratchets Up Drug-Terror Rhetoric," Drug Policy Alliance, November 7, 2002.
86. "Remarks by President Bush at Signing of USA Patriot Act of 2001," U.S. Newswire, October 26, 2001.

## Chapter 12

1. Editorial, "Terror Firma; Reagan vs. Terrorism," *New Republic*, November 19, 1984.
2. Martin Peretz, "Israel, the United States, and Evil," *New Republic*, September 24, 2001.
3. Lawrence Kudlow, "Bullish on Bush," *Washington Times*, December 9, 2001.
4. Samuel G. Freedman, "We're All on the Front Lines Now," *USA Today*, September 13, 2001.
5. Paul Greenberg, "When the Enemy Is Hidden from View," *Washington Times*, September 15, 2001.
6. "William Bennett, Empower America, Gives His Views on the Attack on America and What Actions Should Be Taken against the Terrorists," *Hardball with Chris Matthews: Attack on America*, CNBC, September 12, 2001.
7. The Netanyahu statement was quoted in a later interview with him on National Public Radio. "Continuing reactions to events in the aftermath of the attack on the World Trade Center and Pentagon," *Talk of the Nation*, National Public Radio, September 21, 2001.
8. Benny Avni, "U.N. Moves Swiftly to Ban Terror, but Gets Bogged Down Defining It," *Forward*, October 5, 2001.

9. Todd S. Purdum, "What Do You Mean, 'Terrorist'?" *New York Times,* April 7, 2002.

10. For an excellent analysis of recent Middle East history and the failures of U.S. policies, see Sheldon Richman, "'Ancient History': U.S. Conduct in the Middle East Since World War II and the Folly of Intervention," Cato Institute, August 16, 1991.

11. Jerome Slater, "Israel, Anti-Semitism and the Palestinian Problem," *Tikkun,* May 2001.

12. Albert Einstein et al., "'New Palestine Party,' Letter to Editors of the *New York Times,*" *New York Times,* December 4, 1948.

13. Benny Morris, *Israel's Border Wars, 1949–1956* (Oxford: Oxford University Press, 1993), p. 245.

14. Morris, *Israel: Border Wars,* p. 245.

15. Morris, *Israel: Border Wars,* p. 247.

16. Samat Gideon, "Deja Vu All Over Again," *Haaretz,* May 3, 2002.

17. Martin van Creveld, "Israeli Defence Forces Will Inevitably Lose to the Palestinians," *World in Focus,* ABC-TV, March 20, 2002.

18. "Excerpts from Begin Speech at National Defense College," *New York Times,* August 21, 1982.

19. Martin van Crevald, *The Sword and the Olive: A Critical History of the Israeli Defense Force* (New York: Public Affairs, 1998), p. 340.

20. "Israeli Violations of Human Rights of Lebanese Civilians," B'Tselem, January 2000.

21. Ibid.

22. Associated Press, "Mideast Truce Demanded 101 Refugees Slain as Israel Shells UN Post," Toronto Star, April 19, 1996.

23. David Usborne, "We Did Not Kill Deliberately, Israel Ssays," *Independent* (UK), May 7, 1996.

24. Associated Press, "Mideast Truce Demanded 101 Refugees Slain as Israel Shells UN Post."

25. Associated Press, "U.S., Israel Condemn UN Report on Shelling," *Chicago Tribune,* May 8, 1996.

26. "Unlawful Killings During Operation 'Grapes of Wrath,'" Amnesty International, July 1996.

27. Reuters, "Israeli Gunner's Quote: Just Arabs," *Newsday,* May 11, 1996. The quotes originally appeared in *Kol Ha'ir.*

28. Ibid.

29. Ari Shavit, "How Easily We Killed Them," *New York Times,* May 27, 1996. (This article was first published in *Haaretz*).

30. Barbara Demick, "Israel Supreme Court Orders Release of Lebanese Held as 'Bargaining Chips'" *Philadelphia Inquirer,* April 13, 2000.

31. Aliza Marcus, "Lebanese Prisoners in Israel Held as Bargaining Chips," *Cleveland Plain Dealer,* February 17, 2000.

32. William Claiborne, "Israeli Invasion Brings Quiet to Galilee," *Washington Post,* June 8, 1982.

33. Richard Sale, "Israel Gave Aid to Hamas," United Press International, February 24, 2001.

34. Boaz Ganor, "Hamas—The Islamic Resistance Movement in the Territories," Institute for Counter Terrorism, February 2, 1992.

35. Richard Sale, "Israel Gave Aid to Hamas," United Press International, February 24, 2001.

36. Richard Sale, " Hamas History Tied to Israel," United Press International, June 18, 2002.

37. Michal Sela, "'Resistance is a Moslem Duty'," *Jerusalem Post,* May 26, 1989.

38. Ibid.

39. Michael Parks, "Rabin Talks to Right Wing to Strengthen Coalition," *Los Angeles Times,* March 4, 1994. Italics mine.

40. David K. Shipler, "Israel Considering Curbs on Settlers," *New York Times,* March 14, 1983.

41. "Israeli Settler Massacres 40 in West Bank Mosque," Facts on File *World News Digest,* March 3, 1994.

42. Ibid.
43. Ibid.
44. "ADL Research Report 'Extremism in the Name of Religion: The Violent Legacy of Meir Kahane'," U.S. Newswire, February 16, 1995.
45. "Israeli Settler Massacres 40 in West Bank Mosque."
46. Editorial, "Hatred Stalks the Settlements," *New York Times*, March 1, 1994.
47. Clyde Haberman, "West Bank Massacre; Israel Orders Tough Measures against Militant Settlers," *New York Times*, February 28, 1994.
48. Doug Struck, "Israel Plans Crackdown on Settlers," *Baltimore Sun*, February 28, 1994.
49. Susan Sach, "Rabid Talk Plants Seeds of Massacre," *Newsday*, March 7, 1994.
50. "Hebron Unit Hamstrung by Orders," *Baltimore Sun*, March 11, 1994.
51. Bob Hepburn, "Israeli Army Scrambles to Restore Image," *Toronto Star*, March 20, 1994.
52. Ibid.
53. Mark Matthews and Peter Hermann, "Militancy Alive in Jewish settlement," *Baltimore Sun*, July 21, 2001.
54. Suzanne Goldenberg, "Battle for Land Spawns a Brutal New Group of Jewish Vigilantes," *Observer* (UK), July 22, 2001.
55. Amos Harel and Jonathan Lis, "Minister's Aide Calls Hebron Riots a 'Pogrom'," *Haaretz*, July 31, 2002.
56. Charles A. Radin, "A Top Israeli Says Settlers Incited Riot in Hebron," *Boston Globe*, July 31, 2002.
57. Akiva Eldar, "People and Politics: Hold Off with the Laurel Leaves," *Haaretz*, January 23, 2003.
58. Martin Sieff, "Hebron's Hatreds Threaten World," United Press International, April 2, 2001.
59. Jack Kelley, "Vigilantes Take Up Arms, Vow to Expel 'Muslim Filth'," *USA Today*, September 4, 2001.
60. Charles A. Radin, "Hebron's Jewish Extremists Protected Despite Actions," *Boston Globe*, November 23, 2001.
61. "Settler Gets 6 Months for Killing Child," *Haaretz*, January 22, 2001.
62. Ibid.
63. Joel Greenberg, "Jewish Settlers' Zeal Forces Palestinians to Flee Their Town," *New York Times*, October 21, 2002.
64. Ibid.
65. Andrew Cockburn, "Lines in the Sand: Deadly Times in the West Bank and Gaza," *National Geographic*, October 2002.
66. "Land Grab: Israel's Settlement Policy in the West Bank," B'Tselem, May 2002.
67. Ibid.
68. Sara Roy, "Ending the Palestinian Economy," *Middle East Policy*, December 1, 2002.
69. Ibid.
70. Ibid.
71. Danny Rubinstein, "A Land of Roadblocks and Barriers," *Haaretz*, November 04, 2002.
72. "Lethal Curfew—The Use of Live Ammunition to Enforce Curfew," B'Tselem, October 2002.
73. Barbara Demick, "Israeli Rights Group Denounces Army," *Los Angeles Times*, October 17, 2002.
74. Stephen Farrell, "Cameraman Records the Slaughter of Bicycling Children," *Times* (London), July 8, 2002.
75. Barbara Demick, "Israelis Open Fire in Jenin, Killing 4," *Los Angeles Times*, June 22, 2002.
76. John Ward Anderson, "Israel Shells Market in West Bank; 3 Children Among 4 Dead; Tank Fire Called 'Error,'" *Washington Post*, June 22, 2002.

77.  Ibid.
78.  "Land Grab: Israel's Settlement Policy in the West Bank."
79.  Press Release, "House Demolitions hit 12,700 in West Bank and Gaza Strip," United Nations Relief and Works Agency for Palestine Refugees, May 7, 2003.
80.  Ibid.
81.  Ben Lynfield, "Rights: Israel Demolishes Houses in the Name of 'Security,'" Inter Press Service, June 29, 2001.
82.  Barbara Demick, "No Olive Branches in the Grove," *Los Angeles Times,* November 7, 2002.
83.  Stephen Kaufman, "Study Says Malnutrition Poses Humanitarian Emergency to Palestinians," Voice of America, August 9, 2002.
84.  Ramit Plushnick-Masti, "Palestinian Study Finds Nearly half of West Bank-Gaza Children Suffer Malnutrition," Associated Press, August 1, 2002.
85.  Gregg Greenough and Gilbert Burnham, "Disrupting the Flow of Food," *Baltimore Sun,* January 11, 2003.
86.  "Israeli Official Says 'No Famine' in Territories," BBC Monitoring International Reports, April 14, 2002.
87.  Benjamin Netanyahu, "Today We are All Americans," *New York Post,* September 21, 2001.
88.  Barak Cohen, "Democracy and the Mis-Rule of Law: The Israeli Legal System's Failure to Prevent Torture in the Occupied Territories," *Indiana International and Comparative Law Review,* 2001, p. 75.
89.  Ibid.
90.  Ibid.
91.  Ardi Imseis, "'Moderate' Torture on Trial: Critical Reflections on the Israeli Supreme Court Judgment Concerning the Legality of General Security Service Interrogation Methods," *Berkeley Journal of International Law,* 2001, p. 328.
92.  Ibid.
93.  Ibid.
94.  Michael Gross, "Just and Jewish Warfare; Israeli Soldiers Seem to Disregard Rules of War," *Tikkun,* September 2001.
95.  Ibid.
96.  Robert Kaplan, "The Return of Ancient Times," *Atlantic,* June 2002.
97.  Cohen, "Democracy and the Mis-Rule of Law," 75.
98.  Imseis, "'Moderate' Torture on Trial," 328.
99.  "Israel Stands Behind Policy of Physical Interrogations," CNN, November 19, 1996.
100. "Routine Torture Interrogation Methods of the General Security Service," B'Tselem, February 1998.
101. Catherine M. Grosso, "International Law in the Domestic Arena: The Case of Torture in Israel," *Iowa Law Review,* October 2000, 305.
102. Grosso, "International Law in the Domestic Arena," 305.
103. Imseis, "'Moderate' Torture on Trial," 328.
104. Jessica Montell, "Israel's Lesson Is That Torture Doesn't Work," *Sunday Gazette Mail,* (Charleston, W.Va.) December 9, 2001.
105. Ibid.
106. "Israel's Assassination Policy: Extra-judicial Executions," B'Tselem, January 2001.
107. Alexander Cockburn, "Israel's Torture Ban," *Nation,* September 27, 1999.
108. Imseis, "'Moderate' Torture on Trial," 328.
109. http://www.stoptorture.org.il/eng/about.asp?menu=2&submenu=1
110. Dov Waxman, "Terrorizing Democracies," *Washington Quarterly,* Winter 2000.
111. Imseis, "'Moderate' Torture on Trial," 328. The court declared, " If it will nonetheless be decided that it is appropriate for Israel, in light of its security difficulties to sanction physical means in interrogations (and the scope of these means which deviate from the ordinary

investigation rules), this is an issue that must be decided by the legislative branch which represents the people. We do not take any stand on this matter at this time."

112.  Grosso, "International Law in the Domestic Arena," 305.

113.  "Torture of Palestinian Minors at the Gush Etzion Police Station Information Sheet," B'T-selem, July 2001.

114.  Elizabeth Olson, "Israel Denies Groups' Charge That It Is Torturing Detainees," *New York Times*, November 21, 2001.

115.  Jessica Montell, "Operation Defensive Shield; The Propaganda War and the Reality," *Tikkun*, July 2002.

116.  For a critique of the idea that Israeli prime minister Ehud Barak made Palestinian leader Yassar Arafat a very generous offer that Arafat refused out of spite or malice or sheer ill will towards Israel, see Hussein Agha and Robert Malley, "Camp David: The Tragedy of Errors," *New York Review of Books*, August 9, 2001. Malley served as Special Assistant to President Clinton for Arab-Israeli Affairs. See also Jerome Slater, "What Went Wrong? The Collapse of the Israeli-Palestinian Peace Process," *Political Science Quarterly*, June 2001, p. 171.

117.  "Events on the Temple Mount—29 September 2000," B'Tselem, October 2000.

118.  "Illusions of Restraint—Human Rights Violations during the Events in the Occupied Territories, 29 September–2 December 2000," B'Tselem, December 2000.

119.  Ibid.

120.  Amos Harel, "Wildly Throwing Punches," *Haaretz*, December 12, 2002.

121.  Avi Shlaim, "Sharon's Dangerous Designs; A Career of Terror," *International Herald Tribune*, April 5, 2002.

122.  "Israel's Sharon: Palestinian Statehood Resolution Would Be 'Dangerous Mistake'," BBC Worldwide Monitoring, May 12, 2002.

123.  "Palestinians: Thousands in Mass Graves," United Press International, April 12, 2002.

124.  Aluf Benn and Amos Harel, "Peres Calls Jenin Operation a 'Massacre,'" *Haaretz*, April 9, 2002.

125.  Ibid.

126.  Laura King, "Israel Will Bury Palestinian Dead," Associated Press, April 12, 2002.

127.  "Israeli Court to Take on Issue of Jenin Killings," CNN, April 13, 2002.

128.  "Briefing by Major General Dan Halutz, Israel Air Force Commander; Mr. Danny Ayalon, Political Advisor to the Prime Minister," National Media Center, Jerusalem, April 6, 2002.

129.  Ellis Shuman, "IDF Now Estimates 45 Palestinians Died in Jenin Fighting," *Israel Insider*, April 14, 2002.

130.  "Briefing by Brigadier General Ron Kitrey, IDF Spokesman," National Media Center, Jerusalem, April 9, 2002.

131.  Ellis Shuman, "IDF Now Estimates 45 Palestinians Died in Jenin Fighting," Israel Insider, April 14, 2002.

132.  Ben Lynfield, "Jenin Residents Had No Chance to Run," *Scotsman*, June 14, 2002.

133.  John Lancaster, "Ill-Prepared For a Battle Unexpected," *Washington Post*, April 26, 2002.

134.  Ibid.

135.  "Jenin: IDF Military Operations," Human Rights Watch, May 2002.

136.  "Briefing by Major General Dan Halutz, Israel Air Force Commander; Mr. Danny Ayalon, Political Advisor to the Prime Minister," National Media Center, Jerusalem, April 6, 2002.

137.  Uri Avnery, "Something Stinks," *Gush Shalom*, April 20, 2002.

138.  "Occupied Palestinian Territory Update—Urgent Needs in Psycho-Social Counselling, Education and Health Care and Development," UNICEF, April 26, 2002. Available at www.unicef.org/emerg/Country/OPT/020426.PDF.

139.  Amira Hass, "Operation Destroy the Data," *Haaretz*, April 26, 2002.

140.  Gideon Levy, "Twilight Zone—'I 'm Sorry for Your Loss,' the Officer Said," *Haaretz*, May 22, 2002.

141. Ibid.
142. "Trigger Happy: Unjustified Shooting and Violation of the Open-Fire Regulations during the al-Asqa intifada," B'Tselem, March 2002.
143. Ibid.
144. Ibid.
145. Ewen MacAskill, "Israeli leftwingers astonished and outraged by new commander's blunt," *Guardian,* August 27, 2002.
146. *Ari Shavit,* "The Enemy Within," *Haaretz* August, 30, 2002.
147. Editorial, "A Brutal Routine," *Washington Post,* January 03, 2003.
148. Jon Sawyer, "'Road Map' Will Hinge on Reciprocal Concessions," *St. Louis Post-Dispatch,* May 4, 2003.
149. Editorial, "Unbridled Force," *Haaretz,* March 17, 2003.
150. Ibid.
151. Amos Harel, "Wildly Throwing Punches."
152. "Whitewash—The Office of the Judge Advocate General's Examination of the Death of Khalil al-Mughrabi, 11, on 7 July 2001," B'Tselem, November 2001.
153. Ibid.
154. Dan Fisher and John M. Broder, "Value of Israel's Assassination Policy Debated," *Los Angeles Times,* April 22, 1988.
155. Greg Myre, "Mideast Lingo Tries to Skew World's View on Violence," Associated Press, August 25, 2002.
156. "Dead Israeli Commander Headed Up Much-Criticised Special Unit," Agence France Presse, February 15, 2002.
157. Edward Pilkington, "Israel Admits F-16 Attack Was Flawed," *Guardian* (UK), May 23, 2001.
158. Ibid.
159. Ibid.
160. "Briefing by Major General Giora Eiland, Head of the IDF Operation Branch, to the Foreign Press Association," Jerusalem, May 20, 2001.
161. Deborah Sontag, "When a Tough Sharon Gets Tougher, Israelis Get Nervous," *New York Times,* May 21, 2001.
162. Ibid.
163. Chemi Shalev, "Gaza Attack Sending Shrapnel Flying through Israeli Society," *Forward,* July 26, 2002.
164. Aviad Kleinberg, "Oops!" *Haaretz,* September 8, 2002.
165. Chemi Shalev, "Gaza Attack Sending Shrapnel Flying Through Israeli Society."
166. Joshua Mitnick, "Debate Stirs in Israel after Gaza Air Attack," *Washington Times,* July 25, 2002.
167. Ross Dunn, "Sharon Shifts Blame for Civilian Deaths," *Sydney Morning Herald,* July 25, 2002.
168. Joshua Mitnick, "Debate Stirs in Israel after Gaza Air Attack."
169. Ross Dunn, "Sharon Shifts Blame for Civilian Deaths," *Sydney Morning Herald,* July 25, 2002.
170. Ibid.
171. Associated Press, "Israeli Commander: Airstrike on Gaza Was Morally Correct," *USA Today,* August 21, 2002.
172. Ibid.
173. Quoted in "Israel's Assassination Policy: Extra-judicial Executions," B'Tselem, January 2001.
174. Vincent Cannistraro, "Assassination Is Wrong—and Dumb," *Washington Post,* August 30, 2001.
175. Neve Gordon, "Israel Must Face Threat from Within," *Baltimore Sun,* January 23, 2002.

176. Douglas Davis and Gil Hoffman, "British Chief Rabbi Defends Newspaper Interview," *Jerusalem Post,* August 30, 2002.

177. Ori Nir, "Bush Seeks Israeli Advice on 'Targeted Killings,'" *Forward,* February 7, 2003.

178. Lawrence Joffe, "Rehavam Zeevi—Unsentimental Toughness Was the Hallmark of Military Commander Turned Rightwing Politician Who Advocated 'Transfer' of Palestinians," *Guardian* (UK), October 18, 2001.

179. Ben Lynfield, "Israeli Expulsion Idea Gains Steam," *Christian Science Monitor,* February 6, 2002.

180. "Christians Hail Rightist's Call to Oust Arabs," *Forward,* October 18, 2002.

181. Ibid.

182. "Transcript Hardball with Chris Matthews," CNBC, May 1, 2002.

183. Ben Lynfield, "Israeli Expulsion Idea Gains Steam."

184. "The Logistics of Transfer," Gamla, July 2002. http://www.gamla.org.il/english/article/2002/july/b1.htm

185. Ibid. http://www.gamla.org.il/english/article/2002/july/b1.htm

186. Will Youmans, "Preempting Transfer," *CounterPunch,* October 9, 2002.

187. Martin van Creveld, "Sharon's Plan Is to Drive Palestinians Across the Jordan," *Sunday Telegraph* (UK), April 28, 2002.

188. Ibid.

189. www. Professorsofconscience.ort/Israeli_letter.html

190. "Growing Popularity of a Transfer in Israel," National Public Radio, Morning Edition, October 21, 2002.

191. Aluf Benn, "Israel Strives to Import America's War on Terror," *Haaretz,* December 18, 2001.

192. Greg Myre, " In Other Words, They Mean Death and Destruction," Associated Press, August 25, 2002.

193. "Briefing by Major General Dan Halutz, Israel Air Force Commander; Mr. Danny Ayalon, Political Advisor to the Prime Minister—National Media Center," Jerusalem, April 6, 2002.

194. Leah Harris, "It's the Occupation, Stupid," *CounterPunch,* December 28, 2002.

195. "Security Brass: Targeted Killings Don't Work; No Military Solution to Terror," *Haaretz,* December 19, 2001.

196. Richard Sale, "Analysis: Hamas History Tied to Israel," United Press International, June 18, 2002.

197. Molly Moore, "On Remote Hilltops, Israelis Broaden Settlements," *Washington Post,* December 8, 2002.

198. Harvey Morris, "Israeli Press Attacks Sharon over Violence in Jerusalem," *Financial Times,* August 6, 2002.

199. Jackson Diehl, "The Catastrophe of U.S. Inaction," *Washington Post,* March 31, 2002.

200. Lev Grinberg, "State Terrorism in Israel?" *Tikkun,* May 2002.

201. Neve Gordon, "Living in a Prison," *Jerusalem Post,* May 23, 2001.

202. "Remarks Prior to a Meeting with Secretary of State Colin Powell and an Exchange with Reporters," *Public Papers of the Presidents,* April 18, 2002.

203. Robert Novak, "Sharon and the Senators," *Washington Post,* June 17, 2002.

204. Gideon Samet, "Uncle Sam's Cabin," *Haaretz,* February 8, 2002.

205. Robert Fisk, "Arafat Bypasses Courts to Execute Palestinian 'Spies,'" *Independent* (United Kingdom), August 9, 2001.

206. Lior Yavne, "Keeping Israel Righteous," *Jerusalem Post,* November 5, 2002.

207. Khaled Abu Toameh, "Lawyers Say Arafat Is Undermining Palestinian Authority Judicial System," *Jerusalem Post,* January 9, 2003.

208. Gila Svirsky, "The Price of 35 Years of Occupation," *IsraelInsider,* May 29, 2002.

## Chapter 13

1. "President's Remarks at the United Nations General Assembly," White House Office of the Press Secretary, September 12, 2002.
2. "Address Before a Joint Session of the Congress on the State of the Union," *Public Papers of the Presidents,* January 28, 2003.
3. "Text: Bush's 2003 State of the Union Speech," *Washington Post,* January 29, 2003.
4. "Remarks at the National Religious Broadcasters Convention in Nashville, Tennessee," *Public Papers of the Presidents,* February 10, 2003.
5. "Remarks at Carl Harrison High School in Kennesaw, Georgia," *Public Papers of the Presidents,* February 20, 2003.
6. "Remarks to the American Enterprise Institute Annual Dinner," *Public Papers of the Presidents,* February 26, 2003.
7. Douglas Turner, "U.S. Sent Iraq Germs in Mid-'80s," *Buffalo News,* September 23, 2002. Turner's article was based in part on U.S. Senate committee testimony from 1994.
8. "Text: Bush's 2003 State of the Union Speech," *Washington Post,* January 29, 2003.
9. "President Bush Addresses the Nation," White House Office of the Press Secretary, March 19, 2002.
10. David Leigh and James Wilson, "Counting Iraq's victims," *Guardian* (UK), October 10, 2001.
11. For an analysis of some of the overstated claims of sanctions fatalities, see Matt Welch's article, "The Politics of Dead Children: Have Sanctions against Iraq Murdered Millions?" *Reason,* March 2002.
12. Ibid.
13. Richard Garfield, "Excess Deaths among Children In Iraq: How Many Children Have Died?," working paper, February 8, 2003. Garfield has published widely in scholarly and medical journals on the subject of sanctions.
14. Thomas J. Nagy, "The Secret Behind the Sanctions—How the U.S. Intentionally Destroyed Iraq's Water Supply," *Progressive,* September 2001.
15. Ibid.
16. Ibid.
17. Ibid.
18. Ibid.
19. Barton Gellman, "Allied Air War Struck Broadly in Iraq; Officials Acknowledge Strategy Went Beyond Purely Military Targets," *Washington Post,* June 23, 1991.
20. Ibid.
21. Ibid.
22. Ibid.
23. Colonel John Warden III, "The Enemy as a System," *Airpower Journal,* Spring 1995.
24. Sarah Zaidi, Mary C Smith Fawzi, "Health of Baghdad's Children," (Letter to the Editor), The Lancet, December 2, 1995.
25. James Wall, "Deadly Silence," *Christian Century,* October 25, 2000.
26. Cameron McWhirter, "Iraq Health Care Crisis Brings more Pain, Death," *Detroit News,* October 18, 2002.
27. Peter Baker, "Iraq's Shortage of Medicine May Grow More Severe," *Washington Post,* December 19, 2002.
28. Frances Williams, "Child Death Rate in Iraq Trebles," *Financial Times,* December 12, 2002.
29. Quoted at http://www.amazon.co.uk/exec/obidos/ASIN/1903488222/202–4282062 –4218262—the Amazon.com book page for *Sanctions on Iraq: Background, Consequences and Strategies,* a book produced by the Campaign against Sanctions on Iraq.
30. Caitlin Talmadge, "Systemic Misery," *Harvard International Review,* Winter 2000.

31. "The Impact of Sanctions," U.S. State Department, 1999. Posted at http://usinfo.state.gov/regional/nea/iraq/iraq99a.htm.

32. Joy Gordon, "Sanctions as Siege Warfare," *Nation,* March 22, 1999.

33. Matt Welch, "The Politics of Dead Children," *Reason,* March 2002.

34. "Iraq: A Decade of Sanctions," International Committee for the Red Cross, December 1999.

35. Robert Naiman, "The Economic and Social Toll of U.S. Policy," *San Francisco Chronicle,* January 18, 2001.

36. Philip Shenon, "Washington and Baghdad Agree on One Point: Sanctions Hurt," *New York Times,* November 22, 1998.

37. Barbara Crossette, "For Iraq, A Doghouse with Many Rooms," *New York Times,* November 23, 1997.

38. Eric Schmitt and James Dao, "Iraq Is Focal Point as Bush Meets with Joint Chiefs," *New York Times,* January 11, 2001.

39. Joy Gordon, "Cool War," *Harper's Magazine,* October or November 2002.

40. Editorial, "When Sanctions Don't Work," *Economist,* April 8, 2000.

41. Robert Fisk, "The Dishonesty of this So-Called Dossier," *Independent* (UK), September 25, 2002.

42. Nicole Winfield, "U.N., Diplomats See No Evidence of Change in U.S.-Iraq Policy," Associated Press, February 26, 2000.

43. Ibid.

44. Ibid.

45. "Iraq Slams 'Smart Sanctions'," Associated Press, February 27, 2001.

46. Carola Hoyos, "US Lifts Block on Russian Contracts With Iraq," *Financial Times,* April 3, 2002.

47. Joy Gordon, "Cool War," *Harper's Magazine,* October-November, 2002.

48. "Remarks on the Iraq Threat to America," *Public Papers of the Presidents,* October 7, 2002.

49. Matthew Rothschild, "Now They Cite the Toll of Sanctions," *Progressive* (online), March 28, 2003.

50. Ibid.

51. "Press Briefing by Andrew S. Natsios, Administrator, U.S. Agency for International Development—U.S. Humanitarian Relief and Reconstruction Efforts in Iraq," State Department Office of Public Affairs, March 25, 2003. Also cited at Rahul Mahajan, " The New Humanitarianism Basra as Military Target," Counterpunch.org, March 27, 2003.

52. Statistics from "Patterns of Global Terrorism," U.S. State Department, 1990–2002.

53. Eric Schmitt and James Dao, "Iraq Is Focal Point as Bush Meets with Joint Chiefs," *New York Times,* January 11, 2001.

54. "Remarks on the Iraq Threat to America," *Public Papers of the Presidents,* October 7, 2002.

55. Stephen C. Pelletiere, "A War Crime or an Act of War?" *New York Times,* January 31, 2003. Pelletiere was the CIA's senior political analyst on Iraq during the Iran-Iraq war.

56. Bob Woodward, *Bush at War* (New York: Simon & Schuster, 2002), p. 61.

57. Ibid., p. 83.

58. Ibid., p. 99.

59. Glenn Kessler, "U.S. Decision On Iraq Has Puzzling Past," *Washington Post,* January 12, 2003.

60. The letter is posted at the website of the Project for the New American Century at http://www.newamericancentury.org/iraqclintonletter.htm.

61. David Wurmser, "Middle East War—How Did It Come to This?" American Enterprise Institute, January 1, 2001.

62. Joe Hagan, "President Bush's Neoconservatives Were Spawned Right Here in N.Y.C.," *New York Observer,* April 29, 2003.

63. Thomas E. Ricks, "Briefing Depicted Saudis as Enemies," *Washington Post,* August 6, 2002. Also, see Jack Shafer, "The PowerPoint That Rocked the Pentagon," Slate.com, August 7, 2002.

64. Ari Shavit, "White Man's Burden," *Haaretz*, April 5, 2003. The article noted that Washington's "belief in war against Iraq" was "disseminated by a small group of 25 or 30 neoconservatives, almost all of them Jewish, almost all of them intellectuals."

65. John Fund, "Where Today's Big Ideas Come From," *Wall Street Journal*, March 14, 2003.

66. Robert S. Greenberger and Karby Leggett, "Bush Dreams of Changing Not Just Regime but Region—A Pro-U.S., Democratic Area Is a Goal that Has Israeli, Neoconservative Roots," *Wall Street Journal*, March 21, 2003.

67. Michael Kinsley, "What Bush Isn't Saying about Iraq," *Washington Post*, October 24, 2002.

68. David Frum, "In the Cold," *National Review*, January 20, 2003.

69. Editorial, "Comfort and the Protesters," *New York Sun*, February 6, 2003.

70. Jonathan Steele, "Israel Puts Pressure on US to Strike Iraq," *Guardian* (UK), August 17, 2002.

71. Benjamin Netanyahu, "Conflict with Iraq—An Israeli Perspective." Testimony presented to the House Committee on Government Reform on September 12, 2002. Posted at http://www.netanyahu.org/con1.html.

72. Robert Novak, "Sharon's War?" *Washington Post*, December 26, 2002.

73. Robert Kaiser, "Bush and Sharon Nearly Identical on Mideast Policy," *Washington Post*, February 9, 2003.

74. Akiva Eldar, "They're Jumping In Head First," *Haaretz*, September 30, 2002.

75. "Remarks to the American Enterprise Institute Annual Dinner," *Public Papers of the Presidents*, February 26, 2003.

76. Matt Spetalnick, "Israel to Palestinians: Learn Lesson of Iraq War," Reuters, April 10, 2003.

77. Daniel J. Wakin, "A Prominent Rabbi Reconsiders His Recent Antiwar Remarks," *New York Times*, March 28, 2003.

78. Michael Kinsley, "The Pro-Israel Lobby: Anti-Semitic Propaganda Turns Up in the Unlikeliest Places," Slate.com, March 13, 2003.

79. Steve Holland, "Bush Offers U.S. Troops to Help with Terrorists," Reuters News Service, December 21, 2001.

80. James C. Moore, "Karl Rove: Counting Votes while the Bombs Drop," *Los Angels Times* or *Atlanta Journal Constitution*, May 7, 2003.

81. Dana Milbank, "For Bush, the Military Is the Message for '04," *Washington Post*, May 2, 2003.

82. Colum Lynch, "U.S. Seeking Broad Control of Iraqi Oil, Funds," *Washington Post*, May 9, 2003.

83. Michael Elliott and James Carney, "First Stop, Iraq," *Time*, March 31, 2003.

84. Ibid.

85. Howard Fineman, "Bush and God," *Newsweek*, March 10, 2003.

86. "Text of a Letter from the President to the Speaker of the House of Representatives and the President Pro Tempore of the Senate," White House Office of the Press Secretary, March 19, 2003.

87. Greg Miller and Bob Drogin, "U.S. Renews Claims of Hussein-Al Qaeda Link," *Los Angeles Times*, January 30, 2003.

88. "Text of President's State of the Union Address," *Washington Post*, January 30, 2002.

89. "Remarks by President Bush and President Alvaro Uribe of Colombia in Photo Opportunity," White House Office of the Press Secretary, September 25, 2002.

90. Mike Allen, "Bush Asserts that Al Qaeda Has Links to Iraq's Hussein," *Washington Post*, September 26, 2002.

91. "Bush Administration Links Iraq, Al Qaeda," Associated Press, September 26, 2002.

92. Ibid.

93. "Remarks on the Iraq Threat to America," *Public Papers of the Presidents*, October 7, 2002.

94. " Remarks in Portsmouth, New Hampshire," *Public Papers of the Presidents*, November 1, 2002.

95. "Text: Bush's 2003 State of the Union Speech," *Washington Post*, January 29, 2003.

96. "The President's News Conference with Prime Minister Tony Blair of the United Kingdom," *Public Papers of the Presidents*, January 31, 2003.

97. Greg Miller and Bob Drogin, "U.S. Renews Claims of Hussein-Al Qaeda Link," *Los Angeles Times*, January 20, 2003.

98. Nancy Gibbs and Michael Duffy, "Trust Me, He Says," *Time*, November 3, 2002.

99. James Risen and David Johnston, "Split at C.I.A. and F.B.I. on Iraqi Ties to Al Qaeda," *New York Times*, February 2, 2003.

100. Elizabeth Drew, "The Enforcer," *New York Review of Books*, May 1, 2003.

101. Linda Feldmann, "The Impact of Bush Linking 9/11 and Iraq," *Christian Science Monitor*, March 14, 2003.

102. "Selling an Iraq-al Qaeda connection," CNN.com, March 11, 2003.

103. Martin Merzer, "Americans Are against Unilateral War in Iraq," *Philadelphia Inquirer*, January 12, 2003.

104. Nancy Gibbs and Michael Duffy, "Trust Me, He Says," *Time*, November 3, 2002.

105. Linda Feldmann, "The Impact of Bush Linking 9/11 and Iraq," *Christian Science Monitor*, March 14, 2003.

106. Anne Kornblut and Charles Sennott, "Saddam the new Hitler, Bush Tells Europeans," *Sydney Morning Herald* (Australia), November 22, 2002.

107. Maureen Dowd, "The Empire Strikes First," *New York Times*, January 29, 2003.

108. "Saddam's Rule 'Worst in World History,'" Reuters, April 1, 2003.

109. "Text: Bush's 2003 State of the Union Speech," *Washington Post*, January 29, 2003.

110. "President Says Saddam Hussein Must Leave Iraq within 48 Hours," White House Office of the Press Secretary, March 17, 2003.

111. "President Bush Addresses the Nation," White House Office of the Press Secretary, March 19, 2003.

112. "President Says Saddam Hussein Must Leave Iraq within 48 Hours," White House Office of the Press Secretary, March 17, 2003.

113. Ibid.

114. Warren P. Strobel, Jonathan S. Landay, and John Walcott, "Officials' Private Doubts on Iraq War," *Philadelphia Inquirer*, October 8, 2002.

115. Dana Milbank, "For Bush, Facts Are Malleable—Presidential Tradition Of Embroidering Key Assertions Continues," *Washington Post*, October 22, 2002.

116. Dana Milbank, "U.S. Officials Make It Clear: Exile or War," *Washington Post*, March 17, 2003.

117. Walter Pincus and Dana Milbank, "Bush Clings To Dubious Allegations About Iraq," *Washington Post*, March 18, 2003.

118. Seymour Hersh, "Who Lied to Whom? Why Did the Administration Endorse a Forgery about Iraq's Nuclear Program?" *New Yorker*, March 31, 3003.

119. Ibid.

120. Ibid.

121. Ibid.

122. Ibid.

123. Veteran Intelligence Professionals for Sanity, "Not Worth the Paper It's Written On? Intelligence Fiasco," Counterpunch.org, May 1, 2003.

124. Nicholas D. Kristof, "Missing in Action: Truth," *New York Times*, May 6, 2003.

125. Colum Lynch, "Iraqi Defector Claimed Arms Were Destroyed by 1995," *Washington Post*, March 1, 2003.

126. Ibid.

127. "DoD News Briefing—Secretary Rumsfeld and Gen. Myers," Department of Defense, February 12, 2002.
128. Edward W. Lempinen, Wolf in Sheep's Clothing," Salon.com, December 7, 2002.
129. James Pinkerton, "Bush's Blind Spot Could Put Us in a Very Dark Hole," *Newsday,* December 12, 2002.
130. Maureen Dowd, "Powell without Picasso," *New York Times,* February 5, 2003.
131. Jim Garamone, "Seeing a Smoking Gun Means It's Too Late, Rumsfeld Says," American Forces Press Service, September 18, 2002.,
132. Reprinted in the Congressional Record, March 4, 2003, p. E363.
133. James Bamford, "Maintain CIA's Independence," *USA Today,* October 24, 2002.
134. Warren P. Strobel, Jonathan S. Landay, and John Walcott, "Officials' Private Doubts on Iraq War," *Philadelphia Inquirer,* October 8, 2002.
135. Warren P. Strobel, Jonathan S. Landay and John Walcott, "Officials' private doubts on Iraq war," Philadelphia Inquirer, October 8, 2002.
136. "President Bush Addresses the Nation," White House Office of the Press Secretary, March 19, 2003.
137. Glenn Kessler, "United States Puts a Spin On Coalition Numbers," *Washington Post,* March 21, 2003.
138. Dana Milbank, "Many Willing, But Only a Few Are Able," *Washington Post,* March 25, 2003.
139. Ibid.
140. Ibid.
141. Alan Perrott, "Coalition of the Willing? Not Us, Say Solomon Islanders," *New Zealand Herald,* March 27, 2003.
142. Dana Milbank, "Many Willing, But Only a Few Are Able," *Washington Post,* March 25, 2003.
143. "Press Briefing with Ari Fleischer," White House Office of the Press Secretary, April 10, 2003.
144. David Von Drehle, "'Shock and Awe' Author Uneasy With New Fame," *Washington Post,* March 22, 2003.
145. William Bunch, "U.S. Plan for Saddam: Shock and Awe," *Philadelphia Daily News,* February 26, 2003.
146. "Address to the Nation on Iraq from the U.S.S. Abraham Lincoln," *Public Papers of the Presidents,* May 1, 2003.
147. "President Bush Outlines Progress in Operation Iraqi Freedom," White House Office of the Press Secretary, April 16, 2003.
148. Rory McCarthy, " Iraq: After the War: Campaigners Count Bodies to Ensure US Compensation," *Guardian* (UK), May 17, 2003.
149. Peter Ford, "Surveys Pointing to High Civilian Death Toll in Iraq," *Christian Science Monitor,* May 22, 2003.
150. Niko Price, "AP Tallies 3,240 Civilian Deaths in Iraq," Associated Press, June 10, 2003.
151. Laura King, "Baghdad's Death Toll Assessed," *Los Angeles Times,* May 18, 2003.
152. http://www.Iraqbodycount.net. Accessed on May 23, 2003.
153. Charles J. Hanley, "Civilian Toll, War's Underside, Mounts as U.S. Forces Approach Baghdad," Associated Press, April 3, 2003.
154. Ibid.
155. Laura King, "Baghdad's Death Toll Assessed," *Los Angeles Times,* May 18, 2003.
156. All quotes taken from Dexter Filkins, "Either Take a Shot or Take a Chance," *New York Times,* March 29, 2003.
157. Peter Ford, "Surveys Pointing to High Civilian Death Toll in Iraq," *Christian Science Monitor,* May 22, 2003.
158. http://www.defenselink.mil/transcripts/2003/tr20030425-secdef0126.html.
159. Michael Weisskopf, "The Bombs that Keep On Killing," *Time,* May 12, 2003.

160. Interview with Michael Weisskopf, "Live Sunday," Cable Network News, May 4, 2003.
161. Elizabeth Becker," The American Portrayal of a War of Liberation Is Faltering across the Arab World," *New York Times,* April 5, 2003.
162. Ibid.
163. Bradley Graham and Dan Morgan, "U.S. Has No Plans to Count Civilian Casualties," *Washington Post,* April 15, 2003.
164. Ibid.
165. Ibid.
166. Barton Gellman, "Frustrated, U.S. Arms Team to Leave Iraq," *Washington Post,* May 11, 2003.
167. Barton Gellman, "In Search for Weapons, Army Team Finds Vacuum Cleaners," *Washington Post,* May 18, 2003.
168. Alan Elsner, "Bush Officials Change Tune on Iraqi Weapons," Reuters News Service, May 14, 2003.
169. "Here Come the Thought Police: US Official, Iraqi 'Intellectual Capacity' Justified Invasion," Global Security Newswire, May 24, 2003. Global Security Newswire is a "National Journal Group daily online publication covering weapons of mass destruction and terrorism."
170. Dana Priest and Walter Pincus, "CIA to Review Intelligence," *Washington Post,* May 23, 2003.
171. Seymour Hersh, "Selective Intelligence," *New Yorker,* May 12, 2003.
172. Ibid.
173. William Broad, "The Impossible Task for America's Spies," *New York Times,* May 11, 2003.
174. Harold Meyerson, "Enron-Like Unreality," *Washington Post,* May 13, 2003.
175. Dana Milbank and Jim VandeHei, "No Political Fallout for Bush on Weapons," *Washington Post,* May 17, 2003.
176. "Address to the Nation on Iraq From the U.S.S. Abraham Lincoln," *Public Papers of the Presidents,* May 1, 2003.
177. Dana Priest, "Analysts Discount Attack by Iraq," *Washington Post,* October 9, 2002
178. "Letter from Agent Colleen Rowley to FBI director Robert Mueller" (dated February 26, 2003), reprinted in the *Minneapolis Star Tribune,* March 6, 2003.
179. Richard Lugar, "A Victory at Risk," *Washington Post,* May 22, 2003.
180. Anne Q. Hoy, Timothy Phelps, and Ken Fireman, "Pushing U.S. Toward War," *Newsday,* March 16, 2003.
181. Joshua Micah Marshall, "'Practice to Deceive,'" *Washington Monthly,* April 2003.
182. "Iraq War Helped Boost Al Qaeda," *Toronto Star,* May 20, 2003.
183. Ibid.
184. "Address to the Nation on Iraq From the U.S.S. Abraham Lincoln," *Public Papers of the Presidents,* May 1, 2003.
185. James Kuhnhenn, "Congress Feels Bush's Force on Iraq," *Philadelphia Inquirer,* October 7, 2002.

## Chapter 14

1. "Remarks at the President's Dinner," *Public Papers of the Presidents,* June 19, 2002.
2. "Remarks to the Republican Party of Alaska in Anchorage," *Public Papers of the Presidents,* February 16, 2002.
3. " Remarks on the Terrorist Attacks at Barksdale Air Force Base, Louisiana," *Public Papers of the Presidents,* September 11, 2001.
4. "Statement by the President in His Address to the Nation," White House Office of the Press Secretary, September 11, 2001.

5. "Remarks at the National Day of Prayer and Remembrance Service," *Public Papers of the Presidents*, September 14, 2001.

6. "Address to a Joint Session of Congress and the American People," White House Office of the Press Secretary, September 20, 2001.

7. "Remarks By The President To U.S. Attorneys Conference," White House Office of the Press Secretary, November 29, 2001.

8. "Remarks at a Dinner for Senatorial Candidate Norm Coleman and Congressional Candidate John Kline in Minneapolis," *Public Papers of the Presidents*, July 11, 2002.

9. "Remarks to the Community in Louisville, Kentucky," *Public Papers of the Presidents*, September 5, 2002.

10. Remarks at Eden Prairie High School in Eden Prairie," *Public Papers of the Presidents*, March 4, 2002.

11. http://www.rsf.fr/article.php3?id_article=4116

12. Lawrence M. O'Rourke, "UN ranks U.S. 13th in freedoms," *Chicago Tribune*, May 24, 1991.

13. Robert G. Kaiser, "The Long and Short of It; The War on Terrorism Began So Well," *Washington Post*, September 8, 2002.

14. Sarah El Deeb, "Arabs Dislike America but Not Democracy: Poll," *The Age* (Australia), November 1, 2002.

15. Ibid.

16. Barton Gellman, "In U.S., Terrorism's Peril Undiminished," *Washington Post*, December 24, 2002.

17. "Remarks to the Troops at Elmendorf Air Force Base in Anchorage, Alaska," *Public Papers of the Presidents*, February 16, 2002.

18. "Remarks at a Dinner for Senatorial Candidate James M. Talent in Kansas City," *Public Papers of the Presidents*, June 11, 2002.

19. "Remarks by the President at Coleman/Kline/Minnesota Republican Party Victory 2002 Dinner," White House Office of the Press Secretary, July 11, 2002.

20. "Remarks to the Troops at Fort Hood in Killeen, Texas," *Public Papers of the Presidents*, January 3, 2003.

21. Bob Woodward, *Bush at War* (New York: Simon & Schuster, 2002), p. 327.

22. "Remarks to Airline Employees in Chicago, Illinois," *Public Papers of the Presidents*, September 27, 2001.

23. "Remarks to Department of Homeland Security Employees," *Public Papers of the Presidents*, February 28, 2003.

24. "Remarks at the National Republican Senatorial Committee Dinner," *Public Papers of the Presidents*, September 25, 2002.

25. "Remarks at a Luncheon for Gubernatorial Candidate Mike Fisher in Pittsburgh, Pennsylvania," *Public Papers of the Presidents*, August 5, 2002.

26. "Commencement Address at the United States Military Academy in West Point, New York," *Public Papers of the Presidents*, June 1, 2002.

27. "Remarks at a Republican Luncheon in Greenwich, Connecticut," *Public Papers of the Presidents*, April 9, 2002.

28. "Message to the Congress Transmitting Proposed Legislation To Create the Department of Homeland Security," *Public Papers of the Presidents*, June 18, 2002.

29. "Address Before a Joint Session of the Congress on the State of the Union," *Public Papers of the Presidents*, January 29, 2002.

30. "Remarks to Employees at the Army Tank Plant in Lima, Ohio," *Public Papers of the Presidents*, April 24, 2003.

31. "Address to the Nation Announcing Strikes against Al Qaida Training Camps and Taliban Military Installations in Afghanistan," *Public Papers of the Presidents*, October 7, 2001.

32. "Remarks at the University of Pittsburgh in Pittsburgh," Public Papers of the Presidents, February 5, 2002.

33. "Address to the Nation on the Anniversary of the Terrorist Attacks of September 11 From Ellis Island, New York," *Public Papers of the Presidents,* September 11, 2002.

34. Posted at the website of the Future of Freedom Foundation, www.fff.org/freedom/0893e.asp. Quoted from James Madison, Letters and Other Writings of James Madison, 4 vol., (Philadelphia, PA: Lippincott, 1865).

35. John Phillip Reid, *The Concept of Liberty in the Age of the American Revolution* (Chicago: University of Chicago Press, 1988), p. 65.

36. Quoted in Friedrich Hayek, *Constitution of Liberty* (1960; reprint, Chicago: Henry Regnery, 1972), p. 246.

37. "Remarks at Logan High School in La Crosse, Wisconsin," *Public Papers of the Presidents,* May 8, 2002. Italics mine.

38. "Remarks on Improving Counterterrorism Intelligence," *Public Papers of the Presidents,* February 14, 2003.

39. Alisa Solomon, "Things We Lost in the Fire: The Assault on the Constitution," *Village Voice,* September 11, 2002. Attorney General Janet Reno, in a 1995 speech vindicating federal actions at Waco, informed a group of federal law enforcement officers, expressed a similar sentiment: "You are part of a government that has given its people more freedom . . . than any other government in the history of the world." Speech by Attorney General Janet Reno, Newark, New Jersey, May 5, 1995. Quoted in James Bovard, "Waco Must Get a Hearing," *Wall Street Journal,* May 15, 1995.

40. George W. Bush, "Securing Freedom's Triumph," *New York Times,* September 11, 2002.

41. Quoted in Jacques Ellul, "Politicalization and Political Solutions," in Kenneth S. Templeton, Jr., ed., *The Politicalization of Society* (Indianapolis, IN: Liberty Press, 1979), p. 232.

42. "Commencement Address at the United States Military Academy in West Point, New York," *Public Papers of the Presidents,* June 1, 2002.

43. Sonja Barisic, "Judges: U.S. Must Explain Detention," Associated Press, July 18, 2002.

44. G. W. F. Hegel, *The Philosophy of Hegel* (New York: The Modern Library, 1954), p. 282.

## Chapter 15

1. "George W. Bush Delivers Remarks to the Carpenters' Union Conference," Federal Document Clearing House, June 19, 2002.

2. Shannon Mccaffrey, "Specter Criticizes FBI on Taps Congress Oversight on Surveillance Asked," *Pittsburgh Post-Gazette,* March 3, 2003.

3. Jake Tapper, "Senate Report: FBI Still Unprepared," Salon.com, March 3, 2003.

4. Shannon Mccaffrey, "Specter Criticizes FBI on Taps Congress Oversight on Surveillance Asked," *Pittsburgh Post-Gazette,* March 3, 2003.

5. "FISA Implementation Failures," Interim Report on FBI Oversight in the 107th Congress by the Senate Judiciary Committee: Senator Patrick Leahy, Senator Charles Grassley, and Senator Arlen Specter, February 2003.

6. Greg Gordon, "Minneapolis FBI Agent Told She Will Be Fired for Hurting Bureau's Image," *Minneapolis Star Tribune,* May 1, 2003.

7. "Remarks on Departure for Waterford, Michigan, and an Exchange with Reporters," Public Papers of the Presidents, October 14, 2002.

8. Susan Schmidt and Patricia Davis, "Investigators Not All in Loop, Some Complain," *Washington Post,* October 23, 2002.

9. Bob Dart and Rebecca Carr, "Sniper Shootings: Frustration with Police Escalates as Toll Grows," *Atlanta Journal and Constitution,* October 24, 2002.

10. Susan Schmidt and Patricia Davis, "Investigators Not All in Loop, Some Complain," *Washington Post,* October 23, 2002.

11. Ibid.
12. Tony Allen-Mills, "Money Might Have Been Only Motive of the Urban Snipers," *Sunday Times* (London), October 27, 2002.
13. Craig Whitlock and Josh White, "Police Checked Suspect's Plates at Least 10 Times," *Washington Times*, October 26, 2002.
14. Ibid.
15. Stephen Braun and Mark Fineman, "Sniper Suspects Slipped Past Authorities Time and Again," *Los Angeles Times*, November 30, 2002.
16. Robert O'Harrow, "U.S. Hopes to Check Computers Globally; System Would Be Used to Hunt Terrorists," *Washington Post*, November 12, 2002.
17. Stephen Braun and Mark Fineman, "Sniper Suspects Slipped Past Authorities Time and Again," *Los Angeles Times*, November 30, 2002.
18. Adam Clymer, "Big Brother Joins the Hunt for the Sniper," *New York Times*, October 20, 2002.
19. Dan Eggen, "GAO Criticizes System for Tracking Terrorists," *Washington Post*, April 30, 2003.
20. Noam Scheiber, "Number in the News: 5,000 Al Qaeda Operatives in the U.S.," *New York Times*, February 16, 2003.
21. "Statement by U.S. Attorney General John Ashcroft on the Arrest of Abdullah Al Muhajir," Justice Department Office of Public Affairs, June 10, 2002.
22. Dave Boyer and Bill Gertz, "Questions Irk White House," *Washington Times*, June 13, 2002.
23. Kevin Johnson and Toni Locy, "Threat of 'Dirty Bomb' Softened," *USA Today*, June 12, 2002.
24. Dan Eggen, "Ashcroft's High Profile, Motives Raise White House Concerns," *Washington Post*, June 17, 2002.
25. Elaine M. Grossman, "Military Outside Pentagon Report Possible Terrorist Surveillance," *Inside the Pentagon*, June 27, 2002.
26. Kevin Johnson and Toni Locy, "Threat of 'Dirty Bomb' Softened," *USA Today*, June 12, 2002.
27. Dave Boyer and Bill Gertz, "Questions Irk White House," *Washington Times*, June 13, 2002.
28. "No Proof of Plot by Dirty Bomber: Law Enforcement Official," Associated Press, August 13, 2002.
29. Dan Mihalopoulos, "U.S. Rebuked Over Padilla," *Chicago Tribune*, March 12, 2003.
30. George Clark, "The Unsung Genius of Red Green," *London Free Press* (Canada), March 8, 2003.
31. Ibid.
32. Editorial, "Duck and Cover," *New York Times*, February 12, 2003.
33. Michele McPhee and David Saltonstall, "Mike: Don't Duct and Cover," *New York Daily News*, February 14, 2003.
34. Mark Lane, "Understanding the Limits to Power—and Duct Tape," Cox News Service, February 17, 2003.
35. Dana Milbank, "Market Testing for Homeland Security," *Washington Post*, February 15, 2003.
36. Michael Isikoff, "The FBI Says, 'Count the Mosques,'" *Newsweek*, February 3, 2003.
37. Ibid.
38. "FBI Request for Mosque List Condemned by CAIR," PR Newswire, February 20, 2003.
39. Yemisrach Benalfew, "Rights—U.S.: FBI Plan to Count Mosques Stirs Protests," Inter Press Service, February 17, 2003.
40. Kelly Brewington, "FBI's Mosque-Counting Policy Worries Nation's Muslims," Orlando Sentinel, February 7, 2003.

41. "Statement of the Honorable John Ashcroft, Attorney General," United States Department of Justice, Senate Judiciary Committee Hearing on War against Terrorism, March 4, 2003.

42. Mark Fazlollah, "Reports of Terror Crimes Inflated," *Philadelphia Inquirer,* May 15, 2003.

43. "Attorney General John Ashcroft Speaks about the Challenges since September 11th, 2001," National Public Radio (Morning Edition), September 11, 2002.

44. Ibid.

45. Bob Woodward, *Bush at War* (New York: Simon & Schuster, 2002), pp. 351–352.

46. "National Security Strategy of the United States," White House National Security Council, September 2002, at http://www.whitehouse.gov/nsc/nss.html.

47. "National Security Strategy of the United States," White House National Security Council, September 2002. At http://www.whitehouse.gov/nsc/nss.html.

48. Ibid.

49. Ibid.

50. "President Rallies the Troops in Alaska," White House Office of the Press Secretary, February 16, 2002.

51. Quoted in John T. Correll, "Verbatim," Air Force Magazine Online, September 2002.

52. Marc Perelman, "Israel, Activists Train Sights on Syria Lobby to Focus on Preventing Missile Transfer," *Forward,* April 4, 2003.

53. Eric Boehlert, "Islamism is Fascism—An Interview with Daniel Pipes," Salon.com, November 9, 2001.

54. Norman Podhoretz, "In Praise of the Bush Doctrine," *Commentary,* September 2002.

55. Ari Shavit, "White Man's Burden," *Haaretz,* April 5, 2003.

56. Ran HaCohen, "Killing and Taking Possession," Antiwar.com, May 4, 2002. HaCohen is a columnist for Israel's largest-circulation newspaper and a lecturer at Tel Aviv University.

57. David Francis, "Economist Tallies Swelling Cost of Israel to US," *Christian Science Monitor,* December 9, 2002.

58. "Remarks on the National Economy and an Exchange with Reporters in Crawford," Public Papers of the Presidents, April 26, 2002.

59. Timothy M. Phelps and Knut Royce, "The Mideast Arms Race," *Newsday,* April 20, 2003. See also, Seymour Hersh, *The Samson Option: Israel's Nuclear Arsenal and American Foreign Policy* (New York: Random House, 1991).

60. "Remarks to the Community in Louisville, Kentucky," Public Papers of the Presidents, September 5, 2002.

61. Carlotta Gall, "As the Iraq War Goes On, Afghan Violence Increases," *New York Times,* April 15, 2003.

62. Andrew Gumbel, "America Admits Suspects Died in Interrogations," *Independent* (United Kingdom), March 7, 2003.

63. "No Compensation for Afghan Bomb Victims: US Military," Agence France Presse, April 10, 2003.

64. April Witt, "After the Airstrikes, Just Silence," *Washington Post,* April 28, 2003.

65. Ron Fournier, "Bush Advisers Draft Re-Election Agenda," Associated Press, December 29, 2002.

66. Eric Boehlert, "How the GOP Struck Gold with its Permanent 'War on Terrorism,'" Salon.com, May 8, 2003. Also, Matthew Engel, "Claim of Bush Exploiting September 11," *Guardian* (United Kingdom), May 16, 2002.

67. Anne E. Kornblut, "Bush '04 Fund-Raising Cites War on Terrorism," *Boston Globe,* May 25, 2003.

68. Maureen Dowd, "Chest Banging, Here and There," *New York Times,* April 23, 2003.

69. Edward Wyatt, "Goal Is to Lay Cornerstone at Ground Zero During G.O.P. Convention," *New York Times,* June 13, 2003.

70. Quoted at the website of the Future of Freedom Foundation: http://www.fff.org/freedom/1001e.asp.

## Chapter 16—Conclusion

1. "Remarks Following Discussions With Business Leaders," Public Papers of the Presidents, April 15, 2003.
2. *U.S. v. Jannottie,* 673 F. 2d 578, 614 (1982).
3. "Traces of Terror; Excerpts From the Ruling Against Secret Hearings," New York Times, August 27, 2002.
4. "Bush mocks Bush," BBC News, March 25, 2001. Bush said he had gotten this advice from former Democratic Party heavyweight Robert Strauss. Bush made the comment in a speech to the Gridiron Club.
5. Bob Woodward, *Bush at War* (New York: Simon & Schuster, 2002), p. 338.

# Index